SCHOLASTIC
JOURNALISM

ONLINE RESOURCES

These additional resources for students and instructors are available at www.wiley.com/go/scholasticjournalism.

STUDENT MATERIALS

- Glossary of all key terms
- Library of useful links from the text
- Contact information for professional and student organizations
- List of additional resources

INSTRUCTOR'S MANUAL

- Introduction
- Learning objectives for each chapter
- Narratives for the end-of-chapter exercises
- Answers to test your knowledge and quick exercises by chapter
- Key terms defined by chapter
- Additional exercises for each chapter

SCHOLASTIC JOURNALISM

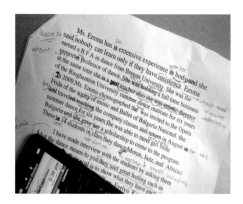

12th Edition

C. DOW TATE AND SHERRI A. TAYLOR

WILEY

This twelfth edition first published 2014
© 2014 John Wiley & Sons, Inc.

Edition History: Iowa State University Press (9e, 1996); Iowa State Press (10e, 2001);
Blackwell Publishing Ltd (11e, 2007)

Registered Office
John Wiley & Sons Ltd, The Atrium, Southern Gate, Chichester, West Sussex, PO19 8SQ, UK

Editorial Offices
350 Main Street, Malden, MA 02148-5020, USA
9600 Garsington Road, Oxford, OX4 2DQ, UK
The Atrium, Southern Gate, Chichester, West Sussex, PO19 8SQ, UK

For details of our global editorial offices, for customer services, and for information about
how to apply for permission to reuse the copyright material in this book please see our website
at www.wiley.com/wiley-blackwell.

Library of Congress Cataloging-in-Publication data is available for this book.

9780470659335 (hardback)
9780470659342 (paperback)

A catalogue record for this book is available from the British Library.

Cover images used courtesy of Sherri A. Taylor
Cover design by Simon Levy

Set in 9.5/11pt ITC Century by SPi Publisher Services, Pondicherry, India
Printed in Singapore by C.O.S. Printers Pte Ltd

2   2015

BRIEF CONTENTS

 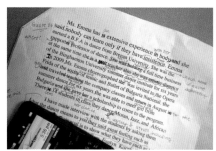 

Contents vi

About the authors xi

Preface xii

Acknowledgments xiii

Walk through xvi

Timeline xxii

1 Understanding news 3

2 Interviewing and reporting 29

3 News writing 51

4 Writing specialty stories 81

5 Writing feature stories 111

6 Sportswriting 139

7 Opinion writing 165

8 In-depth reporting 189

9 Coaching writers and editing copy 215

10 Writing headlines 245

11 Typography and production 263

12 Newspaper layout and design 291

13 Yearbook design 323

14 Online journalism 347

15 Visual storytelling: pictures, art and graphics 371

16 Advertising in newspapers and yearbooks 405

17 Student press law 427

18 Ethics for student journalists 451

19 Careers in the media 471

Professional and student organizations 485

Glossary 488

Index 498

CONTENTS

About the authors xi

Preface xii

Acknowledgments xiii

Walk through xvi

Timeline xxii

1 | Understanding news 3

Where does news come from? 6

News value 6
Timeliness 6
Proximity 7
Prominence 8
Audience impact 9
Surprise or oddity 10
Human interest 10
Conflict and drama 10
Visual impact 10

The importance of audience 11

Beat reporting 12

Featurizing news 15

News in other contexts 17

Sourcing news 17
Primary sources 17
Secondary sources 20

Other factors affecting coverage 22

Conclusion 25

2 | Interviewing and reporting 29

Interviewing 30
Developing questions 31
Organizing the interview 32
Setting up the interview 32
Conducting the interview 33

Observation 40

Reliability of sources 42

Internet research 44

Conventional research 47

Conclusion 48

3 | News writing 51

News writing 52

The news lead 54

Alternative news lead approaches 55

Feature leads 59
Contrast lead 59
Vignette lead 61
The descriptive lead 62

Developing a news story 63
Body of a news story 66
Flow and organization 69

Potential weaknesses in news writing 69
Vagueness 69
Wordiness 71

Jargon and pretentious vocabulary 71
Editorializing 72
Numerical distortions 72
Passive voice 74

Online news coverage 74
Using quotes and attribution 75
A news writer's checklist 75
Conclusion 77

4 | Writing specialty stories 81

Health writing 82
Academic writing 85
Death coverage 87
Speech stories 87
Poll story 94
Selecting respondents 94

Civic journalism 97
Yearbook writing 99
Unique story angles 101
Alternative copy or sidebar writing 101

Conclusion 106

5 | Writing feature stories 111

The feature story Idea 112
The feature-writing process 113
Conclusions 116

Elements of feature writing 116
Precise writing 117
Details 117
Pace 118
Examples 118
Dialogue 118
Voice 118

Feature story types 124
Profiles 124

Human interest story 126
Informative feature story 130
Other types of features 131
Conclusion 132

6 | Sportswriting 139

Writing the sports story 140
Sports slang and sports language 141
Developing a sports story with statistics 142

Types of sports stories 143
Advance story 143
Trend story 145
Sports news story 146
Game story 146
Sports feature story 151

Feature leads for sports stories 152
Packaged coverage 154
Sports webcasting 155
Getting started 155
The webcast staff 156

Conclusion 158

7 | Opinion writing 165

Developing editorial ideas 168
Role of the editorial 168
Opinion vs. fact 169
Editorial writing: the formula 169
Editorial leads 170
Developing the argument 172
Editorial cartoon 172
Columns 175
Blog writing 176
Review writing 178
Reviewing tips 178
Packaged opinion coverage 183
Conclusion 183

8 | In-depth reporting 189

Finding topics for in-depth coverage 192
School governing boards 193
Athletics 193
Curricular areas 193
Extracurricular and other areas 194
Beyond the school 195
Localizing national and state trends 195

Getting started 198
Full-page coverage 198
Double truck coverage 200
Beyond the double truck 200
Special issues 203
The yearbook 203

Writing the in-depth story 204
Anonymous sources 209
Layering information 211

The need for accuracy 211

Conclusion 211

9 | Coaching writers and editing copy 215

The coaching process 216
Planning stage 216
Collecting stage 216
Writing stage 217
The lead 217
Body organization and flow 217

Proofreading and correcting a story 218
Fact check 218
Clarity and conciseness 220
Detail 220

Common editing mistakes 225

Using journalistic style 226
Names and identification 226
Capitalization 227
Abbreviations 228
Numbers 229
Punctuation 229
Italics 232
Computer-related terms 232
Spelling 232
Screening sexist language 234
Problem words 236
Race, ethnicity and other terms of identity 236

Coaching writing continues 237

Conclusion 237

10 | Writing headlines 245

Headlines: the basics 246
Teaser and teller headlines 246
Getting the words to fit 246
News website headlines 248

The appearance of headlines 248

Writing a headline 250
Writing a teller 250
Headline construction rules 253

Feature headlines 255

Conclusion 258

11 | Typography and production 263

Type: the basics 264
Type terms 265
Categories of type 267

Choosing type 272
Factors to consider 272
Contrast and creativity 274
Consistency 277

Production and printing 281
Digital toning for printing 281
Printing 283

Conclusion 286

12 | Newspaper layout and design 291

The importance of design 292
Changes in news presentation 292
Elements of design 292
Information packaging 301
Grid and column considerations 301
Modular design 306
Preparing for design 306
Special considerations for design 310
Using color effectively 317

Pacing the newspaper's design 317

Conclusion 319

13 | Yearbook design 323

Speaking the language 324
Getting ready to design 327
Designing the pages 331
Special considerations 335
DVD and interactive coverage 341

The use of color 343

Conclusion 343

14 Online journalism 347

Creating web publications 348
Website hosting and privacy policies 350
Assembling a publication website 351
Creating online content 353
Multimedia content 354

Involving the readers 358

Enhanced yearbook content 360

Design of the website 361

Cooperative efforts 368

Conclusion 368

15 Visual storytelling: pictures, art and graphics 371

The importance of visuals 372

Photographs 374
Technical parameters 374
Content and composition 375

Telling stories through images 380
Picture packages or groups 380
Picture stories 381

Digital shooting 384
Lenses 384
Flash 386
Camera bodies 387

Captions and cutlines 387
Cropping photographs 389

Photo editing 389
Abuse of images 391
Photo alteration 396

Art and illustrations 396

Information graphics 400

Other graphic forms 400

Conclusion 401

16 Advertising in newspapers and yearbooks 405

Creating an advertising program 406
Preparation 406
Advertising policy 409
Business knowledge 411
Preparing for the sales call 411
The sales call 411
Telephone sales 414

Creating an advertisement 414
Define the message 414
Creating the advertisement, one step at a time 417
Some other considerations in ad design 418

Conclusion 421

17 Student press law 427

Who, what, where, when and how – and student press law 428
The law 428

The First Amendment 430
Unprotected speech 431

The Supreme Court and speech in school 436
Tinker 437
Fraser 438
Morse 438
Hazelwood 439
Post-Hazelwood cases 442

Conclusion 448

18 Ethics for student journalists 451

What is ethics? 452

Ethics, the law and the First Amendment 452

Media ethics 453
Newsgathering ethics 454
Publishing ethics 456
Post-publication ethics 457

Common ethical issues journalists face 458

Quotes 458

Anonymity and confidentiality 459

Conflicts of interests 460

Crimes, victims and the suspect 460

Photo integrity 461

Using someone else's photographs or artwork 461

Ethical lapses – gaffes, quandaries and journalistic felonies 461

Fabrication 462

Plagiarism 463

Lies, deception and undercover reporting 463

Stolen materials and unauthorized access 464

Identification of groups/stereotyping/sexist/racist/personal details 464

News vs. opinion 464

Obscenity, profanity and vulgarity 464

Web reporting 464

Journalism codes of ethics 467

Conclusion 467

19 | Careers in the media 471

Studying media in high school 472

After high school 474

After college 475

Advertising 475

Public relations 476

News organizations 476

Magazines 477

Multimedia photography 478

Wire services 480

Broadcasting 482

Freelancing 482

Other opportunities 482

Conclusion 483

Professional and student organizations 485

Glossary 488

Index 498

ABOUT THE AUTHORS

C. Dow Tate is a journalism teacher at Shawnee Mission East High School in Prairie Village, Kansas, and the director of the Gloria Shields All-American Publication Workshop sponsored by Dallas County Schools. In 2011, he was named a Kansas Teacher of the Year finalist. He was inducted into the Scholastic Journalism Hall of Fame at the University of Oklahoma and was named a Texas Legend, as one of the most influential people in the state's 75-year scholastic journalism history. His students' publications – the newspaper, yearbook and news website – have earned the nation's highest honors, including the National Scholastic Press Association's National Pacemaker and the Columbia Scholastic Press Association's Gold Crown. Tate has been named the Dow Jones Newspaper Fund's National High School Journalism Teacher of the Year as well as the Texas Max R. Haddick Teacher of the Year.

Sherri A. Taylor teaches graphic design in the Multimedia, Photography and Design Department of the S.I. Newhouse School of Public Communications at Syracuse University. She is also Director of the Empire State School Press Association at Syracuse University, and Director of the School Press Institute, a summer journalism workshop for high school students. As a high school teacher in Irving, Texas, she advised a state and national award-winning yearbook and newspaper. She has been inducted into the Scholastic Journalism Hall of Fame at the University of Oklahoma, was named a Pioneer from the National Scholastic Press Association and received a Gold Key from the Columbia Scholastic Press Association. She also received the Max R. Haddick Teacher of the Year award, and named a Texas Legend. She has judged the Society of News Design's international competition and judged the Katie Awards for the Dallas Press Club. She advises a magazine at Syracuse University, MPJ, which has won both Associated Collegiate Press Pacemakers and Society of Professional Journalists regional and national Best College Magazine awards.

Roy S. Gutterman (author of Chapters 17 and 18) is an associate professor of communications law and journalism and director of the Tully Center for Free Speech at the S.I. Newhouse School of Public Communications at Syracuse University. He started in journalism at *The Fanscotian*, the student newspaper for Scotch Plains – Fanwood High School in New Jersey, and went on to work as a reporter for the *Cleveland Plain Dealer*. He practiced law and writes and speaks on First Amendment and free speech and free press issues.

PREFACE

A GROUP OF FRIENDS CHATTER OUTSIDE the band hall. The phone buzzes heralding a new text. Sirens scream outside the chemistry lab windows. So what are they talking about? What does the text say? Where are the police going? These are the questions any student would have.

Students may not realize it, but their inborn curiosity is a huge asset. If they like to ask questions and get answers, they have a journalist's instincts. Their hands may not shoot up as often as they did in second grade, but we know that those questions still bounce around in their heads. Scholastic journalism provides an outlet, a forum that encourages students to explore and apply their natural curiosity.

This textbook builds on our desire to know what is going on in the world around us. Students will learn how to collect information through interviewing and research. They'll learn to communicate through text, design and photos. They'll learn to create stories that are relevant, accurate and important for their school, their classmates, their audience.

While we've seen numerous newspapers shut down in the last decade, we understand that journalism isn't dying, it's merely evolving. The range of media at our fingertips is constantly growing. In this tumultuous era of 24-hour news, enhanced by the opportunities of social and new media, the need for scholastic journalism training is also growing. The skills that young journalists learn – writing, designing, questioning, problem-solving, computing – are as valuable now as ever. Giving young people the skills to think for themselves will serve the generation and the public well.

Good journalism is alive in student journalism programs across the country. In the following pages you'll find a wide array of examples showcasing articulate, insightful and creative student writing, photojournalism and design in school websites, newsmagazines, newspapers and yearbooks. High school reporters across the country are tackling relevant stories that impact their classmates and communities. The school reporter can tell the story of the softball player with the stamina to battle through cancer, highlight a teacher's musical success on YouTube or enlighten an audience to the dangers of prescription drug abuse.

This textbook, the latest edition in the book's 60+ year history, embraces the changes that the Internet has brought to journalism. Students will learn the basics of journalism to be used in blogs or webcasts, online galleries and online posts.

This book is written for the 21st-century classroom. It's for the classroom filled with students who are constantly bombarded with texts, tweets and fast-moving information. And it's for the teachers who have to prepare those students to be competitive in an ever-changing marketplace. This edition has been revised to include more user-friendly features. The Test Your Knowledge questions and Quick Exercises break up the text into manageable chunks and offer readers the chance to check their comprehension and apply their new skills throughout each chapter. The weblinks provide quick references and resources for interactive and extended learning possibilities. An instructor's manual and wealth of supporting online resources to accompany the book can also be found at www.wiley.com/go/scholasticjournalism.

Whether the information comes through a mimeographed paper or a podcast, we will always have an interest in the life around us and there will always be a need for curious minds to inform, educate and entertain us. And beyond scholastic journalism, we believe the skills students learn from this textbook will benefit them – in journalism or in whatever career they pursue.

In the fast-changing world of technology and mass media, vibrant fresh ideas often come from the next generation. We encourage students to have the confidence to be creative visionaries. We believe this book will provide the foundation for strong scholastic journalists who can become active, thoughtful and responsible members of the media and society.

ACKNOWLEDGMENTS

WE'D LIKE TO THANK A long list of teachers, colleagues, friends and corporations who helped us in the preparation of the 10th, 11th and 12th editions. Their support, insight and help in providing permission to use material from their newspapers and yearbooks have been invaluable in producing this textbook.

Kathryn Abbruzzese-Browning, Bishop Snyder High School, Jacksonville, Fla.

Wasim Ahmad, School of Journalism, Stony Brook University, Stony Brook, N.Y.

Logan Aimone, National Scholastic Press Association

Martha Akers, Loudoun Valley High School, Purcellville, Va.

Genaro C. Armas, Associated Press, State College, Pa.

Dan Austin, Casa Roble High School, Orangevale, Calif.

Crissie Ballard, Anderson High School, Austin, Texas

Michelle Balmeo, Monta Vista High School, Cupertino, Calif.

Elizabeth M. Barberio, Wiley

Javonna Bass, Boyd High School, McKinney, Texas

Robert and Penny Belsher, Ferris, Texas

Sue Blackmon, Klein Forest High School, Houston, Texas

Jason Block, Prospect High School, Mount Prospect, Ill.

John Boogert, The Wichita Eagle, Wichita, Kan.

Wayne Brasler, University High School, Chicago, Ill.

Jen Bray, Wiley

Deanne Brown, Westlake High School, Austin, Texas

Reneè Burke, William R. Boone High School, Orlando, Fla.

Jennifer Buske-Sigal, (formerly) Washington Post, Washington, D.C.

Chaz Busuttil, Woodlands High School, Hartsdale, N.Y.

Robert Butler, Butler's Cinema Scene, http://butlerscinema-scene.com/. Kansas City, Mo.

Andy Cantrell, Findlay High School, Findlay, Ohio

Keith Carlson, Naperville High School, Naperville, Ill.

Erin Castellano, Clayton High School, Clayton, Mo.

Angela Cave, The Evangelist, Albany, N.Y.

Dave Cheng, St. Elizabeth Catholic High School, Thornhill, ON, Canada

William G. Connolly, The New York Times

Judi Coolidge, (formerly) Bay Village High School, Bay Village, Ohio; Balfour Yearbooks, Dallas, Texas

Ashlee Crane, Shawnee Mission Northwest High School, Shawnee, Kan.

Nicolet Danese, Monta Vista High School, Cupertino, Calif.

Brennan Davis, Irmo High School, Columbia, S.C., Ohio

Charles Davis, University of Missouri, Mo.

Mike Davis, One28 Media, Syracuse, N.Y. (formerly) The Oregonian, Portland and The Albuquerque Tribune, New Mexico

Lane DeGregory, St. Petersburg Times, St. Petersburg Fla.

John Dent, Dos Pueblos Senior High School, Goleta, Calif.

Steve Dorsey, (formerly) R + D, Detroit Media Partnership, Detroit, Mich.

Mary Kay Downes, Chantilly High School, Chantilly, Va.

Drake University, Des Moines, Iowa

Jennifer Dusenberry, Washington, D.C.

Mitch Eden, Kirkwood High School, Kirkwood, Mo.

Michelle Edwards, Montgomery Blair High School, Silver Spring, Md.

Patricia Fels, Sacramento Country Day School, Sacramento, Calif.

Cynthia Ferguson, Oxford High School, Oxford, Miss.

Brenda Field, Glenbrook South High School, Glenview, Ill.

Robert Flores, ESPN.com

Kriti Garg, Monta Vista High School, Cupertino, Calif.

Katherine Gazella, St. Petersburg Times, St. Petersburg, Fla.

Jon Glass, S.I.Newhouse School of Public Communications, Syracuse University, Syracuse, N.Y. (formerly) Palm Beach Post.com, Palm Beach, Fla.

Andrew Goble, Kansas City, Mo.

Anthony R. Golden, S.I. Newhouse School of Public Communications, Syracuse University, Syracuse, N.Y.

Sophie Gordon, Francis Howell North High School, St. Charles, Mo.

Karl Grabaugh, Granite Bay High School, Granite Bay, Calif.

Sue Grady, Hindsale Central High School, Hinsdale, Ill.

Mark Graney, Wiley

Kim Green, Columbus North High School, Columbus, Ind.

JiaYu Griegel, Seattle, Wash.

Charlotte Grimes, S.I. Newhouse School of Public Communications, Syracuse University, Syracuse, N.Y.

Kathy Habiger, Mill Valley High School, Shawnee, Kan.

LaJuana Hale, Marcus High School, Flower Mound, Texas

Sandy Hall-Chiles , Yavneh Academy, Dallas, Texas

Charla Harris, Pleasant Grove High School, Texarkana, Texas

Bobby Hawthorne, Austin, Texas

Susan Houseman, Conestoga High School, Berwyn, Pa.

Rod Howe, Westside High School, Omaha, Neb.

Dean Hume, Lakota East High School, Liberty Township, Ohio

Cynthia Hyatt, Conestoga High School, Berwyn, Pa.
Kim Isbell, Humboldt High School, Humboldt, Kan.
Paul Kandell, Palo Alto High School, Palo Alto, Calif.
Frances Johnson, Armed Forces Services Corporation
Jim Jordan, Del Campo High School, Fair Oaks, Calif.
Linda Kane, (formerly) Naperville Central High School,
    Naperville, Ill.
Joel Kaplan, S.I. Newhouse School of Public Communications,
    Syracuse University, Syracuse, N.Y.
Crystal Kazmierski, Arrowhead Christian Academy,
    Redlands, Calif.
Lori Keekley, St. Louis Park High School, St. Louis Park, Minn.
Marilyn Kelsey, Bloomington High School, Bloomington, Ind.
Jack Kennedy, (formerly) Iowa City High School, Iowa City, Iowa
Jason King, ESPN.com
David Kirkpatrick, MarketingSherpa
Jessica Klebanoff, Wiley
David Knight, Lancaster, S.C.
Nancy Kruh, Dallas Morning News, Dallas, Texas
Ian Lague, (formerly) Oakland, Calif.
Corey Lau, Orangevale, Calif.
Pete LeBlanc, Antelope High School, Antelope, Calif.
Frank LoMonte, Student Press Law Center
Gary Lundgren, Jostens Yearbooks, Minneapolis, Minn.
Leland Mallett, Legacy High School, Mansfield, Texas
Dan Mancoff, Riverside Brookfield High School, Riverside, Ill.
Aaron Manfull, Francis Howell North High School, St. Charles,
    Mo.
Jeanette Marantos, Wenatchee High School, Wenatchee, Wash.
Sharon Martin, Wichita East High School, Wichita, Kan.
Susan Massy, Shawnee Mission Northwest High School,
    Shawnee, Kan.
Stacy Mathew, Montgomery Blair High School, Silver Spring, Md.
Sharn Matusek, Lowell High School, San Francisco, Calif.
Chip Maury, (formerly) Indianapolis Star, Indianapolis, Ind.
Jeff Mays, DNAinfo.com, New York City, N.Y.
Tamra McCarthy, Enochs High School, Modesto, Calif.
Cindy McCurry-Ross, The News-Press Media Group, Fort
    Myers, Fla.
Mike McLean, McLean Photography, Dallas, Texas
Ellen McNamara, KSTP, Minneapolis, Minn.
Andrew Meachum, St. Petersburg Times, St. Petersburg, Fla.
Karishma Mehrotra, Monta Vista High School, Cupertino, Calif.
Barbara Meier, Episcopal School of Dallas, Dallas, Texas
Elizabeth Merrill, ESPN.com
John Moore, Getty Images, New York, N.Y.
Jessica Mugler, Francis Howell High School, St. Charles, Mo.
**My High School Journalism, American Society of
    Newspaper Editors**
Jeff Nardone, Grosse Pointe South High School, Grosse Pointe
    Farms, Mich.
National Press Photographers Association, Durham, N.C.
Libby Nelson, Washington, D.C.
Kathy Neumeyer, Harvard-Westlake School, Studio City, Calif.
Jairo Nevarez and Lee Perkins, The ReMarker, St. Mark's
    School of Texas, Dallas, Texas
The Newseum, Washington, D.C.
Mark Newton, Mountain Vista High School, Highlands Ranch,
    Colo.
Casey Nichols, Rocklin High School, Rocklin, Calif.
Sarah Nichols, Whitney High School, Rocklin, Calif.
Joye Oakley, Norman High School, Norman, Okla.
Lori Oglesbee, McKinney High School, McKinney, Texas

Jane Pak, Dallas, Texas
Gary Pankewicz, Hasbrouck Heights High School, Hasbrouck, N.J.
Sung Park, University of Oregon, Eugene, Ore.
Ann Peck, Cupertino High School Cupertino, Calif.
Cheryl M. Pell, School of Journalism, Michigan State University,
    East Lansing, Mich.
Jeremy Pelofsky, Reuters
Adam Penenberg, New York University, N.Y.
Meghan Percival, McLean High School, McLean, Va.
Joe Pfeiff, Mountain Ridge High School, Glendale, Ariz.
Pizza Hut, Inc., Dallas, Texas
Amy Poe, McLean High School, McLean, Va.
Betsy Pollard Rau, (formerly) H.H. Dow High School, Midland,
    Mich; School of Journalism, Central Michigan University, Mount
    Pleasant, Mich.
Jillian Porazzo, Wiley
Professor Ralph B. Potter, Jr., Harvard Divinity School, Mass.
Rebecca Potter, Texas High School, Texarkana, Texas
Mary Pulliam, (formerly) Duncanville High School, Duncanville,
    Texas
Louise Reynolds, Walt Whitman High School, Bethesda, Md.
Carol Richtsmeier, Midlothian High School, Midlothian, Texas
James Rogers, Slocum, Texas
Tom Rosenstiel, The Project for Excellence in Journalism
Darren A. Sanefski, The Meek School of Journalism and New
    Media, The University of Mississippi, Miss.
Rod Satterthwaite, The Squall, Dexter High School, Dexter, Mich.
Laura Schaub, Emerita, University of Oklahoma, Norman, Okla.
School Newspapers Online
Tracy Anne Sena, Convent of the Sacred Heart High School, San
    Francisco, Calif.
Tim Shedor, Overland Park, Kan.
Brian P. Shelton, Hebron High School, Carrollton, Texas
Elizabeth Slocum, Philadelphia Enquirer, Pa.
Kevin Z. Smith, Society of Professional Journalists
Mia Smith, Torrey Pines High School, San Diego, Calif.
Margaret Sorrows, Bryant High School, Bryant, Ark.
Howard Spanogle, Asheville, N.C.
Randy Stano, University of Miami, Coral Gables, Fla.
Bob Steele, The Janet Prindle Institute for Ethics at DePauw
    Universtiy, Ind.
Dot Stegman, (formerly) Kapaun Mt. Carmel High School,
    Wichita, Kan.
Greg Stobbe, Fresno Christian High School, Fresno, Calif.
Robin Stover, Rock Bridge High School, Columbia, Mo.
Lynn Strause, Herff Jones Yearbooks, East Lansing, Mich.
Jim Streisel, Carmel High School, Carmel, Ind.
Edmund Sullivan, Columbia Scholastic Press Association,
    New York, N.Y.
David Sutherland, S.I. Newhouse School of Public
    Communications, Syracuse University, Syracuse, N.Y.
Becky Tate, Shawnee Mission North High School, Overland Park,
    Kan.
Eric Thomas, St. Teresa's Academy, Kansas City, Mo.
Judy Thomas, Kansas City Star, Kansas City, Mo.
TLP Advertising, Dallas, Texas
Cindy Todd, Westlake High School, Austin, Texas
Lori Todd, Hillcrest High School, Dallas, Texas
Melissa Wantz, Foothill Technology High School, Ventura, Calif.
Professor Stephen J.A. Ward, University of Wisconsin, Wis.
Ashley Watkins, Kapaun Mt. Carmel High School, Wichita, Kan.
Chris Waugaman, Prince George High School,
    Prince George, Va.

Alan Weintraut, Annandale High School, Annandale, Va.

David Weisenburger, Gahanna Lincoln High School, Gahanna, Ohio

Ray Westbrook, St. Mark's School of Texas, Dallas, Texas

Leslie White, Dallas Morning News, Dallas, Texas

Jason Whitlock, Fox Sports News

Samuel Williams, Lowell High School, San Francisco, Calif.

Tony Willis, (formerly) Carmel High School, Carmel, Ind.

Brian Wilson, Waterford-Kettering High School, Waterford Township, Mich.

Scott Winter, Assistant Professor, College of Journalism and Mass Communications, University of Nebraska–Lincoln, Neb.

Esther Wojcicki, Palo Alto Senior High School, Palo Alto, Calif.

Doug Wonders, S.I. Newhouse School of Public Communications, Syracuse University, Syracuse, N.Y.

Mitch Ziegler, Redondo Union High School, Redondo Beach, Calif.

Tom (Thomas) E. Rolnicki (1949–2009) was an author of this textbook from the 8th edition through the 11th. Tom was the executive director of the National Scholastic Press Association and the Associated Collegiate Press for 26 years. During that time, he wrote many and edited all of the association's publications. A career educator, he taught at high schools, colleges and universities in Wisconsin, Iowa and Minnesota and spoke at journalism conferences, workshops and conventions throughout the United States and Canada and in other countries, including Croatia, South Korea, Germany, the Czech Republic, Finland and Slovenia. Rolnicki was honored with the Carl Towley and Medal of Merit awards from the Journalism Education Association and the Gold Key from the Columbia Scholastic Press Association.

WALK THROUGH

UNDERSTANDING NEWS | 1

> *News is what affects the greatest number of people with the greatest intensity. Telling my community the news lets me tell people what's likely to affect them and how much it will affect them. If people don't know something is happening and don't know how it will affect them, they can't do anything to change or stop what affects them. If people know something is likely to happen to them, then they have a choice of what do about it. The news and journalists give people choice about how to shape their lives, their neighborhood, their community, their world. The news allows people to change the bad and promote the good.*
>
> Charlotte Grimes, Knight Chair in Political Reporting, S.I. Newhouse School of Public Communications, Syracuse University

LEARNING OBJECTIVES After completing this chapter you will be able to:

- determine the core values that create interest in news
- understand the role of audience in making news decisions
- make informed decisions about covering and publishing news, in both print and online editions
- understand how using a beat system will help you cover your school in an organized way
- understand how to find the sources that will provide the best information for your stories
- provide coverage of your school's diverse populations.

Scholastic Journalism, Twelfth Edition. C. Dow Tate and Sherri A. Taylor.
© 2014 John Wiley & Sons, Inc. Published 2014 by John Wiley & Sons, Inc.

Chapter opening page

Each chapter begins with a thought-provoking and instructive quotation and a list of key learning objectives to help the reader navigate the text.

Timeline

The timeline traces the development of journalism and scholastic journalism in America and provides the reader with valuable historical context.

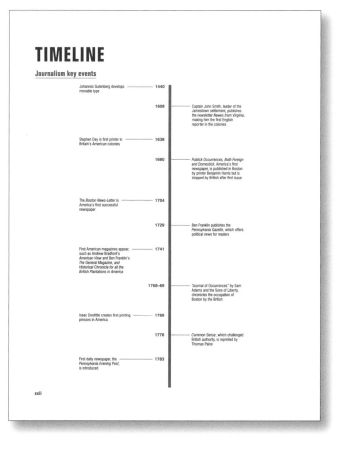

TIMELINE

Journalism key events

1440	Johannes Gutenberg develops movable type
1608	Captain John Smith, leader of the Jamestown settlement, publishes the newsletter *Newes from Virginia*, making him the first English reporter in the colonies
1638	Stephen Day is first printer in Britain's American colonies
1690	*Publick Occurrences, Both Foreign and Domestick*, America's first newspaper, is published in Boston by printer Benjamin Harris but is stopped by British after first issue
1704	*The Boston News-Letter* is America's first successful newspaper
1729	Ben Franklin publishes the *Pennsylvania Gazette*, which offers political news for readers
1741	First American magazines appear, such as Andrew Bradford's *American View* and Ben Franklin's *The General Magazine, and Historical Chronicle for all the British Plantations in America*
1768–69	"Journal of Occurrences" by Sam Adams and the Sons of Liberty, chronicles the occupation of Boston by the British
1769	Isaac Doolittle creates first printing presses in America
1776	*Common Sense*, which challenged British authority, is reprinted by Thomas Paine
1783	First daily newspaper, the *Pennsylvania Evening Post*, is introduced

xxii

Helpful tips

Helpful Tips boxes include useful checklists of dos and don'ts as well as a wealth of easy-to-apply guidelines and advice aimed at assisting students in making the transition from reading about scholastic journalism to practicing it.

CHAPTER 5 WRITING FEATURE STORIES   127

HELPFUL TIPS

Tips for writing successful human interest features

- Select only the details necessary to develop the story's dominant emotion or theme. Don't overload your story.
- Try to present your story in an original, clever way to hold reader interest.
- Consider writing to a particular reader, not just to anyone. This technique can help you develop a conversational tone.
- Avoid presenting your story in the form of a condensed summary, which will not let your reader become engaged with the material. A reader must become a witness to events if the story is to be successful. Do not say someone was angry, for example. Let us see the person in an actual scene.
- Follow the lead with concrete, specific details and examples.
- Try to include some dialogue if possible. The story becomes more personal because your readers will "hear" the persons involved.

Keen observation and intellectual curiosity will guide you toward many human interest stories. Keep an eye out for interesting little events, traditions, oddities and surprises as possible stories. No doubt there are a variety of minor incidents and situations in many of your classes that could be developed into good human interest stories that would amuse your paper's readers.

Look for possible story ideas in:

- any situation or incident that makes someone smile or laugh
- any situation or incident that arouses someone's sympathy
- any situation or incident that is unusual.

The human interest feature is not usually written in the inverted pyramid order. Many human interest stories use a narrative or chronological order or some combination of these.

In the following human interest feature, the author gives the reader a glimpse of the physical and mental struggles of dealing with a rare form of cancer. Look for the strong use of anecdotes about a fantasy novel and a grilled cheese sandwich, which the writer uses to give real and personal insights that are characteristic of a human interest piece.

She isn't attached to her hair. Never has been. She always considered herself kind of a tomboy, and she had worn it pageboy short early in life. So when senior Rachel Hoffman began to lose hers, she wasn't fazed.

"When it started coming out, I just thought it was so cool," Rachel said. "I remember going out to the nurse's station holding a lock of it and going, 'Look what happened; this is so cool!'"

But Rachel shouldn't be here to talk about it today. At age 12, she was diagnosed with myelodysplastic syndrome with monosomy 7, often referred to as pre-leukemia. Rachel's body was unable to make normal blood cells.

"The cancer cells in bone marrow take over everything," Dr. Jignesh Dalal, Director of Bone Marrow Transplant at Children's Mercy Hospital, said. "They don't allow normal blood cells to be made in bone marrow, and you need your blood cells to survive."

The prognosis wasn't good. Rachel didn't want to know what her chances of survival were, but her mother, Torie Clarke, wanted to hear it. She wanted to know what Rachel was up against.

Rachel had a 15 percent chance of making it past five years.

"She shouldn't be alive," Clarke said. "There's no reason – medically, clinically, logically – that she should be alive."

There might not be any explanation for her escape from death, but in life, Rachel Hoffman has always searched for the good in a bad situation.

[…]

Newsflash

Newsflash boxes throw a spotlight on specific aspects of scholastic journalism, allowing the reader to explore them in greater depth.

NEWSFLASH

CHAPTER 9 COACHING WRITERS AND EDITING COPY   219

Resources for copy editing

A good copy editor needs to have quick access to a wide range of resources, including:

- A current journalism stylebook, such as those published by the Associated Press or *New York Times*, as well as the student publication's more specific style sheet. Online subscriptions to major style guides can offer search features and reflect updates to the style.
- A dictionary and thesaurus, even if both are built into your wordprocessing program. An online subscription to the *Oxford English Dictionary* (at oed.com) will be useful. The text review within a wordprocessing program should be customized to reflect your publication's style sheet, frequently used names and other words common to high school events and topics.
- A school directory that lists all students, faculty and staff, so the reporter and editor can verify the spelling of

names and, for faculty and staff, titles. This information may be available electronically in some schools through the registrar or data clerk.
- Local business and residential telephone books (or access to online versions) to verify the spelling of names and to check addresses.
- An almanac and biographical dictionary, useful for verifying facts and the names and accomplishments of well-known persons who may be cited in stories.
- A grammar handbook with a quick reference section, helpful for both reporters and editors. The copy editor may want to prepare a list of the most common grammatical errors to post in the newsroom.
- Back issues of the school newspaper and recent school yearbooks and magazines, to verify information in story updates and for ongoing coverage.

- Check all figures and statistics, especially to see that parts add up to the right total and that all percentage breakdowns add up to 100 percent.
- Be especially careful of dates and times. Check every date, month and day with the calendar.

The copy editor should evaluate each story to make sure it provides the most important relevant information. If not, he should research the missing factual information or return the story to the reporter. The copy editor should not make a guess about any assertions of fact and should double-check all such assertions before changing them.

The copy editor should make sure the writer has cited the proper source for each piece of information. If a science teacher says three teachers are retiring, the copy editor should have the writer double-check this news by interviewing the principal.

Journalists should typically avoid encyclopedias, weekly newsmagazines, books and newspapers as sources for research. The writer should use these sources as background, then go straight to people for interviews.

For depth in the story, the copy editor should suggest the reporter consider these as possible sources:

- Students
- Student polls
- Teachers
- Parents
- Alumni
- District statistics
- Local doctors/psychologists
- Regional education administrations
- Municipal/county statistics
- Professional sources
- Building or local administrators
- Local college professors
- Teens at other schools

IN ACTION

Clarifying the news story focus

Most high school publications hold regular meetings, where the staff members' story ideas for upcoming editions are discussed. Such meetings often generate lists of story ideas, where possible pieces are sketched out and compiled for editors to comb through at a later date. In preparing for such a meeting, it is important to write out clearly focused story ideas, with specific details. Make sure that your ideas are more than just topics, such as "recycling" or "standardized testing." Make sure there are specifics in your story idea, preferably with a local angle. You should always ask yourself the following basic questions to decide if a story idea is feasible and sufficiently focused:

- Is something new, changed or different?
- Do we have solid and accurate sources for the news tip?
- Do we have verifiable facts from which to build the story?

Here are some examples of story ideas:

Poor: "School store. Heard it might be opening."

This is merely a topic without any development.

Better: "The school store is reopening next Friday. The store closed last year after losing a lot of money. The business teacher said the principal approved the reopening. The story should cover the entrepreneurial class plan to oversee cash flow and inventory to improve sales."

This story idea has a definite time peg – the reopening date. The reporter also has a reliable source in the business teacher. As a result, the story is more than rumor. It's the start of a plan for what to cover. A good specific list of sources might strengthen this story idea.

the administration cancel the first basketball game? Where is the monthly dance we usually have in the gym going to be held?

For a more political focus to the story, Selena might also ask: How much did the new flooring cost? How much will repairing the damage cost? Where's that money coming from? What part of the budget is going to be cut to pay for the damage?

The development of the story beyond the lead should answer these questions. The reader should learn something new with each successive paragraph. As shown in Figure 3.3, the remaining information will be presented in descending order of importance. A good reporter will weigh her collected information on the basis of audience impact and interest, and organize the story accordingly.

While a straight news lead on the story above would, like a tweet, highlight the flood damage to the new gym floor and note the source of this information, the next paragraphs should develop other issues, such as the possible cancelation of next week's basketball game. The discussion of the dance would probably come next. Why? Because these last two topics impact the teen audience directly and immediately.

The key to developing a news story is a writer's ability to think through all the relevant questions that need to be answered and to seek out legitimate sources to use and quote.

The sources within a story should all be qualified, relevant sources as discussed in Chapters 1 and 2. Writers should ask themselves: "Who is going to make an impact on this story?" or, "Who will the story make an impact upon?" In the gym flooding story, the original information comes from the assistant basketball coach. A more authoritative source for information on the gym floor and its consequences for the game might be the head basketball coach. The head custodian would be a relevant source for clean-up efforts. The principal might be able to address long-term plans for the gym and activities held there. The superintendent or district public relations representative might speak to the costs of the renovation and the repairs. To confirm such information, the district insurance company's representative could also be contacted. Basketball players impacted by the flooding would be relevant sources, as would Student Council officers who might have to change plans for the dance. Seniors looking forward to their last gym dance and displaced physical education students could add further perspectives.

News writers should avoid one-source stories. The saying is "there are two sides to every story," but the reality is there are many more, and reporters should try to draw on as many as possible.

In action

In Action boxes take the reader through the thought process of making key decisions and explore worked examples.

Words of wisdom

In *Words of Wisdom* boxes industry professionals and teachers share helpful secrets, tips and advice that will both instruct and inspire readers.

 **WORDS of WISDOM**

Whether you have five minutes to interview someone, or all the time in the world, it is important that you establish a connection with the person you are interviewing before you start rolling a camera or go on the record. If you go to the interviewee (which I prefer because you catch the subject in an environment that is comfortable) look for things like photos, school logos or anything that your interviewee has around them that is important to them. Ask the person about a few items and try to find something in common. The more you make a connection with the interviewee before you go on the record, the more open the person will be with you on the record.

Ellen McNamara, Anchor/Reporter, KSTP Minneapolis-St. Paul

Take notes, even when recording an interview. Voice recorders may fail or batteries run out. Taking notes can provide assurance to the subject that the reporter is engaging with the information and has a backup if the recorder doesn't work. An efficient reporter will also make use of the timer on the recorder or smartphone. She will make note of the times of good quotes, so that they can be easily located later on, when she is **transcribing** parts of the interview, typing them out word for word.

A good reporter will make sure to identify and write down the best direct quotes from the interview. A **direct quote**, or the exact words a person says, will be useful to recreate a real sense of the subject's experiences or insights. Direct quotes should always be accurate and enclosed in quotation marks. Each direct quote should include **attribution**, a phrase explaining who said it. Other answers from the interview may be important for the story but not so important that the information needs to be repeated word for word. In this case, reporters can **paraphrase**, or provide an **indirect quote**, by summarizing the information in their own words, without quotation marks, but still attributing it to the source. Journalists are often told to "paraphrase fact, quote opinion" when discussing direct and indirect quotes.

Examine the differences between the following two versions of a story about a student who lost both parents within the same year. In this section of the story, the girl describes the weeks leading up to her mom's death. What does the direct quote communicate that the indirect quote does not?

Direct quote

"We didn't know how much time she had when she first got sick so she made a point to tell [us daughters] we're not gonna fight about dumb things, we're not gonna go to bed angry, we're just gonna love each other," junior Maddie Cardell said. "I remember her telling me, 'You're gonna be happy, you're gonna be fun and we're gonna have a good relationship instead of fighting with each other and just love each other.'"

indirect quote or paraphrase

Junior Maddie Cardell said she didn't know how much time her mother had to live so they agreed not to fight or go to bed angry.

A good reporter will begin identifying good quotes as the interview proceeds. **Clichés**, or over-used phrases, can be left aside and vague language may be worth only a line or two on a reporter's notepad. Good quotes must be recorded accurately, since they may form the heart of the story.

In some cases, neutral reporting methods may offer more sensitive methods of topic coverage. For instance, rather than using anonymous, first-person accounts of student drug use or sexual activity, interviews with professionals may provide less controversial, though perhaps not as interesting, coverage. Student journalists must make sure they cover topics responsibly and appropriately for their audiences.

Many topics that can be covered in depth are far less controversial and serious. Schools continue to face the same difficulties as the community in general and community publications may provide a good source of inspiration. However, reporters should focus on the concerns of their specific readers as primary topics for in-depth coverage. Drawing on the beat system already in place on most publications staffs (see Chapter 1 for more information on covering beats), student journalists can keep an eye out for areas of concern. Assessing the local news value of each story is as important for in-depth coverage as it is for straight news reporting. Issues that affect urban schools may not affect suburban schools. Issues of concern to small schools may not affect larger schools.

School governing boards

The decisions made by the school board or the school's governing body affect every student at your school. Is the district considering a change in graduation requirements, a change in the length of the school day or year, requiring students to wear uniforms, allocating money for new facilities, debating whether to hold a bond election or a tax levy for a special project? All of these topics would be of concern to student readers. Someone from the student newspaper staff should attend all school board meetings, especially when policy changes are being discussed. Debate over major policy shifts starts well in advance of the actual change. Reporters carefully following these discussions will be on top of the issues before the decisions are made and can already be gathering relevant information.

Beyond the local school board, your state's educational governing body will also make decisions that affect your school. Many of these decisions are studied for months in advance. Monitoring the decision-making process will offer opportunities to share possible changes with readers and report their initial reactions. National educational trends and federal policies may also have an important impact on your school community.

When the school board began studying the importance of summer school in the context of budget cuts in the Clayton High School district, the *Globe* newspaper reported the changes that might be coming if the board adopted a plan. The story was reported in the winter, preparing students for the possibilities while the board's discussion was going on.

Athletics

Athletic programs in schools are rich areas for in-depth reporting. How does the athletic department monitor use of illegal substances such as growth hormones and steroids among athletes? Does the school have an athlete who is being heavily recruited by colleges or professional programs and is getting a lot of attention? Is the school restricting participation of athletes who suffer concussions? Who decides how much funding is provided for sports in the school, and is it equitable among major/minor sports and men's/women's sports? Do programs share equal facilities for equal amounts of time? Is the school or the state athletic governing body considering redistricting, which would change the scheduling of your teams and their opponents? Is there an honor code for athletes? Reporters should speak frequently to coaches and athletic directors in the school.

At Francis Howell North High School (FHN) in St. Charles, Missouri, the *North Star* newspaper and FHNtoday.com website reported in April 2012 on the district's plans to build new baseball and softball fields by fall of 2013. These fields were additions to its only facility, a turf stadium for football. Knowing the plans were in the works allowed the reporting.

Curricular areas

Maintaining contact with the heads of curricular programs, school department heads and others who make decisions about academics will enable student journalists to monitor changes in

WWW

WEBLINK Check out
www.investigatingpower.org

This site presents noteworthy coverage of topics from civil rights to Watergate in video interviews with some of the reporters who covered the stories. It also features interviews with reporters on topics of concern to investigative journalism.

WWW

WEBLINK Check out
www.nfhs.org

Students who cover sports can obtain significant information on high school sports governing bodies throughout the United States at this site. The site also includes information on state high school fine arts associations.

Weblinks

Weblinks direct the reader to online references and resources for interactive and extended learning possibilities.

Quick Exercise

For the following story, develop a source list with lines of questions for each source.

Two sixth-grade girls were suspended for three days after violating the new district-wide hugging ban. An assistant principal caught them hugging in the cafeteria. The girls had just found out they had placed first and second in a county-wide essay contest. One of the girls has two sisters in high school. You've heard from your friends that one of the sisters said her parents are seeking legal help in the case.

Each paragraph in a news story:

- should usually cover just one idea – news paragraphs are written for a busy reader who might skim and needs to pick up as much information as efficiently as possible
- should advance the story, giving the readers fresh information different from that of the previous paragraph
- should generally be one to three sentences, although exceptions are possible
- should be relevant to the overall focus of the story.

In the body of the following *Harbinger* story on the rise in cyberbullying, Shawnee Mission East's Andrew Goble gives an example of a Twitter site used to post anonymous comments. Within the first two paragraphs he helps the reader understand the reasoning of the Twitter account's creators. He also, by giving the number of posts and followers, shows how public and potentially-humiliating its posts can be.

Wilson started his account with a friend last fall. It posts "gossip" such as rumored party mishaps and potential parties; as of press time, it had posted 40 times and had 303 followers. When they started last fall, their goal was to just make people laugh.

"We thought it would be funny if no one knew who was writing it, just ridiculous events were reported on, in kind of a laughable manner," said Wilson. "Yeah, [getting tweeted about would] be embarrassing, but it's supposed to be like, 'Yeah, my antics were reported on.'"

News stories should provide objective development of the story. While the standard of **objectivity** is generally taken to mean that a writer shouldn't put his own opinion in a piece, it also means that writer should show both if not multiple sides to an issue. While some readers may agree with Wilson that the comments are just jokes, the writer also explores the perspective of those who object to the negative impact the tweets could have. Not everyone feels it is harmless. Sophomore Julie Sanders* was devastated when she was mentioned on a post on SMEGossipGurlz.

"I just remember not wanting to go to school," Sanders said. "It was like the first week of freshman year, so I didn't know anyone and I called [friend's name omitted to protect identity] crying, 'What am I going to do?' You feel like everyone is staring at you … you feel like the whole school is talking about you."

News sources need to be relevant to the focus. They should generally be identified by first and last name with some explanation as to why they are relevant. In the previous example, the writer decided to change the names of the sources and mark them with asterisks to protect their identity. Anonymous sources should be the exception rather than the norm because concealing

---

* denotes name changed to protect identity.

Quick exercise

Quick Exercise boxes appear throughout each chapter and give students the chance to apply their knowledge through short individual and group projects.

Test your knowledge

Test Your Knowledge questions provide readers with the opportunity to check their comprehension of the material they've just encountered.

- School organizations or clubs
- Book authors
- Advocacy organizations, such as Mothers Against Drunk Driving or the National Rifle Association.

Clarity and conciseness

Once the copy has been corrected for reporting errors, the copy editor should ensure that each sentence and paragraph is clear, direct and well-organized. If the copy editor thinks to herself, "Huh? I don't get that" or "Wait, I need to reread that sentence," the writing probably isn't clear. If she finds herself thinking, "I really want to stop reading now," then the writing probably lacks concision. More than likely, the writer needs help reorganizing paragraphs or recasting sentences.

Both experienced and novice copy editors can use the following list of tasks to guide their work:

- If any paragraphs need to be rearranged, do so.
- If paragraphs are repetitive, combine them or delete one.
- If paragraphs are too long, divide them.
- If the copy has long lists of names, put them into a sidebar or replace them by summarizing the contents.
- Emphasize an important idea by placing it at the beginning of a sentence or paragraph.
- Tighten the writing by eliminating unnecessary words, phrases and clauses and by combining related expressions.
- Simplify complicated sentences.
- Energize sentences by changing passive voice verbs to active voice. Occasionally, the passive voice may be desirable. In the following sentence an active-voice verb is better.

  The Wampus Cats played a strong defensive game. (*Not:* A strong defensive game was played by the Wampus Cats.)

  In the next sentence a passive-voice verb is better because it features the subject.

  Tom Lynch was reelected Student Council president. (*Not:* The student body reelected Tom Lynch Student Council president.)

Test your knowledge

List three types of sources, in addition to students and teachers, that a copy editor could suggest reporters draw on for a story.

- Eliminate trite expressions.
- Strive for sentence variety.
- Improve diction by using specific and precise words: *quibble* is different from *argue* or *debate*; *nice* is general for *affable, kind, pleasant* or *desirable*; *candid* is a synonym for *frank, impartial, open, sincere, straightforward, truthful* and *unprejudiced*, but with its own special meaning; *tree* is general, while *pine, oak* and *elm* are specific.
- Eliminate editorial commentary unless the story is a column, an editorial or a review.

Detail

While a copy editor may correct spelling, style and grammar mistakes along the way, the possibility is always there that errors will be introduced in the copy editing process itself. A final careful review of the story is essential. The credibility of the writer and the publication depend on it. The reader who sees three spelling errors in one paragraph will doubt the accuracy of the reporting in the rest of the story.

Key terms and glossary

Key terms are introduced in bold and clearly defined both in the text and in a complete Glossary at the end of the book.

GLOSSARY

Academics section the part of the yearbook covering classroom and learning activities both at school and outside of school

Actual malice legal term of art which means libel was published either with known falsity or reckless disregard for the truth

Advance story announcement-type story for coming event

Advertising director the staff member chosen to lead the advertising program; person who collects and organizes advertising information for salespeople to arm and train salespeople

Advertising policy a written policy that details the publication's guidelines concerning ad sales and use in the publications

Advocacy editorial editorial that interprets, explains or persuades

Agate type the smallest point size in type a publication uses; traditionally used for sports scores and classified ads

Air white space ("fresh air") around type and illustrations

Align instruction to bring type into straight line

Alignment bringing lines of type or design elements into common starting and/or ending points

Alley see **internal margin**.

Alternative copy space use of a different form of content, often visual or presented in a different form from a traditional prose story

Ampersand symbol for *and* (&)

Anchorperson principal person in charge of newscast

Anecdote interesting short stories that help bring an experience to life

Angle point of view from which something is written

Anonymous source source whose name is changed or omitted in a story to protect the source from harm or because the story's subject is sensitive or controversial

Aperture the size of the opening on a camera lens

Apology type of correction published in cases of extreme or outrageous behavior or mistakes

Art illustration(s) to accompany stories or ads

Art head specially designed headline that may break away from consistent typefaces or styles used in the rest of the publication

Ascender stem or loop that extends above x-height of letters; includes the letters *b, d, f, h, k, l* and *t*

Assignment book (sheet) record of reporters' assignments kept by editor

Associated Press cooperative wire news service owned by its member newspapers and radio and television stations. See **wire service**.

Attribution a statement fixing the source of information in a story

Audience the people who read, view or consume the news

Auto leading computer setting that adds a percentage of the point size of the active typeface to the space between lines

Backgrounding the process of reading and doing research in preparation for asking questions and interviewing sources for a story

Balance in writing, refers to facts in stories being given proper emphasis, putting each fact into its proper relationship to every other fact and establishing its relative importance to the main idea or focus of the story; in design, refers to the weight of the page appearing even

Banner (streamer) one-line head that extends across top of page

Bar thick rule used for decoration or to reverse a line of text

Baseline the imaginary line upon which all type letters sit

Beat (run) reporter's specified area for regular news coverage; scoop or story obtained before other media can print or air it

Beat system a plan to cover routinely all potential news sources in a specific area

Big on the body typefaces with large x-height proportions to capital letters

Biweekly publication that appears once every two weeks, as distinguished from semiweekly (twice a week)

Black letter type commonly known as Old English typefaces, these types are of Germanic origin and are used primarily in newspaper nameplates or flags

Bleed illustrations and type extended beyond regular page margins to outside page edges

Blog online commentary, usually dealing with a specific area of knowledge and appearing on a regular basis

Blur in a photograph, indicates movement by the photographer during the exposure

Body copy the text that verbally tells the story on the page

Body type type used for main text, as distinguished from headlines; generally between 9 and 12 picas in height

Boldface (bf) heavier, blacker version of type style

Book in magazine terminology may mean magazine (as in "back of the book")

Border line or frame that surrounds element in design

Bounce flash diffused flash softened by aiming the direction of the flash at a low, light ceiling or wall and allowing the flash to shower the subject with light

Breaking news coverage of an event as it is actually happening

Broadsheet full-size newspaper, often measuring 14×21 inches

Budget list of content for newshole (non-advertising space) of newspaper

Bullet visual or typographic device, usually at beginning of paragraphs or before items in list

Burning in a traditional darkroom or through computer imaging software, adding tone to an area of a print that would print without detail

Byline author's credit printed with the story

Scholastic Journalism, Twelfth Edition. C. Dow Tate and Sherri A. Taylor.
© 2014 John Wiley & Sons, Inc. Published 2014 by John Wiley & Sons, Inc.

Figures

Vibrant images showcase excellent examples of creative student writing, photojournalism and design in school websites, newsmagazines, newspapers and yearbooks.

Exercises

End-of-chapter exercises provide students with assignments and projects that can be done in class or at home, and which offer an opportunity to apply their knowledge in practical and creative ways.

TIMELINE

Journalism key events

Johannes Gutenberg develops movable type —— **1440**

1608 —— Captain John Smith, leader of the Jamestown settlement, publishes the newsletter *Newes from Virginia*, making him the first English reporter in the colonies

Stephen Day is first printer in Britain's American colonies —— **1638**

1690 —— *Publick Occurrences, Both Foreign and Domestick*, America's first newspaper, is published in Boston by printer Benjamin Harris but is stopped by British after first issue

The *Boston News-Letter* is America's first successful newspaper —— **1704**

1729 —— Ben Franklin publishes the *Pennsylvania Gazette*, which offers political news for readers

First American magazines appear, such as Andrew Bradford's *American View* and Ben Franklin's *The General Magazine, and Historical Chronicle for all the British Plantations in America* —— **1741**

1768–69 —— "Journal of Occurrences" by Sam Adams and the Sons of Liberty, chronicles the occupation of Boston by the British

Isaac Doolittle creates first printing presses in America —— **1769**

1776 —— *Common Sense*, which challenged British authority, is reprinted by Thomas Paine

First daily newspaper, the *Pennsylvania Evening Post*, is introduced —— **1783**

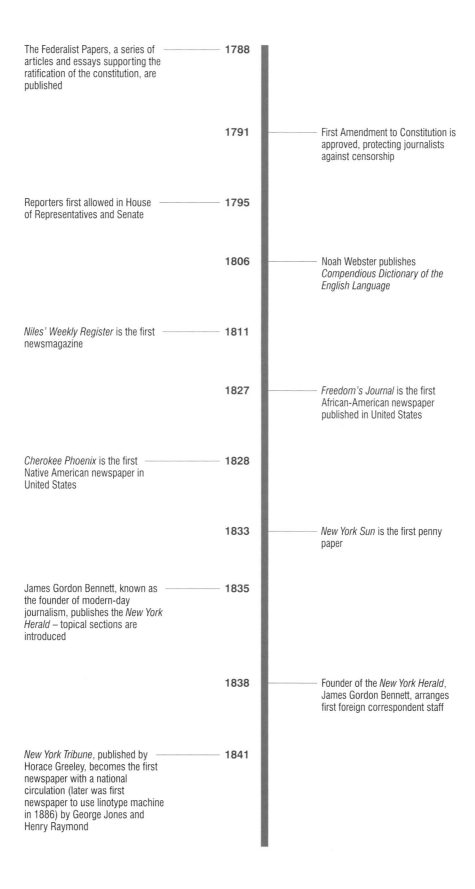

The Federalist Papers, a series of articles and essays supporting the ratification of the constitution, are published —— **1788**

1791 —— First Amendment to Constitution is approved, protecting journalists against censorship

Reporters first allowed in House of Representatives and Senate —— **1795**

1806 —— Noah Webster publishes *Compendious Dictionary of the English Language*

Niles' Weekly Register is the first newsmagazine —— **1811**

1827 —— *Freedom's Journal* is the first African-American newspaper published in United States

Cherokee Phoenix is the first Native American newspaper in United States —— **1828**

1833 —— *New York Sun* is the first penny paper

James Gordon Bennett, known as the founder of modern-day journalism, publishes the *New York Herald* – topical sections are introduced —— **1835**

1838 —— Founder of the *New York Herald*, James Gordon Bennett, arranges first foreign correspondent staff

New York Tribune, published by Horace Greeley, becomes the first newspaper with a national circulation (later was first newspaper to use linotype machine in 1886) by George Jones and Henry Raymond —— **1841**

Groups of newspapers come together to create news-gathering service to supply foreign news by ship and telegraph (what would become AP, Associated Press) —— **1849**

1851 —— *The New York Times* is founded, best known for its high-quality writing

Associated Press receives first cable transmission of European news through transatlantic cable —— **1858**

1870–1900 —— Number of daily newspapers quadruples while the US population doubles; introduction of telephone and typewriters change the newsroom; cables linking United States to the UK and Asia increase speed of news; photographs start appearing in newspapers

The Daily Graphic publishes first halftone (not engraved) reproduction of news photograph —— **1880**

1890s —— Circulation battles between Joseph Pulitzer's *New York World* and William Randolph Hearst's *New York Journal* lead critics to coin the expression "yellow journalism" and accuse both of sensationalizing, exaggerating, even faking news in order to drive up circulation

The Linotype typesetting machine, which can produce an entire line of metal type and therefore increases the speed of typesetting and composition, revolutionizes newspaper publishing —— **1890**

1893 —— Color is introduced for comics and other sections in Sunday editions

1898 —— Spanish–American War is the first conflict in which military involvement is embellished by the media specifically for the purpose of selling more newspapers than the competition

President Theodore Roosevelt coins the phrase "muckraker" to describe investigative journalists who fueled the progressive era crusades ——— **1900s**

Political cartoons become popular ——— **1900**

——— *The Nation*, a newsmagazine founded in 1865, becomes a current affairs magazine with a liberal slant

1905 ——— *The Chicago Defender*, founded by Robert S. Abbott, is one of largest African-American newspapers

United Press Association and international news service compete with Associated Press ——— **1907–9**

1910 ——— The first newsreels, shown in theatres before the main feature, begin to appear

Jazz Journalism tabloids are popular, covering topics such as Hollywood, money and violence and featuring more photography than writing. Two examples are Joseph Patterson's *New York Daily News* and William Hearst's *New York Daily Mirror* ——— **1920s**

1920 ——— Station 8MK broadcasts first radio news program in Detroit, Michigan and radios now used in the home. Radio competes with newspapers and magazines

Time magazine, the first weekly newsmagazine, is published by Henry Luce ——— **1923**

1925 ——— The 35mm Leica camera is developed (contributing to photojournalism) and documentary photography becomes popular way to disseminate the news

National Broadcasting Company, formed *by RC*, has first broadcast ——— **1926**

1927–30 ——— First flash bulbs used (ultimately contributing to photojournalism)

Gossip columns first appear in papers; the use of a new printing method, offset lithography, replaces letterpress printing making production faster and cheaper; the emergence of photography technology makes photography a dominant force in yearbooks, replacing art and illustrations; the era of photojournalism begins ——— **1930s**

Fortune magazine, which focuses on business and economy, is started by Henry Luce ———— **1930**

1936 ———— *Life* magazine is launched by Henry Luce. The magazine really begins the genre of photojournalism

American broadcast journalist ———— **1938** Edward R. Murrow starts to broadcast reports of war in Europe; WWII would become first war to be broadcasted daily to U.S. audience

1940 ———— May 19, Prime Minister Winston Churchill delivers his "Be Ye Men of Valour" wartime speech over British Broadcasting Company radio

On Feb. 23, President ———— **1942** Franklin D. Roosevelt used a radio broadcast to give details on the progress of the war – his 20th "Fireside Chat"

1950 ———— Most people watch television for news (taking over from the radio and newspapers, especially in terms of advertising)

Sept. 26, the first televised ———— **1960** presidential debate takes place between John F. Kennedy and Richard M. Nixon, reaching 70 million American viewers

1970s ———— Niche magazines become popular; yearbooks try experiments with everything from multiple volumes in a slip cover to the use of spot color; copy is more seriously written

Computers change newspaper ———— **1970s–1980s** production (newspapers are going from mechanical to computer production systems), which evolves new media

Hunter S. Thompson writes first ———— **1970** article categorized as Gonzo journalism – a form written without objectivity, favoring style over the facts, often as first-person narrative, making heavy use of sarcasm and humor

1970 ———— An Associated Press bureau in Columbia, South Carolina sends news copy to Atlanta, Georgia – the first reported use of a computer terminal, and transmitting a story to a news room

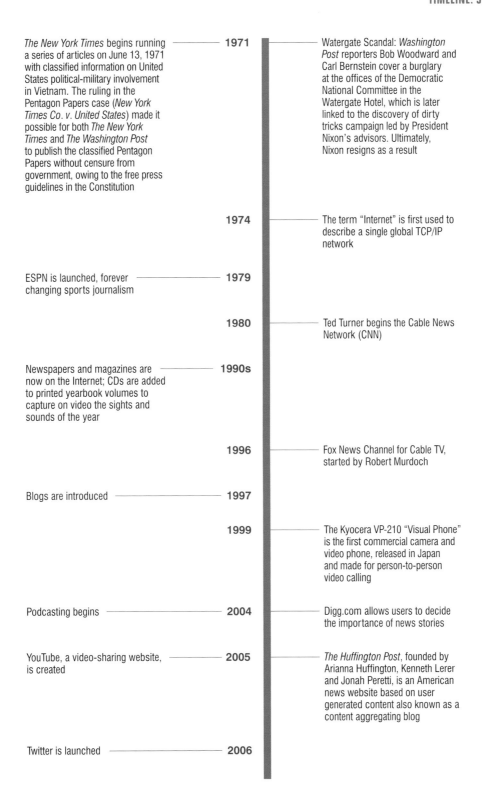

1971 — *The New York Times* begins running a series of articles on June 13, 1971 with classified information on United States political-military involvement in Vietnam. The ruling in the Pentagon Papers case (*New York Times Co. v. United States*) made it possible for both *The New York Times* and *The Washington Post* to publish the classified Pentagon Papers without censure from government, owing to the free press guidelines in the Constitution

Watergate Scandal: *Washington Post* reporters Bob Woodward and Carl Bernstein cover a burglary at the offices of the Democratic National Committee in the Watergate Hotel, which is later linked to the discovery of dirty tricks campaign led by President Nixon's advisors. Ultimately, Nixon resigns as a result

1974 — The term "Internet" is first used to describe a single global TCP/IP network

ESPN is launched, forever changing sports journalism — **1979**

1980 — Ted Turner begins the Cable News Network (CNN)

Newspapers and magazines are now on the Internet; CDs are added to printed yearbook volumes to capture on video the sights and sounds of the year — **1990s**

1996 — Fox News Channel for Cable TV, started by Robert Murdoch

Blogs are introduced — **1997**

1999 — The Kyocera VP-210 "Visual Phone" is the first commercial camera and video phone, released in Japan and made for person-to-person video calling

Podcasting begins — **2004** — Digg.com allows users to decide the importance of news stories

YouTube, a video-sharing website, is created — **2005** — *The Huffington Post*, founded by Arianna Huffington, Kenneth Lerer and Jonah Peretti, is an American news website based on user generated content also known as a content aggregating blog

Twitter is launched — **2006**

SOURCES

http://www.wnylrc.org/documentView.asp?docid=138
http://ehub.journalism.ku.edu/history/1900/1900.html
http://www.poynter.org/latest-news/business-news/transformation-tracker/28803/new-media-timeline-1969–2010/
http://www.uncp.edu/home/acurtis/Courses/ResourcesForCourses/JournalismHistory.html

http://www.animatedatlas.com/timeline.html
http://www.j4ip.org/J4IP/pg003.html
http://www.si.edu/Encyclopedia_SI/nmah/timeline.htm
http://www.class.uidaho.edu/jamm445hart/Timeline.htm
http://library.thinkquest.org/27629/themes/media/mdtimeline.html

Major historical events

Declaration of Independence is adopted and signed by Congress —— **1776**

1783 —— The Paris Peace Treaty ends Revolutionary War

The Constitution is ratified —— **1787, 1788**

1793 —— Eli Whitney patents the cotton gin

Alien and Sedition Acts (four separate bills) are passed by the Federalists, in order to prevent any enemy aliens and to protect from any seditious attacks against the government. More specifically, the Sedition Act makes publishing false writings against government officials a crime —— **1798**

1837 —— Samuel F.B. Morse invents the telegraph, transforming the way people communicate

Railroads and steamships increase distribution of newspapers; telegraph used as well —— **1840s**

1844 —— America's first telegraph line is used to send a message from Washington D.C. to Baltimore

Photoengraving developed, which allowed photos in newspapers —— **1860s/1870s**

1861–65 —— American Civil War: disseminating news becomes essential

Photographers receive passes to cover war, reporters now in the field and headlines of war action. Matthew Brady, a pioneering photographer, documented the war with photography and is known to have taken 3,500 pictures of the war

Reporters could use the telegraph to send stories from the battlefields —— **1861**

Emancipation Proclamation is issued Jan. 1 —— **1863** —— On Nov. 19, President Abraham Lincoln gives the Gettysburg Address

The first commercially successful ——— **1867**
typewriter is invented by C. Latham
Sholes, Carols Glidden and Samuel
W. Soule in Wisconsin

1876 ——— First telephone call is made
between Alexander Graham Bell
and his assistant, Thomas A.
Watson

Communication goes international ——— **1901**
when Guglielmo Marconi sends the
first radio transmission across the
Atlantic Ocean

1903 ——— On Dec. 17, the Wright Brothers fly
the first successful airplane

Thomas Edison invents electric ——— **1908**
light

1912 ——— Passenger liner *Titanic* sinks,
leading to The Radio Act of 1912,
mandating all radio stations in the
United States to be licensed by the
federal government

World War I: ——— **1914–18**

Created need for more print war
correspondents. Richard Harding
Davis was first American war
correspondent to cover the
Spanish–American War, the
Second Boer War and World War I.
Floyd Gibbons was a war
correspondent for the *Chicago
Tribune* during World War I

Propaganda used to influence
American opinion about the war

1917–18 ——— Government censors newspapers

World War I is ended with signing ——— **1919**
of the Treaty of Versailles

1920–33 ——— Prohibition

1929 The stock market crashes on Oct. 24, 1929, initiating the Great Depression

1932 Franklin D. becomes President

1937 The crash of the German passenger airship, *Hindenberg*, is first major catastrophe covered by on-the-spot broadcast reporting

1939–45 World War II:

Life magazine is significant in reporting on news of World War II

1941 On Dec. 7, the Japanese attacked Pearl Harbor

The following day, Roosevelt declares war on Japan on the radio to inform the American population

1944 D-Day, The Normandy Invasion

1945 The Cold War begins

1948 Regular commercial network television programming begins in United States

1950s Communication system created that will become Internet when the USSR's launch of Sputnik makes the United States create the Advanced Research Projects

Agency to surpass the USSR in technological advances; Jostens, a school product company, creates the American Yearbook Company division to produce yearbooks

1963 On Aug. 28, Martin Luther King, Jr. delivers his "I Have a Dream" speech during the Civil Rights Movement

Assassination of President John F. Kennedy

1964 The Civil Rights Act

1969 Neil Armstrong is first person to set foot on moon

This is the most watched event in history at that time

Americans Stephen P. Jobs and ——— **1977**
Stephen G. Wozniak founded the
Apple Computer Co

1988 ——— Internet is available for
commercial use

Tim Berners-Lee implements the ——— **1989**
first successful communication
between a Hypertext Transfer
Protocol (HTTP) client and server
via the Internet – the World Wide
Web is born

1990–91 ——— Iraq invades Kuwait, and Gulf War
ensues

The first World Wide Web browser ——— **1993**
is released and is called Mosaic

1994 ——— World Wide Web is public

O.J. Simpson is acquitted of two ——— **1995**
charges of first degree murder,
ending a widely publicized
nine-month trial

1998 ——— Google is started

The US prepares for the predicted ——— **1999**
consequences of the Y2K bug in
computers

2001 ——— 9/11 Terrorist Attacks, four
coordinated attacks on the United
States by al-Qaeda

Facebook, social networking ——— **2004**
platform, is launched

2005 ——— Hurricane Katrina becomes the
most costly natural disaster in
United States history

Barack Obama becomes the first ——— **2009**
African-American President of the
United States

2010 ——— The Deepwater Horizon oil rig in
the Gulf of Mexico explodes – the
worst oil spill in American history

Scholastic journalism events

First handwritten school publication, ——— **1777**
The Student Gazette, is produced
by the students of Friends Latin
School (now William Penn Charter
School), Philadelphia, Pa

1806 ——— Yale University becomes the first
college to publish a yearbook

The Evergreen at Waterville ——— **1845**
Academy in New York publishes
what is credited as the first high
school yearbook

1846 ——— Hopkins Grammar School in New
Haven, Connecticut publishes a
yearbook

Section organization and the use of ——— **1926**
division pages begin to emerge in
yearbooks including athletics,
organizations, features, humor and
ads; other schools choose to
organize by season

1939 ——— Taylor Publishing Company (now
Balfour), creates a company that
could deal with all aspects of
yearbook publishing in one facility
in Dallas, Texas

Yearbook production classes ——— **1940s**
began to be integrated into English
or journalism classes

1960s ——— Yearbooks reflect the revolution
sweeping the nation; summer
supplements added to printed
books often delivered in the
summer; design heavily influenced
by *Life* and *Look* magazines,
two dominant publications of
the time

New York Times v. Sullivan case ——— **1964**
initiates an actual malice standard
which must be met before reports
about public officials can be
considered libel or defamation;
ultimately supports freedom of
the press

In *Tinker v. Des Moines Independent School District*, the Supreme Court holds that a school district violated three students' First Amendment rights after they were suspended for wearing black armbands to school in protest of the Vietnam War ——— **1969**

1973 ——— In *Miller v. California*, the Supreme Court establishes a three-part test that, when passed, deems graphically sexual content obscene

The Student Press Law Center, an ——— **1974** advocacy group for student press rights and against censorship, is founded

California Student Free Expression ——— **1977** Law is passed

1977 Washington State enacts Washington Administrative Code: Student Rights; grants students freedom of speech and the press as well as the right to assemble peaceably

Supreme Court ruled in *Smith v. Daily Mail* that reporters who ——— **1979** lawfully obtained and truthfully reported the identification of a teenage murder suspect would be legally permitted to publish the juvenile's name

1980s The computer age revolutionizes the yearbook through desktop publishing on Apple computers using PageMaker software; summer yearbook workshops draw thousands of students to get a head start on the school year by studying trends

The *Ollman v. Evans* court case ——— **1984** establishes a four-point test for determining whether a statement is an assertion of fact or the speaker's opinion; ultimately protects opinion and editorial content

1984 In *Bethel School District No. 403 v. Fraser*, the Supreme Court rules it is well within the authority of a school to determine the appropriateness of speech within classes and school assemblies

On Oct. 4, the first National ——— **1987** Yearbook Week is officially created by a joint resolution of both houses of Congress

1988

The Supreme Court, in the landmark case *Hazelwood School District v. Kuhlmeier*, rules that a school district may censor a student newspaper for a variety of reasons; ultimately becomes the standard for future cases

Massachusetts Student Free Expression Law is passed

1989

In *Romano v. Harrington*, the court ruled that extracurricular student journalism does not fall under a school district's authority

Iowa Student Free Expression Law is passed

1990

Colorado Student Free Expression Law is passed

1991

Planned Parenthood of Southern Nevada v. Clark County School District ruling defends a school district's authority to exercise control over advertising in school publications

Masson v. New Yorker Magazine case reaffirms the legal significance of quotation marks; allows journalists to alter words inside quotation marks to fix grammar, syntax or spelling

1992

Kansas Student Publications Law is passed

1994

In *Desilets v. Clearview Regional Board of Education*, the New Jersey Supreme Court holds that censoring a student's reviews of two R-rated movies violated the student's First Amendment rights

1995

Arkansas Publications Act is passed

2000s

Yearbooks become full-color volumes produced digitally and submitted to publishing companies electronically; senior ads replace community ads; DVDs replace CDs

2003

Ruling in *Draudt v. Wooster City School District* case greatly expands the legitimate pedagogical standard

2004

In *Dean v. Utica Community Schools*, the Supreme Court applies the principles established in *Hazelwood* to rule against censorship of student journalism when motivated solely by a "difference of opinion with its content"

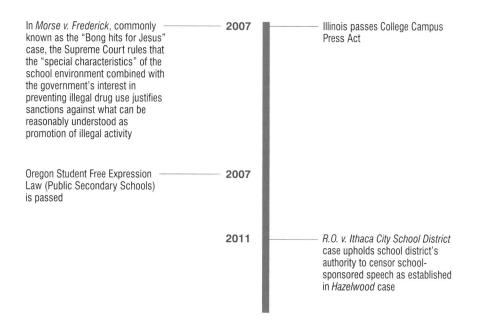

In *Morse v. Frederick*, commonly ———— **2007** ———— Illinois passes College Campus
known as the "Bong hits for Jesus" Press Act
case, the Supreme Court rules that
the "special characteristics" of the
school environment combined with
the government's interest in
preventing illegal drug use justifies
sanctions against what can be
reasonably understood as
promotion of illegal activity

Oregon Student Free Expression ———— **2007**
Law (Public Secondary Schools)
is passed

2011 ———— *R.O. v. Ithaca City School District*
case upholds school district's
authority to censor school-
sponsored speech as established
in *Hazelwood* case

SOURCES

John Cutsinger, Mark Herron, Mary Saracino (eds), *History Worth Repeating: A Chronology of School Yearbooks* (Jostens, 1996).

Mary Arnold and Beth Duffy, "Is the High School Yearbook Tomorrow's Dinosaur? A National, Historical Overview and an Iowa Survey," Paper presented at the 74th Annual Meeting of the Association for Education in Journalism and Mass Communication (Boston, Mass., Aug. 7–11, 1991).

UNDERSTANDING NEWS

1

> *News is what affects the greatest number of people with the greatest intensity. Telling my community the news lets me tell people what's likely to affect them and how much it will affect them. If people don't know something is happening and don't know how it will affect them, they can't do anything to change or stop what affects them. If people know something is likely to happen to them, then they have a choice of what do about it. The news and journalists give people choice about how to shape their lives, their neighborhood, their community, their world. The news allows people to change the bad and promote the good.*

Charlotte Grimes, Knight Chair in Political Reporting, S.I. Newhouse School of Public Communications, Syracuse University

LEARNING OBJECTIVES After completing this chapter you will be able to:

- determine the core values that create interest in news

- understand the role of audience in making news decisions

- make informed decisions about covering and publishing news, in both print and online editions

- understand how using a beat system will help you cover your school in an organized way

- understand how to find the sources that will provide the best information for your stories

- provide coverage of your school's diverse populations.

Scholastic Journalism, Twelfth Edition. C. Dow Tate and Sherri A. Taylor.
© 2014 John Wiley & Sons, Inc. Published 2014 by John Wiley & Sons, Inc.

Test your knowledge

Can you think of a topic of conversation you've had with friends recently or heard classmates discussing that could result in a story on your website or in the newspaper?

YOU'RE WALKING DOWN THE HALL in your high school and you overhear a conversation among several members of the student debate team. It turns out that the principal has canceled an upcoming debate trip because of district budget cuts. The students are dismayed and disappointed. They have spent months practicing and strategizing for this yearly trip to the state debate tournament. They don't understand how this last-minute cancelation could have happened and they didn't see it coming.

As this example makes clear, news is all around you. Sometimes you hear it in idle classroom conversations, sometimes in the cafeteria or the hallways. Or you might read about a pressing issue being discussed on a social networking site such as Facebook or Twitter. Sometimes you may not realize that a casual conversation could be the beginning of a story with far-reaching implications. If your friends are talking about it, it may be news.

For instance, if your friends are complaining about not having access to parking in the school lot despite paying a parking fee, or about having to pay a new fee to participate in clubs and sports or about not having enough time to eat after lunch periods are cut by five minutes – in each case, you're hearing potential news. All of these topics appeared as news stories in high school newspapers. As a reporter, you're empowered to report and write these stories. You'll provide the context and perspective for these news items, providing the answers to basic questions that your friends can't access. You can interview the people who made the decisions and provide factual information to sort out the gossip and rumor that surround any controversial issue.

The school newspaper and its website can give you a chance to impart important information to the school community, and to help find constructive solutions to difficult problems. High school journalists are trained to gather information, interview the relevant sources and to provide credible, timely stories about the news that matters most to their school communities.

Though high school newspapers usually publish less frequently than municipal or national papers, most still have an opportunity to publish timely news. This means that the newspaper staff must be alert to time-sensitive information and be ready to provide context or other supplemental features if an event occurs a week or two before the paper goes to press. Depending on when an event occurs, time-sensitive news may be covered on the newspaper's website and updated in the print edition. Such stories may have long-lasting implications that can generate months of coverage and analysis in both print and online editions.

Many professional newspapers focus on **hyperlocal news**, events and information that are most important to their immediate and local audience, rather than trying to keep up with the pace of the 24-hour news cycle. Most school newspapers publish even less frequently than daily papers, often weekly, every other week or once a month. Ensuring that the print edition of your high school paper is relevant and timely can be a difficult task. But a well-maintained website can provide you with opportunities to keep the news fresh, with updated coverage continuing between print editions.

Quick Exercise

From a recent copy of a local newspaper, find an example of a hyperlocal story focusing on a specific community. Would this story be covered in any other newspaper? Why is the news important to this publication's readers?

"" WORDS of WISDOM

Never, ever be afraid to ask questions. In time, you'll figure out the best way to go about it.

Should you grill that official accused of corruption under the glaring lights of a press conference?

Would it be best to pull aside an aide behind the scenes to get a response no-one else

may get? Or do both? Intimidating situations can turn into exhilarating learning situations when

you get that answer or funny look you may not have expected to get.

Genaro C. Armas, Correspondent, The Associated Press

FIGURE 1.1 *Lance*, Westside High School, Omaha, Neb., Vol. 56, Issue 3, April 4, 2011. Reproduced by permission of Rod How.

The *Lance* front-page focuses on a change in the grading system at the local middle school to conform to new state grading standards. The story includes a sidebar detailing an explanation of the number-based standard from the previous letter-based standard. The second story focuses on visitors to the school observing a modular scheduling system already in place. Both stories are local, hyperfocused stories of interest to the students in this school and their educational experiences.

PULL OUT
in-depth
Is Westside really "Hollywood High?"

PAGE 10
a&e
The entertainment staff reviews local hotspots

Lance

8701 Pacific St. Omaha, NE 68114 Volume 56 Issue 3 November 4, 2011

MIDDLE SCHOOL
change in grading system implemented

By Aaron Calderon
NEWS EDITOR

"A one? How could you get a one?"

Instead of being reprimanded for F's, that's what some students may be hearing now.

In place of the traditional A, B, C grading system, Westside Middle School (WMS) has switched to a 1, 2, 3 system.

Standards-Based Reporting (SBR) was implemented in the elementary schools last year and in the middle school this year.

There is a simple explanation for this change, according to WMS Principal Steve Schrad.

"The elementary schools changed last year because all students are required to meet state and district standards," Schrad said. "Research says if we use standards, which every school does, then we should grade by standards."

That's exactly what SBR does. Students are given ones for "not yet progressing to the standard," twos for "progressing to the standard" and threes for "meets the standard."

Teachers set concepts, or indicators, for their students to master. These indicators are how teachers gauge the learning of their students.

Just as with the previous A, B, C system, there are "cut scores" which determine what grade a student receives.

"In ways it's not a lot different [from the A, B, C system]," Schrad said. "We're doing the same curriculum, actually using more rigor."

But teachers have a problem with the cut scores: they undermine the system of Standards-Based Reporting. SBR, in its purest form, does not use percentage scores.

"We're doing both the old and new systems, not one or the other," middle school instructor *Dexter Johnson** said. "It doesn't work."

Even with a new grading system, the curriculum is the same, and the same concepts are taught.

"Nothing has changed in terms of teaching," Schrad said.

Nothing except time. Teachers had to revise their standards to make them more attainable at the middle school level.

"[The standards] forced teachers to go in and rewrite the indicators because they weren't specific enough," Schrad said.

In addition to creating new indicators, teachers must grade for each of these new

see **WMS** page 3

what do the numbers mean?

1 not yet progressing toward the standard
The student shows little understanding of grade level skills and concepts and needs frequent assistance and/or support.

2 progressing toward the standard
The student is developing an understanding of grade level skills and concepts and may need assistance and/or support.

3 meets the standard
The student demonstrates mastery of grade level skills and concepts.

High school officials visit to observe modular scheduling

By Maddie Goodman
MANAGING EDITOR

The same classes every day, the same seven-period structure. Every moment scheduled.

Westside students are different. With modular scheduling, students are allowed more time to do what they please.

"I have to choose whether to do homework or go to the café to hangout with friends," freshman Hannah Bohacek said.

According to the district website, Westside switched to a modular schedule in the fall of 1967.

Administrators implemented modular scheduling after realizing the traditional six-period day did not give students opportunities to make their own decisions about how to spend their time at school.

"That's always been the number one overriding thing for graduates, that they've always felt, as freshmen in college, that they were much more able to handle their freedom," scheduler Mark Stegman said.

Other schools are curious about modular scheduling.

"There's at least a few schools every year that visit us for modular scheduling," Assistant Principal Tony Weers said.

Representatives from these schools come from all over the country. This year, Westside has hosted schools from South Carolina, South Dakota and Nebraska.

"There were 300 plus kids in an auditorium there at Westside and seeing one teacher deliver a lecture to them, it simulated to me a college experience," said Luke Clamp, principal of River Bluff High in South Carolina. "How enlightening that was to see a school provide that experience for students with the purpose for them to have college experiences on a high school campus."

River Bluff chose to explore modular scheduling with the hope of making its future student body more independent.

Clamps seeks to spread modular scheduling to the other high schools in the district.

"This school has the opportunity to redesign a path and a culture of not just one high school, but also duplicate this in the other four high schools in our district as a potential instrument," Clamp said.

Even schools around the Omaha metro area are interested in Westside's unique system.

"We're looking into different options," Marian math instructor Rochelle Rohlfs said. "It's not that we feel there is anything wrong with our scheduling now as it is, but we also don't want to rule out anything because of not going out and looking at what others are doing."

Westside provides variety for students by offering different types of classes.

"Kids can take a wider variety of classes," Weers said. "Kids have the opportunity to take more classes over a high school career."

Having more class options means the demand for classes could be uneven from semester to semester. Westside tries to fill the needs of the students.

"The way we schedule it goes entirely off student request," Stegman said. "Not every teacher's schedule looks the same from semester to semester, even if they're teaching the same

see **MODS** page 2

WHERE DOES NEWS COME FROM?

WWW

WEBLINK Check out

www.journalism.org

A website produced by the Pew Research Center for Excellence in Journalism, this site contains a wealth of good resources for journalists especially under the Journalism Resources link.

It has been said that the word "news" stands for north, east, west and south – the full compass of directions and topics that a newspaper must cover on a daily basis. According to linguists, though, the word "news" is a plural variant of a French word, "nouvelles," and a German word, "neues," both meaning that which is novel, or new. **Breaking news** has come to mean coverage of an important event as it is actually happening. With today's access to 24-hour media sources, breaking news has become a continuous stream of information from multiple sources and locations around the world.

High school papers usually have to report breaking news some time after it occurs. A gas smell causing a school-wide evacuation was reported in *The Lowell*, the student newspaper of San Francisco's Lowell High School, four days after the event took place. The paper's website, however, was able to post the news online just two days after it occurred, and included a gallery of photos from the event. Fortunately, most high school news is not quite so time-sensitive, and can interest readers for longer periods of time. Such news is appropriate for both the print and online editions of your paper.

NEWS VALUE

It is important that the newspaper staff determine the news value of each potential story. This means evaluating such factors as a story's timeliness, proximity to your school community, prominence of the people involved and size of the potential audience – as well as such elements as conflict and drama, surprise or oddity and emotional and visual appeal. Such factors are essential to how readers interact with the information and how long they stay with a story before losing interest.

As editors determine the news value of potential stories, they help determine what information reaches the public. In this way, the newspaper staff become **gatekeepers of information**, a very important responsibility in journalism. By choosing to cover some stories rather than others, they give life and credibility to particular topics and perspectives.

Where to place each story is another important news value decision. The greater the news value of a story, the more space and more prominent position it should receive in the print edition. The front-page is the first thing a reader sees, and should therefore be reserved for topics most important to your audience. In many professional newspapers, local news appears on the front-page while less timely world and national news is often relegated to inside pages because it's less timely. News is also prioritized on websites, where the timeliest news often takes the top position in a feed or blog. On a website, important and updated news might also be featured in a special banner or distinct multimedia package.

News value goes hand in hand with the elements of a **news lead**, which includes the *who, what, when, where, why* and *how* of a story (see Chapter 3 for more on news leads). In determining the news value of a story, the reporter may determine that the *why* and *how* may need to be emphasized over other facts that may not be as relevant or important.

The more news value a story has, the more important and interesting it will be to a broad audience. More readers will relate and care about what they are reading. The news value of a high school story often determines whether it will interest the local community, in addition to the paper's primary audience of students, teachers and parents. Below you'll find a more detailed discussion of the key factors to keep in mind when assessing the news value of a story.

Timeliness

It goes almost without saying that news travels fast. Information that is current is of greater interest than older news. When something important happens at your school, students and staff will talk about it and will pass on the information they have heard, even if it isn't accurate. A newspaper staff trained to identify the relevant facts can quickly clarify these events through the newspaper's website, as well as through social media such as Twitter.

Reporting old news in the print edition of your newspaper is unlikely to interest readers in an age of continuous Internet and cable news. Your newspaper's website can be used to bridge the gap between print editions, especially through the use of **news briefs** – short articles that report the basic facts of timely news stories. Rather than printing information that has already been

News briefs on this page expand beyond school to include community and state items of interest to student readers. In addition to the briefs, relevant art heads each story adding visual interest. A vertical panel of photos of the week also adds visual interest and includes captions for each image. In addition to news briefs, many newspapers include sports and entertainment briefs.

made public, a striking photograph can also be used, with a long caption summarizing the story. High school papers often publish several pages of pictures from major school events, and offer slideshows or video footage on their websites.

Proximity

News that happens in or near your school will be of interest to students, parents, staff and administrators. Such stories should be a primary focus for a school newspaper, which may be the only official record of the information.

As students, high school newspaper reporters have access to sources and information that may not be available to outsiders. For example, at Virginia's Chantilly High School, the *Purple Tide* newspaper reported on the removal of the senior class president and treasurer from their positions after they were caught drinking before a football game. The story quoted the treasurer admitting to the offense, while school officials would not comment on the reason the two were disqualified. Clearly, the student reporter had access to the students accused in the incident.

FIGURE 1.3 *Spark*, Lakota East High School, Liberty Township, Ohio. Reproduced by permission of Dean Hume.

After district voters struck down a tax levy for the third consecutive time, staff of *Spark* newspaper analyzed in a series of articles what the impact of the district's spending deficit would be. Staff coverage included a series of stories, detailed in an explanatory box on the right page. A visual infographic at the bottom of the left page graphically shows the impact of the past votes dating from 2004.

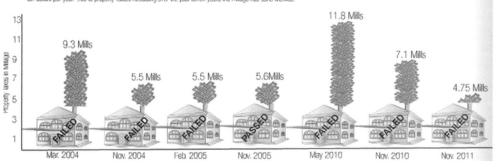

Covering events that happen far from the school, such as the tsunami that hit Japan in 2011, will need to be localized for a high school newspaper. In this case, schools with large Asian populations could have interviewed students who might have friends and relatives living in Japan and covered the story from their perspectives. No news story should take reporting from an already published account in a professional publication, even if the source is attributed.

Prominence

People of prominence will add interest to any news story. A school visit by First Lady Michelle Obama, accompanied by the first lady of the Republic of Korea, made front-page news in *The A*

FIGURE 1.3 *(continued)*

revenue because we won't be able to collect in 2012, we have lost a year of collection."

Lakota Superintendent Karen Mantia said that the decision of whether or not to go back on the ballot is part of many decisions on the horizon.

"The Board will have to ask where will we go from here," she said. "If we do go back, how much do we go back for? Will it be with the same services or wills services have to change here in Lakota? We're evaluating all of that."

Unlike in the Nov. 2010 levy, the Board did not release a list of objectives to be cut in the event of the levy's failure. As of press time, details regarding specific cuts have not been released. According to Logan, there is no set number for how much cuts must amount to, because future levies could affect the how much needs to be cut.

Board vice president Ben Dibble spoke to the fact that where the inevitable cuts will come from is largely up in the air at this point.

"We haven't said exactly what [those cuts] will be," Dibble said. "We can't at this point. The obvious things are already cut. Things like busing—already cut. It will be more of cutting into what we are actually offering. You keep hearing analogies of cutting into the muscle and into the bone because there is no fat. We cut into the muscle so I guess it's back into the bone where we're cutting into the structure of the thing."

According to Dibble, one of the reasons the Board did not release a list of specific

| This issue is the first piece in *Spark*'s series of post-levy budget coverage |

cuts to be made was because of the arrival of Mantia as the new superintendent. Mantia was new to the district and she was deciding where her priorities for the district were and thus she could not outline specific cuts to be made.

To approach the task ahead of making cuts in the schools, Mantia is relying on a data-based decision making model, one that analyzes costs and benefits to all programs. Dibble said that she has gone through a process already to determine where Lakota's costs are and she will use that when making her decisions.

Mantia said, "We'll match the cost to the service as provided. We want to ask the question of the value that it brings to students and what students need."

While the areas from which cuts will be made have not yet been announced, it is the clear message of the NoLakota group that the district should start with a conversation with the teachers.

Rich Hoffman, spokesman for NoLakota, said that Lakota should come up with 5

Lakota levy supporters gathered at Champs on Nov. 8 to watch the election returns.

percent savings out of the teacher's contract.

"I'd like to see the superintendent sit down with the LEA [Lakota Educator's Association] and ask them if they would be willing to work within the budget and come up with five percent savings," Hoffman said. "That way nobody has to lose a job, no electives need to be cut. They need to figure out how to work in the budget that the community set the constraints for [on Nov. 8]."

After the last levy failure, cuts were felt in all grade levels, across all areas: transportation, class offerings and sizes and athletics. While the Board does not know what exactly the next round of cuts will look like, they will most likely come from personnel expenditures, where approximately 77 percent of the general fund is spent on wages and benefits.

"There isn't much else to cut other than personnel," Logan said. "Not in a budget of $1.55 million when 77 percent of the expenditures are in personnel. But that doesn't mean we won't look at everyting. We renegotiate negotiate contracts. We try to save dollars with anything and everytjing we can look at but that is not going to fix our probems. The spending deficit is $9 million and there's not enough of those expenditures to solve $9 million."

Community outreach coordinator for the Lakota Levy Committee Kelly Casper reiterates that while it is painful, cuts will likely come in the form of personnel reductions.

"Unfortunately, the biggest place that we can cut is personnel and I hate to see that happen," Casper said. "I hate to see teachers loosing their robs but I have tremendous, tremendous faith in Dr. Mantia. She is trying to get Lakota back on track."

With the failure of the levy and the certainty of cuts, Manita said that district will use the failure as an opportunity to re-evaluatethe the district's situation. Her plan

was to make cuts regardless of a levy passage or failure and she said this failure is a chance to take a deeper look at Lakota.

"[After talking to the community], the second step is to step back and reprioritize," Mantia said. "We'll have to answer a lot of questions. Will we go back on the ballot, what will we do with the shortage of money? I don't have answers for [those questions]. But there are a lot of questions circling around. We're regrouping."

With all of the factors that go into how voters make decisions, there are any number of causes that lead to the mandate for Lakota to regroup. Dibble expressed his concern that the other issues on the ballot might have taken away from the levy.

He said that levies do not commonly go on the ballot at the same time as board elections and that may have contributed to the failure, while Casper thinks it is a sign of a lack of concern for good schools in the community.

Hoffman disagrees with both of these points and argues that this levy was voted down because people feel that they are taxed too much

"[The levy failed] because the taxes are too high and [the community] is frustrated and there isn't any plan to bring the budget together, even though it might not sound that way in the school system," Hoffman said.

Mantia said that the issue is not about why the levy failed but rather that a new dialogue must begin in Lakota between the school district and the community in order to move forward.

Mantia said, "We need to find out what the community wants from us. This is their failure and we need to ask the questions and develop an understanding of where our community is. I don't think it's about liking kids or not liking kids, it's about the climate. We need to understand the community better." ■

Blast, the student newspaper of Annandale High School, in Annandale, Virginia. The story included additional links to a slideshow and video footage from this event.

Prominence differs with context. Student leaders, teachers, coaches and administrators are prominent in all schools, and much news will center around these figures. Organizations such as the school's student government or principal's council can also be important in shaping news.

Audience impact

A story that influences or affects a large number of readers will have greater news value. In high schools, news may impact on a single set of students, students in certain classes and age levels or the entire school. A story's importance may also extend beyond the school to the broader community. When the voters rejected a tax levy for the Lakota, Ohio Schools for the third time, *Spark* newspaper staff took two pages to examine how their high school would be forced to cut back its programs, an issue of relevance to the entire community. The issue had such impact that *Spark* staff extended it into a series of stories, analyzing how the budget situation would affect everything from academics to sports.

Surprise or oddity

A story that reports on something surprising, unusual or mysterious can spark interest and draw in new readers. While such stories may have less news value than others, they are often topics of discussion and may generate publicity for the paper when people talk about them. *The Harbinger* newspaper of Shawnee Mission East High School in Kansas, reported on a student's project to construct a dress from folded Starburst wrappers as a costuming project for her school's fashion show on Earth Day.

Human interest

Stories about people, their struggles, triumphs, passions and accomplishments will often be of interest to readers. Human interest stories are often those that people relate and respond to on a personal level. In many newspapers, human interest stories generate such reaction that readers may want to offer help, join in a cause, donate money or provide some appropriate help. In *The Campanile* newspaper of Palo Alto Senior High School, a front-page story paid tribute to a loved head custodian retiring after 29 years at the school. The story told of a campaign by the school to raise money for a trip to Hawaii for the employee and his family, the generosity of a teacher in offering her family home to him for the visit, and a letter-writing campaign thanking him for his hard work and dedication to the school.

Conflict and drama

When a story reports on a conflict, the news value is high. People choose sides, squaring off against each other, often with one side possibly unhappy with the outcome. Emotions can flare, adding drama. Conflict in schools often crops up among groups of students, between students and administrators or between teachers and administrators. Students who joined the Occupy San Diego movement in 2011 to protest about inequalities in wealth were interviewed and photographed by *The Falconer* of Torrey Pines High in California. This story had the additional benefits of timeliness and proximity, which helped justify its front-page placement.

Visual impact

The news value of a story can also be enhanced if it has a striking visual component. People will often be the primary focus of accompanying photos or videos, but occasional scene-setting pictorials can also be effective. Schools abound with opportunities for strong visual presentations. Good editors will ensure these images have strong camera angles, a range of people, as well as good pacing and variety. Homecoming, dances, traditional school events, the prom and graduation are obvious choices for visual stories. Good visual journalists look for ordinary, unnoticed and behind-the-scenes images to broaden this list. They should also consider providing multimedia presentations and slideshows of still images for the newspaper website.

Striking images are also useful for capturing the drama, conflict and emotion of a story. The surprise on the homecoming queen's face, the excitement of the band members winning a marching competition or an athlete's tearful reaction to a loss or victory are all visuals that are both memorable and informative.

WEBLINK Check out

www.spj.org

The website of the Society of Professional Journalists has a link to Generation J's Reading Room which contains advice on a variety of topics related to becoming a better journalist, and a Journalist's Toolbox under the Resources link.

FIGURE 1.4 *Harbinger Online*, Shawnee Mission East High School, Prairie Village, Kan. Reproduced by permission of C. Dow Tate.

High school life is full of emotion running the gamut from pure excitement to great disappointment. These pictures are among the most dramatic ones for readers or online readers. Photographer Jake Crandall wisely followed the football team into the locker room after it defeated a crosstown rival to get this emotion-filled moment of excitement of a player hoisting a wooden trophy.

THE IMPORTANCE OF AUDIENCE

Just as a local or regional newspaper must be responsive to its entire community, so must the school newspaper. The audience includes students, teachers, staff, administrators, the school board, parents, alumni, taxpayers and other community members, including local businesses, especially those that interact with the school. All of these audiences should be covered and drawn on as sources of information. Establishing relationships with each segment of your audience is important in making this happen.

The **primary audience** for a school newspaper is the students, staff and teachers within the school and, of these, students are the most important. The school newspaper is the voice of the students and most likely the only media outlet devoted to their perspectives. While many students communicate through social media, the messages aren't publicly distributed. Serving the student population is a huge responsibility with far-reaching implications. The newspaper staff must be responsive to the full range of student voices in its coverage. Staff members must avoid catering to certain factions, cliques or segments, but must strive to represent the entire student body. For each issue, the school's various groups and populations should be considered when story assignments are made.

The **secondary audience** for the newspaper and website are people in the local community, particularly parents, taxpayers, alumni and local businesses. Your paper and website could also be accessed by a wide network of interested readers from surrounding communities, school alumni, other student journalists and friends and relatives of people in your school community.

Serving the newspaper's different audiences isn't easy. Newspaper reporters and editors are constantly called upon to make judgments about possible stories presented in editorial meetings and on their beats. Without a structure in place, students left to brainstorm story ideas may look only to those activities and events with which they are familiar. Editors must be vigilant about making sure that the newspaper serves the entire school community. Recruiting underrepresented student populations to the staff is one good strategy. Or, the staff can seek to include a broader range of voices through submissions, in the form of guest columns and editorials, entertainment reviews, collections of student quotes and through reader-submitted photos and videos.

Quick Exercise

Using a print or online newspaper, find examples of five news leads and identify the news value of each. Why is that news value of interest to the reader?

Test your knowledge

How does visual impact play a role in news reporting? When can it replace traditional prose as a form of storytelling?

BEAT REPORTING

News coverage will frequently be developed by staff members assigned to **beats** – specific people, groups, activities, academic departments, administrators and other areas of interest. Beat reporters will have regular sources on their beat whom they will visit frequently or periodically for updates and potential stories.

Two kinds of stories will often emerge from these beat conversations. One kind of story that may emerge will have immediate news value – upcoming events and student or club awards, for instance. The beat reporter can help the staff determine if this information becomes a news brief (see above) or expanded into a print or online story. Another kind of story might provide the reporter with information to be developed, discussed and possibly used later. This information is referred to as a **future story**. While it's possible to use such information immediately as an **advance story** – a story about something coming up in the future – the information could be kept in a database of ideas that might be covered later, when more information or context might be available. Database entries should be chronological and include the possible story idea, the date it is tentatively scheduled, contact sources, possible visual ideas, website connections and any other information that will help in planning coverage. Maintaining a beat database prevents the stories from getting lost, and gives staff a starting point for coverage in each issue.

Say, for instance, that during the fall semester a student reporter interviews the school's drama teacher, who mentions that he plans to bring a professional Shakespeare company to perform for the entire school the following spring. At this point he doesn't know which play will be performed, when the assembly will take place or how it will be organized. As the school year progresses, though, his plans become more detailed and firm. After the initial interview, there isn't enough information to write a solid story. The reporter makes a note in her beat database to follow up with the teacher and emphasizes that this is a story she'd really like to write. When the performance plans are established, she can write an advance story. Collaborating with the web team would help them plan for multimedia coverage.

WORDS of WISDOM

Beats are the backbone of a good publication. Like a cop covering a beat, journalists need to keep on top of things – because newsmakers, especially high school newsmakers, forget how important it is to publicize information. If we are keeping the student body informed, we are talking to the newsmakers every week.

For my staff, I have the Beginning Journalism students cover beats and report back each week to the newspaper staff. It's important for them to learn the basics. Plus, it's a huge predictor of their future involvement in the paper. Students who work hard and get their beat done every week are driven. Eventually, these driven students almost always write the best stories and make the best editors on the newspaper staff.

Jeff Nardone, Adviser, The Tower, *Grosse Pointe South High School, Grosse Pointe Farms, Mich.*

I think the other things are perks and additions that come with it. There's that pride."

Van Sickle also understands that varsity jackets are a tradition for a lot of students.

"I hope people are investing in something that is meaningful to them and that they can wear," Van Sickle said. "It's part of that high school experience and in time, when you decide to pack it away with all of your yearbooks, and special photos, and memories, and prom ticket, whatever your friends put on your locker that you save as souvenirs, it's part of those things, but it's really something you can wear for a lifetime."

Van Sickle wants students to show their school spirit while at a school events or somewhere outside of school.

She earned her varsity letter, but never got a jacket.

"My mom was a stay at home mom and my dad was retired, as well as disabled. He was a veteran and blind, so [buying a varsity jacket] was not something that I wanted to ask my parents for. I still have my varsity letter. I was in Track."

The students who have met with Van Sickle understand why the district has made this rule.

"She came to a Student Council meeting and she told us about it and it sounded pretty reasonable," Armstrong said. "I just think that it's important to prevent anything bad from happening. I think that the school is kind of complacent because nothing bad has happened yet."

Armstrong thinks that if there was a problem at school, the students would change their minds about the rule.

Root, who feels she has the right to wear her jacket is upset about the rule, but doesn't plan on causing any problems in order to get her point across.

"I'll obey the rules," Root said, "but I'm not happy about them."

Regardless of students' and teachers' opinions on the matter, Armstrong is still convinced of one thing.

"It's just a jacket," Armstrong said.

[partial left-edge column fragments:]

...say fairness is ...rsity jacket, like, ...r school. You're ...ing else, you're ...ol, your academ- ...ts, your awards, ...wouldn't you let ...?

...ot said

...e because we're ...ater on anyways ...re important is- ...n just a jacket. I ...ways going to be ...ay we can be the ...ow we just have

...strong said

Lesley Van Sickle SPEAKS OUT ABOUT THE RUMORS AT WKHS

news 3

Principal Lesley Van Sickle held a press conference with the Murmur staff to address rumors and other topics of discussion

By Allie Shaner

Rumor
Powderpuff is canceled next year because of unsportmanship, incidents at the game and upset parents

Reality
"I haven't heard that rumor at all about parents being upset about it nor have we talked about canceling it at all."

Rumor
Wristbands are to be worn during Prom and other dances

Reality
"I don't have any clarification on the wristbands outside of what we originally talked about, my assumption is that the dance code will be in effect for prom, middle school dances, high school dances, and yes that should be what it currently is."

Rumor
Boots and Moccasins are Banned

Reality
"Not sure where the rumor of moccasins and Ugg boots came from, you just aren't allowed to wear slippers, you have to have a hard sole on the bottom of your shoes for safety purposes."

Rumor
The dress code is going to change at the dances

Reality
"The only dress code restriction that I recall from it is that your dress or dresses need to be fingertip above your knees and [you need to be] in shoes. Outside of that regard to rumors about the strapless and open backs and those sort of things, it's a district wide policy, and it was first implemented at Mott's Homecoming."

FIGURE 1.5 *The Murmur*, Waterford-Kettering High School, Waterford Township, Mich. Reproduced by permission of Brian Wilson.

A high school newspaper staff can regularly meet with its principal and other administrators to help answer students' questions and clarify issues in the paper. In this column, Principal Lesley Van Sickle met with *Murmur* staff to clarify the rumor vs. reality of several issues among students in the school.

After the show, the production could be reviewed by a writer for an entertainment **review**, and might include a slideshow or video on the paper's website. If the paper's print edition is being finalized soon after the production, a story with student reaction quotes could be included. Or, photographs could be used with captions and might refer students to coverage on the website or elsewhere in the paper. A video interview with the school's drama club, interviews capturing

WWW

WEBLINK Check out

**www.myhighschool
journalism.org**

Hosted by the American Society
of News Editors, this site features
a national edition of stories from
across the country as well as
links to high school newspapers
they host. A good source for
story ideas.

student reaction to the event or an interview with the visiting professionals would all add different dimensions to the coverage.

In order to serve their student audience, beat reporters should schedule regular meetings with the school principal to keep abreast of what is going on with the school, and to get comments on specific areas of student concern. Having a regularly scheduled meeting with the principal is crucial to identifying important information for coverage. The principal could be invited to write an occasional guest column, or simply respond to student concerns brought out in a meeting with reporters. Many school newspapers also regularly assign students to cover school board meetings as a beat. School boards make policy decisions which can have significant impact on students at all the schools within their jurisdictions.

Other important sources for beat reporting could include the school PTA and booster groups, the state board of education, local governments (particularly if they share a tax base with the school), and state athletic organizations (especially if they define school athletic districts). While

HELPFUL TIPS

Covering a beat

Being a good beat reporter is more than running into a source in the hall and asking, "Hi, got any news for me?" While you know what news is and what might work for upcoming coverage, your beat contact may be busy or may not understand the potential of information. Here are some tips for good beat coverage:

→ Try to work with editors to get a beat assignment that matches your interests and prior knowledge. Students involved in specific activities will have a base of knowledge about them, and will already know the organizers and participants. This paves the way for good coverage.

→ Go and visit your beat sources early in the school semester, introduce yourself and explain what you'll be doing. Provide the sources with your contact information and establish a good time to touch base on a regular basis. How often you meet with each source should be appropriate for both your schedules and the newspaper's publishing schedule. Once you've established yourself as the relevant reporter, other sources on your beat may contact you when they have news to pass on.

→ Ask questions. Use information you've heard or found on websites to start the conversation. For example, "I hear the math department is starting an after-school tutoring program. Can you tell me when that program will be set up?" Take notes during the meeting and save those notes so you can go back and review them. Be sure to clarify anything that might be just rumor circulating in the school.

→ If your newspaper has a database of future events, add what you've learned so it doesn't get lost. Revise the database when details are firmed up. Add potential resource needs: audio, video, photography or informational graphics, so editors can plan accordingly for these assignments.

→ Ask your source for suggestions for all kinds of possible stories: achievements, interesting classroom activities, guest speakers, presentations. Think visually as well as verbally. While a class might be celebrating Black History Month by wearing period clothing and having readings, these events may not be a good match for your publishing cycle. In that case, they might be better covered on the newspaper's website, both through a story and a slideshow or video.

→ Establish good relationships with your sources by practicing smart public relations. Thank each source by email after meeting, and keep reminding the source how interested you are in gathering relevant information. Make sure to let sources know when their stories and visuals are published or posted, so they'll be sure to see them, whether in print or on the website. Drop off copies of the newspaper or send them links to the coverage online. After a story is published, write a quick email thanking sources for helping you with the information.

→ Don't drop the ball on your beats or you'll miss out on potentially good stories. Your beat sources may not have something for you at every meeting, but providing information to you periodically should be enough to ensure that this beat gets thoroughly covered. In most cases you'll be dealing with people who seek publicity for their program and events. They'll appreciate your work.

the people who run these organizations are harder to contact and might take more time to interview, their impact on the educational process is far-reaching. Establishing relationships before crucial information is needed should be a goal of all beat reporters.

Beat reporters should frequently consult local news and other websites to keep tabs on potential stories and to learn as much about the issues before contacting sources. With local, state and national government organizations, much relevant information can be easily accessed online. With private organizations, sources may be harder to reach and potentially take more time to contact. Starting early is often a key to reaching a source.

FEATURIZING NEWS

Most news published in the print editions of high school papers is **featurized news**: stories with some basic news value, but lacking a strong aspect of timeliness. A story without a strong time connection is sometimes referred to as **evergreen news**: it could be printed today, a week from now, next month or even later without losing importance or relevance. Since most high school newspapers don't publish frequently enough to include breaking news, reporters must emphasize a different **angle** of the story's news value and might need to relate it to a broader topic. Explaining the *how* and *why* of the news is a key service that a high school paper can provide with such features. For instance, a story might have several potential news value elements such as timeliness, conflict and prominence. The writer might choose to emphasize one value over another, avoiding an older timeliness factor in favor of conflict or prominence. This would allow the writer to construct the story around that angle.

In a front-page story, *The Charger*, the Oxford (Mississippi) High School newspaper, used both words and images to report on an increase in student piercings and a new school policy curtailing them, to be implemented at the beginning of the following term. The story involved some time-sensitive news, but was also important in a broader sense because the policy was controversial. In the past, the school had allowed students to cover piercings with bandages, but that policy was being abused and therefore changed, according to the article.

Note the way the story, "Enforced policy limits jewelry in piercings," begins:

> When senior Eliot Miller stabbed his ears, he was not bent on self-mutilation – he was merely piercing them.
>
> "If you do it my way, ice and needles," Miller said. "You hold the ice on your ear for 30 seconds, then you take the earring and – without hesitation – poke it through."
>
> Miller says he got the earrings because, "they're different." When he debuted his new studs, he got good reactions.
>
> "I was just doing something at first," Miller said. "A couple of girls said they liked it, so I kept it in."
>
> School nurse Tracy Shawn says before getting a piercing a person should first consider why he/she wants one.
>
> "These decisions will not go away, and if visible, can cause others to form opinions about the way you look," Shawn said.

The story doesn't start with a traditional news lead, doesn't necessarily have a timeliness angle and uses a writing style more typical of a feature story. But lower in the story, comes the news angle:

> Beginning in January, trouble may come when the school rule dealing with jewelry in piercings will be enforced.
>
> According to Superintendent Kim Stasny, piercings in places other than in ears tend to be disruptive to the learning environment.
>
> "Eliminating or decreasing distractions is important to teachers, administrators and parents," Stasney said.

A story such as the one above can offer journalistic work with depth and breadth, which anchors the material around it. On the same front-page of *The Charger*, the paper published two pieces of timely and more traditional news, and a horizontal bar of photos from the school's medieval faire.

Quick Exercise

Compile a list of beats that you think should be covered throughout your school. Include academic areas, clubs, sports and other relevant areas. Compare your list with other students' lists. How could you organize the coverage of these beats?

Test your knowledge

What are some ways in which beat coverage helps improve the diversity of news coverage in print and online?

FIGURE 1.6 *The Charger,* Oxford High School, Oxford, Miss., front-page, Vol. 30, Issue 3, Nov./Dec. 2010. Reproduced by permission of Cynthia Ferguson, adviser.

Many high school newspapers print feature stories and news on their front-pages often giving more space to features. In this feature on a new school piercing policy, the story appears in a prime position at the top of the page and features a non-standard typeface which helps separate it from the news stories also running on the page. The story also has four visuals showing various forms of student piercings.

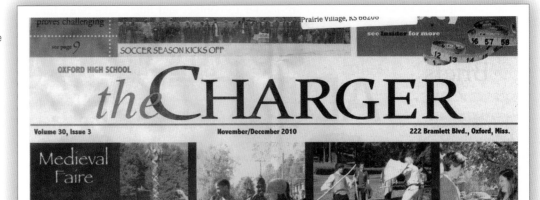

proves challenging
see page 9
SOCCER SEASON KICKS OFF
Prairie Village, KS 66208
see Insider for more
56 57 58
12 13 14

OXFORD HIGH SCHOOL

the CHARGER

Volume 30, Issue 3   November/December 2010   222 Bramlett Blvd., Oxford, Miss.

Medieval Faire

students explore the past

Photos by Katie Krouse and courtesy of Marquece Miller

Students get 'invitations' to Saturday school

ROSALIE DOERKSEN
Staff Writer

After a week of suffering from strep throat, junior Wade Lindley returned to school only to realize that he had a day of Saturday school looming before him.

The latest session of Saturday school met on November 13.

"(The supervisors) were really mean, and they made me do work," he said.

Not just makeup work for his classes, but, according to Lindley, "useless busywork." If a student didn't have any work to make up for a class, he says the supervisor gave them other "random" work to complete.

Amy Beckham, the Saturday school coordinator says, however, that all the work for each student is prepared by their teacher. If they finish making up the work they missed, the teacher provides additional work that the student completes for an extra grade.

English III teacher Kim Austin was one of five teachers who applied to supervise Saturday school.

She says her jobs included taking regular attendance and issuing students' work that teachers left for them to do, including worksheets, study guides, and novel reading.

Several of Austin's students were in attendance that Saturday.

"I left plenty of work for them and graded every single page of it," she said. "If they completed the work correctly they were given the grade for it, which helped several of them raise their grade."

According to Austin, Saturday school is not mandatory. She says the administration "invites" students to attend, for their own benefit.

"We call it an invitation so that (the students) can see it as an opportunity to help themselves," she said.

The school attendance policy says students may only miss six days of school for semester classes and twelve for year-long courses in order to receive credit.

Saturday school and, Beckham says, a few days of summer school, are an opportunity for students to essentially make up days of school.

When a student reaches five, nine, or twelve absences, Beckham issues an intent-to-attend form to them, which the students sign. She then distributes the seven hours of that school day to replace missed class hours, beginning with the semester courses.

Beckham says she gave out a total of 123 invitation to Saturday school this semester.

Junior Tal Toole was absent from school for seven days during the first semester, five of them due to a bout of pneumonia.

He says the administration informed him and the other attendees that they were "invited" to Saturday school. But, he says the invitation is simply a "cover up" to make it look like the administration was working with the students.

"If I declined the 'invitation'," he said, "the school would fail me in (Trigonometry) for missing seven days of school even with my make up work all made up and a passing average."

Toole says the extra educational time is most beneficial for those who skip school for unnecessary reasons and for those in need of raising their grades, but should not be required of those who missed school due to sickness.

enforced policy limits jewelry in
PIERCINGS

Piercing trend among students

DORA CHEN
Staff Writer

When senior Eliot Miller stabbed his ears, he was not bent on self-mutilation –he was merely piercing them.

"If you do it my way, ice and needles," Miller said. "You hold the ice on your ear for 30 seconds, then you take the earring and –without hesitation – poke it through."

Miller says he got the earrings because "they're different." When he debuted his new studs, he got good reactions.

"I was just doing something at first," Miller said. "A couple of girls said they liked it, so I kept it in."

School nurse Tracy Shawn says before getting a piercing a person should first consider why he/she wants one.

"These decisions will not go away, and if visible, can cause others to form opinions about the way you look," Shawn said.

Sophomore Donya Alqasas decided to get her nose pierced last year while she was in Egypt. The piercing became infected because the piercers used a needle gun, typically not used for noses.

"You're not supposed to do that," Alqasas said about the needle gun. "It was really bad."

Although she does not condone certain body piercings, Shawn says going to certified piercing salons will reduce risks of these infections and other harmful effects of piercings, such as keloid build-up, reactions, and allergies.

"Make sure you are using a licensed place and not some unsterile backdoor person because they can tell you anything they want to and not actually properly sterilize their equipment," Shawn said.

Sophomore Mary Catherine Hall currently has her nose and ears pierced. In past years, however, she has had her tongue, septum, lip, and nose pierced – all done at home.

"Doing it yourself isn't really smart because you have a bigger risk of getting an infection, but that doesn't stop me," Hall said.

To pierce her tongue, Hall purchased a sterilized piercing kit from eBay. Aside from proper equipment, though, Shawn emphasized that a piercer must have knowledge of the nerve lines and veins in the area he/she is piercing.

"If these areas are pierced though, you will have great trouble with swelling, decreased circulation, pain, infection, and at times irreversible damage for life," Shawn said.

Beginning in January, trouble may come when the school rule dealing with jewelry in piercings will be enforced.

According to Superintendent Kim Stasny, piercings in places other than in ears tend to be disruptive to the learning environment.

"Eliminating or decreasing distractions is important to teachers, administrators and parents," Stasny said.

To Miller, the claim that jewelry in non-ear

See **Piercing**, page 3

Upper Left: Senior **Sammy Rippon** inserts her nose ring. Rippon has had her nose pierced for one and a half years. **Left:** Junior **Dondre Gatlin** shows off his lip ring. Gatlin took his sister's car after work to get his lip pierced. **Bottom Left:** Senior **Meemee McGuirt** took off her bandaid to show off her eyebrow ring. **Right:** Senior **Dallas Nutt** wears a small silver stud in her nose. This silver stud is usually replaced by a clear one for the school day.

Photos by Jake Williamson & Katie Krouse

Teacher gets custody of Coleman brothers

ROSALIE DOERKSEN
Staff Writer

On October 28, Denise Collier, the school's behavior specialist, got an urgent phone call from her student, sophomore Jesse Coleman. He had just discovered the dead body of his mother, and wanted her to come get him and his brother.

Considering the circumstance, Collier says Jesse was extremely brave.

he says he did suffer from depression during that time, "for about a day and a half."

"It was awful," he said. "I felt pretty sad, and surprisingly, not a single drop of tears came out of my eye, but I still love her."

The Mississippi Department of Human Services gave Collier temporary custody of both Jesse and Drake. Collier says she has worked with both boys extensively since she first met

into the new one pretty easily, but Jesse has had a little more trouble.

"Foodwise, (the transition was) extremely difficult, but otherwise, not that hard," Jesse said.

Learning to eat vegetables, especially broccoli, is difficult for Jesse, according to Collier, but every week she gives the boys a reward for their effort known as "Free Form Friday." On that day, Jesse and Drake are allowed to eat whatever they want: chips, french fries

ments," she said.

However, Collier says both Jesse and Drake have blossomed in the "really stimulating atmosphere" of her home. She says she can learn from them as well.

"They force me to expand my perspective," she said.

Jesse and Drake are both talented with computers and are extremely intelligent according to Collier. Jesse regularly works with a computer pro-

NEWS IN OTHER CONTEXTS

When you hear the word "news," you might think of information that will appear only on the front-page or in the traditional news sections of a paper or website. But other sections include stories that should be considered news, owing to the various factors that give them news value. For instance, sports news includes timely information about games, conflict and drama. Occasionally, a sports team might be playing for a regional or state title, which might demand a front-page treatment in the print or online editions. Sports briefs columns are good ways to keep readers updated on various sports without devoting space to stories that are old news (see Chapter 6 for more on this topic).

Entertainment pages often include information about upcoming concerts, movies and events, all of which are timely and newsworthy. Entertainment stories might also have stronger news ties if other news value elements are present. Many entertainment stories feature people who are well known and popular with the school audience, adding prominent figures to the mix.

In *The Prospector* – high school newspaper of Mount Prospect, Illinois – a 2011 front-page photo featured Haley Reinhart, who had made it to the final three of that season's *American Idol* and had appeared locally for a hometown visit. Reinhart attended high school in the district, so her success had generated a lot of local interest. A small story that ran with the photo referred readers to the newspaper's website for more coverage.

The paper also noted that Lee DeWyze, another local high school student, had won the *Idol* competition the previous year. The newspaper also extensively covered DeWyze when he returned to his hometown as one of the show's top three contestants.

High school newspaper staff need to be frequently reminded about the importance of covering their own community. When important national or state news takes place, it will only be newsworthy for the school paper if a local connection can be established. This is known as **localizing news** – making it relevant to the immediate audience. Trying to cover national or state news without localizing might result in using information gleaned from **third-party sources**, people interviewed by other publications and attributed to those publications in your story. (This should be avoided whenever possible.) It's always better to localize the story through your own reporting.

SOURCING NEWS

News stories should generally feature quotes and information from one of two types of sources. Sources provide authoritative, informed facts which may also include opinion. Opinion should appear only in quotes, and not in the reporter's writing. Sources provide both **direct quotes**, which appear in stories in quotation marks with **attribution**, the name and source identification information in stories and **indirect quotes** in which comments might be summarized or shortened by rewording so the quote is no longer in the speaker's actual words, but with the information still attributed to the source.

Primary sources

Primary sources are generally those people who are actually interviewed for a story. Preferably, an interview should be live and face-to-face although Skype, telephone or online interviews may be necessary when time is limited or the source isn't available for a meeting. Primary sources should be those individuals most informed about or most closely related to the topic of the story, who can clarify the issues or provide opinions. In most cases, primary sources should be selected from your school or local community. Quotes can also come from professionals or people not associated with your school, when appropriate, and when they are the ultimate source for that information.

Quick Exercise

Identify five topics currently in the news. Identify ways in which these topics could be localized for coverage in your school newspaper and online site. Who would you interview to localize the information and make it relevant to your readers?

Test your knowledge

Why is using information from third-party sources a weak reporting technique?

FIGURE 1.7 *The Prospector*, Prospect High School, Mount Prospect, Ill, back page, May 27, 2011. Reproduced by permission of Jason Block.

A back-page sports news story on a new pay-to-play policy garners an entire page of coverage including two sidebars and an illustration photo. The story takes a look at the impact the new policy will have on students, compares the new policy to those at other nearby schools and questions whether non-sports groups will eventually be covered by the policy.

SPORTS

Friday, May 27, 2011

Bringing back the title

The baseball team reclaimed the MSL Championship title for the first time since the last championship win in 2003 — the fifth in Prospect history — on May 21. For the story on the team's finish, go online.

On Prospectornow.com...

The price to play

Graphic by Ian Magnuson and Heather Dove

District 214 charges all co-curricular activity participants $25 fee to continue playing

By Alyssa Zediker and Jack Mathews
Executive Sports Editors

Junior Maura Benson will not only be spending time at gyms and camps over the summer, but she will also be spending money to be there. Benson plays volleyball, basketball and badminton, and she has to pay $96 for a two-week volleyball camp and $176 for a three-week basketball camp.

Benson also participates in a summer basketball league, which adds expenses for uniforms and a sign-up fee. On top of the camp and league fees, Benson and her sister, freshman Trisha Benson, are also doing a team camp at the University of Notre Dame, which costs around $200. Benson said it is expensive to play sports, and even though her family can afford it, she still wants to help cover some of the costs.

Everything seems to have some monetary value and, as a result, nothing is truly free — even public schools. Parents pay for registration fees, bus fees and cafeteria lunches, and now students in all District 214 schools will be required to pay $25 for every activity they join.

Activities affected by this change are the same as those affected by the academic code policy. These include all sports, music programs and clubs. The district is implementing the fee for only

OUTSIDE ATHLETICS

The music hallway is no stranger to fees, and students involved in music programs will also see the $25 increase in their fees because of the new district policy. The district is applying the fee increase to all co-curriculars that fall under the no pass, no play policy.

Band director Chris Barnum feels it won't affect participation, but at the same time, he does not like to dwell on fees with his students and prefers to focus on the music.

In times of economic hardships, students have been forced to quit music activities, but there are scholarship opportunities to help cover fees for students who would not have been able to participate.

DISTRICT COST COMPARISON

Barrington - Registration fees are $138 higher than District 214, plus an additional $50 charge for band or orchestra
Downers Grove - $105 per activity; $22 for band or orchestra
Elmwood Park - $50 per activity; $100 for band or orchestra
Glenbard - $130 per activity
Glenbrook - Registration fees are $100 higher than District 214
Maine 207 - Registration fees are $129 higher than District 214
New Trier - Registration fees are $137 higher than District 214, plus $15 per activity
Highland Park - Registration fees are $190 higher than District 214, plus $100 per activity
Lake Forest - $195 per season with a family maximum of $780
Oak Park-River Forest - $50 per activity
Stevenson - $65 per activity
Woodstock - $92 per activity
Prospect Heights District 23 - $125 per activity with a family maximum of $375

those who participate in activities in order to prevent students from paying for services they don't use.

While the fees could put an economic strain on some families, the district has set a limit so no family will have to pay more than $100.

If a family cannot afford the activity fee, they can apply for a fee waiver along with the registration fee. The fee waiver is based on parent's income level. There are also opportunities to set up payment plans that divide the total cost into smaller payments that can be made over a period of time.

The money from the fees will go directly to the district office, where Associate Superintendent for Finance and Operations Deb Parenti will handle the distribution.

In the past, parents were actually surprised by the lack of fees because they were used to paying for various activities at the elementary and middle school levels.

The District 214 Board of Education decided a year ago to add a fee in order to offset the cost of running each schools' activities.

For the past 17 years, the Board of Education has been able to balance its budget with increasing taxes, but with recent economic problems, the state owes District 214 $4 million. Since the state is $15 billion in debt, it cannot pay its bills to the public schools.

"We haven't really hurt the class-

room for the students [with the fee change], and that's our basic focus," board member Bill Dussling said. "Let's control the budget with minimal effect on the classroom."

Associate Principal Greg Minter feels the only benefit students will see from the fees is the coverage of any competition transportation, hotels and meals when teams compete at state.

"I want to be able to maintain [our activities] as we have them," Minter said. "I don't believe the district would raise fees if they didn't need to."

Board member James Perkins feels there will initially be some disappointment and frustration because families have tight budgets and now have to pay even more.

"I think for the most part, families are accepting of the fact that it is expensive to play sports, and so they will be accepting of the fact that there is a fee associated with having those programs," Perkins said.

Athletes in multiple sports will be required to pay the fee more than once. Juniors Nick and Chris Meersman are involved in track and football, and they will be two more students affected by the new extra-curricular fee. For football players, fees are nothing new be-

cause they have been fundraising to cover the cost of the program for years.

Chris feels some students should be exempt from fees because they already have high fees to pay.

The Meersman family will be required to pay for each activity, and since each boy participates in two sports, this will just reach the $100 limit.

Catherine Mataloni, mother of sophomore Alec Mataloni, said her family will not be too affected by the fee change because she had experience with similar fees from when Alec was in middle school. She said other families, however, might feel strain from the fee.

Alec is on the robotics team and speech team, as well as being involved in school plays. While these activities aren't sports, they are included in the extra-curricular fee. Catherine feels the extra expenses will not affect Alec's participation, but at the same time, she suspects some families will have to be more selective.

Dussling said the board hopes that the new fee won't hurt student participation, but either way, the district has to cover the costs they have.

"I hope [students] understand costs are going up across the board, and we just have to cover that," Dussling said. "Somewhere, you have to fund the activities you want to have."

Minter said he didn't think most families would be too affected by the change, but he agreed that some families in less affluent areas might feel more of a burden.

Ultimately, the board is trying to give the students the best experiences possible, both through the classroom and extra-curricular activities.

"It is the first time we are charging anything, and we get that [the fees] are different," Superintendent Dr. David Schuler said. "[But] what is really important, from my perspective, is looking for ways to raise revenue in a manner that does not prevent students from participating in activities."

> "Let's control the budget with minimal effect on the classroom."
> - District board member Bill Dussling

FIGURE 1.8a *The Prospector*, Prospect High School, Mount Prospect, Ill. Reproduced by permission of Jason Block.

The *Prospector* front-page includes a promotional website link to a story about Haley Reinhart, a finalist in *American Idol*, shortly after she came third in the competition. The online story **1.8b** provided details of her hometown visit. Though she attended another school in this district, she was well-known and drew a lot of interest, boosting this mention on the front-page.

FIGURE 1.8b

Haley comes home

Submitted by Prospector on May 27, 2011 – 7:19 am   No Comment

By Miranda Holloway

Executive Online Editor

On May 14 Mount Prospect residents had a flashback. They remembered the warm May day where former resident and American Idol season nine winner Lee Dewyze came home for his hometown visit. He paraded down Central road and held a free concert at Arlington Park Race Track.

When they woke up from this flashback however, it was not them who had a new sweetheart. It was neighboring Wheeling who could now boast about having a resident become an 'Idol' finalist.

'09 Wheeling High School graduate Haley Reinhart made it to the top three on 'Idol's' season ten which brought her home to Wheeling.

Reinhart did not have the time to enjoy all of the comforts of home however, she had a packed schedule doing promotional events and filming material to be shown on 'Idol'.

Her day started her day in front of 200 fans at a Deer Park AT&T store. According to the Daily Herald, she teared up

at the store seeing all of her supporters, which was just a preview of the emotional day that faced her.

After making a few sentimental stops at old work places and favorite restaurants she then made a stop at her alma mater to promote Ford's "Drive One 4UR School" fundraiser. The program allowed people to test drive a Ford for a $20 dollar donation to the school's music program.

The fundraiser ultimately raised $10,000 for the music department. During her appearance Reinhart made speech to her hometown supporters and to current Wheeling students.

"For me, it started here. I hope this inspires you to do whatever you want to do in life," Reinhart said to the crowd according to the Daily Herald.

Secondary sources

Secondary sources are typically those that provide your story with factual information second-hand, such as a reference book, government records resource, credible Internet website or documentary film.

In a story on eating disorders, a student reporter might obtain state or national statistics on the current percentage of high school students with eating disorders from the National Eating Disorders Association, a credible secondary source. Citing these statistics and attributing them to the organization would give contextual breadth and factual depth to the story. Calling local or regional clinics for eating disorders and interviewing directors or doctors would provide primary source information for the story. Interviewing students in the school who are recovering or suffering from eating disorders would be the primary-source key to making this story work. What a student reporter should avoid is quoting a magazine article or professional newspaper story as a source for the story. That isn't original reporting (see Chapter 2 for more on interviewing and reporting).

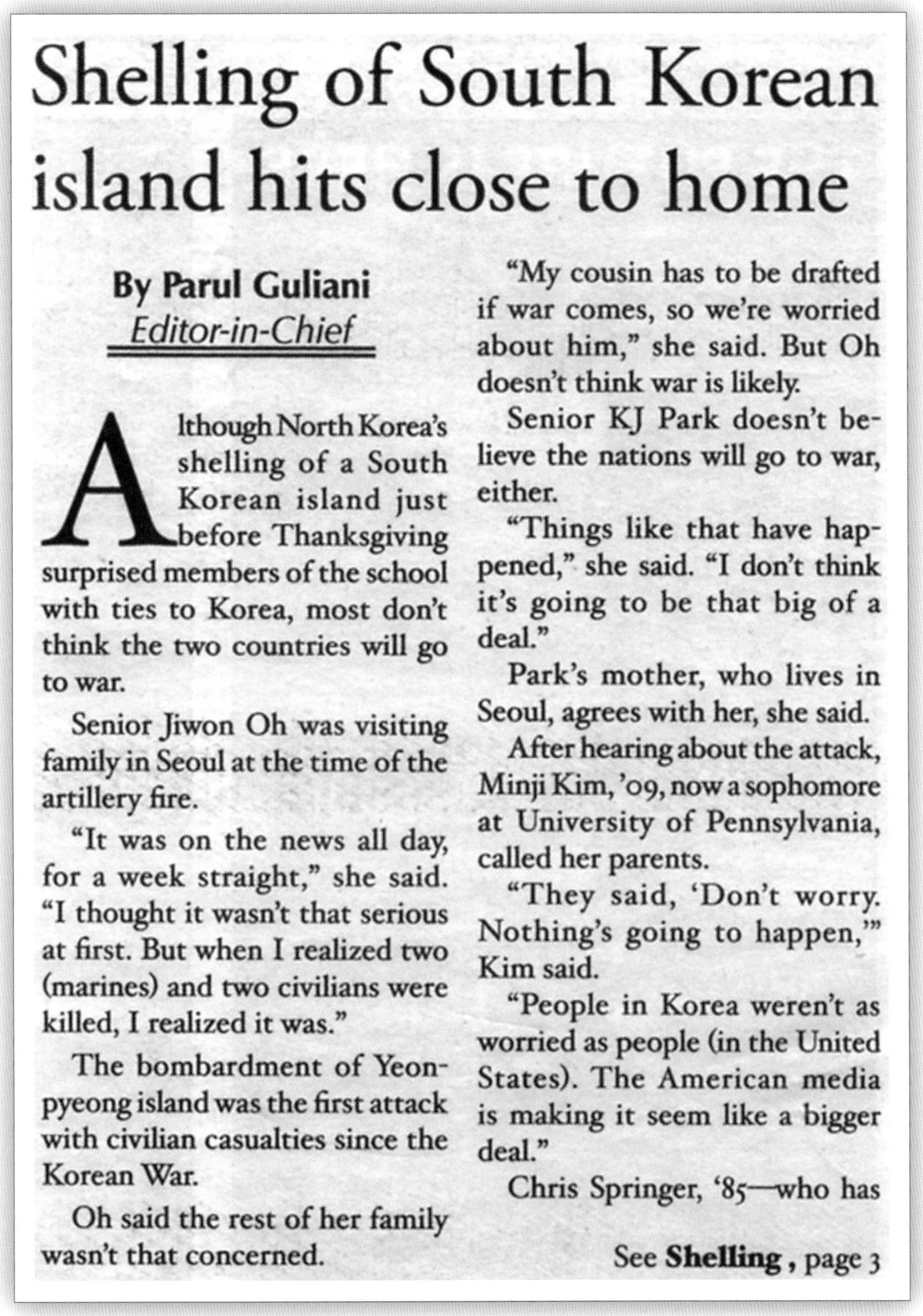

Shelling of South Korean island hits close to home

By Parul Guliani
Editor-in-Chief

Although North Korea's shelling of a South Korean island just before Thanksgiving surprised members of the school with ties to Korea, most don't think the two countries will go to war.

Senior Jiwon Oh was visiting family in Seoul at the time of the artillery fire.

"It was on the news all day, for a week straight," she said. "I thought it wasn't that serious at first. But when I realized two (marines) and two civilians were killed, I realized it was."

The bombardment of Yeonpyeong island was the first attack with civilian casualties since the Korean War.

Oh said the rest of her family wasn't that concerned.

"My cousin has to be drafted if war comes, so we're worried about him," she said. But Oh doesn't think war is likely.

Senior KJ Park doesn't believe the nations will go to war, either.

"Things like that have happened," she said. "I don't think it's going to be that big of a deal."

Park's mother, who lives in Seoul, agrees with her, she said.

After hearing about the attack, Minji Kim, '09, now a sophomore at University of Pennsylvania, called her parents.

"They said, 'Don't worry. Nothing's going to happen,'" Kim said.

"People in Korea weren't as worried as people (in the United States). The American media is making it seem like a bigger deal."

Chris Springer, '85—who has

See **Shelling**, page 3

FIGURE 1.9 *The Octagon*, Sacramento Country Day School, Sacramento, Calif. "Shelling of South Korean Island hits close to home," by Paul Guliana. Reproduced by permission of Patricia Fels.

In a news item of international interest involving a shelling by North Korea of a South Korean island, *Octagon* staff localized their coverage by interviewing students, one of whom was actually visiting family at the time of the event. Other students with Korean ties including alumni were also interviewed giving the story local focus. One alum, an author with two books on Korea, was also quoted extensively.

Similarly, many school publications try to cover events such as professional and college sporting events, often by using already published information or quotes from professional sources. This undermines the integrity of their work, in part because professional news sources have access to primary sources that most student publications can't get. The better way to cover such events is through localizing, getting student and staff reactions and opinions on events such as the Super Bowl, the World Series or the Final Four.

Many school publications cover the Oscars, the Grammys and other important entertainment events by interviewing students involved in drama or music, who have specialized knowledge

FIGURE 1.9 *(continued)*

Shelling: Escalation to full-scale war unlikely, Korean sources say

(Continued from page 1)

written two books about North Korea and has visited the country three times—agrees with Kim.

"When we read about incidents like this in the news, we get the impression that we're on the brink of another Korean War," he said.

"I think that's very alarmist."

He pointed out that since the end of the Korean War there have been hundreds of border incidents.

Korea, annexed by Japan in 1910, was divided at the 38th parallel after World War II by the United States and the Soviet Union. The latter occupied the area north of the border while American forces took responsibility for the area south of it.

"Each country set up a regime, and the 38th parallel became a Cold War border," Springer said. "Each one felt that it should administer the entire area."

North Korea felt so much so that it invaded the South on June 25, 1950.

"A repeat of the Korean War strikes me as extremely unlikely," Springer said.

Andy Furillo, '09, a sophomore at UC Berkeley, is a political science major with a focus on North East Asian politics, has taken Korean history and language classes and is a member of the Korean political discussion club.

Furillo said his Korean language class talked about the attack the day after it happened.

"All of my Korean friends were shocked that (North Korea) fired on civilians," he said. "They were really worried about their relatives."

However, Furillo's friends agreed life was going on as usual in the South Korean mainland.

But Furillo believes South Korea should retaliate more strongly.

"They can't let the North keep attacking them," he said. "At some point you have to go in and let them know they can't get away with it anymore."

Senior Daniel Edgren's grandfather Sam Lim—a Korean War veteran and émigré—thinks Furillo is right.

"If you're afraid of all-out war, you'll have all-out war. If you're not afraid of it and you defend really strongly, there won't be an all-out war," he said.

But he isn't against going to war—even nuclear war.

"If (there is) an atomic war, let them nuke once or twice. A million soldiers might die from it, but eventually, we will win," he said.

"But if you go piecemeal, little by little, a couple million will die."

in those areas. The coverage will be more appropriate and more interesting for the high school audience when local angles are covered and local sources are consulted. Student perspectives will often only be available in your school's publications.

Test your knowledge

Find examples of direct and indirect quotes in two news stories. Identify the sources of those quotes as primary or secondary sources.

OTHER FACTORS AFFECTING COVERAGE

What's important in news coverage can also be affected by a variety of factors unique to different schools and their locations. If the school is private and affiliated with a religious organization, news related to that affiliation will always be important. Issues such as tuition, uniforms, required chapel or other services might all be ripe for coverage. Magnet schools are usually established with a special focus: the visual arts, music, engineering and science, to name a few examples. News in those specialized disciplines will always be important for those magnet school communities. The pressure to succeed, to gain acceptance into prestigious universities, or into specialty programs are other common issues for students at such schools. Student expertise can also serve as a resource when reviewing entertainment, local services or technology products.

WORDS of WISDOM

Cultivating sources is one of the most important tasks a journalist must master because without sources, there is no story. Journalists need to be able to pick up the phone and call a source within minutes when news breaks. Sources are needed to make a story balanced and accurate and are also crucial if you want to do any investigative reporting. When sources trust journalists, they are more apt to alert them to an upcoming story, talk off the record or provide other background knowledge and leads.

To build a database of sources, prove to be an accurate and fair journalist. Keep off the record conversations out of print and follow up with sources even when there is no story in the works. Be personable; share something about yourself and also learn a little something about them that you can ask about whenever you talk. Prove you can be trusted and you will be surprised how much people start opening up to you.

Jennifer Buske-Sigal, Former Reporter, The Washington Post

Other schools might be part of consolidated districts made up of students from two or more nearby towns. Consolidated schools might have unique news coverage needs, based on the different communities they serve. School transportation might be a bigger issue and require a beat reporter. If the school is located in a rural setting, finding and traveling to games with competitors might be issues for sports coverage. Shared resources such as specialized teachers could require students to change campuses during the day. Students' interests outside of school might be distinctive if the community depends on an agricultural economic base. All of these factors could generate special beats and coverage.

Schools in urban settings have their own unique coverage opportunities. In the heart of a large city, students mix with professional workers, might commute to school on public transportation and might be vulnerable to factors such as crime. Urban schools often bring together students from a wide geographical area, who come from radically different communities. Such schools may have fewer after-school activities or meetings to cover, although demonstrations and political rallies might be more accessible for coverage, especially if students are taking part in them.

The demographics of the school population and community are always important in school news coverage. As community populations age and gentrify, school populations can increase or decrease, affecting the school populations, class sizes and sometimes whether or not schools in the district are closed. Schools made up of ethnic majorities are often most interested in issues affecting their particular cultures, such as traditional holidays and celebrations, ethnic foods and styles, as well as local political struggles and conflicts. Religious majorities will have similar interests, which will also affect how the students feel about national and world issues.

In private school settings, where schools might have greater legal ability to censor student journalists, some controversial topics may not be allowed in coverage, particularly if the topics go against the tenets of the private affiliation. In a Catholic school, an article exploring the topic of abortion might be disallowed or censored owing to the beliefs of the church (see Chapter 17 for more information on censorship).

If an important news event occurs in, or dramatically impacts, the school community, students might choose to publish a **special edition** out of their publishing cycle. Written by and for students,

Quick Exercise

In groups, discuss factors that make your school unique. How can these factors affect coverage in your newspaper and online content? Find an example of how one of these factors is represented in coverage from previous editions or online stories.

FIGURE 1.10 *ReMarker*, St. Mark's School of Texas, Dallas, Texas. Reproduced by permission of Ray Westbrook.

In a private school, relevant news might be unique to the school. In this featurized, local story, newspaper staff took a look at a required weekly chapel under a new chaplain who had changes in store for the service. The story takes up the major space on the front-page but is framed by inside page summaries and a more timely news story on a commencement speaker. To add visual interest, staff include a panel of visual references to stories inside the paper across the top.

thursday MAY 17, 2012
ST. MARK'S SCHOOL OF TEXAS
DALLAS, TX 75230
VOLUME 58, ISSUE 7

remarker

Junior Danny Koudelka p. 17 · Cum Laude ceremony p. 4 · Athens band p. 10 · Waleed Rashed p. 3 · Sophomore Sam Khoshbin p. 19

Author Gus Lee scheduled to speak at Commencement

by RACHIT MOHAN
special projects director

NINETY SENIORS, DRESSED IN bright white tuxedo jackets, will walk across the stage May 25, shake the headmaster's hand and receive their diplomas.

As each boy-turned-man steps off the stage, diploma in hand, he puts an end to his time at St. Mark's. But at the same moment, he commences a new journey, one that takes him well beyond the boundaries of 10600 Preston Road.

"I think most of us are ready to move on," Senior Class President Ross Crawford said. "I'm excited, but I'm more sad to leave than excited because this is a pretty awesome place, and I've pretty much known this my whole life so it's tough to actually be leaving."

Commencement speaker will be accomplished author Gus Lee, who writes on topics relating to ethics and leadership. He has also been a resource to development of the school's Leadership and Ethics Program.

He was chosen to address the Senior Class because he has a deep understanding of the community and its goals, so his speech can offer a more direct connection for the graduates.

"Gus Lee is speaking, and he's been around and knows the kids," sponsor J.T. Sutcliffe said. "Which is nice because it's always nice when you have somebody who doesn't come in and gives a bland, generic speech and hopefully tailor it a little bit."

commencement
headliners
- Guest speaker is noted leadership expert and author Gus Lee
- Student speakers include Senior Class President Ross Crawford and class valedictorian (to be named)
- Awards to be presented include Headmaster's Cup, the School Flag and Citizenship Cup
- Begins at 8 p.m.
- Reception follows in the Great Hall

Along with Lee, Crawford will address his class at commencement, as will the class valedictorian, who has not been named as of press time.

But while the seniors may be leaving campus, they have certainly left a trail of accomplishments and successes on the field, classroom and stage.

"The SPC victories, the academic leadership, the wonderful musical performances, they all attest to the achievement that this class has reached," Sutcliffe said. "So in many ways, that's what stays here."

Beyond accolades and awards, the senior class has set the tone for spirit and community support.

CONTINUED, PAGE 6

THE CHANGING ✝ CHAPEL

up&coming

TAKE A SCHOOL OF TEENAGE BOYS EAGER FOR CHANGE AND A NEED FOR A NEW CHAPLAIN. ADD ENGAGING WEEKLY SPEECHES AND PLANS FOR A REVITALIZED CHAPEL SERVICE. WHAT DO YOU GET? REV. MICHAEL DANGELO, OF COURSE.

AS SOPHOMORE JACK PIGOTT WALKED INTO THE DIMMED CHAPEL AMID THE HORDES OF UPPER School students for his March 14 edition of weekly mandated half-hour of respite, his grumbles of apathy and indifference were replaced by a hush of anticipation.

There was a new face atop the altar — a new face that already had large expectations.

When new chaplain Rev. Michael Dangelo first began to speak, a rare aura of personality and charisma was emitted from his every pore, one that captivated Pigott as soon as the minister abandoned the pulpit to homilize from the nave itself. There was something different about him. CONTINUED, PAGE 15

▶ by Paul Gudmundsson, managing editor

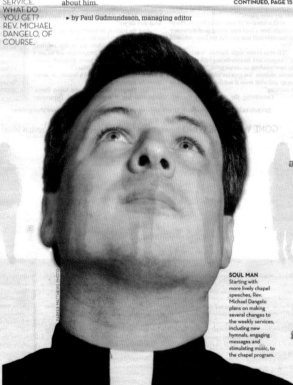

SOUL MAN
Starting with more lively chapel speeches, Rev. Michael Dangelo plans on making several changes to the weekly services, including new hymnals, engaging messages and stimulating music, to the chapel program.

inside

news
▶ By the time he turned 18, senior Roland Salatino had accomplished what only a few Boy Scouts had ever done before: he had earned his 17th palm award. **Page 5.**

scene
▶ Whether it's through his piano concerts at Carnegie Hall or his contagious smile at school, senior Roderick Demmings has touched the lives of countless people. Read his story. **Page 8.**

centerspread
▶ Did you know that in Texas it is illegal to milk another person's cow? We take a look at some of our own little-known rules. **Pages 12-13.**

sports
▶ After the 60th anniversary of SPC this year, we take a look back at some of the best moments in Lions sports. **Page 16.**

commentary
▶ When the deadline for Blue and Gold Day event signups passed, many students did not know where or by when they were supposed to sign up. See the Editorial Board's suggestions to improve communication. **Page 21.**

ahead

today
▶ Last day of classes for grades 9-12
▶ AP exams
▶ Athletic Banquet in Great Hall, 6:30 p.m.

tomorrow
▶ Reading day for grades 9-11
▶ AP exams

saturday
▶ Exams for grades 8-11
▶ Marksmen Ball, 6:30 p.m.

index

News	2-7
Scene	8-11, 14
Centerspread	12-13
Up & coming	15
Sports	16-20
Commentary	21-23
Fun Day	24

❝❝ WORDS of WISDOM

As a religion writer, I think about finding the faith angle in current events or localizing a larger trend in religion news. For enterprise story ideas, never turn off your curiosity. Try to discover the reasons behind facts and ask experts to predict the implications. For instance, why is your cafeteria switching food services? Was there a problem with the old company or its products? Will the new one help students maintain a healthy lifestyle? What will this mean for the overall functioning of your community? Will it save your school money? What can be done with a few extra pennies?

The answers could lead to more questions and unearth information vital to students, parents, faculty, staff and visitors. Always try to consider and give a voice to all players involved in a topic, and your sources may shape your story. Don't try to pigeonhole a story into the blueprint you initially imagine.

Angela Cave, Reporter and Web Coordinator, The Evangelist, *Albany, N.Y.*

❞❞

the special edition might frame the news event from the perspective of the student audience, providing context and school-oriented viewpoints. Many school publications chose to present special editions after the events of Sept. 11, 2001. Other schools have published special editions after natural disasters and serious weather events in their communities or when tragic crimes such as school shootings occur.

Alternatively, a **special section** of coverage might be included in the next print edition, particularly if the coverage is still timely and ongoing in its effects on the school and community. This kind of coverage isn't limited to news events, but could take a look at larger issues such as those of race, gender, sexual orientation, economics, politics, health or labor. In all cases, coverage should center on the people in the school and community, and should examine broader issues from a local perspective. Many schools publish special sections before political elections, particularly presidential ones, with coverage focused on student polls and perspectives, and on local candidates. Interviewing students active in political campaigns or with strong political affiliations can provide a local angle while drawing on their knowledge and analysis (see Chapter 8 for more information on in-depth reporting).

In all reporting, student journalists should strive to ensure their coverage is fair, broad-based and sensitive to their readers. Student journalists should frequently evaluate their coverage to make sure they are being inclusive to all school populations.

CONCLUSION

Though news is still at the heart of a newspaper's mission, technology has altered the way in which traditional news is presented. The core elements of news value remain important in choosing and presenting information to readers and viewers. Without a timeliness angle, journalists rely on another value, often emphasizing a feature angle. Information presented to readers should be chosen and organized based on audience interest.

Test your knowledge

Can you think of an upcoming event, anniversary or special occasion that would make a good topic for a special section of coverage?

SUMMARY

- Reporters should be inquisitive and sensitive to discussions with friends and throughout the school in identifying topics that would make good stories.

- Hyperlocal news and reporting about your specialized school audience will be of primary interest to readers.

- Journalists must take seriously their role as gatekeepers of information.

- News value helps reporters order news in placement in print and online.

- Organized beats help newspapers broaden coverage across the school.

- Featurizing news helps keep it current.

- News sources should primarily be local, school and community based.

- News appears throughout the print edition and website in sections such as news, sports and entertainment.

KEY TERMS

advance story	featurized news	primary audience
angle	future story	primary sources
attribution	gatekeepers of information	prominence
audience	human interest	proximity
beats	hyperlocal news	review
breaking news	indirect quote	secondary audience
conflict	localizing news	secondary sources
coverage	news brief	special edition
direct quote	news lead	special section
drama	news story	surprise or oddity
emotion	news value	third-party source
evergreen news		timeliness

EXERCISES

1   Do a demographic survey of your community and your school population. Using the latest U.S. Census figures from www.census.gov, analyze the make-up of your neighborhood, city, county and state in terms of population, ethnicity, age/sex and housing status. Visit the website for your school district and see if you can compare similar data for your school or district. Or, see if your school keeps data on these demographics.

2   Using the data you collected in Exercise 1, go through a copy of your newspaper and the website and note how many stories relate to this data. What other story ideas can you think of that might draw on, or relate to this demographic information.

3   Find five examples in stories of news value from print or online editions and explain how the value affected the story's placement and space.

4   Analyze five leads from online or print editions. Mark each to identify the *who, what, when, where, why* and *how* elements. Which news element was featured in each lead?

5   In a group, find two examples of featurized news from print or online editions. Share and discuss your examples. What is the timeliness factor? Why was the news featurized?

6   Identify three examples in past editions of your print paper or online edition in which strong visual impact is present in a photo, online slideshow or video. How does the visual impact increase interest in the story?

INTERVIEWING AND REPORTING

2

> *Our greatest asset in journalism is our credibility. Take extra care to get every detail right: the facts, the date, the analysis, the quotes and the context.*
>
> Cindy McCurry-Ross, Managing Editor, The News-Press Media Group, Fort Myers, Fla.

LEARNING OBJECTIVES After completing this chapter you will be able to:

- prepare thoroughly before conducting an interview

- develop questions to elicit thorough answers

- employ a range of interviewing techniques to evoke elaboration and detail

- implement strategies to examine the validity of sources and information

- explore uses of the Internet for journalistic research.

Scholastic Journalism, Twelfth Edition. C. Dow Tate and Sherri A. Taylor.
© 2014 John Wiley & Sons, Inc. Published 2014 by John Wiley & Sons, Inc.

GATHERING INFORMATION IS A JOURNALIST'S primary job. Young reporters should understand that they must have accurate, thorough and developed information before they ever sit down to write. This chapter will cover the process of gathering such information through talking to people and researching facts. Students may be good writers, but they will not be good journalists until they understand the basics of the information gathering process.

INTERVIEWING

Interviewing, or asking questions to get information, may seem easy. Watch first graders' hands shoot up to ask questions. Human beings seem to be born curious. Talking to others seems natural. So when you sit down with another student for an interview, tossing out questions to get her to talk should be simple.

> **"What's your favorite color?"**
> **"Do you like school?"**
> **"Do you have any pets?"**

But now look at the students' answers to these questions.

> **"Blue."**
> **"No."**
> **"Yes. One. A dog named Wiggles."**

Even seven or eight more questions that can be answered with "Yes", "No" or a three-word phrase would not elicit enough information for the reporter to write a story about this student. A good interview requires planning, thought and development.

Before sitting down with a subject, it is important that the reporter knows what she wants to get out of the interview. Here are some common reasons why reporters conduct interviews:

- to gain an understanding that enables the reporter to explain the issue to readers
- to understand a story from different perspectives
- to gather real-life examples that illustrate a topic or a person's character
- to observe details or experiences related to the topic or person
- to fully understand how people feel. A reporter may watch a senior win second in the state pole vault but not understand the athlete's disappointment until an interview reveals that he cleared the first-place height 10 times during the year but failed to come close in the state final round.

Without a good interview or solid information, the reporter does not have a story. A skilled reporter understands that gathering the information through interviews and research based on reliable sources is critical before ever sitting down to write. Too often, young reporters struggle when they begin to write, claiming writer's block. The real issue, more often than not, is that the writer simply doesn't have enough information to write with. The interview was poor, the research inadequate or the story is not properly focused.

The interview process begins by identifying a good story idea – a clear focus on something that people are interested in reading about. (The development of a good story idea is discussed in Chapter 1. Interviewing as it relates to the different types of stories, such as news or features, is covered in news and feature writing in Chapters 3 and 5.) Once the reporter has a focus, **backgrounding**, or gathering information prior to interviewing, is the next step.

Background research will help the reporter understand the story well enough to develop insightful questions. For example, a young journalist doing a story about Ritalin use by those with Attention Deficit Disorder might not think to ask about nightmares unless he'd read about the drug and discovered that nightmares are sometimes a side effect.

A reporter can pursue background information through a variety of avenues. He can research the topic he's interviewing the person about, or the person himself, or both. If a reporter is assigned to write a story about a competitive snowboarder who has already been covered in the local newspaper, the reporter should start by reading that story. If no publication has covered this snowboarder before, then the reporter should prepare by reading as much as he can on the sport of snowboarding.

Background sources might include the following:

- magazine articles
- books
- subject relevant websites
- school newspaper "**morgue**," the archive of previous years' newspapers
- interviews with the subject's friends, colleagues or competitors
- preinterviews with the subject.

Test your knowledge

What is backgrounding?

Developing questions

Journalists should think of themselves as the voice of the people when it comes to asking questions. If you don't ask, then who will? A reporter's job is to find out the information that the reader needs to know. Forming questions properly will ensure that readers get the clear and developed answers they deserve.

How you ask a question will have much to do with the quality of the answer you get. The basic **5 W's and H** are the foundation of a good interview.

- Who was involved?
- What happened or is happening?
- When did it happen?
- Where did it happen?
- Why did it happen?
  and
- How did it happen?

The journalist's work doesn't end with these six questions. A good interview is a conversation with the subject doing most of the talking. Remember that the yes/no questions used at the start of the chapter stop conversations.

Good young reporters should write out and organize their questions. This process should start by identifying different topics for questions. The writer should, by thinking about the focus, create a bullet list that maps out the different parts of the story.

Let's see how this could work. The reporter is assigned a profile on a girl, on the cross-country team, who has no hands. She moved to the United States from Sierra Leone, a West African nation that suffered a decade of civil war. During the conflict, rebels attacked the student's village, cut off her hands and left her to die. So what topic areas do these facts suggest?

- her life in Sierra Leone
- her move here
- her life since she's moved
- the incident that took her hands
- her rehabilitation since the incident.

A good reporter may even break these topics up further. For example, the last topic might include sub-topics such as:

- emotional struggles during the rehabilitation
- physical issues she's dealt with since the incident.

Quick Exercise

Where could you find background for the following stories?

1 A cancer patient support group granted sophomore Vanessa Davis her wish to meet Coldplay.

2 At its next meeting, the school board is considering a schedule change to a four-day school week.

When the basic topics for the interview have been identified, the reporter should start developing the questions for each topic and organize the interview into sections.

Organizing the interview

Organizing each step logically will help ensure that the interview is successful. The reporter and subject will understand the flow better and both will relax.

The easier questions should come early. It is standard practice to start by confirming the spelling of the subject's name and his or her position or title. (Never assume the spelling of even common names, such as John.) Another good approach at the start of the interview is to double-check the background information with the source. Interview subjects often fear students are going to make them look bad in print or won't get the story right. Starting the interview with simple, non-confrontational questions that demonstrate that the reporter has done her homework will help the interview subject loosen up. This will help produce a relaxed, conversational and informative interview.

In the scenario involving the student from Sierra Leone, the reporter might begin by double-checking some information about the student's homeland. Or perhaps the reporter could ask the student how cross-country practice is going. The more sensitive topics – the incident in which she lost her hands and the struggles of rehabilitation – may come later, after she's more comfortable.

Starting with easier questions and moving to tougher ones later on is one logical structure for the interview, but many other organizational strategies can be effective. A reporter could ask about problems first and move to solutions. The journalist could choose a chronological order, with questions about earlier events coming first followed by those that occurred later.

In developing the detailed questions beyond the 5 W's and H, reporters need to think through exactly what information they want from the subject. An inexperienced reporter might ask the question, "What did you do this weekend?" The answer, more than likely, will be a quick list. However, if the subject is asked to: "Describe what you did this weekend," the answer will be a slower, more detailed account.

If a reporter is trying to get specific stories from a person's work days, an inexperienced reporter might ask, "What's an average day babysitting triplets like?" The answer to this question will likely be an "average" – a general, often vague list of activities. A better way to phrase the question might be, "Take me through your last Thursday babysitting the triplets;" or, "Describe your most memorable day of babysitting the triplets." Asking about a precise day increases the odds of getting a specific description because you have chosen a certain occasion, preferably a recent one that the subject will remember and recall more easily. Point-in-time questions will be useful for creating a scene or making sure the example is specific.

"Take me back to when you lost last year's state championship. What did you do when you got home? What was trying to get to sleep like that night?" are better ways to phrase the question than, "How did you feel after last year's state championship loss?"

When tackling a particularly complicated story, the reporter may better comprehend the topic if he frames questions to elicit simplified answers. For a school budget story, ask: "If you were talking to a fifth grader, how would you explain the impact the tax rate increase will have on students?" Don't worry about appearing stupid. The goal is to get understandable information so the topic can be clearly explained to readers who have various education and reading levels. A reporter can always ask a follow-up question for elaboration.

On the other hand, don't ever ask the subject to, "Just give me a quote." The answers will be forced, unnatural and often clichéd.

Setting up the interview

After mapping out the questions, the reporter's next step is to set up the interview. Give the subject a sense of the time it will take. The interview should be in a setting with few distractions. Avoid noisy cafeterias. While a student's home might seem conducive, the interview subject may end up distracted by siblings or a favorite TV show. If hanging out with a group of friends, the subject may be prone to put on a show for them rather than answering your questions honestly or seriously. Don't be afraid to politely ask the subject to turn off the TV or move away from the distractions.

Some interviews should be conducted while the emotions and thoughts are fresh. A reporter covering a student fashion show would be wise to try to visit the make-up room where the first-time runway models might discuss how they are feeling 30 minutes before the show. Their thoughts would be real and raw compared to what might be a weak recollection, if the interview is conducted two weeks after the event.

Interview the subject face to face. Phone interviews are a solid backup plan, but they don't allow for physical observation, which will be discussed later in this chapter. Email interviews should be a last resort. People often fail to answer the entire question in writing, and you have no way to elicit a more thorough response in the moment. (Since email interviews potentially give subjects more time to think about responses, papers often note that quotes were "stated in an email interview"). Texting interviews provide even less information than emailed ones and are unacceptable unless used to clarify a detail, such as the name of a relative or the make of a car. No matter what medium you conduct interviews in, make sure all subjects know they are being interviewed for a story.

Conducting the interview

The best interviews are conversational. Don't read questions robotically. Talk to the subject. Your natural curiosity and sincere interest will pay off. In many cases, interview subjects are talking about their favorite topics – whether themselves or something related to their life's work or passion – so they will be happy to talk to a listener who seems genuinely interested.

Body language plays an important role in making a connection with the subject. A journalist should demonstrate undivided attention and interest. The interviewer who leans in suggests that the information being conveyed is important and valuable. On the other hand, if the reporter averts her eyes, checks her phone for texts or glances at the clock, the subject may cut answers short, because the reporter seems uninterested.

Make sure your interview subjects know you're talking to them for a story. The language can be as simple as: "For this story I'm writing about the grading policy changes, I'd like to ask you a few questions …" For ethical reasons, sources should be informed that their words may be published. If you're recording the interview, ask the source if it's okay to do so. In certain states, it's illegal to tape someone without his or her consent.

In some interviews, making small talk or interjecting your own personality into the exchange can help you connect with the subject. Still, you should keep your own talking to a minimum and avoid taking over the interview. The interview is about your subject, not you. Also, if you plan to use recorded clips on your publication's website, you will want to avoid talking over or interrupting your subject.

WWW

WEBLINK Check out

http://www.rjionline.org/ news/mobile-journalism-reporting-tools-guide

The website offers the mobile journalist a breakdown of the numerous apps and equipment available for interviewing and reporting.

Quick Exercise

Identify two good places in your school where you and a subject might meet for an interview.

HELPFUL TIPS

Interview preparation checklist:

- appropriate dress, without going overboard – a suit and tie is a little much for a teacher profile interview; a ragged shirt would be condescending for an interview with homeless teens

- clear interview focus

- good understanding of your subject through background research

- questions with space left for answers and pages numbered for clarity

- plenty of paper and working pens or pencils

- confidence to ask questions loudly and clearly

- working voice recorder with fresh batteries or a fully charged smartphone with recording capabilities. Try out the recording quality before starting the interview. A loud overhead air conditioner can drown out the subject's voice.

WORDS of WISDOM

Whether you have five minutes to interview someone, or all the time in the world, it is important that you establish a connection with the person you are interviewing before you start rolling a camera or go on the record. If you go to the interviewee (which I prefer because you catch the subject in an environment that is comfortable) look for things like photos, school logos or anything that your interviewee has around them that is important to them. Ask the person about a few items and try to find something in common. The more you make a connection with the interviewee before you go on the record, the more open the person will be with you on the record.

Ellen McNamara, Anchor/Reporter, KSTP Minneapolis-St. Paul

Take notes, even when recording an interview. Voice recorders may fail or batteries run out. Taking notes can provide assurance to the subject that the reporter is engaging with the information and has a backup if the recorder doesn't work. An efficient reporter will also make use of the timer on the recorder or smartphone. She will make note of the times of good quotes, so that they can be easily located later on, when she is **transcribing** parts of the interview, typing them out word for word.

A good reporter will make sure to identify and write down the best direct quotes from the interview. A **direct quote**, or the exact words a person says, will be useful to recreate a real sense of the subject's experiences or insights. Direct quotes should always be accurate and enclosed in quotation marks. Each direct quote should include **attribution**, a phrase explaining who said it. Other answers from the interview may be important for the story but not so important that the information needs to be repeated word for word. In this case, reporters can **paraphrase**, or provide an **indirect quote**, by summarizing the information in their own words, without quotation marks, but still attributing it to the source. Journalists are often told to "paraphrase fact, quote opinion" when discussing direct and indirect quotes.

Examine the differences between the following two versions of a story about a student who lost both parents within the same year. In this section of the story, the girl describes the weeks leading up to her mom's death. What does the direct quote communicate that the indirect quote does not?

Direct quote

"We didn't know how much time she had when she first got sick so she made a point to tell [us daughters] we're not gonna fight about dumb things, we're not gonna go to bed angry, we're just gonna love each other," junior Maddie Cardell said. "I remember her telling me, 'You're gonna be happy, you're gonna be fun and we're gonna have a good relationship instead of fighting with each other and just love each other.'"

Indirect quote or paraphrase

Junior Maddie Cardell said she didn't know how much time her mother had to live so they agreed not to fight or go to bed angry.

A good reporter will begin identifying good quotes as the interview proceeds. **Clichés**, or over-used phrases, can be left aside and vague language may be worth only a line or two on a reporter's notepad. Good quotes must be recorded accurately, since they may form the heart of the story.

So what makes a good direct quote? Good quotes will often feature some or all of the following:

- Words that are more descriptive than the writer could use. This quote package comes from a story about a student who was severely injured in a car accident. He later died, but the boy's friends and family went into the hospital room moments before he was taken off a respirator.

  "I just walked in, and you gotta take deep breaths before you walk into that room, because you can't control tears from coming out of your eyes when you walk in there and see your best friend lying on the bed, completely, just gone," junior Adam Levin said. "There's no way to describe that feeling. I didn't know what to say. I had to sit there for a few minutes and just look at him. Held his hand, and touched him, and finally, I don't even remember what I said. I said good-bye and told him I loved him and then I left. I can't even remember what I said to him, it's just overwhelming to see that."

  Levin's words express a feeling of helplessness and pain that the writer's paraphrase could not.

- Words that convey a unique voice, even though their meaning may be ordinary: In the following story about the head football coach's battle with cancer, the athletic director describes the impact the coach's struggle had on players.

  "We were doing a particularly hard running drill and a player came up to me and was like 'coach, my knees hurt.' And I just kinda pointed over at Coach Sherman who was running hard with the team and said, 'What do you think he's feelin'?' And the kid said, 'I think my knees are okay, coach.'"

  The athletic director's example conveyed a distinctive voice through a relatively commonplace quote. If others were asked what they thought of the coach's struggle, they may have said "He's an inspiration" or "We admire his courage." While those may be true statements, the quote that frames the issue with a unique voice is more likely to capture readers' attention.

- Words that the reader needs to hear from the subject word for word: In this quote from a story about increased use of the illegal drug "Molly" at area schools, the school resource officer speaks to the cases at his own school:

  "It wouldn't surprise me if [Molly] is here and if it's not here, I would expect to see it show up," school resource officer Joel Porter said.

  Although the word choice isn't particularly unique, the officer is a source who knows the subject and school well, and his conviction that the school will see its share of this drug is worthy of a direct quote.

Avoid directly quoting clichés and unclear statements. Even if a coach is pounding the table saying "There's NO I in TEAM!" or "It's do-or-die time," the reporter shouldn't waste his time writing it down. A quote such as, "Yes, I liked it a lot" or "I didn't like it. The music was disappointing," doesn't tell the reader much. Instead of writing down vague statements and moving on to the next question, a good reporter might ask a **follow-up question** – a question in response to a source's statement designed to evoke greater specificity or a clearer explanation.

The reality of most interviews is that the subject will not speak in vivid detail or engaging elaboration without some prodding on the part of the journalist.

The reporter should use follow-up questions in the natural flow of conversation, to prompt the subject to provide more information. If the senior who left the prom early says, "The music was disappointing," the intelligent reporter will follow up with questions such as:

"What was disappointing about the music?"
"What did you not like about the music?"
"Give me an example of the songs that you found disappointing."
"So what did you and your date say about the music and why did you decide to leave?"

FIGURE 2.1 *ReMarker*, St. Mark's School of Texas, Dallas, Texas. Reproduced by permission of Ray Westbrook.

When an older event is critical to a story, a journalist will want to work to get enough information and details to accurately recreate the scene. In this *ReMarker* story, the reporter asked for the details leading up to the key moment to help place it in the everyday context in which it occurred. Those details then provide a sharp contrast with the exploding window and twisting metal of the accident that changed this first grade instructor's life.

JOURNEY OF FAITH

When doors fly open

As the second anniversary of her diagnosis with breast cancer approaches, first-grade instructor Valencia Yarbrough reflects on all the times she's been in times of trouble. Some people might credit luck after making it through the hardships, but she believes in help from above. According to Yarbrough, "God opened doors."

SACRED SPOT Standing in the school chapel, where she was married in 2010, first-grade instructor Valencia Yarbrough looks back on the tough times she's been through, including a near-fatal car wreck, an internal religious struggle and cancer.

It happened on the freeway.

The 19-year-old needed to fill her brand-new 1979 car's tank. Maybe she'd get a milkshake at the gas station. Worn out after the long drive under a cloudless sky, she approached her exit and turned the steering wheel.

A tad too much.

The vehicle flipped as it flew off the freeway, then tumbled across the grass. Windows exploded. Metal twisted.

Inside, first grade instructor Valencia Yarbrough, then an aspiring engineer, screamed and clutched the seat beneath her.

She wasn't wearing her seatbelt.

"I should not have survived that car accident," Yarbrough said. "I had been blessed with a miracle."

She crawled out of a shattered window, unscathed.

Years later, when Yarbrough told her husband, an engineer, about the accident, he couldn't believe she had survived.

"There is not enough strength in your arms to hold you in that car," husband Willie Yarbrough told her. "That wasn't your power. That was God protecting you."

Yarbrough believes in help from above. She almost lost her faith. She almost didn't become a teacher. And, she has survived breast cancer.

"From the very beginning," she said, "God opened doors."

• • •

A teenage Yarbrough trudged past the pews, following her parents.

A freshman at Hockaday, she had taken a class on ancient civilizations that challenged her beliefs, and she hardly wanted to go to church anymore.

As the service began, Yarbrough squinted at the pulpit. A teen, about Yarbrough's age, adjusted his glasses and started to speak. He delivered a sermon that "really impacted" Yarbrough's life.

"It wasn't just the words of the Bible that affected me," Yarbrough said. "It was the fact that he was a kid."

After the sermon, Yarbrough thanked the speaker. Turned out

he was a Marksman who lived two blocks away from her. That's how she met Michael Walker '75.

"[Delivering sermons] was a real practical way of changing the world," Walker said.

His time at 10600 Preston Road influenced him to become a pastor, and he now preaches openness to all religions in Massachusetts.

"Love of God, love of people," Walker said. "I'm still working on that today."

Yarbrough started going to church with Walker and other neighborhood kids. Suddenly, religion became personal, not a ritual.

"I was eating it up because these weren't old people — people the age I am now," Yarbrough said. "Michael Walker's making it applicable to my life and making it real to me."

• • •

Arriving at Stanford University's campus, Yarbrough headed

to the dorms.

She was happy to see her roommate, a friend who showed Yarbrough "how the message of the Bible impacted her life and permeated everything she did."

"God paired me up with her," Yarbrough said.

But she was disappointed at the same time.

She'd called Walker, hoping to join his Bible study, but Walker's group had already finished. Luckily, the day she arrived back on campus, she met someone who invited her to a Bible study.

"Once again, God provides," Yarbrough said, looking up. "And that's actually where I met my husband."

• • •

Yarbrough decided to become an educator after volunteering at a religious organization, YoungLife. She applied to a graduate program for people with degrees in fields other than education. If she was accepted, she could become a teacher.

But she was hiking with a YoungLife group in the Sierra Nevada Mountains when the college program called her back to Dallas for an interview that couldn't be rescheduled.

After prayer-filled hours of travel, she barely made it.

"And when I got to my interview," Yarbrough said, "the [interviewer] and I just had a connection."

Once again, she credits the supernatural—on the bus to the mountains, Yarbrough happened to read a book about disciplining children.

"And everything [the interviewer] asked me," Yarbrough said, laughing, "I could answer based on what I had read in this book."

• • •

Diagnosed with breast cancer in March 2010, Yarbrough planned to get married four months later. She reflects on those tough days as the second anniversary of her diagnosis approaches.

"I was planning to celebrate a joyous occasion," Yarbrough said. "All of a sudden—bang."

All the events fell perfectly and Yarbrough beat the disease, so she didn't have to cancel the wedding, which was held in the school chapel. But why would God give her cancer?

"Honestly? To tell people about Him," Yarbrough said. "Perhaps God allows negative situations to arise in the lives of believers so that we can demonstrate His love to those around us."

It all started when she crawled out of her car's smashed windows in 1979. That's when she realized "God had a purpose" for her life.

"I pray that my work as an educator is doing what He called me to do," Yarbrough said. "And I trust that it is."

" PERHAPS GOD ALLOWS NEGATIVE SITUATIONS TO ARISE IN THE LIVES OF BELIEVERS SO **THAT WE CAN DEMONSTRATE HIS LOVE TO THOSE AROUND US.**

— First grade teacher Valencia Yarbrough

WHEN DOORS FLY OPEN story by Vishal Gokani, staff writer | photo by Richard Eiseman, staff photographer

These questions should draw out details that will help the reporter understand the music the subject didn't like, why he didn't like it and the disappointment he felt.

Follow-up questions can also help elicit **anecdotes**, or interesting short stories that bring an experience to life. The reporter who asks for an example or probes to get the subject to take him back to a specific time may get a good anecdote with some details. However, there is little likelihood that the subject will describe all the details clearly enough for the reporter to accurately retell the experience in a story.

A reporter should work for those details through a series of follow-up questions. In examining the following interview, assess what you think the reporter got from it and where follow-ups were needed.

RAINA THE REPORTER: So I hear you raised a cow for your Future Farmers of America project?

SAM THE SOPHOMORE: Yep.

RAINA THE REPORTER: What was it like?

SAM THE SOPHOMORE: It was cool most of the time.

RAINA THE REPORTER: Most of the time? When was it not?

SAM THE SOPHOMORE: You know. The times when it drug me. It was just so big. He'd pin me again the fence. It was scary.

RAINA THE REPORTER: When was it cool?

SAM THE SOPHOMORE: I liked when he won and stuff.

RAINA THE REPORTER: Wow! What'd you win?

SAM THE SOPHOMORE: Reserve grand champion.

RAINA THE REPORTER: That's cool. Congrats.

The reporter asked a few questions and found out some basic information. But she missed a real opportunity for some great stories connected with raising an animal that is more than likely four times Sam's weight.

Look at the interview and see what information the reporter lacks. Also look to see what the reporter might be assuming she understands. The reporter makes reference to a "cow." But what breed? A Shorthorn calf may weigh 300 pounds whereas a full-grown Longhorn may weigh 1,200 pounds. The breed and age make a visual difference, especially if Raina intends to report that the animal dragged Sam and pinned him against a fence.

Besides lacking a good specific description of the times when he was dragged and pinned, Raina also doesn't have a clear sense of what this felt like for Sam. Scary? No big deal? Was he apprehensive about getting hurt? Or was he so traumatized by the experience that he did not think he could go back to the barn? Did he actually fear for his life?

Before Raina writes a story on Sam, she will want to go back to reinterview him. Even though Sam might not be the most talkative interview subject, this time Raina knows she needs to do a better job of listening for vague language and asking follow-up questions, until she is able to get a better grasp of Sam's experiences and perspective.

RAINA THE REPORTER: Please describe the cow you raised.

SAM THE SOPHOMORE: Well, he was a steer.

RAINA THE REPORTER: What kind?

SAM THE SOPHOMORE: A Hereford.

RAINA THE REPORTER: One of those red and white faced ones? How big?

SAM THE SOPHOMORE: Yep, he was white-faced and weighed 1,300 pounds at the sale.

RAINA THE REPORTER: Describe what it was like when you first got him. Were you scared?

SAM THE SOPHOMORE: A little. I mean, he could jerk his head and he'd pull me around. I learned to control him a little better after that.

RAINA THE REPORTER: Really! How so?

SAM THE SOPHOMORE: I'd just dig the heels of my boots in and keep my hand right at the top of the rope next to his halter.

RAINA THE REPORTER: Describe what happened the day you were dragged.

SAM THE SOPHOMORE: Well, I was walking him along the railroad tracks and he just spooked.

RAINA THE REPORTER: Did he hear something?

SAM THE SOPHOMORE: A train whistle in the distance, I think. I barely heard it. Then it was just out of nowhere, he bucked and ran.

RAINA THE REPORTER: Did you hang on?

SAM THE SOPHOMORE: At first. I held onto the rope flying across the grass. I thought he'd stop. Then I saw he was running for the road. I just let go. I didn't want to get scratched up on that pavement or get hit.

RAINA THE REPORTER: How close to the road were you?

SAM THE SOPHOMORE: About 10 feet.

RAINA THE REPORTER: Were you hurt?

SAM THE SOPHOMORE: Bruised and scratches on my arms. And I dug mud out from behind my belt buckle.

RAINA THE REPORTER: Were there cars on the road?

SAM THE SOPHOMORE: A few. Mostly folks headin' home from the packing plant.

RAINA THE REPORTER: Last time you said you were scared. How so?

SAM THE SOPHOMORE: I was just glad we sold him that week. I didn't want to walk him anymore after that. I knew if he spooked, I couldn't control him.

IN ACTION

Reporting and interviewing at work

Sensitive and complex stories will challenge the reporting and interviewing skills of a journalist. In the following example, this reporter shows a keen ability to ask the questions in order to get details to develop scenes so the reporter can see the image for himself. She also demonstrates an understanding of the complicated medical topic, enough to give readers clear explanations and examples so they comprehend what the family is going through.

FIGURE 2.2 *The Hawk Eye*, Hebron High School, Carrollton, Texas. "Daughters connected through paternal loss," by Erin Hotchkiss, pp. 8–9, Jan. 20, 2012. Reprinted with permission.

1 The reporter gathered nice detail and dialogue for the opening scene to help illustrate a simple task that the Wegman girls' father couldn't accomplish because of his ailment. "Show, don't tell" is a phrase used in journalistic writing to remind reporters to use examples and anecdotes to illustrate key points.

2 In a complicated medical story, this reporter elicited a clear explanation for the medical phrase, "free floating tumor." Asking a source to explain or simplify a complex topic will help a reporter convey complex information.

3 A reporter is always looking for the most descriptive direct quote to use in a story. Here the writer uses a quote that captures the intensity of the moment through a powerfully concrete direct quote.

4 Good follow-up questions help to get specifics that add

January 10, 2012   In Focu

Daughters connecte

Death is inevitable. And at some point, everyone has to face it. Though the passing of a loved one tends to come later in life, these two families were forced to embrace loss much sooner. Regardless of the circumstances and amount of preparation, it's never easy.

BY ERIN HOTCHKISS, EDITOR-IN-CHIEF

photo by Erin Hotchkiss

provided photo

FIGURE 2.2 (*continued*)

ve Lost   *The Hawk Eye*

through paternal loss

TOP LEFT- Graduate Carsyn, freshman Shelby and senior Brooke Wegman wear their Charlie's Angels shirts that were designed for an annual lymphoma walk dedicated to their father.

BOTTOM LEFT- The Wegmans' Christmas card from 1998.

CENTER- The Wegman's memorial plaque and tree for their father, Charlie, in their backyard. "We usually decorate the tree for holidays and the anniversary of his death," wife Kay Wegman said.

TOP RIGHT- The Greenwood family traveled constantly as their daughters grew up. "Even before we were married, he was traveling everywhere," wife Kim Greenwood said. "He was such an adventurous person."

BOTTOM RIGHT- Junior Natalie Greenwood and sister graduate Lauren look upon the bible of their late father Tom. Tom, an avid church goer, used to make numerous notes in it to further understand sermons and his faith.

CHARLIE WEGMAN

photo by Erin Hotchkiss   provided photo

photo by Deanna Moon

BY DEANNA MOON,
ENTERTAINMENT EDITOR

Hours had passed since junior Natalie Greenwood had last spoken to her father Tom. With a systematic dial of her phone, she waited with the patterned ring for him to pick up. At the sound of an unfamiliar "Hello?" she responded, "Who is this?" The shaky voice at the other end answered, "Natalie, I was playing racquetball with your dad. He just had a heart attack, but the ambulance is on its way."

It was July 10, 2010; Natalie was about to enter her sophomore year, and her sister, graduate Lauren, was about to be a senior. As soon as she ended the call, Natalie and Lauren sped to the hospital, phoning their mother Kim who had already gotten the call and promised to meet them there. Accompanied by two friends, the sisters sat silence through the car ride as thoughts of what might happen filled their heads. Knowing friends' parents that have survived heart attacks before, a subtle sense of reassurement lingered within her as she clasped her hands to pray.

He'll be okay. He'll be okay. He'll be okay. Although the words were ingrained into her brain, Natalie had no idea what she was in for.

"At the time I was really scared," Natalie said. "I didn't know what to expect, but I was being optimistic and hoping for the best."

It was only a short 20 minutes later that the doctors informed the Greenwoods that Tom passed away while they operated on him. As word of his heart attack quickly spread, the sight of concerned close friends and family at the hospital quickly followed. The sudden rush of people surprised even the nurses, including one emergency room nurse stating that she had never seen so many people show up for one person in 15 years of working there. Without any major preceding health problems beside a properly-medicated mildly high blood pressure, his death was an event that no one could have predicted.

"There's just such a shock when someone dies suddenly -- you don't have any preparation," Kim said. "When people are sick, which is just as hard, it seems like you've kind of dealt with it. You contemplate what could be the outcome and have hope that they're going to make it through, whatever the sickness. But when it happens so suddenly, you don't have a chance to say goodbye. You have nothing."

The next morning, the Greenwoods awoke to a house busier than ever before. After sleeping over, their friends were busy cooking away in the kitchen, tidying up the home or offering shoulders to cry on in the wake of their loss, never leaving their sides. Hour by hour, friendly faces flooded in into their house, offering their condolences, but despite the great amount of support, nothing could lessen the shock that overtook the family.

"There were a ton of people here," Kim said. "I was like, 'OK, I've got to do this.' I just knew that I had to carry on because I have to be strong for these two kids. I had to carry on because that's what he would've wanted me to do. That's what keeps me going even today. If he were here and I were gone, he would've done the same."

Still stricken with disbelief, the Greenwoods found it hard to reach acceptance and come to terms with what happened. There was nothing that could fill the absence their home. As the weeks passed, they slowly made their way to understanding how much their lives had immensely changed.

"For weeks, we would have people at our house nonstop," Natalie said. "At that time, it was just kind of a big blur. Soon, they began

to trickle off and started to leave, and then it was just us. The house got a lot quieter. I think that's when it really started setting in. We won't have him there to walk us down the aisle. That's when we realized that he was really gone."

The Greenwoods have always been a close-knit family, attending church together weekly and having family dinners at every opportunity. Ever since they could remember, the sisters were tucked in almost every single night by Tom. A tradition exemplified by a childhood photo adorned on Natalie's bedside, the nightly ritual always ended with a prayer from their father. Whether the girls were awake or not, he always made sure to pray over them, thanking God for their family's blessings.

"He was a very religious person," Kim said. "His bible was always filled with notes and his thoughts. In fact, our pastor even used to it to prepare for [Tom's] funeral service."

From time to time, he surprised his family with small notes placed around the house, always bringing a smile to even the darkest of their days. From encouraging tidbits to a "Miss you!" to thoughtful bible verses, he never let a day go by without letting his family know how much they meant to him. Over the years, Kim has held onto many of them, now keeping them in her late husband's bible.

Living by the phrase, "Today is the first day of the rest of your life," Tom was adamant in the stressing that every day was an opportunity to do great things and excel. At every event or game Natalie or Lauren had to perform in, their parents were always there, cheering them on.

"My dad always supported me," Natalie said. "I always think, 'He would want me to do this. He would trust me to do this.' He was always standing by, encouraging me."

Through the passing of time, the support of friends and a strong church, coping has become easier for the Greenwoods. From what was once a paralyzing loss, they've grown from his passing. Natalie and her family could never truly understand the importance of a goodbye until they missed out on their last chance.

The family makes sure to never let a day go by without an "I Love You." Though his death brought upon a long grieving process, Tom's family chooses to live in memory of him and grasp every moment they've been granted.

"It just makes me want to live like him," Natalie said. "Being loving to everyone, having no regrets, not holding anything back. You're not guaranteed tomorrow, and life is so short. You just have to tell people that you love them and how much you care about them— it could be your last time."

[Left column fragments:]

outcome, the church also nursery to be remodeled place he volunteered for al-

rvice would be the hardest ave been better," Kay said. by people's respect for me pected maybe 300 people. I erything went perfect."

ssing, it took the Wegmans e new atmosphere of the had to tiptoe around. They could cook at home. Their hem a tree to plant in the a plaque for Charlie. They with the small things, like st, which were his favorite. as an open spot. Sometimes, o see him on the couch, the months while he was sick. rlie fought with everything ou learn to live with it and you did have. We became his little head, just barely llows on the couch. Every that remind you of him. I'll him."

[Right margin text:]

depth to the story. Rather than just say that Mr. Wegman's sickness changed life at home, this reporter gathered details to show the changes. The bags for the feeding tube are powerful details to help the readers understand the Wegmans' altered life.

5 The story is a difficult topic to begin with. However, the topic demands the reporter ask the family about the painful experience of Mr. Wegman's death. In agreeing to do the interview for such a difficult subject, the sources know that the roughest moments will be a part of the interview. The reporter's commitment should be to accurately capture the information and the moment.

Test your knowledge

What does transcribing mean?

Quick Exercise

Write at least three ways to ask follow-up questions for the following quotes from a story about a profile on a school police officer.

1 "I know it's my job, but I just don't like writing tickets."

2 "I like spending time talking to kids and helping them through a rough time in life."

Raina's conversational style of follow-up questioning paid off. She gained a better understanding of Sam's experience and certainly gathered better details. Although she may not have found many strong direct quotes to use in full, she has the details she needs to recreate an anecdote that will help the reader understand why raising a 1,300-pound Hereford can be scary.

As an interview progresses, it will be helpful to keep the following points in mind:

- Do not be afraid of the pause. If a source stops short of completely describing something, do not feel obliged to ask another question immediately. Some subjects will feel the need to fill the silence so they will jump back in and continue developing their thoughts.

- The subject may stray off your focus or lines of questioning. That's not always bad. You may get relevant information you did not even consider asking about. But if the subject strays too far, stop writing. Then, to redirect the interview, you might say something like, "Now back to what I mentioned before …" Then pick up your pen and ask a relevant question.

- Do not be afraid to politely ask the subject to slow down or clarify something if he is going too fast or has lost you.

- If the subject mentions something that can be produced for observation, ask to see it or get a copy, if that is possible. The object or document might provide good details for the reporter or might even elicit further discussion from the subject. Sam's Future Farmers of America (FFA) photo album might suggest other experiences to question him about.

- Ask the subject for other sources. The person you are interviewing will usually know others connected to the story. If the interview is issue-related, the subject may know others who disagree with him on the topic. Talking to those sources will give your story balance.

To close an interview, always ask if there is anything else the subject would like to add. The source may say something crucial that you never considered asking about.

At this point, the best reporters know that a reinterview will most likely be necessary to get more information or confirm facts or quotes. Ask for a phone number and check the subject's availability prior to **deadline**, the time by which published content must be completed. Thanking the source for his or her time is also important and appropriate.

OBSERVATION

Though a reporter can get many details by asking follow-up questions, first-hand observations provide another source of detail. During the interview, write down relevant observations about the person, his environment and his activities. Calling the cross-country coach passionate is not as effective as noting how he dyes his beard in the school colors during state meet week, and watching as he leads his pack of runners on a 10-mile run in the rain.

Observation may mean everything from taking notes on what a person is wearing to the tone of her voice in conversation to describing in detail her room or workstation. A collection of relevant storytelling details will enable the writer to give the reader a full sensory background to the story. (Observation is discussed further in Chapter 5 on writing feature stories.)

You can find good opportunities for observation in many different settings:

- Watch a video of a snowboarder's tricks from her last competition.
- Sit in on one of the grueling practices of the girls' soccer team prior to a big game.
- Accompany a senior as he volunteers at a nursing home and take notes on his interactions with the residents.
- Hang out with a senior who does spray paint art at a street fair. Watch him create a piece and review his portfolio for significant details.

10 · Personality Profiles

The ROCK

Family of 14 embraces chaos

Kaitlyn Marsh

As the cheesy, synthesized '80s tune "Pop! Goes My Heart" filled the living room of the Belzer household, five-year-old Judah began to bounce one shoulder up and down, wiggling both of her legs to the beat.

She grabbed a metal whisk and sang into it like a microphone, while her father, Joe, danced in the kitchen with one-year-old Gracie and three-year-old Corrie .

The remaining nine of the Belzer children gathered in the living room, singing to each other and giggling at their homemade entertainment.

For the family of 14, this isn't an uncommon occurrence.

"There's always someone to play with," said Jennie Belzer, the family's matriarch. "There is not a loneliness issue. You can always go outside and play a board game or have someone to talk to and be with."

In addition to the three youngest, the Belzer clan consists of 21-year-old Josiah, 19-year-old Mariah, RBHS senior Andy and twin sister Maggie, sophomore Sarah, 13-year-old Lydia, 11-year-old Noel, 10-year-old Esther and seven-year-old Micah.

The house is "not very quiet. There's usually always somebody [making noise], and we have to do our chores every day otherwise the house gets out of control," Jennie, homeschool teacher and stay-at-home mom said. "At one time we had a house with eight kids and only one bathroom and no shower, just a bath tub, and we lived there for a long time, too, and finally I was like, 'I can't do this anymore.'"

After both growing up in families with five children, Joe and Jennie thought they wanted to have four or five kids in their own family when they married, but after having a few, there wasn't a set number of kids they felt would complete their family unit. The parents would sit down at the dining room table with all their children and feel as if someone was missing, and that was a sign a new baby should be added to their home.

The two oldest, Josiah and Mariah, attend college while the rest, with the exception of Andy and Sarach, are homeschooled. Andy decided he did not want to be homeschooled past the fourth grade, and Sarah started public school in the third grade. She bounced in and out for five years, but decided to permanently attend public school her sophomore year.

However, these full-time students may need some solitude from time to time at the end of the day, and a request for privacy can be a lot to ask for in the Belzer household.

"I've never had my own room or really my own area; it's always been sharing pretty much everything," Andy said. "But I think I've learned how to be a better person because of putting up with complete lack of personal space."

In a two bath, six bedroom house, the youngest three girls share a room; Noel and Esther split another, while Lydia sleeps on a mattress in the cor-

> ## "
> I think I've learned how to be a better person."
>
> **Andy Belzer**
> *senior*

ner of the basement and Andy and Micah share a storage space. Instead of being asked to clean their rooms, the children are asked to tidy their areas.

"You're never truly alone," Sarah said as her little sister Lydia loudly sang Justin Bieber's "Baby" in the background. "Things get borrowed without permission, your room gets messed up and just random stuff in my room is out of place."

In addition to privacy and personal space issues, the Belzers have to provide food, clothing and transportation, so making ends meet with one single income could seem impossible. But Joe, a Christian Campus house minister at the University of Missouri-Columbia, and his wife stick to their motto that God will bless their family, even if they do spend more money on milk than electricity in a day.

"Everybody in the family sees that we pray that God will provide, and we see all sorts of miraculous provisions," Jennie said, folding a pair of sweatpants, placing them on one of the 12 piles of laundry on the dining room table. "We always have enough no matter what it is. We wrecked our van and totaled it, and the person that hit us didn't have insurance, and then someone in our Sunday school class gave us $10,000 to buy a new van. We've never not been able to make it

through."

The Belzers have been fortunate; people have donated clothes to their family, and they are frugal with these, passing them down so that they can be worn again by the younger children. As for food, Jennie still has to make three to four trips to Sam's Club a week, where she buys everything in bulk, from giant rice crispy boxes to 24-ounce Parmesan cheese containers.

Even though they might face financial difficulties, the parents believe the rewards are well worth the sacrifices.

"We think as far as character, the older kids wouldn't be who they are if they didn't have the younger kids," Joe said. "There's something about having responsibility of another person besides yourself that is permanent throughout your life."

Even though Jennie and Joe are finished having children, the meaning of family will be treasured for the rest of their lives. They feel content in their family size and look forward to several more years seeing their children grow up, Jennie said.

For Sarah and Andy growing up in a family of 14 has taught them to cherish every moment with their large family, with whom they will celebrate family get-togethers in the future surrounded by their siblings and their own families, and they couldn't ask for anything better, Andy said.

"My family is my life; if I didn't have them I wouldn't be who I am now," Andy said, "I would know how it would be any different [not having a big family]. ...They give me support when I don't have any, and they help me out."

A day in the life: While bonding with his younger sibling, Gracie, senior Andy Belzer does not think having 12 siblings is unusual. To assist his mother, Jennie, around the house, he and his siblings help in their daily chores. Belzer finds the full house enjoyable.

photos by Asa Lory

FIGURE 2.3 *The Rock*, Rock Bridge High School, Columbia, Mo. "Family of 14 embraces chaos," by Kaitlyn Marsh, p. 10, March 22, 2012. Reprinted with permission of *The Rock*.

A reporter who takes the time to observe for his story will often gather massive amounts of information and detail to use with the story. The reporter from *The Rock* begins with a lead that captures the boisterous life of a family of 14. Later in the story, the reporter uses more observation – the 12 piles of laundry on the dining room table and the 24-ounce Parmesan cheese containers – to help the reader understand what it takes to clothe and feed a large family.

Quick Exercise

Brainstorm observation opportunities for the following scenarios:

- Seniors are required to give "Hero Project" presentations, summarizing their 15–35 hours of community service on projects that range from funding teacher education in Africa to training service dogs.

- Weeklong try-outs for the upcoming musical, "Beauty and the Beast."

- Administration and police are cracking down on smokers who cross the street and smoke behind the convenience store before and after school and during lunch.

RELIABILITY OF SOURCES

Good journalists tend to be skeptical about the information they gather. People may answer a question, even though they don't really know the answer. Such sources are not necessarily lying, they are often just trying to feel knowledgeable or helpful. However, their assertions may simply be incorrect. For example, your principal may try to answer a question about your 70-year-old school's original name because she sees herself as the person who should know the story of the school. But because she was not around when the school was named, a school history book or a newspaper story from the time might be more credible.

One of the key considerations a journalist makes is determining whether sources will be primary, secondary or third-party sources (as discussed in Chapter 1).

When interviewing a primary source, consider the source's position or connection to the story. Your principal may be a good source for forecasts about how budget cuts can affect a school. But a district budget director or a superintendent, who has a more direct role in creating the budget, might be a better source for specific numbers. While a junior guard on the basketball team would seem to know about this season's game scores, the coach or the scorekeeper would be a more authoritative source. The junior guard, who thinks his team won their last game by 15 points, may not know that a last-second basket by their opponent counted, making it a 13-point win instead.

An astute reporter should listen for pauses and hesitations, which may signal a source's uncertainty about key points. For example, imagine you ask your school's drama club president who won the annual Best Actor award at Friday night's banquet. If she responds by pausing, tilting her head and saying "Well, uhh … I think it was Adam Lowe," you should check her assertion. Even though she's the drama club president, her pause and body language suggest that she's unsure of her answer. A good reporter will find a better source, and double- or triple-check the fact to assure its accuracy before printing it.

Uncertainty requires action. A reporter must verify any parts of a story that have been cast into doubt. Whether checking requires a second interview source or a printed resource, a reporter should always look for independent verification of the information. A publication should avoid running one-source stories. More sources are preferable, especially when the first two sources are not particularly knowledgeable on the subject.

For example, if both the drama club president and another member say that Adam Lowe was the award recipient, a reporter would probably feel fairly comfortable with the validity of the fact. However, a reporter would still prefer to have the club's sponsor as a source to assure the fact's reliability.

Test your knowledge

Why would a source answer a question to which they didn't necessarily know the answer?

Assassins game triggers Code Red

JESSE ZHOU
features editor
LAURA KAO
opinions assistant

On Monday, Feb. 6, custodian Luis Fraga spotted a student crouching behind a car in the band parking lot while holding an object that resembled a firearm. Fraga immediately notified the administration of the potential danger, and Principal Kami Tomberlain promptly issued a Code Red on the intercom.

"This is not a drill," Tomberlain said.

After the arrival of 42 police officers and a tense confrontation, the student was found to be holding nothing more than a Nerf-brand toy gun. However, further analysis revealed that the student was part of a Nerf "Assassins" game, which the student had joined via Facebook. The goal of the game was to "kill" other students by hitting them with a Nerf dart; the last person standing was to be the winner. Many other students involved in this particular game were called in after the Code Red and some were found to have Nerf guns in their possession as well. Those found with guns faced repercussions on which the administration declined to elaborate, and all students were warned not to play the game on school grounds.

The warnings and punishments given by the administrators incited angry responses from various students. Senior Tobias Shin, who was part of the game, expressed disdain for the administration's actions.

"[The administrators'] reaction to the emergency was understandable and appropriate, but what of their behavior after they realized it wasn't an emergency?" Shin said. "The students were obedient, respectful and consented to having their property searched and confiscated. It's [the student's] fault that he got caught, sure, but it's not his fault that the administrators clearly overreacted."

However, Tomberlain feels that the administration's actions were justified.

"The images [of Columbine] were immediately in my head. You just hope you never have to respond to a situation like that," Tomberlain said. "We don't need those guns on campus, regardless of how toy-like they are."

The administration did not take this incident lightly. Many of the administrators expressed clear dissatisfaction with the students involved, but also felt relief when they realized that the school was not in danger.

see CODE RED, pg.2

FIGURE 2.4 *Prospector*, Cupertino High School, Cupertino, Calif. "Assassins game triggers Code Red," by Jesse Zhou and Laura Kao, pp. 1–2, March 22, 2012. Reprinted with kind permission.
   A good reporter will ask questions of multiple sources to build a story. In this story, reporters from *Prospector* staff talked to multiple administrators to help explain the story. An opposing student view helps balance the story. Notice that the reporters didn't just report the rumors but dealt with their validity.

FIGURE 2.4 *(continued)*

..NEWS THE PROSPECTOR MARCH 2, 2012

THE PROSPECTOR
2011-2012
STAFF

Cupertino High School
Established 1958
Vol LIII., No.V | 2012

editors-in-chief
harini jaganathan
eric jang

news editor
azadeh rongere

opinions editor
sindhu gnanasambandan

features editor
jesse zhou

lifestyles editor
natasha sharma

sports editors
sunwoo jeong
abhishek zaveri

flip side editors
alya omar
michelle cheung

copy editors
kevin chu
victoria duan
madhuri sathish

business manager
virena galotra

news assistants seong hwan yoon, anna huang

opinions assistants nikhil kanthi, laura kao

features assistants virena galotra, katie martin

lifestyles assistants hong suh, jason chen

sports assistants chris tracey, anand hemmady

flip side assistant chris cai

adviser
ann peck

editorial policy

"The Prospector" is an open forum of expression for student editors to inform and educate their readers. It will not be reviewed by or restrained by school officials prior to publication or distribution. Advisors may and should coach and discuss content during the writing process.

The staff of "The Prospector" seeks to recognize individuals, events, ideasand bring news to the Cupertino community in an accurate, professional and unbiased manner. "The Prospector" will not avoid publishing a story solely on the basis of possible dissent or controversy.

If you believe an error has been made, or wish to have your opinion expressed in "The Prospector"please contact us via mail or e-mail. Letters sent become tbe sole property of "The Prospector" and can be edited for length, clarity or accuracy.

"The Prospector" editorial board reserves the right to accept or reject any ad in accordance with its advertising policy.

Contact Us
The Prospector
10100 Finch Avenue
Cupertino, CA 95014
prospector.chs@gmail.com

Code Red:

(cont. pg1)

"When the call comes in that a student has a gun, the immediate reaction is to protect your students," Assistant Principal Andy Walczak said. "It was a sense of relief that no one was hurt. We weren't in a situation in which a person would really be injured."

> It was a sense of relief that no one was hurt. We weren't in a situation in which a person would really be injured
>
> - *Assistant Principal Andy Walczak*

The revocation of the involved students' college recommendation letters was a widespread rumor that was not clearly addressed. The administration, upon hearing this rumor, stated that it was not true.

"We would never do something like that," Tomberlain said.

Another rumor that has been refuted by the administration concerns the customization of the Nerf gun seen by the custodian. Many believed that the Nerf gun was painted black, but according to Walczak, the gun was not customized in such a way. Although other county shootings have involved real guns being painted other colors, but the particular Nerf gun that the student was carrying was not changed in any way.

This particular game of "Assassins" is the first to indirectly cause a Code Red in the school district. Although there are many other games simultaneously being played around the school district, partaking in such an activity, whether using toy guns or any other fake weapon, may lead to consequences if not played in the appropriate place. ■

AP Physics: a hurdle for students and teachers

NIKHIL KANTHI
opinions assistant

When it was announced at junior Parent Night on Feb. 2 that AP Physics would be offered next year, parents and students present applauded the school's decision. However, as time passed, students began to realize the difficulties of taking the class, while staff members encountered the procedural difficulties that came with offering the course.

AP Physics C is a calculus-based laboratory science class. The primary reason for offering the course is to ensure that all high schools across the district have the same classes, but the high demand for the class is also an incentive.

"The key word is equitable," chemistry teacher Larry DeMuth said. "The four other schools in our district are offering AP Physics, and we feel there is now sufficient student demand to offer the the course at Tino as well."

Thus far, enough juniors have signed up to fill two to three classes, and the sophomores have not yet submitted their science class choices. There is a possibility, as with any AP class, that some students may be overwhelmed and drop the class.

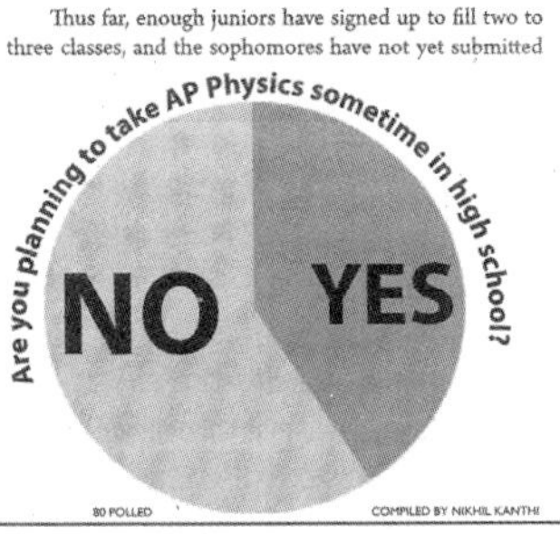
Are you planning to take AP Physics sometime in high school?
NO
YES
80 POLLED
COMPILED BY NIKHIL KANTHI

"There is always a worry of students underestimating an AP science class," DeMuth said. "This is where guidance is critical."

AP Physics C requires several hours of lab work per week. The science department and school want to make this possible, and hope to provide this opportunity for students in the event of a new bell schedule. On top of being a college level science class, however, it is also taught in a shorter time frame than for which it was designed. Given its difficulty, the faculty does not want students to take the class simply for the AP boost.

Said guidance counselor Michelle Avvakumovits, "My biggest question to interested students is, 'Why are you taking the class?'"

In addition to the difficulties faced by students thinking about taking the class, AP Physics C also presents certain challenges to the teacher who will teach it. The College Board, using a lengthy process, must audit the class for students to receive AP credit after the AP test. The College Board requires a detailed written report by the teacher explaining the syllabus, curriculum and pace of the class. This report is usually over 40 pages long. For AP Physics C, the teacher must also complete a separate lab report and attend an AP course on how to teach the class. There are still a significant number of preparations that remain before school begins.

"As of right now, the only thing certain is that the course is being offered," Avvakumovits said. "We still have a lot of work left ahead of us." ■

FEMALE STUDENTS BREAK THROUGH THE GLASS CEILING *(cont. pg1)*

inquiry on how male students spend their time. Luk believes that many now put all their efforts into video games, smaller group activities or academics.

"Time spent gaming is a part of it. Also, guys traditionally take the classes and go for the majors that require more academic work, especially with the maths and sciences, like engineering," Luk said.

There is currently a total of six girls out of 48 students in Eric Ferrante's two Computer Science classes.

Regardless of the reason for which females at school are becoming increasingly prominent in leadership, this same trend is not so pronounced in the real world. A glass ceiling seems to exist for females outside of the school environment; less than 20 percent of top managers and executives in corporate America are women.

Senior Shona Hemmady attributes some of this to lingering gender role expectations. She feels some of these pressures in her high school leadership experiences as well.

"I don't think a lot of guys see me as a girl," Hemmady said. "I don't think I have ever been stereotypically feminine in the first place and maybe that's why people started listening to me more. Honestly, girls who fit the female stereotype a lot more are not taken seriously and it's really sad."

Senior class president Rebecca Tsai has a relatively positive outlook on this situation, though, and it is rooted in history.

"The amendment for colored people came before the amendment for women and I feel like that is how it is going to go — all men first and then women will get equal rights," Tsai said. "We have a colored president now and I feel like that is opening possibilities for women."

The difference in the gender imbalance between the school and the United States may simply require a couple more decades to balance itself out.

"People in power still live under the old model where guys are supposed to be the boss," Morse said, "but I see that your generation is more tolerant of just about everything. Whether it is regarding gay marriage, religious tolerance or even sexism, your generation is going to break a lot of those things down. And it's already starting to happen. But your generation, even the older ones who are 20 to 25 years old, are not in those leadership positions yet. Also, they say there are more girls in college than guys and that's all going to translate."

Morse and Rosado share the belief that the trends at school are a positive sign for what is to come; they believe that it may be the current students' generation that breaks this corporate glass ceiling for females aspiring to be leaders.

"Based on what I see in leadership, clubs and high achieving academic classes, each include very different sets of people," Hemmady said. "People who want to get a good solid job and make a lot of money tend to focus on their high achieving academic classes while the leadership people are generally more sociable [and] outgoing ... That's why leadership gets more girls and in high achieving academic classes, especially in math and science, there are a lot more guys." ■

Alumni portray the pressures of seniors in high school with NYU short film "17"

SEONG HWAN YOON
news assistant

New York University senior and former CHS student Esha Rao, along with her fellow alumni, current CHS students and the rest of Cupertino's community, is raising funds to shoot a shor film, "17," in the Bay Area, which tell the story of high school seniors facing paranormal situation.

"A thesis film at NYU is somethin that a person spends years preparin for, and I always knew that I wante to return to my hometown to mak this film," Rao said. "My desire was t turn it into an experience I could shar with my friends and family as well a my friends and fellow film students a NYU."

The film, which is scheduled to tak place in Santa Cruz and Cupertino — including on campus — is schedule to begin shooting on location this sum mer, from June 19 to July 3. Due t the nature of the film, Rao must rais approximately $12,000 through dona tions to make "17" a reality. Becaus this film is not being produced at NYU Rao and her team must raise their ow money to fund the project. Rao is usin the film's main website, *www.indiegog com/17*, to reach out to the Cupertin community and run the fundraisin campaign.

"I'd like to think that I'm represen ing both CHS and Cupertino, not onl visually on camera, but as a filmmak to whom both the school and city a very important," Rao said.

Rao has currently involved ma alumni and students from CHS a even the city of Cupertino, which h given her and her production team pe mission to shoot here.

Sophomore Jason Shuieh and fres man Caroline Jacquet auditioned th past December for one of the suppo ing roles in the film. Though the st dents do not know their actual role the film, they are very excited to be pa of this project.

The film centers around three gra uating seniors, two of whom are play by Thalia Moshtagh and Maithy Vu both alumni of CHS and close frien of Rao — who decide to make the be of their last night of high school a drive down to Santa Cruz beach. Ho ever, as they speed down Highway they get into a tragic car accident a do not survive. Miraculously yet my teriously, the teenagers wake up on t ground the next morning and find t they cannot interact with the peo they most want to see.

"It's a story that anyone who gr up in Cupertino can relate to, as it cuses on a lot of the challenges I a a number of my peers were faced w during high school," Rao said.

The film brings out characters t are easily relatable to students at C because it focuses on the pressures t face at school and the uncertainty their future.

With such a large number of loc participating in the production of film, Rao truly wants to make this a community event over this summer.

"I want this to feel not like a film making in the city of Cupertino, like a film that the city of Cupertin making," Rao said. ■

INTERNET RESEARCH

While conducting interviews should still be a reporter's primary research method, the Internet has certainly expanded the resources for relevant information. Nevertheless, reporters need to be careful when wading through the massive amounts of data available online.

A reporter should not report the first thing she finds on a Google search, a Twitter post or a Wikipedia page. Why? Because the information may not be reliable. All of those sources, however, may be useful in the news-gathering process, and any of the three may provide good background information (as discussed earlier in this chapter). A thorough reporter will consider information from these sources, but will also try to verify the facts through interviews or multiple sources.

Just because the information is on a website, it doesn't mean that it's true. When a reporter finds information on one website, a second website might not provide credibility simply because websites sometimes link or paste the same information. For example, at 7:13 p.m. on Feb. 11, 2012, five different websites ran articles reporting singer Whitney Houston's death. By 7:17 p.m., there were 24 different posts. By 7:26 p.m., 355 articles were posted and eight minutes later that number had doubled to 726, most of which were copied from the same original postings. While Whitney Houston did indeed die, a reporter should assess a website in various ways before deciding to publish or link something from it.

- Can anyone edit the website, including those with an agenda or ulterior motives? The ability of anyone to edit Wikipedia entries should at least make reporters second-guess assertions they find there.
- When was the website last updated? Information on older websites may not be current.
- Who created and maintains the website? If a study on a new product is published by the product's parent company, the reporter should be wary of a slant or bias in the study.
- Does the site provide clear sources and justifications for its factual assertions? If it features statistical or other technical information, does it explain the methodology behind the conclusions? Does it provide references for its claims? Reporters should be cautious about sites that fail to provide sources for the information they present.
- Is the website full of misspellings or other errors? If so, the reporter should certainly be skeptical of any and all facts within the website.

FIGURE 2.5 Web grab of Twitter feed, http://twitter.com/#!/nhstribune. *NHS Tribune*, Norman High School, Norman, Okla. Reprinted with permission of *NHS Tribune*.

Twitter has become a great tool for high school journalists to get brief but good information to their readers. Publications such as *NHS Tribune* can give regular, real-time updates for sporting events. Without an editor pouring over the words before they're published, journalists must make sure of the accuracy of the information before tweeting.

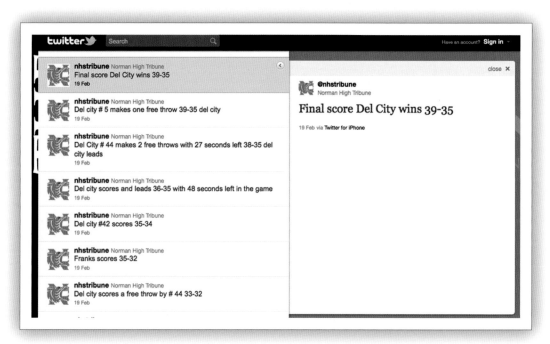

Skepticism about factual reliability should not, however, cause reporters to avoid the Internet or social media. The resources available now provide journalists with a vast and valuable array of information at the push of a button.

The world of social media and the Internet changes rapidly but offers student journalists rich reporting opportunities and tools. Innovative reporters and publications will keep up with the latest apps and technology designed to make communication quicker and more efficient.

Internet resources offer student reporters quick access to national and international sources. For example, a student journalist may contact a well-known national cyberbullying source online and conduct an email interview to get some in-depth perspective for a local story on Facebook harassment. An inspired reporter in Kansas can conduct a Skype interview with a Syrian teenager about life in the middle of a national uprising.

Twitter feeds can also provide journalists with story ideas and sources. A school organization may post results from a national competition that the school's website may re-tweet or use as a foundation for a more in-depth print story about the competition. Searching Twitter for relevant topics or hashtags can produce the latest information trending on school news topics. Following a recent student shooting, one school news website identified multiple leads for the story. They identified the time frame, rumored causes, key witnesses and preliminary information about victims and perpetrator(s). Although the publication needed to verify all this information, the search gave the staff multiple ways to start reporting.

Applications such as Storify allow a publication to gather multiple social media posts that can be included in the news website coverage. Such tools can provide an instant barometer of public opinion on a new law or as a sample of the public's reaction to a state play-off football game.

Facebook posts can offer a similar source of information, but reporters will need to be extremely careful not to violate anyone's privacy and their paper's ethical standards. If a Facebook post was aimed at a limited audience of select friends, the reporter should talk to the source before disseminating it further. Those posts aimed at a wider audience have less expectation of privacy, although a reporter should still verify that the person in question really did post the information on Facebook.

Facebook groups can also serve as a useful tool for identifying story sources. A reporter can ask news feed subscribers if they are planning to attend an event or if they have bought a new product and would be willing to be interviewed for the story. Reporters can do even more comprehensive reporting through Facebook groups depending upon the number of students with a page. One school paper compiled seniors' post-graduation plans as part of the Facebook group, getting responses from 200 of a 421-member senior class.

Internet polls through such services as polldaddy.com or surveymonkey.com can provide a sample of school opinion. However, most Internet polls aren't statistically valid because the integrity of the sample is hard to control. While some surveys can be configured to limit one vote per Internet address, a computer user can get around the limitations by clearing cookies or responding from multiple addresses.

Mobile phone apps allow journalists instant coverage of events. Tweeting the latest score for the district championship bowling tournament offers a service to readers who can't make it to the meet. Although a reporter can immediately tweet a school news event, he should always make sure that the information is accurate. With just 140 characters, a tweet can be a powerful tool for distributing information quickly to an audience, but these limits sometimes mean that information is disseminated without sufficient context or clarity. This can lead to distortions and outright errors.

Audio distribution apps such as Soundcloud and Audioboo offer a quick way to post interview clips from such events as school board meetings, school assemblies and interviews with prominent figures. Reporters should make sure to refrain from interrupting sources during the interview so as to keep the sound edit clear of voices other than that of the subject.

Immediate posting of still and video images can give readers a sense of being there in the moment. Wireless memory cards allow websites to instantly post first-half images from the homecoming game. Video posts of the award-winning floats from the parade earlier that day offer the reader an even richer multimedia experience. If accompanying a written story, the video should complement, not merely repeat the written content.

Tips for researching on the Internet

As an investigative reporter for the *Kansas City Star* Judy Thomas has found that digging beyond a simple word search on the Internet can provide a wealth of information to develop stories. What follows are her tips for making the best of the Internet as a reporter.

Google: When you're conducting background on a subject or a person, Google is a great starting place. You can find articles that have been written by or about your subject, locate their biographies, learn what organizations they're involved with, find out if they've been the subject of any lawsuits and find their blogs or Facebook pages. You can click on "Google Images" to see if there are any pictures involving your subject, and you can sign up for "Google Alerts" if you want to be notified whenever the name of the person or subject you're researching comes up. Keep in mind when you're searching that anybody can post anything on Google, so you should always make sure your sources are legitimate.

Social media: Facebook, Twitter, LinkedIn and blogs can help you learn all kinds of details about your subject – everything from a person's likes and dislikes to the kinds of organizations they belong to and their contact information. If you can't find someone's phone number, try looking them up on Facebook and you can either send them a message or possibly find their email address or phone number on their page. Many publications have a policy that prohibits the use of pictures posted on Facebook without permission, but the photos can be useful in helping you get an idea of the person's interests and activities. And remember that it's not just individuals who have Facebook pages. Organizations do as well, so you can find information on companies and groups, too.

YouTube: This is another great tool for researching a person or a group. For example, if you go to YouTube and search for a specific person, you might find a video of that person either being interviewed or talking about an issue you're researching. You might also find performances by that person or group, and you can find informative presentations as well, which also can lead you to more sources to contact.

Finding people: Through online searches, you can locate specific people, experts to talk to about your topic, or people to interview who have had experience with an issue you're researching. Some good online directories are **www.switchboard.com**, **www.anywho.com**, **www.whowhere.com**, and **www.infospace.com**. These sites allow you to search for a business or a person, and they also have reverse look-ups so you can search by phone numbers as well. For locating experts, try **www.sources.com** or **http://scholar.google.com/**, and for tracking down someone who has experienced a situation that is similar to one you're researching, try **www.googlegroups.com**. Here, you will find discussion groups where people post opinions about certain issues or stories about their experiences.

Court records: Many counties now have their records available online. The County Recorder or Register of Deeds websites contain property records, and the Clerk of Court sites have criminal and civil cases as well as lawsuits filed against individuals, organizations or businesses.

Crime reports: Lots of police departments post their crime reports online. Go to their individual websites to check. For example, the website for the Overland Park Police Department's police blotter is **www.opkansas. org/Newsroom/Police-Blotter**.

Prison and sex offender registries: When backgrounding people, you might want to make sure they're not a convicted criminal or a registered sex offender. Many states have searchable databases for prisoners, as does the federal prison system. You can Google the state you're interested in to see if they have a prisoner database. To search for prisoners in federal custody, go to the Federal Bureau of Prisons inmate locator site at **www.bop.gov/inmate_locator/index.jsp**. For sex offenders, you can conduct a national search at the National Sex Offender Public Registry site, **www.nsopr.gov**, or go to your state's registry.

Business records: A good place to find information about a business is the Secretary of State's office in the state in which the business is registered. Most states have online searchable databases. You can search for the name of the company then look up its annual report to find out the identity of its officers and whether the company is in good standing. In some states, you also can search by a person's name to see if that person is associated with any companies.

→ **Car crashes:** Traffic wrecks in many jurisdictions are available online. Just Google the name of the state and the words "crash reports online" and you should be able to find them if they're available.

→ **Personal or company websites:** Some people and many companies and organizations have their own websites. If you don't know their website address, you should be able to locate it through a Google search. On the websites, you can find their newsletters, mission statements, biographies of their leaders, staff directories, annual reports and videos. Many organizations have online archives on their websites, where you can find back issues of newsletters and pictures.

→ **Guidestar:** This is a great place to conduct research on charities and other nonprofit organizations. You can find out how much they receive in donations, how much they spend, the names and salaries of their officers and the names of related organizations. Go to **www.guidestar.org**

→ **State regulatory boards:** In most states, licensed professionals are regulated by a board or agency. Many of these regulatory groups post information online if sanctions are issued against a professional.

CONVENTIONAL RESEARCH

Reporters should understand that all research isn't conducted on the Internet. Libraries, governments, districts and many other organizations still create and house public information that is available to reporters but is not published on a website. A good reporter will take the time to research studies, reports and statistics that are relevant to each story. A high school reporter has as much right to the information as a professional reporter. A good reporter will make himself aware of the availability of such resources. An in-depth discussion with a source about resources available from his organization can be enlightening. Reporters should also be aware of **Freedom of Information laws**, or laws that guarantee public access to data held by the government, and the steps he will need to take to acquire information covered under those laws. (FOIA requests are discussed more thoroughly in Chapter 17.)

Since public schools are funded by taxpayers' money, the public has access to many records although the school district may not post them on the Internet. Student journalists have access to everything from club account balances to principal salaries to cafeteria food's nutritional content. Board meetings are public as are the agendas and minutes for those meetings, which may provide useful information for story ideas and reporting.

Outside of the school district, a journalist has many other opportunities for conventional research. Recent court documents are available at local and state courthouses. Arrest and accident reports are available at area police stations. Government agencies have cafeteria, building and fire inspections on file. These are just the start of a list of agencies, most funded by public money, that have databases or records open to the public.

High school journalists may find such reporting will help to get specifics and to confirm information from interviews. While witness accounts of an accident in front of the school may offer good information and description, a police report may provide confirmation of details of the time and circumstances. While a school public information officer may explain criminal sexual abuse charges filed against a teacher, the court documents give you more details about the charges as well as the name of the teacher's lawyer for a potential interview. In many cases, the use of conventional research methods may lead to Internet research or to interview possibilities and back. A good reporter understands that one source may lead to another and it may take all of the research to create a clear and accurate understanding.

Although the Internet may provide a gateway to massive amounts of information, a journalist may still find a librarian to be a valuable friend to speed up the process. A librarian, who has extensive knowledge of resources, may help to point a journalist to the exact source or suggest backgrounding possibilities. Still, expect to spend some time doing some digging when it comes to conventional research, but the wealth of information may well be worth it for giving the reader clear and accurate stories.

Test your knowledge

List two questions you should ask about a website to assure you of its credibility.

WWW

WEBLINK Check out http://www.spj.org/foi-guide-students.asp

The website offers a student guide for filing an FOIA request and handling denials.

Quick Exercise

Using three of the Internet or conventional sources, list what public information you can find about a family member.

CONCLUSION

The fundamentals of this chapter will carry through the rest of the book. The ability to report and interview will often dictate how successful a journalist will be. The goal in this process is to collect information from reliable sources that is accurate and thorough. No matter what form a reporter chooses to deliver such information, the fundamental goal in good interviewing and reporting is that the public will get good information.

SUMMARY

- Without a good interview, or good information, a reporter does not have a story.

- Background research will help the reporter understand the story well enough to develop insightful questions.

- The 5 W's and H are the fundamental questions for an interview. Follow-up questions are often a necessity to get developed and specific answers.

- Interviews need to take a conversational tone, not a robotic reading of written questions. Interviews should be conducted face to face in a comfortable environment.

- An interviewer's goal is get developed information through direct quotes, anecdotes and examples.

- Observation can provide a journalist with strong sensory details to use in her writing.

- Although Internet research sometimes makes gathering information easier, a reporter should still work to make sure the source is accurate.

KEY TERMS

anecdotes	direct quote	interviewing
attribution	follow-up question	morgue
backgrounding	Freedom of Information (FOI) laws	paraphrasing
cliché		transcribing
deadline	indirect quote	5 W's and H

EXERCISES

1 Develop sources and lines of questioning for these story topics:

(a) A student's parent has been injured or killed in a military conflict.

(b) A student magician wins a regional talent show.

(c) The school district board votes to begin using a breathalyzer at all school dances.

(d) A star athlete is being recruited by 10 different Division I schools in both football and basketball.

2 Choose 15 minutes of an activity to observe (for example: a choir practice, a science class experiment or skateboarders who try out tricks at the local skatepark).

(a) For the first 10 minutes, write down as many specifics as you can observe, noting details about both the environment and the people.

(b) For the next two minutes, write down a series of single words or phrases that describe your observational focus. Circle the most appropriate focus word or phrase. For the last three minutes, note any additional observations that fit that focus.

3 Choose a partner in the class to interview, one on one, about any of the following subjects. Make sure to ask follow-up questions to get details and anecdotes.

(a) A time in your life when you had to deal with an emotionally difficult situation.

(b) A time in your life when you were involved in a victorious team effort.

(c) The best time you had with your family.

(d) A time when you really learned from a failure.

4 Information scavenger hunt. Identify the following information by interviewing sources within your school community, making sure to have a valid source with first and last name and relevant title for each, or by doing Internet research and making a note of the simplest forms of the website addresses.

(a) teacher with most experience

(b) school's first principal

(c) school tax bill for a $100,000 home in your district

(d) next SAT testing date and deadline

(e) school's total student population reported to the state last year

(f) nation's second wealthiest person under 40

(g) three items on the agenda of the next school district board meeting

(h) last sports team at your school to win a state title

(i) names of four U.S. Supreme Court justices

(j) number of students on free and reduced lunch program within school.

5 Pick a story from a daily news website or newspaper. Choose the three best quotes from the story. Pair up with another student and decide which of your combined six quotes is the strongest. Explain why.

6 Write out four follow-up questions for the following quotes:

(a) For a story about a girl who made her prom dress from candy wrappers: "I had a great time collecting all the wrappers."

(b) For a story about a 14-year-old boy rescued atop a 250-foot waterfall: "I don't know why I climbed out there. I just thought it'd be cool."

(c) For a story on senior football players who have lost 20 straight games: "I still enjoy the game. I think we're still committed to each other and to winning."

(d) For a story on the student musical "The Lion King": "We really worked hard on creating the animal masks. Those were the biggest challenge."

NEWS WRITING

3

> *When you write stories, don't be afraid to start over from scratch if you feel the story is not necessarily shaping up the way you want. I have found it incredibly valuable when writing stories that it is worthwhile to start over sometimes. In the wire world, we update constantly and I find it valuable at times to just start from scratch.*

Jeremy Pelofsky, Correspondent, Reuters

LEARNING OBJECTIVES After completing this chapter you will be able to:

- develop a strong news story idea

- identify the differences in straight news and feature lead styles

- research, interview and write a news story

- employ the variety of writing elements used in news writing

- understand how to organize a news story so that it flows

- explore online media use for news stories.

NEWS WRITING

To upgrade the school's image, your new superintendent decides that students will be required to wear uniforms on campus. Since the story has many of the news value components discussed in Chapter 1 – a broad audience, timeliness, proximity and conflict – you decide that it's clearly worth covering.

The high school publication that decides to publish a **news story** on this new uniform policy will need to create an objective report emphasizing the timely impact of the story for its readers. However, there's a good chance that with a story such as this, the readers may have heard about the change on their own.

Before covering an issue such as this, a student reporter will need to address the following questions: What will be new information for the audience? What does the audience need and want to know? The answer will partly depend upon how the reporter is delivering the information and how quickly.

For a student newspaper that publishes every six weeks, covering the creation and details of a month-old policy can be frustrating. By the time the "news" about the uniforms comes out, students may already be wearing the required collared shirts and khaki pants or skirts. Others may have faced suspension over the issue and some may be resisting the policy with rolled up shirtsleeves or other modifications of the mandated uniform.

The best student reporters will investigate these and other developments, to look for the timeliest angle possible. News writing, especially in the case of breaking news, is about getting readers the most current information that genuinely impacts them. This is the information that will usually be presented in the opening paragraphs of the news story.

In recent years, student newspapers have gained access to a broader range of media to deliver information to their audiences. News websites allow coverage to begin as soon as a newsworthy event occurs, such as the day the superintendent introduces the uniform policy. An enterprising student reporter may send out this basic information to readers via the newspaper's Twitter feed. He may go on to write an online story that includes the basic facts administrators provided in an interview. Such timely reporting gives readers a clear understanding of the issue from the start, rather than letting them rely on the distortions and exaggerations of rumors or lunchroom gossip.

Many good reporters will cover such stories via electronic means on the day of the policy announcement – or, even better, when the uniform policy is still being discussed in departmental meetings or school board retreats. However, the reporter who approaches such a story a month later still has many options for excellent coverage. This reporter should research the latest developments and new information on the uniform policy. Are parents protesting the change because of the high costs of clothes that meet the dress code? Maybe some are even scheduled

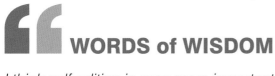 **WORDS of WISDOM**

I think self-editing is even more important in the online world. It's a weird contradiction to have all the space in the world knowing that readers will only read so much online. These days, I try to keep my articles to about 400 to 500 words. After a few hundred words, readers tend to get distracted. There are so many different news sources that readers have many articles to sort through.

But I will do 900 words on an interesting news feature. I don't have a fear of the longer stories because many readers, when I first began writing for an online publication, told me that they liked my articles because they were real articles in length and content.

Jeff Mays, Senior Reporter/Producer for DNAinfo.com

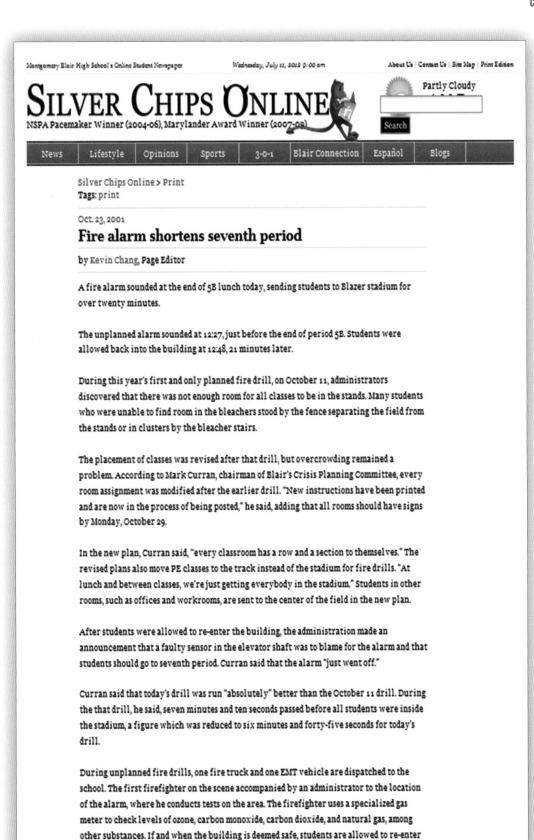

FIGURE 3.1 "Fire alarm shortens seventh period," by Kevin Chang. *Silver Chips Online*, Montgomery Blair High School, Silver Spring, Md, Oct. 23, 2011. Reprinted with permission of *Silver Chips Online*.

The *Silver Chips Online* story is an excellent example of how websites can be the perfect vehicle for breaking news. A brief story the afternoon after a fire alarm sounds can clarify misinformation spread by rumor. The story used an interview with a valid source, the assistant principal, to cover the basic questions about the cause and origin of the fire, as well as the extent of the damage.

FIGURE 3.2 Lucy Chen, theblackandwhite.net, Walt Whitman High School, Bethesda, Md. Reprinted with kind permission.

Black and White demonstrates how high schools have begun covering news events live. Through the technological advances of liveblogging and livestreaming, high school news websites have given their readers and viewers timely information on events of the utmost importance. In the *Black and White* liveblog, high school reporters continually posted the latest information from a budget meeting where major cuts were expected.

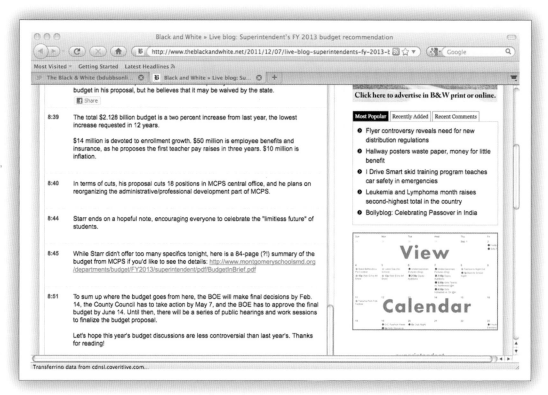

to speak during next week's board meeting. What about the local businesses that are now selling school uniforms downtown? How much are businesses benefiting? Are more jobs available for students? How many students have been put into in-school suspension for violating the new dress code? Why and how have they violated the policy?

For a news-feature angle on the story (see Chapter 5), a reporter should look at the impact of the new uniform policy. Teachers may believe the halls are quieter because students dress more formally. Some parents may have had to cut back on other expenses to cover the costs of the uniforms, especially if they have multiple children at the school.

As reporters look for the most relevant angle to cover, they should always consider the story's planned date of publication.

THE NEWS LEAD

Once the reporter determines the most appropriate angle for the school uniforms story, he will need to identify sources, write questions and conduct the research and interviews (see Chapter 2). From the collected material, the reporter then selects the most important information to convey to the reader. This is usually presented in the **lead** – the opening paragraph or paragraphs of the story – which should be written to grab the reader's attention. The **straight news lead** clearly and directly presents the reader with the story's most important news in the story. The straight news lead is often used in a breaking news story as part of the **inverted pyramid** structure, in which the most important information comes at the top of the story while the rest of the facts and details are organized in descending order of importance (see Figure 3.3).

In the straight news lead, the writer's task is to evaluate which of the 5 W's and H (*Who*, *What*, *Where*, *When*, *Why* and *How*) are most important to the reader and work those into a single sentence, or sometimes two. The writer should open the lead with the **feature fact** or the most interesting and important information of the story. However, detailing all 5 W's and H will often make for a cumbersome or excessively long first sentence. Those basic journalistic questions not answered in the first sentence should be addressed as quickly as possible in the story's opening paragraph or paragraphs.

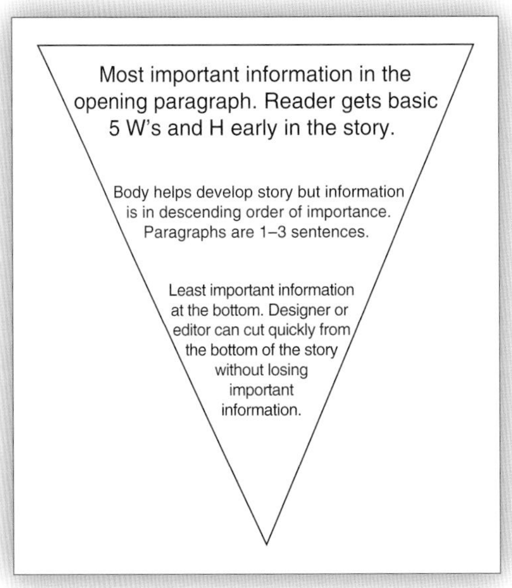

FIGURE 3.3 Inverted pyramid graphic.

In the following lead, the writer decided to emphasize the *What* as her lead's feature fact:

> Tuition for the 2012–2013 school year will rise by 3.3 percent to $31,350, the smallest percentage increase in 25 years, Chief Financial Officer Rob Levin said.
>
> Chairman of the Board of Trustees Christine Hazy (Steven '00, Charissa '03, Trenton '05, Courtney '11) announced this number in a letter on the Parents' Portal that opened re-enrollment in February.
>
> *Rebecca Nussbaum,* The Chronicle, *Harvard-Westlake School, Studio City, Calif.*

The writer could have started the lead with the *Who* as in, "Chief Financial Officer Rob Levin announced a 3.3 percent tuition increase …" However, the fact that there is a tuition increase coming is more important to the student body than who said so.

In the following lead, can you explain why the writer chose to make the *Who* the most important aspect of the story?

> Media Academy Principal Benjamin Schmookler has cut his own position due to the budget crisis and says his day-to-day duties will be turned over to fourth-year teacher Sarah Mazzotta on July 1.
>
> *Alia Furnes and Kim Mejia-Cuellar,* Green and Gold, *Media College Preparatory High School, Oakland, Calif.*

In this case, the *Who*, the principal, comes first, because he is cutting back his own position – a relatively unusual move for an administrator facing a budget crisis.

Leads can also begin with the *How* and *Why* of a story. (Good reporters more rarely lead with the *When* and *Where* because those aspects are typically less important than the answers to the other basic questions.) In the following example, the writer leads with this online story's *Why* element:

> In a first step toward a one-to-one computer model, wherein students will bring or be provided with a personal computing device to use at school, iPads are being distributed to faculty and staff as soon as practicable, Head of School Jeanne Huybrechts said in an email to the faculty Monday.
>
> "We are at a crossroads, and the path that leads to a one-to-one computer model seems the right one to take," Huybrechts said.
>
> This announcement follows the release of the iPad 3 last Wednesday.
>
> *Lara Sokoloff,* Chronicle Online, *Harvard-Westlake School, Studio City, Calif.*

While the other key questions are answered within the opening paragraph, the reporter understands the excitement of the *Why* – the iPad distribution as a step toward providing a computing device for each student. The writer then uses the principal's statement of that goal as the feature fact. Good writers understand that the start of the sentence will get the most reader attention and should therefore showcase the most relevant or exciting information.

Test your knowledge

What's the most important consideration when selecting the angle of a news story?

ALTERNATIVE NEWS LEAD APPROACHES

News leads don't have to be a straight presentation of the facts, especially when a different approach is more likely to catch a reader's interest. The traditional approach to news leads involves identifying and directly stating the 5 W's and H of the story. This section will offer different ways to think about the news lead, often using fascinating details that will be most intriguing to you and the reader.

Very early admission benefits 13 seniors

By Natalia Arguello-Inglis

A COLLEGE offered admissions interviews to seniors this month and admitted thirteen seniors on-the-spot, the first time on-the-spot college admissions have occurred at Lowell.

The Massachusetts College of Pharmacy and Health Sciences decided to offer this opportunity for the first time to students at the school after being impressed by Lowell graduates who attended in the past, according to counselor Jeffrey Yang.

According to Yang, the college will most likely return to Lowell to hold on-the-spot admissions interviews in the future. Lowell is the first school on the West coast that MCPHS has chosen to make on-the-spot admissions available to.

The opportunity was announced both on SchoolLoop and in the senior bulletin, and students were required to sign up with Yang for an interview. Students were also asked to bring a copy of their personal statement, common application, transcript and standardized test scores.

Students were informed of their admissions and scholarships decisions immediately after the interview and all thirteen of the Lowell students who applied were admitted, according to Yang. Yang began discussing the possibility of holding on-the-spot admissions interviews three years ago with MCPHS associate director of admissions Alan Beaudoin.

This is the first time on-the-spot college admissions have ever been made available to Lowell students, Yang said.

Many students find that on-the-spot admissions gives them an advantage over those who apply regularly. "For me it was more beneficial just because I consider myself a better interviewee, so I get an advantage because I can actually talk to the admissions people instead of just being another number in the thousands of applicants," said senior Nicole Gee, who was accepted to MCPHS after her interview with Beaudoin on Oct. 18.

Getting ahead in the race for college admissions allowed the accepted seniors increased their peace of mind. "It feels good to be accepted to one college already, because now I know I at least have that," Gee said.

A VERSION OF THIS STORY FIRST APPEARED ON *WWW.THELOWELL.ORG*

FIGURE 3.4 *The Lowell*, Lowell High School, Cardinal Edition, Vol. 216, No. 3, April 11, 2011., www.thelowell.org. "Very early admission benefits 13 seniors," by Natalia Arguello-Inglis. Reproduced by permission of Sharn Matusek.

To make this a strong straight news lead, the writer includes the specific number of on-the-spot admissions and explains the oddity of such recruiting in the opening sentence. The reporter then answers the next-most important question: why the administration has started instantly admitting Lowell students. News stories written in the inverted pyramid structure give the reader the most important and interesting information early in the story with the least important information later. Notice how the last paragraph isn't an editorialized summary, but an objectively reported quote about a non-essential but interesting reaction to the on-the-spot admissions.

Here is an example of an alternative news lead that makes good use of striking details:

Family members, strangers, oddly-shaped bell peppers and cats are among the subject matter of the senior photography show, "The Best of Three," which began on Monday.

Ingrid Chang, The Chronicle, *Harvard-Westlake School, Studio City, Calif.*

The writer could have simply included the exhibit's title and viewing schedule, but instead included the intriguing mix of subject matter in the show, to get readers' attention and spark their interest.

Here is a different example of an alternative approach to a news lead:

With a goal to raise $3,000 for breast cancer research, the volleyball team will host its second Volley for the Cure game Oct. 13 again Marion Harding.

Lexi Perrault, Blue & Gold, *Findlay High School, Findlay, Ohio*

The inclusion of the financial goal for the fundraiser makes this lead stronger. Reporters who break down the 5 W's and H to write their leads should also ask themselves, what makes this story interesting?

Another alternative approach news writers should take for leads is to ask: How does this story really impact the readers?

Starting this semester, seniors may take online courses to fulfill certain graduation requirements.

Caitriona Smyth, The Lowell, *Lowell High School, San Francisco, Calif.*

The writer could have used a longer lead with facts about the new Cyber High program that is now open to all seniors after last year's pilot program. Instead, the writer decided to answer the question: How are my readers affected by this program?

Quick Exercise

Explain what important questions are not answered in the following straight news leads.

1 Some boys were arrested following Friday night's soccer game.

2 The state passed tougher teen driving laws.

3 A new fundraising effort to raise more than $5,000 will begin Monday.

FIGURE 3.5 *The Kirkwood Call*, Kirkwood High School, Kirkwood, Mo. Reproduced by permission of Mitch Eden.

The Kirkwood Call addresses an upcoming school bond referendum by profiling the different people and organizations impacted by the proposed bond. News websites can cover area, state and national issues by localizing them for the student audience. An important role of news writing in school publications is to help students understand issues beyond the school walls that impact their lives.

14 In-Depth

Prop 1 & 2: In the eyes of...

Pools and kindergarten classrooms are all on the line Nov. 2 as Proposition 1 and 2 wait to be passed for the Kirkwood School District. Advocates for and against the two bond issues have come in the form of high school swimmers, middle school science teachers and concerned taxpayers. In the middle of thousands of arguments and yard signs expressing resident's feelings about Prop. 1 and 2, *The Kirkwood Call* tried to make sense of it all. We tried to read beyond the numbers and financial information of the issue and focus on the most important outcome of the bonds: people. Here are their stories.

...an NKMS science teacher

Joe Weber
in-depth editor

With clustered bumper stickers, crowded tables and not a single gas jet to be found, Ruth Baldwin cannot stand her classroom.

"Space is an issue," Baldwin said, surveying her room.

Baldwin, a science teacher at North Kirkwood Middle School, has taught for 20 years in the school's science facilities. Every day she teaches eighth graders about the complexities of the universe while dealing with the complexities of an out-of-date science classroom.

"This classroom was basic in 1957," Baldwin said. "In 20 years, it has gone below basic."

Built-in gas jets used to show students the effects of heat expansion, but now cheap candles do the job. An everyday faucet stands where lab sinks once gave students handling science equipment a safe place to dispose of scientific material. After decades of use and an un-pluggable leak, the essential piece of equipment had to go. When two new computers and a giant orange and white ActivBoard were placed in the room, Baldwin could no longer use the electrical outlets for turning on hotplates.

"If you don't have the space and you don't have the time, you can't do as much," Baldwin said. "It really hampers what we think of as science."

For a teacher as dedicated and enthusiastic as Baldwin, hampered science is not on the agenda. If passed, Proposition 1 will offer new renovations and changes to the middle school science rooms that would allow teachers like Baldwin to teach in up-to-date facilities with the current science-education standards. Instead of creating heating devices out of baby food jars, sand and candles, middle school students would simply turn a knob and have access to essential tools for science education.

Pulling dirty bins and cramped beakers out of an old supply closet, Baldwin can only laugh in frustration.

"In the last 20 years we've lost gas, we've lost electric, we've lost the lab sink. And as great as technology is, that takes up space in a classroom that's already too small."

jweber@thekirkwoodcall.com

Meredith Bouchein photographer
Ruth Baldwin, NKMS science teacher, helps eighth grade students during her seventh hour class. Baldwin has taught in Kirkwood for 20 years.

Photo courtesy of *Ruth Baldwin*
A rusted sink pipe shown above led to the recent flooding of a NKMS science classroom.

Meredith Bouchein photographer
New technology barely squeezes into the front of Ruth Baldwin's room. Her original demonstration table was put on wheels to make room for an ActivBoard.

...the swim team

Annie Travis
features editor

If Proposition 2 passes in November, it will provide an indoor swimming pool for physical education classes, public swimming and school and club swim teams. Currently, KHS water polo and swim teams conduct their practices at the Meramec pool, built in 1969, which has athletes saying they swim in disgust.

"Right now we have to share the pool with old people who do water yoga classes," Zach Hawkins, senior and water polo player, said. "[The classes] leave the pool and deck really dirty. At practice last year there was a huge hairball at the bottom of the pool that we needed to use a net to fish out."

Hawkins said the pool deck is sweltering and chemicals put into the pool are so strong swimmers' eyes burn and they cannot breathe. Hawkins even reports athletes with asthma have had to sit out of practice because of attacks. David

Niemann, junior and member of boys' swim team, said a teammate vomited during practice because of the harshness of the chemicals.

"The fumes become so pungent it is necessary to take 15-minute breaks during practice to go outside and drink water and breathe fresh air," Billy Fries, junior and former boys' swim team member, said.

Fries said the addition of an aquatic center at KHS would give the swim teams an opportunity to hold invitationals and host home meets without leaving the school. Having a pool on campus would also prevent parents from having to drop off younger students at practice, making transportation easier.

Hawkins hopes for better maintenance and communication about scheduling changes with the addition of an aquatic center at KHS. Niemann simply wants a pool that is not more than twice his age and lacks a leaking roof.

atravis@thekirkwoodcall.com

> " The fumes become so pungent it is necessary to take 15-minute breaks during practice... "
>
> **Billy Fries, junior**

Dylan Brady photographer
Kirkwood boys' swim team practices at Meramec Community College in Kirkwood. For many, the pool's chemicals are infamous for causing irritation in the swimmers' eyes and lungs.

FIGURE 3.5 *(continued)*

...a retired taxpayer

Nancy Ellis has lived, enjoyed and paid taxes in Kirkwood for 34 years. Coming from a family of educators, she cares deeply about the well-being of students and faculty in the Kirkwood School District. Propositions 1 and 2, however, make her feel uneasy.

Joe Weber
in-depth editor

"If money was unlimited, we would all want it," Ellis said, "but money is not unlimited."

As a retired teacher and IBM employee, Ellis helped create the Kirkwood Citizens for Fiscal Responsibility (KCFR), a group opposed specifically to the upcoming bond proposals on the upcoming Nov. 2 ballot. Worried that recent tax raises for Kirkwood residents have become too high, Ellis believes KSD must start judging changes to schools on a need versus want basis.

"They have quality education, and I'm thrilled with that," Ellis said, "but there's quality education, then there's fluff."

Jim Miller, a 30-year Des Peres resident and fellow KCFR member, recently completed a five-year analysis on his own tax payments to KSD.

"In those five years, my taxes to the Kirkwood School District increased 48 percent," Miller said. "I only want to invest in the things I feel are absolute needs."

Both Miller and Ellis have spent most of the last three months doing extensive research on Kirkwood tax raises, listing their findings on www.kcffr.com,

a website dedicated to opposition of the bond issues. According to Miller, another bond proposal reflects the district's lack of recognition to the needs of taxpayers not directly affected by the school improvements.

Though Miller wants the best for the students and faculty, he has no children or family who attend the schools. After willingly agreeing to significant tax raises over the years, he sees another bond initiative as the tipping point.

"The school board, in my mind, should balance the needs of the student, the staff and the taxpayers. We all have needs," Miller said. "I have lost confidence and my trust in the school board in being able to weigh and balance those needs."

With such a diverse range of financial stability of Kirkwood residents, Miller and Ellis worry most about citizens who love living in Kirkwood, but struggle to keep up with tax increases.

"You look around Kirkwood and you see these beautiful homes, but you also see little bitty houses," Ellis said. "Those people are very loyal Kirkwood citizens. They need to have some consideration when it comes to spending their money."

For the hours of number-crunching, attending school district meetings and sign-giving KCFR has undergone throughout the stressful months before election day, Miller and Ellis still smile and laugh

Maggie McWay photographer

when reflecting on their work. Both believe the only way to achieving their goal is to keep personal anger and argument out of the debate and simply stick to the facts. In a community as close-knit as Kirkwood, disagreements can only leave hard feelings for so long.

"I have a neighbor down the street, she's got a sign that says vote for Proposition 1 and 2," Miller said. "I have a sign in my yard that says don't vote for Proposition 1 and 2. We are still friends."

jweber@thekirkwoodcall.com

...a KHS senior

Sarah Schwegel, senior, has spinal muscular atrophy type 2, forcing her to travel by wheelchair. Proposition 2 would affect her directly, as it includes plans to make Lyons Stadium more handicapped-accessible.

Maggie Hallam
co-editor-in-chief

Although Schwegel believes KHS is fairly handicapped-accessible, with the exception of the power doors malfunctioning and classes being on the second floor, Lyons Stadium is not. Currently, simply getting into the stadium is a hassle.

"I have to go around to the visitor's entrance, and that sidewalk is still not the best, and I have to [go] all the way around to the home side," Schwegel said. "Since it's so crowded around the bleachers, I have to sit on the track. There are no seats accessible to us on the bleachers except for at the top."

Schwegel feels the stadium's accessibility should be improved, regardless of the proposition passing.

"It's not fair if the proposition doesn't pass that the field won't be accessible," Schwegel said. "There's going to be a lot of kids with disabilities coming up within the next few years, and it's not fair to us. We should be able to sit in the bleachers like everybody else."

mhallam@thekirkwoodcall.com

Maggie McWay photographer

Buzz Gerstung, works on painting lines on the upper grass athletic fields for the field hockey game that day.

Photo courtesy of *Johnny Frohlichstein*

...a KHS field technician

Though the possibility of turf on the upper athletic fields have soccer and field hockey players pushing for a "yes" vote on Proposition 2, new fields would

Joe Weber
in-depth editor

also affect faculty members who work on all KHS fields, including Bill "Buzz" Gerstung, athletic field technician. Before any team can get into the game, Gerstung is there preparing. As far as the difficulty of maintaining a grass field versus turf, Gerstung sees the two as different types of maintenance.

"[Working on the turf] is more labor-intensive right now," Gerstung said. "You can't let anything sit on there. It all has to be cleaned off."

The duty of constantly painting new out-of-bounds lines and growing new grass would no longer be an issue, but tedious jobs such as completely clearing off the turf of any foreign substances adds a new responsibility. Ideas of always-green turf fields may excite most KHS athletes, yet Gerstung has his own preferences.

"Personally, I'm a grass guy," Gerstung said.

jweber@thekirkwoodcall.com

FIGURE 3.6 "The First 100 Days of Victoria Swartz," by Michaela Marincic, *Blue & Gold*, Findlay High School, Findlay, Ohio. Reprinted with permission.

Blue & Gold takes a packaged approach to this news story, following up on the new principal's programs to address school issues. Many publications typically cover only the arrival of a new principal. Follow-up stories provide important answers to questions that the first story didn't address. *Blue & Gold* achieves a balanced assessment through quotes from the principal, assistant administrators and students, along with survey responses on the principal's first 100 days.

FEATURE LEADS

While the emergence of high school news websites provides a new venue for straight news leads, the feature lead is still an essential tool in high school publications, especially those that publish only monthly or bi-monthly. The feature lead generally comes in the form of an intriguing statement, a contrast, a description or an anecdote. The feature lead will frequently offer the reader a personal or narrative presentation of the news. However, when the news writer chooses to use a feature lead, the **news peg** or that which is new, changed or different about the topic, should immediately follow the lead in a "**nut**," "**focus**" or "**wrap**" **paragraph**.

The following feature lead categories represent only a few of the lead types that educators and journalists teach and use. The reality is that feature leads can take many forms as long as they fit the tone of the story, are free of clichés and are driven by real reporting and facts – avoiding anything that's fictionalized or editorialized. The following examples of feature leads are instead offered to inspire a range of creative approaches to beginning a news story.

Contrast lead

Homosexuality was originally listed in the World Health Organization's compilation of diseases and disorders until 1992. Prior to the 19th century, death was a common penalty for homosexuals. By the 1950s, gay rights in America had improved, but not to the point of equality. Only 60 years later, junior Christopher Fiscus, who is openly homosexual, said he can walk through the halls of CHS without encountering a single instance of intolerance.

WWW

WEBLINK Check out

www.journaliststoolbox.org

This website provides a wealth of links for journalists on everything from expert sources to mobile resources to urban legends.

Generating news story ideas

As discussed in Chapter 1, a good beat system should help generate news story ideas. However, if your paper is still in search of story ideas, the following list might help lead you to important and interesting news stories taking place at your school:

- School policy changes

- New club activities

- Student council activities

- Student contests and honors

- Generational changes (comparing current activities to those reported in the previous decade's newspapers and yearbooks)

- Class projects

- Fundraising efforts

- State and national academic testing trends and changes

- New local, state and national laws relevant to teenagers

- Local business growth

- Driving law changes

- Other changes afoot in your school or local community.

Uproar

by the numbers

732	148	75
Total applications submitted to colleges by this month's deadline	Different colleges and universities sought by this year's seniors	Number of seniors who applied to at least one school during early admission

PREACHING TO THE CHOIR Senior Telos Group member **Joe Bush** speaks to Middle School chapel. Bush spoke Jan. 24 during the second chapel in a series of presentations led by the Telos Group focusing on leadership and ethics.

ANDREW GATHERER PHOTO

Math team succeeds in area competition

Sixteen Upper School students participated in the ninth annual Metroplex Math Competition Jan. 21. Led by co-captains **Jason Altschuler** and **James Rowan**, the team earned a total of 22 top-eight finishes, including sweeps of the top three in the Geometry and Algebra II categories. Rowan and Altschuler additionally took first and second in calculus. The competition, initially started by St. Mark's, was held at Parish Episcopal School this year.

Coat drive comes to a close

The eighth grade Community Service board, assisted by Upper School Co-chairmen **Dylan Clark**, **Andrew Goodman** and **George Law**, ran the Coat Drive from Jan 9-13. Three hundred coats were collected and sent to five charities: Austin Street, David's Place, Gooch Elementary, Jubilee Center and North Dallas Share Ministries.

Eighth grader wins MS Spelling Bee

Eighth grader **Brent Weisberg** won the Middle School Spelling Bee that was held Jan 10. Weisberg will now advance to the next round, the Dallas County Private School Bee to be held Feb. 7 at UTD. Contestants consisted of the winners of humanities class winners, grades fourth through eighth. If Weisberg cannot attend the next round, alternate **Zak Houillion** will take his place.

Storytelling scholar to visit school

Willard E. Walker, Jr. '66 Visiting Scholar **Dr. David Gonzalez** will come to 10600 Preston Road Feb. 28-29. Gonzalez, a storyteller, musician and public speaker, will speak during Middle School assembly and advanced Spanish classes. He will also speak to Lower School students and the Spanish and DADYO Clubs. The Caduceus Club has also arranged for guest speaker **Dr. Stan Goldman** to speak about testicular cancer during Thursday's Upper School Assembly.

FIGURE 3.7 *ReMarker*, St. Mark's School of Texas, Dallas, Texas. Reproduced by permission of Ray Westbrook.
ReMarker staff create an attractive news brief section each issue to cover short, but important and relevant stories for their audience. The coverage allows them to highlight honors, upcoming events and activities that warrant some space, although not that of a full story. The "By the Numbers" graphic is a visually interesting way to provide more information. The photo and full headlines for each brief finish off a professional, informative package.

HELPFUL
TIPS

News brief coverage

While issues such as drinking and driving, budget cuts and local elections may dominate the front-page of your newspaper, shorter news stories covering day-to-day events in your school community can often play an important role in a high school publication. While daily intercom announcements may feature the upcoming art club meeting or academic decathlon results, daydreaming students may miss such events in a noisy classroom.

High school publications should have a briefs section to quickly cover such events, short news items and announcements. Such coverage can help build a daily readership for a high school publication's website. The briefs can come from the paper's beat reporting as discussed in Chapter 1. But briefs can also offer an opportunity to cover community, state and national news in a condensed format, to give the reader whose primary source of news is the high school publication a way to get caught up on the world outside the school walls.

Some topics for brief news coverage might include:

→ Upcoming club meetings

→ Fundraisers

→ Deadlines for scholarships or organization membership applications

→ Contest results

→ Neighborhood events

→ Upcoming speakers

→ Club officer election results.

"You won't find outright homophobia here," Christopher said. "It's not like someone will walk up to you and outright hate you. You'll find a lot of people who are apathetic toward it. They don't really have an opinion; it's just something they're accepting. That's been my experience here."

A variety of research indicates Christopher's experience with growing tolerance toward his sexual orientation is not limited to Carmel. A CNN Research Opinion Poll published on Aug. 11 showed that, for the first time, more than 50 percent of Americans believe gays and lesbians should have a constitutional right to marry and have their marriage recognized as legally valid.

Victor Xu, HiLite, *Carmel High School, Carmel, Ind.*

The **contrast lead** emphasizes the variance, change or contrast in a story. Here the writer contrasts views toward homosexuality in the past and present. The simple fact of a student's walking down the hallway without incident would seem to have little news value, until his experience is compared with those of homosexuals decades and generations earlier, who faced persecution and even death for their sexual orientation. The description of Fiscus's localized experience is followed by a "nut" paragraph with a more general news peg – the shift in attitudes toward gays and lesbians as reported in the recent CNN Research Opinion Poll.

Vignette lead

Senior Marcus Robinson lost more than 10 relatives and friends, many to violence. One of the 10 was his close friend, Mandela High School sophomore Lovell Hadnot, who was killed in January of last year.

"His death made me think that every day, I can be a victim of violence," Robinson said.

Robinson is only one of many students affected by the 110 homicides that took place in Oakland last year. Those murders marked an increase over the 95 in 2010.

Kim Mejia-Cuellar, Green and Gold, *Media Academy, Oakland, Calif.*

The **vignette lead**, or an anecdotal lead, describes a personal example of a larger issue, using a strong narrative to draw readers into the story. In this case, the reporter localizes an increase in the number of murders in Oakland by addressing the impact of such violence on one student at the school. To put a local face on a broader social issue, the writer leads with the deaths of 10 of the student's friends and family members, many through violence. Readers may not be able to comprehend the 110 murders recorded in the city in 2011. However, reading about a fellow student who has experienced the trauma of murder at first hand brings the issue into sharp focus.

In the next example of the vignette lead, the writer dramatizes the impact of new school district fees through a narrative description of one family's dilemma.

Junior Olivia Ko has certainly made the most of her high school experience. In addition to competing in three seasons of sports, she is currently enrolled in six International Baccalaureate classes and on her way to getting the IB diploma. However, her high achievement is putting an extra burden on her parents' shoulders, as the budget for Fiscal year 2011, which was adopted on May 20, is putting the financial responsibility for some academic and athletic fees into the hands of parents.

Next year, students will have to pay $75 for all Advanced Placement (AP) or IB tests and $100 per VHSL sport. This means that Ko, who intends to have a similar schedule next year, will be responsible for approximately $750 in new fees.

Emily Fruchterman, The A Blast, *Annandale High School, Annandale, Va.*

The length of the vignette lead may vary, but like other feature leads, it should always transition smoothly into a "wrap" or "nut" paragraph that includes answers to the basic news questions. In the story above, the writer uses the wrap graph to answer the basic *When, Who* and *What.*

The descriptive lead

The **descriptive lead** draws readers into the story's setting and context, often through an extended narrative description.

During Knights' Way training day, Superintendent Dr. David Schuler had some surprising news for the new crop of leaders.

Last year, he said, three students had requested transfers out of Prospect because of bullying. In his six years as superintendent, Schuler had never before had anyone from Prospect make that request.

"I was shocked," said Sam McArdle, senior Knights' Way leader, "and I think everyone else was [too]."

McArdle, who was one of the committee members given the task of planning the first Knights' Way topic on bullying, used the fact to help highlight the importance of the issue.

Neel Thakker, The Prospector, *Prospect High School, Prospect, Ill.*

The writer creates suspense by delaying key facts until the second paragraph, and saves the full context for those facts until the fourth paragraph. This extended description helps the reader share in the surprise and shock the student leaders felt as they were given the task of trying to change the culture of bullying at their school.

A straight lead describing the task force and its efforts to address bullying could have conveyed much of the same information, but would be unlikely to engage readers to the same extent as the characters and events presented through this descriptive lead.

As you may have noticed, descriptive leads may sometimes overlap with vignette leads, and both may employ the comparisons of a contrast lead. These categories are not mutually exclusive, nor are the broader categories of straight and feature leads.

The death of cursive

With 44 of 50 states phasing cursive out of their curriculum, the Lower School's stance on teaching the art of handwriting is evolving.

It's used every day.

For writing checks. For signing receipts. Or just jotting down a few notes.

But nowadays, some people don't see the practicality in mastering the art of handwriting.

In 44 out of 50 states, public schools are adopting the Common Core curriculum, which does not require the teaching of cursive. But at 10600 Preston Road, cursive is still an integral part of the Lower School curriculum.

Head of Lower School Barbara York believes that one of the reasons cursive should still be taught is so that kids have the option to write in either print or cursive writing.

"You never know which children will respond best to print or cursive writing," York said. "For some kids, the flow of the cursive writing makes that much easier and they can do that more easily and quickly. For other kids, even after learning cursive, prefer to print."

A reason that cursive is being phased out is the rise of keyboarding. Instead of teaching cursive, schools are taking time to teach how to type and use computers. But York does not agree with the overuse of computers or else she thinks people will become dependent on them.

"There are some changes I think we should do with technology," York said. "I think we should use technology as a tool. But I think that that's what technology should remain. I don't want it to take over other parts of our lives. Now there's a good deal of research that's showing too much use of technology and using it too early is detrimental to kids. I don't want technology to be a necessity to think or produce a piece of work."

Second grade teacher and cursive instructor Susan Morris has another reason why cursive must be taught across the country.

She believes cursive should be kept in curriculums because studies show "children formally taught handwriting improve their sentence construction and increase the complexity of their thoughts."

Morris says cursive also helps students become written communicators, and it allows students to read cursive in historical documents and handwritten letters.

"It's a more personal way to communicate," Morris said. "I hope St. Mark's will continue to keep it."

As a second grade teacher, she sees students' attitude toward cursive firsthand.

"They do look forward to [cursive]," Morris said. "It's a little bit like a right of passage at St. Mark's that they know in second grade they are going to be taught cursive."

Junior Max Naseck, who learned cursive in Lower School, never came to use it often.

"Cursive is more tedious to write and more tedious to read," Naseck said. "Since second grade, I've transitioned to using mainly print."

To art instructor Max Wood, handwriting is an art and a direct translation of who one is. Wood, who believes the teaching of the fine motor skill is imperative, emphasizes the role of handwriting on her classes, and she is also the sponsor of the new handwriting club.

"If I have any political power, I would urge [politicians] to reinstate cursive because not teaching cursive is one of the biggest mistakes in our own education," Wood said.

With cursive being phased out across the country, York believes people will still use handwriting, either cursive or print.

"I don't think in the foreseeable future we're going to be able to get along without any kind of handwriting," York said.

But even if children don't embrace the use of cursive handwriting, York still hopes Marksmen will be able to use the skill when necessary.

"I would like for all kids to be able to sign a contract in cursive," York said, beginning to grin, "whether it takes them awhile or not."

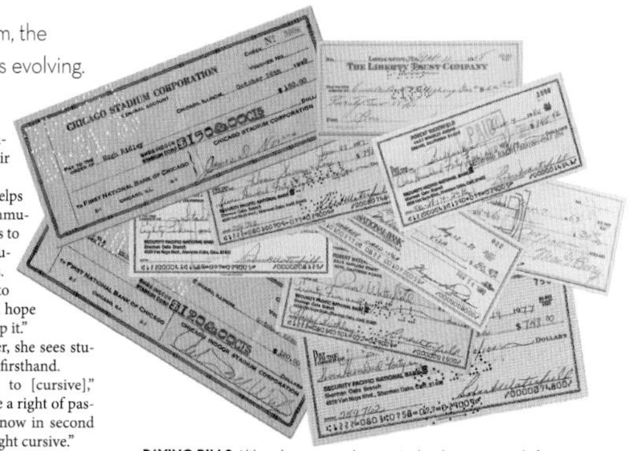

PAYING BILLS Although some people use print handwriting instead of cursive, most people use at least some sort of cursive to sign their names on checks and receipts.

sign here

Although print handwriting is more popular for school and daily activities, cursive is more common for signatures. Here are examples of Marksmen's signatures.

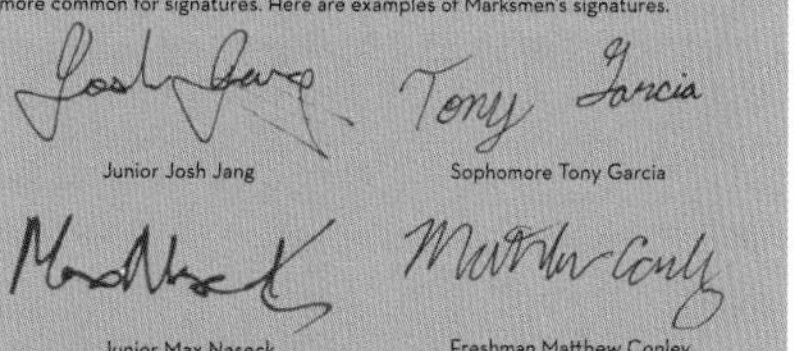

Junior Josh Jang

Sophomore Tony Garcia

Junior Max Naseck

Freshman Matthew Conley

Junior Taubert Nadalini

THE DEATH OF CURSIVE story by Alan Rosenthal, scene editor | photo illustration by Nic Lazzara, graphics direcor

FIGURE 3.8 *ReMarker*, St. Mark's School of Texas, Dallas, Texas. Reproduced by permission of Ray Westbrook.

This *ReMarker* story takes a descriptive lead approach to a news story on the elimination of cursive writing nationally. The lead reminds readers of the widespread use of cursive writing, to set up a discussion on the impact of eliminating it. While the lead is in a feature style, the writer quickly ties it to a news peg on the national trend. In the same paragraph, he also covers the local school angle by noting the district's decision to keep cursive in the Lower School curriculum.

Don't get too caught up in trying to classify each of your leads. The more important point is to recognize the different ways to get the reader interested in the facts of the story through narrative, anecdote, contrasts, descriptions and other creative strategies.

DEVELOPING A NEWS STORY

Consider the following situation:

The renovation of the gym is one week away from being completed. The first basketball game of the season is set for two days after the scheduled end of the construction. Construction workers have been installing new stands and a new floor, but heavy rains have just caused flooding throughout the area, including the gym. Selena, a reporter for the school's paper, hears from her math teacher (who is also an assistant basketball coach), that the flooding has ruined the new floor.

As an online reporter trying to get the information out to her readers quickly, Selena might send this Twitter message out to her paper's Twitter feed: "Heavy rains flood, ruin new basketball floor in remodeled gymnasium."

The word is out, but what other questions will the readers have? Twitter and Facebook posts have given reporters and other users the ability to instantly convey short bursts of information to a large audience. Still, readers will have questions that go beyond a 140-character tweet or a brief status update. The straight news lead offers little more than the average social media

Test your knowledge

What's a news peg?

FIGURE 3.9 "Right-to-work legislation eliminates fees for students," by Rochelle Brual, p. 4, March 22, 2012. *HiLite*, Carmel High School, Carmel, Ind. Reproduced by permission of Jim Streisel.

Through a strong vignette lead, *HiLite* gives readers a personal look at the impact that labor union legislation has upon students. Students won't necessarily go online and read about this legislation. However, a good news writer can help the reader understand the issue by putting the story in concrete terms featuring real people. The writer uses the lead to attract the reader but provides the news peg – the approval to right-to-work legislation – in the focus or wrap graph right after the lead.

Right-to-work legislation eliminates fees for students

New bill prevents unions from requiring dues

BY ROCHELLE BRUAL
rbrual@hilite.org

Although Kyle Tosh, Kroger bagger and junior, is a labor union member, he said he doesn't remember the name of his own labor union, and he doesn't pay much attention to it either. It sends him emails he never responds to, and it leeches $7.40 out of his paycheck a week. Other than that, Tosh said he receives minimal contact and unapparent benefits from his labor union, which makes him want to cease membership.

Tosh isn't the only one. Some supermarket chains like Kroger and Meijer require all of their employees to join the labor union United Food and Commercial Workers (UFCW)—or at least pay the fees to join. However, in January 2012, Gov. Mitch Daniels signed a bill that made Indiana the 23rd right-to-work state, which prohibits unions from forcing workers to pay mandatory representation fees.

"(The union was) like, 'We're going to fight (the right-

to-work law). We're going to help our Kroger employees.' It was total bologna. I don't really care because you're not helping me at all. I could watch it sink, and I wouldn't care," Tosh said.

According to Karen Taff, union member and social studies teacher, the right-to-work legislation was labeled in a way that makes it sound benign. However, Taff said it actually prohibits workers from being able to exercise their legal rights. It will kill the part of the labor contract that requires employees to join unions, and it stifles bargaining with corporations.

Taff said via email, "Since the late 19th century, the labor movement has played a significant role in American history. They were essential in helping to create the broad expansion of the economy and the middle class in the middle of the 20th century. In the last 25 years, much of the power of organized labor has been eroded by industrial and manufacturing jobs being moved overseas. In general, the same economic, social and political factors that have

CONTINUED ON NEXT PAGE

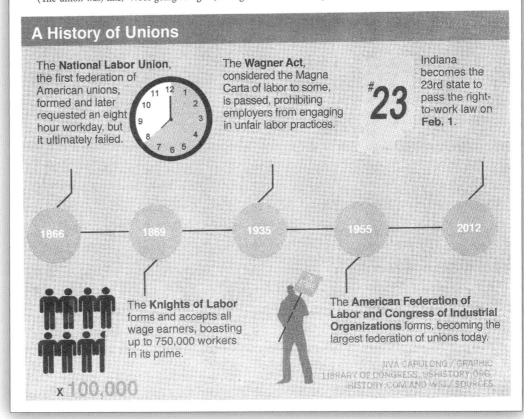

A History of Unions

The **National Labor Union,** the first federation of American unions, formed and later requested an eight hour workday, but it ultimately failed.

The **Wagner Act,** considered the Magna Carta of labor to some, is passed, prohibiting employers from engaging in unfair labor practices.

#**23** Indiana becomes the 23rd state to pass the right-to-work law on Feb. 1.

1866   1869   1935   1955   2012

The **Knights of Labor** forms and accepts all wage earners, boasting up to 750,000 workers in its prime.

The **American Federation of Labor and Congress of Industrial Organizations** forms, becoming the largest federation of unions today.

x 100,000

JIVA CAPULONG / GRAPHIC
LIBRARY OF CONGRESS, USHISTORY.ORG,
HISTORY.COM AND WSJ / SOURCES

message. Developing an in-depth news story is one important way that serious journalists can provide something much more useful than the average Tweet or blog post.

A serious news writer such as Selena will ask and report answers to a number of key questions. These might include: Is the rumor from the math teacher true? How bad is the flood damage? Will

IN ACTION

Clarifying the news story focus

Most high school publications hold regular meetings, where the staff members' story ideas for upcoming editions are discussed. Such meetings often generate lists of story ideas, where possible pieces are sketched out and compiled for editors to comb through at a later date. In preparing for such a meeting, it is important to write out clearly focused story ideas, with specific details. Make sure that your ideas are more than just topics, such as "recycling" or "standardized testing." Make sure there are specifics in your story idea, preferably with a local angle. You should always ask yourself the following basic questions to decide if a story idea is feasible and sufficiently focused:

● Is something new, changed or different?

● Do we have solid and accurate sources for the news tip?

● Do we have verifiable facts from which to build the story?

Here are some examples of story ideas:

Poor: "School store. Heard it might be opening."

This is merely a topic without any development.

Better: "The school store is reopening next Friday. The store closed last year after losing a lot of money. The business teacher said the principal approved the reopening. The story should cover the entrepreneurial class plan to oversee cash flow and inventory to improve sales."

This story idea has a definite time peg – the reopening date. The reporter also has a reliable source in the business teacher. As a result, the story is more than rumor. It's the start of a plan for what to cover. A good specific list of sources might strengthen this story idea.

---

the administration cancel the first basketball game? Where is the monthly dance we usually have in the gym going to be held?

For a more political focus to the story, Selena might also ask: How much did the new flooring cost? How much will repairing the damage cost? Where's that money coming from? What part of the budget is going to be cut to pay for the damage?

The development of the story beyond the lead should answer these questions. The reader should learn something new with each successive paragraph. As shown in Figure 3.3, the remaining information will be presented in descending order of importance. A good reporter will weigh her collected information on the basis of audience impact and interest, and organize the story accordingly.

While a straight news lead on the story above would, like a tweet, highlight the flood damage to the new gym floor and note the source of this information, the next paragraphs should develop other issues, such as the possible cancelation of next week's basketball game. The discussion of the dance would probably come next. Why? Because these last two topics impact the teen audience directly and immediately.

The key to developing a news story is a writer's ability to think through all the relevant questions that need to be answered and to seek out legitimate sources to use and quote.

The sources within a story should all be qualified, relevant sources as discussed in Chapters 1 and 2. Writers should ask themselves: "Who is going to make an impact on this story?" or, "Who will the story make an impact upon?" In the gym flooding story, the original information comes from the assistant basketball coach. A more authoritative source for information on the gym floor and its consequences for the game might be the head basketball coach. The head custodian would be a relevant source for clean-up efforts. The principal might be able to address long-term plans for the gym and activities held there. The superintendent or district public relations representative might speak to the costs of the renovation and the repairs. To confirm such information, the district insurance company's representative could also be contacted. Basketball players impacted by the flooding would be relevant sources, as would Student Council officers who might have to change plans for the dance. Seniors looking forward to their last gym dance and displaced physical education students could add further perspectives.

News writers should avoid one-source stories. The saying is "there are two sides to every story," but the reality is there are many more, and reporters should try to draw on as many as possible.

FIGURE 3.10 Victoria Reick-Mitrisin, *Spark*, Lakota East High School, Liberty Township, Ohio. Reproduced by permission of Dean Hume.

This *Spark* news story gives the reader an in-depth look at the Carteens program though a mix of interviews and research. The anecdotal lead provides a strong personal perspective on the program. The interview with the county official is important because of his role as the program's director. The county statistics showing a decrease in teenage driver fatalities, along with the figures on Carteens participants' reduced likelihood of receiving a second ticket, expand the story to the program's broader impact.

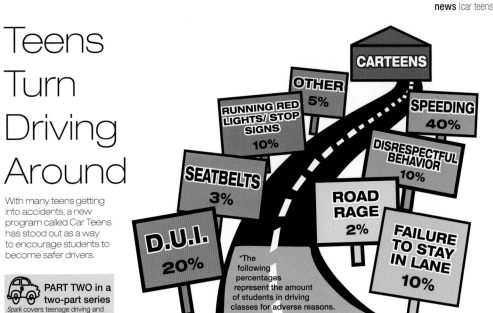

Teens Turn Driving Around

With many teens getting into accidents, a new program called Car Teens has stood out as a way to encourage students to become safer drivers.

PART TWO in a two-part series
Spark covers teenage driving and the various programs that attempt to help teens be safe on the road.

story **victoria reick-mitrisin**
infographic **sara patt**

*The following percentages represent the amount of students in driving classes for adverse reasons.

information-car teens ohio

There are multiple ways in which teens can find themselves
On the Road to Carteens

A tall, 18-year-old girl steps to the front of the small room, which is filled with teenagers like herself. Her demeanor is somber. For the past several Tuesdays, she has relayed the same story—she tells other teenagers about the day that she killed a man.

Each Tuesday between 6 and 8 p.m., teenagers who have violated traffic safety laws gather to learn the truth about the dangers of driving. Butler County courts mandate that first-time traffic offenders and one of their parents participate in the Carteens program for six weeks.

Often, teenagers who attend Carteens meetings are between 16 and 18 years old and have received their first traffic safety violation, depending on how extreme the infraction is. The Carteens meeting is taught by teen and adult volunteers who explain the possible consequences of driving.

East senior Lindsey Naughton recently graduated from the Carteens program. She feels that the six required sessions were an eye-opening experience.

"The one that really hit-home was the video of the family that was hit by a truck," said Naughton. "It made me realize what I could do if I continued to drive recklessly."

Naughton was in Carteens because of a speeding ticket that she received at the beginning of her senior year. She has not received another driving ticket since that time.

Carteens has been helping Ohioan youth realize the dangers of driving since 1987. The Butler County division was founded in 1998 by James Jordan, who is now the Carteens Extension Educator for Butler County. Currently, 58 teen volunteers are a part of the program, most of whom have previously graduated from the program.

"Some parents bring their teen drivers through the program before they receive their

> It [Carteens] made me realize what I could do if I continued to drive recklessly.

first citation," said Jordan. "They do this because of their knowledge of the program and the effective method of teaching done by 4-H Carteens volunteers."

According to Jordan, driver fatalities of people 16 to 18 years old have declined from their initial 10 percent between 2005 and 2010 in Butler County. Jordan attributes this to the Carteens program. The rate at which teenagers received their second ticket after attending Carteens went from 25-35 days to 111 days, based on research done by Judge David Nehaus.

"Based on research that I have done for my dissertation, the 4-H Carteens program has an impact on reducing risky driving behaviors in 33 different categories, [such as texting and changing the radio station]," said Jordan.

Annually, 800 teenagers and their parents enter the class, which consists of one of four different sections that cover preventing specific dangerous activities while driving. One class is generally dedicated to a movie about a deadly crash, while another involves the teenagers using drunk goggles. The class always closes with personal stories from the volunteers.

East Principal Dr. Keith Kline supports the mission of Carteens and believes that it is a necessary part of the community. Last fall, East had an assembly for sophomores in which Carteens volunteers came to explain the dangers to the new and future drivers.

"Anything that we can do to help our students be safe in cars is something that we should try to do," said Kline.

Jordan believes that for high school students to become safer drivers, they need to prevent themselves from becoming distracted.

"[Teenagers] are inexperienced drivers," says Jordan. "[They] need to focus on the task at hand, which is driving cautiously, so they can get to their destination in a timely manner and safely." ∎

www

WEBLINK Check out

www.coveringcommunities.org

This website offers a wide range of topics geared toward training citizen and student journalists in the basic skills.

Body of a news story

The body of the news story will cover aspects that weren't important enough to be in the lead but should be developed for the reader. The news body paragraphs will also provide specifics to help clarify different sides of the issue at hand.

Quick Exercise

For the following story, develop a source list with lines of questions for each source.

> Two sixth-grade girls were suspended for three days after violating the new district-wide hugging ban. An assistant principal caught them hugging in the cafeteria. The girls had just found out they had placed first and second in a county-wide essay contest. One of the girls has two sisters in high school. You've heard from your friends that one of the sisters said her parents are seeking legal help in the case.

Each paragraph in a news story:

- should usually cover just one idea – news paragraphs are written for a busy reader who might skim and needs to pick up as much information as efficiently as possible
- should advance the story, giving the readers fresh information different from that of the previous paragraph
- should generally be one to three sentences, although exceptions are possible
- should be relevant to the overall focus of the story.

In the body of the following *Harbinger* story on the rise in cyberbullying, Shawnee Mission East's Andrew Goble gives an example of a Twitter site used to post anonymous comments. Within the first two paragraphs he helps the reader understand the reasoning of the Twitter account's creators. He also, by giving the number of posts and followers, shows how public and potentially-humiliating its posts can be.

> Wilson started his account with a friend last fall. It posts "gossip" such as rumored party mishaps and potential parties; as of press time, it had posted 40 times and had 303 followers. When they started last fall, their goal was to just make people laugh.
>
> "We thought it would be funny if no one knew who was writing it, just ridiculous events were reported on, in kind of a laughable manner," said Wilson. "Yeah, [getting tweeted about would] be embarrassing, but it's supposed to be like, 'Yeah, my antics were reported on.'"

News stories should provide objective development of the story. While the standard of **objectivity** is generally taken to mean that a writer shouldn't put his own opinion in a piece, it also means that writer should show both if not multiple sides to an issue. While some readers may agree with Wilson that the comments are just jokes, the writer also explores the perspective of those who object to the negative impact the tweets could have. Not everyone feels it is harmless. Sophomore Julie Sanders* was devastated when she was mentioned on a post on SMEGossipGurlz.

> "I just remember not wanting to go to school," Sanders said. "It was like the first week of freshman year, so I didn't know anyone and I called [friend's name omitted to protect identity] crying, 'What am I going to do?' You feel like everyone is staring at you … you feel like the whole school is talking about you."

News sources need to be relevant to the focus. They should generally be identified by first and last name with some explanation as to why they are relevant. In the previous example, the writer decided to change the names of the sources and mark them with asterisks to protect their identity. Anonymous sources should be the exception rather than the norm because concealing

---

* denotes name changed to protect identity.

FIGURE 3.11 *The Apple Leaf*, Wenatchee High School, Wenatchee, Wash. "Absence of chocolate milk causes uproar" by Nicole Jackson, Sept. 22, 2010. Reprinted with permission.

This *Apple Leaf* news story provides readers with the latest information through a good straight news lead that includes the specific number of petition signatures. Reporting on the actual petition gives the story a stronger news peg than simply reporting a few opinions from people who don't like white milk. The body of the story provides related information on other petitions and the reaction of district officials.

WEDNESDAY, SEPT. 22, 2010 • THE APPLE LEAF • WENATCHEE HIGH SCHOOL
KRISTEN STONE, NEWS EDITOR

News 3

Absence of chocolate milk causes uproar

BY NICOLE JACKSON
MANAGING OPINION EDITOR

Sophomore Tanner Odle has collected about 1,100 signatures in his petition to bring chocolate milk back to Wenatchee High School.

Odle and others began the "Protect Chocolate Milk" campaign the third day of school, after discovering that the Wenatchee School District stopped serving chocolate milk this fall.

The decision was made to improve the nutrition of school menus, said Food Services Director Ken Getzin.

"It's just really a matter of trying to do the best thing for kids with our menus," Getzin said.

Odle plans on taking his petition to Principal Michele Wadeikis once he's done collecting signatures. He also has a meeting with Getzin on Sept. 28 to present his case for the benefits of chocolate milk.

"It's a great drink. It's nutritious, tastes good, has 16 different nutrients, including calcium, vitamin D, magnesium, potassium and there are others," he said.

Freshman Caleb Lewis, sophomores Heavan Henderson and Austin Peart, and junior Jasmine Garcia are a part of the committee fighting for chocolate milk. The group is even selling T-shirts for $10. (To purchase, contact Odle through his Facebook account.)

High schoolers are not the only students protesting the loss. Elementary schools are speaking up for themselves, including but not limited to Sunnyslope Elementary and Lewis and Clark Elementary.

Angel Ornelas, a fifth grader at Lewis and Clark Elementary, has collected 69 signatures, but plans on getting 100 because of the high school.

"I was going for 75, but since I heard the high school got 1,000, I'm going to go for 100," said Ornelas.

He also plans on mailing a letter to Getzin in order to further his school's request for chocolate milk. "I'm writing a letter to him right now and as soon as I finish it I'm going to send it to him and get the chocolate milk back if I can," said Ornelas. According to him, kids do not enjoy the white milk.

"I've been seeing white milk everywhere on the ground and on the cart. Some people are drinking the white milk but most of them are throwing it down, getting rid of it, throwing it away. They're sick of the white milk," said Ornelas.

Getzin does not think chocolate milk will ever be fully reinstated to the schools but is also flexible in his approach.

"Am I completely dead set against ever reconsidering or even having a moderate approach to it? Not necessarily. I want to see how it goes. Maybe after awhile we bring it back a couple times a month as a special thing," said Getzin.

According to Odle, "there are more pros than cons when it comes to chocolate milk. We should have a choice."

PROMOTING THE CAUSE CRASH KETCHAM/THE APPLE LEAF
(Left to right) Sophomore Tanner Odle, and juniors Jasmine Garcia and Jonathon Casillas look over the petition that Odle began to challenge the removal of chocolate milk in Wenatchee public schools. So far, the petition has over 1,000 signatures from WHS.

an identity may cast doubt upon the authenticity of the source and the information. In the paragraphs above, Sanders is a better source than a random high school student because she's been the subject of a negative tweet. The writer made a decision to protect her identity because he did not want to re-victimize her and believed her perspective was sufficiently important to include without attribution.

Writers achieve depth in news stories through talking to multiple sources. Professional sources can add insight to an issue because of their background or training with regard to a particular issue. In the following section of the cyberbullying story, the writer uses quotes and information from the co-director of the Cyberbullying Research Center to show how harmful the effects of these online posts can be.

> Along with Co-Director Dr. Justin Patchin, Dr. Hinduja has identified that cyberbullying is tied to loss of self-esteem in the victim, and that victims of cyberbullying are more likely "to have suicidal thoughts and engage in suicidal actions" than those who have not been. He generally describes cyberbullying as kids "being jerks to each other using technology."
>
> "[When you're an adolescent] you care so much about peer perception, so what everyone else is saying about you and thinking about you, even if honestly they're not," Dr. Hinduja said, "So when there's gossip or rumor-spreading or name-calling or insults or being portrayed in a negative light on Facebook or in a YouTube comment or something like that, it just takes over your world and it really wrecks you."

Good news writers will outline all the different points that need to be covered in the story. If the news story is about a new school policy or plan, are both strengths and weaknesses covered? If the story is about a problem, did it cover the possible solutions? If the story is about a proposed change, does the story cover the reasoning behind it? Does it cover the potential impact or difference it might make? In another section of the cyberbullying piece, the writer addresses potential solutions to the problems raised in the story. The writer also understands that the solutions aren't easy, so he covers potential difficulties as well.

> The District Guidelines give the administrators a range of actions to take. The guidelines say that a first offense could range from a conference with student or parent to a short-term suspension. Repeated offences could result in an in-school or out-of-school suspension, depending on the severity.

The trouble, according to Royce, is catching students. Although she has seen an increase in reports of cyberbullying, it is difficult to prove that it happened "while utilizing school property, on school property, in any vehicle used to transport students for district purposes or at a school-sponsored activity or event," as the district policy states. She guesses that 90 percent of it happens from home.

"We are always happy to investigate, talk to kids, call parents, just to let other parents be aware, but in terms of suspending a student from Shawnee Mission East because of something he did Sunday afternoon in the privacy of his own home," Royce said, "the courts don't look very favorably on that."

Flow and organization

As mentioned earlier, news stories are often organized in an inverted pyramid structure, in which the most important information is presented at the top of the story and the least important at the bottom. If the writer provides smooth transitions among the key facts and ideas that make up this structure, the story will be clear and interesting for the reader.

Developing an outline can help ensure that a story is well structured and intuitively accessible to readers. Start by making a simple list of points to cover in the story. Then work to find connections and transitions between various points, to help you find a logical organization and flow for your writing.

Look for natural connections between different paragraphs and pieces of information. A few examples include:

- action to reaction
- cause to effect
- problem to solution
- time sequence (although be careful not to organize chronologically when more recent events are more important than older ones)
- for to against.

POTENTIAL WEAKNESSES IN NEWS WRITING

Beginning writers tend to make the same mistakes. The following points should help young reporters identify the problems to avoid.

Vagueness

Good reporters avoid leaving unanswered questions in their stories. When reviewing the first draft of a story, these reporters often realize that they didn't get all questions answered. The key to handling this situation, as discussed in Chapter 2, is to reinterview or research the needed information rather than "writing around" the problem, using vague language such as "recent," "a lot," and so on.

> WEAK: The increase in the abuse of prescription drugs is because of the low cost, Det. Brady Sullivan said.
>
> BETTER: The reason for the increase has been traced back to several origins, according to East student resource officer Det. Brady Sullivan. One of these is cost. On the streets, OxyContin goes for about $30 to $40 a pill and heroin sells for between $50 and $100, according to Sullivan. Sullivan noted that Prairie Village's undercover drug unit is buying more prescription pills like OxyContin from drug dealers than ever before.
>
> *Logan Heley,* The Harbinger, *Shawnee Mission East High School, Prairie Village, Kan.*

Test your knowledge

What does objectivity in a news story mean?

Quick Exercise

In an inverted pyramid story, what information would flow naturally after the following introduction?

1 (from an accident story)

Three freshmen riding in the back of the pickup were ejected and taken to the hospital by air ambulance.

2 (from a story about a new fee to participate in an extracurricular activity)

Board member Sara Benson supports the new $50 fee because it will help build a new football field.

Transitions

Finding natural connections between the facts and information will give your writing a logical flow, making the development of a story easy to follow. The use of transitional words and pronouns will also help ensure that readers will grasp the structure and flow of your story.

In the following story, the writer uses logical organization and multiple transitional words and phrases to help the story flow. Good writers will strive to help the reader move effortlessly from paragraph to paragraph and idea to idea.

Other examples of transitional words and phrases to consider:

For emphasis: "as an illustration," "in short," "such as," "specifically"

For sequencing: "First … Second … Third …," "additionally," "besides," "another," "initially," "when," "later," "meanwhile," "next"

For similarity: "Like," "just as," "likewise," "so," "also," "again."

HELPFUL TIPS

1 Answering logical follow-up questions makes for a natural transition here. After indicating that the stricter policies "didn't help," the next paragraph answers the logical question "How so?"

2 *General to specific.* Following up "Many" by explaining "an estimated 40" moves the story forward.

3 "Instead" is a good contrasting transitional word. Using words such as "although," "but" and "despite" can smooth transitions that shift from one action to another.

4 *Action to reaction.* Good news stories don't merely stack facts on top of each other. This paragraph follows a policy discussion with a quote to represent student reactions to the policy.

5 *For to against.* The contrasting transitional word "But" helps connect opposing reactions to the policy.

6 Following "dances" with the specific dance names help transition to new information about the reasoning behind the dance.

7 The equivalent descriptions "students left" and "mass exodus" serve to make the transition to this paragraph on the administration's reaction.

8 Again, equivalent phrases such as "what's appropriate and what's not" and the "dance policy" move the story forward to new information about the reasoning behind the stricter policy.

9 "Upperclassman" is followed by specific "Senior" reaction.

Harsher dance policy drives students away

BY MARIA ZAMORA
STAFF REPORTER

Chaperone training may have helped enforce WHS's stricter policies during the Summer Breeze dance on Aug. 30, but it didn't help attendance at the first dance of the year.

Many of the 315 students who bought tickets apparently left the dance shortly after entering.

An estimated 40 students migrated to the Pioneer Middle School parking lot to have their own spontaneous dance to escape the volunteer chaperones, who were trained for an hour before the dance about how to maintain appropriate behavior. One rule: No warnings were to be given for unacceptable actions such as grinding. Instead, offending students would be immediately removed.

"Summer Breeze was like a straight-jacket," said Grace Peven, junior. She said the uptight atmosphere and un-lively music drove her across the street to Pioneer's parking lot where students could dance as they wanted.

But others, such as ASB President Mallory Gillin, said the dance was fun. Students who grind at dances are driven by "raging hormones," Gillin said, but such behavior isn't necessary for a good time.

"I love dances and I don't grind," she said.

Summer Breeze was organized by the Apple-Ettes Dance Team, which plans to use any profit from the dance to purchase new uniforms and a team workshop. Sophomore team member Brianna "Breezy" Bennett said she felt insulted by the people abandoning the dance. She and her fellow teammates believe that if people had come into the dance with open minds they would have had more fun. Bennett said that that's okay, because even though students left, they paid.

Assistant Principal Kory Kalahar said he "noticed a mass exodus" departing the dance but did not find out about the Pioneer party until afterwards.

It's "a two-way street" Kalahar said, in order for dance restrictions to loosen; students have to step up. "I think people know what's appropriate and what's not."

The dance policy has become stricter after the infringements of the past two years. Drinking, illegal activity, and grinding resulted in angry parents and harsher consequences.

If students continue to violate the dance policy, future dances will be cancelled, he said. Fortunately, Kalahar said, there is a four-year cycle of students. Incoming classes are unaware of how dances used to be run. Only upperclassmen remember what dances used to be like.

Senior Caden Stockwell said Summer Breeze was a waste of $5. He understands why restrictions are placed upon student behavior, but thinks they should loosen if students are to have fun. "I had a dance party on Saturday (Sept. 11), and we had more fun there than at Summer Breeze."

Stockwell claimed 170 people attended his dance, a number he estimated was equal to the students who actually stayed at Summer Breeze, even though his dance required some of the same restrictions as a school function in that no drugs or alcohol were permitted.

Even though some students were unhappy with Summer Breeze, they plan on attending future dances. The first dances of the year are usually strict, Peven said. "I don't think the other dances will be as bad."

FIGURE 3.12 *The Apple Leaf*, Wenatchee High School, Wenatchee, Wash. "Harsher dance policy drives students away" by Maria Zamora, Sept. 22, 2010. Reprinted with permission.

NEWSFLASH

Tighter language

Wordy	Concise
Reached an agreement	Agreed
Arrived at the conclusion	Concluded
Be aware of the fact that	Knows
Conducted an investigation	Investigated
Held a meeting	Met
In spite of the fact that	Despite or Although
Absolutely necessary	Necessary
Biography of her life	Biography
Estimated at about	Estimated
A former graduate	Graduate or Alumnus
Gathered together	Gathered

Wordiness

Readers don't have much time. A writer's space is often limited. Tight writing, or eliminating needless words, is an important technique to engage and inform the busy reader. A good news writer will always opt for one word over five when it is sufficient to make the point.

WEAK: The school district's security staff, in an effort in conjunction with the administration staff, has immediately started requiring non-students or staff or those not affiliated with Harvard-Westlake to have in their possession identification cards to show when using the upper school track.

BETTER: The security staff, in conjunction with the administration, will now require people not affiliated with Harvard-Westlake to carry identification cards when using the upper school track.

> *Michael Rothberg,* The Chronicle, *Harvard-Westlake School, Studio City, Calif.*

Jargon and pretentious vocabulary

Journalists should write for the masses, who have varying education levels. Avoid writing to impress a reader with obscure vocabulary and specialized knowledge gleaned from the thesaurus or Wikipedia. Instead, write simply. Write clearly.

WEAK: In the principal's third endeavor this month to clear the halls and hasten young scholars to their course of study, he formulated and released a new tardy policy.

BETTER: In an attempt to keep kids from hanging out in the hallways, the principal announced his third new tardy policy this month.

Editorializing

Editorializing, or using the writer's opinion in a story, should be avoided in news writing. Proper attribution can help the writer maintain objectivity. By telling the reader the source of each piece of information, the writer will make it clear that the views expressed are not her own. Word choice is also critical. Opinionated words such as "hopefully" or "surprisingly" are examples of language that give hints as to the writer's opinion and should generally be omitted.

> WEAK: Early release on Fridays, a policy put in place as part of the district-wide initiative Positive Behavior Interventions Supports, or PBIS, succeeded in improving attendance last semester.
>
> BETTER: Early release on Fridays, a policy put in place as part of the district-wide initiative Positive Behavior Interventions Supports, or PBIS, succeeded in improving attendance last semester according to associate principal Jennifer Smith.
>
> *Alyne Roemerman*, The JagWire, *Mill Valley High School, Shawnee, Kan.*

Attributing the success of the improving attendance rate to PBIS is certainly debatable, as even the word "succeeded" is opinionated, so attribution is necessary. Without attribution, the reader may believe the writer is presenting her own judgments about the policy.

> WEAK: Whitman thankfully raised the second-highest amount of money in the nation for this year's Leukemia and Lymphoma Society high school challenge, as announced during a fun-filled celebration in the courtyard during sixth period April 19.
>
> BETTER: Whitman raised the second-highest amount of money in the nation for this year's Leukemia and Lymphoma Society high school challenge, as announced during a celebration in the courtyard during sixth period April 19.
>
> *Katie Guarino and Isaac Rubin*, Black and White,
> *Walt Whitman High School, Besthesda, Md.*

Numerical distortions

When a friend tells you he placed second in the regional Pet Guinea Pig Makeover contest, your first response may be to wonder what sort of dress a guinea pig wears. Your second response may be to say, "Congratulations! Second place is pretty impressive." But what if you find out that there were only two guinea pigs in the contest? Or that there were 532?

The point here is that numbers are relative and good news writers should remember that. Financial statistics or polling results may find their way into news stories. To present them responsibly and accurately, the story should include a comparison or, at the least, a source's explanation as to the meaning of the numbers.

> GOOD: Last year, the school's energy consumption totaled 1.65 million kilowatt hours. This figure is 0.6 percent of the entire country of Haiti's 1997 total usage, according to the *CIA World Factbook*. The same amount of energy could help light 27,600,000 60-watt light bulbs for one hour. According to Proven Energy, it would take 107 constantly operating seven-meter tall wind turbines a full year to reproduce our annual expenditure. Though it may seem massive, this number is actually a decrease from preceding years.
>
> *Simone Shields and Alessandro Maglione*, The Standard,
> *The American School in London, London, U.K.*

These writers do an impressive job of putting the numbers in perspective. Not only do they compare the district's energy consumption to a small nation, they also give us an insight into the decline of energy consumption. The rest of the story goes on to look at how the school's green initiative is beginning to work.

FEATURE

The *Falconer* takes a look at TPHS' school spirit, A12

Sleep disorders and lack of sleep plague students, A16

Pump Until It POPS

by Natalie Dunn and Daniel Liu

According to an analysis published in the Teachers College Record, the average percentage of students receiving A's in colleges has increased 28 percentage points since 1960. This growing trend of grade inflation has inspired much controversy among teachers and students alike, prompting the question, has inflation has trickled into the high school education system, and what potential effects may it have on students today?

According to English teacher Robert Caughey, grade inflation has "definitely" become apparent in high schools.

"I know that [grade inflation] exists at TPHS," Caughey said. "I get a lot of students who have always received A's in English, and when they enter the AP program, they struggle to get a three or four or even a five on an essay. A quick look at their previous grades will reflect that they've gotten all A's ... and that's not a true reflection of what they've learned if their grades [have shown] A's and their writing skills don't."

The effects of grade inflation in high school are most commonly seen in students' academic performance in college, and this can shape how a college or university views a high school in the admissions process.

"Over time, a school, public or private, in the eyes of a university, produces or supports a clientele," Principal Brett Killeen said. "[This clientele] can either do well at the collegiate level or it cannot. Universities are quick to catch on, so if you have students coming out with straight A's and are either not passing AP tests or not successful [in college], why are they going to keep tapping that resource?"

But according to Killeen, the overall integrity of TPHS is still strong, allowing colleges to look at the school with a firm belief that its successful graduates will also thrive in college.

Although grade inflation seems to hurt more than it can help, Caughey described its effects on students as a kind of "dichotomous experience."

"You will rarely find students complaining about grade inflation because if they get a class that is easy ... they're not going to complain, because they didn't have to do any work, and their GPAs have been inflated, and as such they are going to have a better opportunity to get into college," Caughey said. "[But I also think] there are students that crave challenge ... [who] get upset, and rightly so, when they aren't challenged. And those students might also complain when they receive a B in a class even though they've worked [so hard]."

In an intense academic environment like that of TPHS, the line between inflated grades and a course that is simply easy can be blurred.

According to counselor Brennan Dean, the notion of inflated grades at TPHS is largely misconceived; many mistake differences in teachers' judgments in grading as grade inflation.

"I don't feel that or know of any teachers that are purposely creating a grade inflation situation in their classes," Dean said. "I believe that teachers here are grading students on what they believe is accurate criticism or evaluation of the students' work. Now if you gave that student's content to a different teacher, they could grade it differently, and I think that that's where we have the judgment issue."

A continuous debate over the differences between the schooling at private schools and the schooling at public schools also exists.

"It's particularly challenging [for brand new or even established private schools]," Killeen said. "You're competing with the public school down the street, and people are paying you lots of money for you to go to that private institution. You have to do something that's going to set yourself apart ... so I am sure there are temptations. I like where Torrey Pines High School is because we're right in the middle of a community where families can often get a private education, but many of them are shrewd and say, 'Why would I pay $15,000 when I can probably get a potentially more rigorous education at TPHS?'"

According to TPHS student Anthony*, who went to a private school for two years before coming to TPHS, the notion that private schools inflate grades is not completely inaccurate.

"I went to a private school, and I personally didn't see it, but my brother would always tell me about how the people who gave a lot of donations were usually the kids who got good grades, even though they did not deserve them," Anthony said. "My brother had a friend whose grade was inflated because his family donated a lot of money to the school, and he went off to college and by his second year, he was back at home ... He would go in after school, and the teacher would know his family and ... the teacher would bump his grade up."

The simplest way to combat grade inflation, according to Killeen, is through certain kinds of calibrating assessments and a more enforced standard in course syllabi.

"For example, in AP classes, the greatest calibration is the assessment itself, the AP test," Killeen said. "So if a student in the AP class is getting an A and doesn't pass the AP test, you may have an example of grade inflation. I think syllabi are really important in terms of defining expectations for the course, and then adhering to them through your grading policy. There should be alignment there."

Although teachers are not specifically taught in any way to standardize their grades to limit the potential for grade inflation, the lack of existing standards helps teachers create more unique curricula.

"I don't believe in standards because that means you have to standardize the way kids learn," Caughey said. "And you guys don't learn the same. I think when we create this idea of standards, then we're sort of going into this homogeneous idea — that we're all the same. And it's clear that we're not. I do teach AP, which is a standardized examination, but it's not a standardized curriculum; there's a difference."

However, according to Antoni Lee (10), a lot of teachers differ in the way they grade based on the amount of work they have, a primary contributor to grade inflation.

"Some teachers are lazy, so instead of spending hours on grading their assignment, [just inflating grades helps them] spend less hours," Lee said.

Even an increase of 28 percentage points is not grounds enough to claim the sudden presence of grade inflation, but as times change, the evidence that it is in fact working its way into an educational trend is unmistakable. The effects of this trend however, remain to be seen.

*Name changed to protect identity

Grade Inflation

ART BY HEATHER CHANG/FALCONER

FIGURE 3.13 "Pump Until it Pops," Natalie Dunn and Daniel Lu, *The Falconer*, Torrey Pines High School, San Diego, Calif. Page A11, Feb. 16, 2011. Reprinted with permission.

Sharp-minded news writers will take note of trends that are relevant and newsworthy to their audience, using credible and authoritative sources to analyze them. *Falconer* reporters used a college study as the starting point for asking questions about grade inflation at their own school. The reporters got interviews with the principal and counselors as well as honest in-depth interviews with students to develop a thorough, insightful story.

Quick exercise

Story development

Write out a list of sources and questions relevant to your school and student body for a news story on the following subjects.

1 A cellphone company that's a block away from the school announced it will shut down operations in a month. The company employs 1,000 people.

2 A major national health center found that cases of skin cancer among women ages 18 to 39 have increased eight-fold in the last 40 years. Researchers say tanning might explain this trend.

Passive voice

Writers should opt for active rather than passive voice. Passive voice tends to be wordy and recent studies show it's harder for readers to understand. In active voice sentences, the subject performs the action expressed by the verb. In passive voice sentences, the subject receives the action expressed by the verb.

WEAK (PASSIVE VOICE): The tournament was won by the debate team.

BETTER (ACTIVE VOICE): The debate team won the tournament.

WEAK (PASSIVE VOICE): After a three-hour closed session, the English teacher was fired by the school board.

BETTER (ACTIVE VOICE): After a three-hour closed session, the school board fired the English teacher.

Test your knowledge

When a statistic is used in a news story, what should accompany it?

ONLINE NEWS COVERAGE

Planning for multimedia news should begin at the same time that you develop a story idea. The more the writer thinks through the multimedia and interactive potential of each story, the richer and more understandable the resulting online news package will be.

If the story has audio or visual possibilities, be sure to capture them. A visual clip of the naming of the Homecoming king can accompany a news brief on the dance. An audio recording of the winning singer at the school talent show can go with a written story about the contest results. The reader's online experience will be enriched through the publication's attention to multiple storytelling platforms.

For example, say that a group of students plans to lead a protest march outside the school over the firing of a popular biology teacher, who deviated from the curriculum on evolution and included biblical references. Video clips of the protest might be part of the coverage to capture the size of the group as well as the sights and sounds of the afternoon. A podcast could provide a degree of emotion not conveyed or extended quotes that may not fit in a short written story. Within an online story, links to biblical passages referenced in the class, legal discussions regarding the separation of church and state, as well as to serious discussions of evolution versus creationism will all give the reader an opportunity to pursue a more complete understanding of the issues. Interactive reader polls on evolution and creationism or the justice of the teacher's firing might help provide context and explore the attitudes of the broader community.

When creating podcasts, record interviews with a handheld voice recorder. Noting or time-stamping the locations of good quotes or discussion can make audio editing considerably easier. Avoid talking over your source to help facilitate the presentation of extended quotes from the interview.

Natural sounds can be used to enhance podcasts or audio clips. In the previous example, the reporter might have captured the students chanting as they march outside the school. The shuffling feet and honking cars might give the listener a vivid sense of the scene.

High school publications can now offer instant coverage of breaking news events, through a range of technological tools. Photographers can use a wireless memory card to send photos directly to the paper's website. Audio-related websites such as Audioboo and Soundcloud can make on-the-spot audio editing and uploading possible for reporters in the field.

USING QUOTES AND ATTRIBUTION

News writing is built on information gathered from interviews. The following story demonstrates the basic formatting for that information.

Some other considerations to keep in mind when quoting sources include:

- As discussed in Chapter 2, use only the most insightful and powerful quotes from your interviews.
- Quote two or three strong sentences that closely relate to each other rather than including five or six rambling sentences with digressions and other topics. You can paraphrase, or omit these irrelevant quotes with ellipses.
- After you've attributed multiple consecutive graphs from the same source, it's okay to omit attribution for additional quotes, if it's clear that the same person is being quoted.

A NEWS WRITER'S CHECKLIST

After preparing a draft of a news story, good writers should reread, edit and rewrite the draft. The following checklist will give you a good list of questions for evaluating your draft.

- Does the lead convey the latest and most interesting and relevant information with powerful, clear language?
- If you use a straight news lead, does it contain the story's key news?
- If you use a feature lead, does the news peg immediately follow the lead?
- Are multiple sides covered?
- Does the story have multiple sources (if possible)?
- Are the sources balanced?
- Are all the names spelled correctly?
- Do you fully identify each source with a relevant identifier, as well as a first and last name?
- Are all assertions of fact backed by clear attributions?
- Does the story avoid editorializing?
- Are all the factual assertions verifiable and correct?
- Does the story include strong and vivid direct quotes? Is one of the best quotes included in the first few paragraphs of the story?
- Does the story use difficult or technical language that needs to be clarified?
- Does the story explain the issue to your readers in a way that is relevant for them?
- Do you give concrete examples for technical or hard-to-understand concepts?
- Does the story generally contain no more than one idea per paragraph?
- Are the paragraphs short?
- Do you separate paraphrases and direct quotes in different paragraphs?
- Do you still have unanswered questions after reading the story?

1 **Attribution**, or telling the reader where the information came from, is important to keep the story objective and to avoid giving the reader the idea that the story is a mere product of the writer's opinions.

2 A **direct quote** is a verbatim or word-for-word account of what the source said.

3 A **paraphrased quote**, which summarizes the source's words, is one way to set up a direct quote. The paraphrase uses the reporter's words to make the story more concise but should be true to the source's meaning. The writer should still attribute the information. "According to," is acceptable once or twice in a story – but overuse may cast doubt upon the source's believability. Words such as "claimed" should be avoided since they suggest that the source isn't credible.

4 The attribution for direct quotes usually appears after the first sentence of a quote. Avoid attributions before the actual quote, since it the quoted statement is almost always more important than who said it.

5 The word "said" is the preferred choice for attributing a quote. While this word may seem bland or repetitive, readers will accept it as a neutral word. Avoid showy or literary words such as "smiled" or "chuckled," which are liable to distract readers and call attention to the writer.

6 In first references to each source, the writer should provide an identifying phrase. The person's title or grade is often used to help the reader understand the relevance of the source (this issue is discussed in greater detail in Chapter 9).

7 News writers may also provide context for a quote or information by giving the reader information about the source.

8 The verb "states" is used only because the information is taken from a formal written statement– the schools' handbook. "States" should generally be avoided with spoken quotes because it may be seen to grant more validity to this quote than one attributed with "said."

9 Notice the preferred order for attribution in "Havener said," which has a more natural rhythm than "said Havener." The sole exception to this ordering rule is if the name is followed by a long identifier or qualifying phrase, as in, "said Havener, a local pediatrician who has seen three similar cases."

Punishments for tweets raise questions

Claire Salzman
opinions editor

Josh Spiller was angry. One of his teachers sent him to the office after he refused to hand over his phone in class. Thursday, Feb. 2, during the school day, Spiller, junior, fired off a Tweet, cursing at his teacher. He thought that was the end of the situation. But Monday, Spiller said, Mike Gavin, junior class principal, called him to his office alerting him his teacher saw the Tweet. The teacher then brought the Tweet to the administration, and Spiller was given three days of out-of-school suspension.

"I felt that it was a violation of my rights," Spiller said. "It was wrong of me to say it, but I still had the right."

That Tuesday, administrators went on the announcements to discuss social media regulations at KHS, stating anything posted on Twitter would be considered the same as a face-to-face conversation. According to Dr. Michael Havener, principal, the administration felt it was reminding students what behavior is appropriate as described by the school handbook.

"We wanted to make sure students knew two things," Havener said. "One: Twitter's a good tool. Two: it also can be a tool that can be used the wrong way, and vulgar language toward a staff member or threats is just like saying it to staff member. When you use it in a negative way toward staff members, it's just like you're saying it in the classroom."

Mike Hiestand, Student Press Law Center (SPLC) consulting lawyer, an organization that advocates student First Amendment rights, disagrees that Twitter is a personal conversation.

"[Administrators] can't just say that Tweets are the same as face-to-face communication because, well, it's not the same as face-to-face communication," Heistand said. "If they can prove that a particular Tweet had the same sort of impact as a face-to-face meeting that seriously disrupted some normal school activity, then maybe they can justify their punishment. But most Tweets, obviously, aren't that powerful."

Mike Wade, sophomore class principal, understands why students may say the emotional and potentially hurtful things they post online. However, he warns them of the lack of privacy due to the constant possibility that someone could see it.

"I think you're frustrated and you're angry, and you spurt. But guess what? You're spurting to the world. You're not just spurting to your friends anymore," Wade said. "In a school where we can all have our iPads and our iPhones and our computers, all bets are off. It's a different world. There are so many good things this could be used for academically, but it's not for complaining about a teacher."

Including Spiller (who has since returned to school), two students have been punished within the last month for using Twitter in what the student handbook deems an inappropriate way. The handbook, which contains guidelines for how social media should be used, states if conflict occurs on the Internet and creates a disruption in the classroom, the administration will evaluate them according to disciplinary guidelines. According to Gavin, the definition of a disruption has been left "intentionally vague." This allows administrators to judge each incident case by case, leaving the decision on whether to become involved in the incident up to the administration's discretion.

While 64 percent (89/134) of students feel the administration's supervision of Twitter violates the First Amendment, Havener said the principals are looking out for the good of the student body.

"It's not about taking away First Amendment Rights. It's about using a tool in an appropriate manner and keeping everyone safe and secure," Havener said. "We're a strong believer in First Amendment Rights here at Kirkwood. However, with that comes responsibility."

Timeline

@KHSAdministration
Three weeks ago
Administrators go on morning announcements in order to discuss online conduct and behavior

@KHSAdministration
Three weeks ago
The student was given in-school-suspension as a punishment, which was revised to out-of-school suspension

@KHSAdministration
Three weeks ago
A junior sends a Tweet cursing at a teacher after an incident between the two occurred during class

@KHSAdministration
Six years ago
Administrators and lawyers work to create a policy for online conduct

@KHSAdministration
Six years ago
Students suspended for ranking other students' attractiveness online and disrupting the classroom

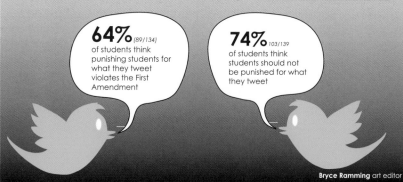

64% (89/134) of students think punishing students for what they tweet violates the First Amendment

74% 103/139 of students think students should not be punished for what they tweet

Bryce Ramming art editor

remembering the '90s

oto courtesy of **MCT Campus**   pg. 8

Ever wondered what goes on behind the scenes of KHS's theater productions? Check out Zach Beuckman's behind-the-scenes feature at **thekirkwoodcall.com**

FIGURE 3.14 Tweeting punishment story from *The Kirkwood Call*. Reproduced with permission of Mitch Eden.

WORDS OF WISDOM

Always remember – no matter what you are writing about, your source probably doesn't know what part of their knowledge is most important for your story or will have the biggest impact for your readers. Don't be afraid to really get down and dirty when asking for details. What might be mundane or ordinary for your interviewee could be the key element that 'makes' the story you are writing.

David Kirkpatrick, Reporter, MarketingSherpa

- Does the story flow smoothly from one idea to another?
- Does the story contain needless information or wordiness?
- Do you feel confident enough in the story's information and quotes to have your name printed in the byline?

CONCLUSION

The news story is the staple of any news publication. Getting the latest information to the reader clearly and concisely provides a critical public service. High school journalists have more options than ever for delivering news to multiple audiences. However, the fundamentals of well-developed objective reporting remain the same.

The strategies covered in this chapter provide a foundation for many of the other writing forms covered later. The varieties of feature style leads will be useful for writing a range of articles and features. Such issues as flow, organization, attribution, depth, concision and active voice are key considerations for every kind of journalistic writing.

SUMMARY

- The news story should get the reader the latest information, based upon how quickly the story will be published.

- Straight news leads and the inverted pyramid structure are often used in breaking news stories to get the reader the 5 W's and H quickly in the opening paragraphs, and the least important information at the end of the story.

- Alternative leads such as a vignette or contrast can be used in news stories to grab readers' attention. In those cases, the basic news questions should be answered in a "focus," "wrap" or "nut" paragraph almost immediately after the lead.

- The body of the news story gives information, details and quotes not included in the lead, in descending order of importance.

- News writers develop their stories through multiple sources to be balanced, objective and accurate.

KEY TERMS

contrast lead	lead	paraphrased quote
descriptive lead	news peg	straight news lead
direct quote	news story	transition
editorializing	nut, focus or wrap graph/ graf	vignette lead
feature fact	objectivity	
inverted pyramid		

EXERCISES

1   Find three good examples of straight news leads from a daily newspaper or news website. Explain why you believe the writer selected the feature fact in the lead. Identify the 5 W's and H in the story. Assess which answers to basic journalistic questions the writer chose to omit from the lead sentence. Explain why you think the writer chose to keep that information out of the lead.

2   Look for two national or state stories that have a localized impact for your high school. Explain the localized angle and whom you would interview to develop each story.

3   First, identify the 5 W's and H from the following three scenarios. Next, write three straight news leads that each begin with a different aspect of the story. Work to tighten the language in each lead and make sure each lead is concise yet informative and interesting. Circle your best lead and be ready to explain why it is the strongest.

(a)   The National Honor Society had their induction ceremony Thursday. Principal Grant Kendall and first-year NHS adviser Emily Perkins-Rock attended. Perkins-Rock began requiring 10 hours of community service this year for induction. Most NHS members simply had to have a grade point average above a 3.65 before this year. Senior and National Honor Society president Brendan Dulohery led the induction. This year only 25 students were inducted. Last year, 50 students were inducted. Perkins-Rock said she thought the drop in inductees was because of the new community service requirement.

(b)   The band went to the Sandy Pond Band Festival yesterday. This was the first year the marching band attended the festival. The band placed first. Fifteen bands competed. The band performed a collection of Lady Gaga songs. The band had worked on the contest routine for the last month.

(c)   The sophomore class held a fundraiser this past weekend. The fundraiser was a walk-a-thon that started and ended at Duncan Maclachlan Park. Seventy-five juniors participated. They raised $7,000 for the Cystic Fibrosis Foundation. Juniors completed distances of 3K, 5K and 10K. Before the event, sophomore class president Grant Heinlein estimated the walk-a-thon would raise $3,000.

4   From the following set of facts and quotes, write both a straight news lead and two different types of feature leads. Make sure that you follow the feature lead with a wrap or nut graph that includes the news peg.

Facts

Your school has an 82 percent attendance rate. This is the third year the school has had an attendance rate below 85 percent after three straight years of an 89 percent attendance rate. The school board has been studying the issue for the last year. Principal Jake Crandall proposed a plan to the board that will tie school attendance to admission to the high school prom, beginning with next year's prom. All four classes, 9th through 12th grade, are allowed to attend the prom.

The board will consider the plan at the next board meeting Tuesday. Your publication is coming out on the Monday before.

The "no-class, no-dance policy," which means if students have one or more unexcused absences, they won't be allowed to attend the prom, mirrors a plan at a high school in Iowa. Crandall moved here from a town near the Iowa school last year. In the first year of the policy's enforcement, it improved the attendance rate at the Iowa high school by three percentage points, from 88 percent to 91 percent.

Interviews

Principal Jake Crandall

I know the board was looking for ways to improve our attendance. I just thought we needed to do something that would get students' attention. Prom is not a right, it's a privilege. If students want to enjoy that privilege then they need to come to school. I watched this policy improve attendance in Iowa, so I know it could do it here.

It used to be that kids wanted to make sure they didn't miss school for fear of having to make up lots of work. Four years ago, teachers said there were rumors of a senior skip day, but only 10 people would skip. This year, we had two senior skip days. The first one, we had 30 seniors with unexcused absences. The last one, we had 50 unexcused.

Junior Andrew Beasley

I sure wouldn't miss school. My girlfriend would kill me if I skipped a class and couldn't go to the prom. I bet people would make sure they got up in the morning and got to class if they pass this.

Junior Molly Halter

I didn't go to prom freshman year. I was sick sophomore year. And this year, my family is going to a family reunion so I won't be able to go. I think next year it'll be the biggest event in my high school career. I can't imagine not being able to go my senior year. I don't like the policy. I know I've been marked absent by a substitute when I was there. I just wouldn't want the biggest event of my senior year to be ruined because of a simple mistake by a sub.

Senior Danielle Norton

This won't really impact me. I know I think it's a bad idea. The prom is something I look forward to and I certainly wouldn't want to miss it because of one absence.

Board member Holly Hernandez

We'll certainly look at the proposal. I think we need to be creative in finding ways to encourage kids to get to school. I don't know if parents understand that our funding is impacted by our attendance rate. We lose state funding if kids don't attend school.

5. Get a copy of your school's weekly or daily announcements. Write two news briefs from the information, in straight news lead form. List what questions, if any, go unanswered.

6. Choose a news story from a major daily newspaper or news website. Circle at least 10 transitional words or natural connections the writer used to help the story flow from point to point. Explain how each of the natural connections worked to link different aspects of the story.

7. Choose a news story of more than 10 paragraphs from a daily newspaper or news website. To evaluate the depth in the story, complete these tasks:

   (a) count the sources within the story

   (b) summarize the different sides to the story.

8. Select a news story from a daily newspaper or news website and make or print two copies. Cut one into separate paragraphs, shuffle the paragraphs, then pair up with another student. Exchange your stacks of cut-up paragraphs and attempt to organize and recreate the original flow of each other's stories (without seeing the originals). Focus on what information is most important and the logical flow of topics. Show each other your original stories and evaluate your recreations, discussing where your organization departed from the originals. Identify key expert or professional sources within the story.

9. Brainstorm potential online packaging from two different scenarios:

   (a) The choir is planning what they are calling their "Yesterday" tour. The choir will travel to three different nursing homes in the area to perform a 25-minute concert at each facility. A month ago, the choir teacher polled the nursing home residents for three song requests that brought back good memories for them. They'll be performing those songs at the concert.

   (b) The graphic novel club has put together a fundraiser local comic con. The comic con will host games for the town's elementary and junior high students. The graphic novel club members plan to dress up as their favorite comic book characters for the event. The events will include a costume contest, which will raise money for their own trip to the national comic con next year.

WRITING SPECIALTY STORIES

4

> *For me, the most important thing is to communicate to readers that I am writing about an actual human being – someone with strengths, weaknesses, phobias, irrational fears and not-so-irrational ones. I want the reader to understand his grudges and be pulling for him to overcome not just the external challenges he faces, but those internal battles, too, the result of which – win or lose – might make him the kind of person he wants to become.*

Andrew Meachum, St. Petersburg Times

LEARNING OBJECTIVES
After completing this chapter you will be able to:

- write a health story, after conducting your own research and interviews

- cover a range of academic stories

- apply appropriate considerations when covering a death

- prepare, structure and compose a story covering a speech

- understand the focus of civic or public journalism

- create and conduct a poll or survey for use in a story

- understand considerations for specialty types of yearbook writing.

TAKE A WALK THROUGH A bookstore and examine the array of specialty magazines – everything from *Newsweek* to *Teen Star Hairstyles* to *Natural Health*. Cable television shows have specialty shows on cupcake decorating and remote island house hunting. New special-interest websites pop up daily. As surrounded as the public is by media, there's a constant battle to reach the viewer, listener or reader. Contemporary media use a wide range of specialty coverage and different story types to reach their audience. High school newspapers, news websites and yearbooks have followed suit. This chapter explores a few of the more significant types of specialty writing.

HEALTH WRITING

For years, acne was the primary health concern of teens. The pimples haven't disappeared, but teens and school publications are now taking an educated look at a wider variety of health issues – both physical and mental. Depression and anorexia, among many other health conditions, have become common topics for coverage. A look at the causes, cures and personal experience of such conditions is now an important part of a publication's role in helping high school students understand their world. Examples of recent health issues covered by high school publications include:

WWW

WEBLINKS Check out

www.healthjournalism.org

The Association of Health Care Journalists website offers a source of story ideas, tips and resources for covering health issues.

- Chemical dependency treatment centers and how they try to help adolescents overcome addictions to everything from marijuana to heroin to inhalants.
- A student's fight with brain cancer.
- Biological brain differences in males and females. The story covers how boys and girls handle their emotions differently, including different interpretations of a kiss and why guys won't cry.
- The physical strains and hazards of wearing a heavy backpack.
- The nutritional values and calories in school lunches.
- The health impact of drinking caffeinated energy drinks.
- How to avoid being bitten by a bedbug.
- How students cope with academic and extracurricular burnout.

Health-related issues must be communicated with the utmost care because so much of the public's health knowledge comes from what it reads in newspapers and magazines, rather than from what it learns from physicians or textbooks. In this arena, a reporter who is inaccurate is not so different from a doctor who gives bad medical advice.

The biggest pitfall for young health writers is approaching subjects they don't fully understand. Delving into the world of medical jargon and complicated concepts can lead to inaccessible writing, such as this:

> Advil relieves pain. Body aches are caused when cells release a substance called prostaglandins, Dr. Foster said. Prostaglandins cause muscle stimulation which causes inflammation in the muscle. Advil is a nonsteroidal, anti-inflammatory drug. It goes to the cells that produce the prostaglandins and inhibits prostaglandins and inhibits prostaglandin synthesis and decreases muscle stimulation.

The writer later admitted he didn't understand what he was writing about. In trying to do a story about how pain medicine actually works, he succeeded only in confusing the reader. The basic lesson this writer learned is best described in a text written primarily for professional writers. The point is useful for journalists of all experience levels.

> Science Writing Rule No. 1: Never try to explain something that you don't understand. Don't be shy about asking your sources to explain something again, if you don't get it the first time. And don't cop out by quoting the scientist's unhelpful explanation. If your scientist source is not a

FIGURE 4.1 hilite.org, Oct. 20, 2010, p. 5. *HiLite*, Carmel High School, Carmel, Ind. "Department of Health issues new vaccination requirements for schools," by Blaine Herbst. Reproduced by permission of Jim Streisel.

To localize the change in state immunization requirements, *HiLite* interviewed the school nurse six months into the school year to find that only half of the students had complied. The writer made the story relevant by including information about a chickenpox outbreak at a nearby high school. The school nurse also made the connection between the outbreak and the urgent need for students to comply with the changes in state health guidelines.

OCT. 20, 2010 | HILITE.ORG | HILITE | **NEWS** | PAGE 5

Department of Health issues new vaccination requirements for schools

BY BLAINE HERBST
bherbst@hilite.org

The deadline for students getting their vaccines was Aug. 10, the first day of school. But nearly nine weeks into the school year, only half of the student body has complied, according to school nurse Carol Gelatt. The IDOH's new guidelines are for three new vaccines this year, that children in all grades six to 12 are required to have; the varicella (chickenpox) vaccine, the meningococcal (meningitis) conjugate vaccine, and the Tdap (pertussis) vaccine.

The IDOH announced new requirements student vaccines on Jan. 26, 2010, for the 2010-2011 school year. After a chickenpox outbreak of 11 students at Zionsville High School, to date, all students have been vaccinated. Since then, there is growing concern over what CHS is doing to protect its students.

"What we're meaning to do is protect kids from vaccine-preventable diseases," Gelatt said.

"Indiana law requires that all students must have on file a completed record of their immunizations with the month, day and year of the immunizations. This must be completed and accurate on the health survey form before the student is allowed to attend classes," Gelatt said. "Some students have already had the vaccine but have not turned in the paperwork. Some students still need to get the vaccine and turn in the paperwork, and some people have done both."

Despite only half the student body complying with this policy, school has resumed as normal. Zionsville schools, on the other hand, have a new policy. If students do not comply with these guidelines by getting the vaccinations, and another student catches one of the three medical conditions, the students who were not vaccinated, and do not have religious exemption, must leave school for 21 days. To date, CHS has not implemented this policy, but is instead giving students more time to get their vaccines.

Students here have mixed reactions to the information.

"I feel like (the vaccines) are a good idea, but how the school informed the students wasn't very considerate," junior Ari Robbins said. "It wasn't considerate because it was really close to the beginning of the year and so everyone had to rush to get them, even though they required you to get at least two to four shots. I just remember my mom getting the notifications and freaking out because we had so little time."

Gelatt said she understands the frustration outbreaks can cause, but said it's really important students get them as soon as possible. Chickenpox, while generally mild when caught as a child, can be more severe with older patients. According to the World Health Organization's website, meningococcal disease and Tdap's illnesses can be fatal as well. The Tdap vaccine protects people against diphtheria, tetanus (lockjaw) and pertussis (whooping cough). The meningococcal vaccine protects people from meningococcal meningitis, a deadly bacterial form of meningitis that comes in four different forms (types A, C, Y and W135, all of which the current meningococcal conjugate vaccine blocks) and can likely cause side effects of meningitis, septicernia and, less likely, carditis, septic arthritis and pneumonia.

"Meningococcal is horrible. Anybody who has meningococcal will say, 'I wish I had gotten that vaccine," Gelatt said. "Meningococcal starts off with flu-like symptoms, but then it develops very rapidly, and some people disregard it and don't get to a doctor in time. Meningococcal symptoms include having a severe headache, fever or a sore throat."

By the numbers

Chickenpox

This viral disease causes itchy blisters to form and can be spread from direct contact or in the air. Symptoms usually last four to five days.

4,000,000
Number of people who contract chickenpox each year in U.S.

Meningitis

The membranes surrounding the brain and spinal cord become inflamed. The viral form is the most common and usually mild.

1,500
Number of cases of meningitis each year

Pertussis

Whooping cough is an infection of the respiratory system. In the past few decades, the U.S. has seen a spike in the number of cases.

30
Number of people who die each year from pertussis

KIDSHEALTH.ORG / SOURCE

Vaccinations will not be offered at the school but elsewhere. The Hamilton County Health Department will be offering vaccinations Tuesdays and Thursdays from 8:30 a.m. to 2:30 p.m. until further notice, at a cost of $5 for one child and $10 dollars per family if people meet certain requirements. Students can also contact their personal physicians and doctors for the vaccinations and can go online to the State Department of Health's website (isdh. in.gov), Hamilton County's website (hamiltoncounty. in.gov), the Fight Meningitis website (fightmeningitis. com) or visit the health center here for more information on vaccinations.

Robbins said, "I think people should be vaccinated, but I think it should be with more rationality behind it. I think the Zionsville incident is just an example of how the school has no control over anything. They can't decide when people get certain sicknesses, but then they scramble to fix it by implementing silly rules."

Despite the frustrations this outbreak has brought students like Robbins, the Health Department still insists students get their vaccinations and paperwork done as soon as possible.

Gelatt said, "I think we need to focus on what's best for you. Let's get it done."

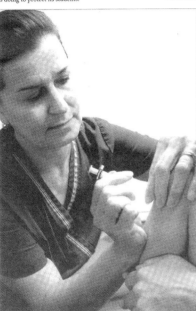

EMILY PUTERBAUGH / PHOTO

SHOT OF HEALTH: *Registered Nurse Lynn Alexander gives a patient a vaccination at the Hamilton County Health Department in Noblesville. The clinic offers vaccinations every Tuesday and Thursday from 8:30 a.m. to 2:30 p.m.*

---

good explainer, ask him or her to refer you to somebody else, maybe one who teaches the field. Once you think you understand something, check yourself by saying it back to the scientist in your own words.

Boyce Rensberger, "Covering Science for Newspapers," A Field Guide for Science Writers, *eds Deborah Blum and Mary Knudson. New York: Oxford University Press, 1997, 13.*

Researching the topic before your interviews will help you understand the doctor or scientist and in turn help you explain the story to the reader. Read books, medical websites or magazine articles on the subject first. For a range of medical subjects from sleep deprivation to Lyme disease, reading background material will provide knowledge of the specialized language and current research. But do not use a lot of secondhand material in reporting the story. Good health writing should depend upon interviews with local physicians, psychologists or students coping with the condition to make it relevant and real to your readers. Use interviews with firsthand sources to make sure you accurately understand the information. Do not avoid asking questions, even ones covering information you have already read about.

No question is dumb if the answer is necessary to help you understand something. There's a difference between not being prepared for an interview and feeling embarrassed about asking a question that you think may sound stupid or silly. Don't pretend to know more than you do in hopes of impressing a source. You need to know the information in order to write an accurate story.

The most important tool a journalist has is the ability to ask questions. Answers always raise more questions and you should keep asking them until you understand the subject.

Ronald Kotulak, "Covering Science for Newspapers," A Field Guide for Science Writers, *eds Deborah Blum and Mary Knudson. New York: Oxford University Press, 1997, 144.*

The point can't be emphasized enough: know what you are writing about before you write about it. The following tips from professional science writers in *A Field Guide for Science Writers* should help the beginning health writer communicate complicated subjects to the reader.

WWW

WEBLINKS Check out

www.ftc.gov/bcp/edu/micro-sites/whocares/index.shtml

This website provides some health care basics as well as a handy list of health issue-related organizations under the heading of "Who Cares."

1 **Do echo interviews** (Ronald Kotulak, author of *Reporting on Biology of Behavior*).
The **echo interview** is a technique where the reporter repeats the key information in his or her own words to the scientist to see if the interpretation is correct. The reporter gets an immediate check on how well he or she is grasping the material. For example, the reporter should listen to an answer and then say, "So my understanding of how Ritalin affects a teenager is …"

2 **Get the face behind the statistic or the issue, but make sure the personal story has revelance** (Abigail Trafford, author of *Critical Coverage of Public Health and Government*).
Showing the reader a student who daydreams during a physics lecture, doesn't do his or her homework but makes an A on the test can help clarify a clinical psychologist's definition of a gifted person. The reporter must understand that the reader can relate to a story of an individual better than to a statistic or a medical description. A story on asthma should include a statistic on the number of people with asthma as well as a description of the challenges of the ailment. But an account of a student's effort to control his breathing disorder while playing baseball gives life to the story.

A reporter should not assume that a student is an example of the larger story but should seek a professional's confirmation that this is the case. Just because a reporter finds a student who seems tired all the time does not mean he or she has found a person who suffers from chronic fatigue syndrome. Confirm the diagnosis with a doctor. A patient's own doctor may talk if the reporter gets a signed permission form from the patient.

3 **Analogies, anecdotes, examples and metaphors are very effective in helping people understand any new ideas and concepts** (Kotulak). Giving the reader specifics he or she can relate to is important to clearly communicate complex information. Here, the writer makes a comparison to clarify the dangers of a relatively unknown herbal cigarette.

However, cloves include 60–70 percent tobacco and twice as much nicotine as the average Marlboro.

In this next example, the author explains how small the chances are of contracting tuberculosis at a school where there is an infected student. Rather than making the vague statement that "the chances are low," the writer follows up with this specific quote.

"You have to breathe the same air as a person with TB in a small area," Dr. Goodman said. "You might contract TB if you lived in the same home as [an infected person] but classrooms are so large that it would be unlikely to catch it because that is a small amount of bacteria in a huge amount of air."

Quick Exercise

Divide into groups of three and list three top health issues facing students at your school. Develop a story idea from each.

XequalsO Student-made engine produces free energy

feature 11

austinnickols
STAFF WRITER

Free energy, independence from oil, increased education and even a stable economy. All of these because of one simple machine. These are just a few of the possibilities for utilizing the engine design of EAST facilitator Charles Holiman, junior BJ Hansen, senior Tim Randall and junior Clint Bowers .

"It can be used to power cars and even whole homes," Hansen said.

In one and a half to two months of devoting time in class and after school, these students with the help of a supportive teacher, designed an engine that creates twice the amount of usable energy it takes to power it.

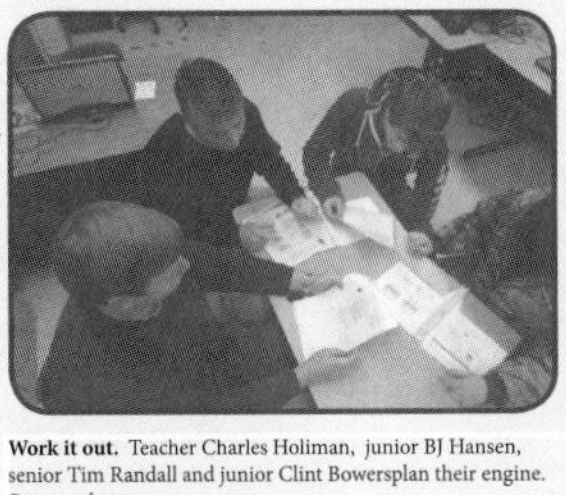

Work it out. Teacher Charles Holiman, junior BJ Hansen, senior Tim Randall and junior Clint Bowersplan their engine.
Bvmers photo

"It's an efficient generator design using a high tech generator built for wind and an efficient drive system. Bottom line is, on paper, it generates more electricity than it takes to run itself," Holiman said. "It's basically free energy, other than repairs and the initial cost of the engine."

Holiman and the entire team are ecstatic about the idea and its possibilities. Holiman stated he was certain that the United States is on the brink of becoming almost independent of oil and that this generation will be able to see the effects within its lifetime.

"It would create jobs, stimulate the economy, give everyone spending money. It would have ecological benefits and it would stimulate education," Holiman said. "When you tell your kids about how the country used to be completely dependent on oil, they will look at you like you're crazy! They'll ask, 'What was the hold up dad?"

The point of the project was not to eliminate the use of oil. There are things oil can be used for efficiently or at the willing expense of the person using it.

"I work on cars, older hot rods. If there's no oil being produced, I'm not gonna be too happy. So the point is definitely not to stop the importing and exporting of oil," Bowers said. "The point is to no longer *rely* on oil. There's no point in a trucker transporting, whatever, paying $3 or more for diesel gas."

Like with any innovative idea, the team faced some roadblocks from those who said it wasn't possible and the actual roadblocks in designing the engine.

One thing the team mentioned was the cost. Holiman guesses that if they built it using high-end products, the cost would be around $26,000. That's if they built it. Holiman and the team have a patent attorney who is curretly searching for a previous patent on the design because if there is then there is no point in building it.

"A lot of the calculations were difficult because there was no prior model and another problem we faced was that with the drive system took a lot of research because some lost a large amount of energy through heat. And something we had to really consider recently is the cost and whether or not there is a patent already," Randall said.

Both Holiman and Bowers said they enjoyed the concept of new thinking, of actual innovation and both of them loved being told that it couldn't be done.

"My favorite part of working on the project was hearing people say it wouldn't work. It channeled into positive energy and motivated the entire team," Bowers said. "We all wanted to prove them wrong."

X is the amount of dollars the average American spends on gas. With Holiman's engine, X is no longer that bite out of the wallet every month. With Holiman's engine, X equals zero.

"Bumblebees and helicopters aren't supposed to be able to fly. So we figure, why can't our design work?" Bowers said.

FIGURE 4.2 "X equals 0: Student-made engine produces free energy," by Austin Nickols. *The Prospective*, Bryant High School, Bryant, Kan. Reproduced by permission of Margaret Sorrows.

The Prospective staff's feature on a teacher and student's invention of a free energy engine is an example of how an interesting class project can be reported in the news or feature sections. In this story, the writer emphasizes the relevance of the invention to readers by discussing its potential value to the student's economic future.

ACADEMIC WRITING

"So what did you learn at school today?"
"Oh nothing."
Conversation between high school student and her mother

If discussions between parents and teens were the public's only source for academic coverage, high school papers might not cover this subject at all. But academics are a huge part of the high school experience that should never be neglected by a paper. A high school reporter's ability to see and cover what's going on in classrooms is an invaluable journalistic asset. Such reporting can help students learn more about their education and help them take responsibility for their own learning. Coverage can also raise critical issues about curriculum, budgets and pedagogy, and help the public evaluate the quality of their community's educational offerings.

Strong coverage of high school academics should include:

- Changes in graduation requirements and standardized testing.
- Updates on student body progress – failure, dropout and graduation rates, test rankings.
- Creative or interesting assignments or projects taking place in specific classrooms.
- Curriculum issues, such as the elimination of a class on jewelry-making or the addition of religious studies courses.
- District- and school-wide issues such as the introduction of block/alternative scheduling or the lengthening of the school year.

Test your knowledge

How should a doctor's medical jargon be handled in good health reporting?

Yearbook **academic sections** or spreads are pages that highlight the most significant classroom activities and issues of the year. They might focus on class assignments, teachers and educational issues, but they should do so through vivid storytelling that revives the reader's memories of the wobbly desk in math class or that faint whiff of formaldehyde in biology class.

Keep the student in mind when covering academics. If the story is about upcoming changes in the science curriculum, make sure to get examples to show the student reader exactly how the classes will be different. Don't simply republish the dry text of the new district policy. If the story is about new science lab computers, get anecdotes from students who say they felt like real surgeons when using the virtual operating room software in anatomy class. Develop the story beyond how many computers the district is installing and how excited the science teachers are.

IN ACTION

Academic story examples

Here are a few examples of academic stories covered in high school publications.

- A feature on the ways grades are weighted – in honors classes, advanced placement classes and the like – combined with interviews of faculty and students

- A feature story on the techniques teachers use to make their classes interesting and engaging

- A news feature story on a science class's study of the school's garbage – what it throws away versus what it recycles

- An informative feature on girls-only classes and whether girls participate more and learn better in these classes

- A how-to piece on college application essays told through interviews with college admissions officers and high school alums

- A feature story on how to work effectively in group projects

- A feature story on a physical science class trip in a hot air balloon to study Charles' Law and the Archimedes Principle.

All of these stories are appropriate in school publications. How effective they are, of course, depends on how well they are investigated, written and displayed. Most are not news stories dependent on a news peg (that which is new, changed or different about the topic), although academic stories are often related to a recent event, such as a school board meeting, or a topic of high reader interest, such as grade inflation. Keep an eye out for original classroom events, such as a mock trial in a civics class or a guest speaker series in a global studies class.

Quick Exercise

Pair up with another student and describe for each other the three most creative exercises you've been assigned by teachers still teaching in your school. Rank which of the three would make the best story.

FIGURE 4.3 *Teresian*, St. Teresa's Academy, Kansas City, Mo. Reproduced by permission of Eric Thomas.

In order to cover academic issues that might not lend themselves to the typical multiple photo coverage, good yearbook staff create informative packages. St. Theresa's staff present their coverage of grading scale changes in two packages: 1) a sampling of opinions about the current scale and 2) a teacher-versus-student Q&A sidebar on the change from reporting letter grades to reporting percentages. By breaking up the information, the staff did more to ensure reader interest.

DEATH COVERAGE

In the midst of all the emotions that surround a death, student publications must maintain a sense of objectivity. Establishing policies before such events occur can help provide ethical guidance for tough circumstances. Guidelines should cover what news-judging criteria to use in deciding whether to do an obituary, a straight news story or a eulogy-like news feature. Considerations may include the deceased's impact on students and the school, the nature of the death and its timing, in relation to the newspaper's publication schedule.

News or feature death coverage should be free of editorialization. Any expressions of sympathy from the writer or staff should be reserved for the opinion section. A reporter should avoid death euphemisms such as "passed away" and "Death's call." Simply use "died," unless the publication is part of a religious-affiliated school with a policy preference for another term.

Factual accuracy is always important, but in an obituary, or notice of a person's death, it is even more so. Common facts included in an obituary are full name (make sure of correct spelling), identification, age, date of death, cause of death, biographical details, survivors and the date, time and place of funeral and memorials. These facts might also appear in a news-feature story along with more anecdotes and quotes surrounding the student's or teacher's life. Those quotes might come from family, friends, teachers or the minister who presided over the funeral service.

Asking for comment on a death, especially from family members, is often awkward for reporters. Chip Scanlan, Director of Writing Programs for Poynter Institute, offers some advice from his own experience of interviewing the parents of a deceased student.

> I said, without thinking, that I was a reporter and that I was very sorry to intrude at this time, "But I just didn't want you to pick up the paper Sunday and say, 'Couldn't they at least have asked if we wanted to say anything?'" It was as if I had said, "Open Sesame." Within moments, we were standing in their daughter's room. On the bed was an unopened package that had come in the mail that day. It was a set of pots and pans for her hope chest. That single detail still haunts me and I think really conveyed what the victim and those who loved her lost. In that way, I think I was able to honor the legitimate journalistic reasons without greatly re-victimizing the family.

High school print reporters often have days to prepare stories for the issue's final deadline. Online reporters have the power to report the deaths of teachers and students within hours after they occur. These reporters need to be careful to post only those facts that they can confirm about the death of a student. The *El Estoque* online posted a story within hours of the death of a beloved water polo coach and teacher. In the In Action feature, Figure 4.4, staff explain the story behind the online and print coverage.

Yearbooks should be wary of dedicating books to a student who has died during the year. The practice can lead to fairness questions if, for example, another student dies after the final deadline. One yearbook staff simply places a gray bar across the student's name in the class section with the dates of birth and death placed underneath. Others would cover such a death as a story and base coverage on news value. Another solution is to allow family or friends to purchase an ad to increase coverage of the death.

SPEECH STORIES

The speech story is not as prevalent in high school publications as it is in professional publications. Nevertheless, such a story should be considered whenever someone knowledgeable speaks to a group about a timely and relevant issue – especially if it takes place on campus or involves members of the school community, for example, if a gubernatorial candidate speaks to a teacher's group or a Vietnam War veteran talks to a history class. Both events may feature insightful points or interesting stories that readers might appreciate.

Preparing to cover a speech, or gathering background, will involve something different for every speaker. The gubernatorial candidate will have a résumé, background information provided

Test your knowledge

Give two examples of academic stories that high school newspapers should cover.

WWW

WEBLINKS Check out

http://topics.nytimes.com/top/news/newyorkandregion/series/portraits_of_grief/index.html

"Portraits of Grief" is *The New York Times's* archive of the brief biographical sketches they ran on every person who died in the attacks of Sept. 11, 2001.

Test your knowledge

What are three common facts that should be included in an obituary?

Quick Exercise

Write an obituary lead for your choice of a comic book or cartoon character.

IN ACTION

Using multimedia to tell a death story

Following the death of a beloved teacher and water polo coach, the staff members of the *El Estoque* at Monte Vista High School in Cupertino, California, began a week of coverage on a man who had touched many in his 30-plus year career. Their online coverage included breaking news stories, columns, a feature story, photo galleries, audio slide shows and a live webcast of his memorial service.

What follows here is a portion of the interviews with the writers, photographer and advisers so readers can gain first-hand insight into the story behind the coverage.

Adviser Michelle Balmeo

It was so powerful. This guy had this Facebook page "In Memorial" and it had 7,000 people on it – and most of them aren't local.

He had a far-reaching impact. I think that one of the things that's important to keep in perspective is that you can't treat every death the same. You know that and somewhere the kids come to learn that. Somebody who's had impact on thousands of swimmers, water polo players and students, where there's an obvious outcry of grief. You just treat it a little bit differently. You don't want to come out and say that every death isn't equal, but at the same time not every death is equal to the community and at that point in time. What made the Livestream make sense is that there are these thousands of people, many of them who can't attend this memorial so [in this way] we could bring the memorial to them."

Karishma Mehrotra

The morning that I heard about it, it wasn't when it happened. It happened the night before. And I woke up at eight and I got

a text. To be honest I didn't know what to do about it … I never heard the first steps to tell you what to do.
[called managing editor]

The first thing (she and managing editor Kriti Garg) did was … we went to Facebook. Just because we know that a lot of our population is on Facebook and we knew that students would probably be talking about it. We thought that was the most ethical verification that it was true. But we had seen stuff on Facebook that it was true, it's true, it's true.

I think we started researching on him just to get some background info because we knew we would have to put in the story about what he'd done not only for the school but other places of his career. We started getting information on him from water polo sites, Googled what he's been doing and where he's taught.

Kriti Garg

We worked it all on Google Docs so we were all online. We had it up and edited by two or three editors within three hours. After that we just waited to make sure his family had heard about it and the principal had sent out an email, or some sort of verification, letting everyone know that this was true for verification and that his family knew about it so we weren't overstepping any boundaries.

[Story was published at 2 p.m. Saturday after coach's death Friday night] We were pretty much the primary news source for a lot of the community. It spread around really fast.

Karishma Mehrotra (on audio slide shows posted Tuesday)

For our audio slideshow what we ended up doing because we found we weren't getting what we needed from reaching

Several teachers began their classes discussing the news with their students and provided the option to opt out of exams and leave class to take part in the counseling opportunities across campus.

♡ RON Freeman ♡

Students, teachers, parents, and alumnus dropped off flowers and other items to mourn and honor Freeman's passing. Photo by Jackie Barr.

Cupertino, CA

Sunny

Wind: N at 0 mph

66°F

MONTA VISTA HIGH SCHOOL

EL ESTOQUE

Google Search

☑ only search elstoque.or

Connect with us

STUDENT NEWS

Home   Top Headlines   News   Opinion   Sports   Entertainment   Bloggers   Print   Multimedia

>>

Coach and teacher Ron Freeman dies

Written by Emily Vu, Karishma Mehrotra and Kriti Garg
Saturday, January 22, 2011 02:32 PM

Loved by many, coach and teacher Ron Freeman died on Jan. 21. The unconfirmed cause of death is a heart attack after the home varsity boys basketball game.

Freeman was part of the MVHS community for over 30 years. He taught World History periodically, but had from the start been an important figure for the MVHS water polo and swimming teams. He also stood as the Athletic Director for MVHS.

"Coach Freeman was the most influential person that impacted my life and made me who I am today. He was a great coach, a caring friend, and my hero," senior Nick Sinzig said. "Coach taught me the importance of responsibility, hard work, respect, and what it takes to have a good heart just like him. Coach was like a father to me."

According to an earlier version of the MVHS boys water polo website, Freeman was previously a coach at the National Junior Olympics, the California State Games, the Men's Senior National Championships, the National Olympic Festival, and the National Youth Team in the Can Am Games.

Counselors will be present at tonight's Winter Ball for students to talk to. To honor Freeman's life and contributions to MVHS, the Leadership class will have purple ribbons available in the Rally Court on Monday before school and during brunch and lunch. Students are also holding a memorial for Freeman at the MVHS pool deck all week and invite students to bring flowers and photos.

The MVHS website Ron Freeman memorial page can be accessed at http://www.mvhs.fuhsd.org/ronfreeman. Community members have

Coach and teacher Ron Freeman passed away on Jan 21. after watching the boys varsity basketball game. He took the boys varsity water polo team to Hawaii for Hell Week during the summer of 2009. Photo courtesy of Patrick Mi.

MOST READ

Coach and teacher Ron Freeman dies
Community mourns loss of alumnus David Kucera
Ron Freeman—the legacy lives on
School reacts to death of beloved coach and teacher, Ron Freeman
Soccer game collision becomes ER trip for goalie

POLL

Which one of the remaining playoff teams would you want to win the Super Bowl?

○ Pittsburgh Steelers
○ Chicago Bears
○ Green Bay Packers
○ New York Jets

Vote   Results

PHOTO BLOG

READ EL ESTOQUE IN PRINT

to. To honor Freeman's life and contributions to MVHS, the Leadership class will have purple ribbons available in the Rally Court on Monday before school and during brunch and lunch. Students are also holding a memorial for Freeman at the MVHS pool deck all week and invite students to bring flowers and photos.

The MVHS website Ron Freeman memorial page can be accessed at http://www.mvhs.fuhsd.org/ronfreeman. Community members have also contributed to a Facebook page in honor of Freeman.

Read more:
Jan. 24: Senior Nikki Danese's tribute to coach and teacher Ron Freeman: "Ron Freeman—the legacy lives on"
Jan. 24: "Students and staff react to death of beloved coach and teacher, Ron Freeman"

Coach and teacher Ron Freeman passed away on Jan 21. after watching the boys varsity basketball game. He took the boys varsity water polo team to Hawaii for Hell Week during the summer of 2009. Photo courtesy of Patrick Mi.

During 5th period on Jan. 24, students took a moment of silence in memory of coach and teacher Ron Freeman around his memorial behind the pool deck. Photo by Karishma Mehrotra.

out to people per se. That Tuesday through lunch, after school and into that evening we had the room open for students and teachers to come in and talk about their favorite memories and what they'll miss about Mr. Freeman. We had a mike set up, connected to the computer and had it record into Garage Band. And that's basically where we collected our stories and used that to make our Soundslides.

Nicolet Danese (on her personal column piece)
I was really close to Mr. Freeman. I've known him since I was born. And I think that some stories kind of covered the basics on him. They say that he's a great person but they don't necessarily tell how he's a great person … I wanted the people at school to understand, especially the freshmen and sophomores who never experienced Ron. I wanted them to know where I was coming from.

Yuna Choi

Dear Yuna,

As each day passes, we can't help but notice what love really means. You've made us realize the true meaning of beauty from the inside out. We miss your kindness and your irreplaceable heart that always knew exactly what to say. Though thick and thin you held us together like glue and you inspired us to get

through the rough spots. Needless to say, you've changed our lives and we're more than fortunate to have known you. Most of all, you taught us to live by the possibilities in life, not the guarantees; you taught that. There's never a time you leave our minds and you will be forever be in our hearts.

FIGURE 4.5a *Echoes*, Wichita East High School, Wichita, Kan. Reproduced by permission of Sharon Martin.

Wichita East yearbook staff were faced with the death of a student Yuna Choi in a car accident on March 15, just days off their final yearbook deadline. Yuna's mother and brother were also killed and her twin sister was paralyzed in the same accident. "Both of the girls were enrolled in the International Baccalaureate program and were well liked," adviser Sharon Martin said. "We have a policy of running a standard obituary when students die which we did as well but several students on my staff wanted to pay for and run the ad and I although I talked to them about appearing to go overboard, when push came to shove, I could not look my students in the eyes and say "No." In spite of the unusually large number of images appearing in the ad, they complied with my request to keep the ad structured and avoid a "scrapbook" appearance so that it would fit in well with the other ad pages. Because we were a spring delivery book and the ad appeared at the end, we were able to accommodate a late addition."

by his campaign staff, news clips from past speeches and, possibly, a copy of the upcoming speech. The Vietnam War veteran may have some of the same prepared information, but the reporter may also have to depend upon the history teacher for background. In either case, the reporter should learn as much as possible about the speech topic, whether it is state standardized testing reforms or a comparison of the Vietnam War with the war in Iraq.

The reporter needs to make sure of the time, day and place of the speech so that he or she can arrive early to cover it. Even if the reporter has a copy of the speech, being there to hear exactly what the speaker says is a necessity, since some speakers change drafts at the last minute. Being in a good position to hear the speaker clearly while taking copious notes is also important. As discussed in Chapter 2, the good reporter will not have to take down every word but can focus on the parts of the speech that have strong news value. Identifying the primary focus and main

Yuna Choi, soph., died March 15, 2010, as a result of a car accident. She is survived by her father, Eun-Seo Choi and her sister, Hana Choi, soph.
Her mother Kyoung-Yeon Chae and brother Seo-Won Choi also died March 15. Funeral services were held for all three at First United Methodist Church, March 19.
While at East, Choi participated in Concert Orchestra, Symphony Orchestra, and Korean Fan Dance club. Choi was also a member of the golf team and the swim team, helping them to win the 2009 City League Championship meet.

FIGURE 4.5b

points is important but may be difficult if the speaker rambles. The quotes the reporter will want to write down verbatim will be the ones that are most striking, controversial, insightful, descriptive or most meaningful to the target audience. Remember that direct quotes mean you record the speaker's exact words. Listening before writing will help you in this task.

Other considerations for assessing what to quote directly include the following:

- Listen for statements that emphasize a speaker's main points. Summarize others in your own words.
- Note references to your school or community. Often such statements, although perhaps of no great importance for the overall speech, do have considerable reader interest.
- Listen for references to topics of current interest to your school community.
- Watch audience reaction carefully. What an audience applauds or jeers at may make a good quotation.

Once the speech is over, ask follow-up questions. The questions can be for the speaker and for members of the audience. Ask follow-up questions about points the speaker made during the talk. Clarify any possible misunderstandings from the speech. Get the speaker's reaction to delivering the speech or to the audience response. Monitor and describe the audience's reaction yourself. Once all reporting is done, read over your notes as quickly as possible to make sure they are clear and understandable. Fill in missing information while the speech is still fresh in your mind.

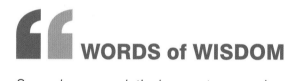 **WORDS of WISDOM**

Speeches are relatively easy to cover because you know in advance who's coming and why, so you can usually do background research on the person before the speech, take good notes during it and write a good story after. When people give a speech, they usually have a point to make, they write the speech in advance and they try to say something worthwhile. The reporter should be listening for the main point, be able to summarize that and should look for two or three good quotes which back up the main point. Or, if there were several main points, have quotes to back those up.

Kathleen Neumeyer, Harvard-Westlake School

FIGURE 4.6 *The Chronicle,* Harvard-Westlake School, Los Angeles, Calif. Reproduced by permission of Kathleen Neumeyer.

When the writer provides the speaker's key credentials in the lead, she bolsters Davis's argument that there has been "little progress for equal representation for women in the media and in films." Notice also the inclusion of key specifics – the ratio of male to female roles and the percentage of females in crowd shots – to back up the speaker's point.

March 24, 2010   THE CHRONICLE | chronicle.hw.com

Actor advocates gender equality

By NICKI RESNIKOFF

Academy Award-winning actor and women's rights activist Geena Davis told upper school students that there has been very little progress towards equal representation for women in the media and in films.

The Women's History Month Assembly on March 8 started off with an introduction by members of Martha Wheelock's Gender Studies class and a video montage feauturing clips from some of Davis' 18 films, including "The Accidental Tourist," "A League of Their Own," and "Thelma and Louise," as well as from the TV show "Commander in Chief."

Davis discussed gender inequality in films.

She helped initiate the most comprehensive research study ever of G-Rated films, which was aptly named "Where the Girls Aren't."

According to Davis, there is a 3:1 ratio of male roles to female roles in films, and in G-Rated films, crowds in group scenes are only 17 percent female.

"The vast majority of females in these movies are stereotyped and oversexualized," she said. "They wear the same amount of sexually revealing clothes in G-Rated movies as in R-Rated movies."

Also, 37 percent of female roles in G-Rated movies in the study were charactors of royalty or entertainers.

"People think women will watch men, but men won't watch women," she said. "That is an assumption I am trying to disprove."

Davis said she noticed when she was younger that on TV, especially in her two favorite shows, "The Rifleman" and "Bonanza," there were very few female characters. She commented on the "Dead Mother Syndrome," where the mother dies in the beginning or is already dead at the start of a show or movie.

Davis also founded the Geena Davis Institute on Gender in Media, whose motto is "kids need to see entertainment where females are valued as much as males."

"The Geena Davis Institute on Gender in Media focuses first on getting more females and more varied portrayals of both female and male characters into movies, TV, and other media aimed at kids 11 and under," according to the GDIGM website. "The Institute is a resource for the entertainment industry (media companies, animators, writers, producers, and others), the next generation of content-creators, and the public."

In February, Davis gave the closing keynote address at the United Nations Economic and Social Council's "Engaging Philanthropy to Promote Gender Equality and Women's Empowerment" event.

Davis explained that she uses the word "actor" to describe both male and female actors because the dictionary definition of an actor, Davis said, is a person who acts. She explained that she does not feel the need for a separate word for females.

"I am a former waiter who became an actor," she said.

CANDICE NAVI/CHRONICLE

ACTOR, NOT ACTRESS: *Academy Award-winner Geena Davis speaks about gender inequality in movies at the upper school Women's History Month Assembly March 8.*

Davis began her speech by proclaiming that she had known since the age of three that she had wanted to be an actor. She spoke of her struggle to fulfill her dream.

As hard as it was, she kept trying, she said.

"I didn't know it was impossible to get into the [Screen Actors Guild]," she said.

Her personal motto is "If a person can do it, I can do it."

As a struggling actor, Davis turned to modeling, joking that it was much easier to become a supermodel than an actress.

However, despite getting jobs as a model, including being on the cover of New Jersey Monthly, Davis had a "profoundly bad self-image."

"I was convinced I was tricking everyone into thinking I was attractive," she said. "I was acting like my butt was cute. It was a sham and one day people would find out."

Davis finally found confidence in herself, she said, when she learned to play baseball for the 1992 movie "A League of Their Own" and a coach told her she had untapped athletic ability.

"I started to feel like it was okay to take up space in this world," she said.

While she previously thought of herself as uncoordinated, Davis went on to learn archery, even becoming a semifinalist to qualify for the 2000 Olympics.

"I have to be careful with what I get involved in, because I am going to want to go to the Olympics in it," she joked.

The writing process begins with organizing the material around the primary focus of the speech. The lead will often come from a striking summary point or anecdote. The lead can also take a summary or feature approach. Engage the reader in the lead with something powerful or surprising about the speech. The basic information answering the 5 W's and H should always be high in the story. Here are a few examples of strong speech story openings:

Academy Award-winning actor and women's rights activist Geena Davis told upper school students that there has been very little progress toward equal representation for women in the media and in films.

Nicki Resnikoff, The Chronicle, *Harvard-Westlake School, Studio City, Calif.*

A Harvard alumnus was making a presentation March 8 to middle school students about treating burn victims when the campus-wide assembly came to an unexpected end. As part of his presentation, Dr. Peter Grossman '80 was showing images of different types of burns. The assembly ended after middle school psychologist Susan Ko asked him to stop showing the images.

"I was concerned about the graphic nature of some of his slides," Ko said. "In particular, I was concerned that many of our students who have been quite upset and experiencing some traumatic reactions in the recent aftermath of a classmate's tragic death, might be especially sensitive to images and discussion about injury."

Sammy Roth, The Chronicle, *Harvard-Westlake School, Los Angeles, Calif.*

Make sure that your lead does not simply state that a given person spoke, as in:

District superintendent Nick Belsher spoke to the National Honor Society Friday.

The reader's response may well be say, "who cares?" and move on to the next story. Typically, you should organize the body of the speech story in order of decreasing importance. The points do not have to be presented as they were in the person's speech. However, make sure not to distort the meaning of the speech if you change the order of the points. Clearly connect the points together and the primary focus of the speech.

Here are a few more tips for speech story writing:

- The reporter should be careful not to distort the speaker's meaning by taking quotations out of context.

- Normally, reporters do not quote grammatical errors, awkward sentences, slips of the tongue or dialect unless there is some significant reason to do so. The reporter should paraphrase passages that include these errors. If there is a reason to use a grammatical error or slip of the tongue, use *sic* in brackets [*sic*] or parentheses if brackets are not available. In Latin *sic* means "thus" or "exactly as stated." This device can annoy your readers; don't overuse it.

- The reporter should avoid letting his or her own opinions and prejudices color the story's presentation of the speech and the speaker.

POLL STORY

After a series of school shootings, a *New York Times* poll showed that 87 percent of teenagers still felt at least "somewhat safe" in their schools. Were students so naive that they believed this wouldn't happen in their school? Were they so resilient that they refused to be frightened by these well-publicized incidents?

We are naturally curious as to whether others think as we do. The **poll story**, or a story based on a survey of the population, is a good way to measure the pulse of the school community. In news and in-depth stories, high school writers often want to write, "Many students believe …" after talking to only two or three students. The only accurate way to assess if "many" believe something is to conduct a poll. The poll story is useful in connection with student body and community elections. Student poll stories often cover issues such as dress code changes, open campus decisions and student tastes, such as most popular TV show.

Accuracy in the polling procedure should be a consideration. A poll of 10 people can be very misleading when there are 900 people in the school. While a poll distributed to two classes may seem sufficient, if both classes are honors classes, the results may be skewed.

Selecting respondents

The **poll respondents** or group to be surveyed must be carefully defined. For example, if the survey is aimed at students who are eligible to vote in a forthcoming national election, the respondent pool can be narrowed by age. If, however, the question involves lengthening the school day or awarding school sweater letters to students who participate in non-athletic extracurricular activities, then many more students should be polled. Since it is not possible to interview everybody, a sample must be selected to represent the large group. Major pollsters such as Gallup have specific guidelines to make sure polls are scientific and report a specific margin of error. The goal in sampling is to give every member of the group an equal chance of being selected. Obtaining a directory or a school roster from the front office makes this process much easier.

Researchers often recommend polling at least 10 percent or 50 individuals, whichever is more. To make the poll more accurate and random, you might choose every tenth name in the school directory. No name should be substituted or specially selected. If the poll is for only one grade level, then again every tenth name should be used, or if there are not enough students in that grade, then every ninth or eighth name could be used. But it is important not to bias the results by singling out friends or favorite teachers. Distributing your poll to general English classes that include the varying demographics of the school is another suggestion. Try to ensure that the sample represents a range of grade levels, sexes, socio-economic groups and races.

Sampling error, or degree of confidence in the accuracy of the poll, defines the difference between those actually interviewed and the opinions of the entire group: the larger the sample, the greater the confidence that the observed difference is real and not the result of chance. In the case of close percentages, such as a 45–55 division, you will need to determine if this is a real difference before making an arbitrary statement about the findings. Professional pollsters often publish sampling error. High schools publish specifics of how the poll was conducted.

Choosing and phrasing poll questions can be tricky. Just because the reporter has a particular meaning in mind when drafting a question does not mean the respondents will interpret the question the same way. For example, one school publication asked teachers, "Do you feel safer in the school now than you did five years ago?" Yes and no were the answer choices. The student pollster interpreted a no answer to mean that the teacher felt unsafe. However, some teachers answered no because they felt the same as they did five years ago. They felt safe then, and they feel safe now.

The best way to make sure questions are clear is to pretest the survey. Choose a variety of people outside the journalism room and ask them the poll questions. After they take the poll, ask them what they thought each question meant and why they answered the way they did. Avoid asking the non-specific question, "So did you understand everything?" Few people would readily admit they did not, for fear of looking stupid.

The questions used in the survey can each have a different function, and can be tailored to different groups of respondents.

Quick Exercise

Pick a famous historical speech from www. historyplace.com/ speeches/previous. htm and write a speech story lead.

Test your knowledge

What should a reporter gather prior to covering a speech?

FIGURE 4.7 *The Campanile*, Palo Alto Senior High School, Palo Alto, Calif. "Campanile poll results reveal cheating at Paly," by Sarah Rizik, Dec. 18, 2003. Reprinted with permission.

Because good poll stories depend on good surveying strategy, *Campanile* staff explain early in its story how the poll on cheating was conducted. Surveying 447 students who were enrolled in a variety of courses at different levels is a key to getting relevant results. The other strength of the piece is that the lead highlights numbers on cheating that may shock and engage readers. The additional reporting from an interview with an assistant principal about the number of cheating offenses and the consequences of those offenses offers a nice balanced approach.

FIGURE 4.7 (*continued*)

Poll yields information on cheating at Paly

Cheating

continued from front page

occurred. The third offense results in an F in the class and suspension from school.

However, most students who cheat aren't caught. In fact, in the past year, the administration filed cheating offenses for less than one percent of all students, according to Assistant Principal Doug Walker.

The poll indicated that of those who cheat at least twice in any given area, a relatively large number have cheated at least six times. In all categories, the number of students who had cheated five times, but not six times or more, was low: ranging from five to zero percent.

In contrast, the percent of students who had cheated at least six times was, in most categories, relatively high: ranging from two to 27 percent.

On some questions, students were slightly more likely to admit to a passive role in cheating than an active one; there was a three percent discrepancy between those who admitted to hearing information about a test at least once in the past year, and those who admitted to telling others information.

On other questions, students were more likely to admit to aiding a peer in cheating than to having personally used others' work; seven percent more students admitted to having allowed others to take answers from their homework than those who admitted to copying someone else's.

Conversely, 21 percent admitted to giving a peer an answer to a test as compared to the 23 percent who had copied answers from another student's test.

In this category, students appear to be less likely to aid their peers cheat because giving answers on a test is treated more harshly by teachers than sharing homework, and the repercussions are the same for both students involved.

Campanile poll on cheating

Poll administered to 447 sophomores, juniors and seniors in November, 2003

1. Are you taking any AP or honors classes? If so, how many?

2. How many times within the past year have you read online summaries as a substitute for reading an assigned book?

3. How many times within the past year has someone else given you specific information about questions on a test you haven't taken?

4. How many times within the past year have you told someone else specific information about questions on a test they haven't taken yet?

5. How many times within the past year have you taken answers from a peer's homework assignment rather than completing it yourself?

6. How many times within the past year have you allowed a peer to take answers from your homework assignment?

7. How many times within the past year have you told a teacher that you turned in something that you hadn't?

8. How many times within the past year have you used someone else's writing (including siblings or friends) in an essay without citing the source?

9. How many times within the past year have you taken answers from a peer's test?

10. How many times within the past year have you allowed someone to take an answer from your test?

- Filter questions are used to eliminate potential respondents who are not in a position to answer meaningfully. For example, attitudes toward the cafeteria food may not be meaningful when provided by someone who does not patronize the cafeteria.

- Background questions provide information to help interpret the results of polling. For example, those who plan to go to college may give different responses to a question about the ideal marriage age than those not going to college.

- **Closed-end questions** are questions answered with a yes or no. While closed questions offer easy statistical results, an open-ended question or multiple-choice question may follow to give more depth to the poll-taker's opinion.

- **Open-ended questions** are questions that often begin with "why" or "how", which are designed to elicit longer, more developed answers. Open-ended questions seek to gather respondents' thoughts about issues and events. The questions encourage detailed answers, and while they may elicit rich quotes for a survey story, they may be difficult to summarize or transform into percentage data.

- A multiple-choice or -range question will give the pollster easier results to tabulate but may not offer as much insight into the respondents' thoughts as the open-ended question. Examples of the answers to this type of question are "strongly agree" and "somewhat agree," all the way to "strongly disagree." Add "don't know" and "no opinion" options when they are relevant.

A poll can be conducted over the phone or by distributing the poll to classes or other gatherings. Online polling through services such as Surveymonkey.com and Google Drive have also been used by some newspaper staff. Design must be a consideration for distributed polls. A survey should have a headline to identify the poll topic. Make sure the questions are sufficiently separated and clear, and that they are short. Too many questions will decrease the chance that the poll-taker will complete the poll.

The poll story itself should offer some insight into the results. For example, one paragraph might highlight the statistical finding that 55 percent of the student body disagree with a proposed change from a block schedule back to a seven-period day. The quote in the next paragraph might illustrate a sophomore's frustration that the change would prevent him from fitting French and athletics into his schedule. An anecdote may be included, but a follow-up interview with the respondent may be necessary to fill in the holes in his or her story. The reporter needs to make sure that the focus of the story accurately reflects the poll results and interprets them correctly. A poll result indicating that 12 percent of students don't feel safe in school should not be the primary story focus, since it's not large enough to reflect the broader school opinion. The number of people selected and how they were selected, the questions they were asked and the sampling error should all be included in the story.

A survey can also be useful in the following:

- Locating people to interview: if a reporter is doing a yearbook feature on people who take self-defense classes, a poll can help the reporter reach beyond his or her small group of friends to increase the diversity of people represented in the story.

- Assessing who is reading your publication and what sections they are reading.

- Assessing the buying habits and power of the publication's readership; information about how much money students make and where they spend it can be useful for an ad salesperson.

- Brightening up the design of the publication by displaying the results in an informational graphic, such as a pie chart.

CIVIC JOURNALISM

Print and broadcast media not only cover the community but are also a part of it. In the same way, high school journalists are also members of the student body, and they have a stake in the well-being of their school. Understanding this connection is at the center of a movement known as "civic journalism" or "public journalism."

Test your knowledge

What is the difference between an open-ended question and a closed-ended one?

Quick Exercise

Pair up with another student and create a five-question student opinion poll over a school-related issue, Have another pair in the room take the poll to test the clarity of the questions.

FIGURE 4.8 *The Stinger*, Irmo High School, Columbia, S.C. Vol. 36, Issue 8. March 26, 1999. Front-page reprinted with permission of *The Stinger*, Irmo High School.

Stinger staff reacted to a letter to the editor by creating a focus group of students to discuss the racial and cultural concerns facing the school. The staff also ran an editorial and poll results on the issue.

Find out what all your night-time thoughts really mean. Dreams are on page 7.

Centerspread
Not sure about what to do over Spring Break? Pages 8 and 9 offer a few ideas.

Take a look inside the huddle at Adrienne Suffridge on page 16.

the Stinger

36 years as the student voice of Irmo High School

6671 St. Andrews Rd. Columbia SC 29212 • Vol. 36 Issue 8 • March 26, 1999

Irmo's diverse environment

Racial diversity: Dialogue begins with focus group

Senior Erin Beasley

Senior Sheena Campbell

Sophomore Ashley Gentil

Senior Namita Koppa

Freshman Miggie Lopez

Teacher John McMillan

Senior Alice Milligan

Junior Robin Otterbacher

Kofi Whitney: You may get confused by the fact that Irmo is a "cliquish" school. Certain groups hang out with certain groups. Things don't mix. You may get that confused with racial tension or separation.

Andy Su: We hang out with people we are like. That's only natural.

Miggie Lopez: I remember when I first moved here people automatically assumed that I would hang out with black people, but I started leaning more toward band people and white people. Everyone was like "What's up with that?" Since I was Hispanic, all the black people assumed I would hang out with them.

Namita Koppa: I hate the loss of individualism that comes in this world because once people say you're Asian, you're expected to be somewhat intelligent. I hate having to deal with that perception over and over again because I'm not like that all the time. It makes me feel like I have to try harder to fit into a group.

Changing race relations

Meghan Walker: When we were younger we didn't really notice races, but as you get older you start to see that maybe a lot of people think you're not the same.

Whitney: There are people in my classes now who treat me totally different than they treat everyone else because of my color. I just figure that's people and that's how people are going to be.

Erin Beasley: People look down on you if you're a black person and you hang around with a lot of white people. They call you a sellout.

Su: You feel, for example, if you're Asian you need to fit in by hanging around with other Asians. You begin to look for people to identify with otherwise you feel like you'll lose your identity.

Interaction between races

Sheena Campbell: If I see someone with a unique skin color or look, then I ask them what they have in them because I'm curious. I don't want to offend anyone. I'm just interested.

Su: I think about 75 percent of my friends met me that way. It all depends on how they ask.

Robin Otterbacher: It's also an icebreaker to ask someone where they're from. A lot of times it's a good way to start a conversation.

Teachers

Gentil: Some teachers definitely look at me differently because I date black guys.

Campbell: Also, with teachers I feel like I have to prove myself and work harder to get over the stereotype of the black person who sits in the back of the room and cuts up, curses, or raps to themselves. I feel like I have to work harder than anyone else to prove I'm intelligent.

Su: I think if any of my teachers feel that way, they do a pretty good job of hiding it.

Gentil: It seems like a lot of teachers hide it, but you still know what they're thinking. It's more noticeable when you work more closely with a teacher. It's not like a teacher does something to you, but more of a feeling you get when you're around them.

Role of parents

Alice Milligan: A lot of people at this school just don't know better because that's the way they were raised by their parents. You can't really hold that against them. That's just how they've been taught.

Wallace: I don't arrive with my set of beliefs because they were passed down to me through my parents or through my culture. I resent that people automatically assume that I think a certain way.

John McMillan: Racism is a learned behavior. You pick it up from your parents or whoever. I believe initially your parents have a big factor in either eradicating it or perpetuating it. If they're walking around using casual racial slurs, you guys pick that up. Parents have to get involved and help alleviate the situation.

Mixing of races

Campbell: America is a lot like a salad bowl now. There are a lot of different groups but they don't mix together.

Wallace: That (salad bowl theory) is so sad. It shows a lack of brotherhood.

McMillan: It's not sad. Everyone's still together but expressing their own flavor and learning from one another. That's the whole concept behind the salad bowl theory.

Solution

Whitney: The only way things are going to change is for people to start being independent and not caring so much about what others think. I think here at Irmo that is going to take some time.

Wallace: If we generalize people as humans, rather than black or white, then we all have come from the same origin.

Koppa: This school has already tried to address this problem and has already failed with things like the Uni-Team, but I think they did try to promote some sort of social equality. You can have people like that trying over and over again but the main problem is larger than that.

Whitney: I don't think they've failed. It's just not going to happen overnight.

McMillan: Whenever you bring people, animals or what have you from different backgrounds or cultures, there's never going to be complete and ultimate unity and harmony. It's just about giving everyone an awareness, making them racially sensitive and eradicating little comments like "Indian Giver." This is something that can seem so innocent but could be really offensive to someone who is an Indian. Communication and making race a casual word are good starting points. You're going to have a lot of different races coming to Irmo. This (focus group) is a start though - talking about it and addressing it.

Whitney: Talking about it will help, but we've got to have other approaches. Here at Irmo we want quick results, but time will change things.

Junior Andy Su

Freshman Meghan Walker

Senior Jonathan Wallace

Senior Kofi Whitney

Editor's note: A Publications Board discussion about a letter that was to run in the February Stinger revealed a growing concern about the racial and cultural atmosphere at Irmo. In order to begin some dialogue among the diverse groups, the Stinger staff asked for input from students and faculty. Following are excerpts from a focus group meeting March 12.

See survey results, page 2; photo collage, page 3; staff editorial, page 10.

Civic journalists believe it's not enough to report on a problem. They must also work to stir community conversation and problem-solving. When covering conflict, public journalists work to "frame" issues in ways to promote understanding and compromise, rather than hostility and intolerance. They also don't limit their work to the opinion page; they figure out ways to encourage civic engagement in every section of the newspaper.

If, for example, a school experiences a rash of physical fights among students, civic journalists would not only cover the incidents but also explore the motivating factors, report on efforts at other schools to decrease violence, and perhaps even convene and cover a meeting among representative group of students to discuss solutions. If the district is hiring a new principal, civic journalists would canvass students, teachers, parents and other members of the community, seeking each group's shared and conflicting perspectives on what qualities a new principal should have. When the school board calls a bond election – a topic that may initially seem like a snore – civic journalists would show how the vote has a direct impact on students' lives and why they should care. Civic journalists do not consider such practices as a special genre of journalism. In fact, they see it as journalism fulfilling its highest calling to public service.

YEARBOOK WRITING

Photos are the core of any yearbook. Most readers – who flip through their new yearbooks looking for pictures of themselves and their friends – would agree. Photos were often the only content in the earliest 20th-century yearbooks. Pages were filled with students dressed in dark wool in the front of the school or helmetless football players with balls tucked under their arms. But writing gradually crept into this medium – perhaps when readers realized they couldn't remember everyone in the group picture or the accomplishments of that year's football team. What began as a thin, printed and bound collection of photos from the school experience has evolved into a more complete historical book, a retelling of the school year through photos, captions, stories and graphics.

The basic tools to create yearbook copy, or written text, were covered in Chapter 2's discussion of interviewing and reporting. The primary forms that make up yearbook writing are covered in Chapters 5 and 6. Headlines are covered Chapter 10 and captions are covered in Chapter 15. But there are several more exclusive yearbook writing forms and special considerations that will be covered here.

Let's play a game. See if you can guess the year or the decade based on the following yearbook story.

> The bell rings.
> It's 8:20 and the last two English students slide into their desks. "Hello, class. My name is Ms. Pennington." And with that, the first day of a new school year begins.

So what's your best guess? It's difficult, isn't it? The writing offers few clues to a decade, let alone a year. Had the writer told you that the students bolted down the hallway listening to their iPods, you would have guessed a decade. Or if the writer had referenced the squeak of the penny loafers or the thump of a boom box, you would have had cultural clues to a different era.

If this vague piece of writing had been placed alongside photos of kids with big hair and bell bottoms or students with Mohawks and oversized shirts, the reader certainly could have narrowed down the decade. However, the yearbook writer would still have missed an opportunity to capture the people, the history and the culture of his or her particular school year through words and stories. The goal of every yearbook writer should be to choose language that captures the sights and sounds of one particular year in the school.

The **yearbook theme**, or the unifying concept for the book, has taken many forms since themes were popularized in the 1970s. Chapter 13 will tackle the visual aspects of yearbook theme development. What will be discussed here is the verbal side of the yearbook theme. The voice of the year and the yearbook is first established with the theme and theme copy. However, good yearbook staff understand that the visual and verbal are intertwined. Good yearbook copy should complement strong photos and design.

FIGURE 4.9 *Lion*, yearbook, McKinney High School, McKinney, Texas. Reprinted with permission of Lori Oglesbee.

The 2010 *Lion* opening and closing theme copy establishes the voice of the yearbook and its theme. The voice of the theme copy should never feel as though it could fit another yearbook, school or year. The writers developed the theme with the specific changes that students dealt with such as swine flu and parking lot painting. When their lives changed, they used the language of their generation – "nevermind" and "Do over" – to describe their adaptation to change.

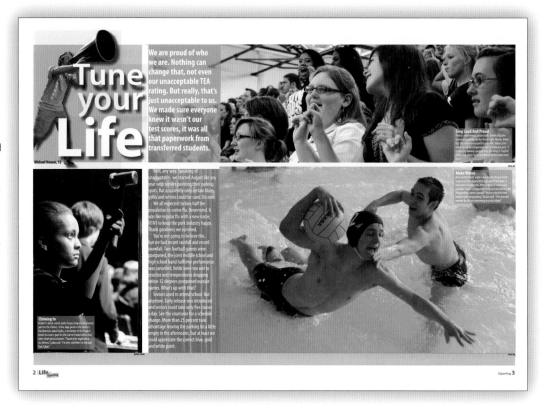

Good theme copy introduces the theme and its relevance to the school year. Theme copy also connects the different sections of the book to the theme. The theme copy will often appear on the opening or first complete spread of the book, the division pages – those pages that separate the book by subject matter or time periods, and the closing pages or last complete spread. Chapter 15 will discuss the design and variations of yearbook organization in more detail. This section will focus on the theme copy writing.

In Figure 4.9, the opening copy from the McKinney High School *Lion* uses the voice of a 16- or 17-year-old narrator telling the story of her 2010 school year. Notice the phrases such as "Do over" and "What's up with that?" which reinforce the yearbook's theme: "Life: Subject to Change."

To better understand the concept of writing voice, think about it this way: "Do those phrases sound like something a 45-year-old businessman from Chicago would say?" Obviously not, in this case. They shouldn't. This theme copy should sound like McKinney High School students in McKinney, Texas in 2010. Should this McKinney High theme copy sound like your own school in 2013, 2015 or whenever you're reading it? It shouldn't, although the differences may be a little more difficult to discern. Identifying the voice of one particular school year can be challenging. Unlike the Texan who immediately recognizes the distinctive word choice and inflection of a native Minnesotan, you will not be helped by obvious regional differences. Like the native Texan who cannot hear the accent of another Texan, you may not notice the unique voice of your area. You must step back from school and friends and listen critically to find the voice of your own school and generation. Asking the following questions will help identify potential language for your theme copy:

- What are my friends this year saying?
- What is the distinctive slang of my generation and region?
- What activities or events are students talking about and which will they remember?
- What makes us different from other classes in other years?

Good theme copy writers capture the people and the events of the year, tying them into a central theme. The best writers hit those events or moments that everyone can identify with. This doesn't mean that every sentence should describe the entire school, and it doesn't mean every moment impacts everyone. In this McKinney example, the writer chooses a variety of events and activities to represent key "changes" that a range of students experienced.

The nationwide swine flu scare certainly stood out in 2010. Mandatory blue and gold paint was an annoyance that all seniors will remember. The addition of a lunch period was a school change that impacted a large number of students – a fact that the image of the shorter lines at Java City vividly illustrates. Good theme copy emphasizes real places, real moments.

Effective theme copy will use the body of the story to subtly show how different elements of the school year are related to the yearbook's theme. In the opening thematic statement of this yearbook, staff announces its own decision to change, which echoes the broader theme. Staff used the theme copy to introduce something readers may not be expecting – the shift in the yearbook's structure from standard sections to chronological coverage. As in the final lines of this excerpt, theme copy should also build to a restatement of the theme at the close of the piece.

The closing theme copy mirrors the opening. Here, the narrator takes a look back at the year, highlighting changes with the same voice. Notice that the language fits the theme but doesn't repeat the same words "change" and "life." Instead the writer says, "Well, that's different" and "Always good to have a backup plan." The prices students paid for smoothies at Java City and for personal pan pizza were great specifics that put a timestamp on the story and the book.

Unique story angles

Yearbook coverage often suffers from the "same old" syndrome. Same old groups and clubs covered or same old topics or student life events represented. The more innovative yearbook staff instead work to build spreads around a unique story angle. In Figure 4.10, *Lair* staff from Shawnee Mission Northwest captured a concrete day-to-day look at life in the classroom by profiling seven different students who sat in the same desk over the seven periods of the day.

The reporter's observation skills were key to the success of this piece. Many writers would have reported that Koenigsdorf's classes did nothing but watch a video. This writer challenged himself to look for the smaller details that tell the readers something about the students in 2010. Jamie Filmore would never have pulled a water bottle out of his bag 20 years before. Jordan Dillon's playful pestering of the English teacher comes alive when the writer describes how student and teacher take turns changing the name of the English 11 lesson plan to the name of a convenience store "Super F-Mart." Michele Beeler's attempt to covertly read a text message and the frequency at which the hay-wire clock created chaos both show how easily high school students are distracted. The reader who may open the book 20 years later will smile at this vivid picture of 16- and 17-year-olds in Shawnee Mission, Kansas, in 2010. This reader doesn't have to have taken Fran Koenigsdorf's class to be transported to the time period. The concrete details will provide the necessary catalyst. Don't believe it? Mention your favorite cartoon from your second grade year to a classmate and see where the conversation goes.

Alternative copy or sidebar writing

The primary difference between alternative copy and sidebar writing is whether the quick read copy treatment is stand-alone copy or whether it accompanies a main story. When a quiz or pie chart is the only form of storytelling other than captions, it's considered alternative copy. When this type of graphic accompanies a main story, it's called a sidebar.

People or class sections are often filled with alternative copy. In Figure 4.11, this faculty spread from *Wings* of Arrowhead Christian Academy in Redlands, California, the extended quotes work to tell short vivid stories about faculty members' high school years. Good alternative copy has a focus. The headlines help package the quotes into three different types of flashbacks: comparisons with current students, memorable first kisses and troublemaking.

Extended quotes work well if the interviewer ensures the answers are developed with specifics. Students most assuredly looked forward to the comparisons of "Most Like You." Nancy Gilmore's answer works because she's open about her own problems with time management, backing it up with a specific reference to Katie Joe Woodrow's inability to make 7 a.m. rehearsals. Lori Breckley's answer has wonderful concrete description of a kiss, and readers will appreciate her honest evaluation her own lips-on-mirror technique – not to mention the humiliation of getting caught by her brother. Yearbook writers may get their best results by asking questions of twice as many respondents as they plan to quote, so they can choose the best anecdotes.

FIGURE 4.10 *The Lair*, Shawnee Mission Northwest High School, Shawnee, Kan. Reproduced by permission of Susan Massey.

Lair staff took a novel approach to classroom life. Through period-by-period observation, the writer gives the reader a sense of the range of students and classes in one school room by telling the story of every student who sat in the "second desk from the left in the front of room 130." The story gives a structure for bringing to life the dialogue and activity of the high school classroom.

one desk

by ed spaunhorst

Seven students sat at the same desk in room 130, but were never aware of all the people they shared a seat with.

1st hour
2nd hour
3rd hour

Imagine all of the people who shared the same desk during different times of the day.

They share the same space, but are never aware of each other. Never know who sat in the seat before they arrived and have no idea who sits there after them.

On an average day, a desk sees seven students. This is the story of the second desk from the left in the front of room 130.

1st hour

Before the bell rang for first hour to begin, English 11 teacher Fran Koenigsdorf asked junior Eric Filmore to move the desk in the back of the room.

"Sure thing," Filmore said with a smile as he picked up the desk and moved it to its proper place.

Filmore was dressed in a black sports jacket, a blue collared shirt and khaki pants for DECA. He dropped his backpack next to his desk and took a seat.

Koenigsdorf explained that the class would be viewing a video about author Henry David Thoreau, and they would be required to take detailed notes. Filmore, after scribbling notes in his planner, retrieved a black spiral from his backpack.

When not writing down facts given in the video, Filmore kept his eyes on the screen and fidgeted with his pen, twirling it between his fingers.

As the video ended, Koenigsdorf asked for the lights to be flipped back on. Filmore opened his backpack and slid his notebook inside. He pulled his water bottle from side pocket of his backpack and took a drink as he listened to Koenigsdorf give a brief follow-up lecture on the film.

As the bell rang, he slung his backpack over his shoulder and exited the classroom.

2nd hour

Upon entering room 130, junior Emily Chambers sat at the desk in the front.

Junior Jaden Gragg, who sat to her right, pointed out that the clock on the wall was moving unusually fast and skipping around. Chambers smiled at the sight and other students began to notice the malfunctioning clock.

Chambers sat with her arms crossed and listened to the morning announcements. When the video began, she opened a black three-subject notebook to the third section where she kept her English notes.

Chambers watched the video with her palm against her cheek, occasionally removing it to take notes.

Between notes, she doodled along the edge of her spiral, her pencil always in motion. As her doodle grew in size, she had to wrap her notes around the drawing in order to fit them on the page.

Once the video was over, she tore out her notes sheet and carefully ripped off the jagged edge of her notebook paper. She then placed the notes sheet neatly in a divider in her notebook.

When the bell rang, she walked out of the classroom while still trying to slide her notebook into her bag.

3rd hour

Junior Jordan Dillon walked into the classroom and sat at Koenigsdorf's desk. When Koenigsdorf entered, she looked at him with furrowed eyebrows.

Dillon stood and changed the title of Koenigsdorf's lesson plan from "English 11" to "Fran Mart," which he quickly erased and revised to "Super F-Mart."

When Dillon finally made his way to the desk, a couple of students pointed out the malfunctioning clock on the wall.

"What's going on here?!" Dillon dramatically exclaimed.

Koenigsdorf explained that the clock had been going "haywire" all morning, then started the video.

Upon hearing the way the narrator pronounced Thoreau's name, Dillon questioned the students behind him.

"Wait, is it Tho-REAU or THOR-eau?" he asked, receiving only shrugs from his peers.

As the video continued, Koenigsdorf interrupted.

"Now, that actually is a woman," Koenigsdorf said, poking fun at the masculine features of the woman.

Dillon smiled at the joke. At the end of the video, he pulled a pair of orange athletic shorts from his backpack to make room for his notebook, then returned the shorts to his bag and zipped it.

In a unique approach to a student profile (Figure 4.12) Boone High School's yearbook staff quizzed multiple people about Fiorella Bertola. Here they asked five of his friends about his personal likes/dislikes and elicited stories. The "right" answers give the reader insight into Michael Sanchez's story. The "wrong" answers can still offer insight into Michael's character or how others perceive him.

In Figure 4.13, Shawnee Mission Northwest chose to break down Snow Day coverage into multiple sidebars. While they all had snow as their focus, the array of sidebars provided good opportunities to vary the coverage.

FIGURE 4.10 *(continued)*

4th hour

Senior Michelle Beeler, clad in a cheerleading uniform and sweats, walked into Room 130 and immediately moved the desk so it formed a circle with the others.

In Writer's Workshop, students wrote creative stories and then read them aloud to their peers. Beeler sat and listened to senior Josh Greene as she bit her nails and fidgeted with the ring on her finger.

Seniors Brandon Barnhill and Alex Franklin were next to read. During Franklin's story, students noticed that the clock was spinning out of control.

"OK, everyone take a second and notice the clock. Now that we've all seen it, we should have no more outbursts," Koenigsdorf said following the interruption.

When Franklin finished reading, Beeler took advantage of the break and stretched her arms up over her head.

Beeler's phone vibrated in her pocket. She discreetly read the text and replied, hiding her cell phone behind her leg and out of Koenigsdorf's sight.

Beeler listened as the next four readers presented their creative works. When the bell rang, students reassembled the desks back into rows and headed toward their next class.

5th hour

Standing next to the desk, senior Emma Malin chatted with seniors Sandy Tickles and Michael Tarne before English 12 IB, taught by Ben Pabst.

"The clock is freaking out!" Tickles exclaimed.

Malin and Tarne glanced at the clock.

"Are you guys going to Planet Sub?" senior Caitlin Fitzgerald asked Malin and senior John Doran.

"Of course," Malin said.

"We haven't missed a Turkey Tuesday in months," Doran said.

While the class was watching a video, the bell for lunch rang and the students scurried out of the classroom.

Malin, Fitzgerald and Doran returned from lunch with Planet Sub cups.

The class watched the end of the play *Rosencrantz and Guildenstern Are Dead*, then stopped to discuss it.

"What's up with the dog howling at the end?" Pabst asked his class.

Malin smirked to herself.

"Did you like the way I asked that?" Pabst asked her.

"What's up?" Malin mocked him.

The class discussed the differences between the movie and the play until the bell rang.

6th hour

In Psychology, junior Alex Wood realized that he had forgotten his book and darted back into the hallway to retrieve it from his locker.

He returned just in time and plopped down in the desk. Only five students sat in the desks scattered across the classroom: two were absent.

Psychology teacher Amy Walker gave the class a reading assignment.

"Oh my God! That's like five pages a day!" Wood said sarcastically.

The class began to read the assigned passage and the room was silent. Wood sat resting his left hand on the back of his neck, holding his Psychology book in place with the other one.

Students began to notice that the hands on the clock were spinning out of control.

"Man, time flies," Wood said, his classmates chuckling. "Wouldn't it be great if the school day actually went that fast?"

Eventually, Wood and the class went back to reading.

He glanced up at the clock, but then remembered it wasn't working and looked at the silver watch on his wrist, restlessly waiting for the bell.

7th hour

In Workshop class, sophomore Toni Britt moved the desk to form a circle with the others.

Koenigsdorf announced to the class that their next assignment would be a review of a film.

"Yes," Britt said as she fist-bumped senior Brendon Fisch.

Shortly after, Koenigsdorf handed Britt an envelope from the school district. Fisch playfully tried to grab it, but she swiped it away just in time.

Senior Tyler Amble read a story about cocaine.

"Darling, that was wildly inappropriate, but quite hysterical," Koenigsdorf said.

When it was senior Nelson Diaz's turn to read, Koenigsdorf pointed out that he used the trick of printing in large "first-grade" font to make it seem longer.

Britt laughed as she examined the paper and then passed it on to Diaz, who sat to her left.

At the end of class, Britt pushed the desk back to its proper place.

As the 2:40 p.m. bell sounded, these seven students hurried into the hallways, wandering toward their next destination. Some had school activities; others were just going home, but all seven would be back the next day to sit in the desk second from the left at the front of room 130.

119

When he stepped into

After entering Writer's

The **Q and A** sidebar, which gives the interviewer's questions followed by the subject's verbatim answers, provided concrete information about how a teacher's leg pain seems to predict snowstorms. By beginning the question using the word "describe," the writer gets a more detailed answer. Notice the good follow-up questions: "How intense is the pain?" elicits more concrete details about Koenigsdorf's "nagging ache." The final question prompts her to describe how the pains related to this year's storm – an important consideration because the focus should always be on the current school year.

The writers broke down different aspects of a snow day well, giving the reader students' views of the perfect amount of snow and whether they had to shovel it or not. A much less experienced

Quick Exercise

List four things people say that specifically distinguish this school year from others.

FLASHBACK

Teachers hope to impart wisdom from their many years of experience. That said, it's probably better to do as they say ... ~~not as they did~~.

MOST LIKE YOU

I'd have say Katie Jo Woodrow because she loves to sing and it's obvious that she loves the Lord. But perhaps the greatest similarity is that poor Katie Jo has a problem getting to early rehearsals on time – 7 a.m. isn't easy. I've always struggled with time management, so I totally understand.

NANCY GILMORE

There is no student with my combination of looks, intelligence, and dance skills. Though, I have heard Justin Bain and I are alike. Will Quanstrom has a slight tendency toward cynicism like I do. Nate Peters and I both like to take a long view of things and not get too worked up over minor problems.

NATHAN TRIEMSTRA

A fun-loving personality like Chaz Lopez. Cool and smooth like Darian Fuyumuro. Physically built like Nathan Wild – not as fast, though. Facial hair like Kyle Smith. Dance [moves] like Joshua Poole, but he's better! Drove a BMW like Jesse Sparks, but mine was actually my mom's. Witty and always ready with a comment like Mitchell Prins. A smile and overall coolness like Paul Glaviano.

DAVID OLSON

I was a mixture of Jenna Geers' humor, Lauren Kennedy's sweetness, and Caleb Light's good looks!

JULIE FREY

KISS AND TELL

There I was ... sophomore year of high school, at Knott's Berry Farm with a young lady for whom I had some level of affection. We were on the log ride. (You know that on that ride you don't sit side by side, right?) She was sitting in front of me when up we went into the dark tunnel to the top of the ride with gravity forcing the back of her head against me. I took my hand and lovingly pulled her chin toward me, hoping to give her a slight peck, but she pulled away. This was the only time a girl ever resisted my advances, of course.

THOM DONEY

I didn't know how to kiss, so I practiced with lip gloss on a mirror. You know what I'm talking about. You look in the mirror, and you can analyze your approach and then evaluate your results. Did your lips land fully on the mirror? Or just half-way? My brother caught me cleaning the mirror, but he was on to me. He saw the lip prints everywhere!

LORI BRECKLEY

I was in the hallway at Fairmont Park Elementary School in sixth grade. Sixth grade – what can I say? I was advanced. When the object of affection did not respond the way I had anticipated, I put her in a headlock. She never spoke to me again and probably never will in this lifetime.

NICK SWEENEY

TROUBLEMAKERS

I never had a detention, ever! But in seventh grade, some boys got into a water balloon fight, and I got caught in the crossfire. Since I was wet, I got hauled into the principal's office (crying) where everyone else received a "swat!" The principal did not give me a swat and told me to keep it a secret. We were best buds after that.

TERRI HARRIS

I was suspended once. I was sitting on the floor in gym class and as my friend walked by I thought it would be funny to yank his shorts down. He scrambled to pull them back up. We all thought it was funny, but the principal didn't. I received an in-school suspension – a full day of sitting in the back office by myself doing homework. It wasn't much of a punishment except for a bit of boredom and isolation.

JOEL POORTENGA

Let's just say I had my own well-worn pathway to the principal's office.

LUTHOR PARKS

148 people

149

FIGURE 4.11 *Wings*, yearbook, Arrowhead Christian Academy, Redlands, Calif. Reprinted with kind permission.

Yearbook copy doesn't have to be a standard 500-plus word piece with an introduction, body and conclusion. Here, *Wings* staff give the readers fully-developed quotes to show what teachers were like when they were in high school. One of the keys to such coverage is a strong interview to assure good anecdotes with specifics.

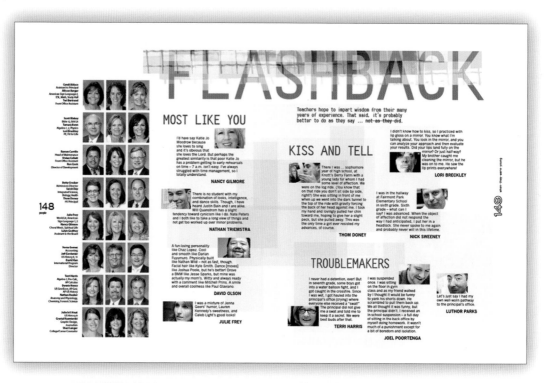

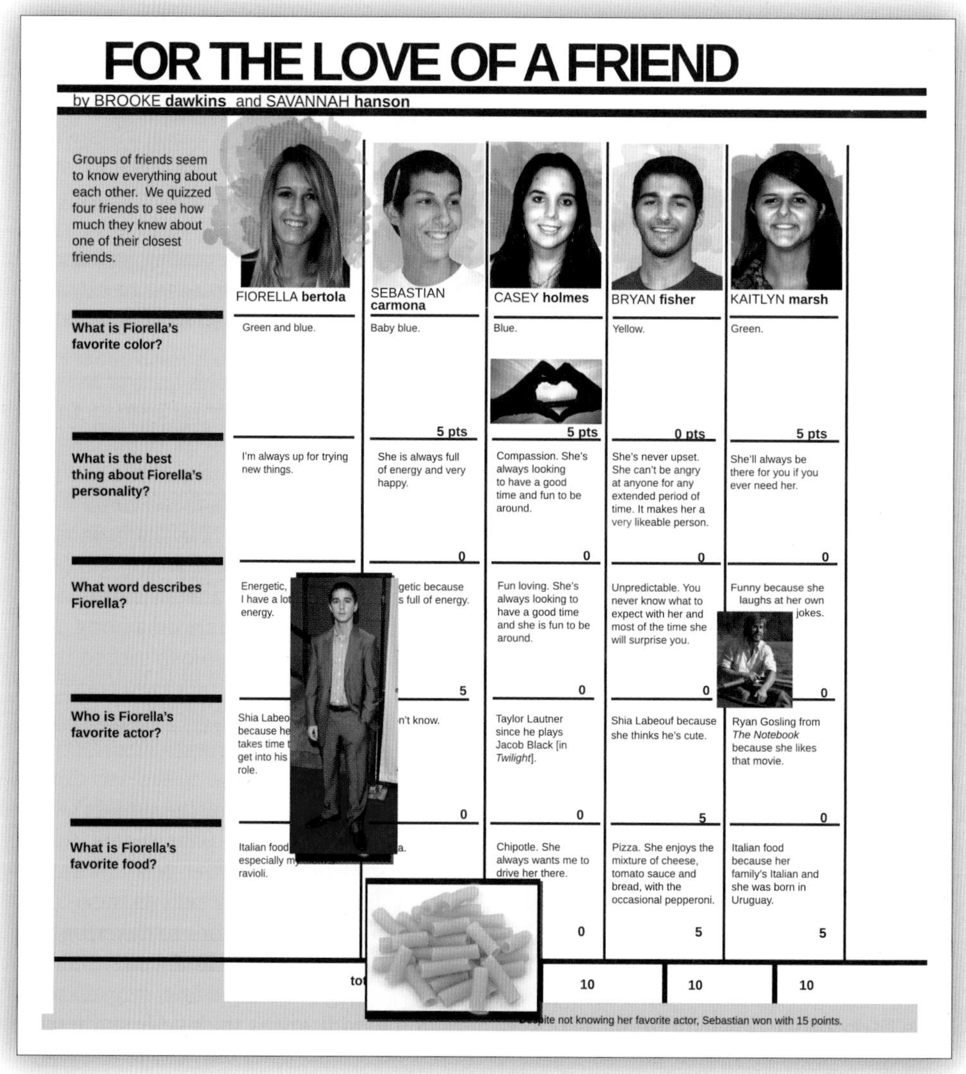

FOR THE LOVE OF A FRIEND

by BROOKE **dawkins** and SAVANNAH **hanson**

Groups of friends seem to know everything about each other. We quizzed four friends to see how much they knew about one of their closest friends.

	FIORELLA **bertola**	SEBASTIAN **carmona**	CASEY **holmes**	BRYAN **fisher**	KAITLYN **marsh**
What is Fiorella's favorite color?	Green and blue.	Baby blue. 5 pts	Blue. 5 pts	Yellow. 0 pts	Green. 5 pts
What is the best thing about Fiorella's personality?	I'm always up for trying new things.	She is always full of energy and very happy. 0	Compassion. She's always looking to have a good time and fun to be around. 0	She's never upset. She can't be angry at anyone for any extended period of time. It makes her a very likeable person. 0	She'll always be there for you if you ever need her. 0
What word describes Fiorella?	Energetic, I have a lot energy.	getic because s full of energy. 5	Fun loving. She's always looking to have a good time and she is fun to be around. 0	Unpredictable. You never know what to expect with her and most of the time she will surprise you. 0	Funny because she laughs at her own jokes. 0
Who is Fiorella's favorite actor?	Shia Labeo because he takes time t get into his role.	n't know. 0	Taylor Lautner since he plays Jacob Black [in *Twilight*]. 0	Shia Labeouf because she thinks he's cute. 5	Ryan Gosling from *The Notebook* because she likes that movie. 0
What is Fiorella's favorite food?	Italian food especially m ravioli.	a.	Chipotle. She always wants me to drive her there. 0	Pizza. She enjoys the mixture of cheese, tomato sauce and bread, with the occasional pepperoni. 5	Italian food because her family's Italian and she was born in Uruguay. 5
tot			10	10	10

ite not knowing her favorite actor, Sebastian won with 15 points.

FIGURE 4.12 *Legend*, yearbook, Boone High School, Orlando, Fla. "For the love of a friend," by Brooke Dawkins and Savannah Hanson. Reprinted with permission.

Legend staff took a creative approach to a student profile in their class section. The quizzes gave us varying perspectives into Fiorella Berola. The staff then packaged it with graphics and colors that fit the theme and attracted readers to a different form of storytelling.

FIGURE 4.13 *Lair*, Shawnee Mission Northwest High School, Shawnee, Kan. Reproduced by permission of Susan Massey.

Lair staff packaged their coverage nicely with a variety of sidebars. In addition to a main story on snow days, the Q and A, polls and extended quotes allow the reader multiple angles to see what students do on their day off. Although they covered sledding and snowmen, good journalists will brainstorm beyond the first two coverage ideas. Here, the writers offered unique angles about students who shovel snow and teachers with body aches that forewarn a change in the weather.

writer might have simply offered percentages about how many students enjoyed snow days. The response would be obvious to most students and offer little variety in the answers.

The writer ensures that the quote selection is strong by asking informed questions to elicit the strongest anecdotes. Again, the best interview strategy is to ask more questions than the number of answers you anticipate using. The end result will provide a surplus of answers so you can pick only the best. Here the proper questioning strategies led to some good specifics about a girl who had to push her car twice on the way to her grandmother's house.

Good sidebars cover specific activities from a specific year. Properly wording your questions to elicit the most concrete answers is certainly a key. Avoid yes or no questions. Choosing creative formats such as the examples displayed here and in Chapter 14 will also help in creating a more interesting final product.

FIGURE 4.13 (continued)

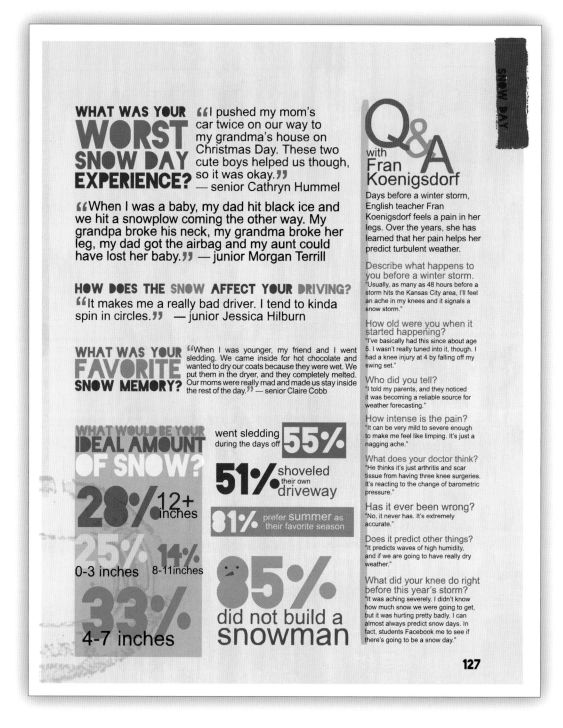

WHAT WAS YOUR WORST SNOW DAY EXPERIENCE?

"I pushed my mom's car twice on our way to my grandma's house on Christmas Day. These two cute boys helped us though, so it was okay." — senior Cathryn Hummel

"When I was a baby, my dad hit black ice and we hit a snowplow coming the other way. My grandpa broke his neck, my grandma broke her leg, my dad got the airbag and my aunt could have lost her baby." — junior Morgan Terrill

HOW DOES THE SNOW AFFECT YOUR DRIVING?

"It makes me a really bad driver. I tend to kinda spin in circles." — junior Jessica Hilburn

WHAT WAS YOUR FAVORITE SNOW MEMORY?

"When I was younger, my friend and I went sledding. We came inside for hot chocolate and wanted to dry our coats because they were wet. We put them in the dryer, and they completely melted. Our moms were really mad and made us stay inside the rest of the day." — senior Claire Cobb

WHAT WOULD BE YOUR IDEAL AMOUNT OF SNOW?

28% 12+ inches
25% 0-3 inches
14% 8-11 inches
33% 4-7 inches

went sledding during the days off 55%
51% shoveled their own driveway
81% prefer summer as their favorite season
85% did not build a snowman

Q&A with Fran Koenigsdorf

Days before a winter storm, English teacher Fran Koenigsdorf feels a pain in her legs. Over the years, she has learned that her pain helps her predict turbulent weather.

Describe what happens to you before a winter storm.
"Usually, as many as 48 hours before a storm hits the Kansas City area, I'll feel an ache in my knees and it signals a snow storm."

How old were you when it started happening?
"I've basically had this since about age 5. I wasn't really tuned into it, though. I had a knee injury at 4 by falling off my swing set."

Who did you tell?
"I told my parents, and they noticed it was becoming a reliable source for weather forecasting."

How intense is the pain?
"It can be very mild to severe enough to make me feel like limping. It's just a nagging ache."

What does your doctor think?
"He thinks it's just arthritis and scar tissue from having three knee surgeries. It's reacting to the change of barometric pressure."

Has it ever been wrong?
"No, it never has. It's extremely accurate."

Does it predict other things?
"It predicts waves of high humidity, and if we are going to have really dry weather."

What did your knee do right before this year's storm?
"It was aching severely. I didn't know how much snow we were going to get, but it was hurting pretty badly. I can almost always predict snow days. In fact, students Facebook me to see if there's going to be a snow day."

127

Test your knowledge

What is the writer trying to capture in good yearbook theme copy?

CONCLUSION

A reporter has to be prepared to deal with all types of stories. A high school reporter will find that some specialty types of stories pop up more often than others and require special attention. When covering health and poll stories, a journalist needs to be concerned with clarifying complex topics while making them relatable through people's everyday life experiences. Death stories require a sensitive touch, especially for a high school journalist. Yearbook writing requires attention to voice and creativity to capture the spirit of the school and year in a brief and readable format.

SUMMARY

- Health-related stories should be covered with the utmost care. Reporters must make sure they understand complex medical jargon and issues well enough to explain them simply to their high school readers.

- High school reporters shouldn't ignore academic classroom coverage. High school publications bear a responsibility to help students understand more about their education and the issues such as curriculum and school budgets that impact it.

- Student journalists must maintain a sense of objectivity when dealing with death stories.

- Gathering information from the deceased's family may be awkward, but it's a necessary step to accurately tell the person's story.

- A journalist covering a speaker should capture the main points of the speech.

- A civic journalist works to "frame" issues to promote understanding and compromise in an effort to solve the problem.

- A carefully written poll given to a representative and statistically valid group of students is the core of writing a good poll story.

- Yearbook copy should be concrete enough to provide a vivid and accurate picture of a specific student body in a specific year.

KEY TERMS

academic sections	obituary	sampling error
civic journalists	open-ended questions	sidebar
closed-end questions	poll respondents	speech story
death euphemisms	poll story	theme copy
echo interviews	public journalists	yearbook theme
hard news	Q and A	

EXERCISES

1   Clip or print a health story from a major daily newspaper or news organization's website. Make a list of the specific terms or medical-related phrases that are used. What did the writer do to make them clear to the public? Was each of the phrases made clear? What could the writer have done to make the story more accessible and clear?

2   Invite the school nurse to discuss a teen health issue. Prepare questions to ensure that you understand the issue well enough to write a story. Work on questions that will elicit clear explanations, examples and anecdotes.

3   Discuss the three biggest academic concerns or issues for students at your school. In small groups, discuss what story ideas could come from those three issues. Pick a story, develop a list of sources for the story and write the questions for the sources.

4   Write your own obituary.

5   Ask a member of a speech class to present a speech before your journalism class. Before the talk obtain the person's name and qualifications. (Your teacher may make up some qualifications to fit the type of speech the person will give.) Take notes and write a good draft of a speech story. Pair up with another member of the journalism class and read each other's stories. Discuss the answers to the following questions with your partner: Is the lead appropriate for the story? Does the body of the story adequately support and expand the lead? Why does or doesn't the story create a unified and accurate impression of the speech? Rewrite an improved draft of the story.

6   Cover a speech at a school assembly or a public meeting in your community. Submit your notes and the finished story to your instructor.

7   In class, discuss several controversial school issues that may lend themselves to a poll or survey. Divide into small groups, with the group's size depending upon the number of issues that seem pertinent. Each group should discuss one issue, develop a questionnaire, pretest the questions and revise them before use. Using an appropriate school directory to decide upon the number of students (and/or teachers) to be polled to give valid results, each group should conduct its own poll. Results of the poll should be shared by the group; members of each group should write individual stories based on the poll. Stories should be discussed within the group. (Perhaps some of these stories can be used in the school paper.)

Some poll and survey topics may not be school-specific issues but may be topics of pressing interest to students. For example: the relationship of high school students to fast food restaurants, diet foods, bulimia and the need "not to look fat"; the concern for a healthy body – depression, carbon monoxide levels in the blood, heart rate, blood pressure, cholesterol level, nutrition and general fitness; the problem of drug use, especially steroids in bodybuilding and athletic performance; part-time jobs and their ramifications; the concerns of minorities and multicultural movements; political correctness issues; sexual harassment; SAT or PSAT scores – or if your state has state exams, what are the results for your school?

WRITING FEATURE STORIES

Everyone has a story and other people's story is what your story should be about. Sure you need to know the who, the what, the when, the where, the why and the how, but you also need to know the personal, storytelling details: the "how did it smell that day when you walked out your front door?" and the "what did your kids say to you when you dropped them off at school?" and the "when did you realize your life would never be the same again?" and the "why did you move to this neighborhood in the first place?" and the "who did you want to talk to first when you found out?" Stay out of your source's way. Let them talk. And talk. And talk. As their story comes out, your story will take shape and the story they tell will be better than any story you could have written.

Frances Johnson, Strategic Communications Analyst with Armed Forces Services Corporation

LEARNING OBJECTIVES
After completing this chapter you will be able to:

- identify the different aspects of a feature story

- develop a strong feature story idea

- write a feature story using research and interview skills

- employ the variety of elements used in feature writing

- explore an array of feature story types.

Scholastic Journalism, Twelfth Edition. C. Dow Tate and Sherri A. Taylor.
© 2014 John Wiley & Sons, Inc. Published 2014 by John Wiley & Sons, Inc.

FEATURE STORIES DIFFER FROM NEWS stories both in style and subject matter. A news story reports that 10 percent of the senior class did not pass the standardized graduation exam. By contrast, a feature story tells how Brent hid his failure notice in the bottom of his dresser to keep his parents from finding out that he will be the first of their eight children who won't graduate. A news story reports the shooting of 15-year-old freshman Mike Bodine outside a local Dairy Queen. A feature story covers the different ways teens cope with death.

The **feature story** is a wide-ranging form of journalistic writing that covers a story in depth and detail. The feature story is strongly based in human interest, as discussed in Chapter 1. The feature appeals to the emotions and entertains. The feature can be informative and timely, but is not considered hard news nor is it generally written using the inverted pyramid structure. However, the feature story may address a recent event and give the reader more context, helping to explain the event's impact through anecdotes, examples and general research. The best feature story, no matter what the form or type, includes accurate storytelling that makes the reader understand and feel. Nevertheless, feature writers should be careful not to get so caught up in making the reader feel that they invent scenes or images that they cannot verify. Feature writing is not fiction.

The feature story is a staple form of copy for monthly high school publications and yearbooks. While deadlines and publication schedules don't always allow such high school newspapers to cover hard news in a timely manner, reporters can spend more time providing depth, detail and context in feature stories.

This chapter outlines a few types of feature stories. As you read, concentrate on specific examples of accurate and interesting storytelling. Let the story types stimulate brainstorming for your own feature ideas. Notice how many different types of stories are in the feature category.

THE FEATURE STORY IDEA

The feature story comes in all forms. The topics can be as serious as date rape and gun safety and as light as a clown class or stupid pet tricks. The feature can be informative, such as a how-to report on buying a car or an investigation of fire hazards in the auditorium. It may also be entertaining, such as a story on the lasting impact of childhood toys or a profile of a sophomore who served as a roadie on a summer concert tour.

All these feature stories nevertheless meet the following criteria:

- They are factual, requiring reporting and interviewing.
- They are not filled with the writer's opinion.
- They have a beginning, middle and end.
- The organization is as varied as the story ideas. (However, the inverted pyramid form, which is typically used in straight news stories, is rarely used in features.)

As with all quality stories, the first step is developing a focused and fresh idea. The feature idea will often come from a keen awareness of life around you. Talking to the kid in the Harry Potter T-shirt who sits on the steps outside the cafeteria might lead to a story on shy or bullied teens. An announcement regarding National Honor Society community service deadlines might lead to a story about juniors who tutor the kindergartners at the neighboring elementary school. Reading a news story on a bus accident in Paradise, Texas, might prompt you to research a story on bus safety, whether Paradise is 10 or 2,000 miles away from you.

Timeliness is still an important aspect of a feature story. A story describing the ways teens cope with death can be printed at any time of the year, because many students can relate to the subject. However, when such a story is published after the recent death of two students, the story will have a more powerful impact on the reader. A teacher who acts out one-man plays in front of the class or dances to old English tunes to teach literature may be worth a feature story. Reporting the story when the teacher has been named as the school's teacher of the year gives the audience one more reason to read the story.

IN ACTION

Feature story examples

Listed below are a number of feature examples written for high school publications. Make notes of story ideas and angles that might be especially relevant for your school.

- Issues in teenage relationships: Drawing on interviews with teen couples, parents and psychologists, the story looks at what holds teen relationships together and tears them apart, and can touch on everything from college to parents to pregnancy.

- A symposium feature with a group of male and female students discussing dating rules.

- One month after a Westside High School senior survived having his throat, ears and legs slashed, the story describes his recovery and mental trauma following the assault.

- A story on students who are wait-listed by colleges: What should the students do to get in? What are their chances of getting in?

- What happens to teens when they get fired? The story includes a discussion of how to keep a job.

- A group of students model dresses for *Quinceañera* magazine: The story covers a sophomore Latina model who is honored and excited about getting paid to model the latest styles.

- Junior ROTC boot camps: A "sights and sounds" piece on the grueling obstacle courses and drills faced by cadets in military service training.

- A how-to story on creating a job resumé.

- A profile of a 16-year-old living on his own: The story covers his struggle to pay bills with a monthly social security check and the impossibility of saving money for college. His loneliness after his mother and grandmother died is also discussed in the story.

- An informative feature on freshman initiation: The story delves into the question of whether the initiation is a valuable tradition or ugly harassment.

- A "where are they now?" piece on past graduates who were voted "most likely to succeed."

- How honest are we? The story investigates students' real feelings and experiences with stealing, lying and cheating. The package includes a sidebar on a "lost" wallet that newspaper staff leave on campus with $30 and an ID, to see if students return it.

- A story on a woodworking class that makes caskets for families who can't afford them: The story covers the emotional impact that the final project has upon students.

THE FEATURE-WRITING PROCESS

Once a reporter collects the information for the story (see Chapter 2), the organization and writing process begins. Given the barrage of information from multiple media sources competing for readers' limited attention, the reporter needs to develop strong, striking leads that capture and keep the readers' interest.

The feature lead is not a summary of the story. The **feature lead** is often an example, an anecdote or a statement that sets the tone for the story. The vignette, descriptive or contrast leads discussed in Chapter 3 can apply when writing a feature story. When the reporter has completed interviews, research and observation, she should develop the lead by answering the following questions:

- What aspects about this story did I react to the most?
- What anecdote would I go back and tell a friend?
- What did I see that made me say, "That's what this story is all about?"

The answers to these questions may be potential leads. The scar on the hand of a freshman girl left when her mother intentionally burned her in anger after her recent divorce may have made you cringe. The description of the scar and the story that went with it may be the perfect lead for a feature story about children caught in the middle of a divorce.

The feature lead (as discussed in Chapter 3) varies in length. While the one-word lead may work in some cases, other stories may require multiple paragraph leads to do justice to the anecdote that will draw in the reader.

Quick Exercise

Create a three-member group to brainstorm a web of story ideas around the topic of cars.

Test your knowledge

How important is timeliness in a feature story? How is this factor different in a news story?

Typically, features will have a focus paragraph following the lead. This **nut, wrap** or **focus paragraph** (as discussed in Chapter 3) helps the reader understand the main point of the story and gives the reader a sense of why he is reading this story. If the feature is tied to a news event, the nut graph will establish the timeliness. For example, the bus safety feature might mention a recent accident in the nut graph.

Read the following opening paragraphs from high school stories and see if you get a sense of what each story is about.

In fifth grade, life made sense to John Brzozowski. He played soccer on Saturdays, attended church on Sundays and did his homework on weekdays. For one assignment, John wrote: "If I could get Santa to grant two wishes … (1) Get rid of all pollution. (2) Get rid of all the drug dealers and tell everyone that drugs kill."

Somewhere down the road, however, his mother Linda said her middle child got lost. On a rainy day, Brzozowski was found dying in his car of a suspected heroin or cocaine overdose, ending a six-year battle with drugs.

Melissa Borden, DeSoto Eagle Eye, *DeSoto High School, DeSoto, Texas*

In the opening sentence, the author alludes to the fact that at some point life no longer made sense for John Brzozowski. Then she paints a picture of a normal child who was very aware of the risks of drugs. The idea that a child so aware of these dangers could find himself in a six-year battle with drug addiction hooks the reader. The writer then subtly transitions to the wrap paragraph. It informs the reader that the story is about a kid becoming lost in drugs for six years. The reader has a focus and is now ready to read the rest of the story.

Another type of feature lead is the startling statement lead. The opening line is a stunning statement that sets the tone. The second sentence is the wrap graph. See if you can explain how each works.

Nothing says "I hate you, Mom" more than a stainless steel bar through your tongue. While most parents look at body piercing as a form of rebellion against them, pierced students tend to say that piercings are a form of expression.

Michael Weisman, Valkyrie, *Woodbridge High School, Woodbridge, Va.*

While **question leads**, an introduction that poses an intriguing question for the reader that's closely tied to the topic, are rare, this next one offers vivid images, especially for a reader who knows the area.

Gastonia – city of redneck farmhands with limited vocabularies, wads of chewing tobacco and Dale Earnhardt T-shirts cruising down Franklin in lowriders? Undeniably, Gastonia is viewed differently by different people. However, a large number of both Gastonia residents and "them that ain't from 'round here'" see the town as farm community populated by pick-up trucks with shot-guns on the dashboard and rebel flags in the windows. On the other hand, others see it as an emerging suburb of Charlotte – one with smalltown charm yet lacking all big city headaches.

John Woody, Wavelengths, *Ashbrook High School, Gastonia, N.C.*

Read and analyze the following leads. For each, answer the following questions (which you should also use to analyze your own leads): What is the tone of the lead? How did the reporter get the lead? What are the best details in the lead?

As soon as the doorbell rings, two barking dogs come rushing to the door. The shrieks of a little girl can be heard through the walls of the house itself. After a few moments, the door opens with a groan.

"Hello – down, Tybo! Ophilia! says a tall dark-haired boy.

"Hi," says the little girl, suddenly shy, peering around her brother's leg. Something inside grabs her attention, and she runs screaming down the hall.

"Kaylee!" calls the boy. "Please stop yelling," but his voice is drowned out in the blare of iCarly, Kaylee's shrieking and yelping dogs.

Stepping carefully through the shoes and backpacks lying in the front hallway, the booming TV comes into view. A couple of neighborhood children sit raptly watching Nickelodeon, along with one African-American boy sitting on a dining room chair only a foot away from the TV set.

Outside a large picture window, a red-haired boy rides his scooter up and down the neighborhood street. Bicycles, waveboards, baseball bats, balls and other toys clutter the front driveway.

Welcome to the Mitts' home.

Doug and Susan Mitts are former foster parents and, over the course of their service, they have opened their hearts and home to three adopted children: Austin, 14, Logan, 11 and Kaylee, 7, along with their biological son, junior Connor Mitts, 16. Each adopted child has a unique handicap he or she lives with every day, adding to the slightly chaotic, fully functioning family dynamic.

Andy Wickoren, The Lair, *Shawnee Mission Northwest High School, Shawnee, Kan.*

Everything about that night makes freshman Andre Bowie uneasy. His voice drops when he talks about it, and he stares at the floor. Twelve years old at the time, he was at his grandmother's house on the phone with his cousin when he heard the whole story. There was a fight, a gun pulled, 11 shots. His close friend, whose name he won't mention, passed away shortly after being taken to the hospital. This was someone Bowie had looked up to, confided in and in the flash of a muzzle – he was gone. This wasn't the first traumatic moment in his life, and certainly not the last, but through writing and recording hip hop music as his alter ego Yung Dre, Bowie has found an escape from a world he desperately needed escaping from.

Bob Martin, The Harbinger, *Shawnee Mission East High School, Prairie Village, Kan.*

Forty-one. This is the number of tiny metal rings and bolts that she must place into the container when she goes thought airport security. While she may be notorious for holding up the lines during screening, East senior Cornelia Lange says she does not mind the added attention.

"People give me strange looks all the time because of my piercings, but I usually just ignore them," says Lange, who has everything from three-quarter inch gauges to four piercings surrounding her belly button.

Devin Casey, Spark, *Lakota East High School, Liberty Township, Ohio*

Observe the group of teenagers sitting around their watering hole, a dingy local coffee shop in Takoma Park. "The Smiths" are playing on a cassette player. The boys wear skintight jeans and plaid, lumberjack shirts; these locals easily blend into their environment. The girls dress in printed leggings and 1960s-inspired frocks. The group lounges, discussing ironic pop culture. These high school students make up a new branch of the Homosapien species: hipsters.

Mandy Xu, Silver Chips Online, *Montgomery Blair High School, Silver Spring, Md.*

The sun stands firmly against the stark Texan sky like a sergeant inspecting the rows of young men and women lined up on the field, until finally deciding to hike the temperature up to a sweltering 110 degrees. It is a whole new level of hell. Despite having woken up at 7 a.m. after spending a restless night sleeping on a gym floor, they were ready to spend the next 13 hours sweating away. Many participants had been forced to take their final exams early, skip prom and miss graduation parties to spend almost an entire summer on this sort of rigorous schedule.

But this is no ordinary boot camp – they are holding brass instruments instead of rifles and preparing for a performance instead of a battle. And for East seniors Marie Knueven, Jacob Niederman and Megan Manley, it is the experience of a lifetime.

The three seniors auditioned for and were accepted by the Blue Stars Drum Corps in the contrabass bugle, baritone horn and trumpet sections, respectively. Blue Stars is a competing member of Drum Corps International, often referred to as "Marching Music's Major League." Every year, over 8,000 students audition for less than 3,500 positions available in this tier of drum corps. However, high school students face a special challenge when competing against other musicians as old as 22.

Test your knowledge

What is a wrap graph?

"Many [of the] people [I was competing against for a position] had been marching for six years while I had only been playing for six years," says Manley, who did not begin marching until her sophomore year of high school.

Victoria Liang, Spark, Lakota East High School, Liberty Township, Ohio

Feature stories can be organized in any form and written at any length. Writers often use fiction-writing devices such as suspense, surprise, dialogue, description, narration and climax in the development of the body of the story, if appropriate to the topic.

The goal is to keep the story and the reader moving. Organize the story so the reader can logically and smoothly move from point to point or anecdote to anecdote.

The organizational possibilities are as varied as the feature story types. The feature story can be told chronologically. Or just as a movie sometimes has flashbacks, feature stories can move around in time, as long as the shifts are made clear to the reader. If the writer is using suspense, the storytelling will build, teasing the reader with bits of information while holding interest–a challenging task. Feature writers should organize and outline their story structures *before* they begin to write.

Conclusions

Unlike news stories where the ending paragraphs contain the least important information, feature stories typically emphasize conclusions or the final paragraphs of the story. Feature writers often consider the conclusion the second or third most important part of the story, behind the lead and the wrap graph.

As with the lead, the conclusion should be written to reflect the focus and tone of the story. A quote, anecdote or simple statement often makes for the best conclusion. (Note the conclusions in Figures 5.1 and 5.4.) Some feature writers may also circle back to an idea or a scene from the lead, reinforcing the central themes of the story. Writers should avoid forcing a conclusion with a jarring editorial comment or a clichéd "moral" of the story.

ELEMENTS OF FEATURE WRITING

Observation or firsthand reporting can help you create an accurate and descriptive written scene. Taking notes firsthand is easier than trying to get a subject to recreate the scene verbally. Good feature writing is *not* done over the phone. Reporting is best done outside of the journalism room, when you visit the subject of the story and use all five senses to describe what you observe.

Say you're assigned a story on agriculture students and their work at a local farm. As a good reporter, you will want to go to the farm and spend part of the day observing the students.

What can you observe with your five senses?

Quick Exercise

Partner with another student to find and print three feature leads from a news website. Exchange those with another pair in the class to rank them for quality–first through third. Write a brief justification of your rankings.

Sight
A 1,000-pound Hereford steer that lumbers toward his owner's blue Ford Ranger pickup.

Feel or Touch
The slick mud in the animal pens sticking to your rubber boots.

Smell
The sour stench of fresh manure mixed with the syrupy sweet hint of feed molasses.

Sound
The whoops and hi-yas of the boys herding the Angus bull.

Taste
The sweet chocolate taste of the Yoohoos, purchased from the drink machine, which the freshmen drink as they sit waiting for their parents to pick them up at the farm.

WORDS of WISDOM

Three tips your editors won't tell you about

Talk to strangers

Be a nosey neighbor, sit by the old woman on the swing, everyone has a story.

Bus director Mark Sheppard: "Route to Independence"

http://www.sptimes.com/2005/01/30/Floridian/Route_to_independence.shtml

Sit the bench

Be a fly on the wall, eavesdrop at beauty parlors, eat lunch alone.

Foster mom Amy Chandler and Lilly: "Good intentions"

http://www.sptimes.com/2006/05/14/Floridian/Good_intentions.shtml

Wonder: Who would ever?

Here's to you, Mr. golf ball picker-upper. Someone has to do it, why is it that?

Rodeo flag carrier Grant Mason: "He's the guy"

http://www.sptimes.com/2007/06/12/Worldandnation/He_s_the_guy___No_ifs.shtml

Lane DeGregory, St. Petersburg Times *staff writer*

An interviewer talking to young agricultural students by phone would have been challenged to ask enough follow-up questions to gather such detail. An observer can manage those details by developing a keen eye and grasping which observations are relevant to telling the story. A good reporter will make note of a great many more details than will actually be used. The story focus should dictate which of the mass of observed details will be relevant.

The following are the elements of a good storytelling feature.

Precise writing

Observation and reporting is best when it is precise. **Precise writing** means choosing accurate and specific words. How important is precise writing? Let's say the writer simply states: "The dog jumped up on the boy." Replace "dog" with the more precise "Saint Bernard," and the scene dramatically changes. Or, let's rework another. The reporter writes: "The officer ran past the gate when the dog turned on him." Rewriting the sentence with more precise nouns and verbs changes the scene. "The officer sprinted past the gate when the Chihuahua turned on him." Precise nouns and verbs help make vivid feature writing.

If the reporter has to use an adjective, it should be a specific one. "The teacher put on his cashmere sweater" is a more exact and concrete image than "the teacher put on his nice sweater."

Details

The small, specific facts help make a larger point or impression. The reporter must choose **details** that add to the overall focus of the story. For example, the use of the cashmere sweater in the example above would be good detail to use if the story is about a teacher who won the lottery

Quick Exercise

Make these sentences precise by replacing the nouns and verbs with precise language. Discuss how the words changed the scene.

1 The student said an awkward phrase in class.

2 He paused as he drank his drink and tugged at his shirt.

3 The girl put on her shoes to go out to shop at the store.

4 The boy stood in front of the group and sang a song.

but still teaches. The cashmere sweater helps to show how the teacher's life changed. The detail may become needless if the story is about the school's heater breaking down.

Pace

A reader needs variety. Variety can be achieved through pacing. **Pace** is the pattern and rhythm created by word choice, sentence length and construction and paragraph lengths. A good pace keeps the reader moving through the story. Read the story aloud to hear the rhythm and pacing. If you have to take a breath in the middle of a long sentence or the writing slows, go back and work on pacing. If all the sentences begin the same way, go back and change sentence construction for variety.

Varied and appropriate pacing can also help the reader experience the emotion of the scene. For example, a series of three short sentences can help recreate the anxiety of a situation. Another way to vary pace is by writing a well-crafted longer sentence, then following it with a short sentence. The use of other writing elements discussed in this chapter, such as details and dialogue, can alter pace.

Examples

Examples are typical cases or samples and should be specific. The basic premise in feature writing is "Show Don't Tell." Don't leave the reader guessing or filling in blanks left by vague words. A beginning writer might tell the reader that, "it's different being home-schooled." But in the following lead, Sadie Grabill from Harrisonville, Md., writes:

> Her freshman year of high school, it took Katharine Steinmetz 10 seconds to get to school. It was a matter of getting from her bed to her kitchen table.

The reader now understands at least one way that Steinmetz's life is different from most students— through an example to which teenagers can relate.

Dialogue

Dialogue – the use of quotes and conversation – is a device borrowed from fiction. It is useful if the sentences say more than the writer can put into his or her own words. The dialogue must be specific and relevant. The quotes can reveal the character of the speaker. The reporter must have a keen ear or use a tape recorder to capture long segments of dialogue. Quotes must be exact. Be wary of dialects. If you choose to try to capture a dialect in writing, be balanced and avoid exaggeration or any hint of mockery. The way you hear the accents of people from another state or country may not reflect the way they sound to themselves. (Think of how difficult it can be to really hear your own accent.)

Voice

In Roy Peter Clark and Don Fry's book, *Coaching Writers: Editors and Reporters Working Together*, voice is described this way:

> Writers often talk about "finding their voice." Readers and editors may talk about how a story "sounds." All are describing the same phenomenon: the illusion that a single writer is talking directly to a single reader from the page. This effect derives from the natural relationship between the writer's speech and prose and from artifice and rhetorical invention. All writing, even newswriting, has a voice, although the voice may be described as objective, dispassionate or neutral.

> *Roy Peter Clark and Don Fry,* Coaching Writers: Reporter and Editors Working Together. *Boston: Bedford/St. Martin's, 2003.*

IN ACTION

FIGURE 5.1 "Into the arms of love," by Katherine Gazella. *St. Petersburg Times*, Fla., Jan. 1, 1999. Reprinted with permission of *ZUMA*.

The *St. Petersburg Times* feature was part of a seven-part series called "Love Stories." This piece captures young love as experienced by a junior high couple from Clearwater, Florida. Though the piece is more than a decade old, the vivid observation still offers an example of how timeless good writing can be. In the following interview, the writer discusses the observation and writing process she used for the piece.

1 *Let's talk about the piece a second here. How and why did you choose that stuffed monkey battle for your lead?*

GAZELLA: [Laughing] It was just sort of a light-hearted scene. Every time I saw them, they were holding hands or trying to be that much closer to each other, so that was a good representation of that. Also, the scene in the car. It was so funny. I mean they were on a date, but they had the dad in the front seat, and they had this little nine-year-old brother that they had to deal with. It was just not exactly the most romantic of scenes, so it seemed perfect for the kind of a relationship that they would have at the age of 14 – that they have to deal with these little kids shooting fake machine guns.

One of the things you do well in the story is you have great use of pace in your writing. When and how do you think about pace in your writing, or is that something you consider?

GAZELLA: I don't think about it ahead of time, but I'll try to read it out loud in my head when I'm done writing it, and I guess I listen for that. And sometimes I'll feel like I'm going "vroom" right through the story, and I'll try and slow it down a little bit if that happens.

2 *Summarize what your typical reporting and writing process is like.*

GAZELLA: For a story like this, try and spend at least a couple of days with the people involved just to get to know them and what their routines are like. As opposed to just interviewing them for a half hour like you might do on a daily story. When you're there, you can interview about the important things, but just to really observe what their life is like is key. I just try to write down everything I can. It's hard sometimes because they are saying something important and you are also noticing some detail about the way they walk or the kind of car that they drive. But those are just as important, if not more so, when you're writing the story than what people say. I just try to write down as much as I can and wade through it later.

For these two, it was like this gift was given to me. They were both very talky. They said a lot of funny things. A lot of things, you would expect a 13-year-old and 14-year-old to say and with the sort of syntax that they have, so the actual quotes were really great. But also the style of clothing that they wore. The way that they looked at each other and joked around with each other turned out to be really great things to write down.

What kind of rewriting and reinterviewing did you go through? Was this one of those pieces where you sat down and sort of blast-drafted the whole thing?

GAZELLA: For me finding the top of the story is one of the last things that I do, and I think that's atypical. So I didn't know

Interview with Katherine Gazella of the *St. Petersburg Times*

As you read the story, determine the point that Gazella is making with each detail she chooses to include. How would you describe her voice?

SAFETY HARBOR – They sit shoulder to shoulder in the back of the white Mercury minivan, her neatly manicured right hand locked in his left. Mike throws a stuffed monkey at Jessica with his free hand; she catches it with hers and whips it back. They won't let go of each other, not even to fight.

The moment is sweet but hardly intimate. In the middle seat, Mike's nine-year-old brother, D.J., and his friend Andrew cackle loudly and spray each other with imaginary machine guns. You can always count on a kid brother to destroy a romantic moment.

Mike's dad is behind the wheel, good-naturedly performing his duties as chauffeur. He is driving the couple to Steak 'n' Shake in Clearwater, where Mike and Jessica will sip milkshakes and Mike will steal strips of chicken from Jessica's plate and Jessica will gently stab Mike's hand with a fork. The last time they were there, they caught Mike's dad standing outside the restaurant, spying on them through the windows.

Let him look. Jessica Replogle, 14, and Mike Sharkey, 13, are in love, and they don't care who sees it – which is a good thing, because they are hardly ever alone. Theirs is a roller-rink-and-Gummi-bear romance. They talk on the phone for hours. He's slender and athletic, so naturally she calls him Chubby. They celebrate an anniversary every month. In classes at Safety Harbor Middle School, he writes her notes that begin, "Hey, Beautiful." She wears a charm necklace, a gift from him. "Taken," says the charm. (Should they ever break up, Mike jokes, he'll give her another charm: "Available.")

Jessica and Mike love being together and being in love.

On this day in the minivan, they have been going out – dating each other exclusively – for precisely four months and nine days, a fact Jessica has at her exquisitely decorated fingertips. It is an endurance record for each of them.

"Things are, like, perfect right now," Jessica says. How many people can say that about their relationships? But like any romance between eighth-graders this one is fragile and probably fleeting. Perfect things often are.

When we began working on this article, we met an eighth-grade girl from New Tampa who said oh, yes, she and her boyfriend would just love to tell us their story. But when we called to set up the interview, she made an excuse and backed out. Her mother later explained why. Ten minutes before we talked to her, the boy dumped her.

Mike has no such plans; he's smitten. Still, if we want to understand where love begins, we need to watch Mike and Jessica now, in this pristine moment.

At last the van arrives at Steak 'n' Shake. When it stops, Mike bolts out so he can open the restaurant door for Jessica, an act of chivalry she has come to expect from him. Their love is one of the sweetest and most uncomplicated they will ever know.

The great wall of hair

The list of perfect things in the relationship includes Mike's tucked-in shirt.

It is Monday afternoon and Mike and Jessica are in his bedroom getting ready for a date. The time they will spend here provides a clear picture of the relationship, right down to the banter about Mike's shirt.

Mike, a snazzy dresser who sometimes changes his clothes three times in a day, twists and turns in front of the bathroom mirror, looking from all angles at the plaid button-down shirt he just put on. He pulls it out of his jeans a little in front, tucks it in a little more in back, checks the mirror again.

Mike is seeking what he calls The Perfect Tuck.

"It takes him, like, an hour to do," Jessica sighs.

While she waits, she obsesses over a few details of her own appearance. She flattens her red shirt against her small waist, glosses her lips and brushes her long, middle-parted, blond-streaked hair.

Finally, Mike puts the finishing touches on the tuck of the century.

"Jessica, do I have it?" Mike asks, holding his arms up like a gymnast after a dismount.

"Nope," she says, then fixes one part of the shirt that was uneven. "There."

In some ways, Jessica and Mike are like an old married couple; they know each other's bad habits and quirks. It drives her crazy when he twitches his knee. He jabs her in the side when she says "like," which is often. And she knows that even if she tells him to wait for her call, he will grow impatient and call her first.

"And have you seen his wall of hair?" Jessica says, poking her finger into his heavily-gelled 'do. They gained this knowledge by spending a lot of time together. They meet in the hallway after fifth period when she's leaving math and he's coming out of language. They study together after school. They attend school basketball games together–Mike as a point guard, Jessica as a cheerleader. Go, Warriors.

At night they talk on the phone for hours at a time, but none of the conversations goes too deep. They usually end these marathons with a debate: "I love you more," she'll say. "No, I love you more," and so on.

They're like an old married couple, yes, but without the lingering resentments, the deep affection, the cycles of pain and forgiveness. Their love is true but it's also lite.

And they know it. When they are out with friends, as they will be today, Jessica will playfully drape her arm around another boy's shoulders and Mike will hug other girls.

"We'll both flirt with other people," Jessica says. "I mean, we're going out. We're not dead."

Me, you – and Pooh

It is Jessica's 14th birthday, and 60 – that is not a typo – of her closest friends are jammed into her living room for a party. These are the children of the mid-1980s, Generation Y. They wear hair scrunchies on their wrists and platform sneakers and low-slung Tommy Hilfiger jeans. Their names are Meghan and Tyson and Justin and Kalyn.

They're a peculiar subspecies, 14-year-olds; somehow, they're both children and adults, yet neither children nor adults. Theirs is a world of love notes passed in the hallways at school and 'i's dotted with hearts. It is also a world of skimpy tank tops, provocative songs, sexual exploration and sultry dancing.

You can see some of that right here, in Jessica's living room. Everywhere you look, kids are grinding their skinny hips to techno music. On a makeshift stage in the corner, other kids sing along to the music of a rented karaoke machine, appearing free of all inhibitions as they perform.

"Oooh! Me so horny," they sing.

At the same time, Winnie the Pooh and Rugrats balloons drift side to side, as if they, too, are trying to keep the beat.

One girl goes into the kitchen, her arms folded across her chest, and asks Jessica's mom to turn off the black light. One of the boys has announced that he can see her bra through her black sweater.

It's unlikely that any couple here has been dating more than a year, and chances are none will be together a year from now. And yet the songs they sing are all about grown-up romance, with all its passion and peril. On the karaoke stage, Jessica and eight other girls line up for one of the big numbers of the night.

"At first I was afraid, I was petrified," they sing.

The song is *I Will Survive*, the anthem of women's heartache and resilience. The girls belt out these words with dramatic flair, squinting to demonstrate pain, shouting loudly to portray passion. Jessica's mom, Beverly, smiles as she watches. She's 42 and surprisingly calm amid all these boisterous teenagers. Five years ago she and Jessica's father were divorced–for the second time. She doesn't want to discuss it.

On stage, Jessica and the girls are still shouting out their song. "I'm trying hard to mend the pieces of my broken heart," they sing. One girl places her right hand over her heart, which is doubtless as pink and tender as filet mignon.

"They have no idea," Beverly says.

Save the last dance for me

One of the kids keeps turning the light on and off, on and off, until finally someone tells him to stop it and the room goes dark.

"Ladies' choice!" one of the girls shouts. Most of the ladies choose to giggle and look at their shoes, too coy or bashful to ask a boy to dance. One girl pulls a girlfriend into the corner, in a whisper, asks whether she should approach the boy she likes.

But Jessica is not shy or uncertain, and just a few notes into the Aaliyah song *One in a Million* she makes her move. She walks over to Mike and playfully butts her head into his chest. He grins, folds his arms around her waist and whispers something only she can hear.

Aaliyah sings: *Your love is a one in a million. It goes on and on and on.*

Several couples join them on the carpeted dance floor. Many of the girls tower over their partners, their arms slanting downward to rest on the boys' shoulders.

what the top was going to be until almost the end. So first of all that came last. The scene at the birthday party, I knew that would be a separate scene, so I just sat down and wrote that. Once you have something on paper, it's sort of a relief that you have a piece of the story done. But that was so lively, so fun and so energetic that I just wrote that one and then added some other details in later like about her mom and things like that. And a lot of that came from phone calls that I made later on. [That's how I] found out how long she and Jessica's father had been divorced.

If there's an easy section to pull out like that, then I'll start with that one. There's no order beyond that, except that [I'm] trying to organize it in a way that makes sense. Some of the stuff on their date fits together with some of the history of their relationship, and so a lot of it I'll just sort of write in pieces, then figure out how to piece it together later. It's not the most organized way of going about things [laughing]. Often I'll have the last line of the story written way before I'll have the top of it written.

Is it just something that stands out at you?

GAZELLA: The kickers usually come to me before the top does for whatever reason. The scene in the car didn't come to me, not long before my deadline.

I was taken back by the wonderful job you did observing for the piece. What was your observation process for this story?

GAZELLA: I actually was in a really good position on this story because it happened to be the one girl's birthday party and her mother invited me to come to the party, so it was

▶

just a matter of writing down all these great details that were there. They played this music that I had to go around and ask the kids who the artists were and what the songs were. I felt old at this thing … The party itself was such a great forum because they had a disco ball and they had all these wonderful details. So for me it was just writing all these things down and later on deciding which ones I had room to use. There were a lot of great things that I just didn't have room for.

How important do you think observation is in your writing?

GAZELLA: I think it's key. I think it's the most important thing. I wanted to be at as many places I could with them in the short time that I had between the time that it was assigned to me and the time that I had to turn it in. It turned out that there were some great opportunities for that. But I think you just have to walk around and do things with people that they normally would be doing. One of the things that people will often say to me, and I said it in this story I believe too, is that they had to make time with me, to spend time with me. I said, "Don't do anything other than you would normally be doing." I just wanted to see them in their normal setting. Just what they're normally like when they get in and out of the car and go to basketball games together and go out on a date.

How do you put them at ease like that?

GAZELLA: They were amazing — these two kids in particular. With other kids it has been more difficult, but with them they liked the idea of having a reporter with them, and they were popular at school, so they were used to

But this is not the case for Jessica and Mike. She is three inches shorter than he is, the perfect height for dancing in the way long favored by teenagers: Her arms clasped behind his neck, his behind her waist, leaving no airspace between them. They shuffle side to side, hugging more than dancing, careful not to step on each other's bare feet.

To have and, like, to hold

For eighth-graders, Jessica and Mike have had their share of experience in love. Asked to count their past relationships, they realize they have both reached the double digits. Off the top of his head, Mike knows how many girlfriends he has had.

"Fourteen," he says after taking a sip of his chocolate milk shake at Steak 'n Shake. "Swear to God."

Jessica has to do some math. Steve was her first flame, in fifth grade. Later, there was that guy who thought they were going out but she never knew it, so she doesn't count him. Then there was the guy who was involved in the kissing accident.

"He didn't actually bite my tongue," she says. "He just scraped it."

In all, she has had ten relationships, most of them lasting only a couple weeks. "That's my usual – two weeks," she says, then turns to Mike and grins. "You got lucky."

Her count of ten includes the first time she and Mike hooked up, back in the sixth grade.

He asked her out – that is, asked her to go steady – over lunch in the school cafeteria. Twelve days later they had their only real date, at an after-school dance. They arrived separately and paid 50 cents each to get in.

The afternoon did not go well for Jessica, who expected Mike to slow-dance with her, or at least acknowledge her existence. He did neither.

"I was just all aggravated with him," Jessica says.

Afterward, they went with some friends to Astro Skate Center in Tarpon Springs, where he continued to neglect her. Well, there's only so much a 12-year-old woman can take. She decided she would break up with him the next day.

But Mike had made a decision of his own. Jessica and Mike were skating on opposite

sides of the rink when Mike's friend Steve – Jessica's fifth-grade boyfriend – skated over to talk to her.

"He came up to me and said, 'Yo, Mike doesn't want to go out anymore,'" she says, rolling her eyes.

Yo!

Now, at Steak 'n Shake, Mike tries to defend himself. "I knew she was gonna dump me the next day, so I got to her first."

Jessica smirks. "Yeah. Whatever."

She exacted her revenge the next year, in seventh grade. She flirted with him incessantly in hopes he would become interested in her again. It worked.

"He'd ask me out and I'd say, 'Nope!'" she recounts gleefully.

Her attitude changed this year. Once, in September, they talked on the phone late into the night. Near the end of the conversation, Mike asked her if she wanted to go out with him. She said she would tell him the next day after school.

"But I had volleyball practice that night, so I had to wait an extra two hours," Mike says. "She made me wait the whole day."

Jessica the secret agent slayer

Jessica and Mike are spending a rainy afternoon in Mike's bedroom, with the door open as always. House rule. Other 14-year-old kids are having babies or doing what it takes to get them, but Jessica and Mike are in a simpler time of life, one filled with talking and wondering but not with doing, not yet.

At this moment they are surrounded by all the things that matter to a 13-year-old boy: posters of Michael Jordan, his tongue wagging, his body defying physics. On the dresser is a gift from Jessica: A Halloween photograph of the couple dressed as Sandy and Danny from *Grease*, with the words "I love you Chubby" painted on the frame. Pictures of Sarah Michelle Gellar, who plays the title character on TV's *Buffy the Vampire Slayer*, adorn three of Mike's walls. There's Buffy on the cover of *YM* magazine, Buffy on a motorcycle, Buffy with big devil horns and blacked-out teeth. The last one was altered by Jessica.

Jessica and Mike sit side-by-side on Mike's twin bed, playing the Nintendo 64 game *GoldenEye 007*, which involves secret agents. Jessica barely knows how to play, and Mike, an expert, is taking advantage of that.

"Hey, wait, which one am I?" Jessica asks. "You keep changing the controls! Am I the guy on the top or on the bottom?"

Seconds later, her secret agent dies. She was, as it turns out, the character at the top of the screen – the one that was blown to pieces by Mike's secret agent.

"No fair!" Jessica says.

They elbow each other, pout and giggle, delighting in this perfect moment when being together is all that matters. And why shouldn't they enjoy it? Someday, whether or not they stay together, things will be far more complicated for Jessica and Mike. If they're like most people, sooner or later they'll build up a little scar tissue on their hearts. It's a hard thing, getting together and staying there. Just ask Jessica's mom. And yet you see Jessica and

Mike and it gives you hope, if you didn't have it already.

Yes, things will be hard. But for now, this is the way it should be: lighthearted and carefree and set to the rat-a-tat-tat soundtrack of a video game shooting match.

After a while, Jessica and Mike put on their shoes to go outside. When Mike bends over to tie his sneakers, Jessica grabs one of the controls and slaughters his unsuspecting secret agent.

Mike lets out a yelp. "Oh! No way!" he shouts.

He gently strangles her, then puts her in a headlock. She pats his stomach and says, "I'm sorry, Chubby."

And with that, all is forgiven.

Gazella, Katherine, "Into the Arms of Love," St. Petersburg Times, *St. Petersburg, Fla. Jan. 11, 1999.*

having attention. Their other friends at school were kind of jealous that they had the reporter. They kind of liked it because it was sort of a status thing for them. They were just really sweet about it too. They were both very nice kids. They were very talkative and pleasant. In that case I didn't have to do that much. The harder thing with this project was getting the parents to be at ease with it. In fact, I had set it up with a different teenage couple, but one of the moms said, "No, I'm not comfortable with my son even having a girlfriend, and I certainly don't want it in the newspaper."

Voice comes from the writer's combination of pace, word choice and use of examples, dialogue and details. Voice in a feature story helps the writer capture the feel of the subject, place and time.

In this *St. Petersburg Times* story, Katherine Gazella gives voice to the experience of young love. As you read, take note of how Gazella crafts the story. Where does she use a variety of sentences to shift the pacing? Which observations are the most vivid and striking?

The feature writer used all the elements discussed earlier: precise writing, details, pace, voice, examples and dialogue all creating a vivid feature on junior high school love.

A lesser writer might have written about this same relationship using vague phrases such as "innocence" or "going out and having fun together." The same writer might have described how "they always hold hands" or "they like to do things such as going out to eat and roller skating." Then the reader would have to work to imagine what Mike and Jessica's relationship is really like. Instead, Gazella provides precise details that let the reader experience this relationship on a moment-by-moment basis.

Let's look at several particular aspects of the story. Notice the pacing of the opening paragraph. Look at how in the second sentence the author uses a semicolon to tie the two thoughts together. The connection of the two thoughts makes Jessica's reaction seem quick and instinctive. The sentence paints a picture of two people who won't let go of each other, physically or emotionally. Then after two long sentences, the third sentence is short to emphasize the point of the opening scene.

Pace is used effectively again in the fourth paragraph. After explaining how the couple caught Mike's dad spying on them through the restaurant window, Gazella follows with the short sentence, "Let him look." This short sentence from the teenagers' perspective captures the proud defiance of a junior high couple. The details and observations are photographic and worthy of a second reading. What details did the author use to show the naivety of the relationship? What verbs are particularly vivid?

Concrete references to superstars of the time such as Sarah Michelle Gellar and Michael Jordan provide insights into Mike's likes and dislikes but they might be seen to date the story. While Gazella's piece is more than a decade old, we include it here because its portrait of a relationship still rings true. Replace those with a current basketball star and TV heartthrob and

Quick Exercise

1 How does the author illustrate the point that Mike and Jessica are like an old married couple?

2 What effect does the pacing help create in the fourth paragraph?

3 What specific images does Gazella capture to contrast the innocent and not-so-innocent nature of the teenagers at the dance?

4 What point do the mother's quotes make in the story?

the story will be relevant for your generation. As with many a good story, the awkward truths of everyday human experience can speak to readers of many different ages and backgrounds.

WWW

WEBLINK Check out

www.lanedegregory.com

Pulitzer Prize winning feature writer Lane Degregory offers some of her best and latest feature stories on this website.

FEATURE STORY TYPES

The breakdown of feature story types is anything but definitive. Instead of taking what follows as a hard and fast set of rules, you should use them to help you brainstorm your own ideas for how to approach features.

Profiles

Consider the following facts: Alex Abnos's favorite color is blue, and he is into Spider-Man underwear and Coldplay. While all this information is factually accurate, it's not clear that readers will care about it. A profile is more than a list of facts about a person, and it is far less comprehensive than a biography. Instead, a **profile** captures a central focus of someone's life that others might find interesting or entertaining (see Figure 5.2). If Alex has the largest Spider-Man underwear collection in the state, this fact could be a primary focus of the profile. Readers may be intrigued by how he got started with his collection, how rare and valuable some have become and how he's handled the ridicule of his classmates.

A profile or personality sketch can also be related to a hard news story. Take the scenario where the school board has appointed a popular faculty member as the school's new principal. The story of the board's action would be news, but here is also a chance for a detailed interview and profile.

Readers will be interested in knowing that the new principal was a high school drop-out who got his G.E.D. after seeing how important education had become. They will be interested to know that he wakes up at 5 a.m. each day to do 500 sit-ups, to make sure he has enough energy for 12-hour school days. Readers would also be interested to hear the new principal's views on education, as well as his plans and goals for the school. The reporter writing this story should use details that enable readers to "see" as well as "hear" the new principal.

The profile is not an encyclopedic listing of the subject's life and accomplishments. Rather, the reporter should select facts that individualize the person and suggest the type of personality he or she has. This account of what makes the subject unique should give readers a vivid sense of the person. Typically, there is one dominant reason the publication is doing a feature profile on this particular subject. The reporter should collect information and details that are relevant to that central reason. The central focus should be summarized in the wrap or nut paragraph of the story.

In collecting the information, the reporter should interview the subject's friends, relatives, colleagues and sometimes his or her enemies. Reading any previous stories about the person will give the reporter a good starting point. Interviews with those who know the profile subject may inspire informed questions for the primary interview. Another teacher's stories about the volunteer work a coach does at a homeless shelter can provide new insight into the coach's character. An All-State actress's mother may have great anecdotes about how her daughter used to dress up their dachshunds and act out movies. Such interviews may inspire a striking lead for the profile or good development for its body paragraphs.

The point of the profile is to bring the person to life on the page or the monitor. The reporter should reveal personality through incident and anecdote rather than through a summary of the person's life and achievements. Permit the reader to see the subject in action. The person's appearance, dialect and conversation patterns; others' words about the subject; as well as his or her actions – should all help give the reader a clear picture of the profile subject.

Close observation is crucial for collecting relevant details for a profile. If a student leans down to just three inches above an English assignment to read five sentences in a large font, the reporter should take note. Recounting such an observation will give readers a better understanding of the student's challenges than using a general description, such as "severely sight impaired."

FIGURE 5.2 *ReMarker*, St. Mark's School of Texas, Dallas, Texas. Reproduced by permission of Ray Westbrook.

ReMarker demonstrates how reporting the details and subtleties help produce a strong feature story. The writer's understanding of the differences in the guitars and sounds are evident in his profile of a teacher who has become a YouTube sensation as a Delta blues musician. Notice how the writer uses detailed comments from the website as a second source to show the teacher's connection to his more than 100,000 viewers.

scene / remarker / march 11, 2011 PAGE **8**

Virtually Famous

Forget the stage — physics instructor Stephen Houpt is proving the way to go is on the web.

SLIDING INTO THE SPOTLIGHT Playing his National tricone slide guitar, physics teacher Stephen Houpt shows why he has amassed nearly 110,000 views on the popular video-sharing website YouTube.com.

You should be famous.
notsoprettynow84 1 year ago 2

It's in your blood man!
DonMoc 1 year ago

absolutely fantastic !
I would give anything for your gift !
imageoptical 3 years ago

I watched this video months ago, and today I feel it in my bones all over again. Fantastic.
aalippiinnee 3 years ago

This is physics teacher Stephen Houpt's audience.

He only knows them by their eccentric usernames, but in a sense, he's closer to them than many other rock stars are with their followers.

He offers advice. He answers all their questions. He doesn't know them, but he's bonded to them by their shared love of the blues.

Houpt, who utilizes video-sharing website YouTube.com to upload his now-widespread guitar videos under the username "houpts," is a rock star in almost every sense.

Houpt has essentially achieved what the hopeless masses of YouTube videomakers—most with merely a few hundred views—strive for: acknowledgement.

His most popular video has an astonishing 110,000 views, a staggering amount for any YouTuber, much more so for somebody whose day job is teaching physics.

In all, Houpt has just over 175,000 views on his 19 uploaded videos.

"It was really pretty surprising [to get that many views]," Houpt said. "I think [my style is] kind of different than how anyone else plays. What I play is all original stuff. There aren't any covers or anything."

While Houpt's success is mainly due to his ability to play the slide guitar better than most in the YouTube community, he attributes the uniqueness of his guitars themselves to many of his views.

"The instruments I'm playing are definitely part of the deal, too," Houpt said. "I'm playing a tricone, which is that metal-body guitar. There aren't very many people who play it and it has a really distinctive sound. I'm also playing a 1935 Dobro in some videos. And so, because the instruments I'm playing are ones that most people don't play, people are curious about them."

Perhaps most striking about Houpt's music is that he doesn't write anything down. Instead, he improvises.

"I'll sit wherever it is I'm playing and sort of come upon a theme," Houpt said. "So, a variation on a theme is sort of what it's like."

Houpt's style of music, the Delta blues — originating from the Mississippi Delta region and one of the earliest forms of blues music — is another reason for his view count.

"The style of guitar that I play lets me play things that more talented guitarists couldn't play," Houpt said. "Some people who are really good at normal guitar-playing just couldn't play slide guitar to save their life because it's a completely different thing. Normal guitar playing, I'm not very good. Slide guitar playing, I'm pretty good.

"The Delta blues is something people are interested in," he continued. "At least older people. Not so much younger people. Delta blues on the tricone is just kinda catchy. I like to think that the songs I'm playing are pretty good, too."

Houpt is good, but the equipment he uses to film his videos is nothing to rave over. His first videos were filmed by his wife, Sherry, in the breezeway of their home using a regular still camera. Those are the better sounding ones, he says.

Newer videos, including some of his instructional ones, are made using iSight on the Mac computer in his room. But one video from last March stands out as most eccentric, both in ambience and in sound.

"I played at my mother-in-law's funeral in this tuning with [the Dobro]. So, we were in Fort Worth and I just went into a sculpture outside the Fort Worth Museum of Modern Art, and my daughter's boyfriend filmed. The sculpture was amazing. Real echoey."

By now, most students on campus know of Houpt's internet accomplishments, but his current students have especially taken notice of his fame.

"I think it's really cool that he has videos with so many views," junior Peter Montgomery said. "It speaks a lot about him, that he can be both a physics teacher and an accomplished musician."

Before YouTube, Houpt had been limited to playing harmonica with his old band but said he would occasionally get nervous playing the guitar in front of crowds. When he films his videos, he feels more comfortable because "there's no one around except me and the camera."

Adorning the "walls" of Houpt's videos are comments. Most of them are praises. The rest are questions. Someone asked what Houpt's guitar was tuned to. Another was wondering about the type of model.

Any consistency Houpt lacks in the amount of videos he uploads — he can usually only get around to making them when soccer season is over due to his duties as assistant coach — he makes up for by responding to every question asked.

Houpt has even been able to cash in on his path to internet stardom through YouTube's "Partner Program" — an exclusive group consisting of YouTube's most viewed members. Through the program, which he says took months to finally join, advertisers are able to put ads next to Houpt's videos.

The only problem? "I didn't look over the contract very well," he admits. "I should probably look over that again."

He either needs "a ton of views or for people to click the ads next to my videos." Either way, he's not making much.

"In a little over a month, I've only made about 15 bucks," Houpt said, laughing.

But it isn't about the money. It's about a music-lover playing the music he loves.

To a crowd that loves him, too, of course.

Other YouTubers in the community

Junior **Thomas Tassin** (DJ214music): The DJ
What he does Creates hip-hop beats and dub-step compilations
Amount of uploaded videos 7
Total number of views 2,089

Junior **Andres Miller** (nectarboy12): The Historian
What he does Explains historical events in his series "Moments in History"
Amount of uploaded videos 7
Total number of views 834

Junior **Jackson Stager** (assistdisplay): The Vlogger
What he does Records video blogs ("vlogs") of his daily life
Amount of uploaded videos 9
Total number of views 1,803

Senior **Daniel Abramson** (BebopProductiOns): The Professional
What he does Uploads videos previously used for film festivals
Amount of uploaded videos 6
Total number of views 1,056

VIRTUALLY FAMOUS story by **Sam Yonack**, staff writer / photo by **Rishi Bandopadhay**, staff photographer / artwork by **Robbey Orth**, staff artist

Such an observation could easily serve as a lead for a story on how a freshman is working to overcome visual impairment. In all cases, the lead must be clearly relevant to the primary focus of the profile. For example, a profile of a teacher who rides bulls on the weekends could begin with an anecdote about her being saved by a rodeo clown – but not with an unrelated anecdote from her biology class.

An indirect quotation, relevant description or pertinent anecdote can make for a strong profile lead. Direct quotations are used less frequently in experienced reporters' leads, because even a strong quote often fails to make a point as tightly and effectively as the reporter's own careful paraphrase. The wrap graph of a profile will clearly identify the primary reason for doing a story about this person. As with most features, the structure of profile's body paragraphs will vary with the topic.

HELPFUL TIPS

Final tips for profile writing

→ Use only the most descriptive or entertaining words of the interviewee as direct quotations. If you can say what the interviewee said more concisely and forcefully, then you should paraphrase.

→ Weave characteristic expressions, mannerisms or gestures into the story, if appropriate. Avoid paragraphs in which you are forced to describe personality with adjectives or other general terms. Instead, *show* personality by including precise descriptive details.

→ Dialect can provide a vivid sense of the subject's personality. However, be careful to use the subject's slang and dialect consistently and carefully, avoiding caricature or exaggeration.

→ Avoid overworking the interviewee's name by using noun substitutes that apply, such as "the noted foreign correspondent," "the author," "the former Council president," "the Heisman Trophy winner," "the well-known educator," "the editor of the local paper," "the former Olympic champion" or "the new lottery millionaire."

---

300 WORDS: Creeping in Club Blood

Modeled after Brady Dennis' original 300 words, this series captures people and moments in 300 words; no more, no less

story by **MORGAN SAID**
editor-in-chief

As she throws on her short, black halter dress over her ripped up tights, she contemplates the night of work she has in front of her.

The screams.

The laughs.

The fright.

The fun.

Yanking on her thigh-high 4-inch boots, she grabs the red corset to wrap around her dress and drapes the big black cape around her shoulders.

Now all that's left is to apply the makeup: dark black eyeliner, bite marks, fangs, maybe even a pair of colored contacts. Once her body is airbrushed white, she's finally ready to head into the club.

To an outsider, Club Blood looks like any regular club—it's got a few couches and some chairs, a bartender and even a jumper—yet to her, it's anything but.

There, she doesn't have to be Rosemary. There, she gets to be whoever she wants, she gets to act however she wants.

As guests weave in and out of the club, she jumps out at them and laughs in their horrified faces.

McGraw

Holding up two pouches of fake blood, she growls in their faces: "0 negative, 0 positive? Make a donation today!"

The men keep their cool, calling her names and pretending like they aren't afraid, although realistically, they're terrified.

The young kids squeeze their eyes shut; the older ones yelp in delight.

But it's the teenage girls that are the best prey, venturing through the club in large groups with hands clasped together.

She relishes in their terror and proceeds to scream "Blood!" at the top of her lungs and chases them out.

In the end, everyone leaves the club alright and may even contemplate coming back again.

Because, afterall, Club Blood is just a haunted house at Worlds of Fun and junior Rosemary McGraw is just a vampire. Only at night, anyway. ★

FIGURE 5.3 *The Dart*, St. Teresa's Academy, Kansas City, Mo. Reproduced by permission of Eric Thomas.
   The Dart features a 300-word profile every issue. In this short feature, the writer vividly describes a student's night as a vampire in Club Blood, an area haunted house. The description of her black halter top, ripped up tights and thigh-high four-inch boots are key observations in creating a brief but crisp picture of Rosemary McGraw's alter ego.

Test your knowledge

What should a feature writer observe for a story?

Quick Exercise

Brainstorm a quick list of people you'd interview for a profile of a student who is a competitive skateboarder. Also include observation possibilities for the story.

HUMAN INTEREST STORY

The **human interest story** usually lacks a hard news angle, while illuminating aspects of life that are unusual, surprising, fascinating or moving. This type of feature appeals to the reader's curiosity, empathy or desire to be entertained. The human interest story can be about almost anything: persons, places, animals, inanimate objects. It can be about the track team's unofficial mascot – a rabbit who makes his home along the practice track; or about how two band students discovered they were distant cousins; or about a rock in front of the high school that each senior class spray-paints to celebrate graduation.

Any major news event has a human interest angle. A new bridge dedication may bring to mind a story on the first person to cross the bridge; the baseball fan who stood in line 18 hours to buy the first bleacher ticket becomes the human interest angle in connection with the start of the World Series.

Tips for writing successful human interest features

→ Select only the details necessary to develop the story's dominant emotion or theme. Don't overload your story.

→ Try to present your story in an original, clever way to hold reader interest.

→ Consider writing to a particular reader, not just to anyone. This technique can help you develop a conversational tone.

→ Avoid presenting your story in the form of a condensed summary, which will not let your reader become engaged with the material. A reader must become a witness to events if the story is to be successful. Do not say someone was angry, for example. Let us see the person in an actual scene.

→ Follow the lead with concrete, specific details and examples.

→ Try to include some dialogue if possible. The story becomes more personal because your readers will "hear" the persons involved.

Keen observation and intellectual curiosity will guide you toward many human interest stories. Keep an eye out for interesting little events, traditions, oddities and surprises as possible stories. No doubt there are a variety of minor incidents and situations in many of your classes that could be developed into good human interest stories that would amuse your paper's readers.

Look for possible story ideas in:

- any situation or incident that makes someone smile or laugh
- any situation or incident that arouses someone's sympathy
- any situation or incident that is unusual.

The human interest feature is not usually written in the inverted pyramid order. Many human interest stories use a narrative or chronological order or some combination of these.

In the following human interest feature, the author gives the reader a glimpse of the physical and mental struggles of dealing with a rare form of cancer. Look for the strong use of anecdotes about a fantasy novel and a grilled cheese sandwich, which the writer uses to give real and personal insights that are characteristic of a human interest piece.

She isn't attached to her hair. Never has been. She always considered herself kind of a tomboy, and she had worn it pageboy short early in life. So when senior Rachel Hoffman began to lose hers, she wasn't fazed.

"When it started coming out, I just thought it was so cool," Rachel said. "I remember going out to the nurse's station holding a lock of it and going, 'Look what happened; this is so cool!'"

But Rachel shouldn't be here to talk about it today. At age 12, she was diagnosed with myelodysplastic syndrome with monosomy 7, often referred to as pre-leukemia. Rachel's body was unable to make normal blood cells.

"The cancer cells in bone marrow take over everything," Dr. Jignesh Dalal, Director of Bone Marrow Transplant at Children's Mercy Hospital, said. "They don't allow normal blood cells to be made in bone marrow, and you need your blood cells to survive."

The prognosis wasn't good. Rachel didn't want to know what her chances of survival were, but her mother, Torie Clarke, wanted to hear it. She wanted to know what Rachel was up against.

Rachel had a 15 percent chance of making it past five years.

"She shouldn't be alive," Clarke said. "There's no reason – medically, clinically, logically – that she should be alive."

There might not be any explanation for her escape from death, but in life, Rachel Hoffman has always searched for the good in a bad situation.

[…]

Growing up, Rachel was an adventurous child. She loved climbing in trees, rock climbing and riding her bike. She was full of energy, full of life.

All that slowly began to change in the summer of 2004, when Rachel was 12.

She began getting colds, and it became harder to shake them. Once one cold went away, another would emerge immediately. She used to ride her bike to her elementary school in Olathe, but as she became more and more tired, the rides got harder and harder.

"My immune system was just not able to cope with anything," Rachel said.

Rachel also began to notice emotional changes as well. She felt less emotion – less worry, but at the same time, less happiness. Her mind and emotions began to slip. School was once fun, but it soon became a chore. She found herself staring off into space more often. When out in public with her mom, Rachel dawdled and had trouble keeping up.

"I couldn't concentrate on where my feet were going or how fast they were going," Rachel said. "I couldn't focus on one train of thought."

Clarke noticed slight differences in Rachel's behavior, but she always had a reasonable explanation for it. Rachel was just tired, she thought. She hadn't been eating enough. She was stressed over a test. Typical teenage stuff, she thought.

It was the other people that Clarke encountered that seemed to fear something more severe.

"We had several friends that would see Rachel and go, 'She's kinda pale,'" Clarke said. "It's almost like they knew better than I did."

Finally, in November 2004, when Rachel's sister, Karin Hoffman, was in for a routine appointment about her asthma, the long road to recovery began. The nurse practitioner took one look across the room at Rachel, and asked how recently she had checked her hemoglobin. After a quick conversation, they set up an appointment for Rachel to get her blood drawn at the beginning of the calendar year, once her father's insurance had switched.

On January 4, 2005, Rachel underwent blood tests so doctors could attempt to figure out what the problem was.

"I had been terrified of needles," Rachel said. "They used a butterfly needle to draw blood, and I thought, 'You know, maybe it's not so bad.' Little did I know, I'd be getting stuck a lot."

The next day, the results came in, and Clarke got a call. They needed to get down to Children's Mercy Hospital as quickly as possible. Ninety minutes later, they arrived at the hospital, and Rachel and her parents listened as the doctors told them what the prognosis was.

The weather outside was snowy, horrible, nasty and Clarke didn't feel much better inside.

"I really wish he'd told me to sit down," Clarke said. "You felt like you got punched in the stomach, and that was just the very beginning."

After all the uncertainty, all the tests, all the confusion, one thing was clear: Rachel had cancer.

"Our world has never been the same," Clarke said.

On January 5, 2005, Rachel Hoffman's battle began.

[…]

Rachel was never a fighter. Clarke remembers seeing kids take her daughter's toys, and Rachel never put up any objection. She had always minded her business in a quiet way.

She had never fought for anything, and now she was forced to learn how to do so while fighting for her most prized possession: her life. Rachel avoided thinking about her fate. To her, it didn't make a difference.

"Either I fall into one category or the other," Rachel said. "There's not a whole lot I can do about either category, so why waste time worrying about it? If I'm going to be in the larger category, I might as well not worry about it and do as much as I possibly can."

She couldn't do much. The chemotherapy weakened her immune system to the point that she was always vulnerable. Rachel spent her days in isolation, sleeping 12 hours a day and watching "House" and "Lost." Her friends were the nurses in the hospital, and she'd talk to them daily.

But above all other diversions, Rachel found her greatest escape to be reading.

"I've always had a book in my hand," Rachel said. "Usually somebody else has a problem, and it's not my problem to think about."

Rachel pored over books of all lengths and authors, but they were mostly of the same genre: fantasy.

"When I read, I want to read something that's not in this universe, because I get enough of this universe as is," Rachel said. "You can do things you want in your head. Things can be other than they are. I look differently in my own head – I look like I did before I was diagnosed."

She says that she read *The Trumpet of the Swan* by E.B. White over and over as a child. After the transplant, she picked it up again. It was a quick read, taking about a day. In those moments, it became her favorite book to read again and again. It comes as no surprise. The story's main character is born without a voice, and is forced to overcome his physical obstacle.

Just like Rachel.

[…]

Beating the odds involved more than just isolation for Rachel. She underwent multiple blood transfusions, a few rounds of chemotherapy and eventually received a bone marrow transplantation from a 32-year-old man.

The process was a tough one on Rachel. Her hair fell out. Her stomach felt upset. She was always tired. Her immune system had been worn down by the chemotherapy, and she was always at risk. She couldn't go to movies, couldn't eat at restaurants and couldn't even go into the sun as often. But the struggles didn't stop at physical pain. About a year after the diagnosis, Rachel began feeling depressed.

"I didn't have any emotions," Rachel said. "You start to become isolated, because you can't do the things that you used to be able to do and you're not allowed to do the things that you used to be able to do."

There were moments that gave the family hope. Just after one of the transfusions, Clarke began to make grilled cheese for Rachel, and then she moved on into the laundry room. Rachel took it upon herself to flip the grilled cheese, and Clarke was shocked.

"That's the smartest thing you've done in six months!" Clarke told Rachel.

Though the road would be long, hope was there. "She had her brain back," Clarke said. "She had herself back."

Rachel endured several setbacks during the recovery process, including cataracts in her eyes and scar tissue in her lungs. Most recently, she is battling a case of grafts vs. host disease, which occurs since her blood is different from the rest of her organs and skin due to the transplant, and the blood attacks them. Her joints have calcified and her skin is stiffened up. Rachel currently can't extend her arms past a 90 degree angle due to the calcification in her elbows.

Despite all the complications, Rachel finally began to receive some good news in 2007. She was undergoing constant blood tests, and the cancer cells were present less and less frequently, until the cells stopped showing up entirely. She had beaten the odds. An 85 percent chance of death, a near certainty, had been defied by a few medical procedures and a 70-pound girl that refused to give up hope.

Rachel continues to defy common logic, and she is even teaching her doctor a few things.

"What I am learning from her is in spite of difficulties, keep on smiling," Dr. Dalal said. "It is so satisfying to see her after going through all of this that she's able to go to school, able to study. I am giving her example to my other patients that with determination, fight and hard work, you can beat leukemia."

After her triumph over cancer, Rachel and her family are working to find a balance between being careful with her health and keeping her from living in a bubble, shielded from everything in the world.

"You need to be cautious, you need to be intelligent, but there's a line where you can't live your entire life in the house with the shades drawn," Clarke said. "There's a point for me where I'd much rather have her live as much as possible, even if it kills her. If getting out and living means that potentially it could kill her, that's God's choice – not mine."

[…]

After transferring to East during the 2008–09 school year, Rachel began working on her GED. She is far enough behind in her credits that she had to push back her graduation from last year to this year. Despite all the work she's doing for herself, she hasn't forgotten about the kids that are in situations similar to the one she endured.

Rachel, Clarke and Karen Anthony, a nurse at Children's Mercy Hospital, are all working together to found RaJa's, a community center and school for immune-compromised children from ages 2 to 18. The center was named with the first two letters of Rachel's name and the first two letters of Jason, a nurse's son who was killed in a car accident. Rachel's role in the center is fundraising. Since the center's total start-up costs expect to be around $1 million, she's helping write applications for grants and looking for connections to large donors. She even set up a golf tournament and is working on a making a run for RaJa's. There is currently a RaJa's Facebook page, and Rachel said that they hope to get a website up and running soon.

FIGURE 5.4 McKinney High School yearbook, McKinney, Texas. Reproduced by permission of Lori Oglesbee.

The yearbook feature on the camaraderie within their own staff shows how a writer can zoom in on scenes in the process of telling a strong story. The focus on the water gun fight conveys how playful, inclusive and close the staff became over the course of the year. The use of Mrs. O's distinctive voice and the details of the game became the foundation for a strong human interest piece.

For Rachel, it was a no-brainer to make a place like RaJa's.

"There needs to be some place for these kids to go," Rachel said. "I was alone. I would have been able to relate to kids much better. I would have had a lot less of the depression that I had, since a lot of it was the isolation and not having anyone to talk to."

Clarke sees her daughter as the perfect person to advocate for those in a situation similar to what she underwent.

"If anybody knows what [the kids] in that position need, it's Rachel and if anybody is going to be capable in articulating that and succeeding in that goal, it's Rachel," Clarke said. "It gives her a goal. I think RaJa's has been one of the best things for giving her something to look forward to, for giving her direction, for giving her a reason to not die."

Dr. Dalal said that Rachel's hair will grow back, and his staff continues to search for treatments to help her joints. The odds of a relapse into cancer are very small, according to Dr. Dalal, and he predicts that she will have a normal life expectancy.

"It's finally starting to get where I can think about the future," Rachel said. "You don't think past a week or two from now. You don't make plans because if I get a fever over 100.5 degrees, they stick me in the hospital for up to a month, and you never know. We're actually starting to be able to plan ahead."

For a girl so fascinated by stories of fantasy and the unknown, Rachel Hoffman is starting to enjoy the benefits of certainty.

Kevin Simpson, The Harbinger, *Shawnee Mission East High School, Prairie Village, Kan.*

Simpson gives us an intimate and touching window into Rachel Hoffman's world. While her classmates may have been reluctant to ask her about her baldness and pale skin, this writer found her and her family open to discussing the inescapable effects of the disease. Through liberal use of quotes, the writer reveals Hoffman's tenacity and courage. Notice the use of powerful quotes from Hoffman's mom and her doctor. In this case, the writer had to put in the extra effort, by getting the family's permission for the doctor to discuss Rachel's case, and was rewarded with insight about her character from a physician who had seen many others face the adversities of illness.

INFORMATIVE FEATURE STORY

Informative features give the readers information about ordinary issues and topics that they may encounter in daily life, both in and out of school (see Figure 5.5). Stories about the college application process, Internet addiction and the best local bike shops are all informative features. While the topic may be timely, the story does not revolve around one central news event.

Quick Exercise

In the story above, what examples do you think show the most about Rachel's character? What do you think are the strongest quotes? Were there other moments in her life that you would like to know about?

Tips for writing informative feature stories

➜ Talk to knowledgeable sources. Use in-school sources if they are informed about the topic, but do not forget area college professors, businesspeople, civil servants and other professionals.

➜ Avoid using secondhand sources such as encyclopedias or books, except to provide background for interviews.

➜ Use student quotes and anecdotes to bring life to the topics and issues explained by expert sources.

➜ Be accurate. Make sure you understand the topic thoroughly before attempting to inform the public about it.

The informative feature sometimes seems to overlap with the news feature. The informative feature may not be as timely as a news feature, but the informative feature may cover a recently-raised issue. Internet addiction is certainly a relevant subject for an informative feature story. However, the same story could be considered a news feature if it follows the school board's call for parents to limit their children's Internet use.

The focus of an informative feature can be as ordinary as taking care of your car or keeping a good friend. Coverage of lifestyle features is becoming more prevalent in professional and high school publications, and informative features often focus on health, exercise and diet. (Health story writing was covered more thoroughly in Chapter 4.)

OTHER TYPES OF FEATURES

A **community feature story**, usually of the informative type, relates the school to parts of the community with relevance to students. Many of today's school newspapers publish features on aspects of the juvenile court, the police department, city hall, the voter registration bureau, hospitals, mental health clinics, local colleges and universities, even nursing homes and assisted living facilities. All of these subjects provide angles of interest for the school community.

Interpretative features explain various aspects of school, such as art exhibits, new courses, changes in graduation requirements, school financial problems and the like. Art displays, for example, often need interpretation to help viewers understand the work at hand. Exhibits of work in home economics and industrial arts departments also lend themselves to interesting features that interpret the functions of the departments. The whys and wherefores of new courses and changes in graduation requirements will interest readers if they are informative and well written. A behind-the-scenes look at the school's financial structure can help readers understand where school money comes from and perhaps why the school is in financial trouble. Some school newspapers have published interesting statistical features on the cost of operating the school for one day, one week and one year. Informative graphics could accompany such stories.

Historical feature stories use research and interviews to bring the past to life. Historical coverage is usually tied to a timely event. For example, the school's 50th, 75th or 100th commencement would lend itself to a "then and now" comparison feature, complete with pictures if records and files are available. Old yearbooks are often an excellent source for historical information.

Symposium interview features are written panel discussions on timely topics of interest to school readers. Some examples are symposia or forums on the counseling system, information kept on student records, merit pay for teachers, graduation requirements, the value of foreign languages, low enrollment in certain courses, censorship or prior review of school newspapers by administrators or community topics such as drugs, child abuse, divorce, police brutality, runaway teenagers, racial problems or movie ratings. Background on each panelist should be included with the story.

Test your knowledge

What's the difference between a news feature and an informative feature?

Quick Exercise

Pick a transportation-related topic for an informative feature story and develop the lines of questions you'd want to develop.

BINGE DRINKING

risky
BUSINESS

90 percent of all teen alcohol consumption occurs in the form of binge drinking — a dangerous statistic that is causing alarm from students, administrators and parents.

▶ by Jairo Nevarez, copy editor and Lee Perkins, special projects editor

PARKER MATTHEWS PHOTO

IN EXCESS According to *Parade* magazine, binge drinking in today's teen culture is on the rise.

He didn't know he would be confronted with a bigger challenge than asking out his first homecoming date.

He didn't know he would feel more nerves than he did the first time behind the wheel.

He didn't know he would be faced with a decision so big so soon, at least not until senior year when he would declare his college choice.

But there was William McGee, then a sophomore, at a friend's house party, being offered a drink.

McGee declined, but it seemed like no one else had.

He looked around and noticed a friend, sluggish, dazed, wonky-legged. Everyone else was too engrossed with their friends, seemingly lulled by the amalgam of beer and hip-hop music.

His friend took one more step, and like a jittery Jenga tower, that last move led to his collapse.

The ambulance came and immediately took him to the hospital.

McGee later found out his friend suffered from alcohol poisoning.

"It was very scary. I had never seen anything like that," McGee said. "I knew I would be exposed to alcohol in high school, but I didn't think one of my first experiences would be like that."

> " I THINK WE HAVE TO ASK THE QUESTION: **WHY IS IT SO MUCH PART OF OUR CULTURE?**
> —Headmaster Arnie Holtberg

Continued on p. 8

FIGURE 5.5 *ReMarker*, St. Mark's School of Texas, Dallas, Texas. Reproduced by permission of Ray Westbrook.

The *ReMarker* story looks at the causes and impact of binge drinking among high school students, as well as potential solutions to the problem. This informative feature is not driven by a recent event, but instead focused on the continued prevalence of the problem at the school. The writer uses a strong range of sources: from the parents of a former student who died binge drinking in college to the school's headmaster to an alum who recalled how he started in the party scene as a sophomore. The article itself will be dealt with in more detail in chapter 8.

There are many other types of feature stories – limited only by the ingenuity and resourcefulness of a newspaper staff. One of the best ways to get ideas is to study newspapers from other schools and communities, particularly those that have been cited for imaginative feature coverage.

CONCLUSION

As you've seen, feature stories – the staple of newspapers, news websites and yearbooks – range widely in their topics and types. While news and feature stories can be more formulaic, the writing style of a feature varies, giving high school journalists the opportunity to explore organizational strategies and literary devices. Narrative, detail, voice and pace all find a vital role in the feature story.

FIGURE 5.5 *(continued)*

BINGE DRINKING | CONTINUED FROM PAGE ONE

risky BUSINESS

It's all about decisions. With alcohol consumption, specifically binge drinking, becoming increasingly popular in the high school social scene, students here must make the right choices.

A statistic published in *Parade* magazine's June 2011 issue suggests 90 percent of all teen alcohol consumption occurs in the form of binge drinking. Binge drinking is the excessive consumption of alcohol in a short period of time. According to gordie.org, a more exact definition of binge drinking is the consumption of five or more drinks for males and four or more drinks for females during one drinking experience in a two-week period of time. Marksmen like McGee are often exposed to this behavior at social events and parties.

NIC LAZZARA GRAPHIC

TOO COMMON Binge drinking, and drinking in general, is becoming increasingly popular among teenagers. Statistics show that teens begin drinking regularly as early as eighth grade.

"Since that time, I have seen more guys drink and have heard of guys binging at parties," McGee said. "I think it's almost become a normality, something kids expect to see at parties."

According to intheknowzone.com, McGee's assumption is accurate among teenagers nationwide. Half of students who binge drink do so more than once a week. Binge drinking among teenagers isn't just a prevalence, it's a regularity. And that regularity can be attributed to the influence older role models have on impressionable underlcassmen.

One family that has suffered because of those influences of older role models is Leslie and Michael Lanahan, whose son Gordie Bailey, a St. Mark's student through ninth grade, died in a hazing incident at the University of Colorado at Boulder in 2004.

Michael Lanahan says it didn't have to happen. A simple phone call would have saved Gordie's life. But that phone call never came.

"Your legs just drop out from under you," Lanahan said. "You can't believe it. You want to get to the hospital to help him. No, he's not gone. You just can't believe it. You just talked to him the day before. You want a second chance. Let me do it different, let me help him. It's like your life's gone before your eyes. I can't believe we lost him."

"It's just so permanent. You don't know what to do."

AS A FRESHMAN, MCGEE REMEMBERS looking up to the older boys in Upper School. He wanted to be like the Student Council leader, the class president, the captain of the football team. Going to his first Upper School party, he was excited to be with those guys he so tried to replicate.

And when one of those guys approached him at a party leaning in with a high five, McGee slapped his hand, feeling for the first time like a part of the Upper School brotherhood.

"Good to see you here, William," the older student.

McGee jerked, startled by the overwhelming smell of alcohol in his breath. He was shocked. Naïve and formable, he didn't know who he could look up to.

In today's culture, Headmaster Arnie Holtberg knows the issue of excessive drinking among teenagers is a sad truth.

"What I have read and what I have learned is that excessive drinking seems to have become more prominent. That is, the issue of binge drinking has escalated in recent years. Not just the last three years but over time," Holtberg said. "And dangerous drinking has become more prominent. Young people drink to get drunk. Drink a lot in short period of time for some reason, and the ferocity of that seems to have increased in both high schools and college."

When it comes to educating students about the effects of alcohol consumption, Holtberg believes the school plays a major role. For that reason, every year the school implements Freedom from Chemical Dependency (FCD) week. During that week in February, a group of men from the FCD organization come to share life experiences as well as scientific facts and statistics relating to drugs and alcohol consumption.

"I think we have a responsibility to [educate students about the affects of alcohol consumption]," Holtberg said. "I think we exercise that responsibility primarily through our Freedom from Chemical Dependency program that we have every year."

As for the Lanahans, following the initial disorient of Bailey's death, Michael resolved to take action against the ignorance that took his son's life.

"Gordie's death was totally preventable," Lanahan said. "As people that had better or more information about the dangers of alcohol, Lanahan and his wife Leslie sort of felt a natural responsibility to not have another kid fall to something that's really so silly and preventable. Our mission really was to help kids navigate the dangers of alcohol, including binge drinking, peer pressure and hazing."

It didn't take long for Lanahan's efforts to manifest into something powerful. The Gordie Foundation has produced a movie, Haze, to educate kids and parents alike about the dangers of alcohol abuse, in addition to holding an annual National Gordie Day, in which over 260 colleges take part.

"We try to reach as many people as we can with the limited dollars that we have," Lanahan said. "One of the elements that's most successful is our film, which has reached about a million and a half people. The colleges that are a part of this program will have a day just to stop and reflect upon the dangers of alcohol and talk about peer pressure and poisoning."

The Gordie Foundation also attempts to raise awareness of their cause through its website, gordie.org. Two of the site's key features, the Hero Wall and Memorial Wall, recognize those who have "made the call," and commemorate the many students who have died alcohol-related deaths.

Holtberg agrees that education is key, and he feels it should be a collaborative effort among all members of a boy's life, beginning with his parents.

"It should start with the parents, quite frankly," Holstberg said. "School has a role certainly. And I would say that one's church or synagogue or place of worship or some other social institutions would have a role in it as well. I think it's an entire community effort to keep young people safe. It has to be a team effort."

While Holtberg believes in educating students, certain distinctions should be made. He also believes the core of the problem needs to be tackled, asking the simple questions, consulting the appropriate experts.

"I think we have to continually talk about the important messages," Holtberg said. "One is that to developing brains and bodies, the consumption of alcohol can be extremely detrimental. What is responsible drinking? Having a glass of wine with dinner? Having a beer while watching a ball game on a Sunday afternoon? How do you teach that while adhering to the law? I guess the question is why do young people drink to excess the way they do? Why is the data what it is? What do the psychologists, what do the medical physicians, what do they say about why this is? What do the psychiatrists say? I think we have to ask the question: why is it so much part of our culture?"

HOLTBERG REALIZES, HOWEVER, PARents can sometimes be the cause of their child's unlawfulness. Though a boy's community tries to foster him in the right direction when it comes to alcohol consumption, those efforts are sometimes futile if a parent is a hindrance.

"Our greatest problems are, one, that kids drink. And sometimes drink enough to harm themselves," Holtberg said. "And another is, and it can be a problem from time to time, is that parents do not adhere to the philosophy of the school, and therefore may serve alcohol to kids in there homes. That's a very serious issue."

For Lanahan, though, the issue is not parental choices but social atmosphere. Ultimately, the goal of The Gordie Foundation is not to eradicate all underage alchohol use but rather to change the environment of today's college and high school social scenes.

"Our belief is that high school and college kids are challenged by the environment," Lanahan said. "It's the environment that needs to be changed, and part of that is the education and making sure everyone is focusing on the right things. The law says don't drink, everyone else says go for it. People don't know about it so they don't think they're doing anything dangerous."

If a student were to get caught participating in the act of underage drinking, the school would always take appropriate action if the behavior took place on campus or at a school-sponsored event. Lion Tracks is clear on this issue. If a student is reported to have consumed or possessed alcohol off-campus penalties would follow, Holtberg says. Punishments, however, are determined on a case by case basis.

"For any occurence, we would always get involved when we have knowledge of improper behavior with someone who has a leadership position or is on an athletic team. If we learn that someone has been consuming alcohol, or some other substance for that matter, then training rules apply as prescribed in Lion Tracks," Holtberg said. "And if behavior were egregious enough, let's say for instance, that a student consumes alcohol, becomes inebriated, goes to a function at another school and causes a disturbance, we would consider that our business for sure. There may be many other circumstances where we would become involved. Sometimes it is simply a matter of judgment."

in fact

- Thirty percent of eighth graders, 58 percent of tenth graders and 72 perent of twelfth graders reported they have tried alcohol in their lifetime.
- Five percent of eighth graders, 15 percent of tenth graders and 27 percent of twelfth graders reported being drunk in the past month.
- Among 12-20 year olds, approximately 6.9 million (18 percent) reported having engaged in binge drinking and 2.1 million (6 percent) in heavy drinking.
- Seven percent of eighth graders, 16 percent of tenth graders and 27 percent of twelfth graders reported binge drinking in the previous two weeks.

*Statistics taken in 2010 every two grade levels from centurycouncil.org.

Holtberg hopes Marksmen will be able to make the right decision when confronted with such challenges, applying the virtues of courage and honor that are so emphasized here. Holtberg hopes this courageous behavior will influence others to do the same.

"I would very much like everyone to refrain from using alcohol, and I say that with absolute conviction," Holtberg said. "And the more guys who don't drink, the more normal that becomes because we know that there's peer pressure, social pressure to join in, right? You go to a party and some other guys are drinking beer and you have a Coca-Cola in your hand and somebody leans on you, and you say no thank you, or do you give in? The easy thing is to give in, the harder thing is to say no thank you, but, that can be done and should be done."

Holtberg also hopes Marksmen who see this behavior are able to take appropriate action.

"Any time any of you sees someone else getting in trouble, that is drinking far too much, people need to intervene, because we know that people all over this country die from alcohol poisoning," Holtberg said. "It is certainly something that happens in colleges, and you know it happened to a former member of this community. You know, intervene, the heck with the repercussions. What's better? Getting in trouble with some official or allowing someone else to die? Do the right thing because not having done the right thing is far worse than getting in some trouble, it seems to me."

And that "right thing" echoes the sentiments of the Gordie Foundation. Its motto? "Save a Life. Make the Call." Gordie never got that call. Through The Gordie Foundation, Michael Lanahan has made it his goal to prevent other kids from falling into his son's fate.

"My real concern is people drinking too much in a short period of time," Lanahan said. "But the overall point is calling for help. The guy who was last with Gordie and went home instead of realizing Gordie was in trouble, and then came back and found him dead the next day, was living with something he's going to live with all his life."

Your legs just drop out from under you. You can't believe it. You want to get to the hospital to help him. No, he's not gone. You just can't believe it. You just talked to him the day before. You want a second chance. Let me do it different, let me help him. It's like your life's gone before your eyes. I can't believe we lost him. — MICHAEL LANAHAN

more info

- View Gordie's website at gordie.org.
- To read the original article which appeared in the November 2004 ReMarker, go to www.smtexas.org/common/publications

We asked members of the Class of 2012 to predict their lives in 10 years. Click to hear them.

FIGURE 5.6 *The Foothill Dragon Press*, Foothill Technology High School, Ventura, Calif., Aug. 3, 2012. Screengrab – http://foothilldragonpress.org/index.php?option=com_content&view=category&layout=blog&id=112&Itemid=253. Reprinted with permission.

The Foothill Dragon Press demonstrates how a feature story can be told with an interactive multimedia approach. The website gave the listener the choice of ten seniors' stories in their own words. The audio clips featured the seniors' visions of lives as everything from a cardiothoracic surgeon to a Peace Corps volunteer to a statistician.

SUMMARY

- The feature story, a form of journalistic writing that goes beyond the news in depth and detail, is a staple writing form for high school newspapers and yearbooks. Unlike the news story, the story structure is not inverted pyramid, but varies in its organization and narrative flow while usually including a lead, body and conclusion. Primary forms of feature stories are the profile, human interest feature and informative feature story.

- The feature story depends heavily upon strong reporting where the reporter uses all five senses. A strong writing voice in a feature comes from the writer's use of pacing, precise word choice, details, examples and dialogue.

- The feature lead is often an example, an anecdote or a statement that sets the tone for the story. The lead is followed by a wrap graph, also called a nut or focus graph, which helps the reader understand the focus of the story. The conclusion is an important part of the feature story, which reinforces the main theme for the reader usually using an anecdote, quote or simple statement, but avoiding clichés and editorializing.

KEY TERMS

community feature story

human interest story

profile

detail

informative feature story

question leads

dialogue

interpretive feature

symposium interview
features

feature story

pace

historical feature story

precise writing

voice

EXERCISES

1   Print or clip five different types of feature stories from school and daily newspapers or print out from websites. Mount them on 8½ × 11 paper and label each. Beneath each type explain in detail what makes it a feature rather than a straight news story and what some of its best characteristics are.

2   Use the following categories to list possible feature story ideas:

   (a) List five topics for informative features. Indicate possible sources for each story. Try to have several that are related to timely events.

   (b) List five persons who would be excellent subjects for personality sketches or profiles. Opposite each indicate the reasons why each would generate an interesting story.

3   Read and evaluate five different leads from a daily newspaper or from a media website. Rank them. Which one does the best job of grabbing your attention? Why? Why do you think the writer choose this particular lead?

4   In small groups create a list of ten topics or issues that interest students most. Now develop at least two feature stories for each item on the list. Consider all types of features: profile, informative, human interest, community, interpretive, historical and symposium.

5   Find a major news story in a daily newspaper that has affected high school students. Create a list of possible feature story ideas based on the news story.

6   Interview a classmate on one of the following experiences and write a feature story:

   (a) first or worst date

   (b) scariest accident you've been in

   (c) the time your parent embarrassed you the most

   (d) best holiday memory

   (e) best or worst job experience.

7   Pick a subject, such as the preparations for a student council bake sale or the antics of the school mascot at a basketball game, and observe. Use all your senses. Write down as much information as you can. Be precise and accurate. Based on your observations, decide what your focus would be for a story and circle the relevant details or dialogue to go with that focus.

8   Write a feature story based on the following information:

The Student Council sponsor Amanda Webb is in her first year of teaching at your school. She attended Eastfield Community College and then transferred to University of North Texas. Five years ago at Eastfield, a friend of a friend asked her if she would like to join the rodeo club. The friend's friend was the club president.

   She started going to the practice arena to learn how to ride a horse. She started riding with rodeo team members. Then one day, the president asked her to try chute dogging, a form of steer wrestling. She went on to become the first female to steer wrestle for Eastfield. She still competes in rodeos on weekends. She's won several competitions that have earned her $750 in prize money, T-shirts and ribbons. Each competition during the rodeo season, she earns points for the grand prize, which is a belt buckle. She's never won a buckle. To pay for riding time, she has worked at the ranch repairing barbed wire fences, painting barns and repairing the rodeo arena's concession stand.

Quotes from Amanda Webb interview

"I guess I've always wanted to do it. Ever since I was a little girl I've wanted to own horses. It's hard to explain; this is just something I love to do. The first time I went to the ranch, I rode a 20-year-old horse named Honey. He only walked in circles. I got bored pretty quickly. I was moved up to a horse named Star, and I would walk, trot and lope in circles with it. I was trying to teach the horse rein control. Walking in circles is good practice. I had to work at the ranch to get more riding time. Whatever it takes to be around the sport, I'll do. You can't be afraid of getting a little dirty. I've gotten manure in my hair so many times, I can't even count."

[On chute dogging:] It's actually easier for me than it is for some guys because of my size. I'm small enough to get up under the bigger steers, and I can use leverage to swing those big son-of-a-guns down. I'll battle one after the other. I'm not afraid of them. I've never been afraid of much. When I was four or five, my mom said I'd walk right up to a barking Doberman.

"Anything a guy could do, I wanted to do. Anyway, it's the big [steers] that are easy. The little ones are the ones that will charge after you."

(The money and the scholarships don't mean anything. You compete for the buckle. It's all about the buckle).

Details

Webb is also the art teacher. She grew up in the city. She's 22. She's 5 foot 1 inch tall and 100 pounds. She wears cowboy boots with dresses to school. The average weight of a steer she wrestles is 600 pounds. She has a scrapbook with her ribbons in it. The scrapbook is decorated with cowhide drawings, cutout horses and cowboy hats made from construction paper. Her favorite song is Garth Brooks' *Rodeo*.

She has to drive 45 minutes to get to the rodeo arena.

In the chute dogging event, the competitor starts in the chute with the steer. The competitor grabs hold of the steer's horns. The gate opens. The steer is prodded with an electric device so that it runs out onto the floor of the arena. The wrestler's goal is to pull the steer off all four feet. The person who does so in the fastest time wins. The average time is five seconds.

9 Write a feature based on the following information:

A group of Key Club members are helping teach kindergarten students. The students are from Virginia Bodine Elementary School. The Key Club is an all-boys club from the junior and senior classes. The main activity the members participate in is reading to a class of 16 kindergartners. They go to Miss Kate Mider's class every Wednesday. Key Club sponsor Mary Tuttle said she has had 21 students who participate. She said four students volunteer to read more regularly than the others. Those who read regularly are Junior James Rogers, Senior Sam Jones, Junior Alan Ricks and Senior Alex Johnson. Some of the books that Key Club members have read in Mider's class are *Green Eggs and Ham*, *Fox and Socks*, *The Foot Book*, *The Armadillo from Amarillo*, *Chicka Chicka Boom Boom* and *The Very Hungry Caterpillar*.

Quotes

From sponsor Mary Tuttle

I have two children. I thought of doing this after James (Rogers) came over this summer for a meeting and started reading a book to my youngest. He was great, and she loved him. So I called Kate and asked what she thought of the idea. She loved it, so we started about the second week of school. It's great for everyone. The kids will sit and listen to every word. These boys are role models for these kids. Afterwards, they want to talk to them. I saw little Kemble showing his football cards to James the other day. Then he wanted to talk about his dog. They hang on these boys' legs and climb all over them.

I think it builds self-esteem for my Key Club kids because they see how much others care about them.

From Kindergarten teacher Kate Mider

These boys are great. When they started, they were a little timid. Then they got into it. My kids' favorite is *Green Eggs and Ham*. James decided one day he'd dress up to read it. He wore a long red and white hat and a red bow tie.

He's quite an actor. He's created different voices for Sam-l-am and for the guy he's chasing around. He's great at bringing the book to life.

Then there's Sam. Here's this guy who's 6 foot 8 inches tall and about 230 pounds, lying stretched out on the floor reading *The Very Hungry Caterpillar*. He may be three times their size, but he really relates to these kids. He gets down on their level, literally and figuratively.

From Junior James Roger

I just remember how my mom used to act out all the books when I was little. I had this Dr. Seuss outfit that I wore for Halloween, so I thought the kids would get a kick out of it. Then I bought these toy eggs and ham and painted them green. We just have a good time. I was surprised that they'd really sit and listen to me. Their eyes get so big when you read to them. I could really see myself as a teacher. It's just neat to think I could help them want to read. They just hang on every word even though they've heard the same book at least five times. Now I'm really getting to know some of the kids. Every time I go, Kemble and I have to talk about football cards. I don't have any brothers or sisters, so it's pretty cool to kind of have a little brother.

From Senior Sam Jones

At first, I was like, naw man. Then I did it once, and it was cool. The first time I did it, I stood up and read. They had to crane their necks to look up to me. So next time I laid down on the floor with them. I think they liked that. It put me on their level. They'll even climb on my back when I read.

I go home and read to my brother now. I'll finish my homework, then I'll sit him on the couch with me, and we'll read. He's only three, but Miss Mider said I should point at the words as I read them and he'll learn to read that way.

James is crazy, but he has great voices for the characters. I get to read *The Polar Express* next week, so I'm going to wear my big coat and hat.

From Kindergartner Kemble White

I like when they come to read. They're funny. I like it when James dresses up. He's crazy.

Details

Miss Mider has been teaching two years.

- Senior Sam Jones is a starting center for the basketball team.

- Junior James Rogers is the president of the Key Club. His mother is a teacher at Martin Luther King, Jr. High School.

- Key Club sponsor Mary Tuttle also teaches English I. Her two children are Heather, five, and Thomas, seven.

- Miss Mider's room is decorated like a rain forest, with lots of green leaves stapled to the ceiling and plants of all kinds sitting around the room. She decorated it like this because she's teaching about wild animals. She lays out blue gym mats for the kids to sit on during the reading time.

- The first book that James read to the Tuttle children was Dr. Seuss' *Fox and Socks*.

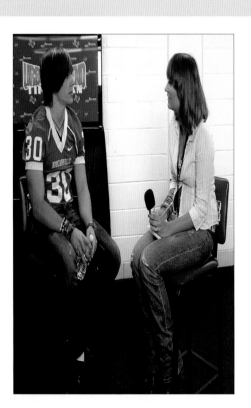

SPORTSWRITING

> *Once I told myself to think of the camera as a friend who hasn't seen the game and it was my job to tell him what happened, then I think I became a more effective broadcaster. Luckily, sports lends itself to a more relaxed approach and I try to take advantage of that when possible. Bottom line, we are storytellers. To be a good one, quality writing must be included; without clichés. Whether it's television, newspaper or blogs there is no substitute for effective writing.*

Robert Flores, ESPN Anchor

LEARNING OBJECTIVES
After completing this chapter you will be able to:

- develop a strong sports story idea

- research, interview for and write a sports story

- explore the different types of sports coverage and choose the one most appropriate for your medium and deadline

- plan and design a sports webcast.

HIS CLIP-ON TIE BARELY COVERED the fourth button on his shirt. Still, the large figure known only as "Coach" standing before the young reporter was rather intimidating. Coach leaned across the desk and pounded his fist on the reporter's spiral notebook, emphasizing each word. "You can quote me on this. We … are … going … to … give … it … one hundred … ten … percent."

Hearing the conviction in the coach's voice, the reporter was sure he had a zinger quote. Suckered. Just like that, the reporter has just allowed another cliché to live on in scholastic journalism sports reporting.

The ultimate goal in sportswriting is to give the reader a fresh look at the hard work, strategies, struggles and triumphs of athletes, and the impact of athletics on the community and society. A reporter who conducts a two-minute interview where the only question is: "How do you feel about the upcoming game?" can expect coaches and players to spit out a series of tired clichés: "I think if we just play our game, we'll be okay." "We had better come to play today."

Reporting that stops at the surface level of a sport won't produce engaging stories.

WRITING THE SPORTS STORY

As with hard news and features, developing a clear focus is the crucial first step in writing a good sports story. Sometimes the editor will assign this focus and other times this process will be up to the reporter. Either way, the focus must be specific. If an editor gives a broad assignment such as "Go write a story about soccer," the writer will have to do research to find a specific angle.

HELPFUL TIPS

Sports reporting tips

In developing a story that goes beyond surface clichés to capture the real spirit of a sport, reporters should consider the following strategies:

→ Read magazine and newspaper stories about the sport or the team to understand what approaches have become trite or overdone.

→ Spend time talking to coaches and players before the season starts and before game days. In a more relaxed setting, the reporter will find out what kind of a game or performance the coach expects and what parts of the game his or her team or athlete is working on during longer practices.

→ Remember that sports are not merely play-by-play recaps and statistics; sports stories are about people.

→ Understand that sports stories should ask *why*. Why was the team more motivated in the second half? Why has the softball team started hitting home runs in the last three games? Why did the figure skater change the last jump she had planned?

→ Look beyond the action on the field for stories. See the stories of relationships off the field that lead to results on the field. A team manager with Asperger's syndrome who motivates players through his intense focus on statistics or the offensive line whose barbecues help build the team's camaraderie off the field – these are both promising off-field story ideas.

→ Understand that winning teams are not the only ones worth covering. A lacrosse team that hopes to win its first game in two years can be a fascinating story of perseverance.

→ Recognize that sport is always more than the game. Professional publications and websites often cover the business and labor side of sports, from contract battles to pay caps. High school newspapers often end up covering the hard news side of sports, as players face pressures to use performance-enhancing drugs or receive illegal payments from college alumni.

WORDS of WISDOM

A good journalist must develop the confidence to be comfortable in situations where everyone else is uncomfortable. Stories that make an impact often make sources, editors and readers uncomfortable. Good journalism is not a popularity contest.

Jason Whitlock, Fox Sports News

A good reporter may, in talking to the team captain, find out about the pressure the team is facing as they go into the playoffs with a 10-game winning streak, and decide to focus on that. With a clear objective for the story, the writer will be able to proceed more effectively through the interviewing and writing process.

Later in this chapter, we cover five different sports story types. In nearly every type of sports story, the reporter will need to use both statistics and sports terminology. Both deserve some special discussion.

Sports slang and sports language

The drama of sports should speak for itself. Using slang terms, jargon, hyperbole and forced language will only distract from the event being reported. Instead of writing, "The 145-pound blazer rumbled through the giant gridders of the goal line for sweet six," the writer should simply focus on a good factual description using clear sports language: "Senior running back Robert Belsher leapt over from the one-yard line for the game-tying touchdown."

HELPFUL TIPS

Know the game

A good sports reporter must be a student of the game. A reporter must:

→ Know sports well: rules, strategy, team and player records and the like. A good reporter will become well informed by reading up on the sport being covered, including rule-books, and talking to coaches, players and managers. He or she should not rely on general prior knowledge.

→ Follow team and participatory sports during practice. It is not enough to secure information secondhand from coaches, players or spectators.

→ Work at detecting the strengths and weaknesses of a team or an individual.

→ Get to know coaches and players as well as possible and interview them.

→ Refrain from attending games or meets as a cheering spectator. The writer has the responsibility to interpret difficult plays and decisions for fans too excited to notice exactly what happened.

→ Observe accurately.

→ Be able to take notes quickly without losing the sequence of play.

→ Be fair and unbiased, even though privately rooting for a particular team or individual.

→ Support all opinions with facts. Although a sports-writer has more freedom than many other news writers, he or she must not make comments without supporting them, even in byline stories.

→ Find a voice that is both informal and original.

Sports clichés

This list is a sampling of the many trite statements and phrases that a sports reporter should avoid quoting. Just because a coach or player said these things does not mean a reporter should use them.

- "We have to play as a team."

- "We have a lot of potential."

- "I think we're going all the way to state."

- "We're going to have to take it one game at a time."

- "We've got our backs against the wall."

- "The best defense is a good offense."

- "It's a rebuilding year for us."

- "Things just didn't go our way."

- "These guys played with a lot of heart."

- "We need to get back on track."

- "The ball just didn't bounce our way tonight."

So how does a sports reporter know the difference between sports jargon and the standard specialized language of a sport? The sports stylebook of the University of Missouri's teaching newspaper, the *Columbia Missourian*, offers the following advice:

> If a word or phrase is so obviously silly that nobody would say it, don't write it. Nobody says "grid mentor" when he or she actually means "football coach," or "cage tiff" when he or she means "basketball game."
>
> Try for interesting or colorful angles in your leads. But do not cram too many images into one lead or story. It can make things confusing for your readers. Adjectives and adverbs crowd stories and leads. Stick to good verbs and genuine description where possible. Use slang sparingly.
>
> A sportswriter should use the specialized writing of the sport that the average reader understands without getting too technical. You're not expected to explain what a jumper is in basketball but you might want a simpler explanation for "swing backside on a low post pick."

Developing a sports story with statistics

Sports are about people; statistics and records are just measures of people. Statistics are an important way to develop a sports story – but they shouldn't overwhelm the reader.

Tips for using sports stats

When using sports statistics, the reporter should:

→ Avoid long lists of scores. More than three numbers in a sentence or a paragraph is typically too many.

→ Choose only those statistics that warrant highlighting, or that develop the focus of the story. Other relevant statistics can be used in an accompanying sidebar or sports briefs section.

→ Double-check accuracy. A reporter should make sure that scores add up and question numbers that don't sound logical or reasonable.

→ Gather historical statistics from old newspaper archives and yearbooks. Some coaches keep files on school records or old scorebooks.

→ Package statistics not used in a story. Sidebars and separate coverage are useful here and will discussed later.

Rather than saying that a running back "had a good day," the writer should demonstrate it with specifics: "He ran for a season-high 220 yards and two touchdowns." The reader now understands how good the player's performance was. The sportswriter needs to know that numbers are relative, meaning that statistics should always be put in the proper context or perspective. If the goalie had 28 saves, an average reader may not realize the significance of the achievement – unless the writer adds that her save total is the second-highest in the district.

Perspective is also important in discussing a team's record. If a team is 10–2 for the season, the reader should be informed that the two losses were against the third- and fourth-ranked teams in the state.

Test your knowledge

Give tips for using statistics in sports stories

TYPES OF SPORTS STORIES

Multiple 24-hour sports networks, rows and rows of sports magazines, team and fan websites and more – sports fans have ample opportunities to stay connected and still can't seem to get enough. The types of sports stories range widely to give readers sports of all kinds at all times. Whether you're updating a news website daily or publishing a student magazine every other month or producing a school yearbook, the variety of story types will give you ideas to keep sports fans of all types and interest levels informed.

Advance story

"How do you think the team is going to do tonight?"

Whether a team is 0–11 or playing for the school's first state championship, people will ask the same question. This kind of public curiosity helps explain why there are 10 hours of pregame coverage for the Super Bowl.

The **advance story** satisfies public curiosity and gives insight into the upcoming game, providing as many specifics as possible. It should always answer the 5 W's and H. The high school advance story can also mirror professional sports journalism where the advance story is often told within a feature story. The advance feature story chooses one specific aspect of the upcoming game to highlight. The story is told through strong quotes, description and anecdotes. For example, the advance story may be about the possibility of a coach getting his 300th win. Another advance story may focus on how the team will replace three injured star players. The game's significance and key matchups can be primary feature focus (see Figure 6.1). In a feature format, the basic 5 W's and H will appear in the nut graph of the story that comes after the lead.

For news websites, the advance story should appear the day of (or the day before) the game, in order to keep the reader informed about late developments. The website sports reporter should explain what the impact of last week's game might be on tonight's game. With the ability

---

Quick Exercise

From the following coach's quotes, write down those that would be good to use, then explain why.

I'd say with three games left we're still in the mix. We're really on a roll. We're peaking at the right time. But in the next three games, we had better put up 85 points in each of them because these next three teams have the three best offenses in the state. We had better be prepared. It's do or die time for us. If Jay has one down game, they'll all be turning in their jerseys and heading to track.

Coach John McKinney

FIGURE 6.1 "Wrestlers hope nine advance to districts," by Michaela Marincic, *Blue & Gold*, Findlay High School, Findlay, Ohio, January, 2010, p. 8. Reprinted with permission.

This *Blue & Gold* story looks ahead at the wrestling team's major meet for the season. Sports writers must make sure to know a story's publication date and choose to cover important upcoming games to give the readers a timely angle. In this story, the writer hones in on the team's expectations and key opponent in the next district match.

Wrestlers hope nine advance to districts

■ By Michaela Marincic

With the Greater Buckeye Conference (GBC) disbanding after next year, the varsity wrestling team wants to hold on to its league title to the end.

Winning the GBC championships last year gave the team and coach Ben Kirian confidence that they can repeat.

"It (maintaining title) is a big goal of our team," Kirian said. "It'd be cool to win this year and next year and be the last GBC champs. We have a good chance to win it again, because we have the strongest team."

Sum it up

4-12
overall record

The wrestlers overcame setbacks due to incorrect body weight and poor health, and are entering the league tourney at their best.

"In the beginning of the season, we had little things like minor injuries and people not at the right weight," senior Michael Alexander said. "But now we are in the right weight classes and we have the strongest line-up possible, ready to compete at full strength."

This strength can carry them into sectionals on February 20, where they will face defending champions, Oregon Clay.

"Oregon Clay is the team that keeps beating us and they are very good," Kirian said. "They're deep top to bottom and very good in the lightweights, whereas traditionally we haven't been as strong in the lightweights, so that gives them the edge over us."

While Oregon Clay will be tough, Kirian

150 Senior Michael Alexander had his 150th win against St. Francis Wednesday night, the most by any wrestler at Findlay. The team beat the Knights, 48-28.

photo by Taylor McGonnell

hopes to send many individuals to districts.

"Last year we had nine (wrestlers) qualify for districts, and this year we could go at least nine again," Kirian said. "Our kids know they have the ability to win."

Alexander not only hopes to win districts, he wants to be the state champ.

"I can definitely qualify for state," Alexander said. "My big goal is to go out and win state. I've been wrestling for a long time, and my brother won state his senior year, so that's been my goal since I started wrestling at the high school."

Test your knowledge

Define "advance story."

to update and post every day or hour, online writers can keep the reader abreast of daily changes – such as injury updates or playoff venue changes that may affect the game. Online writers must keep up with the news from other teams in the league or district, since the results of their games can affect playoff pairings.

Owing to infrequent publication schedules and early deadlines, school newspapers may face special challenges with a sports advance story. When story ideas are being passed out, the sports editor or writer should carefully consider the date of publication. Games played after the deadline date but before the publication date can often change the significance of the game that is the subject of the advance story. Interviewing for the newspaper advance story may require coaches and players from competing teams to think about a game that is three weeks away. These individuals may be reluctant to think ahead of the next night's game. Clarifying the release date of the story may help allay fears about distracting readers from the team's current focus.

Lacrosse team reaches new heights with few losses

Tucker Whitley
Sports Editor

They have the highest goals per game average in Michigan. They have the fewest goals scored upon them.

Most importantly, though, the mens varsity lacrosse team has only lost one game, and they plan on keeping it that way, according to junior Mike Spuller.

With a 16-1 record, the team has only experienced two close games, the first being a 13-12 double overtime win against Saline, and the second a 10-6 loss against Pioneer.

The lacrosse team is ranked 17th in the state. There is some controversy to this though, as other teams are ahead of Dexter that have more than one loss.

"At first, it's not really fair, but then again our schedule isn't the hardest," Spuller said. "We have played some hard teams and stuck with them though. Beating a ranked Saline team and sticking with Pioneer really says a lot."

Ann Arbor Pioneer is ranked eighth in the state.

Senior midfielder Andrew Erber had a positive attitude towards the 17 ranking, however. He said, "I think it's pretty darn good for a second year team."

The team has lost once, and has a lot to be proud of, Spuller said.

"We are doing great, as we have only lost one game," he said. "We are doing a lot better than last year, and that is because the team itself is really strong together."

Coach Brian Callaghan said his team's success is not more than he expected, but he is impressed.

He said, "I go into every season with no preconceived expectations other than that the players play hard. To say that I anticipated the success would not be true. This team has worked really hard, and it has translated to the outcomes of the games."

It's not only the offense that gets the job done either. It's also the play of the defense and senior goalie Carl Baker.

Baker leads Michigan in fewest goals per game, with a 1.16 per game mark.

Spuller said another reason for the team's success is the discipline. "We have tough practices that usually last about three to three and a half hours," he said. "We end at about 7 o'clock each and every day. We will warm up, shoot a lot and we will end with live drilling with the defense."

Spuller also said that he has a lot of respect for his coach as does everyone else on the team.

"To us, his name is Coach Callaghan, and he's a great coach," Spuller said. "He comes from out east, and he has a lot of experience with lacrosse. He motivates us all really well. This is because he is an ex-Marine, as well as an ex-cop. He intimidates us, and that's a good thing."

Callaghan agreed that discipline is important. He said, "One of the foundations that I base my coaching on is discipline. Not only on the field, but in the class room and in the social life."

Erber agrees. "He sure knows how to keep his players in line," he said.

Lacrosse is often called the fastest sport on two feet, and that is just what Spuller likes about the sport, that and lacrosse is a combination of almost every sport. Spuller said that he loves everything about it.

"To me, it seems like a mixture of every sport," he said. "It combines every aspect that I have loved in those other sports."

With this start, a run at the state playoffs seemed very likely to Erber.

He said, "If we can get out of our region, we can win the whole thing."

Though lacrosse is a team sport, it requires individual accomplishment as well. Two players have signed their college letters of intent, and many other players have been recruited by colleges. Erber signed with Virginia Military, and senior Corey Diamond signed with Albion.

"U of D Mercy has scouted me, but I plan on being more heavily looked at out east during the summer, when we go to camps," Spuller said. "I have always wanted to play college lacrosse, and it would be great to go onto the next level. Though I want to perform well, it would be nice to see the team itself win states this year."

When talking about his scoring ability, he said, "I have a good shot, and I'm able to help out the team by scoring a couple of goals every game. This is because I practice shooting for at least three hours every day."

Moving towards the goal: Junior Mike Spuller looks to make a pass as he moves down the field. Spuller has been scouted by colleges such as U of D Mercy.

Photo by Merve Öztroprak

FIGURE 6.2 "Lacrosse team reaches new heights with few losses," by Tucker Whitley, sports editor, *The Squall*, May 25, 2011, Dexter High School, Dexter, Mich. Reprinted with permission.

Newspapers who don't publish frequently will find the trend story a good way to cover their sports teams. In this lacrosse story, the newspaper covered the team's 16-1 winning streak. Rather than write a game-by-game recap, they chose to look into strict coaching style of their head coach and the other reasons behind the streak. Trend stories address a trend in the team's performance since the last publication date. Some publications work in the upcoming game early in the piece to create an advanced trend story.

Trend story

In the month since the last issue came out, the football team has lost 66-0, 74-28 and – in the homecoming game – 49-0. For three weeks, the area daily newspaper has run scores, and in the halls students have talked about the disappointment.

To detail every single scoring play of each losing game in your publication would be repetitive, if not downright painful. A **trend story** is not a rehashing of plays from each game, but instead covers patterns and tendencies that are apparent in the team's play since the last issue (see Figure 6.2.).

In a trend story the big question high school sports reporters should ask is, "What's gone on over the last month and why?" The answers generally come from reviewing statistics, observing games or interviewing coaches. In the losing football season described above, interviews with players and coaches may be critical to a focus on the verbal abuse the players are taking from fans for their lack of offense. The writer may include quotes from defense players who are angry because they have spent three-fourths of the game on the field. Anecdotes of players being booed by band members may be part of the story. Talking to coaches about how dejected they have become after the seven turnovers in the last three games allows you to work in statistics and show exactly how bad the situation has become.

Because high school newspapers rarely come out on a weekly or even bi-weekly basis, the trend story is a good alternative to the game story (see below). Instead of listing the team wins of the 10 basketball games played since the last issue was published, the story may look at the team's increasing use of the three-pointer to win six of the last seven games. A news website isn't as dependent upon the trend story when shorter game stories can be posted daily or weekly. However, trend stories can still find their way into the news website when staff resources don't allow for daily coverage.

The trend story, along with the sports feature (discussed below), is the preferred format for a yearbook story. Covering a high school game two weeks after it has happened is like getting a Zhu Zhu Pet the Christmas after it was hot. By the time you get the news, you've seen it, your friends have all talked about it and everyone has moved on to other things. For some student newspapers, by the time the story comes out on the football team's 66-7 romp, it's already baseball season.

COURTESY OF ALAN SASAKI

HW VS. HW: *Oliver Lowry '10 runs with the ball while Charlie Nelson '14 pursues him during an intrasquad scrimmage Friday. The game against Franklin High School was cancelled due to air quality.*

LAUSD cancels Friday night football game due to air quality

By Ashley Khakshouri

The varsity football team was forced to scrimmage against itself Friday night when the season opener game was cancelled because of concerns over the air quality in the East San Fernando Valley.

Wildfires in the La Cañada Flintridge area had caused poor air quality all week which had disrupted some practices and caused some teams to practice indoors, but the athletic department, using data from the Air Quality Management District, felt the air was safe to play in Friday night.

However, opponent Franklin was forced to forfeit.

"The Los Angeles Unified School District was not allowing any games to be played in the San Fernando Valley east of the 405 because the air quality was not healthy enough," Athletics Director Terry Barnum said.

"Franklin High School wanted to play but they were not allowed to because they are a public school and have to listen who they are governed by, the LAUSD."

Barnum said phone calls to LAUSD from Head of Upper School Harry Salamandra and President Thomas Hudnut were not answered.

"We're monitoring the air quality. We have print outs at 9 o'clock 10 o'clock and so on, that show that the air quality is moderate. Over 100 is when it becomes unhealthy. We are at 60, somewhere in that range, which is moderate which means we could have activities and for whatever reason they had different information," Barnum said. "We've been using AQMD which we've been using from the very beginning. But if the issue is students' health and air quality, it shouldn't matter public or private we are all breathing the same air. I think what this points to is the bureaucracy that is LAUSD.

That's really what is at the heart of this matter. They failed to use common sense in this case."

"I'm very disappointed that LAUSD wasn't able to take case by case," said Salamandra said.

The athletic department presented Franklin High School with the idea that they could play the game here Saturday night to give the air some time to clear.

That was something they couldn't do, Barnum said.

"They invited us to go there but we have some issues sending our kids closer to the fire in the name of health," he said. "That sounds a little contradictory on our part. How come they are allowed to play at Franklin which is closer to the fire and not here? We've been asking everyone we can that question and we have yet to get an answer."

Although Barnum did not dispute that the forfeit was unfortunate, he saw a few positives in it.

"Those guys have been killing themselves all summer to get ready for today and then today is taken away from them," Barnum said. "That's disappointing, really disappointing. But it gives us extra time to prepare for Lynwood. Lynwood tied us last year and they are a very good football team."

The athletics department cancelled all out-of-season practices and moved in-season outdoor practices indoors on Friday Aug. 28 and Monday, Aug. 31. As of Tuesday, Sept. 1, all out door practices continued, Barnum said.

Director of Sports Medicine Sandee Teruya monitors the statistics hourly to determine if practices need to be cancelled.

"It's okay for someone without any type of lung disease to practice outside. None of the athletes who have been practicing outside have had an asthma attack or felt any symptoms," Teruya said.

FIGURE 6.3 *The Chronicle*, Harvard-Westlake School, Los Angeles, Calif. Reprinted by permission of Kathleen Neumeyer.

Although most high school sports are still about fun and games, they aren't immune from issues that call for more serious coverage. In this *Chronicle* story, the writer understood that the story was not simply that the teams weren't allowed to play. Through interviews with key officials, the writer covered acceptable air quality for athletic events and the controversial decision by an urban school district.

Sports news story

Sports are a business at the professional level and have become so at the collegiate level. While some may see the high school level as unspoiled territory, monetary concerns have steadily crept into the secondary sports scene.

Student athletes face questions surrounding recruiter tactics, NCAA eligibility, performance-enhancing drug use and sports funding. These issues have taken newspaper sports coverage outside the realm of sports as "just a game." The **sports news story** is a type of story used to keep the reader informed on the latest issues tied to the sport but often beyond the field or arena. A sports news story may follow the inverted pyramid style. (See Figure 6.3 and the other suggestions in Chapter 2 on newswriting.) Reporters may also choose a news feature format (see Figure 6.4). Reporters should make sure to consider balance and objectivity, as well as libel and ethics issues when writing sports news, just as they would for other newswriting.

Game story

Without the long delay from deadline to newsprint, high school websites are giving new life to the game story. When most sports stories appeared in high school newspapers published three weeks after the actual game, a game rehash was irrelevant to the reader. Game stories are only relevant when news websites are updated regularly or when the print publication gets a very late deadline on a significant game or event. The **game story** offers significant details, game summary and highlights, and player and coach analyses on a timely basis (see Figure 6.5).

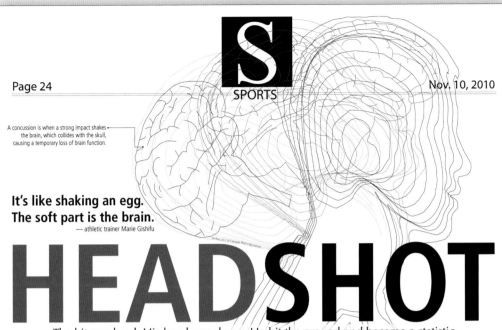

S SPORTS

A concussion is when a strong impact shakes the brain, which collides with the skull, causing a temporary loss of brain function.

It's like shaking an egg. The soft part is the brain.
— athletic trainer Marie Gishifu

HEADSHOT

The hit was hard. His head was down. He hit the ground and became a statistic.

IT TOOK JUNIOR MICHAEL WHITTAKER almost five minutes to get up after delivering a big hit in the second quarter of the football game against Cupertino High School on Oct. 23.

Once he got back to the sidelines, he felt fine—good, even. He was examined by trainers. He chatted with teammates until halftime, when he left the field with the rest of the team.

He didn't come back.

Whittaker was taken to the hospital, diagnosed with a minor concussion.

He doesn't remember the play. He doesn't remember the time he spent on the turf. The only thing he remembers about halftime is forgetting.

"Once we went to half and I was listening to the coaches talking, I was like, 'Try to remember what they are saying,'" Whittaker said. "They would say something and...10 seconds later, I would have absolutely no idea what they were saying."

That's when he knew something was wrong. An MVHS player ran from the locker room to tell trainer Marie Gishifu that Whittaker wasn't doing well. Whittaker's parents rushed back and accompanied their son to the hospital, from which he was released at about 11 p.m. that night.

It wasn't until Whittaker talked to his parents and friends later on that he learned he had been out cold on the field.

"The hardest part was not knowing what's wrong," recalled Whittaker's mom, Dee Johnson, of the ordeal, "and I just wanted to see him get up. The longer he was down and not getting up, it was like somebody was just taking your heart out of your chest and wringing it."

Gishifu knew right away that Whittaker had been seriously injured.

"[I knew] right when I saw him go for the tackle," she said. "He laid there motionless...definitely he had been concussed."

Varsity football head coach Jeff Mueller estimates that he sees one or two concussions a year at the high school level, mentioning the near-fatal injury to San Jose High Academy junior Matt Blea on Nov. 26, 2009.

Yet concussions aren't getting the most attention at the high school level; the biggest concern has been raised at college and in the pros.

"You know when [University of California, Berkeley tailback] Jahvid Best got knocked out when he scored the touchdown, and he had a spasm? They say I sort of did the same thing," Whittaker said, referring to the season-ending injury Best sustained on Nov. 7, 2009.

Best's concussion was one of many in the past few years that captured the attention of the NCAA and the NFL, both of which have seen dozens of such injuries this season. Yet there's no single solution that's agreed upon. Some suggest that equipment should be minimized, as padding and facemasks have encouraged players to be more reckless on the field.

"I think that the helmet has become a weapon, and I think that the facemask has made it even more of a weapon," Mueller said. "You can basically go head-first into somebody and your head isn't going to get hurt if it's protected by a facemask."

The NFL took a different route, cracking down on big hits with fines and suspensions. Critics claimed that the policy would ruin the physicality of the game—and, alas, more points per game (52.6) were scored in Week 7 of the 2010 season than any other week since 1983.

Mueller suggests that removing high school offenders from games could be beneficial. But even though the injury is the same for high-school players, the solutions might not be.

"I don't think we hit hard enough," Whittaker said. "If you tackle correctly, I don't think we're good enough yet to hit hard enough to knock someone out."

Therein may lie the problem—Whittaker blames himself for the concussion, claiming that the injury could have been avoided if he had not dipped his head before the hit. And in most of the pictures Johnson has taken of Whittaker, she observes that her son's head is habitually down as he tackles.

"My opinion—though I don't know a lot of technical stuff about football—is that it would've been nice if there was some kind of instruction... so if the coaches just said, 'When you tackle, don't look down, look up,' maybe that could have avoided it."

Mueller emphasizes the importance of such instruction.

"Our job is to teach our kids how to tackle properly and how to hit properly," he said. "If they don't do that right, they're going to get hurt."

Scientists and doctors also have a crucial role to play, in terms of gaining a better understanding of the injury.

"It's like shaking an egg," Gishifu said. "The soft part is the brain."

Though research centered around athletes and military veterans with brain injuries has increased, discoveries are still being made regarding the nature of concussions and their treatment. On Nov. 1, the American Academy of Neurology issued a statement "calling for any athlete who is suspected of having a concussion to be removed from play until the athlete is evaluated by a neurologist or physician with training in the evaluation and management of sports concussions."

The new standard could be most beneficial to high-school players, who do not often have access to a trained professional at the time of the injury.

"If the kids have a concussion and they go back in, and they get a second shot to the head, it could be fatal," Mueller said. "So it's up to the coaching staff and it's up to the trainers to see if somebody has a concussion."

Whittaker didn't practice the week after the injury—Gishifu explained that players have to go a week without symptoms before returning—but he was back on the field for the Nov. 6 game against Lynbrook High School. He had to bounce back from a broken arm his freshman year, so he doubts that the concussion will change his playing style.

"I'll try to keep my head up next time," Whittaker said, "but it definitely won't make me less aggressive."

And to Mueller, that's not a problem.

"Football is a violent sport," he said. "There are going to be violent hits. As long as we teach the kids how to play correctly, and we punish the people who aren't going to play correctly, hopefully there's going to be a happy medium in between."

Joseph Beyda | j.beyda@elestoque.org

HIT HARD Junior Michael Whittaker watches as his teammates practice before the Oct. 29 game against Los Gatos High School. Whittaker was rested for a week, recovering from the concussion he sustained on Oct. 23 in the game against Cupertino High School.

CONCUSSIONCOUNT

40.5% of concussed high school athletes returned to play too soon

6% of sports-related emergency department visits from 2001-2005 involved a concussion

10% of all contact sport athletes get concussions every year

86% of athletes that suffer a concussion will experience Post-Traumatic Migraines or another type of pain in the future

15.8% of concussed football players in 2007-2008 who lost consciousness returned to play the same day

According to:
Sports Concussion Institute
Center for Injury Research and Policy
Centers for Disease Control and Prevention

BIGGER IS BETTER Page 21 They may be small, but these big men can pin down wins

LIFTING FOR DUMMIES Page 22 Want to buff up for Winter Ball? Time to get your gym on

PRESEASON PAINS Page 23 Varsity boys basketball players are on a mission to condition

FIGURE 6.4 Sports news story. *El Estoque*, Monta Vista High School, Cupertino, Calif.

Sports writers aware of national sports news stories may find ideas they can localize to their own schools. This *El Estoque* story comes after changes in collegiate and pro procedures for treating concussions. A strong anecdotal lead from interviews with a player and his mother serve to develop the issues players face when they suffer such a head injury. The writer advances the story with interviews with the head coach and trainer.

FIGURE 6.5 "Swim and dive win divisional relay carnival," by Sarah Harper. *Silver Chips Online*, Montgomery Blair High School, Silver Spring, Md., Jan. 9, 2011. Reprinted with permission of *Silver Chips Online*.

News websites give high school writers the opportunity for timely game stories posted the next day or even the night of an event. In this *Silver Chips Online* story, the reporter recaps the highlights of a recent meet with times and placings. A coach interview allows readers to get his insight into the meet and the team's performance. Some publications even post live game updates via Twitter or Facebook.

But the game story is not a play-by-play recap. Instead, the game story provides insight into the main storylines behind a particular win or loss.

A good sports reporter writing a game story will look for key statistics, trends or moments to weave into the story. A particularly striking or representative statistic can provide the lead for a game story. A senior's three-run homer that changed the momentum and started a 10-run inning may be worthy of the story's primary focus.

Reporters covering high school games generally have to calculate their own game statistics. Coaches may provide statistics but not quickly enough for deadline purposes. A game story writer needs to understand the sport well enough to record and calculate statistics. For example, a football reporter should know that if a quarterback is sacked for a 10-yard loss, the yards are deducted from rushing yards even though he was trying to pass.

The game story is typically written in inverted pyramid structure. The lead can draw on the variety of leads discussed in Chapter 3 and does not have to be a **summary lead**, a lead that much

IN ACTION

Game story reporting

Whether looking for a feature angle or collecting information for a straight news story, reporters writing the game story may want to pursue the following lines of inquiry:

- Significance of the event, for example, if the league title is at stake

- Probable lineups and meaning of any lineup changes

- Records of the teams or individual competitors during the current season

- Analysis of comparative scoring records of teams

- Tradition and rivalry: how the teams stand in the won/lost figures (a graphic can be effective)

- Weather conditions: how possible changes may affect the game

- Systems of play or strategies used by teams or individuals

- Condition of players, physical and mental

- District, state or national rankings

- Individual angles, such as star players

- Coaches' statements

- Who is favored and the odds, if available

- Other specifics: crowd, cheering-section antics, new uniforms, appearance or condition of playing field.

---

like the inverted pyramid lead captures or summarizes the highlights of the game. If the sportswriter chooses a feature style lead, then the team names, score and primary significance of the game should come in the wrap graph. In whatever form, game story leads should begin with something significant about the game or match.

> After the referee at the San Jose State Event Center declared junior Maddie Kuppe's serve an ace, the Palo Alto High School's varsity volleyball team won its first ever state championship 17-15 in the fifth game of the match on Dec. 4.
> "I'm pretty sure I threw myself on the floor," Kuppe said. "I couldn't scream loud enough. It was unbelievable. It was just an indescribable feeling."
>
> *Hannah Totte,* Campanile, *Palo Alto High School, Palo Alto, Calif.*

Since the game story is not a play-by-play rehash, the story does not have to be organized chronologically. The reporter should give the reader interesting and game-changing moments first, then weave in postgame quotes from players and coaches. The quotes can give the reader insight into a second-half strategy or a record-breaking day, then move on to less important moments or points.

Possible information for a game story:

- Significance of the outcome. Was a championship at stake? Will the standings of the teams change?

- Spectacular plays. How did the last-minute fumble cost the team? How did the mid-court heave change the game's momentum?

- Comparison of the teams. How did their weights and heights compare? In what part of the game did the winners excel? What were the losers' weaknesses? Reporters should make sure to support analysis with facts or coach and player quotes.

- Individual performances. Who were the game's top athletes and how good were their performances? Did the pitcher throw 92-mile-per-hour fastballs and give up only one hit, or did the right halfback run for 230 yards and score on four runs of more than 30 yards?

- Weather conditions. Did mud, sunshine, heat, cold or wind make a difference?

Test your knowledge

Should game stories in monthly publication be play-by-play recaps? Why, or why not?

Quick Exercise

Your school team is headed to its first state championship match in girls' volleyball. Group with two other classmates and develop a plan – at least three story ideas – to cover the team and game in the following publications and time frame.

1 A news website that could change coverage every day in the week before the game.

2 A monthly newsmagazine that publishes the week after the game. (Note: you'll have to plan a week before the game not knowing if they'll win or lose.)

FIGURE 6.6 "Into the game, out of the shadows." by Jasmine Sachar and Devon Miller. Photos by Sarah Sauer and Becca Dyer. *The Marquee*, Marcus High School, Flower Mound, Texas, Sept. 24, 2010, pp. 18–19. Reprinted with permission.

Drama, emotion and struggle abound in sports. Sports can be a feature writer's paradise. In this piece, the writer mixes statistics, observations and anecdotes to let the reader see inside the world of a student-athlete who lives in the shadow of his NFL Hall of Fame father. The writer's use of strong direct quotes and narrative make a longer story compelling.

---

sports

Into the game, out of the shadows

Starting quarterback with a name the world knows strives to lead rush-inclined team and defy expectations

*story by **jasmine sachar and devon miller**
photos by **sarah sauer and becca dyer***

Deion Sanders Jr. knows what they say in the hallways.

They say he'll be a terrible quarterback. That he's too short. That he can't see squat past the six-feet-something offensive linemen. That he's cocky. That he can't complete passes. That he'll never amount to anything. That he'll never be his dad.

But now, as the stands of Standridge stadium clear and grinning families, cheerleaders and Marquettes swarm the field to greet exhausted players, Sanders' eyes glance over the scoreboard. Marcus 33, Garland 13.

It wasn't supposed to happen. The previous day, eight out of nine Dallas Morning News sports analysts had cast their vote for the Owls. Garland went 9-2 in district last year, and their quarterback Dawson Hadnot was an immovable 240 pound 6-feet-1-inch wall. Garland was supposed to crush by 12.

But then there was Sanders. He nimbly dodged blitzes, discreetly handed off to running backs Rufus Mason and Dagan Newsome, then got pinned to the turf by a pile of stocky Garland defense men mere seconds after throwing a 33-yard touchdown in the second quarter.

"Everybody in the school, everybody outside of the

school thought we were going to lose," Sanders said. "That we didn't even have a chance. We proved everybody wrong."

His dad, Deion "Neon Deion" Sanders, is an athletic megastar. He won Super Bowls with both the Cowboys and the 49ers. He played outfielder for the Yankees, the Reds, the Braves and the Giants. He has the fastest recorded 40 meter dash in the history of all NFL players and is a commentator on NFl network.

It's the shadow cast by his father that Deion's trying to outrace.

And this unexpected victory is the first step.

> **You just can't make mistakes. You can't— like all eyes are on you. You can't do anything stupid. People look up to you.**
> **DEION SANDERS JR.**

***

Moving in from Cedar Hill where he was primarily a wide receiver and special teams player, Sanders came to the program as a quarterback, a position he hasn't played since he was a freshman.

"You just can't make mistakes," Sanders said. "You can't— like all eyes are on you. You can't do anything stupid. People look up to you."

To Head Coach Bryan Erwin, Sanders moved in at the right time. The 5'7" quarterback entered the program just when career leading running back Stephan Hopkins left to play for Michigan. Sanders was fast in pads. He was elusive, he could run 40 meter in 4:55. He had "his little dance steps" according to Erwin that confused the defense and helped him run a 59 yard touchdown against Grapevine in the second quarter. He was an ideal fit for the rush-happy empire Erwin had been trying to perfect since his arrival in 2007.

"He's smiling and he's loosey goosy," Erwin said. "He's not real emotional. He's always poised and under control and I don't see any fear in his eyes."

On the field, Sanders is solemn, contemplative. He kneels to the side away from the bench, hand resting on this helmet, analyzing the defense. In the huddles, he's serious. Off the field, he's a laugh. He sits at a packed lunch table every day with other football players.

"He's one of those people that everybody loves," running back Rufus Mason said.

Recently Sanders was named the number three celebrity son playing high school football on Maxpreps.com. The school and the media, Sanders acknowledges, see him as just that, Deion Sanders' son.

"My friends, the people I hang out with, the football team, they look at me as their quarterback and their friend," Sanders said. "At first they weren't used to me, but then we got cool with each other. ... They didn't even say, 'Hey, can I have your dad's autograph?' But I'm so used to it by now, it happens everywhere I go."

***

It's Friday afternoon. The conference room of the new football office is abandoned, swivel chairs scattered, a model of a defensive play scribbled on the white board. All boys were dismissed to the locker room half an hour ago, but Sanders sits in the coach Bryan Erwin's office in a cherry red sports jacket, hunched over a cell phone on speaker. The lights are switched off.

"So Deion, what kind of relationship do you have with your father?" said a voice on the phone.

"Me and my father have a great relationship," Sanders replied.

Somewhat unsatisfied, the eager reporter from Rivals.com probes further through the speaker.

"How often do you get to talk to him?"

Sanders laughs half-heartedly. "I talk to him everyday, he's my father."

In truth, his dad, who lives about a 50 minute drive away in Prosper, comes out to almost every practice. He'll sit in the stands, he'll analyze.

On the weekends when he's at his dad's house, they bowl. They play basketball. They go to Luby's, his dad's favorite place, and then sometimes Waffle House. He insists that having an athlete dad isn't pressure. It just helps.

"Since he's good, he's going to teach me what he knows and I'll be even better," Sanders said. "Other than that just football technique, he's taught me most of all how to be a man. I'll have kids one day, so how to be a father, how to treat women, how to treat people."

Sanders watches on the sideline as the defense holds a pass-heavy Lamar offense on Sept. 10. Marcus held Lamar 35-0 until the fourth quarter when they scored, ending the game 35-7.

FIGURE 6.6 (continued)

sports

Sanders talks to junior defensive back LC Wright during the fourth quarter on the Sept. 10 away game against Grapevine. Marcus won the game 56-20.

* * *

It's been raining since 4 p.m., but Sanders sits comfortably on a brown leather couch watching the Tyler Lee vs. Euless Trinity game with his mom and uncle. Practice was rained out and he just got back from treatment. Half-empty pizza boxes cover the glass coffee table and shoes in every style and color scatter across the floor. Sanders dumps a package of parmesan on his slice of sausage and pepperoni. The lighting is low as he takes a bite, focused on the game.

"When you play football, you have to live, breathe, everything football," Sanders said. "It's not just something to do on Fridays, it's a lifestyle."

The walls of his bedroom are stark white and bare. His bed is unmade. Exactly 23 pairs of shoes line up in two rows against the wall.

"I'm really color coordinated," Sanders said. "I love matching. I will never go out of the house without matching."

A trophy sits on the ebony dresser beside Sander's bed amidst half filled water bottles and a red sports jacket --- a faded silver man with a plaque beneath him, "Deion Sanders, Defensive Player of the Year, San Francisco 49ers, 1994." It was gift from his dad but he doesn't remember from exactly when.

On his door are 19 college letters taped in rows. One from LSU, two from Iowa State, two from University of Florida, two from University of Houston, two from Oklahoma, two from Alabama and five from UCLA.

He's still not sure which school he sees himself playing for; he'd rather let them come to him. "It's just motivation," Sanders said. "I got to be doing something right."

Still, Sanders doesn't know if he's to be the football player everyone expects him to be. From out his front door, he can see the rain letting up, the sun sinking beneath a bed of thin clouds.

He's ready to step out of the shadow.

"They just compare me to my father," Sanders said. "They say 'You're never going to amount to him. You're never going to be like him.' They're actually right, I'm going to be better."

Tennis breezes past Flower Mound, still crushed by Plano West

*story by **olivia tarlton***

One word: fierce. With eight teams in the 8-5A district, this is the word that Coach Kelly Langdon uses to describe the tennis team's competition this fall.

Langdon said that Plano West would be the team's toughest rivalry. West has come home with four state titles in the past 10 years. However the team lost 13-6 to West on Saturday Sept. 18.

The team had been working had to "pick up the slack," Langdon said. Last year the top three girl's doubles players and two number one boy's doubles players graduated.

Junior Joseph Rau said the team is doing all that it can to prepare for the fall season .

"On Tuesday (Aug. 31) we had a match against Plano East (which the team won) and really focused on keeping up the enthusiasm on and off the court as well as working hard throughout the whole match and not losing any of our drive or focus."

"If the past is a predictor of the future, we've always risen to the challenge," Langdon said.

*photo by **becca dyer***

Young team sets eyes for first time on state

Freshman Sydney Brown runs in the two mile race for varsity girls on Sat. Sept. 11 at the Samuel Cross Country Invitational held in Mesquite. "It was my first varsity race, so it felt good." Brown said. Brown is one of the several key underclassmen expected to help the team reach state this year.

New district includes state power houses

*story by **alex cain***

Marcus UIL sanctioned events are facing a reputedly tough new district this year after the state's biannual realignment. District 8-5A now consists of Flower Mound, Lewisville and Hebron in addition to largely populated schools such as Allen, Plano, Plano East, and Plano West.

Every two years, the UIL committee board meets to draw out new districts according to changes in population and new school being built. There are eight schools to a district, eight districts to a region and four regions to a state which all depend on school size and location.

Having roughly 2,800 students in just their senior high schools, "the Plano schools are some of the largest in the state" Athletic Director Bryan Erwin said.

A large student population makes the cut for their UIL teams more competitive.

"I feel that this district is going to be more competitive for basketball, especially because we played Plano West in the regional championship last year and we have to play them twice this year," senior basketball player Lucas Golding said.

*design by **breyanna washington 19***

Sports feature story

The head basketball coach who coaches his three nephews and the volleyball player who plays despite the challenge of a prosthetic leg are both good sports feature story subjects. The **sports feature** is a story behind or beyond the game. The sports reporter generates the sports feature idea from the human interest angle or something unusual or surprising he finds on or off the field (see Figure 6.6.) For example, a reporter might overhear football players discussing the "black mask" award for making a big hit on the opposing team. A good sports reporter might find an interesting story in what players are doing to get the mask or a broader story on incentives coaches use to motivate players. In the cafeteria, soccer players might mention how great it will be to see the coach get her 200th win. A story on the coach

" WORDS of WISDOM

I'm not big on using the complex, sophisticated words that send readers scrambling for a thesaurus. Writers who do that are trying to show off and prove how smart they are. I want someone to be able to get through my story without stopping all the time to try to figure out what I'm saying. Plus, this is sports. Not everyone who reads your articles is a Rhodes Scholar. Again, there's nothing wrong with being clever and writing with flair, but don't overdo it. It's OK to be simple sometimes.

Jason King, ESPN.com

and her career highlights may be timely for the next issue. While sports features do not have to be timely, running them while the sport is in-season will enhance reader interest. If the story is tied to a news peg, such as the expectation of the coach's 200th win, that fact should be included in the wrap graph.

Sports features are as varied as the types of feature stories discussed in Chapter 5. Some examples of sports feature stories that have appeared in high school publications include the following:

- A player profile on a 6 foot 8 inch basketball forward who, despite having played the game for only four years, has been named to the All-State team and is being recruited by Division I colleges.
- A human interest feature story on the four-year C-team cross-country runner who has continued with the sport, based on a good attitude and desire to stay in shape, despite never moving up to a higher level team.
- A news feature story on the increasing number of student athletes whose parents hire personal trainers for advice, motivation and health information.
- A human interest feature story on a school's top golfer who, after seeing his game break down in his last two tournaments, walked away from the game.
- A human interest feature story about a group of students who coach Little League teams. The story covers why these student coaches are working with younger kids and how the coaches' advice is helping players on and off the field.

Test your knowledge

What's an example of a sports feature story?

Quick Exercise

A 16-year-old Olympic swimmer who won a silver medal returned to high school and will compete in the same league with your high school. Develop a focus, sources and questions for the story.

The organization of the sports feature story is as varied as that of other feature stories; however, the inverted pyramid form is rarely used. Sports feature development follows the same feature writing guidelines discussed in Chapter 5.

FEATURE LEADS FOR SPORTS STORIES

If the reporter isn't using the straight-news game story lead, a variety of feature lead types can be used, as discussed in Chapters 3 and 5. The following high school sports leads represent a good variety of feature lead approaches:

sports

PAGE 16

FEBRUARY 5, 2010

JUNIOR VARSITY

For many athletes, junior varsity may seem to be some sort of purgatory — the waiting period before moving up to the gloried annals of varsity athletics. Some argue, however, that there may be more benefits than deficits to sitting out the big show for another year.

VARSITY Blues

"Huddle up boys," Head Varsity Football Coach Bart Epperson said at an early August football practice while the freshmen were still on the Pecos. "Time to assign jerseys."

Epperson called all the sophomores, juniors and seniors names that were at the practice to tell them their jersey numbers. All except sophomore Carson Warnberg.

"I miss anyone?" Epperson asked.

Warnberg slowly and nervously raised his hand in the air.

After a moment of pausing, Epperson finally broke the silence. "Carson, JV dude but that's alright. You'll swing."

Warnberg, admittedly a little disheartened, went through that practice like all the other athletes, but when the freshman returned from the Pecos, he joined them on JV rather than continuing practicing with the varsity players.

"Being the only sophomore on JV hurt my pride a little bit," Warnberg said.

Epperson's intentions were not to damage or hurt Warnberg's pride, but to get him more reps and playing time so that he will eventually be a heavy contributor to varsity.

"I put him on JV for his own benefit," Epperson said. "Let's say we pulled him up because we did not want a sophomore on JV, now Carson is going to be sitting on the sidelines not getting the valuable playing time and reps. That would hurt him in the long run. On JV however, Carson got to play and practice."

Although disappointed and disheartened, Warnberg knows that Epperson made the right decision.

"But no matter what I think, Coach Epperson's decisions are the right ones," Warnberg said. "He knows more about the game and life in general than I do and I trust his judgment completely. He thought JV was the right place for me to be, so it was."

In fact, the way the athletics system is set up most sophomores should be making a JV team.

"Freshman and sophomores should expect to be on JV," Assistant Director of Athletics Josh Friesen said. "If they happen to make varsity, and they actually play, then good for them. Our intention as an athletics program is to only play ninth and tenth graders up on varsity if they are capable of and the coach intends playing them in meaningful situations at the varsity level."

But even though most coaches believe sophomores and freshman should make JV, many athletes themselves do not.

"Making JV is always a disappointment at first when you think you have a chance of making varsity," JV basketball point guard Cameron Cole said. "But it is only going to make me better, because I am gaining more experience playing JV with the ball in my hands, and am becoming a better player. However, not making JV as a junior would be a major disappointment."

According to Epperson, the prestige in making a JV team has gone down significantly over the years.

"I feel that nowadays, kids, for some reason, feel kind of like it's a slap in their face if they have to stay on JV for more than one year," Epperson said. "But, in reality it's not, if you're on JV you're getting reps and playing and just because you're not on varsity just yet, it doesn't mean you're not good enough, it just means that maybe you haven't developed as quickly as other people have."

From Friesen's perspective, to be a star on varsity, one must be a star on JV no matter how long it takes.

"Making JV is a stepping-stone for making varsity," Friesen said. "An athlete will not be a star on a varsity team if they have never been a star on previous teams. JV teams provide the opportunity for players to develop in a less stressful environment while still exposing them to the tough game situations they will face once they make the varsity team."

Most athletes want to make varsity not only for the good competition, but for the pride that comes with it.

"A lot of the joy that comes with making varsity is the pride that comes with the honor of earning a spot on a varsity team," senior Andrew Ngo said, who plays two varsity sports, volleyball and baseball, "Because there is such a large talent gap between JV and varsity."

But sometimes, even those who are really good at their respected sport made JV as a sophomore and sometimes even a junior. Friesen, who walked on to the Kansas University's varsity basketball team, played on his high school JV basketball as a sophomore and junior.

"As a junior in high school, I did not make the varsity basketball team at my high school," Friesen said. "I was initially upset because I felt I was a comparable player to several guys who did make the team. Luckily, my high school coaches saw enough potential in me to keep me around on the JV where I played all the time and was a leader of the team."

And in Friesen's senior year, his time at the JV level finally paid off.

"Those same guys who I thought I should have made the varsity over were role players on varsity and played limited minutes," Friesen said. "The following year, I had surpassed them in both skill and confidence which I gained by being a major contributor at the JV level. My role on varsity as a senior was much like my role was the previous year on JV, and so was theirs. Without playing JV as a junior, I may never have had the chance to walk-on to the basketball team in college."

Friesen was not the only coach to play JV as a sophomore. Epperson did too.

"When I was in high school at my public school," Epperson said. "I played two years on JV and that was probably the most fun for me because I knew I was not ready to move up, and I was able to succeed and play a lot."

Epperson's playing time proved to help him thrive in football as he later went on to play college ball at TCU.

Even though there is no prestige playing on a JV team, it is still important to work hard and get better so that one can contribute at the varsity level.

"I don't think there is very much prestige in playing a sub varsity sport," Friesen said. "However, one should be very honored if they put forth a lot of time and effort to accomplish the goal of making the team."

Although the glory or satisfaction may not come with making a JV team, the coaches all agree that athletes make JV for a reason—to contribute at the varsity level in the future.

"Being a part of JV means that you are a part of program with the potential of becoming a contributor at the varsity level at some time in the future," Friesen said. "It means that you are part of a group of young men who are willing to work hard every day to reach a common goal, and you do it for the love of the game, not the glory."

> **'**I feel that nowadays, kids, for some reason, feel kind of like it's a slap in their face if they have to stay on JV for more than one year. But, in reality it's not.**'**
> **HEAD FOOTBALL COACH BART EPPERSON**

JUNIOR VARSITY As is custom in Lion athletics, JV players wear uniforms passed down from their varsity counterparts.

VARSITY Befitting their status, Lion varsity athletes are always dressed in the newest uniforms from the Athletic Department

JUNIOR VARSITY story by **EVAN BERKOWITZ** staff writer, photos by **SAM MALLICK** managing editor

---

FIGURE 6.7 *ReMarker*, St. Mark's School of Texas, Dallas, Texas. Reproduced by permission of Ray Westbrook.

While high school sports sections tend to be dominated by the varsity teams, the number of students involved in freshman and JV teams should warrant coverage. *ReMarker* found a good feature story in those who don't make the varsity team. His in-depth interviews with two coaches who used their JV experience to improve enough to eventually play the sport collegiately were strong examples to develop the advantages of playing JV.

Quick Exercise

Pair with a classmate and develop sources and questions for the following story: "Senior girl has been on the cross-country C-team all four years."

They've been through thick and thin, grass that is. Seniors Tyrell Miller, Quinton Ewer, Jesse McCarren have been hunting together since they were 10 years old. It's made their friendship unparalleled to any other.

"Not many people can say their three best friends live within 100 yards of each other," McCarren said. "We're pretty lucky that way."

Alli Thorson, Century Star, *Century High School, Bismarck, N.D.*

Three dancers tower above a gaggle of black spandex, lacking the grace of the others; they are new to dance, and they can't do the splits. Dressed in their black Under Armour shirts and shorts, varsity football players middle-line backer senior Conor Byrne, center senior Joseph Jarke and left guard junior Bryce Thigpin shimmy and shake along with the rest of the Dance I.

At the end of last year, Conor realized he needed a fine arts credit. After weighing all of his options, he decided to sign up for dance.

"I looked at the options and saw that all you could do really were art classes, and I really don't like that kind of thing," Conor said. "I saw dance and how you can get a fine arts credit for the class. I heard stories about NFL football players like Herschel Walker doing ballet and thought it would be fun. My dad is the president of Ballet Austin, and he's told me about guys [working with the ballet] to train and [work on] coordination. Also I know a lot of dancers, so I thought it would be fun to see what they do. I recruited my friends – Jarke and Thigpin and anyone else who wanted to do it – that's what led us to take the class."

Lauren Nelson, Westlake Featherduster, *Westlake High School, Austin, Texas*

1:30 a.m. He was ready.

Ready for a grueling 16-mile journey that would take 14-and-a-half hours to complete. Ready for a near vertical scramble that would require him to hike 5,000 feet up. Ready to embrace a challenge that has, in the past, claimed the lives of others. And he was ready to do it alone.

Decked in a pair of Timberland hiking boots, jeans, a T-shirt and a supporting a bulging Camelback on his shoulders, junior Charlie Barnard turned his back on Longs Peak Ranger Station. A full moon illuminated the surrounding forest as Bernard began his 5,259-foot hike to the very top of Longs Peak, a Class 3 climb characterized by great steepness, total exposure to open cliff and chance of fatal injury.

Sam Kovzan, The Harbinger, *Shawnee Mission East High School, Prairie Village, Kan.*

As you can see in these leads, good reporting and storytelling is at the heart of every sports story. The techniques discussed in the chapters on news and feature writing apply in sportswriting. Review Chapters 1–3 and 5 to improve your sportswriting strategies.

Many young sports fans see high school sports reporting as a dream job. While having a zealous fan's command of a sport can be helpful, becoming a good sports reporter requires work – to get beyond the hyperbole and clichés of fandom and capture the narrative drama inherent in sports.

PACKAGED COVERAGE

Complete coverage of all sports and all levels – varsity, JV and freshmen – is a worthy goal for every high school publication. In a newspaper, sports briefs sections can help cover all the teams while allowing space for features and special events. The packaged coverage might include game scores with highlighted player performances, district standings, key matchups and area or state rankings. The creation of this type of coverage can be fun and varied. A list of scores from the last 20 years may accompany a preview story about a rival school. A graphic showing the team's game-winning scoring play can give the sports junkie something fun to study. Using a type size that is smaller than the body copy for the lists of scores or district standings can help save space and help the page editor pack more into the section. In the yearbook, a "scoreboard" page can serve as a history of the year's game scores. Packaging all-district team members, statistical leaders and quotes with the scoreboard can give the reader even more of the year's highlights.

FIGURE 6.8 *The Dart,* St. Teresa's Academy, Kansas City, Mo. Reproduced by permission of Eric Thomas.

With so many teams and games to cover, publications often create packages of recent scores, stats and briefs. *The Dart's* scoreboard design gives the readers the latest scores. The callout box adds nice depth by highlighting a game and developing it further through brief quotes. The player profile and winter review stories round a well-designed page to package a lot of information in small amount of space.

SPORTS WEBCASTING

Advances in webcasting, or broadcasting a game online, have given high school reporters opportunities to break into sports broadcasting by streaming live webcasts of games through their publication websites.

Getting started

At an entry level, a minimum of two or three staff members can begin live webcasting with a video camera and a laptop with a wired or wireless Internet connection. Staff will then need to download a free or premium version of video production software and connect to a streaming

IN ACTION

Designing a sports briefs package

Since more sports news occurs than can be covered with full stories, a box of news briefs and statistics can greatly expand a newspaper's coverage. When packaging sports briefs keep these tips in mind:

- **Create a set style**. Save time by designing the package once and using variations of the layout for the rest of the year.

- **Space is the enemy**. Avoid wasteful elements, like bullets and extra white space. Most often type effects, like bold and italic, can replace these.

- **Mix up the sports**. If not every sport can be covered, keep a good mix of freshman, JV, varsity, men's and women's news bites.

- **Use agate**. Agate type is small text used for stats and standings. By shrinking a sans serif to as small as 6–7 points and expanding the horizontal width to 110 percent, the paper can save a lot of space. An example: JOHNSON 6–12, 2 HRs, 8 RBIs, 6 RUNs.

- **Set features**. Come up with 8–15 different pre-designed features and mix and match them each publication. Some ideas include: Player of the month, top performers, division standings, quote box, injury report, team updates, interesting numbers, marquee matchups, next week's big game, strategy highlights.

---

service, which sends a broadcast feed to the Internet. The equipment required is minimal. However, the webcast itself needs producing, reporting and technical preparation, much of which should be done before the night of the game. Since equipment, technology and software evolve rapidly, the first section will focus on the fundamentals of using equipment and taking full advantage of the available resources.

To start, the broadcast will require production software to make the content look professional. For example, the program BoinxTV provides a palette of pre-made layers to select and run over the video input. This content might include the commentators' names, game statistics or an advertiser's logo.

Next, a streaming program is needed to carry the broadcast to the Internet. Popular streaming services such as Livestream or Ustream offer free trial versions, but they also offer premium accounts. Because it provides a broad bandwidth, which allows more data to flow from computer to server, an upgraded premium account will generally reduce **pixelation**, or breaking up of the webcast feed. Additionally, the premium account will allow the school to provide ad-free content viewing or ad-profiting – meaning the publication, not the streaming service, can collect the sales revenue from the ads shown before the content. Another advantage is that premium accounts provide increased interfaces; the user will be able to insert pre-recorded video, switch between cameras and overlay text, pictures and graphics.

The webcast staff

At a bare minimum, the webcasting team should include a producer, technician, videographer and announcers, both play-by-play and color commentators.

Producer
The webcast producer, similar to a newspaper editor, is the leader who organizes the staff scheduled to work the game, to ensure that they function as a team.

Technician
A technician's responsibilities are operating equipment and software during a broadcast and maintaining it beforehand. The technician should be vigilant in updating the score, inserting advertising, changing camera perspectives and starting and stopping the game clock. Before the game, the technician should direct the set-up of equipment for easy access during the broadcast and, after the broadcast, should oversee the "packing up," making sure that no equipment is left behind. A producer may often double as a technician.

Test your knowledge

List two items a sports packaged page might include.

Quick Exercise

The 50th meeting in boys' basketball against your rival school is coming up. Develop three short packaged items to cover the game.

WORDS of WISDOM

If you're involved in a sport or event, you shouldn't write about it, and avoid writing about professional sports. You can write opinion pieces about some significant event if you were a part of it, but you shouldn't write about your team. Also, leave the professional sports to those that cover them more closely than you do. Don't regurgitate information on your readers – stuff you've read from other media outlets. No bowl predictions or March madness previews. You have to understand that you're not educated enough on these topics even though you think you are.

Jeff Nardone, Grosse Pointe South High School Adviser

Videographer(s)

The videographer operates a video camera, looking for good angles and maintaining unobstructed views. The videographer should choose and set up a good base of operations, with adequate power supply and a good vantage point. (Videographers should always have extra surge protectors, extension cords, batteries and camera tripods on hand.)

Announcers/Commentators

Game Day preparation for the webcasting team should begin days before the actual game. A good play-by-play and color commentary team must understand that they can't simply go into the broadcast and wing it because they "know a lot about sports." The on-air webcasting team should follow the sports reporting tips listed earlier in this chapter and head into the game with pages and pages of information such as statistics, game strategies and roster information for both teams. Good commentators will observe practices and interview players to gather player anecdotes and team histories. One commentator should be designated as "play-by-play," describing the game as it happens for viewers, and the other as "color," adding personal analysis and insight as a compliment to the game action.

If the online staff is large, additional positions may be assigned to individuals. Otherwise the skeleton staff might use the job descriptions below to create a to-do list of tasks for a successful webcast.

Runner(s)

Whether pushing statistics to the commentators, finding key floor-level insight or setting-up equipment, a runner can play a critical role. A runner may also coordinate half-time interviews for the commentators or become a sideline reporter if the equipment is available. While this position isn't essential, the runner can certainly be helpful.

Webcasting publicist

Posters and announcements should be part of any webcasting plan. Motivated staff may even send them to the opposing schools so the grandparents, high school graduates away at college or other fans who may not be able to travel to see the game will be aware of the webcasts. Publicity can be as easy as submitting a promotional announcement to the school's secretary or emailing details to a coach so she can inform players and parents.

Equipment manager

This staff member should make sure all the microphones, switchers and cabling are set up and ready to go. The manager should check with the athletic director to be sure that press box or floor space is available for the webcast team. Another consideration in some areas is that an area TV station may have exclusive broadcasting rights, so an equipment manager might need to seek the station manager's permission for a student webcast.

Advertising sales representative

Promoting a business within a broadcast can be as simple as commentators thanking a sponsor and reciting their slogan. The advertiser's logo can also be placed unobtrusively on the output video.

Depending on equipment availability, a webcast staff might include more videographers, a spotter or statistician to assist with running statistics or player information and a sideline reporter for spot reporting.

CONCLUSION

The life and drama of high school sports, along with the sheer number of students involved, gives high school publications plenty to cover. However, publications must work to see past covering month-old games and quoting clichés to give their audience fresh insight into the athletes and games. Writers must pay attention to the timing of their coverage when defining the focus of their stories so that the readers don't simply get something they saw a week ago or heard on the morning announcements.

SUMMARY

Sports writers need to be students of the game and familiar with athletes to cover the subject accurately and clearly. They must have a clear focus in mind with each story so as to write with insight into the people and game and not merely rehash old games or individual performances.

- Sport clichés abound so the sports writer must ask follow-up questions in the interview and work hard in the writing process to avoid all trite quotes and language.

- Sports statistics are important specifics to develop a story with. However, the writer shouldn't use so many numbers that they overwhelm the reader. Remember, sports stories are about people and statistics are only measures of people.

- Sport game stories are valid when they're run in a timely fashion, such as online the day after the game or in a newspaper with a particularly late deadline. Publications without those options will use more advance and trend stories in their coverage. Sports feature and news stories can also be part of the publication's sports section. Packaged coverage gives the publication plenty of opportunities to cover a wide variety of sports and teams without devoting each a full story.

KEY TERMS

advance story	scoreboard	summary lead
game story	sports feature story	trend story
pixelation	sports news story	webcasting

EXERCISES

1   From daily newspapers, websites or sports magazines, print/clip and mount 10 examples of good sports story leads.

    Make a note of what information the writer used in the lead. Was it a particular play? A particular trend? An anecdote? Or something else? Why do you think the writer chose that focus for the lead? Was the lead written in straight news or feature style? Why did the writer choose that style?

2   Watch one of your favorite professional sports teams over a two-week period. Make note of the team trends you could cover.

3   Make a list of 10 clichéd sports quotes or phrases from your high school or community publication.

4   Clip, mount and label 10 descriptive sports quotes from your school or community newspaper or news websites. Explain why the quotes are good ones.

5   Clip, mount and label 10 examples of sports statistics that were used in stories. For each, explain why you think the writer chose to feature the statistic.

6   Write an advance story based on the following information. Your story will run the day before the game.

The Bristol High School Bandits are playing the Ten Mile Creek High School Bullfrogs in a boys' basketball game.

The game will be for the regional championship. Your school is Bristol. Bristol is 23–8 so far. Ten Mile Creek is 26–1. The teams have played each other two times this season. Ten Mile Creek is the defending state champion.

Ten Mile Creek's only loss was to the Hawthorne Bearcats, 88-86. Bristol beat the Hawthorne Bearcats 64-58.

Key players for the Bristol Bandits

Clayton Hunter–position: point guard; statistical averages: 14 points per game average, eight assists per game average; height: 5 foot 10 inches.

Johnny Miller–position: center; statistical averages: 22 points per game (best in the district), 12 rebounds per game; height: 6 foot 7 inches.

Donald Lampier – position: forward; statistical averages: 10 points per game, 9 rebounds per game; height: 6 foot 3 inches.

Key players for Ten Mile Creek Bullfrogs

Geoff Mitchell – position: forward; statistical averages: 16 points per game, 10 rebounds per game; height: 6 foot 6 inches.

James Robertson – position: center; statistical averages: 28 points per game (second best in the state), 12 rebounds per game; height: 6 foot 10 inches.

Game 1: Finals of the Spring Creek Tournament, score 85-83

Highlights: Bullfrogs' Robertson scores 35, including the last eight points of the game. Robertson hits game-winning shot with two seconds left. Bandits' Miller scores 15 points and has five shots blocked. Bandits' leading scorer is Hunter with 30, including six three-pointers.

Game 2: Finals of the Lake Bardwell Tournament, score 72-70

Highlights: Bullfrogs' Robertson scores 24 including the game-winning shot with five seconds left. Robertson also blocks six shots–all of them Miller's. Bandits' Miller scores eight points. Bandits' leading scorer is Hunter with 23, including four three-pointers.

Coaches' quotes

Bandits' head coach Buck Cargal (lifetime coaching record 299–71)

"We just have to go out and play much harder. We've been really close in two big tournaments, but this one's bigger. This could be Bristol's best chance to win a state title, and as you've seen, we're just a bucket or two away from that. We must get Robertson in foul trouble or keep him from getting second shots. You thought Godzilla was big, You thought King Kong was tough. I mean I saw *Halloween* when I was 10, and nothing is scarier than this kid on the court. He has dominated our team in both of the past two games. We will double-team to see if the rest of their team can beat us. I told our kids 'Robertson will not keep us from winning a state championship.' I'm expecting Hunter to have another big game. Hunter's on such a streak now. I'm giving him the green light in this game. He may shoot 20 three-pointers this game.

This game would mean a lot to me. Not just because it would mean our first trip to the state tournament but it could be my 300th win. I can't think of any better way to hit 300 than to beat last year's state champion."

Bullfrogs' head coach Mike Keeney (lifetime coaching record 112–30)

"We just have to go give it 110 percent. Bristol has a good team. They've pushed us to the limit every time we've played this year. We better show up to play. It's not going to be a cake walk."

Keeney on Robertson:

"He's the most dominating kid I've ever coached. He's such a quick jumper. And when you're already 6–10, it makes him a force that can control a game. He's clearly headed to a Division I school. He has been sick with the flu all week though. We hope he's well and ready to go at game time. If I have to rest him for the first half, I'll do it. We need a healthy Robertson on the floor."

Player interviews

Clayton Hunter

"I'm pumped for the game. We just know we can win tonight. We've been so close both times. Coach has said he wants me to take the game over. I felt really good after we beat Hawthorne. Ten Mile couldn't beat them. Our losses to Ten Mile were earlier in the year. I've been shooting a lot better since then. And Johnny [Miller] has been working on making the other guy foul him. I really want to give coach his 300th win too. He takes us home. He spends his whole summer opening the gym for us. The guy deserves it."

Johnny Miller

"Nah, I ain't scared of [Robertson]. The first two times we played them, I was going up too slow. I'm much better now. I get my shot off quicker now, and I have better fakes. He'll foul out this time, and then he won't be around to make those game-winning shots. Clayton will be doing that.

We'll be hyped for coach to get his 300th [win]. Both of my brothers played for him, and they told me 'you better win this one for coach.' I want to see coach get his state championship ring, too."

Additional information

Bandits' team scoring average: 80.0 points; opponent's scoring average: 54.1 points.

Bullfrogs' team scoring average: 78.0 points; opponent's scoring average: 55.0 points.

State rankings: Bullfrogs – number 1; Bandits – number 10. The Bandits are 0–6 in the last three years against the Bullfrogs.

7   **Write a yearbook sports story using the following information. The story can be a trend story with a feature angle.**

You are from Hazard Hill High School. The team mascot is the Lions. The girls' fast pitch softball team finished 19–10 for the year. It was 10–4 and finished third in the district. The team went 7–0 in the second half of district, beating every team in the district. The team opened the district schedule losing its first three games. The third place finish was the team's best ever. The team earned its first playoff berth. It lost 12-6 in bi-district to the Paradise Cougars. The team lost three starters but returned seven for the next year.

Key players: Hazard Hill finished the year with three first-team All-District players, which included freshman pitcher Jennifer Dusenberry, junior catcher Katie Mitchell and senior first baseman Karen Greening.

Dusenberry was also named Newcomer of the Year. Dusenberry pitched every game. She's 4 foot 11 inches and 100 pounds. She throws 58 miles per hour. She played for the Amateur Athletic Union team last year, and the team went to the state championship. Dusenberry struck out 10 batters in the district finale against the Tucker High School Mustangs.

Mitchell averages throwing out three people per game. She has a batting average of .376. In the district finale against Tucker High School, she threw out one base runner in the 3rd inning when the Lions led 2-1. In the top of the 7th inning, she hit a home run, giving the team a 3-2 lead. Then in the bottom half of the 7th and final inning, she threw out another base runner at second and blocked the plate getting the final out. The Lions won 3-2. The win meant the Lions would go to the playoffs.

Greening finished with a .340 batting average. A team captain, she hit three game-winning home runs in the first three games of the team's district win streak.

Player and coach quotes

Head coach James Rogers

[On Dusenberry]: "She's so tiny you would think a big gust of wind would blow her into the outfield. And off the field she's a clown. Those two different kinds of rainbow socks she wears are her trademark. Plus she loves to talk. You can put her in the corner, and she'll talk to the wall. But that's what the other players came to like about her. On the field, though, she takes care of business. She hasn't played long enough to be flashy and flamboyant yet. She doesn't pump her fist when she strikes out someone. She's all business. She's in control. She tells everyone where to line up. If she's going to throw a fastball, she'll move the second baseman to the left and the shortstop to the right because she knows the ball will come directly to them."

"The first game she had to prove herself. We had an honorable mention all-district pitcher coming back. The girls came to me and said, 'Why is this kid up here? Why is she on varsity?' Then she struck out 10 batters, and they finally realized she belonged."

[On Mitchell]: "She single-handedly got us into the playoffs. What an incredible game. She's the real leader of the team. She helped make Dusenberry a part of the team when others didn't want to give her a chance. She makes plays that you don't think she can make. She seems to have a knack for knowing when runners are going to go. Then if they're trying to score, she will not give up the plate."

[On the win streak]: "After a poor district start, we couldn't go anywhere but up. We played good defense. We stopped making mental errors. In the first half we were throwing the ball to the wrong base, and we would step off the base before the ball even got there. We went back and started working in practice. Everyone got 100 grounders a day. Getting you used to doing the same thing over and over makes you comfortable in the game. When the ball's coming at you during the game, you've seen that over and over so you just do it naturally.

It got to where me and my family would eat, sleep and drink softball. I'd wake up, get a cup of coffee and read the paper to see how the other teams did the night before. By the week of bi-district, my wife would have to leave me messages on my cell phone just to reach me."

Jennifer Dusenberry

[On the playoff week]: "Parents brought us balloons. People were telling us how good we were. It was cool. Then, the day of the game, we were scared. No one was saying anything. We didn't understand how much attention we were going to get. We thought we were really focused on the game, but we were really worried about what color of socks we were going to wear, how our hair was going to look."

[On her play]: "No one liked me at first. After I did pretty well my first game out, they started to let me be a part of the team. Karen invited me to eat breakfast with the team. After that we all got along. I'd try to do crazy stuff just to make them laugh. We had a good time. Once we knew we could have a good time and work hard in practice, we started winning."

Katie Mitchell

"Duse made the difference for us. She's a lot of fun to have on the team. She's crazy. She'll braid her hair in little knots, wear different colors of eye shadow just to get people to laugh at practice. Then when she's on the mound, she just wants to win."

"I'll never forget that game against Tucker. I just knew I had to play my best if we were going to win. When that girl came barreling down the line, I kept telling myself, 'this is for the playoffs, this is for the playoffs.' I was looking around for someone to hug after the umpire called the girl out."

Karen Greening

"I got so tired of taking ground balls at practice, but coach said it would pay off. By the time we played Tucker, we knew we weren't going to make the same stupid mistakes that cost us the first game against them. Coach just wouldn't quit on us. You can tell he loves the game. His whole family loves the game. His son would go with him to scout. He'd sit there with his crayons and chart the hitters. His wife would bake us cookies and send them to us during the winning streak. They'd have little messages on them. One would say 'Work Hard in Practice.' Another would say 'We're Thinking about You' and 'Good Luck Tonight.'"

Additional information

Tucker High School was the district champion. Two hundred people showed at the bi-district game. At most district games about 40 people showed up. The Paradise Cougars lost the next week in area competition. They finished the season 25–6.

8 Write a news website story to be posted that night after the game, based on the following information.

Situation: The Goble High School Gobblers (3–0 in district play) took on the Nichols High School Nanny Goats (3–0 in district play) at Kevin Simpson Field. Simpson Field is the Nanny Goats home field. The game was played at 6 p.m. Weather was sunny with a slight five mph wind. Pitchers: Senior Alex Abnos pitched all seven innings for the Gobblers. Junior Tim Shedor pitched the entire game for the Nanny Goats.

Inning highlights

1st inning: Gobblers rightfielder Felix Hernandez singled.

3rd Inning: Nanny Goats first baseman Jeff Cole tripled to lead off the inning. Abnos struck out next three hitters to get out of the inning.

4th inning: Gobblers catcher Bob Martin singled.

5th inning: Nanny Goats' Cole doubled with two outs. Abnos got Nanny Goats shortstop Grant Heinlein to ground out to end the inning.

7th inning: Gobblers second baseman Chris Heady hits solo home run to open the inning. Nanny Goats shortstop Curtis Brinson singled to lead off inning. Nanny Goats Cole doubled to put baserunners at second and third. Last three Nanny Goats last three batters strike out.

Quotes

From Gobblers Head Baseball Coach Tom Lynch

"We needed this one. This puts in the district lead and it feels good."

"I couldn't believe Alex [Abnos] got us out of the jams that we were in. He had trouble with Cole, but most teams do. That kid can hit the cover off the ball. Alex got on a roll getting his curveball over in the first inning. I knew after that, it was going to be a good night."

From Gobblers Pitcher Alex Abnos

"I felt good. I was sweating it a little at the end but I knew we had a lead that I couldn't lose."

" I just get on a roll sometimes. I know it's a pressure game, but I can block that stuff out. Then it's just me and Bob [Martin] playing pitch and catch like we did in Little League."

From Gobblers third baseman Chris Heady

[On home run]: "I knew I had Shedor. He struck me out twice, but I was just ahead of that fastball the last time. I just guessed he'd go at me with it again and I got it good."

Additional information

Season records: Gobblers 12–3; Nanny Goats 14–2

Alex Abnos (4–1 on the season) threw 12 strikeouts. Tim Shedor (3–1 on the season) threw seven strikeouts.

OPINION WRITING

> *Pursue your work with gusto and passion. If you're a columnist, or an opinion writer, do your homework. Outrage will only carry you and your reader so far. Live, read, research and talk to as many real people as you can. Write thoughtfully and provocatively, with clarity and conviction. Then, when you're done, find a littler corner, read your draft out loud and see if it induces a smile, laughter, tears or rage. If so, you just might be on to something.*

James Ragland, Columnist, Dallas Morning News, *Dallas, Texas*

LEARNING OBJECTIVES After completing this chapter you will be able to:

- understand the different types of opinion writing

- brainstorm for editorial ideas

- develop and write an editorial

- investigate a variety of forms for opinion pieces

- understand basic goals and considerations of review and column writing

- explore the variety of styles employed in column and review writing.

Scholastic Journalism, Twelfth Edition. C. Dow Tate and Sherri A. Taylor.
© 2014 John Wiley & Sons, Inc. Published 2014 by John Wiley & Sons, Inc.

FROM FACEBOOK POSTS ABOUT STUDENT council elections, to blogs about girls' makeup, from *American Idol* voting to YouTube dress code rants – mass media provides teenagers with bountiful opportunities to voice opinions. The impulsive comments tagged onto an online story about banning backpacks at school have value because they give the reader a gauge of the community's views on the issue. Genuinely convincing opinion writing, however, requires that writers use the tools of informed argument.

While a news writer's role is to inform objectively, the opinion writer's purpose is to inform and persuade. Opinion stories – editorials, columns, blogs, reviews – all provide an outlet for writers to share their personal insights with the reader. The opinion writer can combine the skills of a dogged reporter, a perceptive scholar, a keen observer and passionate advocate, to bring insights to an issue, an event or the course of everyday life. An opinion writer can educate consumers, help a community grasp a complicated problem, rally citizens to an issue or publicize the perspectives of the voiceless or underrepresented.

An opinion piece is only as strong as the writer's thorough knowledge of the subject. Opinion writers who talk to multiple sources and explore multiple sides of an issue develop persuasive arguments that give readers insight. Let's return to the backpack ban scenario discussed above. Readers will only gain so much insight from one sophomore's angry, knee-jerk response to the ban. A serious opinion writer won't dismiss the girl's reaction, but might put it in a broader context of opinions and facts.

An informed opinion writer does not base her reporting and understanding of the subject to the views of one source. The writer should understand the basics about the ban by seeking the ban's creator and asking key questions. Were the facts in the story accurate? Who initiated the ban? What was the basis for it? The writer should also seek out the school security guard who can explain the difficulties of searching huge backpacks every morning to assure student safety. The assistant principal can tell the writer about how the halls get dangerously clogged by the extra bulk on the backs of nearly 1,400 students. A 102-pound honor student who struggles to lift her back-breaking load of books might offer a personal perspective on the argument over the ban. All of these insights should help inform and complicate the writer's own opinion on this subject. Whatever stance the writer now takes on the issue, the opinion piece will reflect multiple perspectives and a solid grounding in the facts.

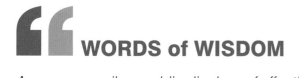

WORDS of WISDOM

Anyone can rail on public displays of affection in the hallways or school dress codes. And every staff has that guy who wants to explain how to solve the crisis in the Middle East because he's a whole lot smarter than most 18-year-olds. But what a reader of a high school publication really wants is a columnist who has the guts to be honest. A columnist who isn't afraid to give something up about herself. Who will admit to the awkwardness of trying on bras while shopping for back-to-school clothes with mom. Or admitting what it felt like to be cut from the sophomore baseball team. As readers, we know what it's like to be in an embarrassing situation, or to have to face failure or broken dreams. We find out that we're not alone. The universal theme of the column keeps us coming back each issue. And that's how a columnist builds readership. Give. Of. Yourself.

Scott Winter, Assistant Professor, College of Journalism and Mass Communications, University of Nebraska–Lincoln

opinion | letters

Forum

Dear *Spark*,

I recently was reading the Pulse Journal and I was astonished to see names of teachers in local school districts with the salaries of those teachers. This floored me because I feel that this is private information that should not be shared with the general public.

The local school districts included: Butler Tech, Fairfield City Schools, Kings Local Schools, Lakota Local Schools, Little Miami Schools, Mason Schools, Warren County Career Center and Wayne Local Schools. From all of these school districts the newspaper only listed those who earned a salary above $65,000. And out of these school districts the one with the highest paid employees was Mason City Schools. Having this private information out in the open makes me second guess becoming a teacher in one of these school districts. This information should remain confidential; information like a person's salary should not be exposed especially published in a local newspaper. This is just wrong.

I cannot believe how privacy has vanished; I guess it is just a sign of the times. One should not be able to look in the local newspaper and see a list of names and teacher salaries. Whatever happened to confidentiality and privacy?
—Olivia Lepper, East sophomore

Dear *Spark*,

I am very impressed with your publication. This is my first year as a *Spark* subscriber and I believe that each issue is better than the last.

This publication has proved that it can report on light topics, such as sleep and dieting, to very serious topics, such as school budgeting, drug use and even same-sex marriage, with a high level of maturity and sophistication.

With great informational graphics and photos to accompany these amazing stories, I am incredibly impressed with not only the publication but also with the hard work put in by

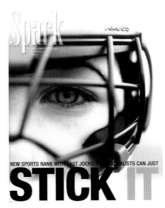

these students every day. I cannot wait for more issues of this astounding publication.
—Ian Castro, East sophomore

Dear *Spark*,

I feel that *Spark* articles are interesting to an extent, but I would target the main articles more towards my age group, considering that this is a school magazine and the main readers are students.

For example, the Nerf wars issue last year was very interesting because we have seen it happen and frankly we would like to know a little more. We want to know about stuff like how many car accidents are Lakota East students involved in every year. It would show us if there needs to be more enforcement in teaching students how to drive.

There are only a few issues that are actually worth reading and spark my interest. You do a great job on your articles each issue, but I don't feel that they spark interest in student minds.

Maybe it does for an older group, but not for the main readers.
—Dustin Miller, East junior

Dear *Spark*,

Spark needs to survey students about smoking weed again because I don't think there are many people who do not smoke weed at our school.

Also the school should bring back the regular cola because ever since they replaced it with diet cola in the vending machine I haven't been buying as many as I used to buy. Plus, they raised the price from $1 to $1.25, and I need to bring in an extra 25 cents to school for a pop, which is very inconvenient.
—Daniel Mansdorfer, East junior

GOT SOMETHING TO SAY?

The Spark, which provides an open forum for students, faculty, subscribers and community members, encourages letters to the editor. Letters can be sent to the publication at the address below or dropped off in the journalism classroom (room 118). Letters must be signed, and the staff reserves the right to edit letters for length, grammar, invasion of privacy, obscenity or potential libel. The Opinion Editors will contact letter writers for confirmation.

Spark
c/o Lakota East High School
6840 Lakota Lane
Room 118 attn: Opinion Editor
Liberty Township, OH 45044
Phone: (513) 759-8615 ext 15118
Fax: (513) 759-8633
Email: lehs.spark.opinion@gmail.com

Spark Notes

The first ever issue of *Spark* debuted on Dec. 18, 1992. It was the first medium in which Lakota High School students could express themselves.

Unlike today's vibrant and illustrative *Spark*, the first issue was black and white and contained only one graphic and 20 pages.

The origin behind *Spark*'s title is explained in this issue. The idea was that its purpose was to

spread a new idea like "wildfire" and that action is sparked through the power of the written word.

An important story in this issue was about the change in grading scale from a 10-point scale to a seven-point scale. The issue included an infographic about other school districts that had similar grading scales, including Indian Hill, Princeton and Mariemont.

FIGURE 7.1 *Spark*, Lakota East High School, Liberty Township, Ohio. Reproduced with permission of Dean Hume.

Good opinion sections encourage and offer space for reader response through letters to the editor and comments posts on websites. *Spark* provides a strong forum for public discussion of student-relevant issues. The letters include the author's name which helps assure that the letter is legitimate. Some publications require, but won't publish, a phone number with each letter to the editor to assure the validity, as well as to follow up if edits need to be made.

Printed opinions have generally been split into two categories: the editorial and the column. In most magazines or newspapers, the **column** is the opinion of one person, while the **editorial** is frequently the opinion of a group of people.

For an editorial, a group of people – usually called **the editorial board** – discusses and debates the issue to arrive at a position and an argument for it that represents the perspective of the publication. An individual writer, often the board member most passionate or knowledgeable about the subject, will craft the story, bringing drafts back to the board to see that the editorial represents their views. To reinforce the idea that the editorial represents the entire publication – and not just the writer – a byline is often omitted. However, the editorial

Test your knowledge

What's an editorial
board?

page should be clearly labeled as such, and editorials are often set off by a different format or design, to help distinguish them from neutral news reporting. In high school newspapers, where the readers may not be aware of the differences between an editorial and straight news reporting, editorials are sometimes labeled with "our opinion" or "an opinion based on 11-2 editorial board vote." (The argument against printing the vote count is that the revelation of a lack of unanimity weakens an opinion piece written to stand for the entire publication.)

An opinion column is often accompanied by a picture of the writer to help distinguish it as an opinion piece and to help the readers make a more personal connection to the columnist. In professional publications, well-known columnists are often featured on the front-page of a sports, local news or feature section. The **op-ed page**, or the page opposite the editorial, often features a number of columns as well. Sometimes editorial board members who don't agree with the other board members are given space on the op-ed page to share their opinions. The editorial or op-ed page will often feature reader feedback through letters to the editor.

DEVELOPING EDITORIAL IDEAS

The chatter in the hallway minutes before first bell is loud and angry today. The late morning freeze iced over the untreated sidewalks and parking lots. Junior Anna Petrow complains about how she fell twice as she shuffled toward the back school entrance. Senior Emma Pennington thinks she bruised her tailbone when she fell. The group is demanding answers to their questions.

"Why didn't anyone put salt on the sidewalks?"

"Why wasn't there a snow day?"

"Does anyone realize people are going to get hurt?"

This scenario should also raise an important question for the student journalist: Is there an editorial here?

Maybe. The first clue should be that kids are talking about this issue. There's certainly a news story if students are getting hurt. Often where there are news stories, there is also a potential editorial.

Like good reporters, opinion writers should start asking questions to understand their subject. The answers to these questions can become the basis for an opinion piece. In this case, basic questions might include: what is the standard procedure for salting the sidewalks during winter storms? Was it followed here or not? How are the decisions about snow-day school cancelations made? What are the criteria? If students are injured due to the ice, who would be legally liable? Answering these questions can be pursued through interviews and research.

After talking to the superintendent, the column writer may craft a story about how difficult deciding to call a snow day can be. The editorial writer should not assume that the custodians were to blame but instead talk to them directly. The custodians may explain that budget cutbacks left them without a full staff for the morning shift and they were able to cover only the front parking lots with salt in the time allotted. The editorial writer may then decide to argue for full custodian shifts, the impact of which parents and students may not have previously grasped.

Again, good editorial writers seek out multiple viewpoints and take the information back to the board before deciding on a final stance. The information may come from both the editorial writer's interviews and those of the news writers – who may use the material for an objective story. The editorial writer should be prepared to take drafts back to the board repeatedly to get feedback and assurance that the piece still reflects the board's focus and opinions.

Quick Exercise

Pair up with another
student and develop a
list of five school-
relevant issues that
could be covered in an
editorial.

ROLE OF THE EDITORIAL

As teenagers mature into adulthood, they may see themselves as having no say in society and government. The editorial can represent these "voiceless" individuals.

Editorials give individual teenagers a chance to strengthen their voices through a larger group and have it heard by their entire school community. A mature, thoughtful, well-argued editorial can go a long way toward discrediting the idea that young people should be seen and not heard.

IN ACTION

Editorial ideas

High school publications can publish editorials on a wide variety of subjects. Student editorial writers should use the following list of examples to help brainstorm ideas relevant to their own school community:

- A congratulatory editorial to the fans for changing their ways and creating a positive atmosphere while cheering for the basketball team. (This change came after the school neared state sanctions for unsportsmanlike chants against rival schools.)

- An editorial calling for the administration to get student announcements back on the P.A. system, to make sure students hear about important events. (The administration had been allowing teachers to read the announcements themselves or show them in a PowerPoint presentation.) The editorial board argued that many teachers didn't understand the new technology or forgot to read the announcements in class.

- After a year of school budget cuts in the midst of a state and national economic crisis, one paper's editorial board called

for a personal finance class as a graduation requirement, to help students understand how to handle their own finances wisely.

- After learning of a neighboring schoolwide community service efforts in which 800-plus students prepared 16,000 meals to send to Africa, renovated a homeless shelter and removed invasive plants from wetlands, the publication asked that their own school follow that lead. The editorial called for a "school-wide social action day so students can actively learn about problems in the community and work together to solve them."

- A school called for improving student–teacher communication by asking teachers to conduct anonymous class evaluations or by putting up suggestion boxes. The editorial asked that students approach teachers with respect. The editorial explained to teachers that these forms of communication would help when lectures weren't entirely clear or let the teachers know when their constant teasing was hurtful.

The editorial board should understand that they speak for the greater public good. Potentially, a board member may personally dislike a stance but may agree to the editorial when he understands the end result will be best for all the readers.

OPINION VS. FACT

All journalists should understand the basic distinction between fact and opinion. Facts are verifiable statements of truth. They are pieces of information that can be checked out and agreed upon. Opinions are subjective. They reflect personal beliefs that can vary with the individual. For example, "the sky is black" is a purported statement of fact, whether true or false. "The sky is scary," is an opinion, because it only describes a subjective experience that not everyone shares. While one person may cringe at the lightning that ripples across the sky, another may enjoy this dramatic sight of nature in action.

The pursuit of facts, through interview and research, is not only important to straight news stories, but is crucially important in opinion writing. Facts are the primary means by which the opinion writer should defend and uphold an argument.

Of course, all statements promoted as facts may not be. What some advocates call a fact, others may see differently. It is the responsibility of a good opinion writer to check each assertion of fact and assess its validity.

EDITORIAL WRITING: THE FORMULA

Editorial writing is often taught as a step-by-step formula. This formula typically includes the following:

1 **The editorial lead.** The lead usually is one of two types. One type establishes the opinion first, either directly, through a description or contrast or as the result of a brief

Quick Exercise

Identify whether each of the following sentences is a fact, an opinion or a blend of both. In sentences identified as an opinion, identify which word makes the sentence subjective.

1 The band won a school-record 10th Stradinger Lake Band Festival championship.

2 Kat's Kafe serves a tasty pecan pie for $3.

3 School board president Ebony Moore lost the election by 27 votes.

4 The offensive line played poorly in Friday's game.

5 After 20 years in the classroom, Mr. Logan Heley has become a dedicated science teacher.

summary argument. Background on the issue is often woven into the lead paragraphs or immediately follows the lead. The other type of lead starts with background on the issue first and then builds to a statement of the writer's position on the issue. Either approach can be effective, depending on the topic.

2 **Clear position statement.** This statement usually appears early in the editorial, often in or immediately after the lead. The position statement is a straightforward articulation of the editorial's focus and the author's opinion on it.

3 **The argument.** Within the body of the story, the writer makes and develops key points to defend the position statement. The points should draw on factual research and a clear explanation of the writer's reasoning.

4 **Refuting the opposition.** A good opinion writer takes time to understand all sides of an argument. In this section, the writer demonstrates an intelligent and open-minded consideration of all sides, but goes on to explain why the other views are inadequate, mistaken or misguided.

5 **Solution.** Anyone can complain. The editorial writer should take a leadership role, just as a superintendent, principal or lawmaker would, and seek to find a feasible solution to the problem or issue facing the school or community.

6 **Conclusion or call to action.** In the concluding paragraphs, the opinion writer should end with a strong summary statement of her argument. The writer may also offer readers suggestions about what action they might take with regard to the issue.

EDITORIAL LEADS

To find the editorial lead, the editorial writer should identify the heart of the opinion that speaks to the readers and engages them in the issue.

Although the purpose of the editorial differs from the news and feature story, an opinion writer can use many of the same strategies to capture the reader's interest that were discussed in earlier chapters. Opinion leads may be straightforward statements, summaries, descriptions or contrasts. What distinguishes the editorial lead is the need to quickly establish the opinion and the reasoning behind it. As in the sample leads provided below, some do so in the first sentence. Others start with background or provide context before building to a position statement.

Drinking under the age of 21 is against the law. This fact is commonly known throughout the public. But it is also widely acknowledged that for high school and college students to drink under the age is not an anomaly by any stretch of the imagination. The first provision of the two-part law states that underage drinkers in Illinois may have their driver's licenses suspended without any involvement with a car or driving: the second stipulates that sober underage drivers with intoxicated underage drivers may also suffer license suspensions. While this recently passed law attempts to fulfill the worthy goal of curbing underage drinking, it goes about that goal in an irresponsible way.

Lion, Lyons Township High School, LaGrange, Ill.

The opening lines of this lead give some background on the issue, but when the writer points out that law-breaking students aren't an anomaly, he starts to suggest his stance. The closing sentences of the opening graph provide more information and also build to a clear and thoughtful position statement.

At home, most parents don't notice what books the students are reading in their English classes because students either don't bring home their books or their parents trust the school in their choice of reading material, which they should. But when the parents do notice what their students are reading, what follows next could be potentially negative, unnecessary and waste of time.

The Update, H.H. Dow High School, Midland, Mich.

The strength of this lead lies in its direct approach to the key reasons for leaving reading list choices to the schools and English teachers.

The scene is reminiscent of Ferris Bueller's Day Off.
A name is called. Silence. No one responds.
The process repeats again and again until one lone student walks across the stage.
The Academic Breakfast took place on Thursday, April 7.
Out of a total of 461 awards that were supposed to be given out that day, only 139 students showed up to accept.
Barely 30 percent showed up at a breakfast meant to recognize and honor their achievements.
Granted, some students who were supposed to be recognized were away on a band field trip. Assuming they would have shown up, that only slightly bumps up the percentage of attendance.
Around one of every three students were invited to the awards ceremony, got a free meal and received an award.
While this is not unexpected or unusual in any way – student have been skipping this breakfast for years – it is still wrong.

Tiger Print, Blue Valley High School, Stillwell, Kan.

The descriptive lead isn't used as often with editorials as it is with feature stories. However, the opening of this piece vividly depicts the poorly-attended award ceremony that is the focus of the opinion piece. "Silence," "no one responds" and "one lone student," all build to the stunning fact that out of 461 awards, only 139 were picked up in person. The writer finishes the lead with a clear position statement: although historically the event has been poorly attended, the students' snubbing of the ceremony is wrong.

The STA and Sion rivalry has gone too far.
The fighting between the schools has leaked beyond our sports arenas and academic fields and has taken a whole new life. It is malicious. It is wrong, and frankly, it is a little hypocritical.
STA prides itself on loving "neighbor to neighbor without distinction," but did we ever consider that our neighbors might extend beyond our own campus? It is hypocritical of us to take such pride in our motto when we stop treating our own sister school with decency. And yes, they are our sister school.

The Dart, St. Teresa's Academy, Kansas City, Mo.

Other considerations for editorial writing

← Editorial writers often use "we" to remind the reader that the story speaks for the newspaper or the board.

← Good editorial writers deal with issues, not personalities. Maturity and restraint should prevail when an editorial board evaluates each issue. For example, a new school board policy should be the focus of critique – not the demeanor of the principal whose job is to enforce it.

← A thoughtful, balanced editorial tone should avoid any hint of ranting or sarcasm. A writer can be passionate about a topic but should still appeal to the reader's sense of reason and civility.

Quick Exercise

Pair up with another student and make a quick list of three points you'd want to research from one of the five school-relevant issues you identified as potential editorials in the Quick Exercise on page 168.

WWW

WEBLINKS Check out **www.markfiore.com**

This website from Pulitzer-Prize winning editorial cartoonist Mark Fiore offers up examples of animated short political cartoons that he regularly posts on the Internet.

WWW

WEBLINKS Check out http://editorialcartoonists.com

This website offers a wealth of examples of recent and award-winning editorial cartoons. Students can study the concept and art of professional and student work from across the country.

The lead offers a simple and strong opinion statement. The last line of the second paragraph outlines the main arguments. The writer's comparison of the school's motto with its students' actions builds to a particularly striking charge of hypocrisy.

DEVELOPING THE ARGUMENT

The body of the editorial provides specific reasoning, to convince the reader of the writer's stance. The editorial writer can't act like a parent who explains an opinion with, "Because I said so." The reader will want to know *why* the editorial reaches the conclusions it does. Good editorial writers explain and analyze their reasoning. They teach with background information and prove points with verifiable facts. The editorials broken down in this section provide good examples of how various high school publications have approached the craft of opinion writing.

The examples provided below draw on the structure from the "editorial formula" discussed earlier. Notice, however, how these writers use vivid and concrete language and examples, and devise creative ways to develop logical arguments. Even though editorials often follow a basic formula, the writing doesn't have to be formulaic.

EDITORIAL CARTOON

An **editorial cartoon** is any drawing, usually humorous or caricatured, that represents an opinion on a newsworthy issue. While editorial cartoons may not play the same prominent role as they did in 20th-century newspapers, such cartoons are still an effective way to deliver a direct, poignant and clear opinion to the reader.

Consider the following points when developing an editorial cartoon:

- Write out a clear opinion or perspective to be illustrated by the cartoon.
- Brainstorm with sketches of the cartoon. Don't settle for the first idea.
- Try out the cartoons on others who are unfamiliar with the issue. Ask, "What do you take from this cartoon?" or "What's the artist saying with this cartoon?" Follow up by asking, "How did you come to that conclusion?" The answers, even though they may not be the ones you want to hear, may create starting points for new and improved sketches.
- Most editorial cartoons are single-panel cartoons getting across the punch-line within a single frame, unlike the comic strip which tells a story over multiple panels.
- Editorial cartoonists often use a brief caption or speech bubble to reinforce their visual point. The caption wording must be tight and sharp. Don't settle for your first caption. Brainstorm others and pick the best.

opinion

HARVARD-WESTLAKE SCHOOL □ VOLUME XIX □ ISSUE 1 □ SEPT. 9, 2009

JOYCE KIM/CHRONICLE

Step away from the Skittles

1

W e are choosing the hard right not the easy wrong, we understand that just because we can doesn't mean we should and that character not circumstance makes the person, but this has gone too far. This is the Pixie Stick that broke the camel's back. We want our candy.

2 A ban on soda and candy in both campuses' cafeterias has been adopted for the students to learn the "self discipline necessary for a healthy lifestyle," according to a letter sent out to parents by Head of Middle School Ronnie Cazeau, Head of Upper School Harry Salamandra and Head of Athletics Audrius Barzdukas.

At Harvard-Westlake, Cazeau and Salamandra strive to "empower" and "enable" their students—or, that's how the mission statement reads. Yes, overall, the school does do an excellent job developing self-reliance in its students. We are trusted to be able to manage our time from seventh grade on during free periods and we are repeatedly told that, every year at Harvard-Westlake, our responsibilities and our academic maturity increase.

3 We are deemed old enough for free condoms at school, but not old enough to make decisions about our lunches. This new campaign against all that is sweet tosses out the idea of building self-reliance.

Apparently, we are so incapable of making the right dietary choices that all temptation must be removed.

4 In the real world, temptation is lurking all around. Working under the premise that this policy is to instill "self-discipline for a healthy lifestyle as we become citizens of the world," should we assume the world is without candy and soda, and if so, how are

we supposed to learn self-discipline when there is nothing for us to discipline against?

It is undeniable that upping the healthy options in the cafeteria is a good idea; however, eliminating all other choices implies that we cannot be trusted to make the right decisions. The new restrictions on our food choices are equivalent to putting restrictions on free periods; a student cannot be trusted to do his or her homework, so he or she must forcibly be placed in the library. It would be a rousing success to be sure.

We understand the administration's goal to promote a healthier lifestyle. However, in a school with such a rigorous curriculum, we deserve some candy and soda. Balancing an in-class essay, math quiz and an AP Biology test in one day warrants a Snickers bar and a Diet Coke.

We propose a compromise. If the school wants to help us be healthier, there should be an increase in healthy choices in the cafeterias, alongside the unhealthy choices.

Limiting our lunch choices does not breed a student ready to take on the dietary traps of the world with discipline, but will only result in sugar-starved teenagers.

As the old proverb goes, you can lead a horse to water, but if it really wants soda, you can't make it drink.

5

FIGURE 7.2 "Step Away from the Skittles" by Anna Etra. Art by Joyce Kim. *The Chronicle*, Harvard-Westlake School, Los Angeles, Calif. Reproduced by permission of Kathleen Neumeyer.

The *Chronicle* staff brings a strong voice to an editorial asking that the school lift its ban on soft drinks and candy machines in the school cafeteria. The editorial writer's strong use of specifics and developed logical points lends credibility to an argument that in some administrators' eyes could be seen as whining. Editorial writers should be keenly aware of issues that impact their readership and speak to those issues.

---

1. In this lead, the last two lines give a clever twist to the cliché, "the straw that broke the camel's back" and then proceeds to a straightforward position statement.

2. The writer follows this paragraph with a brief summary of the new ban, to inform the readers who aren't aware of what has changed. The writer's research produces the quotes from the school's mission statement, which bolster the argument that the ban contradicts the school's stated goal of empowering and enabling students in self-reliance.

3. Good editorial writers don't just present their points; they fully develop each one to enhance its power and scope. The writer's point about giving students responsibility to handle condoms but not their own lunches is a striking extension of the "contradiction" point.

4. The next paragraphs further develop the argument by pointing out that eliminating candy and soda at school won't prepare students for the real world – which is still full of tempting and unhealthy diet choices.

5. Another strength of the editorial comes with the board's proposal for a feasible compromise solution – increasing the range of healthy lunch choices without eliminating the current options. The writer follows with a clever play off another cliché to reinforce the main idea of the story.

1. With these paragraphs, the writer's able to walk the fine line of not being offensive toward the friends of the deceased students while still transitioning to the editorial's point that people need to share their inner positive thoughts and compliments with friends while they're still around to enjoy them.

2. The writer's depth of thought shows here as the writer looks beyond the clichés that students toss around meaninglessly.

3. What a wonderful twist here, tying the wording of the sign with the editorial's basic premise.

4. The conclusion, as discussed in the editorial formula above, should reinforce the argument and give a solution, or urge the reader to act when appropriate. The conclusion can have as much voice as the editorial lead, leaving the reader with a strong, lasting impression. In Figure 7.3, the writer builds wonderfully on a standard phrase "stop and smell the roses," – adding "… and tell the roses how good they smell" to echo the point that we should say how much we love others while they're still alive. The concluding sentence has a wonderful rhythm to it, reinforcing how shocking, sudden and final the death of a friend can be.

opinion

HARVARD-WESTLAKE SCHOOL □ VOLUME XIX □ ISSUE 6 □ MARCH 24, 2010

Slow down for Julia and just B

Two holes were seared into our school in the past three months. Some of us lost a classmate, some of us a friend, but we have all felt the pain of laying to rest two of our own. One of the holes is the size of a 17-year-old science whiz with the heart of gold, just as he was getting ready to graduate and take on the world. The other, a 13-year-old dancer who by all accounts spread optimism and cheerfulness wherever she went.

Brendan Kutler and Julia Siegler share little in common other than that their deaths were devastating blows to the entire school and all who knew them. We lost both Brendan and Julia in senseless cosmic spasms, the kind that make us question our faith in a rational and benevolent universe.

If there is any ray of good to emerge from these successive tragedies, it is the way in which our community rallied together to support each other. Teachers, students and parents alike were rocked by the news, whether or not they knew Brendan or Julia.

The ubiquitous double baseball caps in honor of Brendan as well as the letters of love and support that practically overflow in Julia's bedroom are a testament to the family that is Harvard-Westlake. Purple bouquets fill the corner of Sunset and Cliffwood, now covered in scrawled messages of love and mourning.

Since their deaths, we have heard more beautiful and eloquent things said about Julia and Brendan than we have ever heard anybody say about anybody. These words bring comfort to us as we grieve their loss, but we think another true tragedy is that they never got to hear what people truly thought of them while they were still alive.

All of the beautiful things people have been saying were not planted posthumously. The compliments were in our minds, but we never thought to or summoned the courage to say them until it was too late for the subjects to hear.

We always talk about the uncertainty of life in an abstract, rhetorical manner that borders on cliché. "You better enjoy life because you never know when you'll step into a street and lose it in a flash," or some variation is a phrase said so often that there is only the hollow echo of a trite, vague remark until the violent reminder of the fundamental truth that one second you could be running for a bus and the next, not. It is necessary to try to take something away from what would seem to be a senseless tragedy in order to maintain our own beliefs in a logical existence.

The only lesson we can find from the loss of Brendan and Julia, though, is that we shouldn't bottle up and hide away our feelings about others. If you have something nice to say to someone, say it while you still can.

We shouldn't have to wait until a person is gone to remember them fondly.

Too often we take for granted the idea that the people we love know that we love them. When we criticize our friends, it is rooted in our admiration and affection for them, but usually that part escapes day-to-day conversations. There would be much more happiness in the world if we just vocalized those compliments that we think but don't say.

In honor of Julia, her friends have placed street signs and made wristbands that read "Slow Down for Julia." The phrase, they said, has double meaning: drive with more caution so as to avoid another accident like the one that took Julia, but also take your time in everyday life to appreciate the beauty in the world and people around you. We should decrease the tempo of our lives as well as the speed of our cars. We should stop and smell the roses, and then tell the roses how good they smell.

So Slow Down for Julia and Smile for BK. Spread love while you still can, because you never know when, suddenly, you can't.

FIGURE 7.3 "Slow Down for Julia and Just B." Editorial by Sam Adams. *The Chronicle*, Harvard-Westlake School, Los Angeles, Calif. Reproduced by permission of Kathleen Neumeyer.

This Harvard-Westlake *Chronicle* editorial doesn't fit the stereotype of issue editorial. Following the deaths of two students, the publication worked to help students cope in a difficult time. Editorials can do more than find fault. This one helps readers find lessons and reason to move forward. Editorials can also commend projects and decisions to give positive reinforcement where needed.

FIGURE 7.4 Editorial cartoon. Gabriela Epstein, *The Spoke*, Conestoga High School, Berwyn, Pa. http://www.studentpress.org/nspa/winners/image/cartoon11_001.jpg.
    The editorial cartoon can deliver a powerful message in one panel. This cartoon acknowledges the work of several school clubs' efforts to "pull the plug" on cyberbullying at the school. As it is in this one, the art delivering the message needs to be the dominant element in the frame and should not be littered with irrelevant visual details.

Gabriela Epstein/The SPOKE

- Editorial cartoonists often create the original cartoon at twice the size it will appear in the publication – so that when the image is reduced, lines and cross-hatching will look better.

- Beginning cartoonists sometimes make the punch-line panel too small within the overall cartoon. As a good photographer crops out needless information in the photo and zooms in on the storytelling action, good cartoonists must focus on the central point of the cartoon and make that fill the panel.

COLUMNS

The **column**, an opinion piece by one person, is as varied as any form of journalistic writing. From column to column, the writer can vary the topic, the writing structure, the writing style and the tone.

    Nevertheless, there are some basic standards to which all columns should conform:

- Columns should make a point. The column shouldn't be pointless rambling. The writer should find a focus and stick to it.

- The column should speak to an audience. While column writers may give personal opinions or share personal stories to make a point, the audience must find themselves engaged with the writing. While the column writer may use the personal pronoun "I," the column should never seem like it's all about the author.

- Each column should have a beginning, a middle and an end. The same concepts in earlier discussions of lead, body and conclusion generally apply here. The lead should grab the attention of the reader and be relevant to the focus. The body should follow a logical structure and move the story along to develop the focus. The conclusion

Quick Exercise

Pick one of the following topics and sketch out a visual analogy for an editorial cartoon:

1 recklessness in the school parking lot

2 overprotective parents

3 elimination of all drink machines in the school.

IN ACTION

Column ideas

- A columnist disputed the school's right to punish a girl after she, while off-campus, sent nude photos of herself to other students.

- After not qualifying for the district orchestra, a columnist wrote about how she got through the bitterness and found lessons in her failure.

- A 16-year-old female columnist put on a weighted pregnancy simulation belly, went out in public and wrote about the reactions she faced.

- A sophomore wrote about the chaos and love he experienced growing up in a family of seven children.

- A senior wrote a letter to her freshman self, advising her about her future. The letter served as a call to freshman to be themselves for a drama-free year.

- A writer suggests discussing radical ideas such as suspending Congress for a benevolent dictator, all in an effort to rethink the current American system. The writer contends that the discussion of ideas is one of the few ways to save U.S. democracy that no longer seems to be in pursuit of liberty as it is interested in the pursuit of shopping malls and weekend music festivals.

BY KATE SKOCHDOPOLE
Senior Editor

Age is just a really scary number

Tomorrow I can buy cigarettes. I will also be able to vote, get married, join the navy, and adopt a child. As of March 12, I'm going to be a legal adult.

So why am I so scared about it?

Sometimes I feel like I'm a little Peter Pan. I've never wanted to grow up. While other kids dreamed of being adults so they could eat ice cream for every meal and see PG-13 movies, I valued the structure of my parents' rules. I didn't mind going to bed at 8 every night and only watching *Full House* on TV.

I guess that some would call this acceptance of rules maturity, but I think it has a lot to do with fear.

Because most of my March 11s have been filled with a little bit of trepidation.

The night before I turned 10, I stared at the ceiling, hoping that I wouldn't miss living in single digits. Before I turned 13, I fretted for hours, hoping that come midnight, I wouldn't be possessed with the overwhelming need to loiter outside a Walgreens or graffiti a bridge -- my mom had always blamed these offenses on the teenagers. On the eve of my 16th birthday, I had nightmares about crashing into innocent pedestrians or totaling the car within a couple hours of getting my license.

But this year, my fears have some grounds. I think that it's normal for seniors to feel a little scared about the "I" word: independence. Not Fourth of July independence, but the fact that I'm going to be eating Easy Mac every night for four years instead of sitting down to something that Mom made. Soon, I'll be paying the bills and worrying about mortgages. There'll be no one to depend on but myself.

To be blatantly honest, I'm scared about being out in the real world. I mean, most of us have grown up in this tight little North Dallas bubble.

And I think that the word"adult" is making that imminent reality a little too real for me. I still enjoy reading awkward "tween" novels and watching animated Disney movies. I like jumping off the last step of the stairs and skipping around the house. I find myself humming the "Itsy-bitsy Spider" to myself often.

But tomorrow is coming

I'm going to have to turn 18. I'll be excited. I'll smile, grit my teeth, and blow out that 18th candle.

I'll try to be adult about it.

FIGURE 7.5 *Eagle Edition*, The Episcopal School of Dallas, Dallas, Texas, Issue 5, Vol. 27, March 11, 2010, p. 26. "Age is just a really scary number," by Kate Skochdopole. Reproduced by permission of Barbara Meier. Column writers often give readers a different perspective on a daily event. While teenagers normally celebrate their 18th birthday and all the newfound freedoms, this Episcopal School of Dallas writer takes an insightful look at all the responsibilities. She says what other teenagers may think but won't say aloud: getting older is scary.

reinforces the focus and leaves the reader with a strong sense of the column's main points.

- Like editorials, columns can require research. An ill-prepared argument in a column may be even more obvious to readers than in a news story. Readers tend to respond negatively and sometimes harshly to columnists who toss off opinions without factual or logical support.

- Columns should be developed with specifics. The concrete nouns and verbs, the strong voice and the strategic pacing used in feature writing (see Chapter 6) should all be employed in column writing.

- Good column writers may have the opportunity to put into words those feelings and opinions that their readers are afraid to voice in public.

- Strong column writers are often powerful storytellers, bringing a person's experiences – sometimes their own – to life and using them to shed light on an issue that readers may not have considered.

- Columnists can offer fresh perspective to well-worn issues. Graduation, grades and stress can be clichéd high school topics, but a compelling columnist will find a refreshing or poignant way to address these universal, but no less powerful, experiences.

BLOG WRITING

A **blog** (short for "web log") is online commentary, usually appearing in reverse chronological order, which addresses a specific area of knowledge, and is updated on a regular basis. While column writing is typically a top job on newspaper staffs, the blogger position has been tackled by anyone with a website who wishes to be heard. But only those bloggers good enough to consistently produce interesting, insightful pieces in their areas of interest build a readership. People still differ as to whether blogging is journalism. As Poynter writing coach Roy Peter Clark argues:

Most bloggers are not journalists. Most do not claim to be. Some bloggers who are journalists disdain journalists – they don't want to be associated with the mainstream media. Blogging – like journalism—is a term that contains many different forms of expression. The key … is whether the blogger finds things out and checks thing out. Without that, there is no journalism.

Source: *http://www.poynter.org/how-tos/newsgathering-storytelling/ writing-tools/83326/writing-for-the-web-the-basics-still-apply/*

The blog is a relatively young writing form, still evolving on thousands of websites across the Internet. But when compared to the editorial and column, some basic features about blogs emerge:

- Blogs are updated regularly for the Internet reader who is always searching for the latest information.

- Columns and blogs are similar in their use of voice, structure and development.

- Blogs usually provide abundant links to their sources and related information elsewhere on the web – usually in the text of the blog itself.

- Individual blog posts should be relatively short, to fit on one or two computer screens – but blogs can span months or years of comments, reflections, analysis and research.

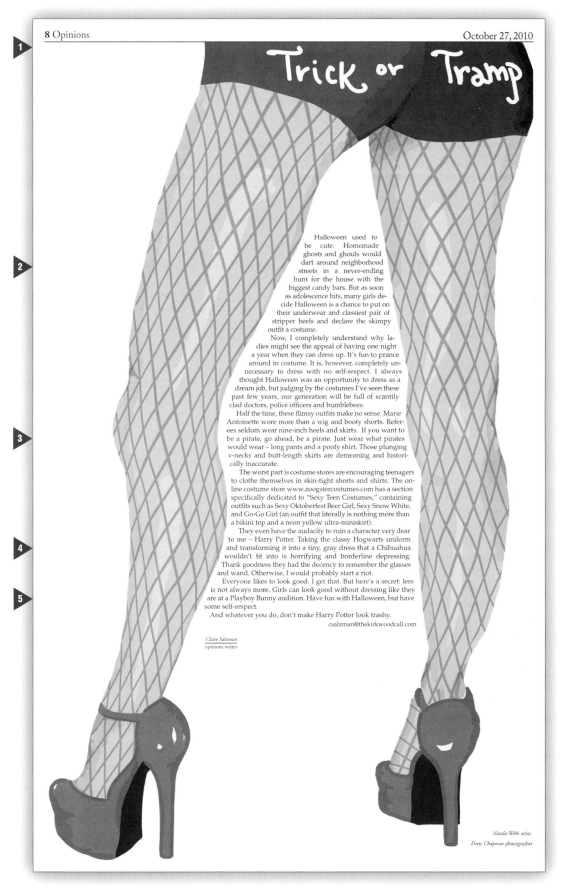

Trick or Tramp

Halloween used to be cute. Homemade ghosts and ghouls would dart around neighborhood streets in a never-ending hunt for the house with the biggest candy bars. But as soon as adolescence hits, many girls decide Halloween is a chance to put on their underwear and classiest pair of stripper heels and declare the skimpy outfit a costume.

Now, I completely understand why ladies might see the appeal of having one night a year when they can dress up. It's fun to prance around in costume. It is, however, completely unnecessary to dress with no self-respect. I always thought Halloween was an opportunity to dress as a dream job, but judging by the costumes I've seen these past few years, our generation will be full of scantily clad doctors, police officers and bumblebees.

Half the time, these flimsy outfits make no sense. Marie Antoinette wore more than a wig and booty shorts. Referees seldom wear nine-inch heels and skirts. If you want to be a pirate, go ahead, be a pirate. Just wear what pirates would wear – long pants and a poofy shirt. Those plunging v-necks and butt-length skirts are demeaning and historically inaccurate.

The worst part is costume stores are encouraging teenagers to clothe themselves in skin-tight shorts and shirts. The online costume store www.zoogstercostumes.com has a section specifically dedicated to "Sexy Teen Costumes," containing outfits such as Sexy Oktoberfest Beer Girl, Sexy Snow White, and Go-Go Girl (an outfit that literally is nothing more than a bikini top and a neon yellow ultra-miniskirt).

They even have the audacity to ruin a character very dear to me – Harry Potter. Taking the classy Hogwarts uniform and transforming it into a tiny, gray dress that a Chihuahua wouldn't fit into is horrifying and borderline depressing. Thank goodness they had the decency to remember the glasses and wand. Otherwise, I would probably start a riot.

Everyone likes to look good. I get that. But here's a secret: less is not always more. Girls can look good without dressing like they are at a Playboy Bunny audition. Have fun with Halloween, but have some self-respect.

And whatever you do, don't make Harry Potter look trashy.

csalzman@thekirkwoodcall.com

Claire Salzman
opinions writer

Natalie Webb artist
Drew Chapman photographer

FIGURE 7.6 *The Kirkwood Call*, Kirkwood High School, Kirkwood, Mo. Reproduced by permission of Mitch Eden.

Good column writers can put words to gut reactions. In this column from *The Kirkwood Call*, the writer breaks down her dislike for the trend of sexy Halloween costumes into vivid, voice-filled points. We've identified some of the strong writing devices the columnist chose.

1. The strong headline and design promise an equally strong and clever column.

2. Lead is short and gives the reader direct insight into the writer's views.

3. The writer makes a wonderful point about nonsensical Halloween outfits. She brings the point alive with the concrete examples of a referee in nine-inch heels and a pirate without a poofy shirt.

4. Notice that the writer looks for a more concrete and interesting way to say "It's skimpy." Good column writers bring a vivid concrete voice to the everyday.

5. The authors concluding two paragraphs play off the cliché "less is more" and use the repetition of the word "have" for some rhythm to the writing.

FIGURE 7.7 *ReMarker*, St. Mark's School of Texas, Dallas, Texas. Reproduced by permission of Ray Westbrook.

In this unusual column, the writer looks inward, finding parallels between his own experiences and that of celebrities run amok. He opens with a clever observation about the common strands in recent stories about David Beckham and Charlie Sheen. The columnist discusses the insanity of his own actions and that of the celebrity-obsessed public, which craves lurid stories of celebrity disgrace.

lee perkins

On David Beckham, Charlie Sheen and God

David Beckham got a new tattoo. Yep, that's international news.

And I don't know what's more disturbing, the fact that his new ink depicts the modest soccer star as Jesus Christ, emerging from the lush undergrowth of heaven accompanied by angelic figures, or that this ground-breaking story has maneuvered its way into every major news outlet.

More ominous were Charlie Sheen's quotes in a Yahoo! news article.

The actor declared that he is "tired of pretending that I'm not special," and de-

> Deep down, I think we all desire fame, or at least some attention and recognition. It's an obsession that manifests itself in the media's thorough coverage of every celebrity move.

scribed himself as having "tiger blood" and "Adonis DNA."

Seriously, when was this transition from celebrity to deity?

But in all truthfulness, the ridiculously egotistical actions of these famous figures — the desperate pleas for attention and publicity —are partially my fault.

I am one of many people with too much free time who sifted through trivial, pseudo-journalistic articles and clicked on the enticing photograph of Beckham's ink-splattered left pectoral.

I read the few sentences about Beck's trip to the tattoo parlor, about how every tattoo he has represents something meaningful in his life, his skin rivaling the Prado and the Bible, and the worst part is, I enjoyed it.

I can't explain why, but I take some

perverse pleasure in reading about these public icons. Steep rises into the public eye, schemes for attention and, of course, crumbling demises — it all interests me.

Maybe I subconsciously seek some time in the spotlight, indulging in this gossip to quench my thirst for fame.

Honestly, I don't know.

Deep down, I think we all desire fame, or at least some attention and recognition. It's an obsession that manifests itself in the media's thorough coverage of celebrities' every move.

It's the reason that Justin Beiber's haircut is a national crisis, and that the talentless Paris Hilton was the seventh most Googled person last year.

Because at the very core, there's a bit of God in all of us.

And a little bit more in Charlie Sheen.

REVIEW WRITING

Lil Wayne's latest music release may be worth the download price. Will Ferrell's next film – an attempt to revive his career – may not be. Teens often dictate what's a hit and what isn't in the world of entertainment and pop culture. As a reviewer, you get a chance to experience a song or a film first and to share your opinion of it with other teens – an influential and rewarding role.

High school publications have long provided **reviews**, evaluations of entertainment, products and services for an increasingly sophisticated and powerful group of consumers.

Two considerations are critical in review writing. First, the writer must ensure that the review is timely. Both Will Ferrell and Lil Wayne may have fallen off the radar by the time this textbook is published. Newspapers that publish once a month or every six weeks face a major challenge in reviewing: how to offer insight into a product or service while it is still relevant to readers. Websites that can post reviews during the opening week of a movie or the day after a music release can provide timely and relevant information for the reader. Print newspapers can research upcoming release dates and plan out reviews to accommodate their publication schedule, but this requires careful planning.

Second, the review writer needs to make sure the review is a genuine opinion piece, not just a summary or free advertising for a service or product. As with all opinion pieces, the writer should offer a sense of his take on the service or product in the lead, and then back it up with specific details, facts and features. The writer may preview a few plot points of a film or provide background information about a new personal electronic device, but the main organization of the piece should be structured to support an opinion. When summarizing any part of a book or film, review writers shouldn't give too much away, to avoid ruining surprises or twists.

Quick Exercise

Develop a list of three topics you could blog about regularly. Discuss your topics with a partner and settle on one that readers would most connect with.

Quick Exercise

Do some research to develop a list of seven products that will be released in the next two months that you are excited about and would like to review.

REVIEWING TIPS

While approaches to reviews can vary as much as the products, services and entertainment options that teenagers consume, the following advice can be applied to most reviews:

- Reviewers should choose to evaluate something they find enjoyable. They will then anticipate interests and concerns of readers who might benefit or have curiosity about the product.

WORDS of WISDOM

1. *What is the artist (writer, filmmaker, playwright, etc.) trying to do?*

2. *How well did he/she do it?*

3. *Was it worth doing?*

You could say that in writing Macbeth *William Shakespeare was attempting to examine issues of ambition and guilt while providing his audience with some gruesome thrills and violence.*

Did he do it? Yeah, 400 years of Macbeth *productions suggest his mission was accomplished.*

Was it worth doing? Yes. These are issues that all people in all times and places must deal with … that's what makes Macbeth *immortal.*

On the other hand, let's say you've just seen Zookeeper *with Kevin James. It's the movie with the talking animals.*

What were the filmmakers trying to do? Well, they're trying to make audiences laugh, certainly. AND they're trying to make a load of money.

How well did they succeed? That can be measured in how many times you laughed and whether the movie was profitable.

Was it worth doing? Well, that's the dealbreaker. Most of today's entertainments aren't really ABOUT anything. They have no real reason for being except to keep people working and audiences buying tickets (or tuning in). Under those circumstances you may conclude that, no, this film, poem, book, etc. wasn't worth doing.

Robert Butler, Butler's Cinema Scene, http://butlerscinemascene.com, Kansas City, Mo.

- Student reviewers should consider the audience at which the product or service is targeted. It's not fair to evaluate Zoe's Fun Burger's low appeal for a gourmet, post-opera crowd, when the café actually caters to the seven-year-olds who have been playing Zombie Tag next door.

- The reviewer should do some research prior to testing a product, eating a meal or viewing a film. Researching an author or chef or director's previous work may provide a basis to evaluate the current offerings.

FIGURE 7.8 Food review by Amy Char and Adriana Millar, thelowell.org, Lowell High School, San Francisco, Calif. Reproduced by permission of Sharn Matusek.

The Lowell's review of a ready-to-cook meal service offers a clear opinion with a lively voice and detailed development. The writers clearly understand their audience as they discuss the value of the service in lieu of eating Nutella at 10:30 at night. They continue that viewpoint with strong specifics, noting the simple instructions for when the pan is hot: "when you see 'wisps of smoke coming off the pan.'" They also provide a vivid sensory description of the food's taste and appearance: "Mixing together the sauce, chicken and rice in my bowl turned it into a hearty stew."

- Just as a good reporter would, a reviewer should take copious notes. Notes might include the key lyrics from the best song on a CD or descriptions of the cardboard characters that the movie's director ignored in favor of visual effects.

- The writer should vary the review's structure. The reviewer's account doesn't have to start chronologically, as he walks through the restaurant door. The three-layer carrot cake served warm for dessert that made the whole visit worthwhile may belong in the lead.

- Reviewers should hit the highlights. They don't have to cover every song or every dish.

- Writers shouldn't give too much away. This is particularly true in movie reviews. Don't give away the surprises that would ruin the movie for the readers.

- Good entertainment writers should have detailed knowledge of their review specialty but still keep a general audience in mind. While a detailed understanding of the development of the *Star Wars* movies will serve the writer well in a review, showing off this arcane knowledge in a review of a new sci-fi TV show will only bore or annoy the reader.

- A review should be fair, honest and reasonable. A writer should never review something she didn't experience and shouldn't go into any review determined to bash someone or something – even if the review is negative on many points.

- The review writer should outline all the important factors related to the product or service. Everything from costs to availability to ambience could be relevant considerations for a review writer.

- Websites can allow high school publications to create links to subjects that are mentioned in the review. Movie reviews might include a link to the movie trailers or a biography of the director. Song reviews might have links to the artist's iTunes page or free downloads from the artist's website.

- Entertainment coverage can be developed through news features and reviews can be presented in alternative formats, such as YouTube videos.

Review topics

What writers choose to review can be as varied as those things teenagers value in their everyday lives. These might include the following, but the options are almost limitless.

→ Movies
→ Music
→ Plays
→ Musicals
→ Restaurants
→ Beverages or food products
→ Websites
→ Phone apps

→ Technology products
→ Coffee, ice cream or yogurt shops
→ Books
→ TV shows
→ Food trends
→ Clothes and clothing stores
→ Sporting goods or sporting goods stores
→ Art shows and museum exhibits

WORDS of WISDOM

Five tips for reviewers

1. *Remember that your objective is to analyze the job of the performance/product in terms of what its creators were wanting to accomplish, not what you think it should be. [Don't judge a high school musical by Glee standards, or a poetry slam to literary festival levels.]*

2. *Only review performances/products that you are an expert consumer of and have a deep appreciation for. [If you don't like heavy metal, don't review a performance by Motley Crüe.]*

3. *Offer constructive criticism, not sarcastic comments. The goal of any good reviewer is to improve the performance/product being offered, not just to write something clever and snarky.*

4. *Evaluate the product/performance. Don't make this a personality piece. Keep your comments focused on what's being offered to the public.*

5. *Be a sensor by proxy for your readers so they know what to expect should they seek the same product/performance. This is a reader service.*

Sandy Hall-Chiles, Yavneh Academy, Dallas, Texas

FIGURE 7.9 *ReMarker*, St. Mark's School of Texas, Dallas, Texas. Reproduced by permission of Ray Westbrook.

ReMarker staff added some creativity to their editorial page with the creation of "the heat index," a recurring short opinion package. The package approach to brief editorials gives the publication an opportunity to applaud or jeer people, events or issues that don't need a full-length piece. Lunch food and a creative new class were perfect topics that needed succinct development and could be designed in a clean tight graphic.

---

commentary

Editorials

The 24-hour solo   A tradition that must be kept

Any Marksman will tell you what the Pecos Wilderness Trip is about: the 24-hour solo — a day of isolation in the serene New Mexican forest — an opportunity for incoming freshmen to reflect on their past decisions and ponder what paths they will take during their high school career. This past summer, the solo was reduced to 12 hours. Administrators cited safety as the primary reason for their decision.

A group of upcoming freshmen hiking through the Pecos

Headmaster Arnie Holtberg will meet next month with wilderness directors Scott Hunt and Nick Sberna to determine whether they will extend their decision for future Pecos trips.

If the mission of the Pecos trip is to foster growth and independence in Marksmen, then we believe this goal cannot be achieved without a 24-hour solo. If the administration hopes to make the Pecos Trip safer with their 12-hour reduction, then we believe they are targeting the wrong aspect of the trip.

Of all the activities on the Pecos Trip, the solo is arguably the safest. There have been plenty of injuries on the Pecos Trip during its 40-year tenure — but over all these years, no Marksman has been injured during his 24-hour solo. After all, one takes more of a statistical risk by riding the Pecos-bound bus than he does by spending a day in quiet reflection a few hundred meters from his camp leader.

If administrators were to provide a legitimate safety concern, we would certainly accept that — the trip is not intended to be dangerous. If they choose to extend their 12-hour solo decision for years to come, however, they are cheating future generations of Marksmen of a full experience here. The independence and refined sense of self that the student gains from the 24-hour solo cannot be taught in a classroom and is undermined in just 12 hours.

The truth is the solo *is* demanding. Being a Marksman is demanding. But this demand on Marksmen defines the school. Marksmen should be allowed to experience the 24-hour solo just like their friends, brothers and fathers before them.

We urge adminstrators, when they meet next month, to restore the tradition of the 24-hour solo.

Scott Gonzalez   Thanks for stepping up — again

When Marksmen and faculty flocked into Hicks Gymnasium for the annual opening convocation Aug. 23, they expected Rev. Richard Towers, as in years past, to deliver the opening prayer.

Scott Gonzalez

Instead, Dean of Campus Scott Gonzalez stood up to speak to the school. The word soon spread that Gonzalez would take the role of interim chaplain — a job very familiar to him.

In the past, when the school has been unable to find a replacement for a significant position, Gonzalez has been there to fill those shoes. Not only did he replace Chris Gunnin as interim head of Upper School after the 2008-2009 school year, but he was also interim head from 2000-2001 and interim chaplain from 2002-2003.

Gonzalez is an example of a true Marksman, whose dedication to the school is boundless. We encourage students to develop interests in activities of various different fields and excel in varied activities like he does.

Gonzalez, with his uncanny versatility as a faculty member, portrays an ideal role model to our students. While a devoted dean of campus and an experienced English instructor, Gonzalez is able to step up into key positions and perform these roles with poise and perfection.

We applaud Gonzalez for this ability and for his dedication to this school.

The heat index
What's hot — and what's not — around 10600 Preston Road

Owens's Science Fiction Class | Super Hot

This is hot. Like 373 Kelvin hot. There is no better sight than to see chemistry instructor Ken Owens trotting through the second floor of Centennial with his lab coat on and — what? — science fiction books in his hand.

Owens's class, exploring the intriguing similarities between the worlds of science and literature, is one of the most popular English electives among seniors. Entering his class is like entering the *Chronicles of Narnia*, and opening into a world of imagination

Brown's Chapel Solo | Hot

Let's be honest. When Master Teacher David Brown stood up and sang "You're a Mean one, Mr. Grinch" during chapel Sept. 14, no one could hold a smile off his face.

Now that Brown has broken the musical ice, maybe the Chapel Committee will finally accept our requests for psalm rap-battles. And if we're really lucky, they'll let us add DJ $penca's dubstep remix of "All Things Bright and Beautiful" to our hymn books.

Lunch Planning | Pretty Chilly

The cafeteria often features all its best items in one lunch, resulting in one day of unbridled stomach ecstasy, often followed by vicious cramps for those audacious enough to tackle chicken tika masala, a Holtberger, red velvet froyo, chocolate milk, yogurt parfait and peach crisp in one sitting.

Unfortunately, the physics of a Marksman's stomach is different from those of a black hole. Perhaps the cafeteria can spread the wealth, and allow us to accept all of our entrees as brethren instead of pitching them into a contest for our affection.

Vuvuzelas | Lukewarm

Vuvuzelas are slippery slopes. During a vuvuzela jam sesh, if you can somehow maintain consciousness despite ruptured ear drums and a lack of oxygen, you won't be able to stop unless you are either sprayed with bear mace or your instrument is clogged with the backup vuvuzela hanging from your landyard.

The vuvuzela's tone also perfectly matches a wide repertoire of exotic animals' mating calls, so play with caution.

The midterm exam

The recent chaos in Libya, including riots, a civil war and an innumerable amount of deaths, has caused much instability in the nation.

With the events in Libya becoming one of the most talked-about topics in the news, we feel that it is important for each Marksman to have a sufficient amount of knowledge this country.

Here are six questions to test and further extend your knowledge of Libya. Don't worry, we won't give you a grade on this. We just want to make sure you're up to date.

Riots in Libya

THE QUESTIONS

1. Which of the following is the capital of Libya?

   a) Tripoli
   b) Doha
   c) Khartoum
   d) Libya City

2. What is the official language of Libya?

   a) Libyan
   b) Arabic
   c) French
   d) Gaddafian

3. Which of the following countries doesn't share a border with Libya?

   a) Chad
   b) Niger
   c) Egypt
   d) Nigeria

4. In what year did Muammar Gaddafi gain rule in Libya?

   a) 1976
   b) 1969
   c) 1993
   d) 2000

5. Which of the following titles did Gaddafi give to himself?

   a) General
   b) Captain
   c) Colonel
   d) President

6. Gaddafi was found to possess an album full of photos of which female U.S. political figure?

   a) Hillary Clinton
   b) Nancy Pelosi
   c) Condoleezza Rice
   d) Barbara Bush

THE ANSWERS

6) c
5) c
4) b
3) d
2) b
1) a

Midterm exam compiled by NAEEM MUSCATWALLA,

PACKAGED OPINION COVERAGE

Opinion coverage can also be expanded through a variety of short packaged sidebars. Not every opinion needs to be a long developed story. Editorial, op-ed and review pages can include a variety of quick collections of opinion that are creatively designed to pull the reader into the page. Editorial and op-ed pages often feature letters to the editor and short quick editorials packaged under the label thumbs up/thumbs down, letter grades, hot/cold, ratings, etc. Review pages have similar packages that can offer short staff picks or even encourage reader involvement through their feedback about the latest entertainment. The entertainment page tends to offer a more creative approach to the package. The sidebars might include:

- Top three tech gadgets that will make high school easier
- Books you wish the school would assign for a English class
- Readers weigh in on the four best songs for a school dance
- Playoff bracket of the best staycation ideas for spring break.

Opinion writers should be reminded that they still need to include opinion and reasoning even in such short packaged pieces.

Test your knowledge

Should a review be a complete rehash of a movie or book?

CONCLUSION

The purpose of opinion writing is to inform and persuade. To develop a convincing opinion piece, the writer needs thorough knowledge of a subject, gained from research or personal experience. Opinion pieces generally appear as either columns, where the view expressed is that of only one person, or editorials, where the opinion reflects the consensus of a group of people representing the publication.

The editorial generally follows a formula. The formula starts with a lead that explains the issue, delivers a clear position statement and previews the reasoning behind it. The body of the story includes an argument backed up by factual and logical development. The writer should refute the opposing side and present a feasible solution. The editorial conclusion should reinforce the argument.

The column is as varied a form as any style of journalistic writing. The column should make a point and speak to the audience with a fresh perspective, developed with insightful points and original research or vivid storytelling from personal experiences. Blogs are similar in structure and variety to columns but are created through short, pithy, web-linked Internet posts.

The review is another major form of opinion writing. The review is a service to the reader, offering evaluations of entertainment, products and services. Reviews should not be summaries or advertisements, but informed opinions supported by specifics.

SUMMARY

● Opinion writers should base their stories on a thorough knowledge of the subject.

● The column is the opinion of one person; the editorial is the opinion of a group.

● Opinion stories, which reflect subjective personal values of an individual, need to be backed up with verifiable statements of fact.

● The editorial is often written along a formula. The writer should start with an opinion, followed by background on the issue and a clear position statement. The writer should defend the argument with specifics in the body of the story as well as refuting the opposing side and providing a feasible solution. The story should end with a strong summary of the argument or a call to act on the issue.

● Columns should have a point and speak to readers with a fresh perspective on an issue or experience.

● Reviews should offer the reader timely insight and opinion on a relevant product, service or entertainment option. Reviewers should have a detailed knowledge of the subject but keep the target audience in mind. Reviews should be fair, honest and reasonable.

● Packaged opinion coverage can offer the reader brief but developed opinion in an attractive, reader-friendly form.

KEY TERMS

blog	editorial	editorial lead
call to action	editorial board	op-ed page
column	editorial cartoon	review writing

EXERCISES

1   Pick an opinion piece and underline 10 opinion words or phrases. Rank the top three strongest opinion words or phrases and develop an argument for your ranking.

2   Editorial page scavenger hunt. From editorial pages or websites, clip and mount examples of these:

(a) letter to the editor

(b) an editorial cartoon that deals with a topic of student interest

(c) solution proposed in an editorial

(d) three facts used to back up opinion

(e) how design is used to differentiate opinion stories from news stories

(f) examples of opposing opinions on the same topic

(g) paragraph from an editorial that refutes the opposing sides.

3 Write an editorial based on the information given in Chapter 3, Exercise 4.

4 Write a column on one of the following topics:

(a) a rewarding or frustrating experience with a parent

(b) a state issue that impacts students

(c) something that others do that makes a positive impact on people

(d) a school rule that you have a better solution for.

5 Read the following column and answer these questions:

(a) Why was the opening paragraph about her D.A.R.E. essay important to the point of the column?

(b) Underline three good uses of specifics or dialogue and explain what point the writer was making with them.

(c) Do you think it took courage to write and publish this story? Why, or why not?

FIGURE 7.10 Kat Buchanan, *The Harbinger*, Shawnee Mission East High School, Prairie Village, Kansas. Reproduced by permission of C. Dow Tate.

This columnist tackled the issue of binge drinking in high school through her own raw and honest experiences. Column writers often try to make readers think differently about a subject by dealing with real and personal specifics. Statistics can be useful in defending an argument, but some readers respond better to strong narrative.

---

08 | OPINION
09-20-10

TIME WASTED
▶▶KatBuchanan

Junior reflects on her past experiences with underage drinking

In sixth grade, I won an award from D.A.R.E. for an essay I wrote.

It was a masterpiece, filled with all of my naïve heart and soul, opening with the hard-hitting line: "My name may be Kat, but that doesn't mean I have nine lives, and I'm not going to waste the one I do have using drugs and alcohol."

I read it in front of the entire Westwood View student, parent and administrative body and I was filled with hope for my future, one that was bound to be illegal-substance-free. I promised myself I'd practice what I preached. It seemed easy enough then, standing boldly at the podium with Officer Sullivan at my side.

After sixth grade, I found myself standing on the threshold of middle school and the nearby Pembroke Hill School proved to be the perfect opportunity for a new experience. So I went for it. I applied for the '07-'08 academic year and was accepted.

As the preteen with the red D.A.R.E T-shirt on, I had no idea that the coming years would bring me closer and closer to rock bottom. No warning signs telling me to stay where I was. To sidestep disaster.

I had to find out for myself.

***

"I don't know how she got like this, Carol, I really do not."

I repeatedly bang my head against my best friend's kitchen door, sobbing, screaming, profanity and gibberish spewing forth, wondering what I've done now and how I can escape this lifestyle, how I can right my most recent wrong.

My mind feels like a PowerPoint presentation with too many pictures and scarce bullet points explaining what's going on. Like I'm having one of those dreams where I show up at school without my backpack, sitting in classes I didn't sign up for, trying to read words in a language I don't understand.

Or, more realistically, like I'm blow-a-.24-into-the-breath-alyzer drunk.

My friend's mother's worried face enters my fuzzy line of vision and I feel my own mom's hand grip my shoulder, a hopeless attempt to calm her out-of-control daughter.

I'm sorry, I'm sorry, I'm so sorry.

"Kat, we need to get you home. Can you hear me?"

My arms, my legs, my fingers, my toes—nothing is connected; nothing is attached to my body. A tingling sensation fills me up in the worst way possible. There are cuts on my forehead that I won't notice until morning and my ankles are giving out from stumbling in high-heeled boots. But for the time being, I really can't hear her.

Images from mere hours before flash through my mind. A production of horror, the Kat Messed Up Again Picture Show.

A bottle of Smirnoff Citron vodka with tap water to chase it down, an unfinished basement floor littered with yellow and black trash bags, an unexpected visit from the host's father. The distorted, angry look on his face as kids cleared out faster than he could recognize them.

I recall my head hitting an off-white cement driveway and Amy frantically searching through the contacts on my phone, looking for someone, anyone, to get us out of the mess I'd gotten us into.

But of course, we were already in it too deep.

***

I was right.

Transferring to Pembroke did bring on an array of changes. These new experiences ranged from cliques of mean girls to pre-shredded Abercrombie jeans and Ralph Lauren polos.

As I got older and approached the end of eighth grade, the changes in my lifestyle became more prevalent. Things took a turn for the worse with the red solo cup of Kettle One vodka mixed with Sunkist that lead to the two-year detour from the path I had envisioned myself being on.

It was the first time I drank myself to oblivion. I was 14.

I cannot blame my faulty behavior on hanging out with the "wrong crowd" or giving into peer pressure. I can't blame it on a pushy boyfriend or problems at home or even a desire to experiment.

I can only blame myself. I blame myself wholeheartedly for seeking some way to get around social niceties and skip to drunken heart-to-hearts with strangers. For losing my best friend and my once-strong relationship with my parents; for leaving my morals behind to discover just how much I could act out.

For trying to be someone who I clearly should not be.

***

I'm on a hospital bed.

I force my eyes open and immediately cringe at the fluorescent lights shining directly above me. My right hand feels heavy, my eyelids droopy, my mouth dry. I try to follow the marquee of news headlines scrolling underneath the CNN reporter but the words move faster than I can read them. The volume seems to be so loud that it's thumping directly against my eardrums. Many decibels lower, I can hear my parents' urgent whispers fluttering around the hallway in front of me.

It feels like a freight train plowed over me and then backed up for good measure.

I look down at my hand and see an IV hooked up to the vein crawling up my pinky finger. My stomach churns, and I'm just lucid enough to note that I have a phobia of needles before my mind goes blank and my vision black.

The next morning, I awake in my bed at home in a cold sweat. More than ever before, I savor that familiar moment of incoherency, that split-second between dream and wake where nothing matters and I've done nothing wrong.

Then the memories flood into my already-pounding brain and I pull the covers over my head, hoping with all my heart that this storm passes as quickly as it came.

***

After that night my freshman year, I was almost done with it.

I began drinking somewhat sparingly, but when I did, it was big—my friends came to know me as a binge drinker. Using the preface of a special occasion, I'd load up on drinks, a beer here, a couple of shots there. And then more. I had quickly become the girl that people warned their friends to keep an eye on, the burden, the one who always took it too far.

My not-so-subtle relationship with drinking continued up until the second semester of my sophomore year. A new friend entered my life at precisely the right time and he showed me that above all else, staying true to myself and to what I believe in would be the most important factor in the grand scheme of things.

He showed me that relationships with people can be stronger than any proof label on a bottle and that leaning on someone when I need help is much more effective than grabbing a handle and guzzling it down. That true friendship is of infinitely more value than any fake ID.

He showed me the life I thought I'd lost for good, and I haven't had a drink since.

***

More often than not, I find myself lying awake at night wishing that I could erase the past.

Drinking and going to parties and talking about drinking and going to parties—it was a cycle that dominated two years of my life, two years wasted. I didn't think I had time for old friends or time to make new ones.

I feel so ashamed of things I've done under the influence, of the people I've hurt and the people I ignored because of the way I was living and the behavior that went along with it. I regret every conversation I missed out on, every family dinner I skipped, every "friend" I never called back.

But in spite of this, I'm glad that it happened to me.

I'm glad that I've realized from experience that life has more to offer than a 12-pack of beer, a trip to the liquor store to see if I'll get carded or a busted party. Money and time can be better spent, especially while I'm still in high school.

I've been to the other side, and I know first-hand that I never want to go back. Artificial fun isn't nearly as great as the real thing.

Since I've come to terms with underage drinking and the consequences that go along with it, I've found myself with more time to spend on the things I enjoy, things that require thought and hard work and laborious nights in room 521 of Shawnee Mission East. I've met many incredible people and learned how to get along with them without throwing back a Bud Light beforehand.

I only have one life, after all. And I'm slowly but surely learning how to live it.

▶▶ GrantHeinlein

6   Pick a topic from the following list and write a review. Make sure to do background research on the genre and artist:

(a) a free download of the day's/week's song

(b) a new app or website

(c) a retro movie that your parents may own but your generation hasn't seen

(d) a new line of clothes.

7   Develop three ideas for blogs that you could write, outlining three different stories you could do for each. Pick and write your favorite.

8   Choose three recent trends in clothing, entertainment or technology and create a packaged opinion piece (a quote collection, rating scale, etc.) from collected opinion from classmates.

IN-DEPTH REPORTING

> The backbone of any good student publication is in-depth reporting and writing. A high school student body must rely on its student journalists to tell them what is really going on. That means digging into the school budget; reporting on school board meetings; examining police records to determine if any students – or teachers – have been getting into trouble and analyzing school test scores to determine how its school compares to other similar local schools.
>
> Although such reporting is difficult and time-consuming, the importance of keeping their fellow students informed is not only invaluable, it teaches both student journalists and student readers the types of information they will need as adults to make informed decisions in a democracy.

Joel Kaplan, Former City Hall and Investigative Reporter, Chicago Tribune

LEARNING OBJECTIVES
After completing this chapter you will be able to:

- identify topics that would be appropriate for in-depth coverage

- understand the resources needed to properly report in-depth stories in both words and images

- utilize the resources available for conducting in-depth background research

- effectively use both print and online resources to report in-depth stories

- update and follow up on in-depth coverage through print and online media.

Scholastic Journalism, Twelfth Edition. C. Dow Tate and Sherri A. Taylor.
© 2014 John Wiley & Sons, Inc. Published 2014 by John Wiley & Sons, Inc.

SCHOOLS FACE MANY OF THE same issues as society in general: substance use and abuse, discrimination, sexual assault, bullying, budget problems, political and religious disagreements. School districts continue to struggle with inequitable distributions of financial resources and social capital. School boards constantly debate how and whether to spend tax dollars. Violence in the schools continues to make national headlines. Charter schools affect public school enrollments and funding dollars. Federal and state government often link school funding with academic performance and place pressure on teachers for improved test scores. Students are required to pass exit exams to earn diplomas in many states. Some parents home school their children or place them in private schools, owing to concerns about quality of public education.

As school communities grow more complex, opportunities for in-depth, long-form reporting abound. But challenges also increase for scholastic journalists as they seek to provide in-depth coverage in both the online and print versions of their newspapers and yearbooks.

FIGURE 8.1 *Globe* newsmagazine, Clayton High School, Clayton, Mo. Reproduced by permission of Erin Castellano.

In a newsmagazine, the in-depth story often starts on the front-page. **a** The story often begins with a strong typographic presentation, as was used in this issue of *Globe* newsmagazine from Clayton High School in Missouri. Tackling a timely and controversial topic – sexual harassment – the staff chose to localize this national issue by focusing on recent events at the school.

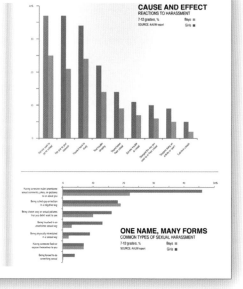

FIGURE 8.1 (*continued*)
b The first inside spread contains a photo illustration, a photo created for the story and introduces a blue horizontal line which unites the visual presentation of the story on subsequent spreads. The headline and preface set up the focus of the story and pique the reader's interest by ending with a question.
c The story begins on the second spread and repeats the blue line and the typography of the headline in drop caps throughout the text. A pull quote borrows a visual highlighting technique from the cover, using a box and all-cap typography.
d The next spread maintains the visual features previously introduced, but adds three bar charts of national statistics. Note how the horizontal blue line is now a vertical blue line in the chart.

FIGURE 8.1 *(continued)*
e The story concludes with one last spread which uses two photo illustrations in the same visual style as the first spread, adds one last chart and finishes with one last large pull quote.

"MY EXPERIENCE, OVER 11 YEARS WORKING IN ST. LOUIS, IS THAT SCHOOLS THAT ARE MORE AFFLUENT AND MORE WHITE TEND TO TALK ABOUT THIS LESS. I THINK IT'S DENIAL."

CHRISTINA MENESES

In-depth reporting is needed to address the subtle and complex issues and situations that arise in the context of secondary education. Coverage of in-depth topics may require a greater commitment of resources – both staff members and time – as well as a greater need for understanding all sides of the issue. A team of reporters, photographers and editors may need to be assembled to properly cover complex topics of concern to the publication's readership. In some schools, a special editor is charged with the responsibility for this special **package** of content. In most cases, in-depth reporters should expect to spend a considerable amount of time gathering information and researching – also known as backgrounding – before they come together to actually report, write, design, visualize and publish the story.

In-depth reporting may take many forms. In a newsmagazine, a feature package may examine an issue over the course of multiple pages, using a distinctive design. It may be a single page of coverage in a traditional newspaper, or a series of articles published over a period of time on a website. An in-depth story might be published on the double truck – where the pages are actually printed on one sheet of paper – which allows different opportunities for layout. Since the pages are a single sheet of paper, headlines and visuals can be brought across the two pages to unify them. (Two pages of related content can also appear on facing pages without actually appearing on the double truck.) An in-depth story might also appear as a special content package, taking up several pages in a specialized presentation. An occasional in-depth section across multiple issues offers another form of in-depth reporting. Coverage in many other forms can appear on the staff's website. Online, a news staff can add video or still photography and sound to continue reporting an important story. **In-depth**, or **long-form reporting**, offers student journalists a sustained opportunity to cover important topics and relate stories of interest to their audience.

In the yearbook, in-depth reporting can also take many forms. The opportunity to cover topics of significant reader interest will not only broaden the depth of the yearbook's reporting, but will also break up the structure and pacing of its presentation. This allows for different kinds of content in different formats.

Test your knowledge

How does in-depth reporting serve the mission of the newspaper or yearbook both in print and online?

FINDING TOPICS FOR IN-DEPTH COVERAGE

Controversial, sensitive topics such as drug and alcohol abuse, sexuality and school violence could be topics for in-depth coverage. While these topics are relevant to high school audiences, reporters and editors need to make sure their selection of in-depth topics is appropriate for their school communities. Coverage of sensitive topics should be discussed thoroughly among staff members, and decisions about how these topics can be covered should be carefully decided.

In some cases, neutral reporting methods may offer more sensitive methods of topic coverage. For instance, rather than using anonymous, first-person accounts of student drug use or sexual activity, interviews with professionals may provide less controversial, though perhaps not as interesting, coverage. Student journalists must make sure they cover topics responsibly and appropriately for their audiences.

Many topics that can be covered in depth are far less controversial and serious. Schools continue to face the same difficulties as the community in general and community publications may provide a good source of inspiration. However, reporters should focus on the concerns of their specific readers as primary topics for in-depth coverage. Drawing on the beat system already in place on most publications staffs (see Chapter 1 for more information on covering beats), student journalists can keep an eye out for areas of concern. Assessing the local news value of each story is as important for in-depth coverage as it is for straight news reporting. Issues that affect urban schools may not affect suburban schools. Issues of concern to small schools may not affect larger schools.

School governing boards

The decisions made by the school board or the school's governing body affect every student at your school. Is the district considering a change in graduation requirements, a change in the length of the school day or year, requiring students to wear uniforms, allocating money for new facilities, debating whether to hold a bond election or a tax levy for a special project? All of these topics would be of concern to student readers. Someone from the student newspaper staff should attend all school board meetings, especially when policy changes are being discussed. Debate over major policy shifts starts well in advance of the actual change. Reporters carefully following these discussions will be on top of the issues before the decisions are made and can already be gathering relevant information.

Beyond the local school board, your state's educational governing body will also make decisions that affect your school. Many of these decisions are studied for months in advance. Monitoring the decision-making process will offer opportunities to share possible changes with readers and report their initial reactions. National educational trends and federal policies may also have an important impact on your school community.

When the school board began studying the importance of summer school in the context of budget cuts in the Clayton High School district, the *Globe* newspaper reported the changes that might be coming if the board adopted a plan. The story was reported in the winter, preparing students for the possibilities while the board's discussion was going on.

Athletics

Athletic programs in schools are rich areas for in-depth reporting. How does the athletic department monitor use of illegal substances such as growth hormones and steroids among athletes? Does the school have an athlete who is being heavily recruited by colleges or professional programs and is getting a lot of attention? Is the school restricting participation of athletes who suffer concussions? Who decides how much funding is provided for sports in the school, and is it equitable among major/minor sports and men's/women's sports? Do programs share equal facilities for equal amounts of time? Is the school or the state athletic governing body considering redistricting, which would change the scheduling of your teams and their opponents? Is there an honor code for athletes? Reporters should speak frequently to coaches and athletic directors in the school.

At Francis Howell North High School (FHN) in St. Charles, Missouri, the *North Star* newspaper and FHNtoday.com website reported in April 2012 on the district's plans to build new baseball and softball fields by fall of 2013. These fields were additions to its only facility, a turf stadium for football. Knowing the plans were in the works allowed the reporting.

Curricular areas

Maintaining contact with the heads of curricular programs, school department heads and others who make decisions about academics will enable student journalists to monitor changes in

WWW

WEBLINK Check out

www.investigatingpower.org

This site presents noteworthy coverage of topics from civil rights to Watergate in video interviews with some of the reporters who covered the stories. It also features interviews with reporters on topics of concern to investigative journalism.

WWW

WEBLINK Check out

www.nfhs.org

Students who cover sports can obtain significant information on high school sports governing bodies throughout the United States at this site. The site also includes information on state high school fine arts associations.

WORDS of WISDOM

It never stops being about sourcing. It's amazing how many kids can comment (or be quoted) on serious and pertinent issues without ever experiencing them first hand. For example, a story about an anorexic student shouldn't rest on an outside publication report and a bunch of juniors and sophomores commenting about it from the bleachers or the lunchroom. The writer should devote all reporting attention and energy to a local source who suffers the affliction. While students may sympathize, they can't empathize. Let the anorexic kid tell the story and then balance it with experts – doctors, psychologists and finally include parents and friends to provide the anecdotal context. Then follow up with a sidebar discussing the life of the psychologist who treats anorexic kids and faces the all-too-typical 20 percent cure rate.

Basically this is a story that can't be reported or written from the journalism room or the school hallways. Sourcing is the key. Difficult to find, yes. But worth the effort when the story revolves around a person. Which paper do you want: a publication with stories about people or a publication filled with people who have stories?

Dean Hume, Spark, *Newsmagazine Adviser, Lakota East High School, Ohio*

www

WEBLINK Check out

www.edutopia.org

A site funded by the George Lucas Educational Foundation, Edutopia contains a wealth of great information on what works in education. It links to information for high schools and other ages. It includes a link to "What are the biggest challenges young adults face today."

curriculum that will affect students. Other areas of curricular concern include elimination of programs, reduction of teachers and consolidation of school resources such as counseling and advising programs. Teacher concerns, such as students buying essays on the Internet or other forms of cheating in the school could also be examined. Do students sign an honor code? Is it uniformly enforced among students and athletes? What about computer resources in the school? Are **filters** used on computers to block access to sites to censor student browsing? Are books censored from the library? Do local citizens with extreme viewpoints show up at textbook adoption time?

The *ReMarker* newspaper of St. Mark's School of Texas, in Dallas, began a front-page with a story on new guidelines on teaching social studies in Texas handed down by a conservative Texas State Board of Education. The story talked about the effect of the board's action on textbooks that would then be rewritten to include the board's mandates and their effects on social studies teaching in schools throughout the country.

Extracurricular and other areas

Changes in student clubs, organizations and other extracurriculars will affect a large percentage of the student body. Some schools have cut funding for clubs and other organizations; others have restricted student field trips and activities because of funding cuts. Some clubs are dropped because of a lack of sponsors. Club hazing or initiation rites have resulted in serious injury and have generated strict policies at some schools. Schools are constantly debating whether or not religious clubs can meet or activities can be held during the school day or in school facilities. Prayer before school activities continues to be a national and local issue.

Issues that concern being a student and teenager also come into play here. Getting into college, cramming for exams, balancing school and work, obeying curfews and dealing with serious issues such as rape and abuse are also important topics.

The *Devils' Advocate* newsmagazine of Hinsdale Central High School in Illinois, took a look at sleep deprivation and its effect on students who were using caffeine and other drugs to stay awake for extended periods of time.

Beyond the school

Community, societal, economic and environmental changes that affect the school should also be examined. Is the school's neighborhood changing in ways that would affect it? Is the school located on a major street that might be dangerous to cross? Are the lights and turning lanes adequate for the numbers of cars that use them? Has the school started safety measures such as installing radar detectors or locking all entrances except the main one during the school day?

The school's effect on the neighborhood should also be considered. Do students gather in stores and fast-food restaurants close to the school? Do these businesses ever restrict the number of students who can be in the store at one time? Have the businesses been in touch with the school or local police about their concerns? Is there an open campus policy that results in dangerous driving situations at lunch? Have students or school personnel been in trouble with the law in ways that may affect their continued enrollment or employment in the school?

The Harvard-Westlake *Chronicle* in Los Angeles, California, reported on the school's participation in the Great California ShakeOut, the largest annual earthquake drill in the nation on a page labeled with a logo, "Expecting the big one," that also included two related stories.

Localizing national and state trends

The last few years have been volatile for many schools, with massive budgetary crises, lagging test scores and graduation rates and the ongoing debate over policies such as No Child Left Behind. Changing times and trends are ripe for in-depth coverage. Offering students the opportunity to voice their concerns about these changes is a valid use of space. Publications can also offer readers forums for discussion of issues as complex as budget cuts, voting rights, drug and alcohol use and abuse, teen pregnancy, texting while driving, body piercing, stress, college acceptance, school rivalries and juggling the stress of school, jobs and activities.

The key to good coverage here is localizing the issues – reporting them in relation to the specific concerns of your audience – and drawing on quotes from students, teachers and other relevant local resources. Stories with a local angle will almost always be of greater interest to your readers. Quotes from local sources will help place the story in context for your audience and help them grasp the relevance of the topic.

Where a school is located can also be important in choosing topics for long-form reporting. In Lakota, Ohio, a suburb of Cincinnati, student journalists localized the weak economy's effect on poverty in their school by reporting that 64 students in their district met the district's definition of homeless.

Local professional sources can also be interviewed and used as sources to help put a topic in perspective for your local community. This is a far more powerful reporting strategy than simply reprinting information obtained from the Internet that has no local connection to the school or community. For instance, in the Lakota homelessness story, the student reporter interviewed a school social worker, the homeless coordinator for the Ohio Department of Education, the school principal, a school transportation coordinator, the school student services coordinator and a former homeless student whose identity was kept anonymous. The reporter also cited figures from the National Center for Homeless Education, comparing figures in Ohio with those nationwide for perspective. Other stories in the package included an interview with a local couple who volunteer at a homeless shelter and a profile of students who volunteer through local community organizations.

In-depth reporting should also pique readers' interests about the diversity of the student body, with topics ranging from differences in race, ethnicity and sexual orientations, to students who categorize themselves as "alternative." In a four-page, special section in *ReMarker*, the newspaper of St. Mark's School in Dallas, Texas, staff took a look at the "entitled generation,"

WWW

WEBLINK Check out

www.studentsfirst.org

This is an online grassroots movement with the intention of reforming education. The movement seeks to mobilize parents, teachers, students, administrators and citizens. It includes a good blog link to topics of concern in education.

Quick Exercise

For each of the following categories, find an example of a story that would be appropriate for an in-depth report in your school's publication:

1 school governing boards

2 athletics

3 curricular

4 extracurricular

5 beyond the school

6 national trends.

In a small group, choose the best, most appropriate and engaging topic for in-depth coverage.

FIGURE 8.2 *El Estoque*, Monta Vista High School, Cupertino, Calif.

Experiencing budget cuts due to a crisis in the state budget, many schools in California have wound up cutting their local budgets to compensate. At Monta Vista High School in Cupertino, editors of *El Estoque* localized the story on the front-page. The story details the school's decision to cut 26 classes in anticipation of budget cuts for the next school year. A visually powerful headline display grabs readers' attention. Note the box at the bottom detailing specific cuts to the school's classes and the monetary results. The story also uses text headings, small headlines at key junctures in the story, to help break up this long story, which continues on an inside page.

Is there a story here?

The best student newspapers in the country today are looking far beyond Homecoming and the results of the debate squad's latest tournament for coverage ideas. They are tackling real issues, presented in incisive, relevant stories – in-depth, investigative – geared toward fully engaging their readers. These stories have substance and provide strong connections to their students and to their community.

Scholastic journalists have every right – and motivation – to tackle sensitive, provocative issues which affect them and their communities. So, for that reason, student journalists need to be trained to continually ask the question, "Is there a story here?" when surfing the Internet, watching television (news programs and regular programs), reading newspapers and looking at magazines. You never know where you'll hear or read about an issue that might be appropriate for us to use. That's one of your main tasks as a journalist: always keeping your "news radar" on, being receptive to finding these issue-driven stories that will be lively, fresh and stimulating.

Example? Even in the most obscure quotes in a national magazine you might find something. Take this quote from the December 2007 edition of *Esquire* magazine:

> We [the United States] have not been educating enough engineers and scientists, people with the skills we will need to compete with China and India. We have not been investing in the kinds of basic research that made us the technological powerhouse of the late 20th century.

That allegation was turned in to a cover story by a private school whose notoriety came from its storied mathematics and science programs. Department chairs, a foreign exchange student, students who hoped to enroll in college as pre-med majors, and former students were interviewed.

Or consider this from *Parade* magazine in September 2012:

> In an interview with former Supreme Court justice Sandra Day O'Connor, the interviewer found that upon retirement, she was now focused on civics education, especially to middle schoolers. The justice told the magazine that more Americans could name an *American Idol* judge rather than the chief justice of the U.S. Supreme Court.

Think of the story possibilities a creative journalist could come up with for in-depth pieces: an overview of the civics program or government education in his school, a look at how former students who are now in the legal fields and public service became interested in their careers, an interactive quiz or poll testing students' knowledge, interviewing professors at nearby universities to get their reaction to Ms. O'Connor's findings.

The key to making a story relevant for your newspaper is finding the local peg. The easiest way to do this is to get someone in authority or with knowledge of the subject (students, faculty members, administrators, parents, members of the community) to react to a certain issue. For a story on nutrition, an appropriate subject would be the director of your campus food services; for a story on concussion, a parent who is a physician or the football coach or trainer at your school.

Ray Westbrook, Advisor, ReMarker *Newspaper and* Marksmen *Yearbook, St. Mark's School of Texas, Dallas*

a term used by a coach during a chapel presentation. At a wealthy, private school, the term struck a nerve and prompted the newspaper staff to examine the economic and social "entitlements" of its school community. The coverage included visually interesting and well-planned photo illustrations, a center spread story entitled, "You lose," a story about coaches fighting the trend toward giving everyone a trophy, a personal column from a student who began his education at an average public school, an interview with an economics professor who is the father of a St. Mark's student and one with an educational reform specialist at StudentsFirst, a grassroots movement to reform education.

How were these stories developed into powerful examples of long-form journalism? To start with, good journalists listen. They observe. They hear. They pick up on conversations among the various segments of the school community. They reflect on these observations through discussion with others, and through newspaper staff meetings, where editors and writers evaluate the news value of different topics. Not every story is appropriate for long-form, in-depth reporting. Evaluating a story's potential and balancing it with available resources is an important part of the process.

Test your knowledge

How could your school's location provide topics for possible in-depth coverage?

GETTING STARTED

An in-depth report will usually require far more time and more newspaper staff members than traditional story coverage. Much of that time will be spent conducting research in different forms – from talking to fellow students and teachers, to learning and reading on the Internet or in the school or local library. Often, in-depth reporters won't even be able to start interviewing until they've done a fair amount of background research, informing themselves about the issue so they can write with authority about the topic in question. If the topic is to be localized for the school publication, reading national reports will give the reporters access to information that will help them form questions and guide them to likely sources and resources. Reporters should be careful to use this backgrounding information only for research and should avoid quoting material that has already appeared in print or online in professional publications. No in-depth story should read like a class project or book report. Current, nationally reported statistics from reputable sources, however, are easy to access on the Internet and can be cited in stories. These statistics provide perspective, especially when broken down by state or locality.

If the publication's staff size allows it, a team of reporters, editors, photographers and others should be assigned to the topic. Even on a small staff, one reporter, editor and photographer can form an in-depth reporting team. The newspaper's online editors should also be part of the team, planning from the outset how the website can add to the coverage. The team should meet early in the process, to discuss the topic and to divide research responsibilities. The team should meet regularly throughout the pre-publication period to share and discuss information, and begin to develop a structure for the coverage. Depending on the school's publishing schedule, this process could extend across one or more upcoming issues.

Once the basic research has been done, the reporting team can begin to anticipate the space commitment they will need for their in-depth report. Making that decision too early in the process may mean that the story is given insufficient space or too much space in the publication. Often, space for in-depth reporting may already be established in the newspaper's structure. It may always appear on a center spread or some other designated page. But also consider the resources of your publication's website for additional coverage and relevant links. If reporters, editors and photographers are working together, a discussion of how the topic will be reported and how the story will be visualized is also key at this early stage, so adequate time can be devoted to making the visuals strong and appealing.

On some publications staff, more than one team may be working on stories simultaneously. Team members may also be working on more than one team, but with deadlines spread out across publishing periods. Some publications designate specific editors or reporters to work exclusively on in-depth or package stories.

Regardless of the space allocation, the publication should help the reader understand the significance of the information through its placement and layout. Identifying the story as a special report, in-depth report, centerspread, front-page feature, special section or other such **label** will help focus attention on the importance of the information. Starting the story on the front-page and continuing it inside the publication is another way of alerting the reader to the special content. This type of story is known as **jump coverage** since it jumps from one page to another. Many yearbooks use jump coverage for serious issue reporting. Smaller sized newsmagazines often feature in-depth coverage on the cover of the publication and devote several pages of coverage to it inside the issue.

Full-page coverage

In the newspaper, a full page of coverage may be all that's necessary to adequately cover a topic. That page could even be the front-page or in another prominent position in the paper. Even with a full page, the reporter should discuss the story's angles with a photographer or visual thinker so the story can be visually interesting as well as adequately reported. Well-written, detailed headlines will help the reader understand the importance of this story. Strong visuals will offer another layer of information that can attract the reader's interest. With a long article, the layout should also offer some visual relief from unbroken text, such as headings or drop caps at natural junctures in the story. Pull-quotes, taken from the story and set off in a larger font, can also aid in the layout. Statistics and number-based information should be appropriately presented in

Copy That

By Elijah Alperin

■ **Students and teachers alike examine what many consider to a growing epidemic at school: cheating.**

DESPITE PENALTIES in place for academic dishonesty, cheating and plagiarism remain a significant part of the school atmosphere. Now the school is taking steps to curb the behavior.

Plagiarism: Getting in trouble for something you didn't do.

Plagiarism in all departments has always been taken seriously. If caught, your grade is likely to suffer and you are liable to receive a referral. For honors and Advanced Placement students, however, the English department's spring semester crackdown on plagiarism has upped the ante for students who are thinking about misrepresenting their assignments.

In response to an increase in school-wide plagiarism, and especially academic dishonesty amongst honors and AP students, the English department voted unanimously to implement a stricter plagiarism policy this semester. The new policy states that if a student in an honors or AP class is caught plagiarizing, that student will be removed from the course and placed in a regular English course for the remainder of the year, according to English department head Bryan Ritter.

Students who are removed from the course may reapply for honors or AP placement the following year, provided the course does not require students to have taken the previous year of honors or AP, according to Ritter. Because of the necessary prerequisites, sophomores who are removed from the 10th grade English honors course will not be eligible to take AP English Language and Composition as juniors. However, they can enroll in English teacher Cathy Innis's AP English Language and Composition, an open class, as seniors. Juniors who are penalized for plagiarism may rejoin the AP Literature track as seniors. However, their access will be dependent on how they perform on the English honors placement exam, as if they were first applying for English honors, according to Ritter.

The policy also affects regular English students, who if caught plagiarizing in their classes, will not be allowed to apply for the honors and AP English track. The ban will be in addition to the established penalties for plagiarism in all classes, which include parent contact and a visit to the dean.

Ritter, who has taught at Lowell since 1998, says that while the new penalty has been long due, it was sparked by a rise in instances of plagiarism during the fall 2011 semester. "From last year to this year, there's been a marked increase," he said. "We had 14 confirmed cases, five of which came from honors and AP students." All 14 students received Fs on the plagiarized assignments, and one student who plagiarized twice was removed from the honors/AP English program after teacher discussion under the past policy, according to Ritter.

At least one English teacher feels that the punishment should be more severe. "I think kids should be kicked out after plagiarizing at Lowell," English teacher Jennifer Moffitt said. "It is a competitive academic school, and other kids would love to get in."

Some English teachers have resorted to alternate teaching methods to discourage plagiarism. "I set up my class so students can discuss essays in groups, ask their friends and have time to write in class," Innis said. "I try to give them time in class so they don't go home and say 'I don't know what to write' and copy off someone else."

Innis even changes the structure of her assignments to prevent cheating. "There is tons of stuff on the Internet about the traditional texts we read," she said. "I try to give assignments with different topics than the standard essay."

Other teachers, such as English teacher and advisor for *The Lowell* Sharn Matusek, teach mini-units on plagiarism to convey to students how passing others work as your own can have serious repercussions, and how to work more authentically. "I have students do research about plagiarism in the real world, and it really brings it home that when people plagiarize, there can be serious consequences, such as losing a book contract or a Pulitzer Prize," Matusek said.

In an effort to discourage and avert plagiarism, the school pays $5,000 annually out of the technology budget for the anti-plagiarism Web service Turnitin (www.turnitin.com). Lowell teachers began to use the resource in 2008 to check students' work against content available online as well as other writing previously submitted to the site. "With access to billions of Internet source documents, students can cut-and-paste entire written passages in seconds," according to the website. "Turnitin's OriginalityCheck helps instructors check students' work for improper citation or potential plagiarism by comparing it against the world's most accurate text comparison database."

Many teachers, particularly from English, social studies and science departments who used to spend time double-checking for sources students might have used to falsify their work, welcome the help. "It's hard to hide from this program," Ritter said. "Plagiarizing in a way to make it look clean would be more work than just writing the piece on your own."

Besides searching the Internet for sites that students may have plagiarized from, Turnitin keeps track of all essays ever submitted to its database, so work from other students or from Lowell graduates can also be flagged for dishonesty.

Although the school pays for a schoolwide license, not all teachers use Turnitin, and so plagiarism may still go undetected in some cases, according to Ritter. He hopes to work toward integrating the Web service into

> **"** Lowell has created an atmosphere in which students have lost their passion for learning and replaced it with a perfect-grades-no-matter-how-I-get-them mentality."
>
> MIA KALO,
> sophomore

all English classes at Lowell, and that more teachers schoolwide incorporate it into their practice.

Ritter acknowledged the possible use of in-class essays as a method to discourage dishonesty, but said that while they are valuable exercises, the standard take-home analytical essay is a skill that all students must learn. The new plagiarism policy and Turnitin, he says, make him confident that students will submit their own work, regardless of the availability of online analysis.

Cheating: An Underside of School Culture

While new technologies have recently uncovered high levels of plagiarism, cheating has been an issue impacting the school's academic atmosphere for much longer. Students, faced with pressure to perform well and the temptation of quick and easy ways to cheat, may turn to academic dishonesty as a way to stay afloat.

According to the results of January 2011's Student Body Council survey on stress and its impact on students, Lowell students are no exception. Only a slim 7 percent of seniors, 15 percent of juniors, 20 percent of sophomores and 37 percent of freshmen said they had never copied homework or cheated on tests. SBC gave the survey to all students during their English classes and based its results on 100 randomly selected from each grade.

Currently, instances of academic dishonesty are dealt with according to the official academic honesty policy, which is attached to a packet on student behavior that incoming freshmen sign. The policy outlines the consequences of cheating on a test or homework. The severity of punishment depends on the student's past record, and with each successive instance of academic dishonesty the repercussions become more serious.

Another student spoke of how the pressure at Lowell changed their views on acceptable behavior. "In middle school I was totally against cheating," the student who requested anonymity said. "But at Lowell, I work so hard but I'm still in danger of getting B's, because of those few assignments I just couldn't get done or a couple of unfair tests. So now I copy some work and occasionally cheat because I have to get an A."

A third student agrees that the high pressure at Lowell exacerbates the problem. "Lowell has created an atmosphere in which students have lost their passion for learning and replaced it for a perfect-grades-no-matter-how-I-get-them mentality," sophomore Mia Kalo said.

While math teacher Wilson Sinn acknowledged that the competitive atmosphere at Lowell might accentuate the problem, he attributed the levels of academic dishonesty to an overall decline in ethics. "It's not just a teenage phenomenon, but part of an entirely new culture," he said. "We cheat from the bankers all the way down to the students."

Some students assert they cheat in selected classes because they feel that the morality of cheating depends on their commitment to the subject or assignment. "I will never be a

chemist, nor will I ever develop a sudden love for the subject. So I don't feel guilty copying the homework," a fourth student, who also requested anonymity, said.

The same student who opined that there was little teacher enforcement also felt that being dishonest in less enjoyable classes was more acceptable. "I do so much busy work that is completely useless, so I have no problem cheating in classes that have no value to me," a student who requested anonymity said. The student explained that more involved assignments would impact the inclination to falsify work. "I'd prefer more projects and interactive learning," the student said.

In addition to academic pressure, the modern student must constantly compete with the temptation that, in today's world of spontaneous information transfer, the answer could be just a couple of clicks, texts or taps away. According to a May 2010 survey from the Pew Internet and American Life Project, 82 percent of Americans 13 and over have a cell phone, and 38 percent of mobile phone users use their phones to access the Internet. The survey also stated that 54 percent of teens text daily on their phones.

A different student spoke of a scenario where a group of students decided to take advantage of being allowed to use cell phones, in place of calculators, on a final exam. "We were set up in rows and beforehand about 15 people agreed to text each other the answers," the student who requested anonymity said. "The teacher walked by my desk several times, and failed to see the 'one new message' sign flashing on my 'calculator'. It was basically a group final."

Some may have heard of the saying "When you cheat you are only cheating yourself." In reality, dishonest students also negatively impact their teachers due to their difficulty of dealing with students who break the academic honesty contract. Honest students also suffer side effects. "I don't give take-home tests anymore, because I gave one two years ago where at least 30 percent of my students had the answers from the other test version," physics teacher Bryan Cooley said. "All students have now lost the opportunity for that kind of test."

Many teachers attempt to discourage students from sharing information about tests with classmates in later periods by penalizing the whole class if there is a discrepancy between its average score and that of the later class. "I always curve to the higher score," Sinn said. "So if the later class scores much higher, the kids in the earlier class do not get as much benefit from the curve."

Biology teacher Theodore Johnson said that although he sometimes catches students cheating, he tries not to let it affect his classes. "It can be a huge stress for the teacher to try and figure out which students are cheating, and it's unfair to honest students to have the teacher not trust you," he said. "I just figure that you will be caught and pay the price eventually. You can't cheat your whole life."

> **"** You can't cheat your whole life."
>
> THEODORE JOHNSON,
> biology teacher

FIGURE 8.4 *The Broadview,* Convent of the Sacred Heart High School, San Francisco, Calif., Dec. 14, 2010, pp. 6–7. "Farm fresh: Organic food is chemical-free option," by Isabelle Pinard and Aniali Shrestha. Reproduced by permission of Schools of the Sacred Heart – San Francisco.

A double truck offers premium space for an in-depth presentation. Using one dominant image across the two pages creates a focal point for this spread on organic food. In the picture, the subject is facing the headline, which takes the reader to both the primary and deck heads. The writers divided the content into two main stories, one on small local farmers and one on organic pre-packaged food. A strong timeline wraps around the left and bottom sides of the layout comparing the days between food's arrival in a local farmer's market with the time it takes to reach a grocery store. An additional sidebar told in numbers is based on information obtained from the Organic Farming Association. The color green ties the photo, headline and timeline together in an effective way.

graphical forms such as charts and diagrams for easier comprehension. Appropriate sidebars can also help relieve text-heavy presentations.

Double truck coverage

If an in-depth story demands more space, the natural location to consider is the double truck or center spread. Most papers will include two facing pages printed on one sheet of paper that offer better options for layout and presentation. Multiple visuals can be used. Information can be presented in a variety of storytelling forms to amplify the main story. Such techniques offer readers a chance to experience a story in an alternative, visually-compelling format – which may draw them back to the main story (see Chapter 15 for more information on visual storytelling). Building the design around a distinctive, interesting, well-planned headline and strong visual will provide a focal point for the coverage and demonstrate its relevance.

Beyond the double truck

When coverage demands more space or if space is pre-set or limited, reporters could consider **series reporting**: stories broken into parts and presented over the course of several issues or in print and online. The challenge in series reporting is to make sure the information lends itself to a series of stories and to make sure the information is logically presented in the series. Complex topics, such as cheating or a series of changes planned for the school's curriculum, work well for a series of reports. A visual device such as a **story logo** or another visual identifier will help readers identify the story as part of a multi-issue series. A series tends to be less effective in a publication printed monthly or less frequently, though the series can be updated more frequently on the publication's website. Even in a bimonthly or trimonthly publication, the series should recap the previous reports before presenting the new information, so the reader recalls the context of the previous report. For publications with limited space for in-depth reporting, a series is often an effective solution.

IN ACTION

Building an effective in-depth design

No one will be attracted to a story that fails to provide some visual appeal, no matter how strong the reporting and writing.

Here are some suggestions for a strong in-depth package design.

Sidebar 8a *North Star* (fhntoday.com), Francis Howell North High School, St. Charles, Mo., April 11, 2012, pp. 18–25. "The Beauty in the Beast," by Sophie Gordon. Design and graphics by Kelsey Bell. Reproduced by permission of Aaron Manfull.

1 It all begins with a strong headline and visual. And if you can create a connection between the two, even better. Here, the strong typography of the primary headline creates a single message embedded with the pink Twitter icon image in the cage. Note how the pink is repeated in "social media." The story begins in a strong way with another deck head and strong drop cap in the text column.

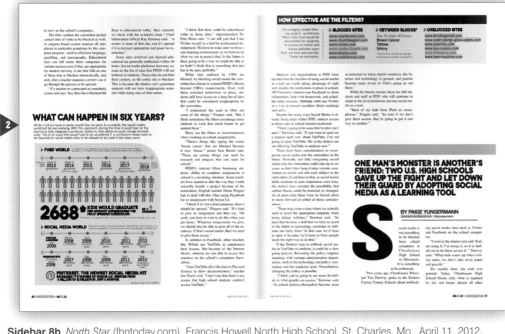

Sidebar 8b *North Star* (fhntoday.com), Francis Howell North High School, St. Charles, Mo., April 11, 2012, pp. 18–25. "The Beauty in the Beast," by Sophie Gordon. Design and graphics by Kelsey Bell. Reproduced by permission of Aaron Manfull.

2 A sidebar effectively compares six years of Internet growth and repeats the pink color from the opening spread. Another sidebar on Internet filters pulls out information from the text. A second story on how two high schools have embraced social media begins here and continues on the next spread. It also introduces a second color, green, in a bar used to introduce a third story. Blue highlights are also used as a third color in the sidebar and as a standard color for all web addresses throughout the newsmagazine.

3 Two more sidebars keep the story moving, focusing here on student/parent quotes and later identifying how social media forms could be used effectively in the classroom. A third story looks at careers in social media. Note how each story and sidebar continues the strong typography and large capital letter introduced on the first spread.

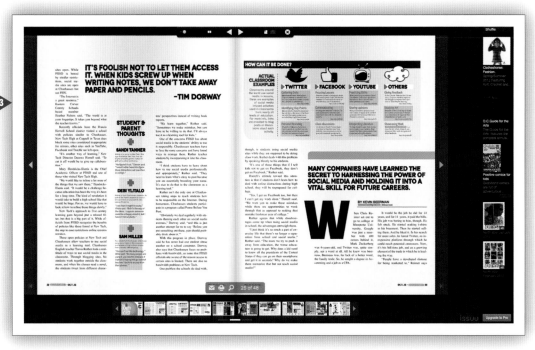

Sidebar 8c *North Star* (fhntoday.com), Francis Howell North High School, St. Charles, Mo., April 11, 2012, pp. 18–25. "The Beauty in the Beast," by Paige Yungermann. Design and graphics by Kelsey Bell. Reproduced by permission of Aaron Manfull.

4 On the last spread, two pull quotes provide perspective for the story and continue the strong typography. A final sidebar presents more statistics in a simple format, picking up the pink and green color palette. A very simple poll result in large type also provides key information, but without interfering with the design.

Sidebar 8d *North Star* (fhntoday.com), Francis Howell North High School, St. Charles, Mo., April 11, 2012, pp. 18–25. "The Beauty in the Beast," by Sophie Gordon. Design and graphics by Kelsey Bell. Reproduced by permission of Aaron Manfull.

Effective design for an in-depth story requires extensive planning and production. Adequate time and resources should be devoted to creating a compelling design for the story, which makes the topic visually interesting for readers.

Series reporting can appear more frequently on a website, especially if the story is still unfolding, with key events between print editions. Updating issue reporting on a website also offers additional storytelling forms not available in print, such as videos and animated graphics. Gathering student reaction to previous reports can add a valuable supplement to the printed content. In a story on a local issue such as community volunteering, a video showing students volunteering at local organizations, or a slideshow of the various students assisting in the local organizations could provide additional visual information and expand the topic's reach beyond print content.

In the newsmagazine format, packages of information will commonly start with a visually striking cover, which connects with the visuals used on the initial and subsequent spreads inside the publication. Using a specific color palette and visual style will link all the packaged content together.

Special issues

In the case of a story with a strong timeliness factor, such as a major school anniversary, a major sports victory, an important school event, the opening of a new school or a breaking news event such as a natural disaster or school tragedy, the staff might consider publishing a special section or edition – especially if the event occurs out of sync with the publication schedule. This coverage could also be used effectively on the newspaper's website if financial resources are limited or if there is a need for frequent updates.

In the case of an important scheduled event, adequate time will often be available to plan for the special section and its content. This would be true of a building renovation or opening, a school anniversary celebration or a team making it to an important playoff competition such as a state championship. In the case of a breaking news event, editors may be able to quickly marshal the staff's resources to report and photograph the event. Cooperative publishing efforts between different schools are another possibility if events impact multiple campuses. If the staff doesn't have the resources to obtain pictures or other visuals, obtaining copies with permission to publish from local media such as community newspapers might also be possible. Such breaking news stories should usually be updated online with fresh content to maintain interest and provide crucial information. This might be the case with a natural disaster, extreme weather, the outcome of an important sports competition or another unplanned event affecting the school community. Social media such as Twitter can also be used to provide updates.

In the event of a scheduled event, good advance planning enables staff to provide special coverage to document a major school anniversary, opening, building project or state/national recognition. Many schools publish special sections to start the year, for freshman orientation or at graduation to honor the senior class.

The yearbook

Yearbook staff should not overlook the in-depth form for coverage. In-depth coverage helps change the pace of storytelling in the yearbook, offering longer stories and different styles of reporting. Covering significant or complex issues that have occurred during the year can amplify coverage in other parts of the book. Sports sections can tackle the same kinds of issues as the newspaper, or can give special coverage to teams that have won championships. Academic sections could cover curricular changes or shifts in teaching policy and procedure. Coverage of issues that helped to define a year can add a new dimension to activity or **student life sections** where yearbooks cover a variety of events and activities both in and out of school. Many schools experiment with magazine format reporting, using topic-oriented coverage for issues such as pressure, achievement or stress. Focusing on personal profiles of interesting or accomplished students is another way to add a different tone. Significant school events during the year that attracted large numbers of students offer other possibilities for in-depth coverage.

Test your knowledge

What kind of topic could be appropriately covered in a double truck and in visual coverage online?

Test your knowledge

What print and online resources would be needed to publish a freshman orientation guide for the first day of school or during orientation week?

FIGURE 8.5 *The Indian*, Shawnee Mission North High School, Overland Park, Kan. Reproduced by permission of Shawnee Mission North Principal Richard Kramer.

In addition to covering the school's events, academics, clubs, sports and people, a yearbook can also take a hard-hitting approach to issues through specialized, in-depth coverage. In a story that could also be covered by the school newspaper, the staff of the *Shawnee Mission North yearbook* interviewed three teen parents and documented how their lives had changed while still in high school. A strong image focuses the story on a mother and daughter, whose pink blouses set the color for the headline.

Quick Exercise

Using exchange publications, look for an example of one of the following in-depth formats: single page, double truck, magazine cover and spreads, special section or issue and yearbook in-depth coverage. For the example you choose, evaluate how the staff used the space to present the story. Is the headline appealing? Did staff plan for a strong visual connection? Is the story given an adequate amount of space? Is the overall presentation inviting and appealing?

WRITING THE IN-DEPTH STORY

Traditional news story forms are rarely successful for the in-depth report. Instead, reporters need to build in-depth stories around the key points and themes that arise from all the information gathered. The depth of the research will make the task of organizing the information more important. Talking through the story with the other team members, such as other writers, editors and visual reporters will help the organizational process. Writing an in-depth story most closely resembles writing a long feature story. As with a feature, the lead needs to grab the reader's attention and make the story's importance clear from the outset.

Note the way this lead begins for a story titled: "For students with ADHD, the hardest part is lack of focus."

It's the end of seventh hour. The minute hand on the clock can't go any slower. I feel myself getting jittery as my medicine starts to wear off. My eyes dart around the room. I feel myself talking incessantly. I can't stop. I've forgotten to write down any of my assignments. Later tonight, I'll have trouble getting a paper written. Too many things will distract me.

From ages 10 to 14, I had to face this disorder every day and cope with the symptoms. I took Ritalin, and as my symptoms worsened, my prescription changed to Adderall, both of which are used to treat ADHD symptoms as well as narcolepsy, a sleep disorder.

My experience isn't as uncommon as people may think. According to the Center for Disease Control and Prevention (CDC), about 1.2 million children ages six to nine were diagnosed with ADHS from 2006 to 2008 in the United States, in addition to about 3.3 million ages 10 to 17.

Ashlee Crane, Northwest Passage, *Shawnee Mission Northwest High School, Shawnee, Kan.*

Would you continue reading this story? Probably. Written in first person, the lead paints a picture and invites the reader into the difficult world of ADHD. The lead is compeling and creates a strong desire to continue reading. Crane's use of the CDC statistic makes the incidence of the problem clear, beyond her own situation. The student went on to interview a fellow classmate and include his personal story. The coverage included a large photo of the student interviewed and a chart comparison of the three major ADHD drugs with short- and long-term side-effects and additional information.

In a special in-depth section on gay rights in the *Eagle Edition* of the Episcopal School of Dallas, student journalists devoted three pages to the topic, including a personal column, two main stories, a timeline and a sidebar on religious views of homosexuality. The in-depth report included a strong typographical illustration.

Over three pairs of facing pages, the staff of Francis Howell Central High School's *Central Focus* published three in-depth stories about students finding balance in managing pregnancies,

WORDS of WISDOM

Know that in-depth stories take time. Lots of time. And probably more time than you're used to taking for other types of stories.

First, reporters need to take time to find a solid angle – what they want readers to think about – and then take time to develop that angle through research. After that, they need to find sources, as many as they can, who are both relevant and credible to the story's angle and spend lots of time talking to those sources, again, probably more than they're used to. Next, they need to take time crafting the story in such a way that makes it as readable and accessible as possible. Along the way, designers and photographers need to work on multiple ways to tell the story visually.

An in-depth story isn't something you can write in a day or even a week. It might take months to put one together properly. Make sure you keep those projects simmering on the "back burner," working on them a little at a time to give them time to develop. Don't take shortcuts and always think about your readers. Be prepared to listen to your sources and adapt your story along the way, and always have a Plan B if your original idea doesn't work out, because sometimes it won't.

Jim Streisel, Adviser, HiLite and HiLiteOnline, *Carmel High School, Carmel, Ind.*

a topic also featured photographically on their newsmagazine cover. The first story, "Planning for the unexpected," told the story of one senior's unplanned pregnancy:

> Minutes passed as senior Hannah Edler anxiously fixed her eyes on a pregnancy test hoping a little red negative sign would appear before her and all of her worries would be over. As the little green plus sign appeared, she sat wishing it were a negative sign – as if all of this was just a dream – but deep inside she knew that was not the truth.
>
> In the United States, approximately 750,000 teenagers become pregnant each year, according to dosomething.org. In 2012, Hannah will be a part of that statistic.
>
> "When I first took the pregnancy test I was at my boyfriend, Grant (Nickle)'s house. I think Grant was scared and nervous when I told him," Hannah said. "My first reaction was just to cry."
>
> *Jessica Mugler,* Central Focus, *Francis Howell Central High School, St. Charles, Mo.*

The second story looked at the support a teen mother received from the school, her parents and the baby's father and his parents. The third story looked at a junior who gave birth at age 14 and chronicled her life in high school with a toddler son. The newspaper staff used its resources to publish all three stories in one issue – though, if space had been limited, this topic could have been a three-part series in subsequent issues or published on a website.

Because reporters will gather information for in-depth reports over a period of time, the deadline pressures of a normal story won't usually apply. This will give the reporters more flexibility in polishing their writing. In addition to an interesting lead, in-depth reporters should make sure they have interesting anecdotes and illustrations, effective transitions, clear writing and strong demonstrations of the topic's relevance for the reader. A good editor can make a big difference in improving the writing of in-depth reports to make sure the story's organization is clear and logical. A meticulous copy editor should always be involved in a package presentation.

Some newspapers start in-depth reporting on the front-page and continue it inside the paper. In the *ReMarker*, St. Mark's School of Texas, Dallas, Texas, the topic of binge drinking started with the following headline and deck: "Risky business, 90 percent of all teen alcohol consumption occurs in the form of binge drinking – a dangerous statistic that is causing alarm from students, administrators and parents" (see Figure 5.5). The story begins:

> He didn't know he would be confronted with a bigger challenge than asking out his first homecoming date.
>
> He didn't know he would feel more nerves than he did the first time behind the wheel.
>
> He didn't know he would be faced with a decision so big so soon, at least not until senior year when he would declare his college choice.
>
> But there was William McGee, then a sophomore, at a friend's house party, being offered a drink. McGee declined, but it seemed like no one else had.
>
> He looked around and noticed a friend, sluggish, dazed, wonky-legged. Everyone else was too engrossed with their friends, seemingly lulled by the amalgam of beer and hip-hop music.
>
> His friend took one more step, and like a jittery Jenga tower, that last move led to his collapse. The ambulance came and immediately took him to the hospital.
>
> McGee later found out his friend suffered from alcohol poisoning.
>
> "It was very scary. I had never seen anything like that," McGee said. "I knew I would be exposed to alcohol in high school, but I didn't think one of my first experiences would be like that."

By starting with an anecdotal lead, the writers, Jairo Nevarez and Lee Perkins, grab the reader from the start. It's an anecdote many of the readers can probably relate to. As the story continues, note how the writers broaden the issue by quoting national statistics and then narrow the focus, returning to William McGee.

> A statistic published in *Parade* magazine's June 2011 issue suggest 90 percent of all teen alcohol consumption occurs in the form of binge drinking. Binge drinking is the excessive consumption of alcohol in a short period of time. According to gordie.org, a more exact definition of binge drinking is the consumption of five or more drinks for males and four or more drinks for females

during one drinking experience in a two-hour period of time. Marksmen like McGee are often exposed to this behavior at social events and parties.

"Since that time, I have seen more guys drink and have heard of guys binging at parties," McGee said. "I think it's almost become a normality, something kids expect to see at parties."

According to intheknowzone.com, McGee's assumption is accurate among teenagers nationwide. Half of students who binge drink do so more than once a week. Binge drinking among teenagers isn't just a prevalence, it's a regularity. And that regularity can be attributed to the influence older role models have on impressionable underclassmen.

One family that has suffered because of those influences of older role models is Leslie and Michael Lanahan, whose son Gordie Bailey, a St. Mark's student through ninth grade, died in a hazing incident at the University of Colorado at Boulder in 2004.

Michael Lanahan says it didn't have to happen. A simple phone call would have saved Gordie's life. But that phone call never came.

"Your legs just drop out from under you," Lanahan said. "You can't believe it. You want to get to the hospital to help him. No, he's not gone. You just can't believe it. You just talked to him the day before. You want a second chance. Let me do it different, let me help him. It's like your life's gone before your eyes. I can't believe we lost him."

"It's just so permanent. You don't know what to do."

As a freshman, McGee remembers looking up to the older boys in Upper School. He wanted to be like the Student Council leader, the class president, the captain of the football team. Going to his first Upper School party, he was excited to be with those guys he so tried to replicate.

And when one of those guys approached him at a party leaning in with a high five, McGee slapped his hand, feeling for the first time like a part of the Upper School brotherhood.

"Good to see you here, William," the older student said.

McGee jerked, startled by the overwhelming smell of alcohol in his breath. He was shocked. Naive and formidable, he didn't know who he could look up to.

Jairo Nevarez and Lee Perkins, ReMarker, *St. Mark's School of Texas, Dallas, Texas*

The reporters then included an interview with the school's headmaster who talked about the school's responsibility to educate its students through a Freedom from Chemical Dependency Week every February. The story also returned to the Lanahans who turned their personal tragedy into an organization, The Gordie Foundation, which produced a movie and holds a National Gordie Day for educating college students about binge drinking consequences.

Another important consideration for in-depth reporting is helping readers keep track of multiple sources. Readers may need reminders to sort out all the names and positions of the sources quoted in the story. Information can become difficult to understand if the readers can't figure out the source of quoted material or remember which last name corresponds to which source.

Complex quotes should be simplified using ellipses or brackets for clarifications. **Running quotes** – those that are too long to contain in one paragraph – are also a viable option for in-depth pieces. Running quotes don't use closing quotation marks until the end of the quote. Each new paragraph of quoted material begins with opening quotation marks.

In this multisource story on their school's lockdown on Internet content, reporter Sophie Gordon, of Francis Howell North High School in Missouri, wrote about the issue from a variety of perspectives. This story appeared both in the print and online editions of *FHN Today*.

Calculus teacher Steve Willott finishes showing an example of a new concept on the board. Can anyone find me a different method to do this? Students search through their textbooks and notes in an attempt to find the answer. According to Willott, the only problem with this is that he would like students to be able to recognize good methods even if they're presented in ways beyond the text book.

"I could see students searching YouTube for particular terms we use in class in order to see different methods or examples," he said. "Then under my guidance I would be able to better equip them to evaluate those sources independently."

All social media sites – including YouTube – are blocked on the school's WiFi and school computers with student access, which prevents Willott and other teachers from using those 21st-century tools in class.

The Francis Howell School District [FHSD] is required to use Internet filters because it receives funding from a government program called E-rate, which provides discounted telecommunications services. In order to receive that funding, the filters must comply with provisions in a law known as Children's Internet Protection Act (CIPA). Basically, schools must block material that is obscene and harmful to minors, such as pornography; however, the law doesn't specify everything schools have to block or allow. In FHSD, a committee of school administrators decides what qualifies as inappropriate for students to view on the school's computers.

The filter method the committee picked caused sites of value to be blocked as well. A category-based system restricts all sites placed in particular groupings by the computer program – such as offensive language, gambling and pornography. Educational sites can fall under these categories for various reasons even if they are appropriate for student viewing. A site that falls on one of these lists is blocked automatically, and only after a teacher requests a review can it go through the process to be opened.

"If a teacher or a principal or somebody comes and says 'Hey, this site is blocked but there is educational value,' then certainly we check with the academic team," Chief Information Officer Ray Eernisse said. "A review is done of that site, and it's opened if it is deemed appropriate and good for instruction."

Some sites reviewed and deemed educational are generally unblocked within 48 hours. Social media platforms, however, remain on the list of sites that FHSD will not unblock to students. Those sites do not filter their content, so the entire site is blocked. This is because the district can't guarantee students will not view inappropriate material while using sites of that nature.

"I think that there could be educational value to those sites," superintendent Dr. Pam Sloan said. "I can tell you that I use Twitter myself as a tool for professional development. We have to make sure we have a safe learning environment, so we have to do what we can to protect that. In the future is there going to be a way we might be able to do both? I think that is something that just has to be seen, probably."

While sites outlined by CIPA are blocked, by blocking social media the committee has chosen to expand FHSD's blocks beyond CIPA's requirements. Even with these extended restrictions in place, students still have access to a long list of sites that could be considered inappropriate by the committee.

"I understand the need to filter out some of the things," Fingers said. "But I think sometimes the filters encourage some students to work that much harder to get around them." Many see the filters as inconveniences when working on school assignments.

"There's things like typing the words 'breast cancer' that are blocked because it says 'breast," senior Sam Renda said. "These certain things you need for research and projects that you need for school."

FHSD's Internet filters hindering students' ability to complete assignments at school is a recurring situation. Some teachers have needed to alter the way they would normally handle a project because of the restrictions. English teacher Diane Fingers had to deal with this when using Facebook for an assignment with Senior Lit.

"I think if it's for school purposes, then it should be opened," Fingers said. "It's hard to give an assignment and then say, 'Oh yeah, you have to wait to do this when you get home.' Whatever assignments we give, we should also be able to give all of the resources. If that's social media, then we need to give them access."

In addition to Facebook, other teachers like Willott use YouTube to supplement their lessons. But because of the Internet blocks, students are not able to access this resource on the school's computers themselves.

"I use YouTube all of the time in Physical Science to show demonstrations," teacher Jon Travis said. "I don't see that there's any reason that high school students couldn't access YouTube."

Students and organizations at FHN have decided that the benefits of using social media as a tool are worth taking advantage of right now despite the restrictions in place at school. AP Chemistry students use Facebook to share information, help with homework and schedule study sessions. Multiple clubs use Twitter as a way to remind members about meetings and news.

Despite the many ways social media is already being used within FHN, student access to those sites at school remains restricted.

"There's going to be some that we just can't open," Eernisse said. "If you were to send me a request right now about YouTube, I'm not going to open YouTube. We at the district are not allowing YouTube to students now."

There have been considerations to incorporate social media into the curriculum in the future. Formally and fully integrating social media into the curriculum could take up to six years, as that's how long it takes various committees to revisit and edit each subject in the curriculum. In addition to that, as social media skills continue to gain importance over time, the district may consider the possibility that certain blocks could be removed or changed. As of press time there were no formal plans to move forward on either of these considerations.

"There may come a time where we actually need to teach the appropriate etiquette when using dating websites," Eernisse said. "So does that become a skill that we have to teach in the future as technology continues to infiltrate our daily lives? In that case we'd have to open it because we'd have to have people teach the right way to do that."

If the District were to unblock social media or YouTube to students, it could be a slow-going process. Revisiting the policy requires meetings with various administrative departments, such as the technology and policy committees and the academic team. Nevertheless, changing the policy is possible.

"I think you're going to see more flexibility in what people can access," Eernisse said, "As school districts themselves become more accustomed to using digital resources, the Internet and technology in general and parents become more aware of what's going on out there."

While the blocks remain, there are still students and staff at FHN who will continue to adapt to the inconveniences and use social media as a tool.

"Most of my kids have iPods or smartphones," Fingers said. "So even if we don't give them access."

Sophie Gordon, FHN Today, *Francis Howell North High School, St. Charles, Mo.*

WWW

WEBLINK Check out

www.depthreporting.com

This personal blog maintained by reporter, editor and digital editor, Mark Schaver, provides an extensive set of links and good contributions from reporters, many of whom discuss using and understanding data.

Gordon's reporting is extensive, and answers questions while presenting different points of view. She accessed important sources such as the school's chief information officer and the superintendent, both of whom might have taken some time and appointments to interview. She provides a range of quotes from different teachers. She provides answers and facts to explain the school's Internet policy and the frustrations it creates. The newspaper might have followed up this in-depth story by revisiting the district policy six months or a year later, especially since technology will continue to evolve and policies could change in response.

Anonymous sources

When reporting controversial or sensitive topics, students may request that reporters not use their real names. Use of a real name or closely identifying circumstances could cause embarrassment or ridicule and may prevent the student from agreeing to be interviewed for the story. Reporters should be sensitive to the need to protect identity when a story is sensitive or controversial, but the publication should have a policy in place for dealing with anonymous

HELPFUL TIPS

Top 10 tips to successful in-depth coverage

→ Focus your content for the space you have or will need.

→ Break content into more than one story when possible.

→ Use text heads, drop caps, pull quotes or other visual devices to break up long stories.

→ Make one visual dominant and visually compelling; don't clutter the page with images.

→ Make your coverage relevant to your readers.

→ Avoid quoting from published sources; obtain your own information.

→ Don't force visual illustrations; consider strong, interesting type when appropriate.

→ Use sidebars, infographics and other alternative story forms to add perspective.

→ Make sure quotes are integrated throughout your text from a variety of appropriate resources.

→ Don't try to fill up the entire space with content; use white space effectively.

FIGURE 8.6 *HiLite* (www. hilite.org), Carmel High School, Carmel, Ind., March 22, 2012, pp. 26–27. "Racing for Recruits," by Bobby Browning and James Benedict. Reproduced by permission of Jim Streisel.

Numbers, statistics and other forms of complex information are often meaningless to readers if buried in a mass of text and quotes. This information can often be better presented through visual forms such as infographics. In this centerspread story on recruiting athletes, a "by the numbers" infographic uses a pie chart to compare the total number of high school athletes, the number who will be recruited and the number who will play professional sports. The pie chart's form dramatically compares these groups in a way that is instantly understandable. The second chart, a locator map, shows locations of schools that student athletes have chosen to play for and attend.

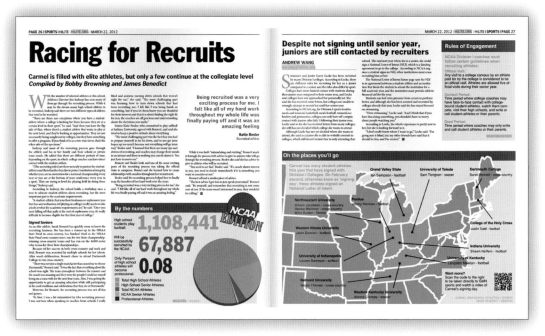

sources (see Chapter 2 for more information on sourcing). In the following online story on teens who choose not to do drugs, the newspaper chose to use only first names for those requesting anonymity, a policy which is explained in a preface to the story. Other students had no problems being identified by name. Mixing anonymous and identified sources can sometimes be a reasonable compromise in order to obtain a variety of opinions.

*Where only first names appear, sources have chosen to remain anonymous

The pressures for high schoolers to take part in different activities are everywhere from the school hallways to current television. While some students' weekends involve drugs, alcohol and sex, there are others who find a way to avoid these situations in an environment where they are commonplace. These students are often known as "clean teens," a phrase coined by the writers of the television series "One Tree Hill." Clean teens are active in school programs, receive good grades, play multiple sports, hold leadership positions and are just like everyone else. They just choose to stay away from what they consider to be risky behavior.

The Blair PTSA's most recent meeting focused on "risky teen behavior." Parents, staff and students discussed issues such as underage drinking and illicit drug use in an effort to raise awareness and provide a forum for discussion for these and other problems often viewed as taboo. Blair's clean teens have different reasons for staying clean, but all understand the dangers of shady behavior.

It's not worth it

For senior Harrison Reed, the motivation to remain a clean teen stems from his parents' Christian religious influence and his early childhood teachings. Reed's conscience allows him to stay true to his beliefs. "I just know what's good for me and what's not," he says. "Drinking doesn't even seem fun to me, I can't stand the smell of smoke and I don't believe the possible consequences of sex are worth it at this age."

Sophomore Briana Villa shares Reed's views and considers herself a clean teen. "There are so many consequences that could results from doing drugs or having sex," Villa says. "To me it's just pointless, why ruin your life in one night just to have some fun?"

Unlike Reed and Villa, Rachel* has never considered the consequences of certain actions as the main factor in remaining a clean teen. Instead, she is not interested in participating in events where drugs, alcohol or sex could be present. "I'm not against these things at all, it's just something I don't feel like doing right now," Rachel says.

Stacy Mathew, Silver Chips Online, *Montgomery Blair High School, Silver Spring, Md.*

Layering information

Beginning with the headline, readers should understand the story's intent: where the story is heading and what its details will provide. Specific deck heads can be combined with clever main headlines to grab the reader's attention from the start. The story's lead should be interesting and relevant to the reader. Visuals, whether photographic or illustrative, should add to the information provided in the story. Alternative story forms such as sidebars, infographics, factoids, quote boxes or question/answer formats should amplify the information in the main story, rather than repeating information from it. Complicated statistics or numerical information should be extracted from the story and presented in an alternative format that can be more easily understood by the readers.

THE NEED FOR ACCURACY

In-depth reporting often involves complicated and subtle information. It may require the journalist to find meaning in numbers, to examine public records, to locate and interview local experts or to condense large quantities of information that may have accrued over a long period of time. Working intensively with a strong editor will ensure that the information is presented logically, clearly and accurately. Numbers and dates should be checked and rechecked for accuracy. Statistics should be obtained from the most authoritative resource and be as current as possible. Complex quotes should be simplified so they are easy to understand.

In-depth reports are among the most important forms of reporting for student publications. Not only do they provide important information but they provide context and texture for the key events that occur each year in a school community.

CONCLUSION

In-depth reporting is an important reporting tool for a high school newspaper and yearbook. Not only does it allow for breadth and depth in reporting, it provides important information to readers about topics of importance to them. In-depth reporting will benefit from an organized staff structure pairing visual journalists with reporters for interesting content both in print and online.

Quick Exercise

From your list of possible in-depth story exercises, compile a list of possible sources within your school. Using a computer, search for an online resource to provide a broader perspective on your topic.

Test your knowledge

When is it appropriate to allow sources to remain anonymous?

SUMMARY

- In-depth topics emerge from a variety of areas including school boards, governing organizations, athletic departments, curricular and extracurricular areas.

- Local and national topics should always be localized to include information relevant for your publication's readers.

- In-depth stories will take longer to research and write.

- In-depth teams can share reporting, backgrounding and visual responsibilities.

- In-depth stories can appear on single pages, on double trucks, in series and in special sections or issues.

- Yearbook staff should take advantage of in-depth stories.

- Reporting the in-depth story will require careful attention to using quoted sources and to attribution.

KEY TERMS

double truck

filters

in-depth reporting or
   long-form reporting

jump coverage

label

logo

packaging

pull quote or callout

running quote

series reporting

student life section

EXERCISES

1   During class changes, lunch periods and time
before, during and after school for a complete
week, make a list of topics that students are talking
about. Write down all topics, including those that
would not, at first, appear to be subjects for stories
in the school paper. Bring your list back to class
the next week and share it in a small group to
create a master list. What topics appear most often
on the lists? What topics have you already
covered? What topics should be further discussed?

2   Using student or professional newspapers or
magazines, find examples of three in-depth
stories. Find one that begins on the front-page (or
cover) and continues somewhere else. Find one
story that only takes up one page (or spread).
Find one story that includes a form of visual
storytelling (see Chapter 15). Analyze the stories
and for each answer the following questions:

(a)   What is the news value of this story?

(b)   How many sources were used in the story?

(c)   What background information appears?

(d)   What anecdotes and personal information are
included?

(e)   Are the sources kept distinct and clearly
referenced?

(f)   If possible, visit the publication's website and
see if online content was added about the topic.

3   Using one of the in-depth story ideas generated in
Exercise 1, brainstorm for a possible headline
idea and for visuals to accompany the story.

4   Using one of the in-depth story ideas generated in
Exercise 1, begin backgrounding the story by
doing some research on the topic. Begin by
consulting resources available in your library or

through the Internet. Prepare a list of information
resources for the topic. Next, make a list of
possible local sources; search online for local
resources. Prepare a list of questions you would
ask your local sources.

5   Using your school newspaper or yearbook, or in
an exchange publication, find an example of an
in-depth story. Analyze it by answering the
following questions:

(a)   Is the topic relevant to the school, and is that
relevance clear?

(b)   Has the story been localized?

(c)   Does the story contain difficult statistical or
numerical information that needs to be better
explained or extracted from the text as a graph
or chart?

(d)   How many sources were quoted? Is the source
information clear and relevant?

(e)   Does the story contain effective anecdotal
evidence?

(f)   Do you lose interest in the topic? If so, at what
point and why?

(g)   Does the story answer all your questions as a
reader? If not, which questions still need to be
answered?

(h)   Does the story provide a strong visual focus?

6   Invite a couple of members of the school board,
your district superintendent or your principal to
class to discuss possible changes or issues being
contemplated by the school board, the district or
the state's educational governing body. Have an
informal discussion with the school officials about
coverage of these and other topics. Discuss

coverage of controversial topics that affect your school or that students are talking about. What suggestions do the school officials have for covering sensitive or controversial topics?

7   Read the following story in which the student's identity was protected by an asterisk by the name used in the attribution. Do you think it was necessary for the writer to change the student's identity? Are there clues provided that would make the student's real identity obvious to a student reader? Is this an instance where it is appropriate to use anonymous sources?

Effects of drinking and driving spill over into adulthood: A night like any other turned into a nightmare for two teens

The sirens flashed and the ambulance came to a deadly halt. The street lights cast an eerie glow on the pavement and a young boy's body lay twisted at the curb. Shards of glass glistened and alcohol laced his breath. It could have been anyone, but on this night, it was him. It was him, and he was only 16.

"We'd done it a hundred times before but just didn't think about it. Someone tried to stop us, but we were like, whatever. We'd seen it on TV, but when you're 16, you think 'It could never happen to me.' That's the world's biggest cliché," Jeff* said.

The night ended with a bad accident and a dead friend. No one knew who was driving, and at that point no one cared.

They were just two average high school boys. Both did relatively well in school, played sports and liked girls. On the weekends, they partied.

He'd only had a few drinks and although no one was supposed to leave, both Jeff and his friend thought they could handle it. "We all put our keys in the hat, but it wasn't like we'd never done it before," he said.

Despite attempts to stop them, the two got into the silver-gray car and rolled out of the driveway. Neither was sure who should drive or which route to take. It didn't matter why they left. As they headed down the main roads and veered onto the side streets, Jeff and his friend began to take driving less seriously. In a split second the car had struck the curb, rolled viciously and Jeff's friend lay silent, just outside his reach.

"I wish I would've known that could have happened," he said. "We just wondered where we could find our next buyer – no second thoughts."

In a single night, it was over, but the pain followed Jeff into the upcoming week and still remains with him to this day.

"The whole time they said, 'Oh no, he's going to be all right,' but they lied to me. I knew they were lying," Jeff said. "The entire time I didn't care about me. I was scared and wanted things to be okay."

Only a few hours after reaching the hospital, Jeff's friend was pronounced dead. "I knew it before they told me," he said.

The days that followed were riddled with guilt, fear and worry. How could anything like this happen to someone so young, so innocent and with so much potential?

At school, some people were dealing well with it while others found it difficult to grieve and even harder to cope. The hallways echoed mourning and Jeff felt sick.

"Some people were like 'What the hell is wrong with you? How could you let this happen?'" Jeff said. "And others tried to tell me it wasn't my fault. But if it wasn't my fault, whose fault was it?"

The emotional wounds were still fresh and Jeff had to face his friend's parents before he could heal.

"The hardest thing I had to do in my whole life was to tell his parents I was driving the car," he said. "They told me they were glad I told them and they were glad it wasn't me."

Though the days at school were extremely difficult to deal with, nothing could compare to the funeral Jeff had to face only a few days after the accident.

"I remember going in there to see him. That was the worst part by far. When you see the person in there and they're dead," Jeff said. "I remember the smell – I'll never forget the way he looked. Seeing him there, dead, was the worst part. You could tell there was a lot of make-up; it didn't look like him."

With the accident behind him, Jeff never did forget. "I never tried to," he said.

For years he didn't drink and was even paranoid when his parents had a glass of wine with dinner. "I've never driven drunk since," he said. "I hang out with some of the same people and they haven't learned anything from it."

"When it's not you, they still think, 'It'll never happen to me,'" he pauses. "And like I said, that's the biggest cliché ever."

Update, *Herbert Henry Dow High School, Midland, Mich.*

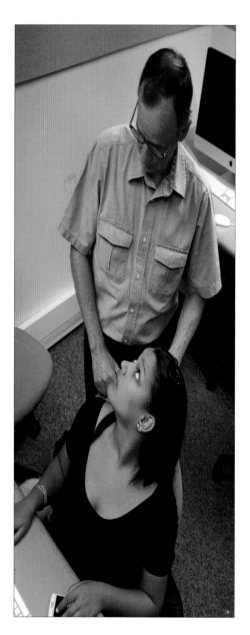

COACHING WRITERS AND EDITING COPY

9

> *A wise editor once told me, "Show, don't tell." Study your subject and your surroundings. Flaunt access. Take the reader places he can't go.*
>
> Elizabeth Merrill, ESPN.com

LEARNING OBJECTIVES After completing this chapter you will be able to:

- understand and apply the basic principles of copy editing

- coach writers through the various stages of the writing process

- formulate questions to help writers clarify ideas and develop stories

- implement the basic conventions and standards of journalistic style

- grasp the basic skills and strategies necessary for editing journalistic writing.

WWW

WEBLINK Check out

www.copydesk.org

This website offers examples of national award-winning headlines and editing articles for copy editors.

GOOD JOURNALISM CAN BE DEFINED as a story that gets torn from a newspaper or magazine and taped inside a locker door, that gets dog-eared in a yearbook or that becomes a the topic of conversation in the cafeteria over pizza and corn.

Powerful writing is composed of sentences that people use, quote and remember. A writer and a copy editor working together should strive to achieve that goal in every story. The **copy editor** works to improve the clarity, logic and consistency of the writer's sentences and paragraphs. To produce stories that respect the reader's interests and intelligence, the copy editor must discuss the story at many stages of the writing process. A good copy editor may not be the best writer on a staff but must be someone who understands the elements of good writing.

Copy editing used to mean capitalizing "Dallas Cowboys" and taking a comma out of "lions, tigers, and bears." Oh my, how copy editing has changed. Much copy editing now involves **coaching** writers, which means discussing the story's structure and style at multiple stages during the writing process. Correcting spelling, grammar and style is still a very important part of copy editing. A copy editor will want to first coach writers on the overall depth, flow and structure of a story, then attend to sentence level clarity, grammar, punctuation and consistent style.

THE COACHING PROCESS

The coaching part of copy editing can prove helpful to a wide range of writers, from a first-year staff reporter to an experienced sports editor trying to improve the writing quality in his section. Every writer needs a sounding board. Discussion can happen outside the lockers during a passing period. The copy editor can raise questions in a five-minute phone conversation. More intensive writing discussions can take place in a quiet hallway outside the staff room during class. Taking copy editing beyond grammar and punctuation errors can be a critical step toward improving the writing in your publication.

One of the keys to good copy editing is to know what questions to ask the writer. The copy editor can help the writer by playing the role of an average reader, asking questions the reader might have when parts of the story are missing, unclear or repetitive. The questioning process should help the writer develop a sense of the story's purpose and focus. The questions can be organized so that the copy editor asks them in three basic stages: the planning stage, the collecting stage and the writing stage.

Planning stage

"So what's the reader going to want to know?"

"What are you, the reporter, going to need to know before you interview? What will help you make sure you understand what's being said in the interview?"

"What do you think the reader is going to find interesting in this story?"

The purpose of coaching questions in the planning stage is to help the writer hone her questions or focus before the interview. The coaching questions also ask the writer to think about what sort of background research she should do before starting to collect the information through interviews. When talking through the planning stage, the reporter should develop an outline of the information needed.

Collecting stage

"What did you see when you went to the rehearsal for the musical?"

"What details do you remember from the valedictorian's room? What do those details say about her?"

"What do you think your best quote is?"

Questions in the collection stage should help the writer sort through the images and information gathered from interviews and observation. The copy editor can also help the writer see what information is needed through reinterviewing or re-observation. During this stage, the copy editor may also help the writer find a lead or the first quote.

Writing Stage

"So what do you think this story is about?"

"What do you think is going to be complicated about this story? What do you think is going to be hard for the reader to understand?"

"What surprised you in what your interview subjects said?"

Coaching questions in the writing stage should be aimed to help the writer sort through the research and interviews. The writer should be trying to decide which are the best quotes to use *verbatim* or word for word. The questions can help the writer decide what parts of the story are complicated enough to require careful explanation or step-by-step treatment.

In any of the three stages, the copy editor should also provide positive feedback, to give the reporter something to build on and to get the writer excited about the story.

"I liked that funny quote from Coach Dupree. That could go high in the story."

"I'm still thinking about the teacher who survived her own bout with cancer and then offered to cook for the coach during his brain cancer treatment. That's a great anecdote and it could be your lead."

Identifying the strongest parts of writers' research and interviewing is crucial to helping them improve each draft. To help evaluate the story, the copy editor should break it down into the following parts.

The lead

The lead makes a crucial difference in whether the audience actually reads the story. This means that copy editors should scrutinize it closely. As covered in the previous writing chapters, leads vary based on the type of writing. A copy editor may need to review the relevant chapter with the writer to make sure she understands the appropriate lead. A copy editor may still need to ask the writer questions to help the writer think through the early drafts.

Key questions may include:

- In a straight news lead, is the most important and timely information provided?
- Could the lead be shortened and remain clear?
- In a feature lead, does the anecdote, image or statement fit the tone and focus of the story?
- Are all assertions of fact verifiable?

Writers are often very sensitive and protective of their leads. Perfecting a lead with a well-placed edit may endear a copy editor to the writer for years to come; shredding a writer's lead could cause hurt feelings and subsequent problems in the newsroom. In some professional publications, a copy editor on deadline is asked to discuss the lead with the writer before making any changes, while edits later in the story can be made without consulting the writer. Coaching a writer through the lead is ideal. However, copy editors should not sacrifice the credibility of the publication. The copy editor should still correct major issues of accuracy, detail and flow (discussed later in the proofreading and correcting section).

Body organization and flow

While most beginning reporters would like a formula for organizing the body of a story, there simply isn't one. As with leads, the copy editor may review the previous writing chapters for the possible ways to organize different stories. In all story types, a copy editor can help by making sure that the writer's focus, established in the lead or focus graph, is developed in the body of the story. A copy editor can then ensure the body is thoroughly developed and organized to flow by helping the writer think through a few questions such as these:

- Does the story leave the reader with unanswered questions?
- Does the organization of the story make sense and follow a logical progression?
- Does the story "flow" smoothly, with clear transitions and pacing, when read aloud?

WWW

Weblink Check out
www.kokedit.com
This copy editor's blog has a copy editors' knowledge base that provides a great list of resources for copy editing.

Quick Exercise

A sophomore reporter is writing a feature story about a head football coach who has cancer. The reporter has talked to the principal who hired the coach and who admires his work ethic. He's interviewed the coach about his chemotherapy experience and his positive outlook. He observed the coach at his 5:30 a.m. weightlifting sessions that he has continued despite the illness. He has also interviewed team captains and observed them shaving their heads in support of their coach. What questions can you ask the reporter in the collecting and writing stages to help him work through the information?

To coach the writer through, the copy editor may underline key words to help to see if the story continually reflects the focus or suggest a quick outline. In their book *Coaching Writers*, Roy Peter Clark and Don Fry list these among their tips for copy editors to give writers:

- Ask what the reader needs to know and in what order.
- Arrange the material into a narrative with a beginning, a middle and an end.
- Write a series of subheads for the sections by visualizing what the story will look like.
- List the players and their motives.
- Type two screensful quickly without worrying about sentences or sense, then print it, underline important things and rearrange them into an outline. Then delete the two screensful.
- Arrange materials into scenes, chapters or both.

Clark, Roy Peter and Don Fry. *Coaching Writers: Editors and Reporters Working Together Across Media Platforms*. Boston: Bedford/St. Martin's. 2003.

Test your knowledge

List three resources a copy editor should have when copy editing.

But now the deadline is approaching. The copy editor has talked the writer through the eighth draft. Time is a factor, and final changes have to be made. As the deadline approaches, the role of the copy editor starts to evolve from that of coaching writers to proofreading and correcting their copy. The proofreading and correcting section will provide concrete advice about how to approach that task.

PROOFREADING AND CORRECTING A STORY

Although most copy editors may make some corrections in the coaching stages, the majority of the proofreading should happen in the final drafts. Copy editors may discuss the following aspects with writers in the early stages, but they certainly may have to correct these areas themselves in the final reads before publishing. The proofreading and correcting part of the process requires that a copy editor pore over final drafts multiple times to check factual accuracy, to improve clarity and conciseness and to polish the grammar and style details of the story.

Fact check

The copy editor should be a master of detail and, if necessary, be ready to challenge every factual assertion, name and word choice. As part of standard practice, the copy editor should:

- Check the facts; identify and eliminate shaky factual assertions.
- Check factual assertions against each other to ensure consistency.
- Verify names and their spellings.

Resources for copy editing

A good copy editor needs to have quick access to a wide range of resources, including:

- A current journalism stylebook, such as those published by the Associated Press or *New York Times*, as well as the student publication's more specific style sheet. Online subscriptions to major style guides can offer search features and reflect updates to the style.

- A dictionary and thesaurus, even if both are built into your wordprocessing program. An online subscription to the *Oxford English Dictionary* (at oed.com) will be useful. The text review within a wordprocessing program should be customized to reflect your publication's style sheet, frequently used names and other words common to high school events and topics.

- A school directory that lists all students, faculty and staff, so the reporter and editor can verify the spelling of names and, for faculty and staff, titles. This information may be available electronically in some schools through the registrar or data clerk.

- Local business and residential telephone books (or access to online versions) to verify the spelling of names and to check addresses.

- An almanac and biographical dictionary, useful for verifying facts and the names and accomplishments of well-known persons who may be cited in stories.

- A grammar handbook with a quick reference section, helpful for both reporters and editors. The copy editor may want to prepare a list of the most common grammatical errors to post in the newsroom.

- Back issues of the school newspaper and recent school yearbooks and magazines, to verify information in story updates and for ongoing coverage.

- Check all figures and statistics, especially to see that parts add up to the right total and that all percentage breakdowns add up to 100 percent.
- Be especially careful of dates and times. Check every date, month and day with the calendar.

The copy editor should evaluate each story to make sure it provides the most important relevant information. If not, he should research the missing factual information or return the story to the reporter. The copy editor should not make a guess about any assertions of fact and should double-check all such assertions before changing them.

The copy editor should make sure the writer has cited the proper source for each piece of information. If a science teacher says three teachers are retiring, the copy editor should have the writer double-check this news by interviewing the principal.

Journalists should typically avoid encyclopedias, weekly newsmagazines, books and newspapers as sources for research. The writer should use these sources as background, then go straight to people for interviews.

For depth in the story, the copy editor should suggest the reporter consider these as possible sources:

- Students
- Student polls
- Teachers
- Parents
- Alumni
- District statistics
- Local doctors/psychologists
- Regional education administrations
- Municipal/county statistics
- Professional sources
- Building or local administrators
- Local college professors
- Teens at other schools

- School organizations or clubs
- Book authors
- Advocacy organizations, such as Mothers Against Drunk Driving or the National Rifle Association.

Clarity and conciseness

Once the copy has been corrected for reporting errors, the copy editor should ensure that each sentence and paragraph is clear, direct and well-organized. If the copy editor thinks to herself, "Huh? I don't get that" or "Wait, I need to reread that sentence," the writing probably isn't clear. If she finds herself thinking, "I really want to stop reading now," then the writing probably lacks concision. More than likely, the writer needs help reorganizing paragraphs or recasting sentences.

Both experienced and novice copy editors can use the following list of tasks to guide their work:

- If any paragraphs need to be rearranged, do so.
- If paragraphs are repetitive, combine them or delete one.
- If paragraphs are too long, divide them.
- If the copy has long lists of names, put them into a sidebar or replace them by summarizing the contents.
- Emphasize an important idea by placing it at the beginning of a sentence or paragraph.
- Tighten the writing by eliminating unnecessary words, phrases and clauses and by combining related expressions.
- Simplify complicated sentences.
- Energize sentences by changing passive voice verbs to active voice. Occasionally, the passive voice may be desirable. In the following sentence an active-voice verb is better.

The Wampus Cats played a strong defensive game. (*Not*: A strong defensive game was played by the Wampus Cats.)

In the next sentence a passive-voice verb is better because it features the subject.

Tom Lynch was reelected Student Council president. (*Not*: The student body reelected Tom Lynch Student Council president.)

- Eliminate trite expressions.
- Strive for sentence variety.
- Improve diction by using specific and precise words: *quibble* is different from *argue* or *debate*; *nice* is general for *affable*, *kind*, *pleasant* or *desirable*; *candid* is a synonym for *frank, impartial, open, sincere, straightforward, truthful* and *unprejudiced*, but with its own special meaning; *tree* is general, while *pine, oak* and *elm* are specific.
- Eliminate editorial commentary unless the story is a column, an editorial or a review.

Test your knowledge

List three types of sources, in addition to students and teachers, that a copy editor could suggest reporters draw on for a story.

Detail

While a copy editor may correct spelling, style and grammar mistakes along the way, the possibility is always there that errors will be introduced in the copy editing process itself. A final careful review of the story is essential. The credibility of the writer and the publication depend on it. The reader who sees three spelling errors in one paragraph will doubt the accuracy of the reporting in the rest of the story.

 **WORDS of WISDOM**

You're either a good writer or a quitter. Skipping revision means you're a quitter. Here are five easy steps to revise your writing.

1. Read it aloud. Use your voice; don't just move your lips. If your tongue is twisted, it's not working. If you have to back up to get it out, there's a problem. Rewrite. Listen for repeated words. This step must be repeated every time you make changes. The last step should always be to read it aloud again.

2. Look for implied dialogue. Don't summarize what was said. Let the people speak. Put the dialogue in. Nothing paints a character better than using the subject's own words. If you didn't hear the exchanges, ask people what was said.

Dead: I had warned the kids not to bring toys on the bus, but I was so shocked when one student told me another rider had a gun, it never crossed my mind that it was real.

Memorable: Every sentence Ontarius uttered began with "OOOOOOOOOooooooooo, Ms. Ogrebee." So, one day he said. "OOOOOOoooo, Ms. Ogrebee. Justin's gotta gun."
And he did.

"JUSTIN. You bring that gun up here right now." I glared at him in my mirror. "How many times have I told you guys not to bring toys on this bus?"

I reached my hand back as Justin slinked up beside me and placed the gun in my hand. When the metal met my hand, I thought this is excessively heavy. I brought it around to the front and looked down at a .22-caliber automatic pistol.

3. Circle all your adverbs, or -ly words. If the adverb enhances the meaning of the verb, get a better verb. If the adverb contradicts the meaning of the verb, you're brilliant – keep it. "Completely destroyed" adds no meaning. Destroyed is destroyed. However, "partially severed" contradicts, so it's worth keeping.

4. Underline your verbs, and then list them straight down a piece of paper. Defense wins championship; verbs drive writing. Look at them naked there on your paper. Did you win a championship?
If you find too many "be" verbs, look nearby for a noun that ends in "-ion." That's the verb. "-ion" is a skirt on a cross-dressing verb.

Bad: The topic of discussion was …

Better: They discussed …   ▶

◀ *Another culprit of useless "be" verbs: wrong tense. "be" verb + -ing verb usually means you're in the wrong tense. Stick to the simple past, present and future.*

Weak – "The cat is sleeping on the sofa." No he's not. He's not still there. If he is, he's probably dead. At some point he got up.

Better – "The cat slept on the sofa." We know he didn't stay there forever so we just need the simple past.

The more words in the verb, the weaker it is.

5. *Use smart grammar/spell check in Word. Run the check and hit options on the first stop. Check the box beside readability statistics. That will tell you at the end what grade level your piece is written on, the readability (you want to be above 80). Now click the word "settings." Look at all the things it will check for – even clichés.*

This process requires that the writer not wait until the last minute. Sometimes, that's the hardest part of this process.

Now you're ready for the help of your peers. Let others read and make suggestions.

Lori Oglesbee, Lion, *McKinney High School*

In the last read-through of a story, the copy editor should:

- Correct misspellings. Use but don't depend on a spell checker. For example, spell-check won't know to suggest "they're" when the writer incorrectly used "there."
- Correct errors in grammar and usage.
- Correct errors and inconsistencies in style.
- Adjust stories to prescribed length:
  - cut paragraphs
  - eliminate unnecessary sentences or paragraphs
  - combine two sentences, making one sentence a subordinate clause or phrase in the other:

    Weak: Photo editor Jake Crandall took photos of the Fido the Show Dog. Fido was a three-time state fair winner.
    Better: Photo editor Jake Crandall took photos of the Fido the Show Dog, a three-state fair winner.

  - change clauses to phrases and phrases to well-chosen words

    Weak: The cheerleader who is standing in the rain yelled for her mom to bring her an umbrella.
    Better: The cheerleader standing in the rain yelled for her mom to bring her an umbrella.

  - use a single vivid verb or noun in place of a less specific verb or noun plus modifiers:

    Weak: The freshman walked up and down the hall before his interview.
    Better: The freshman paced in the hall before the interview.

NEWSFLASH

Copy editing systems

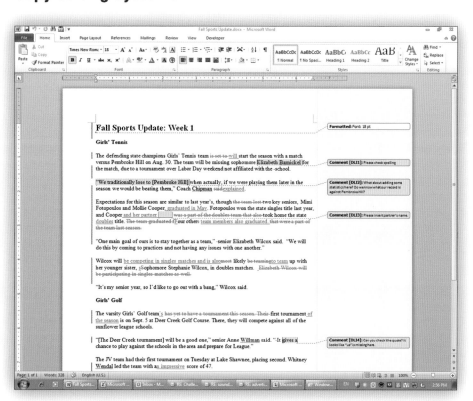

FIGURE 9.1 Microsoft Word allows editors to make and save comments and suggested edits on the original document without changing the copy. The tracked changes appear in the margins of the draft for writers to accept or deny. This process also allows for multiple readers and edits.

FIGURE 9.2 Google Drive allows multiple editors to comment on a draft in real time. Editors can post comments on drafts and watch from other stations as writers work through edits. The process allows high school editors and writers to work from their home computers.

◀ **FIGURE 9.3** These copy editing marks are still used by some copy editors to mark errors quickly in a story. These marks help the editor identify the errors in the tight spacing on printed copy so that the writer can make those corrections prior to publishing. Notice that marks such as inserting a period are made more noticeable to make sure the writer wouldn't read past a small dot placed where the punctuation was needed.

	HOW THEY ARE USED	WHAT THEY MEAN	HOW TYPE IS SET
TYPE SIZE and STYLE	Lansing, mich.---	Capitalize.	LANSING, Mich.---
	College Herald	Small caps.	COLLEGE HERALD
	the Senator from Ohio	Change to lower case.	the senator from Ohio
	By Alvin Jones	Bold face.	**By Alvin Jones**
	Saturday Evening Post	Italicize.	*Saturday Evening Post*
PUNCTUATION and SPELLING	The Spy	Emphasize quotes.	"The Spy"
	Northwestern U	Emphasize periods.	Northwestern U.
	said, " I must....	Emphasize comma.	said, " I must....
	Johnsons	Emphasize apostrope.	Johnsons'
	picnicing	Insert letter or word.	picnicking
	theatre	Transpose letters.	theater
	Henry Cook, principal	Transpose words.	Principal Henry Cook
	days	Delete letter.	day
	judgement	Delete letter and bridge over.	judgment
	allright	Insert space.	all right
	th ose	Close up space.	those
	Geo Brown	Spell out.	George Brown
	100 or more	Spell out.	one hundred or more
	Doctor S. E. Smith	Abbreviate.	Dr. S. E. Smith
	Six North Street	Use numerals.	6 North Street
	Marion Smythe	Spell as written.	Marion Smythe
POSITION	Madison, Wis.---	Indent for paragraph.	Madison, Wis.---
	today. Tomorrow he	New paragraph.	today. Tomorrow he
	considered serious. Visitors are not	No paragraph. Run in with preceding matter.	considered serious. Visitors are not
	But he called last night and said that he	No paragraph.	But he called last night and said that he
	Jones To Conduct or Jones To Conduct	Center subheads.	Jones To Conduct
MISCELLANEOUS	He was not un mindful	Bridge over material omitted.	He was mindful
	one student came stet	kill corrections.	one student came
	or more	Story unfinished.	
	30 or #	End of story.	_____

◄ While pencil and paper copy editing is not obsolete, copy editing onscreen – through **wordprocessing** programs such as Microsoft Word or InCopy, content management systems such as Drupal or cloud computing applications such as Google Drive – has become the norm in many high school newsrooms. Copy editors use these programs to communicate with and coach writers in the early stages of composition as well as during the final drafts. These systems allow the copy editor to enter questions, thoughts or notes that may assist the writing process, but which will be automatically omitted from the final layout. "Tracked changes," in programs such as Word allow writers to see exactly what revisions the copy editor has made to their original work. Those publication staff without access to such systems should develop their copy editing conventions – using all caps, outline text, underlined text or strikethrough letters to distinguish copy editing comments from the main text.

The spelling and grammar checks in some copy editing programs can be useful tools. Some schools use the grammar check preferences to monitor everything from clichés to gender-specific words to serial commas. Still, these functions should be mere tools to assist a copy editor. They don't replace a meticulous and informed review of content, grammar, structure and style. Management of edited story drafts must be handled carefully. A disorganized staff might end up with an early draft full of spelling errors and copy editing comments published in the newspaper or yearbook.

Some copy editors still prefer to read and edit on paper. For that reason, young journalists should still understand the use of copy editing marks (see Figure 9.3). Copy editors use these marks as quick references for identifying everything from transposed letters to missing periods to capitalization errors. The consistent use of these marks makes the copy editing process quick and clear.

Quick Exercise

Fact check the following sentences:

1 In a poll of 224 seniors, 34 percent said they preferred the blue cap and gowns while 27 percent said they preferred black. Forty-one percent said they had no preference.

2 Junior Seth Levy said he was excited about celebrating the 10 days of Hanukkah.

3 Police said the 16-year-old was arrested and convicted in the parking lot after the football game.

4 Junior Marisa Walton was crowned as the 33rd homecoming queen on Sept. 31.

5 Math teacher Julia Poe visited all 50 states including Washington, D.C.

COMMON EDITING MISTAKES

Ask a veteran copy editor and they'll tell you that there are some mistakes they've corrected way too many times. Mention *it's* or *its* to a passionate copy editor and you may hear her scream or rant. While stylebooks, grammar guides and dictionaries are a copy editor's best friends that offer immense detail for correcting copy editing errors, the following list offers a few common copy editing issues for high school writers.

- Using synonyms for *said*. Don't worry about the overuse of the word *said*. The word is neutral enough not to cause problems. Don't force phrases such as "he smiled" or "she chuckled" as attributions for actual speech – they usually won't make physical sense.

- Using the school initials in stories. Most students do not have to run back to the lobby to check the seal on the floor to remind themselves where they go to school. Use of a school's name or initials in its publication is often unnecessary, unless the story is making a comparison with other high schools.

- Inconsistent use of style rules. Do not use *May 29* in one story and *May 29th* in another. Know your publication's style rules and reference guide and stick to them.

- Improper use of *it's* and *its*. The contraction *It's* should be used in place of the words *it is*. By contrast, *its* is used to indicate possession. Example: The car was rated the best in its class. John said it's his plan to buy one next month.

- Including "when asked" to set up quotes. The reader assumes that direct quotes are results of questions from a reporter, so omit the phrase. "When asked" can be correctly used if there's a need for clarification about the circumstances of a quote. One case may be in a speech story where the reporter is including quotes from a post-speech interview. Example: In his Monday speech, the mayor said he would be urging the city to build a new skatepark. When asked afterwards, the mayor said he didn't think it would happen until certain council members were voted out of office.

- Combining several quotes in the same paragraph. When the speaker changes topics, a new paragraph is recommended. The new paragraph helps the reader understand the change in focus. Shorter paragraphs make the text design easier to read and comprehend quickly.

- Misuse of the word *stated*. The word should be used only when the quote is from a written or prepared text. The word *stated* should not be used to attribute spoken words. *Correct*: The law stated that students would not be allowed to text and drive.

- Name misspellings. Never assume you know how to spell a person's name. *John Smith* could be spelled *Jon Smithe* or *Jonn Smythe*. Do not even assume a name in the school records is correct. The reporter should ask each person interviewed for a story to spell his or her name.

USING JOURNALISTIC STYLE

When writing a story for your school newspaper, yearbook or magazine, would you write Nov. 22, Nov. 22nd, November twenty-second or November 22? Number 10 or number ten? Twenty-fifth or 25th? Marathon County, Marathon county or Marathon Co.? Well known or well-known? U.S. Army, United States Army, Army of the United States or army of the United States? Atlanta, Georgia, Atlanta, Ga., Atlanta, GA or simply Atlanta?

The English language permits so many variations that a stylebook, or manual, is necessary to provide consistency in published work. Otherwise, for example, one story might have *Jan. 13, 2007* and another *January 13, 2007*.

Choosing to follow either Associated Press (AP) or *New York Times* style is appropriate for student publications, although some adjustments may be made. Students will then, as career preparation, learn a standard style that is practiced in the professional workplace. Many commercial newspapers depart occasionally from AP style to suit local readers' preferences. The style sheet in this chapter offers some variations on AP style suitable for student publications.

Some suggested style guidelines follow.

Names and identification

The first time a person is named in a story, his or her complete first and last name, along with some identifier, should be used.

Faculty members are identified by position or subject taught, whichever is appropriate for the particular story. Titles can also indicate job, rank or profession (for example, coach, principal, superintendent, nurse, counselor, athletic director, English teacher). Short titles precede names: "English teacher Julia Poe" or "basketball coach James Rogers." Longer titles usually follow: "Mrs. Toni Aguiar, chair of the Language Department," or "Helen Dinkel, School Centered Education committee chairperson."

Students should be identified by class, year of graduation or some other method appropriate to the school (senior Danielle Norton; Ian McFarland, '08; Bryan Dykman, 4). Similarly, alumni are identified by year of graduation (Margie Pak, '90).

In some stories students may be identified in other ways. For example, an editor-in-chief of the paper may be identified by that title if it is appropriate to the story. In sports stories, players are identified by the positions they play or hold (Colin Allred, linebacker; Captain Morgan White). Be sure not to make up titles by mere description, such as "harpsichordist Becky Lucas." Only one identifier is needed on first reference. Do not overdo identifiers, such as "senior forward and team captain Karen Greening." The other relevant identifiers can be used in subsequent references.

A student publication may choose to make no distinction between name references for adults and students, or it may choose to differentiate. Today, major newspapers differ on the use of **courtesy titles** for women and men (Mr., Mrs., Miss and Ms.). Some papers use no courtesy titles, some only for women and some to indicate a married couple. When courtesy titles are used, they frequently appear only on second and subsequent references. These titles are rarely used in sports coverage. If courtesy titles are used for adult women in your publication, request from each adult woman her preference for *Ms., Miss* or *Mrs.* and abide by it. If no preference is sought, use only *Ms.* or *Mrs.* For adult men, use *Mr.* Whether courtesy titles are used is not as important as is a consistent plan for handling them in all stories throughout the year.

One good approach is to use every adult's full name and title in the first reference. Then, in the second and subsequent times the adult is mentioned in the story, use the courtesy title and the last name, or just the last name. For example, the first reference would be "math instructor Jennifer Dusenberry," and the second reference would be "Ms. Dusenberry," or "Dusenberry." If there would be no confusion, the proper name can be alternated with the job title to give more variety. For example, for second and further references, the story could read, "the math instructor said' and then, later, "Ms. Dusenberry said." The job title with the last name may also be used for the second and further references.

There are a number of legitimate ways that reporters can approach the second and subsequent times a person is mentioned in their stories. Some student publications use only the last name in these succeeding references; others just the first name. The former follows most professional style manuals, the latter suggests a more familiar and conversational tone. Either is acceptable, as long as a consistent plan is adopted and followed for every story. If a story mentions many persons, it may be less confusing to follow a policy of using only last names in second and further references.

Accuracy of name spellings should be a priority. Remember, what you think is spelled *John* could be spelled *Jon, Jonn* or *Jean.* If the adult uses only a first initial and a full middle name, then respect that preference. (Do not use only a first name initial and a last name.) Husbands and wives should be referred to by name (Mr. and Mrs. Jeff Mays or Jeff and Shonda Mays, *not* Mr. Jeff Mays and wife).

Capitalization

Capitalization rules are pretty standard among publication style guides.

Always capitalize the following:

- All proper nouns and proper adjectives (Joyce, Shakespearean, Antarctica)
- All titles when they precede names (Principal Vickie Richie, Queen Elizabeth)
- First and all other words, except for articles, prepositions and conjunctions, in titles of books, periodicals, speeches, plays, songs (*A Tale of Two Cities*, *Sports Illustrated*, "Free Speech, Its Problems," "Friends," "Rudolph, the Red-Nosed Reindeer," *Man against the Sea*)
- Holidays and special school events (Thanksgiving, New Year's Day, Homecoming, Senior Day, Spring Swing)
- Sections of the country (the West, the Atlantic States)
- Names of nationalities and races (Indian, German, Ethiopian – also see later discussion for identification of minority groups)
- College degrees when abbreviated (B.A., M.A., Ph.D.)
- Names of clubs, buildings, departments, schools and colleges (Spanish Club, Beardsley Gymnasium (or Gym), English Department, Ferris High School, Cornell College)
- Names of streets (Fifth Street, Oak Avenue, Park Boulevard)

Quick Exercise

Copy edit these sentences. Consider each sentence a first reference in separate stories.

1 At 3 p.m., Terrell Howard, football coach, will give his first press conference since announcing his retirement.

2 Mr. Crandall expects his class to take seven photos at Friday's game.

3 National Honor Society member and senior guard Emily Bruyere scored 27 points last night.

- Geographical names (Hudson River, Lake Tanganyika, Rock of Gibraltar)
- Names of classes only when the term *class* is used and the reference is to a particular class in the school (Freshman Class, Sophomore Class, *but* freshmen, seniors)
- Names of specific courses (American Literature I, *but* the field of American literature; History II, *but* the study of history; Journalism III, *but* journalism as a career)
- Names of languages (English, French, Korean)
- Names of athletic teams (Yellowjackets, Bullfrogs, Green Wave, Blue Blazers)
- Words or abbreviations, such as *No.*, *Fig.* and *Chapter*, when followed by a number, title or name (No. 10, Fig. 4, Chapter 6)
- All other words traditionally capitalized, such as noun references to deities (God, the Father, Allah, Shiva), political parties and the like. Consult an English handbook when in doubt.

Do not capitalize the following:

- Titles when they follow names (Seth Levy, assistant principal; Ryan McGlothlin, director of athletics; Daniel Villarreal, chairperson of the Social Studies Department; Angela Yeung, editor-in-chief of the *Evanstonian*)
- Names of school subjects, unless they are languages or specific courses (He hopes to study chemistry and journalism next year. He is taking Spanish, American History I, Physics M. and Art IV.)
- Directions, unless they mean a geographic place (He lives on the south side of the street. She moved to the South.)
- Designations of time (a.m., p.m., o'clock)
- Seasons of the year, except when personified (fall, winter, but Old Man Winter)
- Names of rooms, offices, buildings, unless they have an official proper name (room 159, the journalism room, the guidance office, the fieldhouse, the library, but Ragland Reading Room, Beardsley Gym)
- The subject of a debate, except the first word (Resolved: That free enterprise is basic to this American way of life)
- Committees (the entertainment committee, refreshment committee)
- Descriptive or occupational words used as "titles" (pitcher Justin Verlander, actress Dakota Fanning)
- Title modifiers such as *former* and *the late* (the late Whitney Houston, former President Bush)
- College degrees when spelled out (bachelor of arts, master of science, doctor of philosophy.

Abbreviations

Normally most publications avoid all but standard, commonly understood abbreviations of accepted titles. Here are some general guidelines for how and when to use abbreviations effectively.

Abbreviate:

- Names that are well-known as abbreviations (YMCA, PTA, AIDS, UN, NASA, NATO). (Note: Write such abbreviations without periods and without spaces.)
- Titles when they precede last names (Dr. Garcia; Rev. Kelly, *but* the Reverend Lynn Kelly; Mr. and Mrs.; all military titles, such as Pvt. and Lt.)

Quick Exercise

Copy edit the following sentences. Consider each sentence a first reference in separate stories.

1 Three days into the school year, principal Grant Kendall announced a $1 million budget cut.

2 Tickets for homecoming will go on sale March 4.

3 Senior Holly Hernandez will bowl her first match at 7 P.M. Saturday.

4 The Social Committee will meet Tuesday on the ramp North of the library to discuss plans for next month.

- Names of states when they follow the name of a city, except very short or one-syllable names, such as Iowa, Ohio, Utah, Maine (Madison, Wis.; Buffalo, N.Y.; *but* Des Moines, Iowa)
- Names of months when followed by a date, except very short months, such as April, May, June, July (Nov. 19, 2014; Oct. 7, 2013 but June 14, 2015)
- College degrees (B.A., M.A., Ph.D., Ed.D., D.D., LL.D.).

Do not abbreviate:

- Names of streets (Eastwood Avenue, Central Street)
- Titles following a name (Susan Ginsburg, professor of history)
- Days of the week
- States when used without a city
- The term *percent* (the symbol % should be used only in tabular material or in headlines when used with a figure)
- Positions when not used as titles (secretary, treasurer, president)
- *Department* (English Department)
- *Christmas* (not Xmas)
- The year, except when used to identify students or alumni (2007; Libby Nelson, '04)
- *United States* as a noun; it can be abbreviated as an adjective (in the United States, *but* U.S. history).

Numbers

- Spell out all approximate numbers and numerals up to and including nine, except for dates, scores, addresses, ages, time and money (about 2,000 are expected; Sept. 4, 2014; Ames, 14, West Des Moines, 7; 7 Wilson Avenue; 5 cents; 3 years old).
- If you begin a sentence with a number, spell out the number and do not use numerals. (Twenty-five students will …; *or* About 25 students will …; *not* 25 students will …)
- Spell out ordinal numbers (from first through ninth) and use figures for 10th and above.
- Do not use *d, rd, st* or *th* in writing dates (May 29, 2012; *not* May 29th, 2012).
- When two numbers are used together, avoid confusion by spelling out the first, whether the number is above or below nine (fourteen 4-year-old children, *not* 14 4-year-old children).
- In a list containing numbers below and above nine, use figures for all. (Those on the committee include 5 from GAA, 11 from the Student Council, 3 from the French Club and 14 from the hall monitors.)
- For sums of money less than one dollar, use figures and the word *cents* (10 cents, *not* $.10; 5 cents, *not* 5 cts.).
- Do not use ciphers when giving the exact hour or an even number of dollars (4 p.m., *not* 4:00 p.m.; $5, *not* $5.00).
- Do not use the date when an event occurs within or close to the week of publication (Friday, next Friday, last Tuesday, tonight, yesterday).
- For numbers of four or more digits, except serial numbers – house, telephone, pages, years – use a comma (4,945; 469,958,000).

Punctuation

No **style manual** includes all the rules for the use of all punctuation marks. A style manual should, however, include any deviations from standard English style. A few special usages are common in newswriting, and they should be included in a style sheet.

Quick Exercise

Copy edit the following sentences. Consider each sentence a first reference in separate stories.

1 Gas prices have already risen $2.00 in three years.

2 The check cashing service will begin charging $20 more on Feb. 10.

3 The Itasca Wampus Cats won 14–seven in their first game of the season.

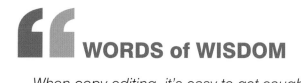

WORDS of WISDOM

When copy editing, it's easy to get caught up in the small details–the grammar, spelling and punctuation – and miss bigger problems with a story. It's important to also take a step back and look at the big picture: Are all questions answered? Is the story fair and unbiased? Is it clear and easy to understand?

Elizabeth Slocum, Philadelphia Enquirer, *Copy Editor*

The comma and the semicolon

- Do not include a comma before the *and* in a simple series. (Those on the committee are Susan Clarke, Paul Block and Dale Jackson.)
- Do not use a comma between a man's name and *Jr.* or *Sr.* (Fred Black Jr.).
- Use commas and semicolons in lists of names and identifying terms. (The committee consists of Gerry Brown, chairman; Shawn Jourdain, vice-chairman; and Cam Carhart, secretary-treasurer.)
- Use a semicolon between the main items in a series when commas occur within the series.
- Use a comma in a compound sentence before the conjunction. (The Key Club led the school in the aluminum can drive, and the Chess Club nearly tied.) When the coordinating conjunction is not present, use a semicolon. (The Key Club won; the Chess Club came in second.) When the coordinating conjunction is present, use a semicolon if there is extensive punctuation in one or more of the clauses. (The Key Club, with 27 juniors and seniors, led the school in the aluminum recycling drive; but the Chess Club, with five sophomore members, nearly tied.) If the clauses are both short, either the comma or the conjunction might be dropped. (The Key Club won and the Chess Club lost. The Key Club won, the Chess Club lost.)

The colon

- Don't use a colon in a list following a *be* verb, such as *are* or *were*. (Those elected were Stefanie Boyar, Suresh Vasan and Bryan Parker.) If she wanted to see good comedy, the teacher suggested she watch reruns of three TV shows: "Seinfeld," "News Radio" and "WKRP in Cincinnati."
- Use the colon to cite time in a track event (3:05.2).

Quotation marks

- A period or a comma at the end of a quotation is always put inside the quotes. (We have just read "The Lottery.") Even when the quote ends with a quote within a quote, periods and commas fall inside the quotation marks. ("I couldn't hear her when she whispered 'I want you to leave now,'" sophomore Morgan Krakow said.)
- A question mark or an exclamation mark goes inside the quotation marks only if it belongs to the material quoted. (Have you read "The Lottery"? She asked, "Have you finished the story?")

- A semicolon or a colon always goes outside the quotation marks. (Incomplete homework assignments may be a symptom of academic "burn-out"; it is a sign of more serious problems.)

- Use quotation marks around the titles of one-act plays, computer games, TV shows, speeches, poems, short stories, songs and articles within publications ("The Telephone Only Rings Twice," "Friends," "Birches," "The Outcasts of Poker Flat," "Tenderly"). In addition, Associated Press style uses quotation marks for titles of books, plays, albums and works of art; however, italics are an acceptable style chosen by some publications for the titles of such works. Some publications choose to follow a literary rule to italicize *wholes* but to put *parts* in quotation marks. By this rule, album titles would be in italics and the song titles would be in quotes. Regardless of which you choose, establish a style and be consistent.

- Do not put quotation marks around familiar nicknames, and ordinarily only use nicknames in sports stories (Babe Ruth, Magic Johnson). Unfamiliar nicknames should be quoted (Kobe "The Black Mamba" Bryant).

- Do not put quotation marks around slang expressions (to do so implies an apology for using them).

- Do not put quotation marks around names of characters in books or plays.

- Do not put quotation marks around the names of animals.

The apostrophe

- In general, form the possessive of all singular nouns by adding an apostrophe and *s* (the boy's book, the fox's den). If the singular noun ends in *s*, add the apostrophe and *s* (hostess's address) unless the next word begins with *s* (hostess' seat). Because stylebooks vary, it can also be correct to use only an apostrophe after a singular proper noun ending in *s* or to add an apostrophe and *s* (Charles' hat, Charles's hat). Consistency requires you choose a particular approach and follow it every time.

- Form the possessive of a plural word ending in *s* by adding only an apostrophe (the boys' books, the girls' uniforms).

- Form the possessive of a plural word not ending in *s* by adding an apostrophe and *s* (men's league, children's party).

- Use an apostrophe in abbreviations of classes or years (Amanda Allison, '06; Class of '11).

- Use an apostrophe followed by *s* to form the plurals of single letters and numbers and of symbols (A's and B's, size 7's, How many *c*'s in recommend?). The apostrophe is not, however, used for plurals of numbers or multi-letter combinations (1990s, ABCs). Note: The plural *s* added to italic letters (or titles) should be set in roman type (three *Newsweek*s).

- Use the apostrophe, not single quotation marks, to indicate omission of letters (wash 'n' wear *for* wash and wear, *not* wash 'n' wear or wash ʹnʹ wear).

- Omit the apostrophe in names of organizations when the possessive case is implied and in certain geographic designations (Citizens League, Actors Equity Association, Pikes Peak).

The hyphen

- Use a hyphen in compound numbers and fractions (forty-eight, three-fourths). Remember a hyphen joins, so no spaces are used before and after a hyphen.

- Use a hyphen with compound adjectives of two or more words (note-taking skills, grade-point average, front-page story, out-of-state student, All-State diver). Note: A hyphen is not used after an adverb ending in *ly* (tightly laced shoes). The hyphen is frequently omitted when two words are joined to function as a noun; see a dictionary for current spellings (makeup *not* make-up; layout *not* lay-out).

- Use a hyphen when combining numbers and measurements to make an adjective (Jones is a 210-pound tackle; Johnson is the 6-foot-8-inch center). AP also uses hyphens to separate figures such as scores and odds.
- Dashes are longer than a hyphen. Some stylebooks draw a difference between the em-dash (so-named since it's the length of the letter m) and the shorter en-dash (the shorter length of a typical n). Those stylebooks that differentiate use an em dash to separate or create a longer pause when a comma will not suffice. En-dashes are used for compound adjectives and relationships. Stylebooks vary on whether dashes are set off by a space on either side.
- Associated Press style does not differentiate dashes and uses a space before and after the dash.

Italics

Some publications use italics for names of books, long musical selections, plays and record albums and may use italics for names of newspapers, magazines and boats or ships. However, widely used AP style puts the names of books, long musical selections, plays and record albums in quotes and capitalizes the names of newspapers, magazines and boats and ships without any quotes or italics. Use italics for emphasis with caution. Readers will begin to ignore italics if they are overused.

In general, you should italicize:

- Words from other languages that have not become an accepted part of English. (The meal was prepared *à la française*; Marie's design has a certain *je ne sais quoi*.)
- A letter of the alphabet or a word used specifically as a word. (The word *letter* has two *t*'s in it.)
- An editor's note accompanying a story
- A word to be emphasized. (He repeated he had *never* been a candidate.)

Computer-related terms

The Associated Press Stylebook has made additions and changes to keep up with technological and social media advances. Preferred forms for prevalent words and phrases include:

> app
> blogs
> download
> email
> e-reader
> Google, Googling, Googled
> Skype
> smartphone
> Twitter, tweet, tweeted, retweet
> unfriend
> Use of fan, follow and friend as nouns and verbs
> website
> widget
> YouTube.

Spelling

Since a number of words have several correct spellings, every paper's style guide should include the preferred forms of those appearing most frequently in news stories. For other words, consult a standard dictionary to determine the preferred form, which should be used consistently.

Test your knowledge

Should a period at the end of a sentence in a quote appear inside or outside of the quotation marks?

Quick Exercise

Copy edit the following sentences. Consider each sentence a first reference in separate stories.

1 "Seinfeld" was one of the biggest hits of the 1990's.

2 Freshman Kate Kulaga bought three cases of cupcakes, cookies and brownies.

3 "I used to work on my jump shot for three hours every night in the park", senior Morgan Tate said.

Skills of a copy editor

Copy editors should have what might be called a "bifocal" mind, one that shifts instantly from meticulous examination of details to the overall story. In the process of poring over stories, copy editors must use a vast array of skills. The following list addresses the primary abilities the job requires.

- Cultivate a broad knowledge base for news and other fields; stories of all kinds will pass the copydesk:

  1 Know geography and history. Be aware of historical shifts. Become acquainted with a wide range of important events and trends.

  2 Understand human nature and social dynamics. Be alert to cultural shifts.

  3 Know your own school and community. Familiarize yourself with legal and governmental structure and procedures as well as political dynamics.

  4 Familiarize yourself with books, plays, magazines and reviews.

  5 Know your own publication and its policies.

- Be able to write clear standard English and to revise poorly written stories:

  1 Be skillful in handling sentences and paragraphs.

  2 Have a strong command of words.

  3 Be able to make redundant or poorly-controlled writing concise.

  4 Be able to edit copy consistently according to a style guide.

- Be able to distinguish editorializing from a sound inference based on fact. Edit out all editorializing. The following is not editorializing since the first phrase is followed by fact:

  Maine will meet its toughest opponent of the season Tuesday when the undefeated Arlington Heights Yellowjackets invade Memorial Stadium.

- Recognize effective, even dramatic writing.

- Have a creative imagination; be able to see a good story in a poor one and to shape it through good editing.

- Exercise great care and patience with each story.

- Gain familiarity with standard reference sources and know how to use them.

NEWSFLASH

The following section lists a number of words that frequently appear in school news stories and are often misspelled. Make your own supplemental list.

Frequently misspelled words

absence	believe	drama
a cappella	biology	eligible
adviser	bookkeeping	embarrass
advisory	business	emphasize
algebra	cafeteria	English
all right	calendar	existence
alumna (f.s.)	captain	experiment
alumnae (f.pl.)	chaperon	faculty
alumni (m.pl.)	cheerleader	familiar
alumnus (m.s.)	chemistry	February
apparatus	choir	field house
arithmetic	chorus	finally
assembly	classmate	football
association	college	foreign
athlete	commencement	foreword (in a book)
athletics	commercial	forty (but *fourth*)
attendance	committee	forward (on a team)
audience	council (student)	fullback
auditorium	counselor	geometry
backfield	criticism	German
baseball	curriculum	government
baseman	custodian	graduation
basketball	defense	grammar

guard	permissible	society
guidance	phase	sophomore
gymnasium	physics	Spanish
halfback	planning	speech
handball	poll *vs.* pole	sponsor
heavyweight	practice	stopping
high jump	preparation	studying
hockey	principal (of your school)	superintendent
homecoming	privilege	tackle
homeroom	professor	teenager
incidentally	psychology	textbook
initiation	quarterback	theater
intramural	quartet	their *vs.* there
its (possessive), it's (it is)	questionnaire	thorough
laboratory	receive	tomorrow
league	recommend	tonight
lettermen	referee	touchdown
library	registrar	treasurer
lightweight	rhythm	tryout (noun), try out (verb)
lineup (noun), line up (verb)	role *vs.* roll	typewriting
literature	runner-up	unanimous
long jump	schedule	university
lose *vs.* loose	secretary	until
lunchroom	semester	upperclassman
mathematics	semifinal	volleyball
misspell	senior	weather
necessary (but *unnecessary*)	separate	Wednesday
occasion	sergeant	weekend
occurred	shining	weird
occurrence	shortstop	whether *vs.* weather
offense	shot put (but *shot-putter*)	writing
opponent	similar	written

Screening sexist language

What we say and write about men and women often reveals attitudes toward gender roles that many find objectionable. Language does reflect and affect our values, especially when we are speaking of persons who belong to groups other than our own. In general, our goal should be to avoid the use of words and phrases that directly or indirectly suggest limited opportunity or discriminatory treatment for members of any group, whether by sex, sexual orientation, race, ethnic description or religion.

In many cases, neutral terms should replace sex-designating ones. Change:

- *Mailman* to *mail carrier*
- *Fireman* to *fire fighter*
- *Policeman* or *policewoman* to *police officer or law enforcement agent*
- *Newsman* or *newswoman* to *reporter*
- *Actor* and *actress* to (only) *actor*
- *Chairman* to *chair or chairperson*
- *Forefathers* to *ancestors, forerunners* or *forebears*
- *Man-hours* to *work hours, staff time*
- *Common man* to *the average person, the ordinary citizen*
- *Lady* (unless that connotation is appropriate) to *woman*

WORDS of WISDOM

On my desk I have …

- *My old, trusty* AP Stylebook
- The New York Times *stylebook*
- Webster's Dictionary
- *Strunk & White*

Among my frequently used links are …

- *CIA World Factbook (LOVE this site): https://www.cia.gov/library/publications/the-world-factbook/*
- *IMDb*
- *AllMusic Guide: http://www.allmusic.com/*
- *Google Maps (I love the street view for checking the spelling of streets and stores on signs)*
- *Wikipedia (used sparingly, of course, but great for background research)*
- *Urban Dictionary (to keep up with the lingo)*
- *M-W.com*
- *In-house stylebook*
- *Lots of local official sites (Pa. City Hall, school district, neighborhood maps, etc.)*

Elizabeth Slocum, Philadelphia Enquirer, *Copy Editor*

- *Man-made* to *manufactured, produced*
- *Coed* (as a noun referring to college women) to *student* (logically, the term *coed* refers to any student at a coeducational college or university).

Job designations by gender should not be mentioned unless pertinent to the story. They imply that the occupations are inappropriate for the individual holding them. Change:

- *Male nurse* to *nurse*
- *Woman* or *lady lawyer* to *lawyer*.

The appearance of a woman (or man) should not be described unless the description is essential for the story. A girl-watching or boy-watching tone – using words or phrases such as *buxom, blonde* or *big hunk* – should be avoided. Clichés and jokes at women's or men's expense such as *typical woman driver* or *dumb jock* should also be deleted.

Problem words

For greater accuracy and less chance of denigrating different groups and value systems, try to find neutral terms on both sides of an issue or (keeping fairness in mind) to identify individuals using the terms they use for themselves. For example:

- Change *right-wing Christian to Christian conservative or religious activist*.
- Refer to someone as a *feminist* or *evangelical* or *Zionist* or other political category only if he or she identifies himself or herself as one.
- Describe individuals as *prolife* and *prochoice*, rather than *antiabortion* and *proabortion*.
- Change cops to police officers or police.
- Change charged words such as extremists when protestors might be more neutral.
- Change *Muslim terrorist* to a more specific group, such as *al-Qaeda*. Avoid using terms such as *terrorist* or *freedom fighter* arbitrarily or inconsistently; if you use them, try to apply such terms based on a single, consistent definition.

Race, ethnicity and other terms of identity

Identifying someone as a member of a particular identity group should be done only when it is essential to the reader's full understanding of the story. The decision to use racial, ethnic, religious or sexual orientation labels should be made only after careful consideration of their news value.

These terms of identity are acceptable if there is a need to use such identification in the story, with labels acceptable to the subjects and conforming to the preferences of official groups representative of the identity group.

Racial, ethnic, religious or sexual orientation stereotypes, like male–female ones, should be eliminated from all writing, art and photography. Some of this bias is subtle and unintentional. For example, if you are doing a story about unmarried teenage mothers, it would be inappropriate to represent, in words and photos, only members of certain racial or ethnic groups, since being unmarried and pregnant crosses all racial, ethnic and economic boundaries.

A good reporter should understand that some words are used within a particular community, but when someone outside the community uses those words, they may have derogatory connotations. Some terms, such as *barrio* started as neutral descriptions but over time have suggested derogatory stereotypes and should be avoided unless part of a quotation.

Labels popular and acceptable in the past may not be acceptable today. For example, the term *Negro* was acceptable for media use in the 1960s, but today *black* is frequently used, and *African-American* is now preferred by many. If a reporter has doubts, a comprehensive, up-to-date style manual should be consulted. When identity terms are relevant, a reporter may ask sources what labels are preferable.

Acceptable labels for some of the major identity groups in the United States include:

- *Asian-American* (adjective); *Asian American* (noun)
- *African-American* or *black* (adjective); *African American* (noun)
- *Native-American* (adjective*); Native* American or *American Indian* (nouns)
- *Hispanic, Latino/Latina* or *Chicano/Chicana* (adjectives); *Latino/Latina, Chicano/Chicana* (nouns). (Note: More than the others on this list, debate continues over these terms and their appropriateness may vary by individual and region.)
- *Native Alaskan* (noun)
- *Pacific Islander* (noun)
- *Gay* (male), *lesbian* (female), *homosexual, transgender* (adjectives).

Some of the subgroups within a large minority group prefer to be identified by more specific labels such as *Chinese-American, Cuban-American* or an exact Indian tribal name (which may not be the commonly accepted tribal name imposed by traders and settlers). The best advice is to be current, specific and do your homework before identifying someone in this way.

Some minority groups have media membership organizations, such as those in the following list. Students and teachers can write to these organizations to request information on programs, learning materials or scholarships.

Asian American Journalists Association, 5 Third Street, Suite 1108, San Francisco, California 94103. Tel: (415) 346-2051; email: national@aaja.org.

National Association of Black Journalists, 1100 Knight Hall, Suite 3100 College Park, Maryland 20742 Tel. (301) 405-0248; email: nabj@nabj.org.

National Association of Hispanic Journalists, 1050 Connecticut Avenue NW 10th Floor, Washington, DC 20036. Tel: (202) 662-7145; email: nahj@nahj.org.

National Lesbian and Gay Journalists Association, 2120 L Street NW, Suite 850, Washington, DC 20037. Tel: (202) 588-9888; email: info@nlgja.org.

Native American Journalists Association, University of Oklahoma, Gaylord College, 395 W. Lindsey St., Norman, OK, 73019-4201 Tel: (410) 325-9008; email: info@naja.com.

The Center for Integration and Improvement website at ciij.org can offer useful advice on dealing with racial, ethnic and other identifying terms.

COACHING WRITING CONTINUES

The copy editor's job should not end even after spelling errors are corrected and the story is published. Set aside a few minutes to discuss the story with the writer without the pressures of a deadline.

"How did you feel about the story?"

"What, if given time, would you have done to improve the piece?"

"What other interviews did you still need?"

An after-publication discussion should aim to evaluate the story and to take lessons from the process. The copy editor can commend a strong lead, provide constructive feedback on habitual problems or reinforce some practices that the writer can use to improve the next story. Making the point that the writer has a good eye for details, needs to do more interviews or needs to double-check facts can only improve the quality of the publication and the writer as the year goes on.

While it is important that novice writers be open to discussion or criticism of their work, both writer and copy editor must set aside egos and focus on improving the product. Writing tends to be a very personal endeavor, so any critical analysis of that work may initially make the writer feel threatened, hurt or angry. Remembering that both the writer and copy editor are there to serve the reader with a clear, interesting story should help to eliminate any tension or the need for anger-management classes.

Maintaining a civil tone eases the pain of critical analysis. The copy editor who barks out, "This stinks" or "What freaking moron wrote this," will not earn the writer's respect or attention. The copy editor could easily begin with, "How can I help you on that story?" or "I think that's a great story you have this deadline. Let's talk about it."

While a copy editor's name may not appear at the top of the story, the lack of such recognition does not reduce the copy editor's worth.

A good copy editor understands that his or her goal is not only to improve the piece on the computer but also to improve the writer's skills. A dedicated copy editor takes pride in the basketball player who actually stops in the gym to read this month's issue. She enjoys the progress of the entertainment writer who can now effectively organize his feature stories. She relishes the positive feedback an improved writer gets from his audience and colleagues. In the end, there's often a bond built between a good copy editor and writer that the writer equally values and appreciates.

CONCLUSION

For too many high school publications, copy editing is almost an afterthought just before turning a story in or just before publishing. However, copy editing should begin early in the writing process and continue up to and after publication. On many papers, the copy editor will also write the headline for the story, as discussed in Chapter 10. In every publication, the copy editor plays a critical role in giving the writer and the reader a clear, polished and accurate work of journalism.

Test your knowledge

List three skills a good copy editor should have.

Quick Exercise

Copy edit the following sentences:

1 Freshman Katie Knight wants to be mailman like her dad.

2 She worked 14 man-hours as chairwoman on the committee to restore the monuments.

3 The cops arrived at the game moments after the shooting.

4 Senior David Choe, an Asian American, won the 200-meter dash Thursday.

SUMMARY

- The copy editor plays the role of writing coach during the writing process and corrects the later drafts for clarity, consistency, grammar, spelling and standard style.

- Writing coaching is the process of discussing the story with the writer. By playing the role of the reader, the copy editor can ask questions the reader might have when parts of the story are missing, unclear or repetitive. Writing coaching should happen at three basic stages: the planning stage, the collecting stage and the writing stage.

- The copy editor double-checks facts and screens drafts for sexist and racist language.

- Each publication should establish a style to follow. Many school papers and websites follow Associated Press style. Major style considerations include: names and identifications, capitalizations, punctuation, abbreviations and numbers.

KEY TERMS

coaching writing	copy editor	style manual
copy editing	courtesy title	wordprocessing

EXERCISES

1   One of the first steps in learning how to edit copy is to study and learn the most common principles of the style manual. Consistency in style often makes the difference between a readable, high-quality newspaper and one that is merely average.

Study your style manual or, if you do not have one, use style tips in this chapter as your guide. Rewrite each of the following exercises on a separate sheet of paper. Some of the cases may not be covered in your style manual. They are included here to promote class discussion and an eventual consensus. If your newspaper does not have an official style manual, these exercises and the preceding chapter may be used as the basis for

forming one. You may occasionally need to consult your dictionary or other style manuals to settle a problem.

(Note: Consider the first time you see a name to be the first reference. If the same person appears in later sentences, copy edit as though the references are the second and subsequent references.)

Names and capitalization

(a) Ferris high school basketball players worked out for three hours Friday.

(b) The Itasca Wampus Cats defeated the Bonham purple warriors 10–1 at Friday's baseball game.

(c) The freshman service club is collecting toys for families who lost their homes in the floods.

(d) Senior Seth Levy did not want to take a History class, even though it was required.

(e) Jeannie Elliott scored two goals in her first soccer game.

(f) Mrs. Whitney Bodine started her lesson by singing the National Anthem.

(g) The children loved Mrs. Whitney Bodine because her teaching style was a little unorthodox.

(h) The birds often nest in the roof of the gym during the Fall.

(i) First baseman Jason King hit two home runs off Starting Pitcher Johnny Seale.

(j) King spent the next three games on the bench of tovar memorial ballpark.

(k) Amanda Webb '08 is recovering from a broken leg suffered during a rodeo accident.

(l) More than 200 students showed up for the class party at bardwell lake.

(m) New students are expected to enroll in at least one class of german or spanish.

Abbreviations

(a) Teachers received a 1 percent pay raise even though they asked for a 10 percent increase.

(b) The play is scheduled for Feb. 15.

(c) Academic Decathlon members will travel to Okla. for their retreat.

(d) Dallas Cowboys running back Tony Dorsett holds the National Football League record for the longest run.

(e) Wed. was the first day students were allowed to return to school after the accident.

(f) The district added eight more portables along Lampier St.

(g) The SCE ruled that teachers would have to remove all tatoos.

(h) Speech teacher Rebecca Bennett is in her fourth year as the head of the Fine Arts Dept.

(i) Two 15-year-old hunters rescued a baby deer in the hills of Asheville, North Carolina.

(j) Six members of the state championship team signed letters with N.C.A.A. Division I schools.

(k) 24. Monday was the last time the boy was late to Doctor Olivia Belsher's class.

(l) The Downhill Ski Club will meet at 5 p.m., Nov. 23, in the library.

Numbers

(a) Calculus teacher Gregg Fleisher started class at 7:00 a.m.

(b) The gymnast fell off the balance beam in her first attempt.

(c) The next game is May 29th.

(d) The boy's father sold the car to his youngest son for one hundred dollars.

(e) The Panthers won the area soccer championship two–one.

(f) Senior goalie Susan Killough made 4 saves in the 6–1 bidistrict win.

(g) The drill team will meet at freshman Tricia Hughes's home at fourteen Churchill Road.

(h) Pianist Pam Murdock, seventeen, will perform a medley of Peter Frampton songs at 6 p.m., Monday, in the concert hall.

(i) Wide receiver Colin Fitzgibbons caught touchdown passes of five, 10, fifty-five and 33 yards.

(j) Admission to the concert is fifteen dollars.

(k) The boy moved to Boston from a town with a population of one thousand five hundred people.

(l) More than twenty-five students were home with food poisoning.

(m) Junior Caryn Statman couldn't stand another day with 20 5-year-olds.

Punctuation and Italics

(a) Freshman Adrienne Lee could not believe that her mom packed her bananas, apples and oranges for lunch.

(b) In Friday's choir concert, soprano Amy Cunningham sang I Love a Parade.

(c) "Why do I have to go to the Coldplay concert with you", Cunningham said.

(d) Leon Solimani, a 224-pound line-backer, joined the team after the second game.

(e) Sophomore Sarah Strauss' goal is to appear on the cover of Rolling Stone.

(f) Senior class president Bryan Parker admitted to getting five Cs and two Bs on his report card.

(g) The workshop's steering committee included: Mike McLean, secretary, Mary Pulliam, president, Chris Modrow, historian and Randy Vonderheid, treasurer.

(h) The Class of 82 will have their 20-year reunion this year.

(i) Sophomore Duane Yee played the lead role in the school's presentation of Hamlet Tuesday night.

(j) I absolutely love the dog "Astro" in the cartoon *The Jetsons*.

(k) President Tanner Bodine, Jr. will speak to the Sketch Comedy Club on Jan. 15.

(l) Freshman James The Real Deal Ragland will start at center in the opening game of the playoffs.

2 We learn to recognize printed words in much the same way that we learn to recognize persons we know. Their overall appearance seems to be enough to allow us to make a quick identification.

Psychologists call the total appearance of an object its *configuration* or the sum of its parts. We can hardly take the time to spell out every word we see in reading copy. We learn to depend on configuration or total form in examining its correctness. We therefore should challenge any word form that raises the slightest suspicion that it is mispelled.

Did you catch it? "Mispelled" is misspelled! This is a troublesome word that should always be examined. Other spelling demons are listed below.

Number a paper from 1 to 50. Let your hunches guide you and rewrite those words you believe are misspelled. Mark *OK* if the word is spelled correctly. (Don't leave any spaces blank.) If you sense a word is incorrectly spelled, mark it with an *X*. If it is actually misspelled, you may add one-half point to your total score, even though you haven't rewritten the word.

(Hint: More than half the words are misspelled.)

1	recieve	26	penicillin
2	alright	27	paralel
3	sophomore	28	elipse
4	berserk	29	embezzlement
5	habatat	30	incidious
6	misjudgement	31	patronage
7	lieutenant	32	athlete
8	restraunt	33	decathlon
9	accomodate	34	potpurri
10	fourty	35	nourish
11	repremand	36	concensus
12	sabotage	37	liason
13	seperate	38	libary
14	protocol	39	Febuary
15	larceny	40	lisence
16	ilegal	41	municipal
17	occured	42	legistlature
18	sponsor	43	indictment
19	elegible	44	peeve
20	corupt	45	hary-kary
21	corparate	46	fallible
22	excell	47	questionnaire
23	succeding	48	misspell
24	commit	49	oponent
25	facsimile	50	integral

3 An Associated Press Managing Editors committee created a list of the 50 most common errors in newspaper writing. Examples of these errors appear in the following sentences. Correct the following errors in word usage, spelling and grammar:

(a) The parents served refreshment afterwards.

(b) The funeral service was held in the First United Methodist Church.

(c) Even though the senior had less errors on the test, he made a better grade than his brother.

(d) More than half of the town went to church on Easter Sunday.

(e) The game will start at 8 p.m. tonight.

(f) The principal agreed to drop the policy prohibiting people from wearing hats in the building and the increase of the number of minutes between class periods.

(g) In the summer months, more than half of the senior class was employed.

(h) I'll never be able to tell who's dog this is without an identification tag.

(i) The sprinter won the race after alluding the former state champion.

(j) The committee, composed of three juniors, five seniors and five teachers …

(k) Junior Hili Banjo headed up the fashion show.

(l) I implied that the speaker was talking about the principal when saying "He was wrong."

(m) The team must improve it's rebounding to win this year.

(n) Freshman Aaron Ofseyer decided to become a meteorologist rather than a Jewish rabbi.

(o) Economics teacher Suresh Vasan closed down his car business to become a teacher.

4 Cut unnecessary words. *Dallas Morning News* writing coach and assistant managing editor Paula LaRocque lists the following phrases as examples of wordiness in newswriting. Your job is to make them more concise. Cut the extra words or replace the phrase with one word that's more precise.

(a) make use of

(b) true fact

(c) personal friendship

(d) conduct an investigation into

(e) on the occasion that

(f) large in size

(g) 12 noon

(h) set a new record

(i) a distance of 35 miles

(j) in the vicinity of

(k) crisis situation

(l) in the event that

(m) a number of

(n) the reason is because

(o) consensus of opinion

5 Edit the following story, written for a daily newspaper. Using all you've learned in this and previous chapters, correct all errors, ambiguities, inconsistencies and so on. (You may also wish to consult Chapter 12, for more on formatting and proofing the piece.)

Sweet Water, Tex – National guard troops patroled yesterday against looter after-tornados carved a 2-mile long, half-mile-wide swath through this east Texas town, killing 1 person, injuring some one-hundred others; and leaving 1500 persons homeless.

Ranging up to $20 million, dollars, officials said the destruction toll could have been worse. They marvelled at the fact that only one person was a fataality.

"After i saw the extent of the damage, I thought we'd have many more inujries and certainly more deaths," said Sweet-water mayor David Maddox. "It was luck. It was a miracle."

As national guardsman patroled the streets to watch for looting, volunteers and salvation army workers served over 2,000 meals to person left homeless by the disaster, said Mitchell Anderson, Public Relations Director for the Salvation Armys' Texas division.

The U. Weather Bureau said 2 tornadoes smashed into the sothern part of the city of 12,00 early Saturday.

Mayor Rick Rhodes sid that about 100 persons were injured and some 1500 left homeless.

Police Chief Jim Kelley said clean up efforts were progresing. "We're getting a lot of volunteer types," he said. "Their swooping in there, and they're helping."

Governor George Bush visited the city yesterday and talked with residents's of the Sun Village Housing Project, a Federally subsidized development for senior citizens which was hard hit. The storms only fatallity ws a 87-year-old man.

One resident, Gadys lane, stood looking through what used to be a side wall of her house asd Bush spoke.

"It was just like I was in a vacum," said Mrs. Lane. I was down on my knees begging the lord to take care of me.

"The only thing I can say is tough times never last, but though people do and we've got a lot off toughj people around here," said Bush.

6 The following sentences contain errors in fact, structure and style. Using copy editing symbols, correct spelling, grammar, punctuation, redundancies and sexist expressions.

(a) Mary has studyied filing, bookeeping and word processing.

(b) Exhausted after the days work, it was difficult for Joan to enjoy the concert.

(c) Bridgetown's 46 policemen in January, February and March, in 27,647 man-hours of work drove 117,786 miles – more than four trips around the earth, or 22,000 miles farther than the maximum distance from the earth to the sun.

(d) The students were given the basic fundamentals of the course.

(e) The sponsers were elated over the finantial outcome which netted a little over one hundred and fifty dollars.

(f) Cattle graze on ranges in the district, and farmers grow cotton, vegetables and citrus fruits, including grapes.

(g) 15 girls from each school will be at the Central high school which will make 150 girls.

(h) After working day and night for the past monthes the 82 piece Central band, under the direction of L. Irving Cradley are ready to do their best to win the district title at Dacon tomorrow night.

(i) My turn finally came to bowl.

(j) She had neither completed her English nor her Spanish.

(k) Plagiarism is where you take the work of another and pass it off as your own.

(l) He was a member of the committee in charge of the making of the student directory.

(m) He hoped to get the true facts of the problem.

(n) Coach Joe Voegle, of Spalding Institute, is the director of the clinic and hopes to have a prominent referee to be appointed by the local refferee's association, appear at one of the sessons to explain the new rules and their affect on the game.

(o) In describing his earliest beginnings he said he had grown up as a child.

(p) Arriving late at night, all the lights in the house were out.

(q) The teacher asked for a brief synopsis of the book.

(r) Housewives are feeling the pinch of inflation.

(s) Jim is a person of strong will and who always gets his own way.

(t) The team had won two straight in a row.

(u) Those elected were Jack Swanson, President, Mary Clements, vice President and Dale Cook, Secretary treasuer.

(v) The cleaning women were already in the building when we left.

(w) After his death he received the award posthumously.

(x) A rattlesnake bite, followed by a series of homemade anecdotes, sent an Almont man to the hospital yesterday.

7 **Approach the following story as a rough draft turned in to you, the copy editor. Using the coaching writing tips provided in this chapter, write out a number of questions to ask the writer to help improve the story. What points would you make to help the writer improve the story for the next draft? What good information does the writer have here? What information does the writer need to go back and get before writing a second draft?**

Junior Eden McKissick-Hawley loves fashion. McKissick-Hawley is getting to do what she loves at Her Majesty's closet, a couture consignment shop in Corinth Square. The store puts an emphasis on the history of the piece.

The store takes in everything from expensive fur coats to old hats and resells them. The have recently created a high school girl's section that the owner has given McKissick Hawley control of.

"We're very happy with her because she'll be here two years and can grow with the business," owner Barbara Bloch said. "Over time, she's shown that she wants a bigger role within the company— and that role has been bringing in a different demographic of teenage girls."

The owner has given McKissick-Hawley a lot of freedom as the public relations representative for the shop. McKissick-Hawley has started doing model shoots for the company.

I got to watch one of the photo shoots and it was really cool. She has them model lots of different types of clothes and gets the models to relax by saying some crazy things.

"It's great for me in terms of creativity, but also responsibility," McKissick-Hawley said. "I like saying crazy things to the models to get them to relax."

"Here I'm respected because I care about the store and care about what I do. And if I make a mistake, then it affects not only me and possibly my paycheck but the company and the customers."

As part of her job, she's been working lots of hours. Within a week, McKissick-Hawley hopes to have the online store up for Her Majesty's Closet— a task that requires taking photos, writing copy and putting online thousands of pieces. McKissick-Hawley hopes that this will expand their market by allowing the beauty of their clothing to be more accessible to girls here in Kansas City and customers around the country.

McKissick has a regular Twitter about fashion. One of the coolest moment she's had in her fashion career is having Elle Fanning, star of Super 8, retweeting one of her tweets.

In working at Her Majesty's Closet, she's loved learning a lot about fashion. She said she's heard some great stories behind the clothes that some people donate. Some people even cry.

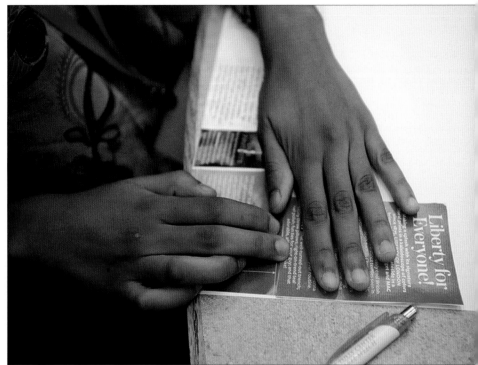

WRITING HEADLINES

Write a sentence that you'd use to describe this story to your mom. Then do the sentence as little damage as possible in making it fit the available space. I hope that's helpful.

William G. Connolly, *Senior Editor (retired)*, The New York Times

LEARNING OBJECTIVES After completing this chapter you will be able to:

- determine the main idea of a story and demonstrate that understanding in the headline

- understand and write both teaser and teller headlines

- understand and write headlines for news websites

- identify proper construction rules and apply those in headline writing

- brainstorm for creative headlines.

Scholastic Journalism, Twelfth Edition. C. Dow Tate and Sherri A. Taylor.
© 2014 John Wiley & Sons, Inc. Published 2014 by John Wiley & Sons, Inc.

HIGH SCHOOL STUDENTS TWEET ABOUT the pajamas they receive for Christmas. They text their parents (sometimes) when they'll be home late. They post status updates when they find errors in their college application essays. More than any other generation, today's high school students find themselves immersed in a world of short-form writing. While high school students certainly have a lot of practice getting messages across using only a few words, doing so clearly and concisely takes thought and practice. This chapter's discussion of headline writing will help hone those short-form writing skills. The headline writing process involves crafting the enlarged type that rests atop a story in a newspaper, news website or magazine; it is also valuable in creating multimedia forms such as broadcast news crawls or breaking news tweets.

HEADLINES: THE BASICS

No matter what the medium, the headline takes two basic forms in an attempt to get people's attention. Headline writers inform and sometimes entertain through relatively few words. Then once they've matched the content of the story, the challenge to make the words fit in a certain amount of space still remains.

Reasons readers value headlines:

- They summarize the important facts of the story. Headlines help readers glance quickly through the newspaper, yearbook, magazine or news website and select which stories to read.

- They provide keywords that Internet search engines will identify and include in a search for relevant topics.

- They suggest the mood of the story and give readers a sense of the story's tone. A feature story's light tone can be conveyed through a play on words. A news or a news-feature story should have a headline with a straightforward, informative voice.

- They signal the relative importance of each story. The headline's role in helping readers decide which story is more important is discussed in Chapter 12. The general rule is that the larger the type, the more important the story.

Teaser and teller headlines

Copy editors refer to headline content as either a "teaser" or "teller." The teller headline grabs the reader's attention by summarizing the story clearly and concisely. The voice of the teller is typically straightforward.

The **teaser headline** pulls in the reader by arousing curiosity or providing entertainment. A play on words such as "Try-athlete" may intrigue readers enough to make them pause at the story. But to make sure readers take the next step and read the lead, the teaser should always be accompanied by a **teller headline** as a secondary headline. In this case, the teller, "Sophomore hopes to finish first triathlon after five attempts" helps to preview the story's content.

In many magazines, newspaper packages and yearbooks, designers make creative use of typefaces on the teaser headline. Teller headlines and sub-headlines are most often designed using clean, readable typefaces. The teaser typefaces often mirror the content of the story in an attempt to entertain visually. Designer headlines are discussed later in this chapter and in Chapter 12, "Newspaper layout and design."

Getting the words to fit

Headlines have to fit into a specific space on the page – that's one of the greatest challenges in headline writing. The larger the typeface size, the fewer words will fit into the space.

Computers with page design, wordprocessing or paint and draw software allow the headline writer to see instantly if the headline fits. In any system, if the headline doesn't fit, the editor will need to add or subtract text or look for shorter or longer words to say the same thing. The

Test your knowledge

What's the difference between a teaser and a teller headline?

IN ACTION

Teaser brainstorming at work

FIGURE 10.1 *Rampages*, Casa Roble High School, Orangevale, Calif. Reproduced by permission of Dan Austin.

The headline on this yearbook spread about all the distractions a high school student has in their life is a clever play on a well-known phrase in the days leading up to the Iraq War. Good yearbook designers will often try to work a visual-verbal connection between their dominant photo and headline. A creative teaser like this has a stronger attraction when tied to a reinforcing image.

"Weapons of Mass Distraction" is a good headline, isn't it? It is, of course, a pun – and we all know that puns are a clever and goofy way to start off a spread. But it also alludes to the culturally relevant phrase "weapons of mass destruction," suggesting that the resistance teachers demonstrate to student possession of these objects mirrors that of Iraqis holding nuclear warheads. It's clever but not hard to understand, and that makes it a good headline.

Headlines are *by far* the most important piece of text relating to the content of a spread. To me, the headline can define the ultimate quality of that spread. It needs to hook the audience and get a reaction – a smirk or agape mouth – out of them while holding a connection to the content. Throwing down a mediocre headline is literary murder – it kills a spread. Headlines are a big deal. Because of their weight, I invest a good amount of effort in headline production. However, I have a lot of difficulty replying when you ask, "How do you attack headlines?" because my methods vary. If I am plugging in a headline to a boxy, templated spread with a dominant shot of two wrestlers grappling each other, I'll write "Grips of Wrath" – a simple pun that gets a reaction while holding a connection between "grips" and wrestling.

How I normally work is rather unconventional. I usually work backwards, starting with a common, well-known phrase, tweaking it until it works as a headline, then allowing content to bloom from there. For the "Weapons of Mass Distraction" spread, I worked this way. We were sitting in the conference room kicking around lame ideas for spread content while flipping through magazines. I read the phrase "weapons of mass destruction" buried somewhere in a *Wired Magazine* and noted how similar "destruction" and "distraction" sounded. "Weapons of mass distraction," I said. Around that freestanding phrase, we built gorgeous content, which *made* the headline perfect. Of course, this method is much easier to employ if your spread is content-driven and you have free reign over what goes in it.

Corey Lau, Rampages, Editor, Casa Roble High School, Orangevale, Calif.

rewriting process is the same when manually estimating space for headlines; however, the process can be slower.

Computers allow the writer to make small adjustments to the type size or **letterspacing**, the spacing between letters of a word, to make the headline fit. But that doesn't mean headline writers should try to squeeze in so many words that they are unreadable or shrink the font size so it is hardly bigger than body type. The minimum and maximum sizes of headlines are discussed later in the design chapters.

The craft of rewriting headlines to extend or tighten the wording to fit a space requires practice, especially when done manually. For the purpose of explaining how to make headlines fit, the count assigned to each letter, space and punctuation mark will be one unit, or character. Note below how the system works. Also notice how each line is counted separately and there are no spaces counted at the end of the lines.

1 1 1 1 1 1 1 1 1 1 1 1 1 1 1 1 1 1 1 1 1 1 1 1 1 1 = 26 units

Senior gains new identity,

1 1 1 1 1 1 1 1 1 1 1 1 1 1 1 1 1 1 1 1 1 1 1 1 1 1 1 1 1 1 = 30 units

access to liquor in 45 minutes

WORDS of WISDOM

Online headlines need not be cute but still need to grab the reader and be lively and interesting. They also should contain as many key words as possible, both for SEO and clarity purposes. One of my favorite tricks: What would I type into Google if searching for this story? Then essentially answer that question with your headline.

John Boogert, Deputy Editor of Interactive Media at The Wichita Eagle

News website headlines

Teaser headlines can be very effective on paper, but they rely on the reader's ability to grasp allusions and appreciate puns – in short, to infer the journalist's meaning. Online headlines, on the other hand, are typically written with Internet search engines in mind so readers can locate the news and information they seek. While the human reader may be amused by a teaser's play on words, the **search engine**, or computer program used to search the Internet for words and provide a list of documents with those words, takes the more analytical approach, looking for keywords related to the topic of the headline.

Therefore, the teller headline is the staple of the news website. These headlines should include specific identifying phrases and avoid vague or general phrases that might suggest a range of possible stories. For example, "Leiter Wins Stratford Student Council Election" would create strong keywords for the story. A more general headline, such as "Sophomore Wins Election" gives few specific keywords that would enable readers to find the story. In the first headline, the writer could have also included the winner's first name to increase the chance that the search engine would locate this story, since many readers will search for the candidate's full name, "Aubrey Leiter." These considerations are more important in large professional news websites competing for a regional or national audience than for a high school news website, whose audience generally goes directly to the website to browse news stories.

News website headlines must also conform to space restrictions imposed by website content management systems. These systems allow journalists to submit content without knowing complicated web coding, but do not allow for the same on-screen flexibility as page layout programs. The counting process described above can be helpful for this type of headline writing since it offers practice in rewriting headlines to fit available space. An additional headache for news website headline writers is crafting their headlines to fit the format of multiple devices – including mobile phones and tablets – to ensure the last words of longer headlines are not cut off.

THE APPEARANCE OF HEADLINES

While teller/teaser labels for headlines refer to content, headlines are also identified by appearance – certain kinds of headlines have certain content qualities. For example, a one-line headline is typically a single, unbroken sentence. The one-line headline is usually a teller.

Quick Exercise

Based on the news website writing guidelines, which headline in each set is better for search engines.

1 Peace of cake

New cake decorating class students find stress relief

2 Senior wins essay contest

Senior Kat Buchanan wins essay contest

Teens numb to gas price increases

FIGURE 10a One-line teller: "Teens numb to gas price increases," *El Estoque*, Monta Vista High School, Cupertino, Calif. http://elestoque.org/2012/08/23/opinion/teens-numb-gas-price-increases/.

A two-line headline is one sentence broken into two lines. Each line is counted separately. For example,

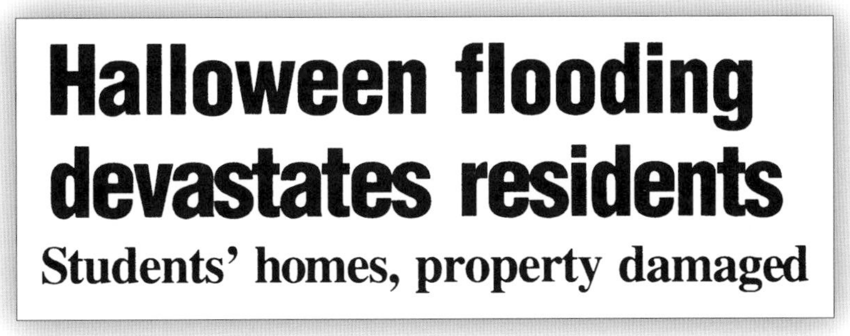
Halloween flooding
devastates residents
Students' homes, property damaged

FIGURE 10b Two-line headline: "Halloween flooding Devastates residents," *Paladin*, Kapaun Mt. Carmel High School, Wichita, Kan. Reprinted with permission.

(A gap of white space is unsightly at the end of one line of a two-line headline. A three-line headline is one sentence broken into three lines.)

Typically these are teller headlines. Remember that each line counts separately.

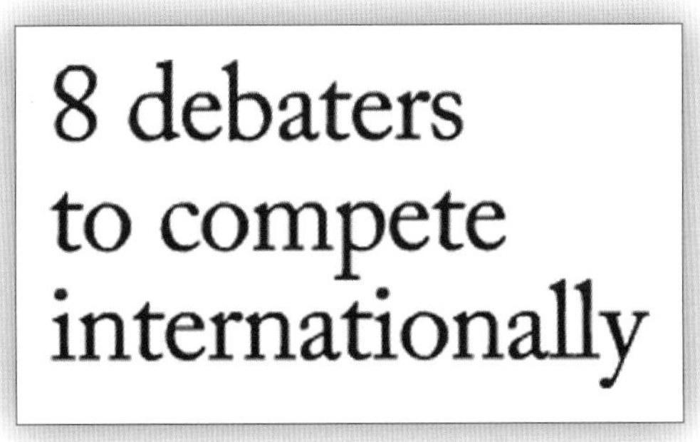
8 debaters
to compete
internationally

FIGURE 10c Three-line headline: "8 debaters to compete internationally," *The Chronicle*, Harvard-Westlake High School, Los Angeles, Calif.

A four-line headline is one sentence broken into four lines. Some newspapers continue to stay away from breaking a headline into four lines but news websites are more apt to use this style.

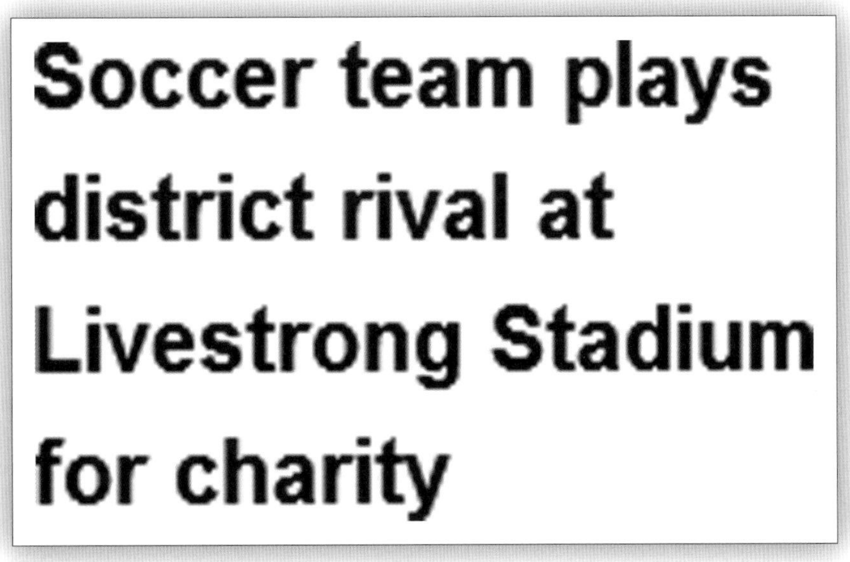
Soccer team plays
district rival at
Livestrong Stadium
for charity

FIGURE 10d Four-line headline: "Soccer team plays district rival at Livestrong stadium for charity," MVNEWS.org, Mill Valley High School, Shawnee, Kan.

Test your knowledge

What's a jump headline?

A **deck** is a **secondary headline** that is positioned under the main headline and is typically a teller. The deck can go under another teller headline. The deck should add information and can be helpful in explaining complicated stories.

Canceled permit foils annual parade

■ Tailgate party to replace Homecoming tradition

FIGURE 10e Deck headline: "Canceled permit foils annual parade. Tailgate party to replace Homecoming tradition," *Edition*, Anderson High School, Austin, Texas. Reprinted with permission.

The **jump headline** accompanies the part of a story that continues on a different page. This jump headline is written as another headline for a story on whether teenagers should be allowed an occasional glass of wine at home. Some publications opt for using only key words as a jump headline.

Wine: Does drinking at home cut down on underage binge drinking?

FIGURE 10f jump headline: "WINE: Does drinking at home cut down on underage drinking?", *The Dart*, St. Theresa's Academy, Kansas City, Mo. Reproduced by permission of Eric Thomas.

Designer headlines, used primarily for newspaper features and in yearbooks and magazines, establish the mood through choice of type. They are also created by adding graphics or manipulating type size. Readability of type should still be a consideration in creating a designer headline. Well-written designer headlines that use type to match the content or message can be extremely effective (see Figures 10.1–10.4).

WRITING A HEADLINE

Writing five or six words seems simple. However, choosing five or six words that summarize a story plainly and briefly may be more of a challenge than you think. The following section gives you a process and rules to follow to make sure the finished product is clear and concise.

Writing a teller

Quick Exercise

Print (or clip) four clever designer heads. Rank them on their visual-verbal appeal. Explain how the design communicates the message of the headline.

Even though the headline has the fewest words of any element in a newspaper or yearbook, it often requires as much thought and care as the lead or the body of the story. While headlines typically are created on deadline, the writer should put maximum effort into creating good ones. If the story was written by someone else, read through the entire story to understand the content. Mentally, or on the computer screen or paper, try to summarize the most important information in the story in one brief sentence. Try it again, this time trimming even more words. Rewrite using synonyms, or by reconstructing the sentence, until the headline fits the space, tone and content of the story.

FIGURE 10.2 *The Indian*, Shawnee Mission North High School, Overland Park, Kan. Reproduced by permission of Shawnee Mission North Principal Richard Kramer.

Teasers often become a place for designers to bring some flair to the type to accentuate a design. This designer used cut out the letters of a font to create a stencil for a mud photo to create a playful, visually appealing headline to match the fun tone of a spread about a religious organization's annual rally to start the new school year.

FIGURE 10.3 *The Harbinger*, Shawnee Mission East High School, Prairie Village, Kan. Reproduced by permission of C. Dow Tate.

This headline plays off the play's title, "The Grapes of Wrath," for a witty teaser that's supported by a clear teller. Designers, like this one from *Harbinger* staff, often emphasize words through larger type. The less important words fit in the flow as the designer right aligns those words to visually connect to the larger, more interesting words.

FIGURE 10.4 "Basketballer Ryan Jackson commits to Lewis," by Bryan Doyle, Dec. 16, 2010. *Clariononline*, Riverside Brookfield High School, Riverside, Ill. Available URL: http://rbclarion.com/sports/2010/12/16/basketballer-ryan-jackson-commits-to-lewis. Reprinted with permission.

News website headlines differ from print headlines because they are not only being scanned by readers but by search engines. This headline from *Clarion Online* uses both the first and last name of the star athlete as well as the name of the university he committed to giving the search engine two specific keywords that are more likely to help narrow the search to this piece for readers. Tellers such as this one tend to be the staple headline of most online stories.

Basic teller headline rules

The headline should follow these guidelines:

→ Be accurate, above all. Specific facts in the headline should be completely supported in the story.

→ Be informative. Try to answer as many questions as a news lead does.

→ Be clear. Although today's generation are practiced writers of texts and tweets, the headline writer must keep in mind that the reader – unlike a friend receiving a text – won't be able to reply with a clarifying question about anything confusing or vague.

→ Be fair. If the story covers two sides of an issue, try to reflect the differences in the headline. Do not editorialize directly or indirectly unless the headline is for an opinion story such as a review or editorial. The headline should convey the same perspective as the body of the story.

→ Do not put anything in the headline that is not in the story.

IN ACTION

Headline writing in action

Watch as this writer works to create a headline for a story about a new Key Club reading project.

A group of Key Club members enjoy weekly reading time with kindergarten class from Virginia Bodine Elementary School.
"Okay, that's the basic idea of the story, but ugh … too long and wordy. Let me try to eliminate some words."

A group of Key Club members share brotherly experience by reading books to kindergarten class.
"Still some unnecessary words."

Key Club share brotherly experience by reading books
"There. Much shorter, but now I lost the point. They could be reading to football players."

Key Club members share experience with kindergarten class
"Now we don't know what the 'experience' is."

Key Club members enjoy reading time with kindergarten class
"Not bad. Gets the point across. Now let's try a couple more."

Key Club reads books to tots
"Haha … I don't guess kindergarteners are actually toddlers."

Key Club bonds with kindergartners through reading time
"Hmm. I like this one because of the stronger verb."

Headline construction rules

Headline-writing rules are continually changing among news websites, professional newspapers and magazines. *The New York Times*, for example, now uses articles such as *a, and* and *the* more often than it used to in headlines.

News websites have adapted their own headline rules, allowing for more flexibility in space and formatting as technology changes,. However, as writers craft more headlines focused on the mobile device reader, tighter space requirements may return headline writing to the traditional elimination of unnecessary words.

Most publications adhere to the following guidelines for headline writing:

- Avoid **padding**. *A, and, the, their, his* or *her* should not be used in hard news headlines. (Notice the deletion of the word in brackets in this and subsequent headlines.)

  Cooper families feel [the] stress of company lockout

- However, use of *the* in the following headline is necessary to keep the headline from sounding awkward.

  All in the family
  Students suffer when mothers battle disease

- Use active verbs in tellers.

  Assassins game triggers Code Red

- Omit forms of the verb *to be*, if possible. Notice the correct deletions of the words in brackets.

  Senior party preparations [are] underway as graduation nears

  Flu bug attacks students; many absences [are] reported

- Opt for the active voice over the passive voice whenever possible. The first headline shows the correct use of the active voice; the second the correct use of the passive voice.

  Debate team ranks first in district, state contests

  Five '10 graduates given top awards at commencement

WWW

WEBLINK Check out
www.allwords.com
The website offers headline writers a whole list of links to websites to help with wordplay.

- Use the present tense to describe past events. This use is known as the **historical present**.

  Council approves $1 million renovation project

- The past tense is showing up in more publications, especially when it enhances clarity. In the following *Dallas Morning News* headline, past tense is used because subject of this obituary headline played an integral role in women's rights during the 1960s.

  Dallas lawyer helped wives get property rights

- Use the infinitive form of the verb for future events. Any other tense would only confuse the reader.

  Crawl-space renovation to begin within month

- Do not separate the following items from one line to the next. Avoid the following breaks:

  1 Preposition and its object

  Security captures monkeys in
  Oak Park Mall bathrooms

  2 Parts of the same verb

  Science club president to
  promote plastic recycling

  3 Parts of names that belong together

  Senior waits 10 hours for final Harry
  Potter premiere in pouring rain

  4 Abbreviations

  Alum wins NC-
  AA top honor

  5 Noun and its adjacent adjective

  HHS Band involves feeder-school
  bands to boost future participation

  6 Compound words

  Texas tourist jumps under sub-
  way to save toddler

- Don't repeat words in the headline.

  Test scores fall
  Students' test results fall for third consecutive year

- Generally use numerals, although numbers through nine may be spelled out.

  Tennis team dominates: Eight head to leagues after an almost
  flawless season

  Senior class collects 123 pints in blood drive

- "Down style," or capitalizing only the first word of a headline and all proper nouns, has become the preferred style of most publications.

  Irmo experiences two fires in two days

 **WORDS of WISDOM**

Never sacrifice accuracy for creativity. Tell readers what is happening, but more importantly, tell them

why they should devote more of their time to the story.

Niko Dugan, ACES Executive Committee Member, Copy Editor, The News-Gazette, *Champaign, Ill.*

- Instead of general words, as in the first headline, opt for specific words that fit the same space. The second headline has been written with stronger, more precise language.

  WRONG: New bill requires increased language requirement
  RIGHT: State may require two years of high school Spanish

- Punctuate headlines correctly; omit periods.

  1 Commas are often used to replace *and*. In all other cases, standard English usage rules that apply to commas should be used in headlines.

  Yellow Ribbon Week reminds friends, family to listen

  2 Use the semicolon to attach two related thoughts.

  Tornado destroys field house; clean-up to take three weeks

  3 Use single quotation marks rather than double.

  Putting 'the boot' down
  Delinquent parking tickets prompt school officials to purchase new tool

- Do not use obscure or unnecessary abbreviations.

  WRONG: New FHS principal changes discipline plan
  RIGHT: New principal changes discipline plan

- Be sure to avoid jargon in headlines, especially those for websites; don't rely on body text to clarify any terms.
- Never abbreviate a day of the week.
- Never use a day of the week and a date together.
- Do not abbreviate months except when a numeral follows (Jan. 27).
- Do not use names unless the persons are commonly known. Using a general description is usually more meaningful. Websites generally don't adhere to this rule because using names in these headlines, including both first and last name, helps create important search keywords.
- Avoid placing headlines and nonrelated photos or other images near each other, especially when an unexpected connection may be perceived.

FEATURE HEADLINES

Entertainment is the goal when writing the teaser headline. Feature editor/writer Nancy Kruh, a 25-year veteran of *The Dallas Morning News*, discusses the process for writing a feature headline and offers tips.

Test your knowledge

When is padding acceptable to include in a headline?

Quick Exercise

Based on the headline construction rules, identify the primary problem in each headline.

1 Yellowjackets lose 4th in a row, quarterback injured

2 Alum named to NA-ACP leadership post

3 Cancer survivor won Miss Bristol contest

With feature journalism now a staple in every section of the daily newspaper, copy editors are called upon to write headlines that sell a story with word play, as well as information.

Crafting a feature headline that's entertaining, compeling and sophisticated requires all of a copy editor's creative skills. The best editors tend to look upon the challenge almost as a word game: How can you make a headline fun – and make it fit the space? The deftest headlines are a delight with or without the story: "She stole his heart, so the police had to write her a ticket," "If all goes as planned, it's an accident," "Hundreds of mice flock to cat's Web page," "It's picture day at school, so make it a snap."

Becoming an accomplished feature-headline writer takes practice but also requires sustained attentiveness to language and popular culture. You simply can't write wonderfully inventive headlines such as, "Nobody troubles the nose I've seen" – as *Dallas Morning News* copy editor Steve Steinberg did for a column about the perils of an oversized nose – without knowing the old song, "Nobody knows the trouble I've seen." Imagine trying to write a feature headline about, say, the "Harry Potter" series without knowing about Muggles, Hogwarts or the Dark Arts.

While wracking your brain is one way to go about searching for appropriate idioms, a far easier approach is to turn to the Internet, which offers access to a growing assortment of searchable idiom and slang dictionaries. Notable sites include sky-net-eye.com/eng/english/idioms/american, which is based on the original book *A Dictionary of American Idioms*, and dmoz.org/Reference/Dictionaries/World_Languages/E/English/Slang/, a compendium of slang terminology. Search engines can point your way to other sites, such as usingenglish.com, idioms.yourdictionary.com and dictionary.babylon.com.

Dictionaries, both online and in hard copy, also often include common expressions in their definitions. (For example, here's some of what *Webster's New World Dictionary* offers for the word "heart": "eat one's heart out, "after one's own heart," "break one's heart," "take to heart," do one's heart good." There also are all these related words: "heartache," "heart attack," "heartbeat" and heartburn.") Many hard-copy reference works also have compiled slang expressions and idioms; check libraries or bookstores for those.

Once you've gathered a few catchphrases, it's time to brainstorm possible headlines. Here, for example, is how Carolyn Poh, another accomplished *Dallas News* copy editor, brainstormed a headline for a feature about the coffee-table books on sale for Christmas. First, she gathered words associated with "books" and "coffee," such as "tome," "binder," "pages," "chapter," "slick," "cream," "sugar," "beans," "grind" and "stir." Then she free-associated her way to these four clever headlines: "Best of tomes, worst of tomes" (a playoff Charles Dickens' "best of times, worst of times"), "Binders keepers," "In the slick of things" and "Cream of the coffee table." The last headline was the one ultimately selected for publication.

Here are a few guidelines that can help you get inspired when you're assigned to write a feature headline (examples have all been written by *Dallas News* copy editors):

1 Freshen a cliché by exploiting its literal meaning. For instance, "A chip off the old block" is a flat and trite headline if the accompanying story is about children who have taken up their fathers' professions. But the same headline is fun and inventive if the fathers happen to be carpenters. Here are other examples: "Kids' tastes get a bit hard to swallow," "Women's soccer team has the world at its feet," "Bartending couple endured two rounds of love on the rocks," "Toilet-seat debate has ups and downs."

2 Turn an idiomatic expression into a catchy headline by switching words: "Sculptor has stones of heart," "You've lain in your bed – now make it."

3 Alter spelling, but not pronunciation: "Cat gives paws to writing career."

4 Alter (very slightly) spelling and pronunciation: "The musician with sax appeal," "Mooch obliged: Author relies on fans' hospitality for national book tour," "Fame thrower."

5 Use a word with two meanings (but only if both meanings are appropriate): "He has few reservations about hotels," "The business of having a baby is all in the delivery," "She has never been hooked by the lure of fishing."

6 Use rhyming words or alliterations: "Saucy Aussie," "Noodling with doodling," "Star-studded dud," "Rough-neck romance," "Intricate intrigue hits home."

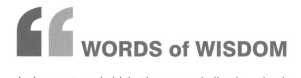

WORDS of WISDOM

I always teach kids that good display decks are like ogres – kids all know Shrek and know that ogres

have layers. The word "ogre" actually becomes lexicon. For example I have an old LA Times *sports page*

with article on Sugar Shane Mosely's first title fight and the headline is "Sugar on Top." Layer one is the

literal reference to the boxer making it to the top. Layer two references the commonly known idiom used

with "pretty please." Layer three references cereal eating. Layer four references the old Aerosmith song.

Dan Austin, Casa Roble High School Yearbook Adviser, Orangevale, Calif.

7 Change a word in a well-known phrase: "Self-adhesive stamps: If you can't lick 'em, buy 'em," "They're only young twice."

8 Employ evocative and subject-appropriate language: "Tale of American West shoots for suspense," "The forceful return: 'Star Wars' blasts into theaters again."

9 Use opposites, such as "up, down" or "rich, poor": "Hard times bring out a light touch," "Novel makes short work of long life."

10 Have your own say. A direct comment on the story or its subject, particularly in the upper line of a deck, can be quite an eye-catcher: "Beat it, kid: Not everyone likes 'Little Drummer Boy,'" "Give 'em yell, mom: Dallas Cowboys cheerleader is 37, married and has four kids," "It's Ms. Cinderella to you, bub: New play toughens a traditional heroine."

A few final thoughts: Word-play headlines have become so popular, editors occasionally stretch puns beyond the bounds of reasonable taste or good sense, inviting groans from readers. You'll have to decide for yourself where you draw the line, but here are a few excesses you can use as benchmarks: "Allergies must have a wheezin'," "There's a lot of finny business going on here," "She's Hillary-ous," "With cows, it's always one thing or an udder."

It's also wise to avoid certain idioms and headline tricks that have become hackneyed over the years. These include playing off the subject's name, "Tom is Cruising to another hit movie"; using parentheses, "Naughty but (n)ice cream"; and employing tired clichés: "Yes, Virginia, there is a Santa Claus," "A sign of the times," "The times they are a-changin'," and "Tis the season." Relying on these crutches is not just unimaginative. It's lazy.

Another no-no in the editor's unwritten code of ethics is repeating the word play that the writer may have employed in the story. That's not only unimaginative and lazy, it's also theft.

Examples of quality feature headlines from high school publications include the following:

- A sports story about two girls trying out for the school's wrestling team

  Wrestling with change

- An entertainment story about the drama club's twisted production of "Alice in Wonderland," where Alice is in an insane asylum

  Alice in ... La La Land

- A sports story about a senior headed to a prestigious school known for engineering to play basketball

  Engineered to play ball
  MIT-bound Dickson extends basketball career through college

- A review of little-known barbecue restaurants

  Off the Eaten Path
  ***The Harbinger* serves up four smokin' barbeque joints you've never heard of**

- A news-feature about the campaign of a mother whose son was killed in a drunk-driving accident

  A drunk driver shattered the lives of a local family. Now in memory of her son, Sue Anderson gives Lakota students...
  A crash course

- A news-feature about social committee preparations for the WPA dance.

  Making themes come true
  Student Council Social Committee Head creates decorations for WPA

CONCLUSION

Today's reader is so inundated with information that a writer's ability to grab the reader's attention with the short writing of headlines, tweets and posts is paramount. A high school journalist must work hard to assure headlines are sharp and articulate while still being concise and accurate. While many writers don't craft the headlines until the story and page is completed, painstaking effort to write crisply and cleverly can make a difference in whether the reader even makes it to the lead of a lengthy story the writer spent hours composing.

SUMMARY

- Headlines are key to helping readers select the stories they want to read by summarizing them in a brief but interesting form.

- The teller headline grabs the reader's attention by summarizing the story clearly and concisely. The teaser headline pulls in the reader by arousing curiosity or providing entertainment.

- Headlines and other such short-form writing such as tweets and posts must often fit within a prescribed amount of space. Headline writers usually work on word choice and information selection to assure they fit.

- The number of lines in a headline often varies based on the layout of the page. Writers should avoid awkward breaks and hyphenations in multi-line headlines.

- A headline should be fair and accurate in its representation of the story's tone. Don't mislead in an effort to grab a reader's attention.

- Teaser headlines are often showcased through creative design. The designer can use layout and type.

KEY TERMS

deck	keyword	secondary headline
designer headline	letterspacing	teaser
historical present	padding	teaser headline
jump headline	search engine	teller headline

EXERCISES

1 Print (or clip) and mount five tellers and five teasers from your area daily newspaper. Explain the difference.

2 Print (or clip) and mount five headlines from your area daily newspaper and rank them for quality. Explain why each grabbed your attention and why.

3 On a separate sheet of paper grade each of the following headlines (a) to (i) on how well it exemplifies the principles of good headline writing. Justify your grade.

(a) A column about the joys and advantages of taking naps

FIGURE 10.5 "Nap Happy" headline. *The Harbinger*, Shawnee Mission East High School, Prairie Village, Kan. Reproduced by permission of C. Dow Tate.

(b) A sports feature story about sophomore who places in national duck calling competitions.

FIGURE 10.6 "Finding his Calling" headline. *The Harbinger*, Shawnee Mission East High School, Prairie Village, Kan. Reproduced by permission of C. Dow Tate.

(c) A story about protesting an assembly film

Commotion is caused by picture

(d) A straight news story about a faculty retirement

Murdock leaves Central faculty; successor named

(e) A football game story for a news website

Team excels in 42-7 win

(f) A new story about a new musical

"Leader of the pack" is named musical

(g) A news-feature on a new program requiring truants to clean up the school

Cleaning up their acts
New custodia enforces community service

(h) A feature story about keeping New Year's resolutions

Resolving problems

(i) A feature story about a special education physical education class

Something special in the air
P.E. class encourages students to learn skills in positive atmosphere

(j) A news website story about an upcoming state poetry contest

Roper to compete for first state title

4   **For the following story write a two-line headline with each line no fewer than 17 and no more than 23 units.**

A Lakota freshman school student has been charged with illegal possession of a deadly weapon after the student was allegedly found with a BB gun in his locker on April 22.

Along with the legal charges, the student has also received a 10-day suspension and a recommendation for expulsion for his illicit activities.

The weapon was found after a school administrator received an anonymous tip that there was a student at the school who claimed to have a gun.

According to Assistant Principal Lee Corder, after the administration called the police a brief investigation of the student was held and the BB gun was found.

Corder feels that the situation was dealt with efficiently.

"I think that it [the investigation] created very little disturbance in the building," said Corder. "It was handled quickly and responsibly without incident."

Lakota freshman Andrea Piri said she was amazed that something like this could happen.

"I was surprised that anybody would bring a BB gun to school. It's obvious that they'd be caught," said Piri.
Lee Delaveris, Spark, *Lakota East High School, Liberty Township, Ohio*

5   **For the following story write a one-line main headline, 16 to 22 units long and a one-line secondary headline of 26 to 32 units.**

"To bee or not to bee." That is the question concerning maintenance personnel who have to deal with the campus bee problem.

The typical lunch has been drastically changed for those students who eat outside, because of the bee swarms around trash cans. Lunch-goers move from table to table and girls scream at the top of their lungs, when pestered by a bee swarm.

"I just sit there and hope the bees leave me alone," senior Bruce Nguyen said.

"We are doing as much as humanly possible to get rid of the bees at this point," plant manager Connie White said. "You're messing with the forces of nature when you leave out food. Students can help by putting trash in its proper place."

Assistant principal Quinn Kellis also emphasized the need for a clean campus. "The problem we have is we can't spray insecticides while students are on campus. So we've been using traps and mild soap that's diluted to kill the bees," Kellis said. "The best solution is to keep the area clean."

"Though the hive has been located, everyone still needs to do their part," White said. "Once a month the kitchen cafeteria area is sprayed by an exterminating firm, but that doesn't stop them from coming back."
Patty Barney, Ridge Review, *Mountain Ridge High School, Glendale, Ariz.*

6   **For the following story, write a one-line main headline, 13 to 20 units long and a two-line headline with each line between 22 and 29 units.**

After two years of discussion, the banning of book bags will become a school policy effective at the beginning of the school year.

There are several reasons that the administration thinks this is a good idea.

"They block hallways, doors and classroom aisles. If we needed to evacuate the school properly, the book bags would be in the way. Fire prevention officer (Dean E. Spitler) did an inspection and recommended that we get rid of them. To continue having book bags would be going against a professional opinion," Principal Dr. Kathleen Crates said.

Another reason backpacks are a problem is that they enable students to bring unnecessary items into the building.

"They allow students to carry in things that aren't healthy in the learning environment. From pop bottles to weapons, they can carry it in without anyone knowing that they have it. They add to the congestion in the halls and are also clinically proven to be bad for students' backs," Crates said.

Hidden objects in book bags are also a concern to Junior Principal Patrick Hickey.

"From the standpoint of security, book bags give students a way to bring contraband into the school. There are hundreds of book bags laying around unattended, and no one questions whose book bags they are. Students could easily leave a book bag that is dangerous laying around in the cafeteria or music wing."

"When purses are left laying around, people bring them down to the office right away. No one would think twice about taking a book bag down to the office," Hickey said.

While administrators think eliminating book bags will increase security, some students are opposed to the whole idea.

"Book bags are supposedly a fire hazard, but I don't understand how a pile of books that could get scattered on the floor is any better than books inside of something. We could find an alternate solution to the problem, like using book bag racks in the classrooms," Junior Amy Chester said.

Yet there are also students who don't really care about the new book bag policy.

"It's not like people are going to have to go to their lockers every period, you take two books and go to your classes and switch books later. There is a big enough place to put them under your desk where they won't be in the way. There are ways to get around without a book bag, but no one wants to work with the system," Sophomore Mike LaRocco said.

Kristin Cramer, Blue & Gold, *Findlay High School, Findlay, Ohio*

7 **For the following story, write a one-line news website headline counting between 26 and 32 units.**

After 30 years with the Duncanville band program and three state champion bands, Dr. Tom Shine announced his retirement to Wind Ensemble students April 26.

"It's just time," Dr. Shine said. "I've been teaching band for 40 years and there's not a single band that competes on such a high level as we do with a band director within 10 years of my age."

Students have been making jokes for years about returning to DHS years after graduation to find Dr. Shine pushing director David Brandon's wheelchair down to the marching field. It's been such a long-standing joke [that] students, like senior Rachel Harvey, find it hard to believe that won't be the case.

"Even if he retires he has to come back and do this," Harvey said. "I mean how else is Mr. Brandon going to get down the field?"

Since Dr. Shine's been with the program, the marching band has become the only 5A band to

advance to state finals every year since 1988 and the Wind Ensemble has become the only 5A band to be chosen as the TMEA State Honor Band three times.

"We have a really great program and all the achievements and awards reflect the dedication of Dr. Shine," senior Sarah Brack said.

Although Dr. Shine wasn't planning on announcing his retirement until the end of the year, rumors surfaced that he's sick or in trouble and he didn't want students to worry.

"I was really surprised," Brack said about Dr. Shine's announcement. "He's the poster-boy for band. When you think of Duncanville Band you think of Dr. Shine."

Although Dr. Shine will be missed, he says he hopes he has everything set up so things will continue on without a period of transition after he leaves.

"Things aren't supposed to be about a director," Dr. Shine said. "It's supposed to be about what we do together."

In spite of his leaving, students are also happy he will be able to enjoy what he loves most."

"I'm really sad, but I'm happy he's doing what he wants and what he feels is right for him and his family," Brack said. "I think we're all just really sad to see him go."

Vanessa Jenkins, Panther Prints, *Duncanville High School, Duncanville, Texas*

8 **Choose a feature story from a newspaper or magazine. Write six different teasers for the story. Keep them short. Be creative.**

TYPOGRAPHY AND PRODUCTION

11

" *I tend to play it safe when choosing type. I'd rather have words that are easy to read, than use an eye-catching (and distracting) typeface. In most cases, I rely on a couple of favorites, like Franklin Gothic and Caslon. When there's a project that calls for more edge, I'll reach for one of those fun novelty typefaces – but only for the display type.* "

JiaYing Grygiel, Creative Freelancer, Seattle

LEARNING OBJECTIVES After completing this chapter you will be able to:

- use and understand typographic terminology

- choose type appropriately to create readable and legible communications in print and online

- explore the creative qualities of type to make powerful and attractive visual – verbal connections in design

- understand the production process of design in print.

Scholastic Journalism, Twelfth Edition. C. Dow Tate and Sherri A. Taylor.
© 2014 John Wiley & Sons, Inc. Published 2014 by John Wiley & Sons, Inc.

TYPE: THE BASICS

When people start reading a story, they rarely think about the typeface. They might be discouraged from reading if the words are difficult to make out, or their eyes might tire quickly due to a poor choice by the type designer. But readers can also initially be drawn to pages based on a strong visual-verbal marriage of words through typography. A beautiful headline display can pull a reader into the text and sustain her attention through an entire story (see Figure 11.1).

FIGURE 11.1 Front-page, *Blue & Gold*, Findlay High School, Findlay, Ohio, Issue 4, p. 1, Jan. 28, 2011. Reprinted with permission.

Blue & Gold creates a striking front-page through strong use of photography and typography. Starting with a feature on declining enrollment, the page then presents the reader with two other stories. The paper's designers help the reader distinguish between the front-page feature and other news through the amount of space allotted to each item; strong, all-cap, sans serif typography; use of blue color; and the arrow graphic.

The front-page package is contained in a black frame and surrounded by extra white space. The package includes a deck, secondary head, a pull quote and a large graphic (the number 175) at the top of the story to indicate the number of students no longer enrolled.

The top banner includes the paper's flag or nameplate, a weather box, an index and teasers to inside story content. Balancing the top, the bottom banner provides self-contained quick-reads, each featuring a visual element. The paper is a broadsheet, similar to many professional newspapers.

NEWSFLASH

Weblinks

So much typography, so much to learn. With dozens of great typeface sites on the web, here are some with links and information for typophiles everywhere to enjoy.

Typefaces convey visual messages about journalistic content. Because these messages must be both readable and legible, type choices are important to the design process. Because typefaces can draw in or deter readers, the page designer can be the best friend or worst enemy of the writer. Good designers understand and appreciate the value of carefully chosen type. They understand how the space between the letters – kerning – and the space between the lines of type – leading – can add to that readability.

Designers have favorite typefaces, and can often identify a typeface just by looking closely for subtle clues in its construction. "Type-aholics" learn to love and appreciate the eccentricities and quirks of letter forms and make use of their features in well-designed type displays.

Typefaces are available for free or by purchase through a variety of online sites, which offer designers a chance to supplement the standard typefaces on their computer software or those offered to yearbook staffs by their publishers. It's best to buy typefaces from companies that specialize in selling type to make sure the typefaces will print and display correctly. Though typefaces for online use are often limited to a core set shared by both Mac and PC platforms, companies are now offering extensive "web-safe" typefaces, which can be used both online and in print.

Type terms

Defining terms that relate to understanding typographic terminology will help the designer in choosing and understanding type.

- **Agate type**: the smallest point size type a publication uses. Agate type is traditionally used for setting sports scores and classified ads in newspapers. The size might range between five and six points.
- **Alignment**: the method used for starting and ending lines of type. **Left aligned** means the type starts on a common left margin but features uneven arrangement on the right. **Right-aligned** features type with a common right alignment, but a ragged left alignment. **Centered type** features ragged edges on both sides and type is set to the middle of a central axis.

  Justified type lines up on both the left and right edges. **Force justified** is a computer alignment that will add space between letters or words of type to cause them to fill up a line of space. This pattern creates awkward "**rivers of white space**," which inhibit readability.
- **Ascenders**: letters that rise above the baseline and include the letters b, d, f, h, k, l and t.
- **Baseline**: the line upon which all the letters sit.
- **Body text**: generally between nine and 12 picas in height, the size in which traditional text stories appear on the page.
- **Bullets**: typographic or graphic devices used to mark entry into paragraphs or text passages. Bullets can be dots, squares, checks or symbols and can be used in color to create repetition.

WWW

WEBLINK Check out

www.ilovetypography.com

The site of a British-born writer, editor and graphic designer, ilovetypography links extensively to other sites. The site's owner also publishes a type journal, Codex, which is available online.

WWW

WEBLINK Check out

www.typographica.org

Typographica is a review of typefaces and type books, with occasional commentary on fonts and typographic design. It includes extensive information on type categories, foundries and designers.

WWW

WEBLINK Check out

www.fontfeed.com

FontFeed is a site full of great articles, and information is frequently updated. Users can subscribe to the site and get email links to new content posts.

WWW

WEBLINK Check out

www.typography.com

This is the site of New York type designers Jonathan Hoefler and Tobias Frere-Jones showcasing their type designs. The pair designed Gotham, a popular American sans serif face. Scroll down to the bottom of the site for a type blog.

Test your knowledge

Using a newspaper or magazine, identify five typeface terms.

- **C/lc:** refers to the use of capitals and lowercase letters in design.
- **Coastline:** the shape made by drawing lines around type set in c/lc display. The rises and falls of the ascender and descender letters help readers process information.
- **Counters:** the open spaces inside enclosed counters in letters such as *a, d, e, g, o, p* and *q*.
- **Descenders:** letters that fall below the baseline, and include the letters *g, j, p, q* and *y*.
- **Display type:** type sizes 14 points and above, used to display information such as headlines, secondary or deck headlines and other graphic information.
- **Down style:** the practice of capitalizing only the first letter of a headline and proper nouns that occur after the first letter. The style is easily read because it mimics sentence style.
- **Drop caps:** letters set in larger sizes at the beginning of sections of text or throughout the text, directing the reader's eye to the beginning of stories. These letters usually "drop" into the first few lines of text – hence, the name. In addition to drop caps, letters can "rise above" the other lines of text, can be set to the side of the text or can be printed beneath the text in a color or shade of color.
- **Em/en space, dash:** a unit of measuring space or dashes in design in which the value is equivalent to the width of a lower case letter m or n in a particular typeface and size.
- **Glyphs:** special character sets that are historically accurate to the typeface. Glyph sets can include fractions, **ligature** pairs (conjoined letters such as *fi, fl, fj, ff*), ornaments, old style figures (non-aligning numbers) and other choices.
- **Hanging punctuation:** punctuation such as quote marks on the left that line up outside the alignment of the type. In Adobe's InDesign software, creating hanging punctuation can be accessed through the menus, Type/Story/Optical Margin Alignment. This allows punctuation to be adjusted outside the left margin alignment.
- **Leading:** the space between the lines of type. Body text is traditionally set with two points of leading (the size of the type plus two extra points of leading; i.e., nine point type/11 point leading). Solid leading means the type size is equal to the leading value (i.e., nine point type/ nine point leading), which could cause ascender and descender letters to merge if they align in the text.
- **Orphans:** the last lines of paragraphs that are pushed to the top of the next column of type, thus separating them from the rest of the paragraph.
- **Pica:** a unit of measurement in type. There are six picas in an inch.
- **Pixels:** Short for picture element, a pixel is a single point in a graphic image. It is also a unit of type measurement on the web in which the size is relative to the resolution of the monitor in which the display is viewed. Monitors display pictures by dividing the display screen into thousands or millions of pixels arranged in rows and columns, which appear connected because the pixels are close together.
- **Points:** a unit of measurement in type. There are 12 points in one pica. Type that is one inch tall in height is 72 points tall.
- **Small caps:** refers to the use of letters that are the height of lowercase letters but have the posture of capital letters.
- **Typeface or font:** a range of type in all the characters in one size and weight.
- **Type family:** a range of text in weights (i.e., light, bold, heavy, extra bold) and postures (i.e., italic, bold italic) for a particular typeface. Some typefaces are versatile, offering as many as 10 or 11 variations of structure within the same type family. Other typefaces might offer only one variation of the face. Generally, sans serif typefaces offer more versatility than serifs.
- **Widows:** last lines of type in paragraphs that end in a single word, a hyphenated part of a word or less than half a line of type.
- **X-height:** refers to the height of the lowercase letters in proportion to the capital letters. Typefaces with larger x-heights are more visible on the printed page, especially in small sizes.

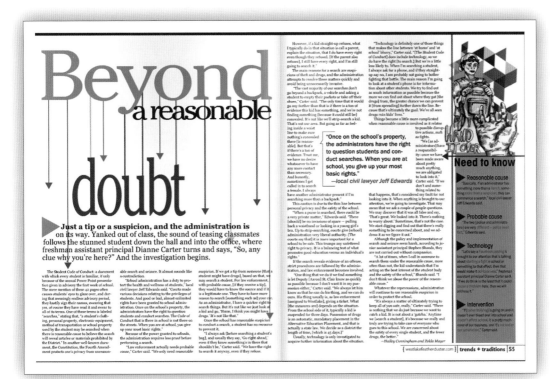

FIGURE 11.2
"Beyond a reasonable doubt," by Hailey Cunninghan and Zelda Mayer. *Featherduster* (westlakefeatherduster.com), Westlake High School, Westlake, Texas. Reproduced by permission of Deanne Brown.

In *Featherduster*, serif typography is used for the headline, deck headline and text. Designers create contrast by using sans serif type in the pull quote and in the sidebar feature's quick reads. Color effectively marries the two pages. Variations of the patterned background colors from the right page's illustration are used in the headline type, the pull quote graphic and in the sidebar background.

Categories of type

Although type could be classified in numerous ways according to its historical origin, placing type within one of six simple categories makes it easier to use and reference.

Serifs

Serif types, by tradition the easiest typefaces to read, are marked by the finishing strokes or touches on the ends of the characters. These finishing touches were indicative of the particular styles of the original designers. Serif typefaces have been the preferred choice for centuries and remain popular owing to their readability. The serifs often help the reader connect the letters visually, resulting in a fluid reading experience in print, but not necessarily online (see Figure 11.2).

Most designers place serif types into subcategories based on the time period in which they were designed. For example, old style serifs (see Figure 11.3a) are noted for consistent contrast, sloped or rounded strokes and slanted and curved serifs. The rounded letters will also exhibit an angled tilt in the swelling. The tops of the ascenders will have a distinctly oblique serif. The serifs angle out from the stems and are rounded and bracketed. Old style serifs are the primary choice for body text, enhancing readability through their consistency and visibility, medium x-heights and open counters.

The transitional serifs (see Figure 11.3b) exhibit more contrast between thick and thin strokes, show almost no tilting in the angle of the swells of the rounded letters, are slightly less oblique at the tops of the ascenders and often have squared off serifs rather than rounded ones. These typefaces also work well for body text.

The modern serifs (see Figure 11.3b) have a pronounced difference between the thickest and thinnest strokes, have completely vertical stress, feature serifs that are squared off and have unbracketed serifs.

Modern serifs are the hardest serifs to use, especially for body text. The thin serifs tend to disappear in small sizes, and the extreme contrast in stroke weight creates inconsistent density of text. They work best for headlines and other large type displays, such as in ads, where the thinnest strokes will not disappear.

FIGURE 11.3
a Oldstyle serif type. Sherri A. Taylor. **b** Transitional serif type. Sherri A. Taylor. **c** Modern serif type. Sherri A. Taylor.

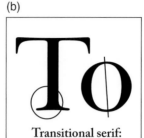

(a)

Oldstyle serif:
Adobe Caslon Pro

Serifs are rounded and bracketed to the stems; stress inside the o is diagonal to the left. Little contrast between thickest and thinnest stroke weights.

(b)

Transitional serif:
Baskerville by Bitstream

Serifs are rounded and bracketed to the stems; stress inside the o is more vertical. More contrast between thickest and thinnest stroke weights.

(c)

Modern serif:
Bodoni by Adobe

Serifs are blunt and attached to the stems without brackets; stress inside the o is vertical. Extreme contrast between thickest and thinnest stroke weights.

NEWSFLASH

What makes Helvetica a workhorse typeface?

A workhorse typeface refers to choices designers rely on because they work for so many applications. Helvetica, a sans serif typeface is just such an example.

Designed by Max Miedinger in 1957 for the Haas type foundry of Switzerland, Helvetica's name comes from Helvetia, the Latin name for Switzerland. When the popular sans serif came to America in the 1960s, it quickly became a go-to typeface for American designers at a time when sans serif typefaces were growing in popularity.

Helvetica is used for logos such as The North Face and Mattel, wordmarks such as Jeep, and JC Penney, signage in the New York subway system and many street signs, in headlines in newspapers and magazines and on countless websites.

Apple included it as one of its four core typefaces along with Times, Courier and Symbol in the early '80s when it developed the PostScript page description language. To show its respect for the integrity of type and designers, Adobe licensed its fonts from the original foundries instead of creating knockoffs.

Microsoft, on the other hand, chose to include a Helvetica knockoff, Arial, in its core set. And since Microsoft owned most of the market, Arial overtook Helvetica as a go-to substitute. It was hard to distinguish the original from the knockoff.

Helvetica has been used so extensively and for so long that many people won't touch it and find it really invisible in design. A newer version of Helvetica, Helvetica Neue, is a redrawing of the entire Helvetica family in the 1980s by Linotype. The family is extensive, ranging from extra light, a thin stroked variation, all the way to black, a heavy weight, with an extensive range in between.

With an explosion of typefaces available for use on today's computer operating systems, Helvetica has been overshadowed by newer, more distinctive choices such as Gotham, which was used in President Barack Obama's signage in the 2008 election. Gotham was created by the New York based type foundry, Hoefler & Frere-Jones, whose designers were inspired by lettering on the New York Port Authority bus terminal.

Sans serifs

Sans serif types (whose name comes from the French for "without") feature stems that do not end in serifs. Geometric, precise and monotonal, **sans serif** typefaces are great for creating contrast between body type and other kinds of information. Many designers rely on sans serif typefaces for headlines, secondary headlines and text heads. Additionally, sans serif typefaces are great choices for information used in alternative story displays. They create contrast with the main story, which is often in a serif typeface, and are easy to read when used in small quantities. Online, sans serifs also display effectively. Magazines hoping to achieve a more modern aesthetic use sans serifs for all body text, contrasting with traditional magazines' use of serif body text.

Sans serifs can also be sub-categorized as primarily geometric, made from circle and straight line shapes (Figure 11.4.a); humanist (Figure 11.4.b), with some contrast in stroke weight and some characteristics of the serif forms; and grotesque, more elliptical than round (Figure 11.4.c).

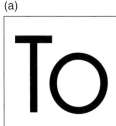

FIGURE 11.4
a Geometric sans serif type. Sherri A. Taylor. **b** Humanist sans serif type. Sherri A. Taylor. **c** Grotesque sans serif type. Sherri A. Taylor.

Sans serif typeface families tend to offer a wide range of weights and postures, including condensed and extended variations, making them versatile typefaces for designers to work with. A single versatile typeface family can be used to create contrast throughout a publication without the designer ever needing to change typeface categories.

Square or slab serifs

Square or **slab serif** typefaces (see Figure 11.5) end in precise, blocky or straight-line serifs. Although difficult to use in text type because of the wide nature of the letters, square serifs suggest a certain ruggedness and stability. They can work for **display type**, type sizes in 14 pt or above generally used for headers and headline displays, and for creating contrast between different kinds of information.

Scripts or cursives

Typefaces that resemble connected or disconnected handwriting, **scripts** or **cursives**, (see Figure 11.6) can provide either a certain formal or informal look, depending on the typeface chosen, and can work effectively in certain kinds of advertising or in displaying specific kinds of information. Their low readability and low contrast make them difficult to work with except in

WWW

WEBLINK Check out

www.philsfonts.com

Philsfonts is a type clearing house linking to a list of type foundries, typefaces and designers whose type it sells online. It includes an occasional free downloadable font offering.

WWW

WEBLINK Check out

www.tendollarfonts.com

This type site sells a range of, primarily, display typefaces for only $10 each.

WWW

WEBLINK Check out

www.fontsquirrel.com

Divided into categories of type, fontsquirrel is a resource for free, hand-picked, high-quality, commercial-use fonts many of which are based on well-known type designs. It also features a link to prepackaged sets which include multiple font formats, CSS and HTML code.

NEWSFLASH

Buying type to add to your type libraries will help extend your choices beyond the core typeface sets that come with your computer and software. It will enable you to have a distinctive look and avoid pedestrian, overused choices.

Buying typefaces is the way to go to add typographic choice to your computers. Typeface resources including foundries and designers will allow you to choose and buy type online.

FIGURE 11.5 *The Royal News* (www.tmwired. com), Prince George High School, Prince George, Va., Vol. IX, Issue 4, front cover, Jan. 21, 2011. Reproduced by permission of Chris Waugaman.

Square serif typefaces have strong voice and presence on the page, and can effectively showcase content, especially in magazine format. Here, the newspaper's flag appears in the same square serif typeface as the teaser headline, directing the reader to the issue's feature presentation inside the paper. The teaser for a religion story under that creates contrast in a condensed, sans serif, all cap type. A geometric sans serif type is used for the "Doodling" teaser. Finally, a humanist sans serif is used for headlines in the three columns across the bottom of the page. The cascading weights and styles of type create strong entry and visual hierarchy down the page.

FIGURE 11.6 *The Hawk*, Pleasant Grove High School, Texarkana, Texas. Reproduced by permission of Charla Harris.

Casual script and cursive typefaces can be appropriately used in publications, especially by yearbook staff looking for contrast in their page designs. Grotesque sans serif type combines effectively with the appealing, casual look of the cursive type used for the word "green" in this yearbook spread. The green color from the dominant image also makes a direct connection to the type's color. The cursive type is emphasized by its size and color, and is repeated in the sidebar's headline, which is also green.

WORDS of WISDOM

To have a good design you need to have typography that is easy to read and to view. The basics of readability and legibility are the same for a typographic design whether in print or electronic. The designer needs to keep in mind which medium they are working with when selecting typefaces and determining their use.

Newer typefaces have been developed for online/electronic viewing or use versus print (Yes, there are typefaces that will work in print that are much harder to read and use electronically); there are typefaces designed for use as display type and not as body copy. You need to have a basic understanding of typography to select the correct typeface use.

All of the basic rules of typography in reference to size, uppercase/lowercase/small capital letterforms, leading, letterspacing, word spacing, baseline use, set width, emphasis, type race/ classification use (serif vs. sans serif/ slab/square serif vs. cursive/script vs. decorative/novelty vs. Old English/Blackletter letterforms), alignment, color and emphasis should all be taken into consideration when determining the use of the type.

Randy Stano, Professor of Practice in Journalism, Knight Foundation Chair Professor 1995–2008, University of

Miami School of Communication

headlines, logos and ads or other strong visual hierarchy displays. The typefaces rarely offer more than one variation in weight or posture, also limiting their use. Some offer quirky letterforms that are difficult to discern.

Black letter

Most commonly referred to as Old English, **black letter types** (see Figure 11.7) are often associated with the nameplates of newspapers such as *The New York Times*. Of Germanic origin, these typefaces have extremely limited readability, especially when used in all-cap form. Black letter typefaces are often used for engraved invitations and to invoke certain moods at Halloween and other holidays. They are helpful in such designs as holiday ads, specialty features headlines or other particular uses. Few scholastic publications have use for any black letter typefaces, apart from their nameplates.

Novelty

Types that can't be easily categorized are often labeled **novelty** or **miscellaneous typefaces** (see Figure 11.8). Exhibiting some "extra" quality, they often display quirky characteristics suggested by their names. Novelty typefaces should never be used for body text and should be limited to display type, if used at all. Too often, designers rely on novelty typefaces to do the job of good design. A well-written and clever headline in a standard typeface can be far more effective than a poorly written one displayed in a novelty typeface. The use of multiple novelty typefaces can create a publication that feels messy and looks like a ransom note.

WWW

WEBLINK Check out
www.dafont.com

If you need free typefaces, dafont has hundreds of them. Primarily display and novelty typefaces, dafont also has knockoffs of well-known mainstream typefaces.

Quick Exercise

In print, find examples of headlines in serif, sans serif and square serif form. See if you can identify which subcategory the serif and sans serifs fall into based on Figures 11.3–11.5.

FIGURE 11.7 *Devils' Advocate*, Hinsdale Central High School, Hinsdale, Ill. Front cover, Oct. 20, 2010. Issue 83.02. Reproduced by permission of Sue Grady.

Following the tradition of many professional newspapers, student publications often use black letter type in their nameplates. However, black letter types can be hard to read. Emphasizing just one letter, the A, *Devils' Advocate* increases recognition and readability for their publication. The publication's entire name appears at the top right corner in a small size and repeats the purple color on Advocate from the A. In all lower case letters with better readability, the headline teaser repeats the black letter type.

CHOOSING TYPE

Page designers are wise to choose serif and sans serif typefaces for most of their type design. Within these categories, bolder variations work best for display type such as headlines. Book, regular or **roman**, weights are terms used in various typefaces to refer to those most often chosen for text. An occasional use of a script or novelty typeface for a logo or in a yearbook theme statement might be effective in conveying the message and in creating contrast with the other type choices. Square serif typefaces can be used effectively in sports sections, where their strong strokes often seem appropriate.

Desktop publishing allows for the commercial availability of a wide array of typefaces. Some of these typefaces are quite visually effective, with smoothed edges that will print and read well. Others are produced by less precise methods, and their digital files could cause problems for printers. It's best to check with your printer before making typeface choices. Remember, too, that saving files as pdfs will embed the fonts into the document so they will print correctly even if the printer does not own the typefaces you use. Alternately, using the "packaging" option under the File menu in Adobe's InDesign will also gather the fonts for correct printing.

Factors to consider

Designers need to consider several factors of type that affect **readability** and **legibility**. Readability is commonly used to gauge how easy type is to read. Legibility refers to the structure of the type choice.

X-height

Typefaces with large x-heights often have large, open counters in their letters and print visibly and easily on the page. These typefaces are known as "**big on the body**." Some old-style serifs have smaller x-heights, smaller counters and eyes (which refers to the inside of the lowercase letter e) and need increased size to be readable.

Text width

Very narrow or very wide lines of text create difficult reading patterns. When designers set type in widths as narrow as five picas, they should choose typefaces that are slightly condensed and should avoid justified lines of type. Narrow lines of type read more easily without hyphenation. Type set in wide lines, generally wider than 20 picas, will be more difficult for the reader's eyes to follow, and over long passages of text will cause the eye to tire.

Alignment pattern

While it's generally accepted that justified type alignment and **left-aligned** type are the easiest reading patterns, some designers choose **centered type** for headline display and right-aligned type for captions placed to the left of a picture. Justified text should never be set "**forced justify**," an alignment pattern that will result in large white spaces between words. Also, when justified is used, hyphenation should be enabled to prevent crowded text and allow lines to properly

FIGURE 11.8 *Spur Magazine*, Boyd High School, McKinney, Texas. "Footloose: Follow the actors from auditions to the stage," by Sierra Smith, pp. 20–21. Reproduced by permission of Javonna Bass.

Novelty typefaces can distinguish particular stories, packages or content. Used appropriately and sparingly so as not to create too much variation, they provide a visual "wow" factor and a welcome surprise. In this double truck presentation – the first of several spreads on the school's musical – the name of the production is displayed in type that looks like stage lights, which visually ties it to the story's content. The blurred background around the letters provides visual separation for this silhouetted image, creating a dramatic and appealing entry into the story. The staff used the same typeface to begin the text on the next page.

justify. Left aligned type – type that is ragged or unjustified on the right side – is a good way to create contrast among varying kinds of text in a design. It's also the best choice when using narrow line widths.

Typeface

Novelty typefaces are often difficult to read and to discern in print, resulting in low legibility. The characteristics suggested by their names can make them hard to read. They should be avoided for text displays. Novelty characteristics can complicate text set in small sizes.

The posture or weight of the type should also be considered. **Italic** type, type that slants to the right and type set in bold weights generally create slower, denser reading patterns for the reader's eye. Use these postures in moderation and for emphasis or contrast. Bold weights also work well in headline typefaces.

Color

Type in color can also slow readability. Color works best when its use is limited, such as in headline displays, bullets, drop caps, headers and pull quotes. **Reversing type** – white on black – also slows readability and tires the eye according to most readability studies. Online type also reads best in black on white or light backgrounds.

In print and online, if a color screen is used behind type, it should always create contrast, either in an opposite palette or toned lighter than the type.

Leading

It is a current typographic trend for designers to use increased leading measures. On a computer, **auto leading** is usually activated. Auto leading will add a percentage of the point size of the active typeface's character to the leading value. When auto leading is being used, the leading value will show up in parentheses in the type palette. Setting your own leading values gives you control over how far apart the lines of your text appear. For instance, type set in all caps is harder and slower to read. A designer can counteract that readability by setting the leading value at a higher percentage, so the lines are farther apart. The extra white space will "air out" the type, making it less dense. Designers should become accustomed to setting pure leading values rather than letting desktop publishing programs make leading choices for them. Most desktop publishing software also allows designers to change the auto leading value in a preferences menu. Increasing leading can also be used in sidebars for contrast.

When setting headlines, auto leading will usually result in too much separation between headline decks. Designers should reduce the leading to bring the decks into a closer arrangement. Some experimentation will be helpful in determining how close lines in a particular typeface can be positioned.

Kerning

Kerning, or the spacing between letters or numbers, can be used to enhance readability. But when designers set headlines in large sizes, desktop-publishing programs' preset leading values can create typographic spacing problems. Numbers, for instance, will usually end up too far apart, especially those adjacent to a number 1, and may require adjustment of the kerning values. These adjustments should be made on individual letter or number pairs, in combination with the program's general settings. Other letter combinations should be adjusted to eliminate uneven white space. Tight kerning will result in dense copy that may be hard to decipher. Alternately, loose kerning will separate the letters, possibly making the words harder to distinguish. Loose kerning can be used for typographic effect in headlines, ads and logos (Figure 11.9).

Some layout software programs offer predetermined or adjustable "tracking" values that can be used in place of individual letter kerning. Unfortunately, these tracking systems don't always fix specific kerning problems and should not be used as a substitute for individual letter kerning. Kerning before tracking is generally a good way to solve type spacing problems.

Kerning is difficult to see accurately on a computer screen. It isn't until the designer prints out a copy of the page that he or she can identify subtle kerning problems. Proper kerning should be invisible and consistent. Though it takes some time and experimentation to master, the rewards will be seen on the printed page.

Contrast and creativity

One of the most interesting and rewarding aspects of type design is the opportunity for visual creativity. The spirit of the design can be achieved through many combinations of type.

A headline should act as a single unit of information on a page. Designers can create contrast within headlines using combinations of type categories, emphasizing certain words by using color and changing the positioning of the type display (Figure 11.10). Creating emphasis words in headlines can be done through size, type posture, letterform and color. Emphasis words should be carefully chosen so they work effectively with the story's content. In emphasis headlines, subordinate words such as articles and prepositional phrases can be lightened through weight, posture and size.

Color can bring the reader to a particular part of a headline. Repeating that color for text heads or story subheads uses the design principle of grouping, which holds that readers' eyes tends to

❝ WORDS of WISDOM

Type is one of the designer's most powerful tools. It's also one of the primary ways we give our publications a voice or personality. Unfortunately, type design is often overlooked or, the other extreme, the design voice is garbled by too many different fonts. Study magazines and other professionally designed pieces. Look at how the pros package their type. When choosing type, match the font voice to that of the publication. And remember that, with fonts, less is more. One large font family used in a variety of ways provides unity. Dynamic, effective headline design not only keeps the readers' eyes on the page but also marries the visual and the verbal, drawing the readers into the story and isn't that what we want?

Lynn Strause, Creative Consultant, Former Yearbook Adviser, East Lansing, Michigan

p.16
Last Friday, before a sea of enamored Marksmen, senior **Andrew Ngo** and Lions varsity volleyball took home their first SPC championship since 2005.

THE remarker friday
NOVEMBER 13, 2009

ST. MARK'S SCHOOL OF TEXAS ▪ DALLAS, TEXAS 75230 ▪ VOLUME 56, ISSUE 2

B A T T L I N G   C A N C E R

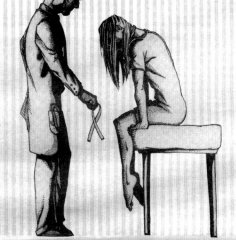

She could be your mom, your sister.
Or, your teacher.
Breast cancer does not discriminate.
Stories of survival provide hope for everyone
impacted by this disease.
A librarian and a mom tell how they fought

the Good fight

TEAR DROPS STREAMED DOWN THE STEERING WHEEL. THE PEDAL, UNTOUCHED, AS CARS MOVED AROUND IT,

THE RED HONDA REMAINED IN PARK. INSIDE, BARBARA KINKEAD SAT ENGULFED IN TEARS. SHE COULDN'T

MOVE, REALITIES OF THE DOCTOR'S WORDS FENCING HER INSIDE HER PARKING SPACE. "I'M NOT GOING TO SAY

ANYTHING FOR SURE," THE DOCTOR SAID AS HE EXAMINED HER, "BUT YOU NEED TO GET THIS CHECKED OUT."

Lower School librarian Barbara Kinkead with cards made by her students, welcoming her back to school Feb. 22, 2007.

Instantly, reality brought the Lower School librarian not only sickness but also immeasurable sadness.

"The whole time, I just knew it was cancer," she recalled. "It was growing in my body every second, and I could hardly stand it."

For over seven years, invasive ductile carcinoma collected and grew inside.

For over seven mammograms, the breast cancer went unnoticed.

But during a summer trip in 2007 to her parents' home in Wisconsin, a golf ball-sized lump plagued Kinkead's body to the point of pain and her mind to the point of unthinkable anxiety.

"I don't even remember that

time," Kinkead said. "All I could think of was breast cancer, breast cancer."

Without a proper diagnosis, Kinkead sat in the dark without information.

In need of support, she called her close friends and colleagues Laura Owens and Valencia Mack.

"She called me, and we were discussing it, and, naturally, as a friend would, I tried to just let her know that everything would be okay," Mack said. "The unknown is scary and unnerving. It is unnerving to be waiting for an outcome, waiting for answers, but all you can do is wait. We are teachers, we aren't medical people."

Even without a definitive answer,

thoughts of disease plagued her mind. When she returned to her parents' house, she packed her bags and left home early with her son Alex.

For the sake of not worrying the then second grade Marksman, Kinkead decided not to inform her son about the possibility of the disease. Instead, she waited until she got home to get more tests.

But Kinkead's quest for the truth lingered as her hope faltered; waiting lists and test results bogging down the process.

"We all wanted answers," she said. "But I had to wait.

CONTINUED, PAGE 12

THE GOOD FIGHT story by **MAX MARSHALL**, staff writer and **ADAM EICHENWALD**, senior writer; artwork by **CHRISTIAN LARRAVE**, graphics staff

agenda

▶NEWS

The Centennial Challenge
The school's latest fundraising campaign, The Centennial Challenge, was launched Monday in a special assembly for the whole student body, faculty and more than 160 special guests. **Page 2.**

▶IN FOCUS

iGeneration: Part 2
In a four-page special section, issues editor Shibi Kannan and special projects editor Shashwat Samudra discuss shifts in the traditional American Dream, especially with respect to entitlement, jobs and healthcare. **Pages 1B-4B.**

▶COMMENTARY

The arrogance of ignorance
Senior writer Adam Eichenwald expresses his disgust with the opinion of a Louisiana justice of the peace, who refused to grant a marriage license to an interracial couple in his parish. **Page 17.**

▶THE WEEK

Today
End of the first trimester

Lower School parent-teacher conferences

Monday
2009 McDonald's Week begins; 7 a.m., Preston-Royal McDonald's; presented by the Class of 2011

▶INSIDE

News	2-7
Scene	8-11
The Good Fight	12
Sports	13-16
Commentary	17-19
Exposé	20
iGeneration Part 2	1B-4B

FIGURE 11.9 *ReMarker*, St. Mark's School of Texas, Dallas, Texas. Reproduced by permission of Ray Westbrook.

This page effectively combines several techniques of good typography. Juxtaposing an ornamented script capital letter with smaller italic serif type creates an interesting headline display. Whenever two typefaces or two sizes are combined designers must pay attention to the kerning, to avoid gaps between letters. A script character, set to the left of the deck headline as a drop cap, is introduced in pink. This evokes the topic (breast cancer), the pink ribbon in the illustration and the color worn by the photo subject. A small label headline across the top of the presentation is kerned loosely, with wide spaces between letters. The deck head's loose leading creates airiness and contrast with the three columns of traditional text below it. The result is a beautifully executed and typographically outstanding feature package.

Type dos and donts

→ Do space only once after periods on a computer to avoid large white spaces between sentences.

→ Don't use tab indents for paragraphs. Set an indent value in the software's type palette or in software type style sheets. A good rule of thumb for text indents is to match the text leading value (i.e. 14 pt. leading, 14 pt. indent).

→ Do use an em dash (—) to replace double hyphens. Access the em dash, as well as other space dashes, in the software's Type menu/Insert Special Characters/Hyphens and Dashes (Adobe's InDesign).

→ Do use typographically accurate fractions, figures and ligatures by accessing Glyphs in the software's Type menu. Typefaces designated as "pro" sets in their names (Adobe Caslon Pro, for instance) include a wealth of special characters accessed by placing the cursor in the text and double clicking on the glyph character you want to add.

→ Do match drop caps to the strongest headline typeface and color, not to the body typeface. Doing so moves the eye from the headline to the text, reinforcing visual hierarchy.

→ Do use typographic quotation marks and hyphens, not prime marks. These are now defaults in most layout programs.

→ Don't use condensed or extended typefaces for body text. Save these options for narrow grids or limited-text sidebar material. **Condensed typefaces** are taller than wide; extended are wider than tall.

→ Don't reduce type readability by placing text on photos (unless the tones of the photo allow consistent contrast and the type doesn't interfere with content), on patterned backgrounds or on colors that blend into the type's color.

→ Do utilize contrast for type used in sidebars, captions, alternative type forms and other small type displays.

→ Don't add strokes to small-sized type. It will close up the **counters** and make the letterforms difficult to read.

→ Don't artificially scale type by using horizontal or vertical scaling in the software's type palette or artificially introduce weights and postures into typefaces that lack these options. In both cases, find a typeface that offers the options you need, even if you need to purchase one.

→ Do avoid overused, common typefaces that lack distinction, such as Arial, Georgia, Helvetica and Tahoma. In print, avoid typefaces such as Verdana, designed primarily for the web. Other typeface variations with web in their names are best suited for online use.

→ Don't choose typefaces that only offer all-capital or small capital letterforms such as Bank Gothic, Capitals or Copperplate Gothic for text. All-cap typefaces are tedious to read and can slow down or discourage the reader. Limit their use to headlines or ad displays.

group elements of similar shape and color. Yearbook staff can use this principle by borrowing a strong color from a dominant photo to lead the reader to the primary headline (Figure 11.11).

Headlines can be woven together in interesting arrangements and patterns. Rotating a headline's baseline by 90 degrees can be effective with bolder typefaces and when only a limited number of words is rotated. Desktop publishing software makes it easy for designers to set type on skews, to baseline shift selected letters of type and to set type into shapes. In general, letters shouldn't be stacked one on top of another because the resulting word or words will be difficult to read. Baselines should be kept intact.

Another creative device, **type wraps** or runarounds are created when the designer interjects a photo, logo or illustration into the type display and contours the type to the shape of the visual. Often, designers may use cutouts, or images with their backgrounds removed. Because these shaped images are visually "active," designers should limit their use. Designers should ensure the lines of type created by the runaround are readable and that hyphenation isn't excessive. In body type, justified alignment is usually most effective when running around an image, particularly a photo or another visual with four sides (Figure 11.12).

Desktop publishing software also makes it easy for designers to create type picture boxes, in which the letters of a headline can be filled with colors, patterns or pictures. This technique might require a bolder type choice and easily recognizable parts of an image showing in the letters. Type can also be set into shapes, but readability should not be compromised.

FIGURE 11.10 *The Edge*, Pleasant Grove High School, Texarkana, Texas. Reproduced by permission of Charla Harris. Skewed slightly and baseline shifted, the letters in "Dangerous" visually evoke the word's meaning, as do the slightly degraded lower case type letters used in "distraction." The positioning of the two words, with little psace between them, adds to the meaning of the headline for a story about students driving while distracted. In the bottom sidebar's "Drive," the black sans serif type is stroked with red, which creates a visual connection to the headline. The double truck lends itself to special typographic treatment.

FIGURE 11.11 *The Abstract*, St. Elizabeth Catholic High School, Thornhill, ON, Canada. Reproduced by permission of Dave Cheng. A colorful illustration showing a student covered with Post-it ® Notes illustrates a yearbook story on students writing notes on every school locker. The designer wisely pulled the colors from the notes on the boy into the headline for the word "Post-it," creating a strong visual-verbal color use on the spread.

Quick Exercise

Find a typeface that you feel visually represents your personality. Typeset your name in this typeface and identify the characteristics that caused you to choose it. Design it into a logo. Then do the same for a local business. Create an ad for the business using the logo you have created.

In using any of these methods of contrast, the designer must consider readability and appropriateness as the most important factors.

Consistency

Creating style templates for the various type patterns in a publication will promote consistency, which is important for ensuring that the publication doesn't have a scattered, eclectic look on every page. Style templates can also save designers a lot of time, since they must import text from various wordprocessing software programs used by staff members.

IN ACTION

Mixing typefaces: a guide

The use of type combinations can be an interesting strategy for creating contrast to emphasize an important word in a headline, in a yearbook theme or on a website. Effective type combinations are artful additions to design.

Here are some guidelines for mixing type for emphasis:

● Classic serif/sans serif variations work effectively in most cases.

● Limit combinations to only two type categories in a single display to avoid confusion. If you need a third emphasis, use a different weight or posture of one of the two categories.

● Combine different weights and postures from one versatile family such as Minion, Univers or Gill Sans. Consider de-emphasizing articles (a, an, the) and prepositions in headlines by making them smaller and using italic posture.

● When combining, make sure neither choice is a quirky, novelty typeface or the type could take over the design and cause distraction for the reader.

● Avoid combining two typefaces from the same category, especially two from the same sub-categories (see Figures 11.3 a–c and 11.4 a–c). Typefaces with similar properties will not provide any contrast and will be too concordant for emphasis.

● Typefaces have distinct personalities: fun, serious, stoic, formal, elegant, casual. Mixing typefaces with disparate personalities will cause distraction.

● Combine typefaces with similar physical properties: x-heights, shapes, serifs (rounded, sharp, blunt) and glyphs.

● Be careful mixing typefaces with too much contrast. An extremely condensed variation of type combined with an extremely bold or heavy weight of type will rarely combine effectively.

● Size variations are important in creating emphasis words and in creating type weaves in which smaller words are tucked into larger words or in spaces created by ascenders (peaks) and descenders (valleys).

● Color is one of the strongest methods of creating contrast. Warm colors add to typographic voice pulling emphasis forward to the eye.

● If you know someone with interesting handwriting, have them create a font. Online, **www.yourfonts.com** allows a person to complete a template, scan it and receive a digitized typeface which is fully editable. The template even includes numbers, punctuation and upper and lower case letters.

● Alternately, using a Wacom tablet – an electronic drawing tablet which works with a stylus – will allow someone to write and create digitized type. Wacom tablets are good for calligraphers.

● Software such as Fontographer, Font Lab Studio and Adobe Illustrator are professional software programs that can be used to create your own unique type designs.

In desktop publishing or web design software, style sheets can define the preferred style for each individual type area on the page. These could include the text type, headline type, secondary headline type, caption type, folio (page number information) type and any other design styles being used by a particular page or section of the publication. Style sheets offer designers the opportunity to choose typeface styles and sizes, leading and kerning values, indents, colors, drop caps, rule lines and many other type specifications. The style sheet information can be input into the desktop publishing software by clicking in a type display and setting the preferred type style. Once set and saved as a template, the styles will already be in place when a designer opens the template and begins designing a page. Yearbook staff can also create templates and style sheets for each section design.

Designers can also use the Library function of the software to save images, unique styles or logos that will appear throughout the publication. These libraries will also save with the template choice.

Elements that should be consistent throughout a newspaper include the body text, folios, standing heads, nameplate, section headers, pull quote designs, captions and secondary or deck heads. Special, stylized headlines set in typefaces not consistently used throughout the publication can be used when the designer decides they will enhance the layout and content. These heads, referred to as "art heads," should not overwhelm page content or interfere with readability.

FIGURE 11.12 *The Edge,* Pleasant Grove High School, Texarkana, Texas. Reproduced by permission of Charla Harris.

A bold, large dollar mark is used as a visual symbol of budget threats in this headline leading a front-page story. The type to the left side of the dollar mark is contoured or wrapped around the curve which helps unite the visual to the text. Using strong justified type on both sides of the text wrap with a pica of white space separation creates a clean and readable span of type with good text line width. Adequate text line widths prevent text with white space holes between words and overuse of hyphenation in type wraps.

Students should use online access to observe award-winning professional newspapers such as *The Boston Globe, Chicago Tribune, Minneapolis Star-Tribune* or any good local or regional newspapers. Notice how creative and attractive headlines can be designed using the limited number of typefaces that appear consistently throughout the newspaper. These publications

Seven type tips

→ Choosing the right type for a publication is probably the most important job a designer has to do. In order to choose, print out and compare several pages of stories with the typefaces you like. Have your staff look at them. Bring in some students to solicit their input.

→ Pay attention to the details. For example, learn the difference between em and en dashes and use them appropriately. Learn about kerning and tracking.

→ Resist the urge to use wacky typefaces, like Oogie Boogie. They draw too much attention to themselves and basically cheapen your work.

→ Follow a typography blog like I Love Typography at http://ilovetypography.com/ or Type Directors Club at http://tdc.org/blog/.

→ Learn the guidelines for mixing type. Your safest bet is to use only one typeface and then the fonts within that typeface. For instance, if you use Helvetica Neue, you could mix the Thin and the Black or the Light Condensed and the Heavy Condensed. Another rule of thumb is that you can mix a serif typeface with a sans serif typeface.

→ Create a style guide for the use of typography in your publication so that all of your type use is consistent. This can really help you create a unified, organized look in your publication, whether it's online or printed. Toss around the idea of using only three typefaces. It takes discipline, but you will be rewarded with a cleaner, more professional look.

→ Learn as much as you can about typography. Consider buying a book about typography such as Ellen Lupton's *Thinking with Type* or Simon Garfield's *Just My Type*.

Cheryl M. Pell, School of Journalism, Communication Arts & Sciences, Michigan State University, Mich.

create attention-grabbing headline displays on feature pages through creative headline content and strong arrangements of type.

Yearbook designers may want to review magazines, which offer myriad feature story displays, for examples of consistent, visually appealing design. Professional magazine pages can also be accessed online through sites such as issuu (issuu.com).

Online, multimedia displays incorporating pictures, videos, infographics and text can be united through a strong type logo or repeated elements, which create a consistent aesthetic.

To ensure consistency in body type, designers should align the **baselines** of adjacent columns. Body text tends to appear in **modules**, or four-sided design shapes, although other patterns can be used, especially contoured around an unusual image.

Captions should be placed under or next to pictures, preferably in one or two point sizes smaller than the body text. Using bolder weights, italic posture or condensed type variations further distinguishes captions from the body text. Yearbook staff often make visual connections between headline and caption elements to help individualize sections of the book.

Visual hierarchy in design ensures that a reader processes information in a logical and coherent way. Designers should choose sizes, weights and postures of type to draw the reader into the largest type display first, and should then set the subsequent type sizes and weights in a logical progression. Text heads, pull quotes and secondary or deck headlines should appear in type sizes that are larger than used in the text but smaller than headlines, and in a typeface whose weight provides contrast with the body text.

Captions and page folios should be among the smallest elements in the visual hierarchy. The smallest size type used on the page might very well be for picture credits. These often appear in type as small as six or seven points, grouped in a caption or placed under each photo.

Placement of elements on a page or spread is another factor in hierarchy. **Visual entry points** such as drop caps, small text heads or similar visual type devices, should be larger and

FIGURE 11.13 *Saga*, Loudon Valley High School, Purcellville, Va. Reproduced by permission of Martha Akers.

Repeating the arrangement, capitalization and color of the headline on each caption area marries the type from the dominant module to the smaller modules of content on this yearbook spread. The staff also matched the color of the dominant module's background to a primary color in the largest photo. That color was then repeated in the capitalized word in each caption. The color changed on each spread throughout the chronological design of the book.

prominently placed. As the reader's eye moves toward the bottom of the page, typographic display (usually headlines) will become smaller, corresponding to stories with relatively less news value (see Chapter 1 for more on news values). Yearbook designers should change headline positions within sections so the reader's eye is kept in motion throughout the book (Figure 11.13).

Visual hierarchy is less important for websites, where readers typically choose content based on their interest in particular stories rather than by story placement. Websites often keep type sizes consistent (Figure 11.14).

PRODUCTION AND PRINTING

With the advent of desktop publishing software, most designers have taken over primary responsibility for the pre-press production of their publications. Files may be sent directly to printers as pdfs, which can be imbedded with the images and the typefaces used in the designs. Some staff still print out their pages on high quality printers with resolutions of 600 dpi (dots per inch) or above and provide the camera-ready pages to the printer to be converted into film for plating and printing.

Schools using laser printers will find improved reproduction of type and image. Laser printers create characters and images by drawing them through a computer language – such as Adobe's PostScript, OpenType or TrueType – on a metal drum with a laser beam. Some schools use ink jet or dot matrix printers. These methods are of lower quality than PostScript and are generally not acceptable for direct reproduction of student publications. Schools can also purchase tabloid printers capable of outputting pages at 11 × 17 inches or larger (tabloid size) and provide those printouts to the printer for reproduction.

When taking electronic files to a printer or service bureau, the designer must make sure to include all file formats, scans and typefaces that will be used in the production of the pages. Most desktop publishing software has the capability to "package" or "collect for output," so the software directly gathers all the necessary files to ensure correct printing and will warn the designers of missing file information. Designers can often access utility checks, called "preflighting," to see if any files are missing that would cause the information to print incorrectly.

Digital toning for printing

Calibrating color tonality on the computer to the output of the printer is a critical issue in accurate digital printing. Color calibration between all the individual printers used in the production process is also important for consistency in printing output. Commercially available

FIGURE 11.14 *The A Blast*, Annandale High School, Annandale, Va. Reproduced by permission of Alan Weintraut.

Using one serif typeface for all story headlines, *The A Blast* uses size to create visual hierarchy on its broadsheet page. The main story's headline is larger than others, focusing attention on the story and its primary position on the page. Three other front-page stories use smaller headlines, and one features an italic variation of the headline type to separate it from an adjacent story. The vertical rail of quick-read information on the left, and the inside teasers across the top, feature sans serif type for headline and hierarchical contrast.

The naked truth

Sexting, racy photos in decline among teens

New school board | All-American again

McLaughlin takes Wilson's seat

Bile finishes 12th in national competition

'Love's Labor Lost' debuts this week

Theatre Without Borders takes on Shakespearian play

FIGURE 11.15 The principle of offset lithography is the pages are inked from an impression blanket or roller that holds an inked image of the print. The blanket comes in contact with the paper and prints the impression directly on it from the ink.

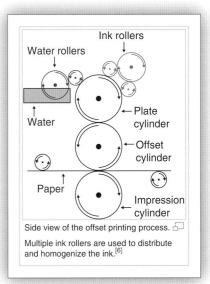

Side view of the offset printing process.

Multiple ink rollers are used to distribute and homogenize the ink.[6]

computer screen calibration devices can be used. Calibration should be performed at regular intervals to ensure accuracy on all computers used in production.

Staff can seek guidance from their publishers in selecting settings to use in their digital photography software to ensure correct toning of their photographs. Or, printers will often provide test runs of sample files to guide the staff in correct toning for the publisher's presses. Photo file resolutions are also important in maintaining quality (see Chapter 15, Visual Storytelling).

Waiting until proofs arrive to worry about color correction and calibration can result in expensive file alterations that may can incur significant and unbudgeted production charges.

Printing

Most printing today is done by the **offset** lithography method, based on the principle that oil and water do not mix. The offset method involves printing from a smooth plate surface onto which the image has been "burned," or exposed, through a large camera (Figure 11.15). The areas to be printed are treated so ink (oil-based) from the printing rollers adheres to them, while the remaining surface is treated with water rollers that reject the oily ink. The inked image is then transferred – offset – to a rubber roller surface, a "blanket," that prints the image on the paper.

In order for photographs to be reproduced through offset printing, they must either be scanned directly into the desktop publishing program and produced as output, or the originals must be screened by the printer and stripped into the pages.

Offset lithography for newspaper printing is primarily done by web presses, which print from continuously fed rolls of paper. Many presses are "perfecting presses" that print both sides of the paper at the same time, making the printing process fast. Most web presses are limited in the kinds of paper they are able to print, and papers with higher pulp content, such as newsprint, are ideally suited. With improved presses, printers can use higher grades of paper, allowing many publications to be printed on paper that is "whiter" and heavier than newsprint. This is often appropriate for newsmagazines.

A popular variation of offset printing is a **flexographic press**, used primarily in newspaper and paperback book publishing. An inexpensive and simple method of printing on a web-fed press, flexographic printing uses rubber plates and water- or solvent-based inks in a two-roller system. The process is considered more environmentally friendly than other types of printing since soy-based or vegetable inks can be used in combination with recycled paper stocks.

Yearbooks and magazines are also printed primarily through the offset method, but often on sheet-fed rather than web presses. Perfecting **sheet-fed presses** take in a single sheet of paper at a time and can print both sides of the paper at once. The single sheets are large, allowing for the printing of several of the publication's pages on each side of the sheet, or form. As discussed above, each side of the paper is known as a **flat** (which might consist of four or eight pages). The entire sheet is called a **signature**, which is then folded and trimmed to allow for normal reading. A printer determines how many forms are required to produce the book's or magazine's total page run (Figure 11.16).

Because the pages on a signature must be arranged in what is known as **printer spreads**, or pages that will print across from one another, printers often use **imposition software** on the electronic files provided by the school. Imposition software takes the file and reconfigures it to print on the flats and signatures the printer uses. Designers find it easier to work with **reader spreads**, the configurations of pages that face each other when reading.

Books and magazines require binding, a method of holding together the printed pages. Magazines are usually bound by **saddle-stitching**, a method of placing metal staples in the gutter of the magazine. Magazines can also be **perfect bound**, in which strips of glue are applied along a flat gutter holding pages together. Some smaller yearbooks are bound by soft covers using a magazine binding such as perfect binding (Figure 11.17).

NEWSFLASH

Short of taking a field trip to a local printer, the videos that can be viewed via the weblinks in this section provide the best solution to help you understand printing and binding from its origins to today.

WWW

WEBLINKS Check out

www.lynnkiang.com/typehigh.html

The site includes stop-motion animation and introduces the grammar of typography using the resources of the Rhode Island School of Design's RISD letterpress shop.

WWW

WEBLINKS Check out

www.fontfeed.com/archives/lovely-video-shows-the-process-of-letterpress-printing

This video shows the process of letterpress printing, a process which preceded today's offset printing process.

WWW

WEBLINKS Check out
www.youtube.com/watch?v=QnulXcfrWho

This YouTube video explains the process of bookbinding used on books such as yearbooks.

WWW

WEBLINKS Check out
www.youtube.com/watch?v=hzMXEpjh5AE

This YouTube video takes you inside a printing plant to demonstrate the modern offset printing method.

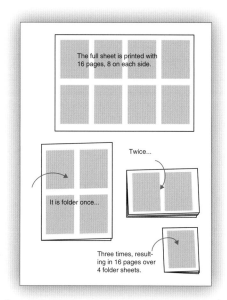

The full sheet is printed with 16 pages, 8 on each side.

It is folder once...

Twice...

Three times, resulting in 16 pages over 4 folder sheets.

FIGURE 11.16 As opposed to the way in which pages are read in sequence, when a printer prints pages for book and yearbook publishing, they are printed on one large, sheet fed piece of paper at a time, eight pages on each side. Each side is called a flat while the entire sheet is called a signature. The pages will read in sequence when folded and trimmed. Yearbook staffs not printing full-color books must plan their use of color based on buying color in flats and signatures to maximize color print pricing. Knowing what pages print on each side is crucial if only buying a flat or signature of color.

These binding methods have a definite effect on page and gutter margins. Saddle-stitched magazines lie completely flat, allowing designers to take information closer to, or across, the gutter without problems. Other binding methods – including mechanical or wire binding, side-stitching and perfect binding – require larger gutter margins because those methods do not allow the open pages to lie completely flat. Using these methods, bleeds across pages will often trap material in the gutter, hiding it from view. In newspaper printing, only the middle pages of the paper will actually be printed on the same sheet of paper. This double truck offers an excellent opportunity for staff to design spreads that span the facing pages (see Figure 11.10).

Yearbooks are bound by collecting and sewing together the various forms or signatures by a process known as **Smythe-sewing**. Binders use big machines that look like sewing machines to stitch a heavy-weight thread across the back of the forms. Then a wide gauze strip is glued to the sewn pages and attached to a hardback cover that has been rounded and backed to allow the book's multiple pages to lie open for reading. The gauze is covered on the inside by heavier end sheets or end papers, often incorporating a design or color. Small, decorative, often colorful, sewn **headbands** are finishing touches at the tops and bottoms of the sewn forms that hide the binding (Figure 11.18).

Before offset became the primary printing form, other methods were used, and are still being used by some printers. These forms include letterpress and **gravure printing. Letterpress**, the standard before offset, is printing from a raised surface. Type characters are cut into metal and pressed into paper. Before metal type was invented in 1450 by Johann Gutenberg, letters were cut into wood. Gravure printing uses a raised or sunken surface into which the image has been etched. Gravure printing is excellent for high-quality reproduction, especially of photographic images, and is used in book publishing, in textile printing and by high quality glossy magazines.

With improvements in desktop publishing and laser printing, many schools produce their pages directly from laser printer output, either photocopied or mimeo-graphed, often in school print shops. Improvements in photocopiers now allow for quality photo-reproduction and can be used effectively in small schools without incurring printing charges for short runs, where a limited number of final copies is needed.

The use of color in printing is referred to as either **spot color**, the use of a single color, or four-color, known as **CMYK (cyan or blue; magenta or red; yellow and black or K)**, the use of which is seen as full color. Owing to advances in digital color printing technology and its decreasing cost, full-color yearbooks and newspapers are standard. The use of very specific color shades or tones can be chosen from patented inking processes manufactured by companies such as the **Pantone® Matching System** (Figure 11.19), the most common color method used in printing in the United States. These colors could actually incur **five-color printing**, adding to the color cost. Four-color printing simply means the paper has to pass through four individual color inking presses that contain CMYK inks – the standard process printing inks – in order to reproduce as full color. Five-color requires the page to pass through an additional color press to apply one or more special colored inks or varnishes.

Yearbook printers often provide their customers with custom color charts for selecting specialty inks such as metallics or pastels. Printers can also match specific colors by mixing percentages of the four-color inks. Most printers can provide customers with charts showing these "process" mixes. Mixes made from the four-process colors usually incur no additional charges on a color page.

Websites define their color by selecting **RGB mode**, or Red/Green/Blue. This color mode is appropriate for viewing color on computers, mobile devices and televisions. The gamut range of color in RGB mode is extensive, offering a range of visible color which cannot be duplicated in printing. Because of that, staffs who are printing may be advised to keep their color images in RGB mode and let their printers convert it to CMYK through customized methods.

In high-quality printing, especially where color is used, designers check proofs of their color before the job is actually printed. Proofs also allow staff to check photograph and type positioning and review the copy for errors. High-end color proofs can be provided by several

FIGURE 11.17 In perfect binding, a flat spine wide enough to cover the depth of the pages is added to the cover's measurement. The spine is glued to the gathered pages. In some cases, the pages may be stitched together to keep them from loosening when the glue eventually dries out. Some school newspapers, magazines and small yearbooks may be bound by this method of printing.

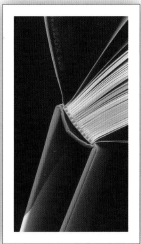

FIGURE 11.18 Woven headbands appear at the tops and bottoms of some books as finishing touches in the printing process to conceal the inside of the spine. Headbands can be matched to colors used in the book's cover material and may incur additional printing costs.

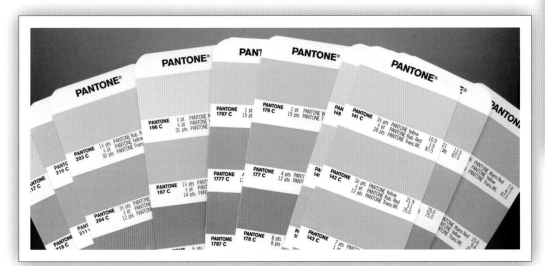

FIGURE 11.19 Using specialty inks such as those manufactured by the Pantone® Matching System could incur additional cost in addition to the four-process colors – cyan, magenta, yellow and black (CMYK) inks. Pantone® inks are precise colors made by combining Pantone® manufactured inks. Printers can make colors by combining CMYK inks, but can only match about 30 percent of Pantone® inks this way.

different processes when required for color proofing and matching. Making corrections to proofs might incur additional charges to the staff's final printing bill. Proofreading should be as precise as possible before the final proofs are checked.

Modern four-color, high-speed digital presses enable a digital file to go directly from the printer's front end, connected directly to a PostScript computer, immediately to the plating process, the last step before actual printing. Low-end printing processes, such as photocopying, also continue to evolve, making short-run printing possible from the local photocopying facility for almost immediate distribution. **On-demand printing** – a single or limited number of copies printed at a time – has become a popular printing option for special or personal projects. On-demand printing is fast, usually reasonably priced and can be done both online and through local printers. Yearbook staff producing end-of-the-year supplements might find these new printing resources helpful.

CONCLUSION

An understanding of typography is essential in producing readable and legible pages and websites that will communicate content with readers. It's essential for designers to choose type effectively for contrast and for creativity, when possible. Creating strong type hierarchy allows readers to move logically through pages and spreads. An understanding of printing also allows designers to make wise decisions when submitting digital files.

SUMMARY

- Good type choices facilitate readability and legibility.

- Understanding type terminology ensures designers will make good choices in preparing type for publication and on websites.

- Knowledge of type categories helps designers make decisions about effective type combinations.

- Designers can use creative techniques and type choices when appropriate.

- Software style sheets, libraries and templates allow for consistency in design.

- Modern print production allows for seamless reproduction of files through an appropriate printing method.

- Spot color, four-color and specialty color use provide effective choices for printed publications.

- RGB color is used appropriately as a color model on websites.

KEY TERMS

agate type	glyph	readability
alignment	gravure printing	reader spreads
ascender	hanging punctuation	reverse type
auto leading	headbands	right-aligned
baseline	imposition software	rivers of white space
big on the body	italic	RGB mode
black letter type	justified type	roman
bullet	kerning	saddle-stitching
c/lc	leading	sans serif
centered type	left-aligned	script
CMYK	legibility	serif
coastline	letterpress	sheet-fed press
condensed typeface	ligature	signature
counter	miscellaneous type	slab serif
cursive	modules	small cap
descender	novelty type	Smythe-sewing
display type	offset	square serif
down style	on-demand printing	typeface
drop cap	orphans	type family
em/en dashes, spaces	Pantone Matching System	type wrap
five-color printing	perfect bound	visual entry points
flat	pica	widow
flexographic press	pixel	x-height
font	point	
force justified	printer spread	

EXERCISES

1   Find examples in print of each of the six main categories of type, including serif, sans serif, square or slab serif, scripts or cursives, novelty and black letter. Cut out an example of each in a headline, ad or logo from a newspaper or magazine and label it. Discuss the use of the typeface within the context of the publication. Was the typeface used in an effective way? How?

2   Using online newspapers from other cities or states, find five examples of logos used in advertising for local businesses, products and services. Try to find an example of a logo for a local restaurant, a service, a children's store, a clothing store and a motel/hotel. Print out and cut out each logo and paste it on a sheet of paper. In small groups, exchange your lists and discuss your impressions of the businesses or services based on the logos. How would you dress to go to the restaurant? Is the children's store exclusive or mainstream? Who would shop at the clothing store? Note how much information you can learn about a business from its choice of typeface.

3   From newspapers or magazines, clip five examples of type uses that fit the criteria for readability and legibility. List the factors that make the type examples readable and legible.

4   Visit the websites of these type houses (companies that make and sell typefaces for use in computer applications):

Adobe Type: http://www.adobe.com/products/type.html

International Typeface Corporation: www.itcfonts.com

FontHaus: www.fonthaus.com

http://www.bitstream.com/fonts/index.html

Lucas Fonts: www.lucasfonts.com

Emigre:www.emigre.com/fonts.php

At each site, browse through the offerings, including free fonts and articles about typefaces and designers. Compare the type offerings and the prices for various typefaces and type packages.

From the different sites, identify a typeface that would be readable for body text and one that would not. Provide reasons for your choices.

Choose a typeface that would work for a headline on the following topics:

- Beauty
- Sports
- Homecoming
- Stress
- Graduation.

Sketch designs combining two typefaces and use of emphasis.

5   On a computer using InDesign software, type your name in a line of type and the year. Choose a serif and sans serif typeface for this exercise and make the type 72 pt. Find kerning problems and adjust the letters and numbers. After kerning, adjust the tracking. Next, set your first name, hit a return and type your last name. Adjust the leading until your two lines of type are close, but not touching. Now set your name in all cap letters and adjust the kerning and leading. Compare your examples for readability.

6   Rent a copy of *Helvetica,* a movie dedicated to the fiftieth anniversary of the typeface. After viewing, discuss reasons why Helvetica is such a typographic workhorse.

7   Find examples of type that use the following techniques for creating contrast:

- a headline in which a word or two is emphasized through size variation
- a headline in which color has been used to create contrast
- a headline with an interesting arrangement and positioning of words
- type that has been set on a skew or where the baseline is shifted from a normal position
- a type runaround or wraparound.

If you have access to a computer and design software, use these samples to create your own headlines in the same styles.

8   Using a local newspaper, examine the front-page and an inside page and discuss the paper's use of visual hierarchy. If you have access to a pica ruler, measure the point size of the headlines on the front-page and write the size next to each headline. Discuss the newspaper's consistency in use of body text, secondary or deck heads, bylines, headlines and captions. Next, look at the way in which the stories appear on the page. Draw boxes around each story unit (it may include a related picture) and see how many fall into modules of four sides. Look for consistency in the placement of text baselines for related columns of text.

9   If you have a local print shop or newspaper press in your town, arrange a visit or invite a printer to talk to the class, bringing examples of the different printing steps. If possible, observe the printing method in action and have the technicians explain the different printing steps from start to finish. Ask questions about any process or procedure you don't understand.

10   Get copies of a newsmagazine such as *Time,* or *U.S. News* and *World Report.* Open one of the covers and locate the staples used in the binding. This binding process is called saddle-stitching. Open to the center of the publication and notice how the pages lie completely flat. Look at pages facing each other at the back of the magazine where elements are printed across the two pages. Observe whether they line up correctly. Next, get a copy of *National Geographic,* a magazine that is

perfect bound. Open to the center of the publication and notice whether the pages lie flat. Look at two pages printed across from each other at the back of the magazine where the elements have been printed across the two pages. Do they line up? Get a copy of the school's yearbook. Look at the end sheets at the front and back of the publication. Notice how the end sheets are connecting the printed pages to the cover. Examine the spine and see how flexible it is in allowing the book to lie open. Look into the spine at the top or bottom of the book and see if the binding is finished with headbands. Find a book somewhere in your classroom that has headbands.

NEWSPAPER LAYOUT AND DESIGN

12

> *Good design jumps off the page, grabs you by the collar and pulls you in. Great design keeps you there until you've soaked up all the content. That means it can't be simply a pretty page. Rather, it has to contain copy that begs you to keep reading, headlines that intrigue and inform you and photos that rock the house. That's why design is a team sport.*
>
> *Betsy Pollard Rau, Retired Adviser,* The Update, *Henry H. Dow High School, Midland and Michigan Instructor of Journalism,*
>
> *Central Michigan University, Mount Pleasant, Mich.*

LEARNING OBJECTIVES After completing this chapter you will be able to:

- understand the importance of newspaper design to the reader

- use the tools of design to lay out attractive and readable pages

- apply the principles of design in an effective way

- be aware of the special design needs of different sections of the newspaper

- supplement print design with well-designed websites.

THE IMPORTANCE OF DESIGN

Stepping back to admire a well-designed page after it's been printed is a wonderful exercise. Good visuals almost sing on the page. Stories are arranged to follow visual hierarchy. The page flows, keeping the reader's eye in motion from top to bottom. Color is used effectively. Typography is strong. The bottom line: effective design showcases that edition's content, attracting the reader to explore, to read and to learn.

It's the job of the designer, sometimes referred to as the **presentation director** at professional newspapers, to make sure high quality stories and visuals get the attention they deserve. Newspaper websites should complement the print edition using a format that is easily navigable and becomes familiar to readers over time, and which provides a steady flow of timely information.

Changes in news presentation

Looking at a newspaper from 10, 20 or 50 years ago can be startling. Few of today's sophisticated readers would tolerate the densely designed, image-scarce pages, with story placement and headline sizes that fail to convey relative importance. Today's news consumers expect direction from their newspapers, just as drivers need a road map for a long trip. Readers seek guidance in prioritizing and making sense of the information presented to them in a newspaper. Additionally, they look to a newspaper's website for additional information in between the paper's publishing cycle. Layout designers are integral partners to writers, editors and photographers in presenting important and interesting content both visually and verbally.

It's not only the appearance of the paper that has changed drastically, but also the presentation of the information as well as the information itself. Today, print newspapers that come out just once a day are often already dated. But today's newspapers aren't just print products, they are accompanied by robust websites that are constantly updated and provide content that goes beyond the printed paper. Even in a high school, the printed newspaper should be supplemented by a web product that provides frequent updates and fresh information in between print editions. The website can also provide multimedia content with audio and visual elements that the printed paper cannot.

Printed high school newspapers traditionally appear in one of three formats: **newsmagazines**, traditionally 8.5 × 11 inches; **tabloids**, traditionally 11 × 17 inches; and **broadsheets**, traditionally 11.75 × 21.5 inches. Depending on who prints the paper, hybrid-sized publications (9.5 × 12.5 inches, for instance) might also be available. Many professional publications are converting their print editions to tabloids or a variety of smaller broadsheets, primarily to save costs on newsprint. Some scholastic publications may also be affected by such changes, especially if the local newspaper prints the high school paper. Newspapers can be printed on standard newsprint or on better quality, whiter grades of paper, again depending on the printer.

Regardless of the printed size, the layout designer can employ the principles of good design to maintain effective visual hierarchy and attractively designed pages.

Elements of design

Designers should begin by considering the elements they will work with on the page or website. If you hang up a page on a wall, stand back and squint you will perceive three visual weights. Text, including headlines, captions and stories, will create gray masses of weight on the page. This contrasts with the "black weight" of images whether color or black-and-white and the "white weight" of white or unused space. Because text can "**gray out**" in long columns, creating long masses of text that can discourage readers, owing to length and lack of visual breaks, designers should pay attention to visual devices that will help break up the text and offer increased readability. Elements such as drop cap letters – large initial cap letters dropped into paragraphs – or **text heads** – small headlines placed within the story that help create transitions at natural junctures – work well as visual breaks. On a website, space can be inserted between paragraphs to facilitate reading. Multiple pictures can be placed with the story or added as a slide show or audio/visual presentation. Hyperlinks to additional content can also be added from the print edition.

WEBLINKS Check out www.snd.org

The home site for the Society of News Design is a resource for all designers. Using the toolbox link will connect you to a variety of information on additional topics. The competition link allows you to view winners of both print and digital archives.

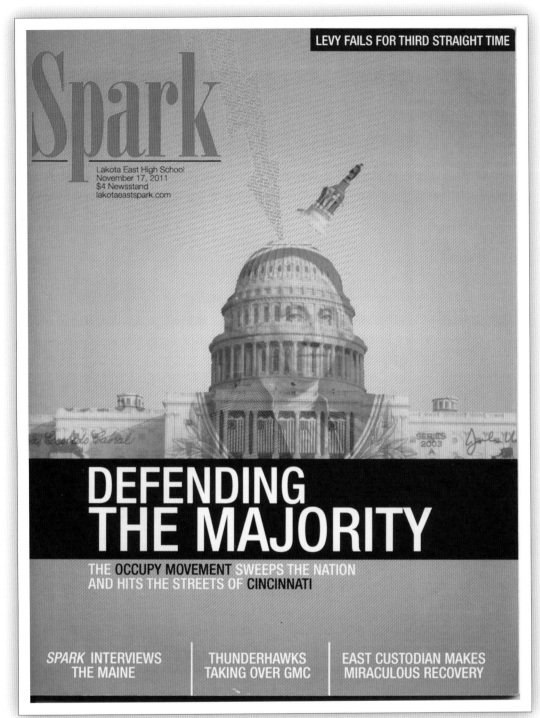

FIGURE 12.1 *Spark*, Lakota East High School, Liberty Township, Ohio. Reproduced by permission of Dean Hume.
Newsmagazines are increasingly popular formats for high school publications. Most newsmagazines employ a traditional "magazine" cover format, featuring a large image that "teases" their primary editorial content. Compelling photographs and illustrations allow designers to create a strong visual approach. Employing cover lines or additional teasers in type help editors promote interior content. *Spark*, the newsmagazine of Lakota East High School in Ohio, also uses color in its cover to give the publication the look of a professional magazine. This image previewed a centerpiece story on the Occupy Movement and its impact on Cincinnati. Lakota is a suburban community of Cincinnati.

Pictures, both black-and-white and color, as well as illustrations and drawings, add visual "black" weight to the page and design. These denser visual areas need to be balanced with both text and the space not used on the page, known as **white space**. This unused space makes up about 50 percent of all pages. It refers to both the vertical separations and **alleys** between design elements, as well as spaces left horizontally between the lines of the text, between the decks of the headlines and between the various other design elements. Even the space left at the ends of lines in unjustified, ragged type adds to the design's white space. White space is an effective device for moving the reader from one element to another on the page, creating separation or connection to nearby content. Surrounding a larger, more important story with a bit of extra

FIGURE 12.2 *The Lowell*, Lowell High School, San Francisco, Calif., front cover, Vol. 216., No. 2, July 10, 2011. Page design by news editor Amy Char. Reproduced by permission of Sharn Matusek.

In a smaller tabloid format, visual hierarchy and page architecture are particularly important components. In an issue featuring a news story about a gas smell causing a school evacuation, a package of content includes a large primary photo used to hold the primary headline, spanning the width of the text. The story jumps, or continues, to an inside page providing additional coverage. Two additional photos used at the bottom of the package show additional perspectives on the event. An index column along the left side of the page also houses the newspaper's flag. Across the top, two teasers provide a summary of two main stories inside.

The Lowell

LOWELL HIGH SCHOOL, RED EDITION, VOL. 216 No. 2, OCTOBER 7, 2011, www.thelowell.org

In the news Today

THE CARDINALS will have a companion in the air today, as the Blue Angels start Fleet Week over the city from 12:30 p.m. to 4 p.m. Keep your eyes on the sky during passing periods when you hike down to the T's; you may spot a screeching, flipping jet hurtling across the firmament.

No free mods to lie on your back on one of the school's grassy knolls? Check out the Angels in their next performances at the same time on Saturday and Sunday in front of a bright blue sky. Be sure to cover your ears!

What's Inside

News Pages 1-9
- Homecoming rally postponed to mid-November
- New English elective class announced for next semester, partly inspired by affectionate chicken

Sports Pages 11-15
- Dragonboat team brings home the gold at Treasure Island
- Unique fitness trends keep workout routines fresh

Columns Page 16
- Girl scoffs at threat of junior year after two weeks in wilderness

Opinion Pages 17-19
- Teen welcomes big-box retailers to city, sees benefit of revitalizing economy

Gas smell prompts school evacuation

AMY CHAR

■ Classes disrupted for an hour, but no gas leak discovered

By Cooper Logan and Spencer Thirtyacre

THE SCHOOL WAS evacuated at around 10:55 a.m. on Oct. 3 due to multiple reports of a gas odor on campus, but after investigation, Pacific Gas and Electric and the fire department concluded there was not an ongoing problem, as they did not find the source.

According to PG&E spokesman Joe Molica, the investigation was terminated due to a lack of evidence of a gas leak. "We used sophisticated natural gas leak detection equipment, but we couldn't find evidence of gas escaping at the school or in the surrounding area, so we wrapped up the investigation," Molica said. "We can't speculate what was the cause of the smell. It could have been many reasons, like the sewer or water treatment plant."

The initial information was only that there was a strong smell of gas and, some students feared the worst, with the 2010 San Bruno fire in mind. "I felt as if something really bad was happening," sophomore Mitchell Szeto said. "I thought my school was going to blow up."

The administration began to receive reports from teachers at around 10:15 a.m. and principal Andrew Ishibashi called PG&E promptly. PG&E then arrived at 11:25. The fire department was called at around 10:50 a.m., and arrived at approximately 11 a.m. according to assistant principal of student support services Michael Yi.

Ishibashi called for the evacuation of the building over the PA system after talking to the fire department and PG&E due to the possible danger. "I radioed security guards to make sure each floor was evacuated," Ishibashi said.

Most students were sent to the soccer field,

but some other classes were evacuated from Eucalyptus Drive to Rolph Nicol Playground. This varied from the normal fire drill evacuation procedure, which calls for students to evacuate to the far side of the fire access road and to the sidewalk in front of the school.

Firefighters worked with Ishibashi to evaluate the situation. "The first thing the fire department did when they arrived was check the fire panel to assure themselves it wasn't a fire," Ishibashi said; a fire with a possible gas leak would have called for a different response.

Ishibashi accompanied the firefighters and PG&E employees as they scoured the school. "The firemen smelled the gas as well, and we walked to where there was a strong smell," Ishibashi said. However, they could not locate a source of the

See EVACUATION on Page 8

CAITRIONA SMYTH   DANIEL GREEN

Teachers brought classes to designated evacuation sites in sports areas at the back of the school and the Rolph Nicol Playground at the beginning of Mods 9-10 on Oct. 3 (**top**). A fire truck arrives at campus at the end of Mods 9-10 to inspect the school for the source of a propane smell (**bottom left**). Later, firefighters walk back from the football field after speaking with construction workers in their search for the source (**bottom right**).

Budget dependent on state revenues

By Elijah Alperin

THE BUDGET FOR the 2011-2012 school year is similar than last year's projection due to California Governor Jerry Brown's May budget revisions that pledge more money to K-12 education, unless projected revenues do not emerge.

The school's budget for the current school year is very similar to the one enacted in the 2010-2011 school year, with a minor surplus of $6,803, which has been allotted for extra hours for the school security guards, according to School Site Council chair Tom

Chambers. No services or teaching positions have been cut since last spring, according to Chambers.

Last year the school planned for a nine percent budget deficit by designing a worst-case budget plan as well as a better-case plan, according to Chambers. In anticipation of the worst-case scenario, the Parent Teacher Student Association and Alumni Association raised upwards of $400,000 to help cover projected shortfalls. Because the school was able to enact the better budget scenario after the May revision by the state government, the money raised will be

saved for next year, according to Chambers.

However, there is concern that the best-case scenario is at risk.

Originally, state education funding seemed to be on track when Brown's proposal — to raise the minimum amount of funding guaranteed to education under Proposition 98 by three billion dollars — was passed in May. Proposition 98, enacted in 1988 in order to regulate education funding, requires that a certain percentage of the state budget be allocated to K-12 education and community colleges.

State politicians tried to keep schools funded by approving Brown's proposal, hence the current amount of education funding is greater than what the legislature approved in last year's state budget. This increase is based on some funds being fronted, with a contingency, due to greater revenue estimates. In May, non-partisan state analysts estimated that the recovering economy would provide the $4 billion windfall in revenue that was needed to balance the budget, according to the California Legislative Analysts

See BUDGET on Page 5

6
People
gives a detailed look into the world of auto servicing and the roles of students taking a tech

8
Lifestyles
outlines the differences in each decade for the past 100 years

10-11
In-Depth
explores how people are affected by first impressions

12
International
tests students' knowledge on international events and leaders

20
Weekend
provides a guide to haunted thing out this Halloween season

ANNANDALE HIGH SCHOOL
4700 Medford Dr. Annandale, VA 22003

the ABLAST
Informing the Atoms since 1954

Visit us online:
www.thea-blast.org

VOLUME #57 ISSUE 3 | TUESDAY, OCTOBER 18, 2011 | (703) 642-4229

Obama spotlights AHS

Around AHS

Last chance for senior pictures in October

Faculty book club begins

The A-Blast sponsors a Halloween costume contest

Korean-American community feels pride

By Angie Curras, Cj Anthony and Nich Conteso
Co-Editors-in-Chief and Managing Editor

First Lady Michelle Obama hugs First Lady of the Republic of South Korea Kim Yoon-ok after Kim's speech to AHS.

Here are the rules:

Online Exclusive

Live blog from PTSA meeting tonight

PTSA hosts candidates

Ten school board hopefuls together

By Angie Curras
Co-Editor-in-Chief

Sandy Evans (left) and Bryong Moon both currently serve on the school board.

Driving recklessly

Racing in reverse on AHS's Four Year Run

By Mario Aguilero
News Editor

New plan for Group IV sciences

Teacher brings in-school field trip idea from Stuart HS

By Mario Aguilero
News Editor

Senior Garssheen Kaur gave her Group IV presentation last school year, before the in-school field trip was added.

A broadsheet format allows designers to maximize content packaging and photo size. In *The A Blast*, primary page space is given to a story and picture combination showing First Lady Michelle Obama's visit to the school, accompanied by the First Lady of South Korea. The large size of the photo provides impact and captures a nice moment between the first ladies.

Three other main stories fill the rest of the page, each with a smaller headline size. The two head shots with the 'candidates' story provide faces for the names, both cropped so the heads are identical in size.

The bottom story includes a well-cropped image allowing it to anchor the bottom of the page and provide visual balance. Along the left side, a column of news briefs includes a picture and a teaser to the website's upcoming live coverage of a meeting. A narrow banner of teasers provides an index to inside coverage. Despite a lot of content, this page doesn't feel crowded or busy. Extra white space separating the stories horizontally helps open up the page. The paper's flag or nameplate is a strong design and is used as a visual connection to the standing head for the news briefs column.

FIGURE 12.4 *The Triangle*, Columbus North High School, Columbus, Ind. Front cover, Vol. 91, Issue 2, Oct. 19, 2011. Reproduced by permission of Kim Green, adviser, *The Triangle*.

A hybrid publication size, *The Triangle* is 9 inches x 12.5 inches. This newspaper is printed on heavier, white paper, which provides better color and photo reproduction than newsprint for this all-color magazine. The cover photo illustration provides a background for the type promoting an inside double-page spread on domestic violence. With center staple binding, each set of facing pages can be designed as a magazine spread, allowing strong visual-verbal storytelling in a variety of forms.

Quick Exercise

Take a copy of your printed newspaper and look at the front-page. Does the page feel crowded and cramped, or open and inviting? Now take a marker and mark up all the white space on the page. Is it about 50 percent of the page? (That's the average amount of white space on a printed page.) Go online and find an image of a newspaper from 50 years or so ago. How much white space would you estimate is on the front-page?

white space will dually serve to draw the reader to that element while creating separation between it and other page elements.

Today's distracted readers also need some visual pacing. Traditional text-heavy stories should be set off and contrasted by stories told in a variety of visual forms. The amount of space these visual stories occupy in the paper can also vary, from parts of a single page to full pages to double trucks – stories laid out across the center facing pages of the paper. Learning to balance text, images and white space allows the designer to create interesting, reader-friendly pages that effectively showcase content and create clear visual pathways for the reader.

On a website, content is usually previewed on a main or home page. The preview might include a large picture or illustration, as well as a short summary of the content. Longer stories,

FIGURE 12.5 *North Star*, Francis Howell North High School, St. Charles, Mo. "The deal with drug tests," by Jordan Bryson, pp. 4–5, Sept. 21, 2011. Reproduced by permission of Aaron Manfull.

White space is one of the best ways for designers to isolate content and help the reader see special content. This newsmagazine story uses visual devices to help break up the text. This side-placed headline stack emphasizes impact words in larger typography, with a narrow visual separating the headline from the deck head at bottom. A 'wrapper head' labels the story as coverage from the school district, and repeats the wrapper in the sidebar, 'The breakdown,' which links these visuals. The text starts with a drop cap matching the headline typography, creating a link between the two. Text heads in the same all-cap typography break the story's length for the reader, making each section almost a mini-story. A strong package of images on the top right provides visual information and balances the text. An additional infographic, 'Time Out,' details the percentage of positive drug tests, the context for the story and repeats the color and typography.

FIGURE 12.6 *HiLite*, Carmel High School, Carmel, Ind. "Fall of the college exam?" by Victor Xu, pp. 16–17, Jan. 27, 2012. Reproduced by permission of Jim Streisel.

White space surrounding the dominant art adds breathing room and invites readers in to this multiple-page cover story on college exams. The stacked headline grouped with a detailed deck head also creates white space in its interaction with the visual. Rather than wrapping the story around the visual's shape, the type is organized in a single column, providing structure and contrast. Blue color from the top book's spine is echoed in the headline, which connects these elements. The books seem to point to the text, taking the reader logically to the beginning of the story.

FIGURE 12.7 *Harbinger Online*, Shawnee Mission East High School, Prairie Village, Kan. Reproduced by permission of C. Dow Tate.

A primary story appears at the top of *Harbinger Online* in prominent size and position. Packaged with a visual, the story includes a headline and a link to the full story. Other prominent stories flash in a slideshow, with a string of thumbnails above the headline. The other story categories appear in vertical columns with blue labels, "News," "Sports," "Multimedia," "A&E," "Featured Video," and "Photo of the Week," among others. The site includes a link to the print edition in pdf format, and includes a link to "most popular" stories as ranked by reader hits. The site also includes links to other sections and a scrolling banner of information on top.

FIGURE 12.7 *(continued)*

Principles of good design

Balance: Balance in design simply means that the page is evenly weighted. This doesn't mean that every element needs to be the same size, but it does mean that the elements should not clash with one another or distract the reader. If all the pictures are placed at the top of the page, the page will look top-heavy. A similar balancing problem will occur if all the pictures appear on the left or right side of the page. A large visual at the top of the page (creating a dense black weight on the page) needs to be balanced with a strong visual somewhere at the bottom. Wide columns of text need to be balanced with narrower columns elsewhere on the page. Justified text columns, even on both the left and right sides, can contrast with columns left ragged, or unjustified, on one side, usually the right.

Rhythm: This often refers to the visual flow of the page: a good system of coordinated typefaces, for instance, or a range of headline sizes that complement each other and work well for the paper size.

Unity: The design must contain elements of repetition that become familiar to the reader over time. Using a consistent style of typography and design for the nameplate as well as for elements that appear consistently throughout the newspaper – such as headings for columns and briefs, often referred to as **standing heads** – is a good way to create unity. Using the same size typeface and leading for most stories or using the same type family for headlines will also give the publication a unified look. The need for unity doesn't mean the designer can't deviate from the newspaper's standard typeface styles for a feature story or for an in-depth piece. Doing so helps to draw the reader's attention to special content in the newspaper. However, using different typefaces for every story in the newspaper will disrupt unity, creating disparate and confusing messages for readers.

Scale: Scale is used in determining how much of the page's real estate will be used for each element. The designer begins a layout with a system of **columns or grids**, or vertical spaces dividing the page. These vertical spaces guide the designer in placing stories and visuals on the page. In addition to vertical columns, some designers will use an intricate series of horizontal rows to maintain alignment across pages and spreads so that baselines or lines of type within story shapes will also align. The grid or column method should create an appropriate and readable width for lines of type, generally between 10 and 20 picas.

FIGURE 12.8 *Blue & Gold*, Findlay High School, Findlay, Ohio. Issue 7, May 20, 2011. Reprinted with permission.

Strong visual hierarchy, consistent typography and dominant picture use are the hallmarks of this front-page. The newspaper's flag, index and teasers are packaged into a strong horizontal box anchoring the top of the page, with a curved shape separating the nameplate from other elements. The nameplate uses color cleverly, with a friendly lower case letter structure. The front-page features a balanced layout and bold, sans serif typography in different sizes to establish visual hierarchy. The primary story uses a dominant image, a horizontal timeline of building projects and a sidebar on eco-friendly technology in a packaged presentation. The other story's photo on the left side of the page provides balance with the primary story's right placement. Three small features span the bottom of the page, adding interest and fun, quick-read content.

Proportion: Asymmetrical designs are far more visually interesting than symmetrical ones. For instance, the proportion of the largest visual on the page should often be two to three times that of any other visual. Similarly, larger, more important stories should take up more space on the page than smaller, less important stories. The designer can also use differing amounts of white space to surround elements on the page.

Visual hierarchy: This is one of the designer's most important considerations, as it helps the reader understand the relative importance of different pieces of information. Stories with greater news value should start above the fold of the page, with larger headlines and more surrounding white space. As the reader's eyes progress from the top of the page to the bottom, the headlines should be smaller, indicating a less important news value (see Chapter 1 for more information on news value). This pattern of visual hierarchy should be maintained on every page to help readers process information and select the content they will read. Shorter text elements, such as summaries or additional, focused content can be integrated into the design of traditional stories. Elements such as columns, briefs, content listings, teasers and other features often anchor corners of pages, rarely straying in position from issue to issue.

features and special reports might be featured more prominently on the main page, and online-only content may be referenced in the print edition. Common link headers may reference the main sections included in the print edition such as news, features, sports and entertainment.

Information packaging

In today's modern designs, packaging should be considered based on the content elements produced for a major story. When an issue is being planned, editors will often identify the major story that will appear on the front-page or on other section fronts. This story might be accompanied by a combination of content forms including sidebars, visuals or **infographics** – information combined with graphic visual forms such as charts and diagrams. But even minor content can benefit from packaging. A designer might start with only a single story without any visuals. By working with an editor, a designer might be able to extract some of the information from the story and present it in a **sidebar** or pullout adjacent to the primary story. A reader might be attracted to these shorter text elements and then be drawn to read the primary story. Or, working with a photographer or an illustrator, the designer might be able to combine photographic and text elements. Something in the visual or in the caption for the visual might attract the reader to the story.

Because readers will have varied interests and some may have short attention spans, information packaging has become a more important consideration in layout and design. Major packaged stories should be prominently displayed in the visual hierarchy, focusing the reader's attention on that content. Such packages are usually placed so they begin above the fold, but don't necessarily need to be at the very top of the page. When a package is not at the top of a page, designers often surround it with a bit more white space to further draw the reader to the content. Other options include using a graphic technique such as a rule line box around the story or a light color **screen** or tint of color behind it to highlight its presence on the page. Narrow columns of white space called **rails** provide additional visual separation for primary packages. Rails are usually wider than the traditional column separations, often three to five picas in width.

Packaging information requires the designer to be flexible and creative. Working with photographers and illustrators can allow designers to devise other effective ways of displaying visual content (see Chapter 15 for more information on using visuals).

Grid and column considerations

As mentioned, designers begin working on pages that are divided into a number of vertical and/or horizontal spaces, with the number and arrangement of those spaces depending on the size of the publication. Traditionally, smaller newsmagazines work with fewer vertical grids or columns, while larger formats such as **broadsheets** offer more options for dividing the page space. In recent years, professional newspaper designers have used as many as 10 to 12 columns as a skeletal grid structure for larger broadsheets. Once a skeletal structure is in place, designers use

WWW

WEBLINKS Check out
www.timharrower.com

Tim Harrower, a former design director, is an author of design books, a consultant and speaker. His site is fun, visual and chock-full of great information. "Ask the Design Dr." and an archive of The Edge, a visual column he designed while at *The Oregonian*, are great links.

Quick Exercise

Find an example of packaged content in your local newspaper, in print or in a PDF of the print edition online. Identify its component parts: sidebar, picture package, infographic or other elements. How do these components extend the story and create interest? Why do you think the editors chose to add these elements?

❝❝ WORDS of WISDOM

Good news design lives at the heart of storytelling.

It is well informed and operates based on a strong understanding of the fundamental principles of good design. But it is not merely an aesthetic consideration – it's also one of product value and usefulness. If the sole value of design were just to make pieces fit on pages or websites or apps, that would reduce "design" to little more than an "assembly line." However, architecting publications to meet reader needs is something more complicated, nuanced and essential.

When good design is in place and active in an organization, it identifies, understands and anticipates user needs and business requirements, conceptualizes solutions and crafts products that directly address those needs.

Good designers are really visual editors who have a mastery in information – graphics, storytelling and story layering forms, illustration, photo editing, typography, use of color as a navigational tool – and bring all of these skills to bear collectively to achieve these goals.

Effective designers make the complex easier to understand. We organize and prioritize information and make it accessible. We are early adopters of technology and therefore valuable teachers, developers and inventors. We have been at the forefront of newspapers' major innovations in printing and new platform development. It is our responsibility to be relevant – and valuable – in our newsrooms.

Steve Dorsey, Vice President/ R + D, Detroit Media Partnership President (2011), Society for News Design

combinations of those narrow columns for content, creating contrast by choosing different multiples of the narrow columns to help differentiate content. Smaller publications such as the tabloid size will rarely divide space into more than five to seven grids or columns, since doing so would create awkward column widths on the smaller sized page.

Standard column widths should be set by the newspaper's design editors at the beginning of the year and be saved on templates in the newspaper's design software. Once set, these standards usually remain in place from year to year. The basic grid structure can be replicated on printed page dummies or sketches, which can be used to plot out a possible design of the page before creating it on the computer.

Multiple-grid formats offer designers a wide choice in creating layouts for stories. When working with numerous grids, combining those grids to create wider columns generally increases readability, which must be a major consideration in design. The more narrow grids can be useful

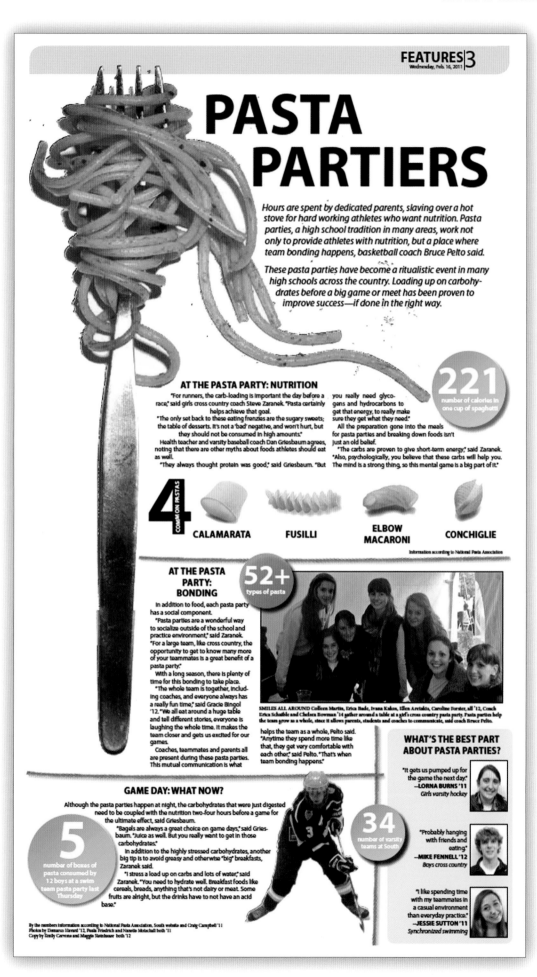

PASTA PARTIERS

Hours are spent by dedicated parents, slaving over a hot stove for hard working athletes who want nutrition. Pasta parties, a high school tradition in many areas, work not only to provide athletes with nutrition, but a place where team bonding happens, basketball coach Bruce Pelto said.

These pasta parties have become a ritualistic event in many high schools across the country. Loading up on carbohydrates before a big game or meet has been proven to improve success—if done in the right way.

AT THE PASTA PARTY: NUTRITION

"For runners, the carb-loading is important the day before a race," said girls cross country coach Steve Zaranek. "Pasta certainly helps achieve that goal.

"The only set back to these eating frenzies are the sugary sweets; the table of desserts. It's not a 'bad' negative, and won't hurt, but they should not be consumed in high amounts."

Health teacher and varsity baseball coach Dan Griesbaum agrees, noting that there are other myths about foods athletes should eat as well.

"They always thought protein was good," said Griesbaum. "But you really need glycogens and hydrocarbons to get that energy, to really make sure they get what they need."

All the preparation gone into the meals for pasta parties and breaking down foods isn't just an old belief.

"The carbs are proven to give short-term energy," said Zaranek. "Also, psychologically, you believe that these carbs will help you. The mind is a strong thing, so this mental game is a big part of it."

221 number of calories in one cup of spaghetti

4 COMMON PASTAS

CALAMARATA   **FUSILLI**   **ELBOW MACARONI**   **CONCHIGLIE**

Information according to National Pasta Association

AT THE PASTA PARTY: BONDING

52+ types of pasta

In addition to food, each pasta party has a social component.

"Pasta parties are a wonderful way to socialize outside of the school and practice environment," said Zaranek. "For a large team, like cross country, the opportunity to get to know many more of your teammates is a great benefit of a pasta party."

With a long season, there is plenty of time for this bonding to take place.

"The whole team is together, including coaches, and everyone always has a really fun time," said Gracie Bingol '12. "We all eat around a huge table and tell different stories, everyone is laughing the whole time. It makes the team closer and gets us excited for our games.

Coaches, teammates and parents all are present during these pasta parties. This mutual communication is what

SMILES ALL AROUND Colleen Martin, Erica Bade, Ivana Kakos, Ellen Aretakis, Caroline Forster, all '12, Coach Erica Schauble and Chelsea Bowman '14 gather around a table at a girl's cross country pasta party. Pasta parties help the team grow as a whole, since it allows parents, students and coaches to communicate, said coach Bruce Pelto.

helps the team as a whole, Pelto said.

"Anytime they spend more time like that, they get very comfortable with each other," said Pelto. "That's when team bonding happens."

WHAT'S THE BEST PART ABOUT PASTA PARTIES?

"It gets us pumped up for the game the next day."
—LORNA BURNS '11
Girls varsity hockey

"Probably hanging with friends and eating."
—MIKE FENNELL '12
Boys cross country

"I like spending time with my teammates in a casual environment than everyday practice."
—JESSIE SUTTON '11
Synchronized swimming

GAME DAY: WHAT NOW?

Although the pasta parties happen at night, the carbohydrates that were just digested need to be coupled with the nutrition two-four hours before a game for the ultimate effect, said Griesbaum.

"Bagels are always a great choice on game days," said Griesbaum. "Juice as well. But you really want to get in those carbohydrates."

In addition to the highly stressed carbohydrates, another big tip is to avoid greasy and otherwise 'big' breakfasts, Zaranek said.

"I stress a load up on carbs and lots of water," said Zaranek. "You need to hydrate well. Breakfast foods like cereals, breads, anything that's not dairy or meat. Some fruits are alright, but the drinks have to not have an acid base."

5 number of boxes of pasta consumed by 12 boys at a swim team pasta party last Thursday

34 number of varsity teams at South

By the numbers information according to National Pasta Association, South website and Craig Campbell '11
Photos by Demarco Havard '12, Paula Friedrich and Natalie Motschall both '11
Copy by Emily Carvone and Maggie Steinhauer both '12

FIGURE 12.9 *The Tower*, Grosse Pointe South High School, Grosse Pointe Farms, Mich., p. 3, March 26, 2011. Reproduced by permission of Jeff Nardone.

Rather than merely writing a story about the school tradition of pasta parties for high school athletes, this broadsheet page featured a package of content with text and images combined into a visual powerhouse. The large fork illustration anchors the subject and headline with the strands of spaghetti leading to the first topic, nutrition. Each subsequent story features an appropriate picture and circle graphic featuring numbers relevant to the story. Finally, a quote collection adds context and faces to the information. This kind of thoughtful storytelling appeals to a wide range of student readers.

FIGURE 12.10 *The Granite Bay Gazette*, Granite Bay High School, Granite Bay, Calif., p. B4, Dec. 16, 2011. Reproduced by permission of Karl Grabaugh.

The versatility of a flexible grid system is important for a broadsheet newspaper. On this inside page with continuations of jumps from news on p. 2, the designer has used a variety of grid widths based on an eight-column grid. The bottom story is in four grids of two columns, the widest text on the page. In the Online jump, three columns provide the narrowest text widths on the page. At the top of the page, three separate features span the grids, providing contrast in the presentation. Varying grids help distinguish content areas and help the readers separate stories.

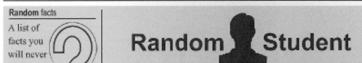

friday OCTOBER 28, 2011

ST. MARK'S SCHOOL OF TEXAS
DALLAS, TX 75230
VOLUME 58, ISSUE 2

remarker

Charlie Garcia p. 17   Amy Pool takes flight p. 7   Cross country runners start strong p. 17   Kendrick Spraglin runs over ESD defender p. 17   Senior Auction p. 4

inside

news
▶As Kim Wargo takes over as headmistress of Hockaday, **news editor Sam Yonack** sits down with her to examine how she plans to strengthen the relationship between the two schools. **Page 3.**

manhood
▶While many students greatly anticipate attaining their driver's license, many do not realize it comes with great risks and responsibilities. **Page 15.**

centerspread
▶Senior writer **Will Moor** and **issues editor Stephen Rambin** explore the behind-the-scenes aspects of how Alumni and Development offices impact life at 10600 Preston Road. **Pages 12-13.**

sports
▶After just one year on the varsity football team, **Will Johnson '11** continued his football career at the University of Texas, playing for one of the most storied programs in the NCAA. **Page 18.**

commentary
▶With college admissions looming in the future, grades are a crucial part of a Marksman's life. The Editorial Board explores the pros and cons of the grading system. **Page 21.**

ahead

today
▶JV volleyball at Greenhill, 4:30 p.m.
▶Varsity volleyball at Greenhill, 5:30 p.m.
▶Varsity football at Greenhill, 7 p.m.

tomorrow
▶Fencing at Lone Star Fencing Center
▶Upper School Fall Play at St. Mark's, 2 p.m. and 7 p.m.

upcoming
▶Upper School Fall Play Sunday at St. Mark's, 2 p.m.
▶Evensong Sunday in the Chapel, 7 p.m.
▶Community Service hours due Monday

index

News	2-7
SAT game	8
Scene	9-11, 14
Manhood	15
Centerspread	12-13
Commentary	21-23
Homecoming	24

STANDARDIZED TESTING

Playing the SAT game

NICK AZZARA/PHOTO ILLUSTRATION

It's something we all dread. But, once the bubbles are filled and the pencils are laid down, what goes in to the test that determines so much of a student's future?

▶ by Max Marshall, managing editor and Ryan O'Meara, staff writer

The night before, it's hard to sleep. Next to the kicked-and-twisted linens, stacks of vocabulary flashcards crumple over wrinkled practice tests scribbled with ink.

Above the sweat-soaked pillow, the mind races through theorems and grammar rules, equations and essay ideas.

Beside the bedside table, the clock flashes closer to the time. Starting at 6:45 the next morning, students will grab their calculators, pack a light snack and head into an anonymous classroom to fill in bubbles that might determine their future.

This is the standardized testing game. And when college acceptances are pending, few things bring more terror to the oxford-clad Marksman.

To some high school seniors, the standardized testing process is an enigmatic, all-powerful machine that seems to eat tests, assign scores and disseminate fate. As some students' acceptances depend on these scores, the mysterious clout these tests hold arouses trepidation and angst in the hearts of college hopefuls.

The testing agencies are as rich as they are powerful. Ac-

cording to Forbes, the CEOs of the College Board and the ACT make over a million dollars a year, more than the president of Harvard.

As these tests seem to determine college fate while garnering power, some are fed up.

The College Board, which administrates the SAT, PSAT, and Advanced Placement (AP) tests, received an F (the lowest possible score) on the Better Business Bureau's customer satisfaction measurement.

But much of the animosity against these organizations comes from mysteries and misconceptions. The SAT enigma sparks fear and loathing in the clouds of mystery. A closer look reveals something different altogether.

Playing the game | Stories on page 8
▶ College Board exec Jim Montoya debunks myths of suits trying to control students' fates.
▶ What do you do when you're the 'perfect' candidate for colleges, but your test scores aren't sky-high?
▶ AP test scores don't dictate teaching style, curriculum here.

Continued on p. 8

School hires consultant as chaplain search is initiated

by AAROHAN BURMA
staff writer

HE GUIDES THE UPPER School through prayers every Wednesday morning, his voice booming above the pews. He teaches multiple classes and works overtime to balance academic and spiritual duties.

When members of the community have births or deaths in their families, he is there to share their emotions. He is one of the most prominent figures on campus.

As of now, however, 10600 Preston Road does not have an ordained minister. But as the search for someone to fill the vacuum left by the previous chaplain, Rev. Richard A. Towers, goes on, Dean of Campus Scott Gonzalez has filled in as interim chaplain, just like in

the 2002-2003 school year.

"I learn something every day," Gonzalez said. "I go home happy 99 percent of the time, and I am needed here. I'll do anything in order to make this school the best institution for young people that I can make it."

Towers chose to leave 10600 Preston Road for Seoul, South Korea in May.

Currently, Rev. George Andrews, an Episcopal priest who

Seniors who started in first grade here will have experienced five different chaplain tenures during their 12 years here, including two stints of interim chaplains.

has served as the headmaster of St. George's School in Newport, R.I. and St. Andrew's School in Boca Raton, FL, is conducting the search for someone to replace Towers. However, the process of evaluating candidates is complex and only in its preliminary stages.

"It's very premature to be sharing names with anyone because we have not vetted them thoroughly," Holtberg said. "They are more prospects than candidates at this point."

To be considered for the position, candidates must go through a background check, be a member of the Episcopal Church and embody virtues established by past chaplains, foremost among them having his finger on the pulse of the youth and respecting other faiths.

"Not only must he have expe-

rience with young people, he must also be enthusiastic about working with young people," Holtberg said. "He must also understand the pluralist nature of the school while being a committed Christian himself."

Although a new chaplain will be selected by the commencement of the next school year, and may even be hired by Jan. 1, Gonzalez is happy to remain as interim chaplain as long as needed.

"I'd love to do it," he said. "However, my hope is that we find somebody because there are some areas in which I have not received training, and I'd rather have somebody who has better ideas and training as to how to go about faith issues. I think that such a person will serve this school and the community so much better than I will."

FIGURE 12.11 *ReMarker*, St. Mark's School of Texas, Dallas, Texas. Reproduced by permission of Ray Westbrook.

In a narrow column of type on the left side of the page, the type under "Inside" is right aligned, ensuring the type won't produce awkward white space given short line widths. The type's light stroke weigh adds to its suitability for narrow grid use. Note, too, that the unjustified text lines in this narrow grid are echoed in the main story's unjustified lines and contrasted in the fully justified lines of type in the bottom story. Other unjustified lines appear in the headline's deck, the boxed "Playing the game" sidebar and in the blue type summary bar at the bottom of the page.

NEWSFLASH

Margins and space

External margins are white space **borders** surrounding the page on all four sides. They are a necessity since newspaper presses cannot print to the edges of the page. In addition, margins provide balance to the page and create alignment for the text. External margins can be as narrow as a quarter or half of an inch, or can be a bit wider depending on the publication's page size and printer specifications.

Internal margins, the spaces between the columns vertically and horizontally, should be generally consistent and even for pages to look balanced and well proportioned. Although exceptions are sometimes made, vertical internal margins tend to be about one to two picas wide. This space allows designers to place text columns next to each other without the lines of text becoming confused. An exception would be made in packaged content where a designer might use three to five picas to create a package margin surrounding the content on the page.

The designer should also maintain consistency in horizontal space separation. To help the reader differentiate between unrelated content, two picas of horizontal separation are suggested. Too much white space, on the other hand, can distract the reader's eyes from the content. Therefore, the designer must plan carefully to ensure that separations, both vertical and horizontal, are consistent throughout the publication.

Quick Exercise

Examine a broadsheet newspaper page and use a colored marker to identify its skeletal structure. Look for a narrow column of type as an indicator, then measure other columns to see if they are multiples of this width. Note how the grid structure creates flexibility for the addition of information.

Test your knowledge

What is the difference between external and internal page margins? What purpose do they serve in design?

for including detail elements such as captions, drop cap letters or nut graf deck heads. Placing story text in grids as narrow as five to seven picas, on the other hand, generally produces low readability, jerky line lengths and problems with hyphenation. When using narrow columns for text, designers should consider using condensed typefaces and unjustified alignment patterns so the text doesn't appear with frequent hyphens or large holes of white space between words.

Modular design

If you were to go back and study news designs from the 1950s and earlier, you would find story layouts that were dense and difficult to follow. Columns of type might extend vertically down a page several for inches and in the next column extend down by a greater or lesser number of inches. This design pattern, often referred to as **dog leg design** for its resemblance to a bent dog's leg, has been abandoned in recent years in favor of patterns of easier readability.

Today, designers primarily use modular design. **Modular design** involves placing information in four-sided shapes such as squares or rectangles. Although designers can't always make design modular, especially on pages with ads of different sizes, the fewer deviations from even text columns, the easier it will be for the reader to follow the flow of the story. Modules include pictures or other package elements. Packages of content will usually follow modular design principles, with all elements lined up within four-sided areas.

Preparing for design

The process of designing might start with a rough pencil sketch of a preliminary plan for the page, often referred to as a **page dummy**. These page dummies, usually drawn in reduced size, allow the designer to explore different options for placing elements on the page before actually sitting down at the computer to formally arrange them. Printed page dummies should reflect (in scale) the external page margins and the grid or column method as well as the internal margins. Preparing pencil dummies allows the beginning designer to determine whether his sketches will reflect solid design principles in completed layouts. Moving elements around on the dummies will offer the designer options for story placement as well as relative emphasis.

Because dummies are a designer's sketch pad, a shorthand method of indicating elements can be used. Headlines might be represented by a series of X's with notes indicating the actual size and typeface. Stories can be represented by arrows drawn vertically down columns indicating both the width and the length of the text. A photo or other image can be represented by a large box with an X drawn in it. Designers can write in a short description of the picture assigned to that spot.

The value of dummies is that they are often drawn well in advance of the completion of stories and photographic assignments. When stories are edited and visuals are complete, designers

page 11 sports

Hawks search for redemption

SeniorDeante Reid dribbles down the court against Atlanta.
— davidbird photo

Despite struggling in district, varsity basketball focuses on long run

by mattdegroot
reporter

He wakes up in a cold sweat. He can't get the images out of his head. Senior Damien Watts hasn't stopped thinking about the Dallas-Madison game ever since the ride home after the devastating loss in the Regional Final last year.

The loss has haunted the Hawks since, and seniors Antonio Graves, Deante Reid and Watts are hoping to redeem that defeat with another long run in the playoffs.

"Our main goal this year is to play them again, except this time, we're not going to lose," Watts said. "We shouldn't have lost the game last year, and we're going to prove it to them."

Last year, the Hawks played hard against the Dallas-Madison Trojans, but in the end they came up short.

"I'm really not sure how they got ahead of us," said senior Antonio Graves. "I remember having a charge called on me after I made a lay up and the Trojans got to shoot some free throws. Then we got up by two and the ref made some crazy call which ended up costing us the game."

That call turned out to be a technical foul on former player Michael Wacha for running out onto the court after the game had resumed. The Hawks had called a

time-out, and when the second horn goes off during a time-out, by rules the players have to return to the court. Wacha wasn't aware of the horn and the game started with only four people on the court for PG. When Wacha realized what had happened, he ran onto the court, which is a technical foul, and Dallas got the ball.

This was a huge momentum change, especially since it was at the end of the game.

"We got bamboozled that game," senior Deante Reid said. "We shouldn't have lost. I'm still really angry about it."

After losing two close games to Liberty-Eylau and Atlanta, the Hawks need to win out to get back to the playoffs.

A recent article in the *Texarkana Gazette* stated that the Hawks were still working out some kinks, but coach Clay Busby said he has confidence in his team even in the face of adversity.

"I don't think any coach needs to get satisfied with where a team is at, but I think we're just fine," he said. "And as for the *Texarkana Gazette*, I wouldn't go as far as to quote them on anything."

The Hawks meet Atlanta for the second time this Friday at Atlanta and have .three more district games before playoffs begin.

Under the radar

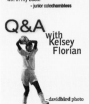

Upcoming games:
JV Soccer
2/9- Liberty-Eylau
2/12- Pittsburg
2/16- Atlanta
JV Girls' Basketball
2/5- @ Atlanta
2/9 Mount Vernon
JV Boys' Basketball
2/9- Mount Vernon
2/12- @ New Boston
2/16- Pittsburg
9th Boys' Basketball
2/11- @ Liberty-Eylau
2/12- @ New Boston
2/16- Pittsburg

Junior Cody Mcgee races towards the ball after he gets by the opposing defender.

JV Soccer
Head coach: J.W Bramlett
Standout: Junior Cody McGee
Team to beat: Texas High. A cross-town rival—every time the teams meet, it is a hard fought match.
Also watch: Freshman Alan Oubre
"I think we are playing really good right now," Oubre said. "We are learning the basic fundamentals that will help us out in district games."

Sophomore Kevin Harris makes his way to the basket against Trinity Christian.

JV Boys' Basketball
Head coach: Todd Elliot
Standout: Freshman Reggie Myrks
Team to beat: Liberty-Eylau has incredible height and they usually have tons of talent.
Also watch: Junior Michael Ward
"It's been a really positive season so far," Ward said. "We've only lost one district game, and the team chemistry is great."

Freshman Samantha Huang listens to the coach before playing against varsity.

JV Girls' Basketball
Head coach: Jenny Coon
Standout: Freshman Claire Rikel
Team to beat: Mount Vernon. They can really shoot the basketball and if we play great defense and make plays, they can be beat.
Also watch: Sophomore Jessica Ross
"I think our greatest strength is the team chemistry," Claire Rikel said. "We also are getting better because everyone gets great playing time."

Freshman Cason Cordray drains a free throw while teammate Alex Alsup watches.

9th Boys' Basketball
Head coach: Justin Watson
Standout: Alex Alsup
Team to beat: Liberty-Eylau. Another crosstown rival —a win would give the Hawks a satisfying season.
Also watch: Nick Cockerell
"Even though the record doesn't show it," Cockerell said. "The practices go really well and the team gives a lot of effort."

Signing on
Four athletes will sign letters of intent this month to play football at colleges and universities across the South

Antonio Graves — Texas Christian
Damien Watts — Central Arkansas
Deante Reid — Trinity Valley
LaMarcus Banks — Trinity Valley

Come by and give us a try!

DISCOUNT WHEEL & TIRE
793-0887   793-0887

3223-A Summerhill Rd.
(903) 793-0887

4810 W. 7th St.
(903) 832-0408

Your Money, Your Way, Your Credit Union!
MOBILE BANKING   BALANCE ALERTS   E-STATEMENTS & NOTICES
Sign up for convenient ONLINE BANKING!
Red River STUDENT CREDIT UNION in Hawk Nation!
903-735-3000 • www.rrfcu.com • 800-822-3317

---

on the edge

The football Hawks not only destroyed the record books on their way to a 9-4 season, but individual players received multiple accolades and all-district honors.

AP All-State Second Team:
LeMarcus Banks
16-3A MVP:
Antonio Graves
First Team all-district
QB/ LB-Antonio Graves
WR-Damien Watts
Second Team All-district
LG-Alex Borrell
DL-Jordan Fazzalaro
LB-Lucas Wacha
DB-Matt Duff
DB-LeMarcus Banks
RB-Nick Reed
TE-Jason Day
WR-Jon Phillips
Honorable Mention
DB-Landon Ashby
OC-Matt Degroot
RT-Len Hammett
WR-Deante Reid
Academic All State Honorable Mention
Len Hammett
Matt DeGroot

Super Predictions
We watched the Colts kill the Jets, then the Saints drill the Vikings in overtime, but before the playoffs we asked students which team they picked to win the Super Bowl. They were only slightly off.

54% picked the Cowboys
"I've watched the Cowboys my whole life and they are playing incredible. Demarcus Ware is a beast and Felix Jones is like Flash."
- teacher stephaniecarpenter

14% thought the Saints would win
"The Saints haven't had a season like this in a long time, and they're playing awesome."
- sophomore jacobbass

12% gave the nod to the Ravens
"The Ravens defense held the dominating Patriot offense to 196 yards. They are good enough to win in my book."
- junior colechambless

Q&A with Kelsey Florian

— davidbird photo

JT: With a new field and the return of some key players, what are your expectations for this season?
KF: My expectation for this season is that our team will play much more aggressive soccer. The team's ball handling has improved and we have much better communication.
JT: Who will be the team to beat this year and why?
KF: I expect Texas High to be the team to beat this year. We both lost key players and we want to avenge a 1-0 defeat to them last year.
JT: What is your team's greatest strength?
KF: Everybody on the team plays for fun and has a heart for the game of soccer as well as their teammates. We are a very unified team.
- compiled by jacksontidwell

In modular design, each content area can be defined by a four-sided container. Using modular shapes prevents awkward columns of type or content legs that don't align. Keeping ads in modular shapes, as was done on this sports page with the two bottom ads, also maintains modular space for story layout. Note the three horizontal modular stories on the left above the ads, contrasted by a strong vertical module of quick-read sports items, including a student poll and Q&A feature.

should re-evaluate the dummies to make sure the designs reflect the edited stories and the strength of the visuals. If story length or picture quality has changed, designers should compensate for these changes by drawing new dummies. For instance, if a photographer's best image is a vertical, but the dummy predicted a dominant horizontal image, the designer should redraw the dummy to utilize the strength of the actual photograph.

Although editors often give writers suggested word counts when making story assignments, story lengths can change during the reporting process. If a story becomes longer or shorter than the assigned length, designers will need to make changes to their dummies or preliminary designs.

Experienced designers will become adept at designing pages and may not need to use dummies, preferring instead to get right to the computer page template. Throughout the design process, the designer must remain flexible and sensitive to changing news value and storytelling potential. Visuals should never be forced into positions that compromise their potential, neither should a story be edited just to fit a space on a dummy. Rather, designers should work from the strength of the reporting, editing and photography when laying out the pages. This process will guarantee the most successful method of bringing information to the reader.

After page dummies have been adjusted and redrawn, designers should take them to the computer to help lay out the pages. Templates reflecting the margins and column grids of the page can be stored in the computer with **typographic style sheets**, organized type systems that will facilitate consistency throughout the publication, and visual libraries containing logos, standing heads and other visual devices that might be useful. Stories written by individual writers and edited on-screen can be imported from wordprocessing programs into the templates, flowed into the design and styled using the pre-set style sheets. Staff using page layout and design software will find endless opportunities for creating interesting designs. Drop caps, text heads and other graphic devices for text relief are easily created through modern layout and design software programs.

Photographs taken with digital cameras can be downloaded directly into the computer and imported into layouts. Care should be taken when cropping to ensure that picture content is not

Avoiding the trap of over-design

Layout software is a great tool for the designer. It facilitates experimentation with various elements right up until the time the design is set. But designers can also get caught up in over-designing or relying too heavily on mediocre design trends. A good practice is to print out the page, hang it up and step back several steps to look for design problems.

While designing, avoid these overused, outdated trends:

→ modifying headlines by heavy shadowing of the typeface

→ distorting type by stretching it vertically or horizontally

→ using random type without regard to an organized type system

→ underlining type for emphasis

→ boxing content with heavy, distracting rule lines

→ placing rule lines too close to text without adjusting inset spacing

→ cutting out the background of picture elements (unless appropriate to the content)

→ using bright or dark color saturations behind reversed or white type, which makes the type hard to read

→ overusing color, which can affect the visual balance of the page

→ adding background shading around pictures or text.

BEST BUDS:
Teachers, administrators develop life-long bonds on and off campus. **B2-3**

HONORING A PLAYER:
Bake sale, baseball signing fundraiser, memorial service pay tribute to classmate. **A14**

THE HARVARD-WESTLAKE
CHRONICLE

Los Angeles • Volume XXI • Issue III • Nov. 16, 2011

IN MEMORIAM: *Alex Rand-Lewis '12, center, comforts Kameron Lucas '12, left, and Michael Wugmeister '12, right, after Monday's memorial service in honor of Chris Robinson. Arden Pabst '13, above, contributes to a memorial by writing a message on a baseball.*

Pool revamp finally begins, Kutler permits still pending

By Eli Haims

The school has received permits and has begun construction on the pool, Head of Campus Operations and Construction J.D. De Matte said. He hopes the City of Los Angeles will grant the permits for the Kutler Center today. The pool permits were granted Nov. 7, and the next day, part of the road next to Taper Gymnasium was ripped up to begin the electrical phase of work.

A new electrical system is being installed to increase the current power four-fold. The first stage of the pool construction will be laying the foundation.

A retaining wall will be built adjacent to the main driveway, and a wall will be continued around the perimeter. De Matte said the pool has to be open by early-to-mid August, in time for the start of the 2012-2013 school year.

There will be about seven months of "hard core construction" and the remaining time will be "fine tuning," he said.

President Thomas C. Hudnut said about half of the funding for the pool has been donated by Peter and Judy Copses (Henry '14, John '14), who turned over the first shovel at the ground-breaking Tuesday.

The construction of the Kutler Center, which bridges Mudd Library and Seaver, will begin as soon as the permits are received.

"Once I get the Kutler permit, we will be immediately inside the building, framing and doing our structural stuff to move forward," De Matte said.

De Matte said that he had hoped to get the permits for the Kutler Center before now.

"It's been difficult getting them," he said last week. "The city is tough to get through, and it's a complicated project with buildings connecting other

● Continued on page A9

Coach, teammates remember 'Bee-Bop' for upbeat spirit

"You were always a reminder to me of how sweet life can be. You make life sweeter for me and my friends. And I thank you."

—*Colburn Pittman '12*

By Judd Liebman

Friends remembered Christopher "Bee-Bop" Robinson at a memorial service Monday for his ability to bring levity to almost all situations, even during his sickness. Robinson died Nov. 9 after battling leukemia for two years.

"I am blessed to have known Chris, because not only did he make me a better person, but he made every place he went a better place," Austin Scholl '13 said at the assembly Nov. 14 in Rugby Auditorium.

Robinson came from Cathedral Chapel School as a new ninth grader in September 2009. Shortly thereafter, he was diagnosed with leukemia, cancer of the blood cells, and took a leave of absence to start treatment in November 2009. Although Robinson never rejoined the Class of 2013 at school, he always considered himself a part of the community.

"Chris, 'Bee-Bop,' really did love Harvard-Westlake," his father Quincy Robinson said. "When he was in the hospital, Chris always wore Harvard-Westlake gear, whether it was shorts or a T-shirt. He seemed to think he got better treatment that way."

Quincy Robinson spoke on behalf of the Robinson family after speeches from four friends, baseball coach Matt LaCour, ninth grade dean Betsy Ilg and President Thomas C. Hudnut. Members of the Chamber Singers sang a rendition of "Somewhere Over the Rainbow," and Max Quilici '12 played "No Woman, No Cry" on guitar.

Long-time friend Aaron Lyons '13 said Robinson's impact on others was "obvious by how many people wrote letters to his parents. It is also obvious based on how many people came to Rugby today."

To help defray the Robinson family's medical and funeral costs, students raised more than $7,000 from a "name-your-price" bake sale and in donations to a memorial by writing messages on baseballs.

Speakers said Robinson was an avid Yankee fan and described his hospital room as decorated with Yankee paraphernalia.

"If you brought up the Yankees, you would be there for an hour," Kameron Lucas '12 said in an interview. "He knew everything about the Yankees."

During hospital visits, Robinson would frequently divert conversation from his condition to baseball.

"He was still wise-cracking, making jokes," Colburn Pittman '12 said of his hospital visits with Chris. "He didn't want to burden us with [his sickness], so he'd push it to the side when he was talking with us."

Christopher Robinson

"He never wanted to talk about what was going on with himself during those visits, how chemotherapy was affecting him, how his body was reacting, how he was feeling, did he need anything," LaCour said. "You would try to ask him a question about his health, and he would just shrug his shoulders and say 'I'm okay.'"

Robinson was a second baseman and pitcher who played with a sense of urgency and took every ground ball at 100 percent, teammate Langston McElroy '12 said.

Sickness sidelined Robinson, but during hospital visits, he and LaCour "put together a covert mission: to get his year of eligibility back once he got back to school," LaCour said.

Robinson was drawn to Harvard-Westlake partly because of the baseball players he knew from Ladera Little League, Quincy Robinson said.

"Chris never got to play a game in a Wolverine uniform," LaCour said. "We use words like toughness and resiliency all the time. Chris embodied those traits each day throughout this process. As a program, we will make sure we embody the things Chris showed us, and forever go on about our business, both on and off the field, knowing that Chris is watching and rooting for us."

INSIDE

END OF THE ROAD:

C4

Loss to St. Paul squashes the football team's playoff hopes.

CASE STUDY:

What happens, step by step, after a teacher reports a possible Honor Code infraction?

A10

FIGURE 12.13 *The Chronicle,* Harvard-Westlake School, Los Angeles, Calif., Vol. XXI, Issue III, Nov. 16, 2011. Reproduced by permission of Kathleen Neumeyer.

The front-page of the newspaper should feature the best content the staff has for that issue, and should look different based on that content. After a memorial service commemorating the life of a student who had died a week earlier, the front-page packaged a feature from the service.

Featuring two strong images of student friends sharing their loss after the memorial, the package also includes a strong story detailing the life of the student, combined with quotes and stories. Narrow rails of white space surround the package, which help separate it from a news story on campus improvement in the right column.

The newspaper's flag runs the width of the front-page and includes essential information such as the date and issue number. Two teasers with small photos promo important inside content. An additional inside content listing anchors the bottom right corner.

Quick Exercise

Using the newspaper staff's dummies or one you create on paper, dummy up a design from a recent copy of the printed edition to show how it might have looked as a sketch before the design was transferred to the computer.

distorted or stretched. Locking proportions or checking to make sure the x/y scaling coordinates retain the same percentages will prevent these problems. Importing the pictures directly into the layouts helps designers see how the pictures will be cropped and helps them evaluate the page's balance by seeing the actual visuals, text density and white space.

Special considerations for design

In addition to using good overall design throughout the newspaper, certain pages have particular concerns that need a designer's attention.

Front-pages

The front-page is the window to the publication. It forms the reader's first impression, and it should look different for each issue. Some elements should be consistent, including the flag or nameplate and other elements such as teasers and index information. Many newspapers use color on their front-pages, either in the nameplate or more extensively in color photographs, or in type. But beyond those elements, the page should look fresh and new each issue. Avoiding a templated look is important.

Front-page content should offer information that readers will find interesting and relevant. Old news, or news that readers will already be aware of, will rarely provide interesting front-page content for readers with access to multiple forms of information, including social media sites. The publication's website is the best venue for timely news content. The print edition's front-page can instead be used to package a feature story, which will give the designer many options to develop a new look for each issue. Most newsmagazines use their front-pages for feature or in-depth packages, often continuing the story on an inside page. Professional newspapers, too, often include a packaged feature story on the front-page as the dominant story.

Front-pages often contrast longer stories with shorter news briefs, teasers and **digests**, short bursts of content in unique presentations such as a numbered list, a fact of the day, a fun fact or a quote. Giving readers multiple visual entry points on a page can attract different kinds of readers – those who scan for information as well as traditional readers.

Something of visual interest should appear high on the page, preferably above the fold. In newsmagazines, a photograph with a cover teaser to inside content might be the only content on the front-page. Regardless of the visual used, designers should vary its size, placement, color and approach in subsequent issues to avoid predictable layout patterns. Even in newsmagazines, teasers are often featured.

Typography used in nameplates should be functional, clean and simple rather than heavily ornamental or over-designed. The nameplate should establish the newspaper's identity without competing with the content of the front-page. The typeface should be readable and distinctive. Because the typeface in the nameplate should be repeated for section headers and standing headlines elsewhere in the publication, it should work well in smaller sizes. The nameplate should also include the date of issue, the volume and issue number (in Arabic rather than roman numerals) and the name and location of the school. The paper's web address and social media sites should also be included.

Quick Exercise

Visit www.poynter.org and take a look at the archive of today's front-pages. Browse through the publications and notice the ways in which front-page packages are used. Discuss the content of a few packages with a small group of classmates. What elements are included in the package? How has the paper included timely news in other content areas?

Inside pages

After the front-page, each subsequent page should include a page **folio line** – information placed at the top or bottom of the page that includes the name and date of the publication, as well as the page number (at the outside edge of the page). It could also include a page label to identify the content of the page such as news, features, editorial or sports. Alternatively, inside pages could repeat the name of the newspaper as it appears on the front-page. This repetition gives the publication a unified appearance. Items such as columns, news briefs, section heads and other content that appear in each issue can be designed to echo the nameplate by using the same typeface, as well as the same style, structure or arrangement.

Designers can employ different grids or column methods in different sections of the paper. Using varying column widths offers visual variety and creates distinctive content areas for the reader. Sections of the paper can start on single right-hand pages to signal content change when it isn't possible to print separate sections.

FIGURE 12.14 *Blue & Gold*, Findlay High School, Findlay, Ohio. Issue 7, pp. 2–3, May 20, 2011. Reprinted with permission.

In these facing pages, there's no confusion in content for the reader. First, the use of four-color on the right side provides strong contrast with the black-and-white content on the left page. Separate section headers clearly label the pages' content and echo the design of the newspaper's flag on the front-page. (See Fig 12.8.) Additionally, the entertainment page features a top 10 index in the top half of the page, while the editorial page's content includes a staff editorial and a column in the top two-thirds of the page. Both sides feature quick-read content anchoring the bottoms of the pages, but each is treated differently and appropriately for its section.

Throughout the newspaper, designers will need to deal with ad placement. Ad space should be designed so it leaves modules of space for content whenever possible. Some publications, especially newsmagazines, fill entire pages with ads, allowing ad content to be separated from editorial content. The only pages on which ads shouldn't appear are the editorial or opinion pages. In most school newspapers, ads traditionally don't appear on the front-page or section fronts inside the paper. However, many professional newspapers print ads on those pages, primarily in narrow horizontal banners across the bottoms or tops of the pages, similar to the way banner ads appear across the tops of websites.

It's also a good idea for the designer to lay out facing pages together to prevent visual problems. Placing banner headlines across the tops of two facing pages will create off-balanced designs and could confuse the reader, as the headlines might seem to run together. Visuals shouldn't appear directly across from each other in the design, which could throw off the balance of the spread.

Feature pages

Feature page design is the heart and soul of the designer's work. Making strong visual-verbal connections through well-designed, well-thought-out illustrations or excellent photographs combined with strong, detail-oriented headlines give designers many opportunities for creating interesting visual units. Feature stories will vary in presentation, often becoming more visual than textual. Surrounding these feature packages with a bit of extra white space brings the reader to the story content and helps separate it from the rest of the page. Alternatively, feature page packages may take up an entire page. Designers should seize the opportunity to be creative, clever and fun when the content dictates, but when the content is serious or complex, should make sure the design reflects the more serious tone. Color should also be used appropriately on feature pages and not be allowed to overwhelm the content.

FIGURE 12.15 *North Star* (fhntoday.com), Francis Howell North High School, St. Charles, Mo. pp. 8–9, Dec. 14, 2011. Reproduced by permission of Aaron Manfull.

In a newsmagazine format, facing pages can be used for feature content. With a clearly labeled banner, "Features," this story on a local teacher's battle with breast cancer is appropriately treated in this design. Anchored by a strong illustration facing the headline, the ribbon of pink color spanning the pages provides an appropriate use of the iconic pink breast cancer symbol in a fresh way. The pages feature white space that isolates the text and attracts the eye to the headline and then to the text. The headline appears in the standard typography of the newspaper, but the tone of the headline and deck are feature-oriented, and directed to the focus of the article. A sidebar of breast cancer facts appears in a contrasting sans serif typography with bullets marking each fact. The sidebar is anchored to the illustration and separated from the main text by a wider rail of white space.

Feature pages offer designers the opportunity to be a bit more experimental with typeface choices. Many newspapers change typefaces for feature presentations to help the reader understand the change in content. Typefaces with visual connections to the story content can be effective, or the designer can choose a different but consistent typeface for feature content throughout the publication. For instance, many professional newspapers switch to strong sans serif typefaces for feature stories despite using a serif type for headlines on other news stories, or vice versa. The arrangement and positioning of type can also be more creative. White space can be more generously used to separate feature content from other types of stories. The leading of the type in the story might be expanded to indicate its special content. Or, the grid system used on the page might be different from that used on news pages. Feature headlines don't have to use a different typeface. Designers can create interesting displays using size, capitalization and color.

Editorial pages

Editorial pages should reflect the opinions of the newspaper's staff as well as other contributors. The designer should mark the change in approach by designing these pages distinctively. Editorials should be clearly labeled as such. Headlines should clearly state the staff's editorial position. Using a different column grid will also help differentiate the editorial content. Many staff editorials appear in the same position in each edition. These editorials can also be set in wider column grids and in slightly larger typeface. Editorial pages typically feature standing heads in a consistent design for the newspaper's columnists. Columns often feature small head shots or drawings of the writers.

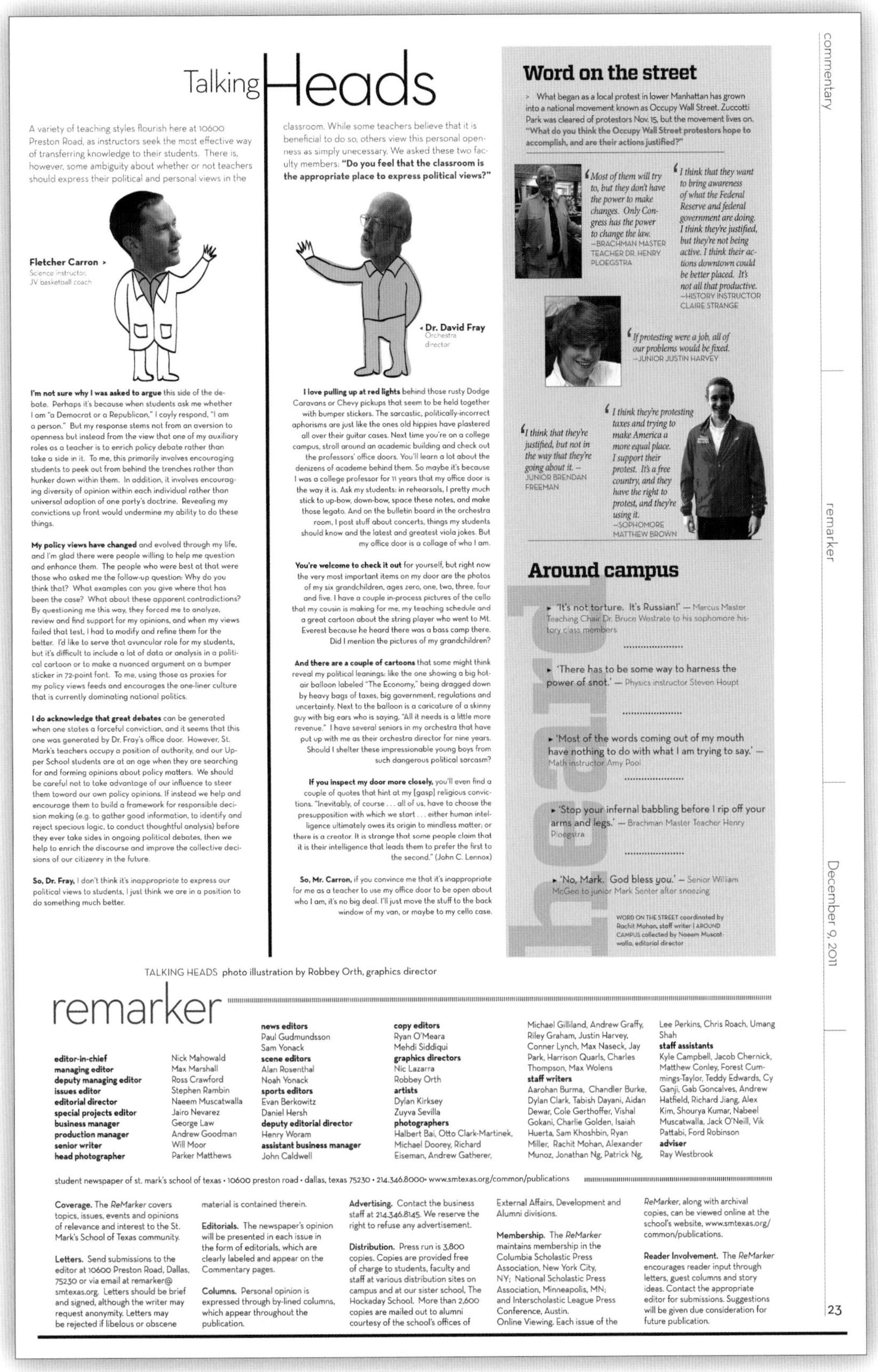

commentary

Talking Heads

A variety of teaching styles flourish here at 10600 Preston Road, as instructors seek the most effective way of transferring knowledge to their students. There is, however, some ambiguity about whether or not teachers should express their political and personal views in the classroom. While some teachers believe that it is beneficial to do so, others view this personal openness as simply unecessary. We asked these two faculty members: **"Do you feel that the classroom is the appropriate place to express political views?"**

Fletcher Carron >
Science instructor,
JV basketball coach

I'm not sure why I was asked to argue this side of the debate. Perhaps it's because when students ask me whether I am "a Democrat or a Republican," I coyly respond, "I am a person." But my response stems not from an aversion to openness but instead from the view that one of my auxiliary roles as a teacher is to enrich policy debate rather than take a side in it. To me, this primarily involves encouraging students to peek out from behind the trenches rather than hunker down within them. In addition, it involves encouraging diversity of opinion within each individual rather than universal adoption of one party's doctrine. Revealing my convictions up front would undermine my ability to do these things.

My policy views have changed and evolved through my life, and I'm glad there were people willing to help me question and enhance them. The people who were best at that were those who asked me the follow-up question: Why do you think that? What examples can you give where that has been the case? What about these apparent contradictions? By questioning me this way, they forced me to analyze, review and find support for my opinions, and when my views failed that test, I had to modify and refine them for the better. I'd like to serve that avuncular role for my students, but it's difficult to include a lot of data or analysis in a political cartoon or to make a nuanced argument on a bumper sticker in 72-point font. To me, using those as proxies for my policy views feeds and encourages the one-liner culture that is currently dominating national politics.

I do acknowledge that great debates can be generated when one states a forceful conviction, and it seems that this one was generated by Dr. Fray's office door. However, St. Mark's teachers occupy a position of authority, and our Upper School students are at an age when they are searching for and forming opinions about policy matters. We should be careful not to take advantage of our influence to steer them toward our own policy opinions. If instead we help and encourage them to build a framework for responsible decision making (e.g. to gather good information, to identify and reject specious logic, to conduct thoughtful analysis) before they ever take sides in ongoing political debates, then we help to enrich the discourse and improve the collective decisions of our citizenry in the future.

So, Dr. Fray, I don't think it's inappropriate to express our political views to students, I just think we are in a position to do something much better.

< **Dr. David Fray**
Orchestra director

I love pulling up at red lights behind those rusty Dodge Caravans or Chevy pickups that seem to be held together with bumper stickers. The sarcastic, politically-incorrect aphorisms are just like the ones old hippies have plastered all over their guitar cases. Next time you're on a college campus, stroll around an academic building and check out the professors' office doors. You'll learn a lot about the denizens of academe behind them. So maybe it's because I was a college professor for 11 years that my office door is the way it is. Ask my students: in rehearsals, I pretty much stick to up-bow, down-bow, space these notes, and make those legato. And on the bulletin board in the orchestra room, I post stuff about concerts, things my students should know and the latest and greatest viola jokes. But my office door is a collage of who I am.

You're welcome to check it out for yourself, but right now the very most important items on my door are the photos of my six grandchildren, ages zero, one, two, three, four and five. I have a couple in-process pictures of the cello that my cousin is making for me, my teaching schedule and a great cartoon about the string player who went to Mt. Everest because he heard there was a bass camp there. Did I mention the pictures of my grandchildren?

And there are a couple of cartoons that some might think reveal my political leanings: like the one showing a big hot-air balloon labeled "The Economy," being dragged down by heavy bags of taxes, big government, regulations and uncertainty. Next to the balloon is a caricature of a skinny guy with big ears who is saying, "All it needs is a little more revenue." I have several seniors in my orchestra that have put up with me as their orchestra director for nine years. Should I shelter these impressionable young boys from such dangerous political sarcasm?

If you inspect my door more closely, you'll even find a couple of quotes that hint at my [gasp] religious convictions. "Inevitably, of course . . . all of us, have to choose the presupposition with which we start . . . either human intelligence ultimately owes its origin to mindless matter; or there is a creator. It is strange that some people claim that it is their intelligence that leads them to prefer the first to the second." (John C. Lennox)

So, Mr. Carron, if you convince me that it's inappropriate for me as a teacher to use my office door to be open about who I am, it's no big deal. I'll just move the stuff to the back window of my van, or maybe to my cello case.

Word on the street

> What began as a local protest in lower Manhattan has grown into a national movement known as Occupy Wall Street. Zuccotti Park was cleared of protestors Nov. 15, but the movement lives on. **"What do you think the Occupy Wall Street protestors hope to accomplish, and are their actions justified?"**

Most of them will try to, but they don't have the power to make changes. Only Congress has the power to change the law.
—BRACHMAN MASTER TEACHER DR. HENRY PLOEGSTRA

I think that they want to bring awareness of what the Federal Reserve and federal government are doing. I think they're justified, but they're not being active. I think their actions downtown could be better placed. It's not all that productive.
—HISTORY INSTRUCTOR CLAIRE STRANGE

If protesting were a job, all of our problems would be fixed.
—JUNIOR JUSTIN HARVEY

I think that they're justified, but not in the way that they're going about it. —
JUNIOR BRENDAN FREEMAN

I think they're protesting taxes and trying to make America a more equal place. I support their protest. It's a free country, and they have the right to protest, and they're using it.
—SOPHOMORE MATTHEW BROWN

Around campus

▸ 'It's not torture. It's Russian!' — Marcus Master Teaching Chair Dr. Bruce Westrate to his sophomore history class members

▸ 'There has to be some way to harness the power of snot.' — Physics instructor Steven Houpt

▸ 'Most of the words coming out of my mouth have nothing to do with what I am trying to say.' — Math instructor Amy Pool

▸ 'Stop your infernal babbling before I rip off your arms and legs.' — Brachman Master Teacher Henry Ploegstra

▸ 'No, Mark. God bless you.' — Senior William McGee to junior Mark Senter after sneezing

WORD ON THE STREET coordinated by Rachit Mohan, staff writer | AROUND CAMPUS collected by Naeem Muscatwalla, editorial director

remarker

TALKING HEADS photo illustration by Robbey Orth, graphics director

remarker

editor-in-chief Nick Mahowald
managing editor Max Marshall
deputy managing editor Ross Crawford
issues editor Stephen Rambin
editorial director Naeem Muscatwalla
special projects editor Jairo Nevarez
business manager George Law
production manager Andrew Goodman
senior writer Will Moor
head photographer Parker Matthews

news editors Paul Gudmundsson, Sam Yonack
scene editors Alan Rosenthal, Noah Yonack
sports editors Evan Berkowitz, Daniel Hersh
deputy editorial director Henry Woram
assistant business manager John Caldwell

copy editors Ryan O'Meara, Mehdi Siddiqui
graphics directors Nic Lazarra, Robbey Orth
artists Dylan Kirksey, Zuyva Sevilla
photographers Halbert Bai, Otto Clark-Martinek, Michael Doorey, Richard Eiseman, Andrew Gatherer, Michael Gilliland, Andrew Graffy, Riley Graham, Justin Harvey, Conner Lynch, Max Naseck, Jay Park, Harrison Quarls, Charles Thompson, Max Wolens
staff writers Aarohan Burma, Chandler Burke, Dylan Clark, Tabish Dayani, Aidan Dewar, Cole Gerthoffer, Vishal Gokani, Charlie Golden, Isaiah Huerta, Sam Khoshbin, Ryan Miller, Rachit Mohan, Alexander Munoz, Jonathan Ng, Patrick Ng, Lee Perkins, Chris Roach, Umang Shah
staff assistants Kyle Campbell, Jacob Chernick, Matthew Conley, Forest Cummings-Taylor, Teddy Edwards, Cy Ganji, Gab Goncalves, Andrew Hatfield, Richard Jiang, Alex Kim, Shourya Kumar, Nabeel Muscatwalla, Jack O'Neill, Vik Pattabi, Ford Robinson
adviser Ray Westbrook

student newspaper of st. mark's school of texas • 10600 preston road • dallas, texas 75230 • 214.346.8000• www.smtexas.org/common/publications

Coverage. The *ReMarker* covers topics, issues, events and opinions of relevance and interest to the St. Mark's School of Texas community.

Letters. Send submissions to the editor at 10600 Preston Road, Dallas, 75230 or via email at remarker@smtexas.org. Letters should be brief and signed, although the writer may request anonymity. Letters may be rejected if libelous or obscene material is contained therein.

Editorials. The newspaper's opinion will be presented in each issue in the form of editorials, which are clearly labeled and appear on the Commentary pages.

Columns. Personal opinion is expressed through by-lined columns, which appear throughout the publication.

Advertising. Contact the business staff at 214.346.8145. We reserve the right to refuse any advertisement.

Distribution. Press run is 3,800 copies. Copies are provided free of charge to students, faculty and staff at various distribution sites on campus and at our sister school, The Hockaday School. More than 2,600 copies are mailed out to alumni courtesy of the school's offices of External Affairs, Development and Alumni divisions.

Membership. The *ReMarker* maintains membership in the Columbia Scholastic Press Association, New York City, NY; National Scholastic Press Association, Minneapolis, MN; and Interscholastic League Press Conference, Austin.

Online Viewing. Each issue of the *ReMarker*, along with archival copies, can be viewed online at the school's website, www.smtexas.org/common/publications.

Reader Involvement. The *ReMarker* encourages reader input through letters, guest columns and story ideas. Contact the appropriate editor for submissions. Suggestions will be given due consideration for future publication.

December 9, 2011

23

FIGURE 12.16 *ReMarker*, St. Mark's School of Texas, Dallas, Texas. Reproduced by permission of Ray Westbrook.

Labeled as "Commentary," these lively opinion pages present a variety of content, providing viewpoints from many people in the school. The left page features two columns with strong, tight head shots and clear labels for the columnists.

Each column also bears a headline relating to the content of that column's subject. The longer column includes a pull quote to help break up the text. A letter to the editor from an alum, a factoid on cellphone use and a staff-drawn editorial cartoon add visual interest to the page. The facing page features pro/con responses to a question posed to two faculty members; the story is accompanied by clever artwork. "Word on the Street" localizes a national news event by highlighting student voices on the topic. "Around Campus" features interesting quotes from classrooms. The staff masthead anchors the bottom of the page.

FIGURE 12.17 *The Octagon*, Sacramento Country Day School, Sacramento, Calif., pp. 6–7, Dec. 16, 2011. "A dangerous doze: Students turn to over-the-counter drugs as sleep aid," by Madeleine Wright. Reproduced by permission of Patricia Fels.

A double truck on the topic of students using drugs as sleeping aids effectively ties together a strong, well-cropped visual with a major story, a factoid sidebar, an advice sidebar and a student opinion bar running across the bottom. The page uses color effectively to connect the content areas across the page. The distinctive headline typography is repeated in all the headlines, creating further visual connection.

FIGURE 12.18 *North Star* (fhntoday.com), Francis Howell North High School, St. Charles, Mo. pp. 32–33, Nov. 16, 2011. Reproduced by permission of Aaron Manfull.

Excellent photo use attracts readers to this story of athletes' bus rides to competitions. The picture package includes a strong dominant image anchoring the spread, showing students having fun on a bus ride. The other pictures broaden the coverage by showing other athletes. A quote collection running vertically along the right side of the spread adds faces and voices to the coverage. Using picture packages of multiple pictures with stories is a great way to add reader interest, as well as visual perspective to the coverage.

FIGURE 12.19 *The Featherduster*, Westlake High School, Westlake, Texas. Vol. 43, Issue 1, front cover, Oct. 10, 2011. Photo illustration credited to Barrett Wilson. Reproduced by permission of Deanne Brown.

The use of four-color printing is common in many newspapers, especially in newsmagazines, which are usually printed on glossy paper. This four-color cover is effective in showcasing a story based on Apple product usage in the school. With faces shown on iPads, the photograph cleverly brings together the visual and verbal focus of the story's content. Without color, the photographic concept would not work as well in displaying the technology now driving education.

Visuals on the editorial pages will be primarily editorial cartoons, which should be used to help break up the text. Other options include **photo polls** in which many people are asked the same question, with responses edited to reflect the most interesting comments. Photo polls can feature small, tightly cropped head shots of the people whose responses are printed. The backgrounds and head sizes in these pictures should also be consistent. Some newspapers print short, 10-second editorials on a variety of issues, using a thumbs up/thumbs down design. Pro/con columns with author photos are another form of editorial contrasting. Letters to the editor or to the newspaper's web site will often appear on these pages.

The newspaper's **masthead**, the box containing a small reproduction of its flag, the school address and contact information and its staff listing should also appear in an organized area on the editorial page. The listing may include only the editors or everyone on the staff with their positions. The masthead should appear in a consistent place without being distracting or taking up too much space. Many staff also choose to include their editorial and advertising policies in small type as part of the masthead box, and may include information about submitting letters or other content to the staff.

The primary concern on the editorial page is preventing the pages from appearing too dense with text or from "graying out." Designers should seek to keep the pages interesting and visually appealing. Recruiting a good editorial cartoonist from the school's art department is often a good way to add visual interest on each editorial page by including a well-drawn, issue-oriented editorial cartoon in each issue.

Double trucks and centerspreads

The middle two pages of the paper are printed on one page surface, offering the designer many possibilities for treating the space as a single design unit. Large headlines can be placed across the **gutter**, the fold between the two pages, and visuals can be used in even larger sizes. Double trucks are usually devoted to topical, seasonal, issue-oriented or other feature coverage that justifies the space. A double truck doesn't have to be included each issue, but can be used when appropriate content is identified and reported.

Double-truck coverage should be built around large and significant visual display. Visual–verbal connections should be strong and appealing. A single, large visual will usually be more effective than a variety of smaller images. Using a flexible grid or column method offers possibilities for changing the width of text in different parts of the double truck to create contrast. Each part of the package should add to the overall presentation. Visual forms can be juxtaposed with strictly textual material. White space should also be a consideration. Filling up all corners of the page from top to bottom, left to right, will result in pages that look static and cluttered. Using extra white space around the visual or around the headline display will help provide balance on the page. Designers often work hand in hand with a team of writers, editors and photographers in making double-truck content engaging and appropriate. It's important to consider how the page topic can be broken up into coverage areas instead of merely using the space for one really long story. Double trucks are excellent space for picture pages especially from important school events such as homecoming, a play or an important school activity.

Sports pages

Sports page designs will often utilize large, action-packed pictures of teams in competitive situations on the field or court. Sports pages can also utilize sports brief columns providing capsulized summaries of teams' seasons as they progress. Features focusing on sports personalities, issues or controversies can enliven the sports pages, providing interesting and diverse coverage.

Picture use

Pictures give readers strong entry points to a page, and because they are important in design, photographs deserve special attention. Pictures in strong vertical or horizontal shapes are far more interesting than square shapes. People in photographs should be large enough so their heads are at least the size of a nickel. Static pictures of people posing for the camera are not as interesting as pictures showing people in natural situations (see Chapter 15 for more information on picture use).

Pictures shouldn't be an afterthought in the design, confined to small spaces in the corners of pages or layouts. Rather, designers should draw on the strength of good photographs, using them in significant sizes and in interesting positions. Careful attention to cropping will make strong pictures even stronger and more visually interesting.

Well-written, detailed captions add to the appeal of good pictures. Some readers will only read the picture caption without ever reading the story that accompanies it. Thin, **hairline** (.25

or .50 wide lines) or one pt rule lines placed around pictures in the design helps give them definition on the pages, especially if the picture's edges are white or light.

Using color effectively

Just as in professional newspapers, color is common in school newspapers. **Spot color** – the use of a single color in design – is a less expensive way of using color than **four-color**. Four-color refers to the four process colors: (1) magenta or red, (2) cyan or blue, (3) yellow and (4) black. It requires the page to be run through four different presses, applying one of the colors each time.

Spot color

Newspaper printers may offer a particular spot color called **run of the press (ROP)** at an even cheaper price. ROP color simply means the printer will use the color already on the press. Unfortunately, the color used will not be the staff's decision, often resulting in weak, less effective color design. For instance, if the printer is already printing a publication with yellow spot color ink and uses it in your publication for the nameplate or for display type, the weak color may not be strong enough to lead the reader's eyes to the type displays that you've designated as color in your design.

When used effectively, planned spot color can create unity through the publication. Warm, strong colors such as red and orange are good choices for signaling important visual elements such as headlines and standing headlines. Cool colors, such as green and blue, will be weaker visual signals. Lighter percentages of warm colors work well to display content in "screened boxes," when the designer is seeking to separate the content and draw the reader's eyes to it.

Designers should be careful to avoid overusing color, particularly spot color, by using it for every headline in the publication, page or spread. Inappropriate use in headlines can affect the reader's perception of the story's content and news value. Body text in color will slow down the reader's processing of information and could reduce readability.

Some colors simply do not work well as spot colors. For example, yellow is difficult to read and will create weaker, less visible content. The most agreeable combination for story text is black on white. Reverse type, white on black, slows down the reader and creates densely inked areas in the newspaper owing to the porous nature of most newsprint.

Four-color

Four-color is expensive to produce and, because of the way a newspaper is printed, can only be used on certain pages without incurring additional costs. It has benefits – four-color photos attract readers, and four-color ads generate more ad revenue – but four-color has drawbacks as well. Color photographs must be submitted as digital files as part of the page designs. Also, the cheap quality of newsprint results in high color saturation, and the off-white color of the newsprint can distort hue and tone. But with almost all professional publications using color consistently, many high school publications strive to use color in every issue, even if just for photographs. Advertisers requesting color for ads can sometimes help bear the cost of color used elsewhere in the newspaper, but news content and value should always be a major consideration when designing with color. In other words, don't use color simply because it's an option. Pictures taken in color but printed in black-and-white should be converted to grayscale and toned appropriately for best printing during production.

PACING THE NEWSPAPER'S DESIGN

Designers should be involved in every step of the content development for each issue. Teams of writers, editors, photographers and designers can improve the publication's narrative power. Publications that feature flexible and varied storytelling forms provide superior experiences for their readers. For example, a photo spread with a succinctly written story and detailed captions may provide all the information necessary and be far more interesting than a traditional textual

FIGURE 12.20 *Central Times*, Naperville High School, Naperville, Ill, Oct. 26, 2010, p.14. Photo courtesy of Russell Harper. Reproduced by permission of Keith Carlson.

    Writers, editors and designers should team up to find opportunities for creative visual storytelling. Doing so helps pace the reader's experience of the publication. The back page of this newspaper is used in a new way each issue to showcase interesting content. Here, the visual relates to a question posed to students about dreams. The visual treatment is both visually striking and relevant to the content.

Design tips to keep in mind

→ Mixing alignments can create visual contrast and draw the reader's attention to particular stories. A primary story in left-aligned type will create contrast and comparison for that story in relation to others on the page or spread.

→ Headlines need a strong visual voice. Using bold, sans serif typefaces will help organize the headline information and create strong reader entry points into story leads.

→ Reverse type and screened type can reduce readability. The use of such devices should be limited.

→ Boxing, framing or screening elements should be employed only when the content dictates their use. Such techniques bring the reader's attention to the story's content in a strong way. Try to avoid boxing more than one story on a page, or the reader will see a conflicting and confused visual hierarchy. Boxing works well for packaged content.

→ Column widths of 10 to 20 picas are generally preferred for ease of readability.

→ Captions are most effective when placed underneath or to one side of the pictures they describe. A contrasting typeface for the caption helps to create contrast with body type.

→ Packaging summary stories such as news briefs and clubs' briefs into well-written, tightly edited reports will result in higher readability than a series of stories separately placed on a page. Adding an occasional, tightly cropped photo adds interest.

→ Every page needs a dominant visual entry point placed prominently on the page, preferably near the top.

→ Screens of color or black behind text slow down the reader's eyes and should be used sparingly. Screens should be kept to lighter percentages, such as 20 to 30 percent. Coarse screens with visible dots per inch will also create reading static. Designers using laser printers should increase the dots or (lines per inch) in the printing command to keep dot patterns light and less distracting.

→ After completing designs, print them and hang them on a wall. View them at arm's length, as readers will do. Evaluate their effectiveness using the design principles. Make sure the design creates clear and logical reading patterns and makes best use of available design elements.

presentation. Or, in a story about the costs of athletic programs, a good informational graphic showing how much money is spent on an athletic uniform, from jerseys to shoes, might be a more interesting way of telling that story without any, or a minimal amount of, traditional text accompanying the presentation.

Creating teams in the student newsroom will improve discussions of content and storytelling. These teams can also help prevent layouts from slipping into predictable story counts or designs from issue to issue, or page to page, within the same issue. Involving different kinds of story-tellers in decision making, from writers and editors to photographers and designers, will ensure that all options are considered. Individuals will feel more empowered in the process, and no one's skills will be under-utilized.

CONCLUSION

Design is as important to the newspaper as is good writing and reporting. Without a strong and consistent visual look, a newspaper simply fails to engage its readers. Newspaper staff who involve photographers and other visual thinkers in the process of initiating stories and content will have multiple options when the time comes for laying out pages.

SUMMARY

● A well-designed newspaper is important in helping readers to process information, understand news value and determine importance.

● Planning before designing can help achieve effective designs under deadline pressure.

● News designers can use software tools to create flexible gridded templates, typography style sheets and libraries to maintain consistency for designers and issue to issue.

● Designers rely on design principles to help achieve interesting, balanced designs.

● Parts of the newspaper need special attention to ensure successful designs.

● Color is an important tool in design that adds to reader interest.

KEY TERMS

alley	informational graphics	scale
balance	internal margins	screen
border	LPI	sidebars
broadsheets	masthead	spot color
columns or grids	modular design	standing heads
digests	newsmagazines	style sheets
dog leg design	page dummy	tabloids
external margins	photo poll	text heads
folio	presentation director	unity
four-color	proportion	visual hierarchy
gray out	rails	white space
gutter	rhythm	
hairline	run of the press (Rop)	

EXERCISES

1 Take an issue of the local or community newspaper and evaluate its use of design principles, including balance, rhythm, unity, scale, proportion and visual hierarchy.

2 Using a local or community newspaper, find examples of packaged content, including a single picture and story; two or more pictures and story; and two or more story forms and illustration. Examine each package and notice how the reader's eyes are brought into the package. Notice what visual design devices were used in distinguishing the packaged content from the rest of the page. Compare the design to how it was handled on the website.

3 In a copy of a local newspaper, indicate the front-page's margins by drawing lines around them. Using a different color pen, indicate the width of the paper's grids or columns. Measure the widths using a pica ruler and mark the widths of the columns on the page. Then measure the widths of the vertical and horizontal internal margins and mark them on the page. Note any variations in these internal margins between unrelated content areas. Draw boxes around each individual story package and note whether the design is modular. Do the same with an inside page that contains ads.

4 Look through several copies of exchange newspapers from other schools. Find examples of pages that you think are well designed. Write a short paragraph explaining what makes the pages successful and attractive. Find examples of pages that are poorly designed. Write a short paragraph explaining what makes these pages less successful in design.

5 Find examples of pages in professional or school newspapers that use strong vertical and horizontal photographs. Analyze each picture's use in the paper: How is the picture's size and content used in the design? Does the picture caption add to the information obtained from reading the story? Is the picture strong enough to serve as a visual entry point for the reader?

6 Find an example of a double truck in your school newspaper or in an exchange newspaper from another school. Answer these questions: Is there a central visual entry point? Is it typographic, illustrative, photographic or a combination? Is the page well balanced? Is the text material sufficiently divided so it maintains interest without "graying out"? Is the content deserving of the space and effort needed to tell the story?

7 Find a page in a local newspaper or in your school newspaper that uses only spot color. Is the color used effectively? Does it make visual connections in its repeated use? Is the color distracting from the content of the page?

Next, find a page that uses four-color. Is the color used effectively? Is the color used in more than just photographs on the page? Where else has it been used? Is the color creating distractions or adding to the appeal of the design?

Next, compare both color pages to a black-and-white page. Which do you prefer? Why?

8 Find a page in a newspaper featuring stories of varied column widths. Measure the widths of the columns with a pica ruler and write their widths on the page. Are the narrowest and widest columns between the recommended 10 to 20 picas? Are the widths readable and attractive in the design? Do they help provide contrast in the content?

YEARBOOK DESIGN

13

> *An effective yearbook design, just like an effective design for any medium, must deliver visual and verbal content in a way that invites readership. Since the target audience for scholastic yearbooks is 13 to 18 years old, the design also needs to be contemporary and energetic, but not at the expense of readability.*

Gary Lundgren, Jostens Publishing Company, Senior Program Manager/Education

---

LEARNING OBJECTIVES
After completing this chapter you will be able to:

- organize and prioritize the reporting and design process for the yearbook

- create visually interesting and factually accurate yearbook spreads

- utilize a variety of storytelling forms for maintaining pacing throughout the book

- represent the varied populations in the school through fair and equitable coverage

- include strong narrative accounts of events throughout the year that incorporate many student voices in quotes and callouts

- supplement the printed yearbook with multimedia content in sound and video, to provide complete coverage of the year's events.

Scholastic Journalism, Twelfth Edition. C. Dow Tate and Sherri A. Taylor.
© 2014 John Wiley & Sons, Inc. Published 2014 by John Wiley & Sons, Inc.

SMALL GROUPS OF STUDENTS LINGER in the hallways and classrooms, gathered around freshly-printed books that still smell of ink. Stopping to admire themselves or their friends, they erupt into spontaneous laughter as they relive memories of the school year. It must be yearbook delivery day, when students catch their first glimpse of these much anticipated volumes.

A historical record of the year, a yearbook seeks to capture the sights, sounds and memories of the school year, in a volume that fairly and accurately represents the diverse interests of the students.

Yearbook designs usually have a contemporary and innovative look. Most schools start fresh each year, drastically changing the book's design. Yearbook staff re-evaluate everything from typeface and photo specifications to the use of alternative visual and verbal storytelling forms. Most state and national scholastic organizations encourage innovation in the yearbook's design in their judging standards.

Despite this emphasis on innovation, the principles of good yearbook design remain intact: quality photographs that capture students involved in meaningful events and activities; well-written, informative copy that contributes to a narrative of the year; complete and accurate caption information and informative and well-designed headline displays.

The organization of the book has become a focus for experimentation by yearbook staff. Many have moved away from clichéd, catchphrase themes and toward graphic or single-word unifiers. Some staffs have rejected the traditional yearbook sections and have chosen to place content in as few as three sections. Using the theme "Three Times Over," the *Deka* staff of Huntington North High School in Indiana divided the book into sections titled "Pleasure," "Power" and "Prosperity." Each of the three sections accommodated two of the book's traditional sections. Other staff have organized sections around different senses, such as sight, smell, touch. Still others have opted to organize the book chronologically, from summer vacation to the last day of school. (For many staff, chronological organization facilitates deadline schedules.)

No matter how your yearbook is organized and unified, it's important to understand the elements that lead to successful and attractive page designs.

SPEAKING THE LANGUAGE

Exploring design terminology will help you understand and implement yearbook design techniques.

WWW

WEBLINKS Check out

www.studentpress.org/nspa

This site maintained by the National Scholastic Press Association (NSPA), a membership-based organization, offers valuable examples of yearbooks at this header: NSPA view/ contests and critiques.

FIGURE 13.1 *Etruscan 2011,* yearbook, Glenbrook South High School, Glenview, Ill., p. 88. Reproduced by permission of Brenda Field.

A non-traditional spread on the use of social media by students is a relevant and contemporary topic for coverage. Though the spread's design lacks a traditional dominant photo and copy block, the coverage and layout provides a nice break from the book's standard design.

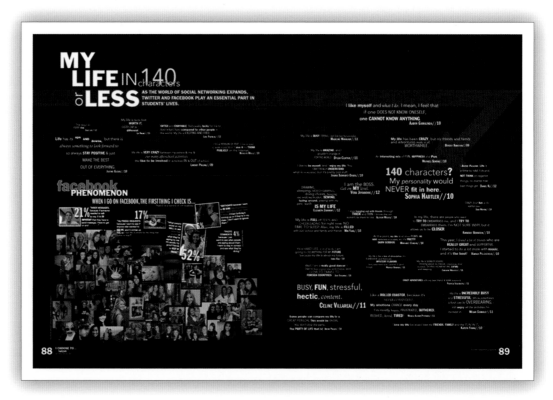

FIGURE 13.2 *The Indian,* yearbook, Shawnee Mission North High School, Overland Park, Kan. Reproduced by permission of Shawnee Mission North High School Principal Richard Kramer.

Page elements found in yearbook spreads are identified in this example: (A) graphics; (B) bleed; (C) headline; (D) body copy; (E) gutter; (F) folio; (G) internal margin; (H) caption; (I) external margin.

- **Body copy:** the main narrative text that verbally tells the story on the page and usually appears near the main headline on the page or spread. Additional, usually smaller, stories can also appear in alternative forms that could include sidebars, infographics, question and answer formats, first-person accounts, bio boxes, charts and diagrams, pull quotes and factoids. Often, these alternative forms of copy are used to supplement traditional text stories. Several forms can appear on a single spread to amplify the overall story. If more than one alternative form is used, each should add additional information and should vary in presentation.

- **Bleeds:** photographs that cover page gutters or that cover external margins and align with page edges.

- **Captions or cutlines:** the text accompanying pictures that describes their content. Complete captions identify the principal people pictured (full name and grade in school), state what they are doing (in present tense) and can add detail, background or results (which can be written in past tense). Captions may include a quote from one of the people pictured (usually following the description). Captions should vary in construction to avoid a predictable, templated construction.

- **Divider pages:** a single page or spread that uses a distinctive design and introduces the beginning of another part of the book. Traditionally, sections of a yearbook include theme, class portraits, student life or activities, clubs and organizations, academics, sports, ads and the index. Many contemporary yearbooks replace traditional sections with a variety of short features blending content from several traditional sections.

- **Dominant image:** the largest image on a page or spread, and the strongest storytelling element of the content. Dominant images should be significantly larger than the next largest photo, generally by a ratio of 2:1 or greater.

- **Drop caps:** oversized introductory initial letters that drop into the first few lines of the story to lead readers to the beginning of the text. The typography in the drop cap should match the largest or boldest type in the headline for strong visual repetition. Other forms of capped letters include **rising caps**, oversized letters that sit on the first baseline of text and rise into white space above the text, and side caps. **Side caps** appear in narrow margins to the left of the beginning of the text.

- **External margins:** the white space on all four sides of a layout used to showcase the content.

- **Eyeline:** an area of alignment that continues across both pages on a spread, helping connect the pages into a single unit. Many designers build eyelines into section templates.

- **Folios and page numbers:** page numbers should go to the outside edges of the pages, but folios can be expanded to include information such as specific page and section content. Some staff add appropriately themed graphics or small student pictures to their folios.

- **Graphics:** lines, borders, screens, colors, textures, illustrations and other elements – all of which create visual continuity when used consistently in design.

- **Grids or columns:** a series of equal or unequal design spaces created between the margins to guide placement of content. Horizontal columns, called rows, can also be defined on layouts to create smaller modules for packaging content.

- **Gutter margin:** the area of space between the pages where the book is bound. Gutter space should be taken into consideration when a photo bleeds or goes across the gutter. Faces and key photo action, as well as typography, should appear outside of the gutters. Templates should be adequately designed to keep content out of the gutters when the book is bound.

- **Headlines:** the largest display of type on a page or spread that focuses the reader's attention on the page content. Headlines are often combinations of **primary headlines** – those that are largest in the design and often created as a design unit – and secondary headlines. **Secondary headlines** should use primarily nouns and verbs to add detail and expand the reader's knowledge. Secondary headlines are often referred to as deck heads in professional design. It is common to see multiple forms of headlines in contemporary yearbook design. A variety of headline sizes and styles helps guide the reader.

- **Internal margins:** margins between columns or grids that separate content.

- **Spread:** two facing pages. Yearbook designers usually design spreads instead of individual pages.

- **Spread unity:** elements that connect two facing pages so they are visually perceived as one design unit. These can include pictures bleeding across the gutter, graphic devices such as color, lines or background textures or headlines that span the pages.

- **Theme:** a verbal statement that is used and repeated in key elements of the book to unify its design. Often a catchphrase, the theme is chosen by the staff because it relates to something about the school or the year's events. The traditional areas in which themes appear include the cover, the **endsheets**, the heavier paper that hides binding at the front and back of the book, the opening pages, the divider pages and the closing pages. Theme

Quick Exercise

Bring copies of several types of magazines to class – men's and women's magazines, special interest publications and weekly newsmagazines. Identify the following items by using a colored pen to draw boxes around the items, labeling each:

- external margins

- internal margins between columns

- headlines

- type columns

- page folios

- dominant visual element

- captions.

WORDS of WISDOM

Yearbooks preserve the history of the school and the personal history of each person who was a part of it in the form of a book. When we create a yearbook, we create a product that people love and cherish forever. Those who buy yearbooks keep them and refer to them throughout their lives. They pass those books to their children and grandchildren.

Although some may argue that online social media have replaced the traditional yearbook, those who buy the book are able to return to that book again and again, remembering those great times they spent with their friends … long after some of the social media sites have disappeared.

Laura Schaub, Journalism Professor Emerita, University of Oklahoma

design can also be integrated into various sections of the book through special features or through "mini-themes" that play off the theme phrase.

In recent years, many staff have experimented with using devices other than traditional catchphrases to unify the book. These devices can include graphics, colors, logos or combinations of these.

- **Visual hierarchy:** a clear sense of size, proportion, scale and content that leads the reader through the design in a coherent way. Readers' eyes should be moved through the content, often following a **Z reading pattern** that starts at the upper left and continues to bottom right.

- **Visual continuity:** design factors that keep a section of the book coherent and unified and which distinguish it from other sections of the book. These factors can include color, graphics, particular typefaces and grid or column structures. The integration of content in a section can also create visual continuity.

Test your knowledge

What tools can a designer use to keep a yearbook contemporary and interesting to the student reader?

GETTING READY TO DESIGN

A yearbook designer begins with a page area set to the size of the finished book. This size ranges from 7.7 × 10.5 inches to 8.5 × 11 inches to 9 × 12 inches. While it's traditional for the yearbook to be printed as a horizontal book, some staffs have even experimented with the standard sizes by turning the books vertically and having the books bound on the narrow side.

Once the designer knows the book's trim size, margins can be created. **Progressive margins** – those narrowest at the gutter and widest on the bottom margin – are traditional in magazine and yearbook design. Margins provide white space that frames page content in a consistent manner and allow for placement of page folios. Folios traditionally appear in the bottom margins but could appear in other locations.

After the margins are set, the designer then decides on a grid or column structure, which will provide the skeletal structure for laying out the content. Generally, a designer should stop an element on every margin at least one time in a spread to define that margin or make it visible in the skeletal page structure. Stopping content between the margin and the outside edge of the page will confuse the reader by blurring the margin's structure. When content (usually pictorial) does extend into the margins, this is referred to as bleeding. Bleeding copy can be a problem for the printer and for the reader, since some of the verbal content could be lost in the gutter when the book is bound.

Most schools use design programs such as Adobe's InDesign or customized software programs, which might include special templates and other features offered by the publishing company or printer of the book. These customized features allow designers to work more easily with the elements of the yearbook's design. They also enable the designers to set their own margins, grids or columns and rows. Rows differ from grids or columns in that they create horizontal guidelines – another option for designers to use to align elements across pages and through sections of the book. Most yearbook publishers offer online design platforms, allowing students to connect directly to work on the same spread from multiple locations.

Not all designers use strict column grids or structures in design. Some choose to create free-form designs in which pictures and other page elements are placed without regard to grids or columns. While this can be a successful design strategy when used by experienced designers, most beginners find it easier to design yearbooks within a grid structure.

Many professional magazines use three- or four-column designs as standard structures throughout their publications. Yearbook designers often find greater freedom by experimenting with a series of narrower grids, often as narrow as four or five picas wide. Using a narrower grid pattern allows a yearbook designer to combine columns and internal margins to create a variety of content widths. Narrower column grids are particularly useful for display elements, which could include:

- **Visual-verbal separators:** use of a narrow column as an **isolation element** void of content
- **Display space:** use of a column to draw attention to a typographic or picture element
- **Alternative copy space:** use of a column for alternative, contrasting content.

In recent years, student designers have created **section templates** for yearbook design. Style sheets for the design of individual sections of the book can include a basic column structure, headline style, alternative copy style and a format for the layout. These style sheets can be turned into templates and saved in the desktop publishing program to aid designers.

FIGURE 13.3 *Hauberk*, Shawnee Mission East High School, Prairie Village, Kan. Reproduced by permission of C. Dow Tate.

A multiple-column grid is evident in this sports spread. The copy at the top of the right page is set in two columns, while the picture area below it shows use of a five-column grid – three columns for the left picture, two for the right. The bottom sidebar uses an eight-column grid. Using multiple grids offers designers a variety of options for placing content in modular, four-sided shapes. Multiple columns also allow for different content widths, creating visual variety. A wider margin to the left of the copy creates isolation for the strong dominant image.

FIGURE 13.4 *Tonitrus*, yearbook, Rocklin High School, Rocklin, Calif. Reprinted by permission of Casey Nichols.

a Covering the school year in a chronological format has become a popular way of organizing yearbooks. In this format, calendar divider pages open spreads of blended section coverage, offering smaller stories on a variety of topics. This opening spread is more than just a divider, providing content of its own based on the popular social media site Facebook and its use of personal status updates.

b Starting with a series of narrow rows and columns helps designers create modular designs. This spread has been created in six modules. Note how each module varies both in copy and picture presentation. Modules vary between horizontal and vertical presentations. Topics provide coverage of sports, popular cultural trends, student dances and a new field turf. Additionally, extra internal space has been used to help separate modules, but within the modules themselves, thinner spaces are used for related content. The left page's module provides a dominant visual area for the spread.

In addition to saving the skeletal page structure, a page designer can create a type template so text brought in from a wordprocessing program can be "styled" to the typeface choices, sizes and alignments for that section to ensure uniformity. These choices can be defined for both character and paragraph styles. Additionally desktop publishing software enables designers to create "libraries," electronic storage areas for visual or typographic elements.

Section templates can save a lot of time for individual designers but can also result in a heavily stylized section that compromises picture quality and creates visual redundancy. Therefore, designers should be careful to keep the templates flexible. They should be able to base their picture placement decisions on the content of pictures, rather than pre-set picture shapes or sizes on the template.

FIGURE 13.5 *The Decamhian,* yearbook, Del Campo High School, Fair Oaks, Calif., pp. 55–56. Reproduced by permission of Jim Jordan.

Experimentation is the topic of this Academics spread of blended coverage. Rather than covering each subject taught in the school, yearbook staff designed content around concepts common to several curricula. Three modules appear on the spread, each one detailing a specific way in which experimentation drives learning. (On other spreads in the section, noun topics included creation, communication and production.) The spread graphics included a lowercase e (for experimentation), which extends to the edge of a red box at the bottom of the page, and a large "experimentation" headline, specifying the unifying topic.

WEBLINKS Check out www.columbia.edu/ccu/cspa

This site is maintained by the Columbia Scholastic Press Association, a membership-based national high school and college press association in New York. It links to images of its crown award winners.

Quick Exercise

What method of organizing your yearbook's sections is used in your most recent edition? Do you think it's effective? Can you think of topics or content that could be included?

Content should be a primary consideration for yearbook designers. Staff must decide how they want to tell stories, considering page allocation and various storytelling forms. Pacing is also an important consideration. For instance, big events during the school year – homecoming, prom, a winning sports season or other school celebrations – might need more than one spread in the book. In those cases, the best way to tell the story might be through two to three carefully planned layouts that continue the coverage just as a magazine might do. This coverage is often referred to as "jump" coverage since the coverage jumps from spread to spread.

Other, daily student life topics such as transportation or after-school jobs, might be better covered through a single page or through a traditional double-page spread. Many schools give clubs single pages of coverage. Tackling a serious issue that is relevant to the school or a big celebration such as an anniversary might call for a special, multi-spread section. Designers need flexibility in the space they assign to different topics.

Content can also be organized around general topics such as school spirit (in Student Life) or field trips (in Clubs/Organizations). Individual stories on a school spirit spread could include different expressions of school spirit, including cheerleading, pep rallies, decorations and a photo poll with quotes from spirited students on game day. A page on field trips could feature blended coverage from several academic groups' and clubs' excursions and include quotes from participants. The spread might also feature pictures taken by those in attendance, including students, teachers and chaperones.

Yearbook designers also have to be aware of storytelling forms. Consider a story on different modes of student transportation. Having photographers take pictures of cars in the parking lot is not the way to tell this story. Good pictures need people in them. Doing a series of individual vignettes of student drivers and their unusual cars with bio boxes of relevant information (such as where the student got the car, how much it costs to maintain and the most unusual thing about it) might make that topic one worth covering. Photographs of the cars either in interesting settings or with very simple backgrounds (to best display the their distinctive features) would be preferable to crowded, busy shots from the school parking lot.

Every event that happens during the year should be considered for its storytelling potential before any attempt is made to design a spread. Content in the book should also evolve from year to year. Cultural trends mark change. Several years ago, yearbook staff started covering trends such as students using MP3 players and shopping online. Now both of those topics are rather dated, and have been replaced by social media and social issue coverage. A careful evaluation of

WORDS of Wisdom

A really great yearbook has a great vision. The vision creates a sense of purpose and focus. When kids "see" the final product in their imaginations and attend to the details, the result is nothing short of extraordinary. Dr. Stephen Covey set forth the principle: The main thing is to keep the main thing the main thing.

Distractions abound in our lives and in our yearbook rooms. A great staff is not distracted from their creative focus.

Judi Coolidge, Education and Marketing, Balfour Yearbooks; Former Yearbook Adviser, Bay Village High School, Ohio

NEWSFLASH

Effective use of white space

Traditionally, internal spacing tends to be consistent, generally about one pica. Leaving consistent internal spacing usually results in more organized and readable layouts. But there might be a reason to increase or decrease this space.

- **Isolation**: To isolate content such as sidebars and make them more visible in the design, a designer might double or triple the internal margin separation between the sidebar material and any other element.

- **Connection**: To connect a small group of photos (usually two or three) as a strong unit, often referred to as a picture package, a designer might want to tighten the internal margins by cutting them in half, leaving less than a pica of separation. Common narrow spacing choices would be .75, .5 or a hairline space, generally .25.

Using available magazines or yearbooks, look for examples of consistent spacing, as well as instances where the designer has changed the spacing to isolate or connect content.

---

the book's content needs should be made by the entire staff at the beginning of the year. Flexibility should also be built into this system so the staff can appropriately cover unforeseen events as they occur during the year. Unexpected and current events that occur outside of school may need to be covered if they affect students. Cultural trends often make their way into yearbooks through polls and surveys. Important to the time period, cultural trends also date the year in ways that grow in importance as years pass.

> **Test your knowledge**
>
> What are three ways to utilize white space on yearbook pages?

DESIGNING THE PAGES

A designer needs to have all the component parts before beginning the design. Carefully edited pictures that show varied content, different people, strong compositional styles and combinations of both vertical and horizontal forms, will help in creating an appealing design. The designer could work from the section template with the typographic styles also defined and saved as part of the template. It's always a good idea to start by sketching a small design on a layout sheet from the publisher or even on a blank piece of paper. Thinking on paper first will often make your final design stronger. Or, printing out the possible pictures for a layout and physically moving them around each other is a good way to begin the design process.

FIGURE 13.6 *The Indian,* yearbook, Shawnee Mission North High School, Overland Park, Kan. Reproduced by permission of Shawnee Mission North Principal Richard Kramer.

Using the extreme horizontal crop of this spectacular wrestling photo to full advantage, the staff created a commanding dominant photo by letting it bleed off three sides of the spread. Flexible section templates that allow designers options in photo placement tend to result in stronger photo displays. This picture commands immediate viewer attention.

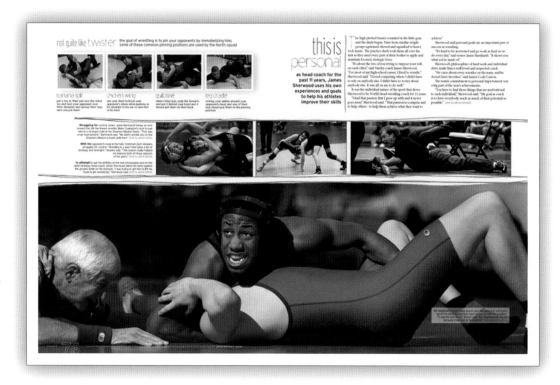

Once the page content has been set, the photographs should be collected, and decisions should be made about their use. These decisions should include the following:

- Choose the dominant image. This should be the most compelling photographic choice. Close-ups, emotion-filled shots, strong angles and interesting content will always draw a reader's attention. Select the picture that best accomplishes this. Photo editing is most successful when done in consultation with the photographer. (See Chapter 15, Visual Storytelling, for more information on choosing and editing pictures.)

- Edit supporting images. Eliminate pictures that show the same or similar content, pictures that show someone who has already been depicted in the same activity and pictures of poor quality, such as those that are out of focus or have backgrounds that interfere with the subject matter. Decide how many images you want to place on the spread – that is, how many you need to tell the story. Additional editing considerations include avoiding the use of multiple pictures with the same number of people in them or those with only one person in them, and eliminating pictures shot from the same camera angle or with the same lens. A good story needs close-ups, super close-ups, detail shots, wide angles, medium shots and long shots.

- Be particularly careful when using small-sized photos. Some staff strive to include more students (a worthy goal) by increasing the number of photos. However, this can lead to some photos becoming "postage-stamped" in size, too small to add any real value to the book. Small-sized photos should be carefully chosen and cropped to best showcase content. Generally, groups of people don't work well in small-sized photos, which reduce their faces to unidentifiable sizes. (See sidebar, "The Nickel Rule.")

- Look for both strong horizontal and vertical images. Avoid square-shaped pictures. Experiment with cropping using a good photo editing software such as Adobe Photoshop. Picture content can often be enhanced by removing "dead" areas of the image, which detract from the subject. This might include cropping to upper body action in sports such as tennis, volleyball and basketball.

- Begin design by choosing the dominant image. In traditional design, a dominant image would be two to three times larger than any other supporting picture. Recent trends indicate that staff are using dominant pictures in smaller size ratios to allow for the integration of more images on the page.

Preferably, the picture's focus should face the gutter rather than off the page, keeping "eyeflow" on the page. Some designers are allowed to ask the photographer to merely "flop" or "flip" the image on the layout if the picture isn't facing into the page. Doing so is an ethical compromise. It's better for the designer to use the original direction of the image. Another content consideration should be whether the picture bleeds across the gutter. The designer must be sure that important content, such as faces or action, won't be printed in the gutter, where it will be trapped in the binding and impossible to see.

- Plan for the placement of the picture's caption. Readers prefer captions placed adjacent to the pictures they describe, generally beneath or beside the picture. Move one pica (or the internal gutter) away from the picture and indicate where the caption will be, and type the caption or import it from its wordprocessing file.

Two captions can be stacked one pica apart, but when three captions are stacked together, the reader will have a harder time matching the captions with their pictures. Designers should also avoid placing captions or credits for the picture's photography directly on top of pictures. Unless there is a consistent, even tonal area for placement, the type could become unreadable. Also, the content of the picture can be compromised when the caption or other type is placed on top of it.

Cluster captions, in which all the captions for a set of images are grouped together in a single block, is usually a weak technique. Readers often have a hard time figuring out which caption goes with which image, and may choose to completely ignore what they perceive as a dense block of small, hard-to-read type. Adding numbering information or color contrasts to mark the beginning of each caption may increase the readability of cluster captions.

Captions should conform to the standard column widths of the spread. An exception might be a caption appearing in a single, narrow column next to a photo. Another option for distinguishing a section's style through captions is to use caption lead-ins, a specifically designed typographical element that provides what is essentially a headline for the caption and visually directs the reader to its contents.

Captions and text should never be placed in the gutter since words trapped in the gutter could become unreadable. Designers who want a headline to move across the gutter should probably design the headline so the words stop at the gutter margin on the

WWW

WEBLINKS Check out www.balfour.com/yearbooks/, www.jostens.com, www.yearbooks.biz (Herff Jones), www.yearbooksLifetouch.com, www.walsworthyearbooks.com

These five sites are links to the five primary yearbook publishing companies and contain a variety of helpful resources. Some content requires a customer sign-on name and password.

FIGURE 13.7 *Pilot,* yearbook, Redondo Union High School, Redondo Beach, Calif. Reproduced by permission of Mitch Ziegler.

Using the same bold condensed, sans serif typeface used in the primary headline, this design connects that typeface to each caption's opening words. Type shape repetition and/or color repetition are both strong visual connectors in design, helping the reader see each caption.

left page and start again at the gutter margin on the right page. Using heads bleeding across the gutter requires careful attention.

- When placing the second photo, the designer typically separates it from the dominant image by only one pica, generally the size of the internal margins. Stay on the column guides and use a combination of columns that allows the photograph to be showcased effectively without compromising its content. Continue to use strong vertical and horizontal crops.

- Continue to place the pictures in the layout until a pleasing arrangement has been created. The designer should also place the body text from the wordprocessing program, making sure that the line lengths are readable and that the story is laid out in modular form. Copy in multicolumn grid formats should use a combination of columns that allows for ease of readability, generally widths between 10 and 20 picas.

Choosing where to position the headline in the layout will be one of the designer's most important decisions. While it is traditional for headlines to be placed above their stories, a headline can appear next to the text, underneath it, jutting into it or dropping into it in a "well" arrangement, sunken between two or more columns of type. If a nontraditional headline placement is chosen, the designer should take advantage of a typographic device such as a strong drop cap that echoes the dominant headline style to focus the reader's attention to the beginning of the story.

As the designer works, attention should be given to placing white space so it appears toward the outside edges of the layout, rather than trapped between page elements, unless isolation techniques are used. Grouping pictures together and placing captions in outlying areas creates strong page eyeflow.

Most schools now use digital cameras to shoot images. Photographers can directly upload their photos onto the yearbook's file server so the designers can place the images in the designs. The value of digital photos is that the designer can preview their actual size and position on screen as the design is being created. Designers can make sure that faces are not trapped in the gutter, that pictures are cropped effectively and that content in the photos works well together on the spread without repetition.

Photographers should make sure they shoot at image resolutions appropriate for the sizes of the images as they will be used in the book. They should also follow yearbook printer recommendations for digital file formats. The preference is usually JPEGS.

FIGURE 13.8 *Wings,* yearbook, Arrowhead Christian Academy, Redlands, Calif., pp. 48–49. Reproduced by permission of Crystal Kazmierski.

Moving headlines to different positions on spreads keeps readers' eyes in motion. Dominant positions and distinctive typefaces also create strong visual hierarchy, attracting readers to headlines. Using modern magazine techniques, yearbooks aren't limited to placing headlines only above copy, but can use other placements including positions in which the headline interrupts the copy. The large, all-capital headline typeface here makes this pattern effective.

IN ACTION

The nickel rule

As yearbook designers have added more pictures to their layouts, picture sizes have been diminished. To help you decide if a picture will work in a particular space, try this exercise. Take last year's yearbook and a dime and nickel. Go through the book and see if you can cover up the faces in pictures with the dime. If the individual faces in a photo can be covered by the dime, the picture is probably too small to have much impact on the page or with viewers.

Now try it with the nickel. If the faces are about the size of the nickel, they will be large enough to have impact on readers.

What does this mean for designers? Small pictures should feature fewer people and tighter cropping.

Think about this, too. Designers often use very small photos just to identify the source of a quote. Such pictures should be tightly cropped around the subjects' heads – right above the top of the hair, below the chin and next to the ears. Try it.

Also, keep the nickel rule in mind when cropping group shots. Those pictures are used to identify team members. Can the faces really be seen? If not, they aren't providing identification for the reader.

SPECIAL CONSIDERATIONS

Some yearbook content needs to be considered in relationship to its unique needs. These content areas will work more effectively in the book if their unique needs are addressed by designers early on in the book's planning stages.

- Portrait pages require designers to work with large blocks of student portraits, usually shot by a studio photographer contracted by the school district. These pictures are generally arranged as a single vertical or horizontal block on each page, with narrow rule lines placed between the photos for separation. Place name blocks to the outside edges of the pictures in first name/last name arrangement.

  If portraits are shot by different photographers in the school's community, it is especially important for the yearbook staff to work with the photographers to keep the head sizes in the pictures consistent. Differing head sizes on the pages will create distracting images.

- In **sports** and **clubs sections**, or in album sections which many yearbooks now use for group shots, pictures should be laid out as horizontals or in the arrangement in which they were photographed, and should be cropped tightly so no extraneous visual information appears with the group. Careful coordination is required between the group-shot photographer and the page designers to ensure the group shot shapes will work on the layouts. If the photographer arranges the group in a strong vertical design, the designer will have to accommodate that shape on the layout, which could pose problems. In attempting to make the pictures larger, to show the individual faces of the club or sport members, many staff have moved the group shots to separate sections. These might be at the ends of clubs and sports sections, at the end of the book or placed within the index or ad sections. These spreads allow readers to thumb through "albums" of images looking for their friends. Regardless of where in the book they are placed, faces in group shots need to be visible and consistent in size.

- The design of theme pages, section dividers and other thematic elements will need special attention. Readers need to know they are looking at special content that sets the tone for the book from the cover to the closing page. Designers should pay attention to consistencies in graphics that will help the readers visually "group" or connect these elements when they come to them in the book. Creating a strong graphic style in the opening and closing sections, and adapting elements of that style to the section dividers, will reinforce this design for readers. The use of color, larger pictures, logos and specially designed text will help readers connect these elements. Designers might also use wider text displays, increased leading or similar typographic devices.

Figure 13.9 *Highlander,* yearbook, McLean High School, McLean, Va., pp. 224–225. Reproduced by permission of Meghan Percival (adviser) and the editors of the *2011 Clan.*

Reference sections containing group shots for clubs and sports allow for expanded coverage traditional or chronological sections. Each club or sports group shot should be clearly labeled and cropped tightly to the content of the photo. Each photo's caption should include complete first and last names and bold lead-ins identifying rows of students, as seen in this spread. Note also that season scores and action shots provide additional information to the package.

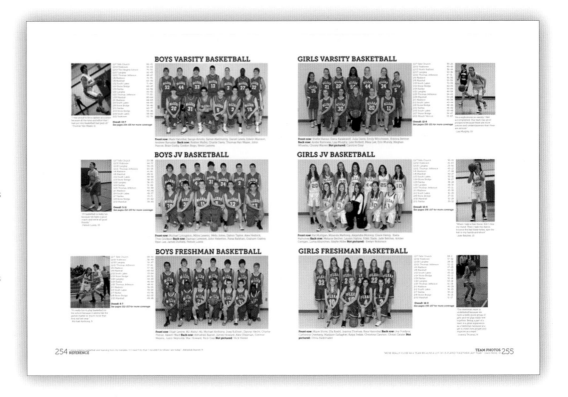

Copy in theme pages needs to be unique, specific and interesting.

Many schools using catchphrase themes will break the theme down into "mini-themes" and incorporate the theme idea.

- The increasing use of photo editing software to cut photos into shapes called COBs for **cutout backgrounds** requires special attention. Without backgrounds, photos follow the contours of the actual photo content. Designers should keep in mind that those active shapes are strong attention-getters. They usually provide visual entry and focus attention directly on these images, and the surrounding design should be simplified to prevent competing visual elements. Photo cutouts also need to be anchored on the page or visually attached to other elements. One way to to do this is to add shadows in an image editing or page design software program. Or, the images can be connected to text, lines or other graphics. Also, when cutting out backgrounds there should be no sharp edges to the shapes.

  Special consideration should be given to cutting out backgrounds in sports action shots. When the context of the sports action is removed, an action shot often loses its meaning.

- The design of the ad section needs to be considered. Display ads from local businesses need to be visually different from each other and preferably reflect what the business is about. Avoid using the same typeface in each ad. Make sure each ad has a strong visual or a strong type message. The ad's price may correspond to the number of columns it occupies. For instance, many staff now sell their ad sections by dividing page space into a series of blocks. Many books offer as many as nine to 12 blocks of space on a page. Advertisers can then purchase a multiple of blocks for their ads. Some schools offer discounts for full-page or larger ads.

  The use of senior ads, friend ads and club ads has enabled many staff to eliminate the outside sale of ad space. These ads can be sold in standard sizes by dividing pages into module shapes and selling them as blocks or combinations of blocks. In the smaller block sizes, the yearbook staff might want to create a standard design style, enabling the parent or buyer to add an individualized message or picture.

  In all cases, careful attention should be given to designing interesting ad sections. Senior ads can be designed with a standard headline design using each student's name.

FIGURE 13.10
Tiger 2011, yearbook for Texas High School, Texarkana, Texas. Vol. 93. Reproduced by permission of Brad Bailey, principal.
A theme placing the visual emphasis on large pictures of students, "look at it this way," combines a lower case, condensed typography in caps and lower case for the two parts of the theme phrase.
a The cover sets the tone by introducing the theme phrase and colors.

Another section that can be used to amplify the book's theme development is the **index**. Every person pictured in the book should be listed in one complete alphabetical index. The index is also an excellent place to list the book's advertisers, clubs, sports and activities as they appear throughout the book. The index should be designed with a column structure. Typographic devices such as dot leaders can be used between the name and the page numbers to lead the reader's eye across the listings. Themes can often be extended into index sections.

Many schools enliven these pages by including candid pictures with captions or by interspersing alphabetized club and sport group shots throughout the index. Making the

Figure 13.10 (*continued*)
b On the front endsheet, the theme statement colors and typefaces introduce each of the traditional sections with student headshots and quotes. **c** On the book's title page, p. 1, the theme is repeated with another strong, carefully chosen photo of a student.

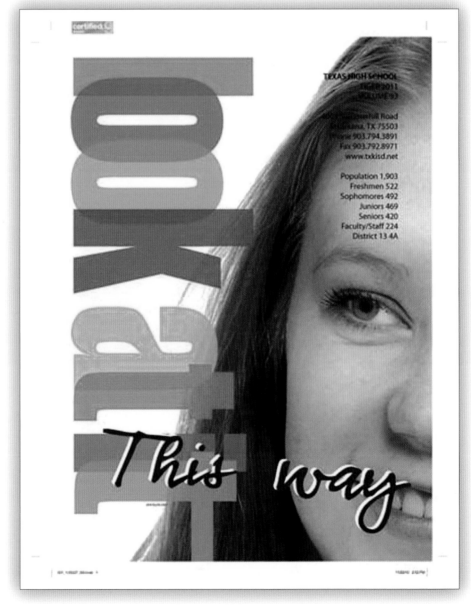

Figure 13.10 (*continued*)
d On the first theme spread, another photo of a student "looking at it" is dominant. The book's tone is set with specific examples in the copy and three additional, smaller photos.
e The second opening theme spread finishes the theme statement in a unique layout showing lots of different perspectives. **f** A section divider spread for "Student Life" carries the orange color banner from the endsheet and the signature type as it transitions into the body of the book.

FIGURE 13.11 *2011 Odyssey,* yearbook, Chantilly High School, Chantilly, Va., pp. 350–351. Reproduced by permission of Mary Kay Downes.

Dividing each ad page into eight modules allows for ads of eighth-page, quarter-page and half-page size. Each of the community ads on this spread has its own identity and look with custom designs. Color helps each ad's identity, too.

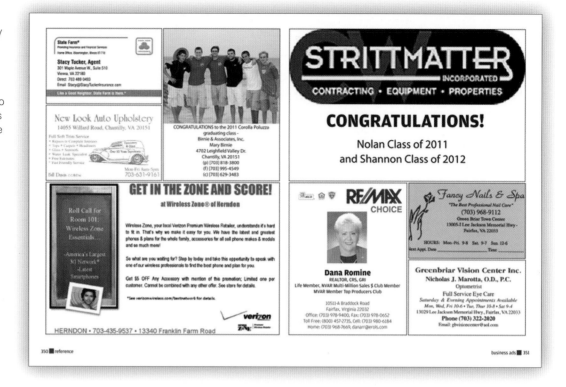

FIGURE 13.12 *Tonitrus,* yearbook, Rocklin High School, Rocklin, Calif. Reprinted by permission of Casey Nichols.

A lively senior ad section allows parents to include multiple personal pictures and messages in each ad space. The staff added interest by including a horizontal feature on each ad page that includes a photo poll of seniors describing their best and worst moments of the year.

group shots large enough for individual faces to be seen is a good rule of thumb for group shot size in the index.

Schools whose yearbooks publish in the spring encounter early spring deadlines, preventing coverage of the complete school year. Many of these schools choose to publish a small special insert called a **spring supplement**, which is usually given to a printer in the local community who can produce the work in a short amount of time to meet yearbook distribution day. These special inserts cover the school activities that occur after the book has been sent to the yearbook publisher. In addition to giving the staff continued design work throughout the spring semester, the special inserts make the yearbook more complete. Many staff use their section design templates and theme styles in these inserts. The special section can be inserted into the yearbook using a special glue strip on the insert. Students can then decide where in the book to place the insert. Or, if the staff does not wish to print an insert, supplemental information could simply appear on the book's web page.

Many yearbook publishers also sell special entertainment and news event sections featuring national interest items that can be purchased by staff and placed in each book to add to the year's coverage. If the staff wishes to provide their own coverage of broader topics, keep in mind that pictures should never be randomly taken off Internet sites and published in the yearbook unless specific written permission has been obtained. This permission should be kept on file. Most Internet content is copyrighted. Because the yearbook publishing companies obtain the permissions for this use, buying their specialty sections to include in the book is a popular choice.

Test your knowledge

What considerations are important in planning group shot coverage in the yearbook?

DVD AND INTERACTIVE COVERAGE

Expanding the coverage of the yearbook by producing DVD additions allows for coverage that supplements the printed book. Many yearbooks have separate DVD staff trained in shooting video and capturing audio and in editing multimedia stories. Supplementing the book allows for expanding coverage and content in interesting ways. Often, the DVD is designed to echo the book's theme and is attached to the inside of the printed book, ensuring each buyer receives a copy. Some schools sell these products separately from the book, although most schools package the product with the actual printed book as a supplement.

DVDs can also capture the sensory experiences of the year's major events – the sounds of the homecoming court being announced at the game with footage from that event, the school fight song played by the band at a pep assembly or an entire special event such as a talent show.

Specialty companies have emerged to offer DVD production services to yearbook staff. Many of the companies offer training and lend equipment for producing the content. They then offer training in the editing and production of the actual DVD using professional programs such as Final Cut.

Establishing a yearbook website or social media site is also a great way to centralize and establish an identity for the book. Adding staff members to manage the site can be crucial, just as having a separate DVD staff ensures the product is properly managed. The site can be used to gather information for stories, to make announcements about the book's sale and to keep students interested in what's going on with the book's content throughout the year. For instance, photo slide shows can be generated and periodically posted using photos that won't necessarily appear in the printed book. This material should never be taken from private social media sites. A public site for the book can include guidelines for reader submissions.

Staff can be creative in designing value-added content for the site. The site can be password protected so only buyers of the book can access it. The entire **portrait section** of the book could be featured on the website in an interactive format, with **rollovers**, responsive content linked to information such as students' names, school activities or awards won or post-graduation plans. An ambitious staff could add audio/video clips of each student.

Senior ads could include audio and/or video of a parent's voice congratulating or reading a message to the senior student and showing photos of the student. The audio/visual supplement could be priced as an add-on to the cost of the printed senior ad.

Club and sports group shots are another natural fit for the web yearbook. Students too often complain about the small size of the pictures used in the printed book. Displaying the pictures from the website on a computer or television screen could enable students to zoom in and see the pictures in even larger sizes and to view the individual faces in the groups. Again, content could be added in rollovers in which information about each club could be included.

Special class presentations could also be added to the site, including science experiments, special class visitors and hands-on work in art and vocational classes. Student reactions could be part of the coverage.

Quick Exercise

Using a recent copy of a yearbook with photos with cutout backgrounds, analyze how effective the photos are in the designs. Has any contextual information been lost? Are the shaped photos anchored on the page? Are the shaped photos complete with no hard edges?

FIGURE 13.13 *Saga,* yearbook, Loudon Valley High School, Purcellville, Va. Reproduced by permission of Martha Akers.

The vibrant colors, pattern and fun theme statement, "equations," are repeated in the design of the book's DVD, which is placed just inside the book's cover in a plastic sleeve. The DVD includes video stories from the year and interviews with a variety of students.

FIGURE 13.14 *Wings,* yearbook, Arrowhead Christian Academy, Redlands, Calif. Reproduced by permission of Crystal Kazmierski.

Most yearbooks use four-color printing for the entire book. When four-color is used, designers must ensure that color doesn't overwhelm the content or take away from the photographic presentation. Red color swoops across the bottom of this Valentine's Day spread and hangs in artistic pieces from the top. The designer also nicely echoed the color of the prominent red and pink balloons in the dominant photo. Red appears in each of the smaller color photos except the one in black-and-white. The use of a black-and-white photo or two was a repeated contrast technique used throughout this book.

The DVD content and a PDF of the printed yearbook could be added to the password-protected area of the website ensuring that buyers could access the book even if they lose or damage their printed copy. There's no limit to content that could be added to the printed book with additional staff members coordinating the web yearbook site.

THE USE OF COLOR

Color has become the standard in yearbooks, as it is in many other student publications. Yearbook publishers commonly offer full-color books, and many schools have taken advantage of this. Most yearbook photographers now shoot digitally in color and later convert their photos to grayscale if the yearbook will be printed in black-and-white.

Using color effectively in design requires attention to detail. Display type used for headlines and secondary headlines works well in color, but smaller type displays such as copy and captions rarely read effectively in color. Colored text type tends to slow down the reader.

Warm colors always come forward in design. Designers can often pull color, or repeat strong color, from a dominant image to create a strong connection between the photograph, the headline and the page content.

Too much color, or overuse of color, can also create confusion in design. When it is overused, the reader is distracted from the content, but when used effectively it can create connections. Pull warm colors – reds, oranges, yellows – to the forefront and let cool colors – greens, blues – recede.

Attention should be paid to color values when choosing which to use. Some colors are hard to work with on white backgrounds, particularly some shades of red, yellow and green. Color contrasts need to be strong and effective. Textured backgrounds with color can also add clutter to the page and distract from the content.

CONCLUSION

The contemporary yearbook is an ever-evolving publication that must adapt to new design and content to appeal and stay relevant to its student audience and stay viable in the school market. Each new edition should aim to provide better coverage of all students and employ innovative design methods and supplemental multimedia content.

SUMMARY

- A strong book begins with a theme – typically based on a catchphrase or graphic motif – that provides a focus for the book in a way that is relevant to the students and to the year.

- The book needs strong content structure. This can be achieved by sections of traditional coverage (Student Life, Sports, Academics, Clubs, People, Ads/Index) or chronological organization, following the flow of the year. Both methods can provide strong structure for the content.

- Well-written copy should provide details, important facts that date the year and feature student voices.

- Pages should be built around strong, dominant images supported by well-written headlines and copy and interesting alternative content featuring student quotes.

- Color can provide unity to sections and to individual spreads through the book.

- A staff-hosted website offers multiple opportunities to gather information and photos for the book. It should also host original content, primarily in audio/video form that supplements the printed book.

KEY TERMS

alternative copy

bleeds

body copy

captions, cutlines

clubs section

cluster captions

cutout backgrounds

display space

divider pages

dominant image

endsheet

eyelines

graphics

gutter margin

headlines, primary and
    secondary

index

isolation element

portrait section

progressive margins

rising caps

rollover

section templates

side caps

sports section

spread

spread unity

spring supplement

theme

visual continuity

visual-verbal separators

Z pattern

EXERCISES

1   Using the layout software provided by the school's yearbook printer, design a standard layout using three or four columns. Start by selecting pictures that have been shot by yearbook photographers that could actually be used in the design. Import relevant text from a wordprocessing file or use the software's text placeholder function. Create style sheets for the copy. Write a headline and a deck or secondary headline for the content. Proof the layout before printing. Hang up your layout and get a classmate to critique its strengths and weaknesses according to the following parameters:

(a) Did you maintain consistent internal margins with only one pica of space separating content?

(b) Are there white space holes and inconsistencies that distract the eye?

(c) Is the dominant image large enough to serve as a central entry point for the design? Is the dominant effective?

(d) Are the supporting pictures of varied shape, size and content?

(e) Is the design visually attractive?

2   Brainstorm at least five different techniques that could be used to create a theme or graphic device that would work for your school's yearbook for this year. Begin by making a list of interesting facts about the year at your school. From that list, generate ideas for each fact. Share the list with classmates and get their opinions on visual and verbal ways in which your ideas could be expressed.

3   Create a graphics file by cutting up magazines or newspapers and looking for at least two examples of each of the following visual treatments:

(a) headlines with secondary or deck headlines

(b) use of color in design

(c) caption starters

(d) graphics such as use of color, lines, screens and textures

(e) sidebars or supplementary copy treatments.

Cut out each example, paste it on paper and write a short explanation of why you think the example works successfully and how it could be adapted for a section of a yearbook.

4   Choose a section of the yearbook and develop a design strategy for the section using the graphics file you created in Exercise 3. Create both a visual and a verbal strategy for the section. Make a list of the typefaces you would choose for the body text, captions, folios and other verbal treatments you have designed. Specify point sizes, leading values and typefaces for each verbal area on the spread. Using your design strategy, paste up a sample of your design using material from magazines. Evaluate the spread's design strategy by presenting it to your classmates and having them critique its strengths and weaknesses.

5   Using a yearbook from your school or an exchange copy from another school, look at the theme or graphic unity of the book. In small discussion groups, critique it using these questions:

(a) Is the theme or graphic unity clearly understandable and relevant to the reader?

(b) Is it presented in a contemporary and interesting way on the cover?

(c) Is the theme or graphic unity included on the endsheets (unless they are white)?

(d) Is the theme or graphic unity clearly developed in both the opening and closing pages of the book?

(e) How do the divider pages continue the theme or graphic unity?

(f) Do you think the staff were successful in developing the theme or unity throughout the book? In what other ways were they able to reinforce the theme or graphic unity in other areas of the book?

6   Get a copy of your state's judging standards for yearbook awards. Evaluate your school's most recent yearbook using the judging standards. How well do you think your school's yearbook fulfilled the standards? What are the book's strengths and its weaknesses? How could these weaknesses be addressed? Discuss any standards you think students on the staff need to pay particular attention to in future volumes.

7   Divide students into teams of three to five with each team taking a different section of the yearbook. Evaluate the content in your group's section in the last three editions of the school's yearbook. Has the content evolved or has it remained consistent? What evidence of cultural trend coverage is in the section? Does the section tell stories in different ways? Is any special coverage included? Could any special content have been included? Is the design different in each of the three volumes?

8   Look through a collection of magazines and newspapers and compile a list of catchphrases that appear in ads, headlines or other content areas. Without choosing a particular product's advertising slogan or using material that would be too closely identified with a product, select some phrases that could be used as themes. Would any of these catchphrases be workable in your school's yearbook? Next, look through a book of idioms or commonly used expressions. Write down expressions that would be relevant to your school this year.

ONLINE JOURNALISM

14

> " A robust website for a newspaper will open opportunities for you and your staff to explore digital storytelling. At times there will be facets of an assignment – a video clip, audio interview or additional photos – that won't technically fit into your print edition. Your website often serves as the link to deliver that content to your audience. Also, your website will naturally lead you to experiment with social media, data visualization and audience engagement – devices that help promote or expand your story. Most of all though, a well-developed website will prepare you and your staff for the technology revolution that aspiring journalists must embrace.
>
> Jon Glass, General Manager of the Newhouse School's Collaborative Media Room, Syracuse University (Formerly Online Content Director for Palmbeachpost.com) "

LEARNING OBJECTIVES After completing this chapter you will be able to:

- understand the importance of a robust website and social media sites for publications that provide content for their readers

- supplement print content with online multimedia storytelling and visual interactivity

- utilize resources to add timely content to a website in both words and pictures

- facilitate collaboration between online and print publication staff

- determine how to effectively use online resources to supplement the print yearbook

- understand the importance of extending online content contributions to others outside publication staff members.

Quick Exercise

You're assigned to write a story on cyberbullying for a future print and online story. Using the Internet, list five resources you find with current statistics and information about the topic. What information would lend itself to your print story? How would you use it? What information would be more appropriate as supplemental web content accessed through a QR code? Is there an interactive feature that would be appropriate for the website? What is an appropriate poll question that could be added to the online story, inviting reader responses?

IT'S SCHOOL NEWSPAPER DISTRIBUTION DAY. The marching band has won a large, nationally prestigious competition. The story is featured on the front-page along with a picture of the band receiving its trophy taken with a parent's smartphone. A **QR code (Quick response code**; a digitized link to information that can be read with your cellphone**)** printed with the story takes the reader to an online gallery of the parent's other photos. A video of the band celebrating its win, shot by another parent, is also featured on the site.

A young soldier, an alumnus, was injured in Afghanistan. A feature story includes an interview with him after he was released from an area hospital, where he had been sent to recuperate. A link in the online version of the story connects readers to a gallery of photos he took in Afghanistan before being injured.

A school blood drive, held in honor of a student fighting an illness, has collected a record number of pints of blood. The student was interviewed and appears in a video on the newspaper's website talking about how much he appreciates the blood drive. An online infographic shows the process by which a blood donation reaches an actual recipient.

Hyperfocused and localized to their audiences, high school publications seem to be doing what many professionals can't do: effectively engage with their readers. Distribution days for many high school newspapers and yearbooks continue to be significant, with engaged students poring over copies. As professional newspapers struggle to survive – cutting their print publishing schedule to a few days a week and moving online content behind paywalls – high school newspapers and yearbooks and their online sites seem to be thriving.

As computer processing speeds grow faster and online services proliferate, the information superhighway has become like the German Autobahn – where speed and access are almost unlimited. Students cruise through expanding information resources both at school and at home, using their computers, smartphones, mobile devices and tablets. Accessing information is almost instantaneous. Tapping the potential of these online resources, student journalists can do research and interviewing for their own reporting, and can offer their student readers supplemental information and additional contact with their publication outside its normal publishing schedule.

Not only can students research and gather information on websites, they can access decades of information that has appeared in print on similar topics. They can even interview and communicate with people, organizations and governmental agencies that might have been unreachable through traditional methods such as calling. Using powerful search engines and limited search requests, student journalists can conduct efficient online research to gather information on topics ranging from entertainment to Ebola. In the professional press, **computer-assisted reporting**, as this process is known, has enabled journalists to write more accurately and thoroughly on a variety of subjects.

Computer-assisted reporting may be enhanced by consulting with librarians or media specialists, who can help student journalists navigate complex sites and information. Consultation with economics or statistics teachers can aid students trying to make sense of complex numbers they have gathered from websites or from online polling.

There are many other possibilities for using the Internet to enhance student journalism. Students may occasionally have access to experts, entertainment figures, political candidates, media personalities and others through live online events such as webcasts. Or, student journalists can use media links on entertainment sites to obtain photographs for reviews. Students can view actual live scenes in places as remote as outer space, can tour museums in locations around the world and can access the online resources of non-local libraries and news-gathering organizations. They can participate in online forums with other student journalists or can conduct online forums to gather information for future stories. Students can use resources such as Skype to interview people in distant locations, such as students traveling or competing in contests.

CREATING WEB PUBLICATIONS

Many publications have active, robust websites which operate seamlessly and in harmony with print publications. Those that don't need to consider several options ranging from who will host the site to the content it will provide. Maintaining and updating websites may require school resources and creation of an online staff.

FIGURE 14.1a My High School Journalism, hosted by the American Society of Newspaper Editors. Screengrab from homepage of www.myhsj.org. Reprinted with permission.

My High School Journalism provides free online hosting and a content management system for youth-generated news, and is connected to more than 3,800 student news outlets. The site hosts stories, blogs, photos, video, audio and other multimedia materials. It also gives out monthly cash prizes to the five school media organizations it hosts that generate the highest monthly traffic to their sites.

FIGURE 14.1b
Screengrab of "Designs & Prices" page from www.schoolnews papersonline.com. Reprinted with permission.

School Newspapers Online is cloud hosted on Rackspace and works on the WordPress content management system. It offers themes and options, and helps schools buy their own domain names. It charges an initial set-up fee, then a yearly renewal fee that includes the domain name.

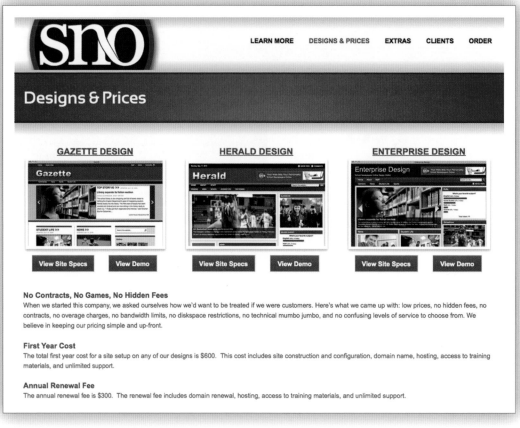

Quick Exercise

Review the privacy policy of both your school or school district's website and your school publication's site. These policies are usually included in a footer bar on the site or may be found through a search. Compare the information. How do they differ? Compare your school publication's online privacy policy to the print edition's editorial statement, which is probably printed on the editorial page. Are the policies clear and reasonable in their intent? Should they be rewritten to include additional information?

Website hosting and privacy policies

Waiting for the next issue of the school newspaper to publish a late-breaking story or announcement is a thing of the past for student journalists with online publications. Student publications can independently, or through web providers, create websites where readers can access information and up-to-date reports, and view still photographs and hear video and audio clips. Student journalists can create a website using available **open source content management systems** such as Drupal or Joomla!, which charge for web hosting. Open source content management systems are usually developed through public collaboration and make the source code available for use or modification by users or as developers see fit. Some open source content management systems are free. Student journalists might also want to consider School Newspapers Onlin*e* (schoolnewspapersonline.com), a site specifically tailored to high school and college newspapers with a simplified pricing system, or My High School Journalism (myhsj. org), a free web hosting service offered by the American Society of Newspaper Editors, but with limited options.

In schools offering web design classes, students can build and manage their own sites using content creation system software. Other sites such as WordPress, which is technically a blog site, are easy to use and offer free, though limited, website hosting. All of these options offer pre-designed themes or templates for site design, simplifying web construction through user-friendly simple built-in content management systems.

The school district might offer to host publications online or provide a link to them, although it might have a strict policy limiting the information that can be posted on the site. Individual school sites may have censorship policies or may require information be submitted to their webmasters before being placed online. Publications staff may find those restrictions too limiting in what they are able to do with their sites.

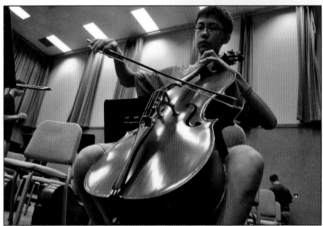

PAGE 14 | STUDENT SECTION | HILITE | HILITE.ORG | MAY 18, 2012

STUDENT SECTION

STUDENTSECTION@HILITE.ORG | TWITTER.COM/HILITE_NEWS

Want more?
Follow this QR code to the *HiLite* Twitter page for quick news all the time.

Music in the City

Sophomore Brandon Xu plans on attending an international music academy in Beijing this summer

Tell Us Your Story:

For every issue, the *HiLite* will ask questions on our Facebook page. Tell us your story, and we will feature you on the next Student Section.

For this issue, the *HiLite* is featuring sophomore Brandon Xu.

We asked:

HiLite Online
How will you be spending this summer vacation? Answer and you may be featured in the next issue of the *HiLite*.
April 30 at 5:05 p.m.

You answered:

Brandon Xu
I will be attending the Beijing Great Wall International Music Academy in Beijing.
April 30 at 5:39 p.m.

HENRY ZHU / PHOTO

MUSICAL FINGERS: *Sophomore Brandon Xu practices on his cello before orchestra rehearsal. Xu said he is not sure if he will pursue a career in music, but it will still be a part of his future.*

BY ROCHELLE BRUAL
rbrual@hilite.org

Sophomore Brandon Xu said when it comes to cello, his greatest strength is finding his weaknesses. Xu plays cello in this school's top chamber ensemble Camerata, which is a part of this school's Symphony Orchestra. This is his fifth year to formally study cello.

This summer, Xu said he plans to attend the Great Wall International Music Academy in Beijing. There he will stay in a resort and receive private lessons, private chamber music coaching and master classes from top conservatory professors from around the world.

Dr. William Grubb, associate professor of cello at Butler University and Xu's private teacher, said, "It's really about training some of the kids that will become the stars of tomorrow in either Asia or the United States. They will just flourish, especially since they can learn from each other."

According to Grubb, the Great Wall International Music Academy is highly selective. Grubb has taught there for about five years now, and he recommended to Xu that he should audition. Since Xu's audition was late, he had to travel to the University of Cincinnati to play for the school's executive director, Stanny Shiu.

However, now that Xu has been accepted, he has the opportunity to work with three to four cello teachers and play in one of the 20 string quartets. After three weeks of intensive work, Xu will perform in a concert. There will also be a National Public Radio program called "From the Top," that will do two broadcasts for the school.

"I think the advantage is that (Xu) will be immersed in a different kind of culture. He will get to be around lots of kids from China and see how that's like and how they study and prepare for things. It's quite different than America. Chinese are more disciplined than American students but sometimes not as creative as American students, so it's a nice mix for Americans to go to China to study, and it's nice for the Chinese students to work with American students," Grubb said. "It's a really wonderful mix of cultures from East and West to make classical music. For us, it's the language of music that brings us together."

According to Xu, practice in China is focused on drilling and intensive work. The methods are based on technicality, which focuses more on intonation and rhythm. In the United States and Europe, teachers encourage their students to develop their musicality, or their musical personality.

The majority of the students at the Great Wall International Music Academy are ethnically Chinese, but they come from all over the world, like from Germany, Singapore, the United States and Taiwan. Students who live in China come from top schools like the Hong Kong Academy for Performing Arts and the Central Conservatory of Music in Beijing. Xu said that although competition is healthy, at the same time it can detract from the learning process.

Although Xu said he is undecided for college, music will still be a part of his future. Grubb said Xu has the ability to double major in music and a science.

Xu said, "You don't have to formally study music to enjoy it. I think that is what really makes it great. You can enjoy it just as much as I do without taking five years of lessons and traveling overseas."

FIGURE 14.2 *HiLite*, Carmel High School, Carmel, Ind. May 18, 2012. Reproduced by permission of Jim Streisel.

HiLite includes its website address in every page folio (top left), an email link to the reporter in every byline, and also features a box called "Tell Us Your Story," seeking comments from readers, with instructions on how to submit an answer online. The box includes the question and a featured answer from the last edition.

Assembling a publication website

Companion web publications can and should be more than mere print PDF archives, or repeats of the printed publication, but managing and updating online information may require additional resources. Publications may need to recruit additional staff members. Or, completely separate online staff may be desirable to keep content flowing. Students with knowledge of web management will be particularly valuable. Or, student journalists can collaborate with students in broadcast or computer classes to provide their readers with fresh, updated information. Publications should have a definite plan for providing online content before beginning to experiment with such efforts. Creating an online site that is never updated or is changed infrequently, especially after advertising it, ensures its failure by frustrating readers. If the publication staff sells advertising in its print edition, it will want to also offer advertising on the website, particularly if it's paying for web hosting. Ads can be bundled for both print and web (see Chapter 16 for more information on web advertising).

Many online newspapers use **navigation content headers** on the website that closely mirror the printed publication's content. These may include news, feature, sports, entertainment, editorial or opinion and in-depth. Many also include navigation links to multimedia stories, videos, photo galleries, blogs and archives of print editions. These links can be connected to host sites such as Flickr and Vimeo or School Tube or YouTube for photos and video, and Issuu for archived print PDFs. The staff may stay connected to readers through a Facebook page, a Twitter account, RSS (Really Simple Syndication), DIGG feeds (a social media news feed) and other methods. When content is being created for the publication, all multimedia forms of delivery should be considered. Print editions should refer readers to the website in page folios and in stories, to reporters through email addresses and should direct readers to additional story content on the web through QR codes.

Because Internet sites are accessible to virtually anyone with a computer, some schools have created strict policies about the content that can appear. For instance, some schools have prohibited pictures of students from being published online, or have disallowed publishing the full names of the students in pictures on the online site. Other schools require that permission forms, known as **photo releases**, be signed by students and sometimes parents before student pictures can be placed on a website.

Online publications should strive to protect sources' First Amendment rights, just as printed publications do (see Chapter 17 for more information on the First Amendment). During the interviewing process, reporters may want to mention to their sources that the information they are providing may be used on a website, just as they mention to sources that they are being interviewed for a story for the newspaper, yearbook or other publication. If the interview is being conducted online, or if information is being gathered via email, online polls or social media

FIGURE 14.3 Screengrab of the polls archive from *The Falcon*, Woodlands High School, Harstdale, N.Y. Reprinted with permission.

Many sites offer clickable surveys using poll widgets. When more than one poll result is available, students can view a poll archive or will be directed to a host polling site to see a bar chart of the results. After students vote, they can click on "see results" immediately. Some polls also allow participants to post comments.

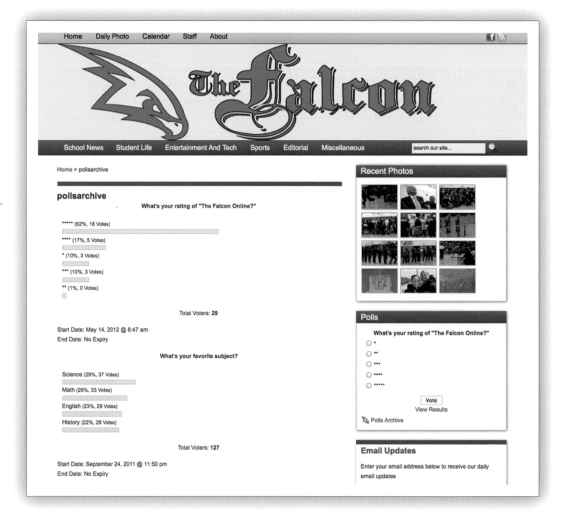

platforms, sources should be informed of the publication's intent to use the responses in print and online. Student journalists should be sensitive to the way in which information obtained from online interviewing or polling can be skewed by repeated contributions from single sources. Some students may make frivolous comments or may not take the interview seriously, particularly if they can reply anonymously to the questions.

Creating online content

A **web editor or manager** needs skills similar to those of the student editor. The person chosen should understand news value, bring an understanding of good news judgment, be organized and exhibit leadership skills. The web editor can work almost as an equal partner to the print publication's editor in determining how stories will appear on the website and how the information will differ from that of the printed publication. The web editor will benefit from the resources of a different group of reporters and photographers who can update printed stories and edit content unique to the site. The online staff will be particularly invested in providing new content on a frequent basis, especially between printed editions.

Websites should encourage reader feedback. Responses to content can be printed as traditional letters to the editor, but publication websites can also set up forums for discussion and dialogue. Each web feature can allow comments, but those comments should be moderated according to standards set by the publication. Readers' online discussions can prove valuable to both the online and printed publication. Editors can gauge reader opinions and interest, which could form the basis of future content. Some commentary may spark leads for new or additional coverage or follow-up. Reporters can research these new story ideas using resources such as online forums or reader responses submitted via email. Social media sites such as Twitter also allow for gathering story ideas and content, but again, with the participants' knowledge of its use.

WEBLINKS Check out

www.webdesignerdepot.com

This site includes downloads, tutorials, links, resources, helpful software information and other resource for web designers in an organized and easily navigable format.

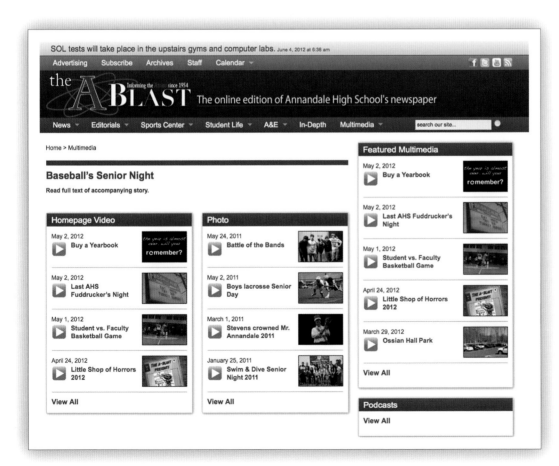

FIGURE 14.4 *The A Blast*, Annandale High School, Annandale, Va. Reproduced by permission of Alan Weintraut.

One of the most useful benefits of a publication's website is the ability to link to videos, audio, slideshows, podcasts, motion graphics and other multimedia forms not suited for print. Working with broadcast programs in the school offers student journalists a collaborative experience for the online content. Submissions can also be encouraged from students who are not staff members. On the *A Blast* site, quick links take viewers to videos, photos, multimedia and podcasts. The site also uses a reduced size version of its distinctive print edition's flag, adding "The online edition of Annandale High School's newspaper" to the banner.

Quick Exercise

With a simple camera or smartphone, go to a hands-on class such as art or cooking, or to a PE class, and shoot pictures of the students in the class. Then download the pictures and do a simple edit of the five to 10 pictures that best tell the story of these classes. Using Adobe Acrobat, or Soundslides software if audio was also collected, sequence the photos into a simple, short presentation. Add a title slide and a credit slide with text. Share your work with others in the class for discussion. Would this presentation be interesting on the website?

Multimedia content

Publication websites offer greater flexibility for multimedia content. The process of picture editing ensures that not all good photographs can be used in the printed publication. A good web photo editor will cull through the edited pictures, looking for additional high-quality pictures to place on the website. Original photographs can also be generated specifically for the website. Many professional sites, such as those of large metropolitan newspapers, supplement stories with navigable slide shows where additional photographs appear, often accompanied by video and audio clips. Creating similar slide shows would be a perfect opportunity for providing a greater number of pictures of students at events such as prom or homecoming. Or, an editor can seek contributions from students and create an online gallery from their submissions. An effort should be made to picture a diverse group of students. Just as in editing for print, the photo editor should make sure the photo content is varied and interesting. Cropping and toning may need to be applied to the photos before they are posted. Technical quality must also be considered. Shoveling weak content onto a website will never be effective. Providing a standard policy for online submission of both words and images and posting that policy on the website will help solve issues with reader submissions.

Professional publications utilize multimedia tools to provide a complete storytelling experience for their readers. If a high school offers a broadcast journalism program, the broadcast staff may want to collaborate with their print partners to offer a broader range of content. Working with videographers, reporters can obtain sights and sounds that can be edited and digitized into short film clips to supplement the printed information. Or, the student publication can make arrangements to broadcast live events on the website. Podcasts of original content can be created and archived for mobile devices, as can webcasts of significant campus events. Multimedia content is a necessary part of a good website since it provides content the print edition cannot provide.

Infographics created for the website, such as maps, polls and surveys can help present complex information to readers. Motion graphics offer interesting ways to present information and might be possible with help from students in art or computer animation classes. Time-lapse animations and videos offering 360-degree views offer interesting visual opportunities. Illustrations provided by talented artists in the school can enhance the website with their unique styles.

Ten good ideas

Online content should be fun, informative, interesting and relevant to student readers. Here are some examples of innovative content:

1. "The College Guide" provides information on admissions and testing for student readers.

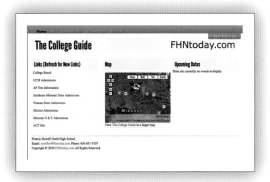

Sidebar 14.1 Under a website link "Exclusives," a sublink to "College 101" provides college information of interest to the publications' readers. *North Star*, Francis Howell North High School, St. Charles, Mo. Reproduced by permission of Aaron Manfull.

Sidebar 14.2 A podcast series includes an audio clip of the student speaking, along with a picture and text. *Trnwired*, Prince George High School, Prince George, Va. Reproduced by permission of Chris Waugaman.

Sidebar 14.3 A page of sports wallpapers is offered to students as downloadable backgrounds for their computer desktops. *North Star*, Francis Howell North High School, St. Charles, Mo. Reproduced by permission of Aaron Manfull.

Sidebar 14.4 Interesting and colorful staff-produced artwork illustrates online stories. Thelowel.org, Lowell High School, San Francisco, Calif., April 26, 2012. Graphics by Jenna Fiorello, Hoi Leung, Eva Morgenstein, Vivian Tong. Reproduced by permission of Sharn Matusek.

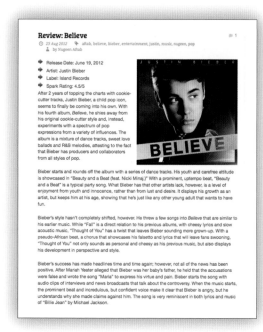

Sidebar 14.5 An entertainment sublink connects to staff members' music playlist selections. *Spark*, Lakota East High School, Liberty Township, Ohio. Reproduced by permission of Dean Hume.

Sidebar 14.6 A feature called, "Last Weekend I…" offers insights into students' activities written in the first person. *The A Blast* online edition, Annandale High School, Annandale, Va. Reproduced by permission of Alan Weintraut

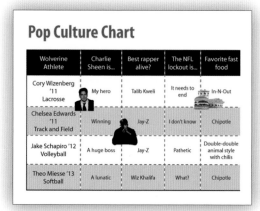

Sidebar 14.7 A pop culture chart compares selections from various sports team members. Created by Alex Leichenger, Judd Liebman and Michael Aronson, Big Red. *The Chronicle*, Harvard-Westlake School, Los Angeles, Calif. Reproduced by permission of Kathleen Neumeyer.

Sidebar 14.8 Vintage movie picks are a weekly feature on this website. *Harbinger Online*, Shawnee Mission East High School, Prairie Village, Kan. Reproduced by permission of C. Dow Tate.

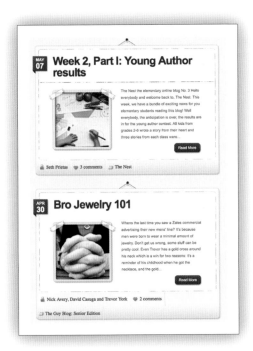

Sidebar 14.9 An active set of blogger links includes logos and titles for each with easy links. Screengrab of links to bloggers from *The Feather*, Fresno Christian High School, Fresno, Calif. Reprinted with permission.

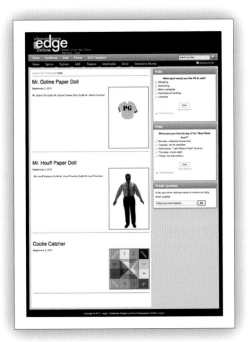

Sidebar 14.10 Sharing a website with the newspaper, this site's yearbook link includes a sublink, "Crafts," which instructs students in everything from making a "cootie catcher" to making a school paper doll with school-themed outfits. *Edge Online*, Pleasant Grove High School, Texarkana, Texas, Sept. 2, 2011. Reprinted with permission.

INVOLVING THE READERS

Newspaper staff can seek to include **citizen journalists**, contributors such as bloggers and reviewers, to expand the voices offered to their readers and to expand online content. For instance, a student who wants to review a new album or movie may be interested in doing so on the website, particularly if it coincides with a local concert appearance or opening weekend. Many students will be interested in reading an online article about a concert that happened the previous night or a DVD that was just released. Linking the reader to the band or entertainer's website, as well as other websites of interest to those readers, will generate even more interest and repeat visits. A concert review printed in a publication two to three weeks after the concert will be old, outdated and uninteresting to student readers, who are thinking ahead to upcoming concerts.

Important events in the school will generate lots of interest but may not be timed to coincide with a print edition. During homecoming week, prom and graduation, galleries of photos can quickly appear online showcasing a wide range of students. A video team can produce pieces in which students are shown at the events and which feature commentary and opinions from the participants.

In some schools, literary magazines have ceased publishing due to printing expense or lack of interest. The newspaper or yearbook can sponsor photo contests or literary writing contests in which students can submit poetry, short stories, art or photographs and publish the works periodically on the website. If the school has a published literary magazine, this project might be sponsored cooperatively with its staff and might supplement that publication's content. Or, teachers of creative writing, art, photography and other hands-on classes could select student work for publication on the website. Students whose work appears on the site could also be tapped as potential staff members allowing them to contribute visual skills online.

Photographers and videographers can post content daily. Offering a gallery of photos from daily events around school will bring viewers to the website on a regular basis. Showing interesting projects from field trips, guest speakers, hands-on classes and other club and academic pursuits reflects a cross-section of the school community and keeps the content timely.

Students and teachers with specialized interests can be valuable resources for creating online content. Seeking them out for help and contributions will be beneficial. Some of these potential

 **WORDS of WISDOM**

The addition of a website to our publication is important for several reasons, as long as it is done with some planning. One key thing is it gives staff members new skills that they will be able to use later in life in almost any job. In our case it revitalized our publication with creative ways to present news by a very veteran cutting-edge staff that was looking for more ways to connect with their audience.

When we made a commitment to do the website the staff did not just want to reprint stories that appeared in the paper. We included new content every day which forced our editors to find new ways to present that information in a variety of mediums. Our website's success, and what our students loved the most about it, was how interactive it was. Students were included in polls, videos, sound slides and photo stories and they felt ownership, which kept them coming back.

Jim McGonnell, Adviser, Blue & Gold *and Blueandgoldtoday.org, Findlay High School, Findlay, Ohio*

In addition to advertising its online site, *Spark* publishes digests of web content not available in the printed edition. On the "Around the School" pages, a banner across the bottom alerts readers to online stories in opinion, sports and news online. A logo with the website address, used in every issue, provides familiar direction for students seeking online content.

FIGURE 14.6 *The A Blast*, Annandale High School, Annandale, Va. May 16th, 2012, pp. 10–11. Reproduced by permission of Alan Weintraut.

This spread features a double truck on censorship issues. Including links to online petitions and the website of a grassroots political movement provides readers with interactive ways to act against government censorship. In addition, the paper provides links to exclusive information related to the topic in a logo-based header, "Online Exclusive."

collaborations can be identified through information obtained from beat reporting (see Chapter 1 for more information on beats). A history teacher could provide a video tour of a historic location. Students interested in fashion can provide seasonal fashion advice, tour shopping areas or host a prom fashion show at a local store. Students who like to cook can write restaurant reviews, recommend special restaurants for homecoming or other events or host periodic cooking segments. A gifted athlete can discuss form and show technique.

Content which wouldn't work as well in print may be perfectly appropriate for the website. Students can document field trips, competitions, club trips and other events through updates to the website in multimedia formats. By using smartphone cameras and videos, participatory journalism is unlimited.

Tablet magazines can now be created using standard and evolving design software that allows for audio, video and interactive scrolling content in addition to traditional words and images. A small group of staff members or interested readers might want to create tablet magazines about specialty topics or for special events throughout the school year. This technology is particularly useful to yearbook staff in supplementing the printed book using multimedia. An entire tablet magazine, spring supplement or special topic could be created.

If news is breaking quickly, print and online reporters and editors can collaborate on how to best present information, utilizing the skills of many students to keep the school community informed.

Creating a dynamic website begins with the publication's staff, but there are many possibilities for engaging readers in content creation.

WWW

WEBLINKS Check out

http://thefastdraw.com/category/on-the-air/

Mitch Butler and Josh Landis combine video, audio, art and humor to break down information into interesting and clever lessons. Their work is frequently used on CBS Sunday Morning.

FIGURE 14.7 *North Star* (fhntoday.com), Francis Howell North High School, St. Charles, Mo. Reproduced by permission of Aaron Manfull.

An article in the print newspaper on alternative Thanksgiving recipes includes a QR code that takes readers to a video providing step-by-step instructions on cooking the published recipes. The other content on this page directs students to use the publication's online resources, including its Twitter hashtag. Icons suggesting letters and comments, a calendar, weather reports and videos appear at the top of the page next to the publication's web address.

ENHANCED YEARBOOK CONTENT

Though newspaper staff have been quick to embrace social media platforms and websites, yearbook staff have been slower to adapt to electronic content. Staff may be reluctant to create websites for fear that **open content** available for free to anyone will discourage buyers. But online ads can be sold to support the online and print yearbook. Since it comes out only once at the very end of the year, maintaining interest in the yearbook before it is published is crucial. A website can keep the buyer buzz going while the book is being produced. The yearbook should also have a Facebook page and other appropriate social media pages through which it maintains a connection to its audience.

A yearbook web editor and staff can edit content and publish it online to provide previews of the printed book or to supplement its content. More pictures will be shot during the year than can ever be shown in the printed volume. The print yearbook can't possibly include candid shots of everyone in the school, though it's a worthy goal of some staffs. Uploading photos from various events as they happen will help keep a wide range of students excited about the coming printed publication. The staff can also sell reprints of photos shown online to add income.

The book's sales campaign can be advertised on the website. Forms for purchasing the printed volume can be provided on the site, and payment options can be provided. Lists of students who have purchased books can be posted so students can verify they've paid for their books. Forms for creating senior ads can also be provided for friends and family. Yearbook staff could experiment with offering online-only senior ads, reducing the bulk of the book and allowing for interactivity. Parents could include short video clips and/or a gallery of images. Or, online and print ads could be bundled for a higher price.

Once the yearbook staff has decided on a theme for the book, it can be previewed on the website to get the students excited about the book. If the staff doesn't keep the design of the cover a secret until the end of the year, the cover could also be posted on the site. Or, the staff could conduct an online vote on possible themes or cover ideas. Giving readers a personal stake in the outcome of the book will make them feel more connected to the publication and will generate buzz and interest in purchasing a book.

Yearbook websites can provide supplemental coverage that is impossible to include in the limited space of the printed book. Even if the book includes a companion DVD (which may be lost or damaged or made obsolete), posting content to a website will keep readers engaged and can provide a permanent archive of content. The website could also include audio/video clips from club events, academic pursuits and school activities. Club group photos could be featured in high resolution with zoom options so faces could be seen more easily. Polls and surveys could be conducted on the site and their results posted using infographics or other kinds of reporting. Minor sports and sub-varsity level sports could receive expanded coverage to supplement limited print content. Video senior portraits and senior diaries could be posted to the site allowing interactivity. Clips of seniors talking about their favorite school activities or memories could be offered. Business ads could provide supplemental income. Inclusion of the web address, QR codes, or other references to online content could eventually link the print yearbook to expanded content on the website.

All of these content add-ons take time and expertise to create. Collaboration with broadcast and web journalism programs is potentially fruitful. Just like the newspaper, the yearbook staff may want to develop a separate online staff with a web editor working closely with the print yearbook's editor and staff. Opening up staff positions to students with skills and interests in web design, management and creation will get more students involved in the process. Once the print yearbook goes to the printer in the spring, the online yearbook can continue to produce content so important spring activities and sports are documented. This supplement could be created using tablet designed software to allow for interactivity.

Quick Exercise

Drawing on a personal interest, plan a video segment you could shoot. Explain why this segment would be interesting to readers of the website. Using an outline, plan the sequence of your shots and what audio you would include. Using quick sketches, create a storyboard to put the scenes in sequence. Use a camera or smartphone to create the video.

Test your knowledge

How does reader/viewer contributed information add value to a website?

Quick Exercise

In small groups, discuss your yearbook's current website to determine how effective it is in attracting students. Is the staff open about the upcoming book's theme and visual look? Do students contribute to the site's content? Does the site engage readers throughout the year? Are the navigation links logical and helpful? What content could be added to the site? How could readers contribute content?

If the current yearbook lacks a website, discuss what features and links could be included on a site. Should it expand beyond the book's traditional sections? Should the print yearbook's unique theme and look be used each year or should a standard web design be used? What kinds of interactive content should be included? What features could be extracted from or used as supplements to the print edition? In outline form, plan a site that could be developed.

On the yearbook website, as on the newspaper website, content could be sought from other students. The staff could solicit photographs, videos, blogs, first-person writing or artwork for online use.

DESIGN OF THE WEBSITE

Most publications will want to make the website's design similar, but somewhat different, from that of the printed publication. Many staff opt to use a variation of the printed nameplate and add 'online' to the title. Other publications give their websites their own distinctive look. Regardless, the publication name should appear at the top of the site in the **header bar**, with identifying information about the school and location.

The yearbook website can use a series of links to sections of the yearbook such as student life, people, clubs or academics, or concentrate primarily on visual content. If the yearbook is using chronological order throughout the book, the links could match the chronology used in the print edition. The newspaper can categorize the web stories according to traditional printed sections such as news, features, sports or other sections. Content unique to the website should also be emphasized, including blogs, polls, multimedia and interactive features.

The website should include a privacy policy and site copyright information, usually in smaller type in a **footer bar**, near the bottom of the site. A searchable archived content database, appropriate links and contact information for staff members should all be carefully planned. **Sub-navigation links**, accessed by clicking on a major link, may make it easier to organize additional, related content such as blogs or columns. An About link can include a brief history of the publication, information on publication memberships and awards and information on becoming a staff member or contributing content. If advertising is offered, there should be a link on the main page that takes potential advertisers to a page with information and downloadable forms.

The readability of the type chosen for the website should be a primary concern. No longer limited to only five or six standard typefaces, websites now have more type options through resources such as Typekit, a website for buying typefaces. Web designers should be aware of the need to keep line lengths short, between 10 and 20 picas for easiest readability, and attention should be given to design elements such as leading, the space between the lines of type. Double-spacing between paragraphs and other design elements such as text heads within longer text will increase readability. Stories on the web may provide content that is different from the printed publication, such as updates, supplements and reader reactions. Live links to additional information and content can be included in the text.

Scrolling, interactive **content banners** of pictures, headlines and short summaries can highlight new content. These banners should be frequently refreshed to emphasize the latest information. Lists of headlines with story summaries or previews can be provided, linking interested readers to the full content. This **digest service** benefits readers scanning content for particular topics or interests. Including pictures with summaries is important in attracting reader interest, as are well-written summary headlines.

Color is another important consideration for web designers. Just as certain colors are difficult to read on the printed page, color can reduce website readability. Black type on white screens

FIGURE 14.8a *Details*, Whitney High School, Rocklin, Calif. Reproduced by permission of Sarah Nichols.

On the website of the *Details* yearbook the staff includes a banner of pictures and uses the typographic style of the current edition. Headers include Home, Events, Sports, Extra, More Time With, About and How To. The How To link provides visitors with information on how to buy the current book or past editions, purchase advertising, contribute photos, get portraits taken, join the staff or learn more.

WWW

WEBLINKS Check out www.typekit.com

This site sells typefaces built around web standards, which gives designers and developers a subscription-based library of hosted, high-quality fonts to use on their websites.

remains the clearest and least tiring color choice. Designers should be very careful about combining black on red or on other bright colors because the type will appear to resonate or move on the screen. Many readers will be discouraged by low readability and will stop reading. Just as the designer is the best friend to the written word in print, the same applies in online publications. Design and readability should go hand in hand.

Photographs should be downloaded at resolutions and in **compression formats** that will enable easy viewing but will keep the files compact enough to allow readers to open them quickly and easily. Photographs already digitized for the printed edition at higher resolutions should be reduced to 72 dots per inch. Photos can be saved as **JPEGs (Joint Photographic Experts Group)**, a picture compression format appropriate for the web.

The site should be easy to navigate and user-friendly. Navigation links to content should be easily accessible and clearly located. Placing links in consistent typographical designs in one

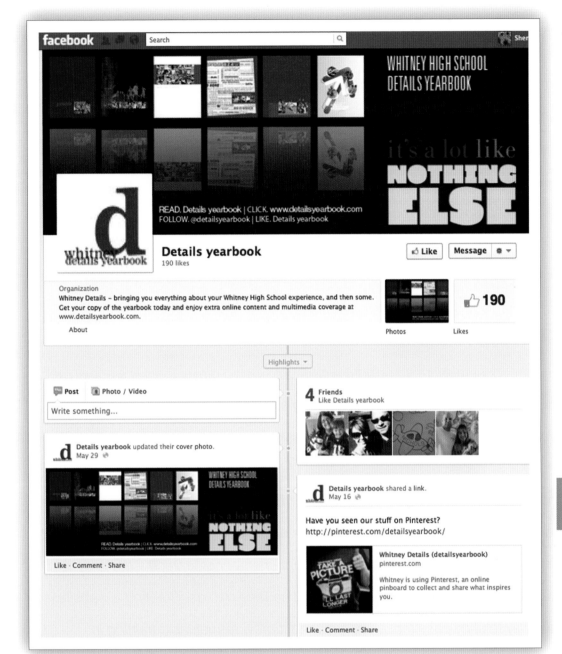

FIGURE 14.8b
The yearbook also maintains
a Facebook page.

location on the site will help readers find them. Including email addresses of the staff will facilitate reader participation. When possible, links to external content can be placed at appropriate places in the text or at the ends of stories. Providing an online search engine will help readers locate specific content. Attaching comment options will allow readers to post their thoughts, but a policy for commenting should be included, and comments should be moderated.

Video and audio clips should open easily and should be digitized in standard compression software and formats. Careful attention to editing will make best use of the space and memory necessary to include these clips on the site. The website can also link to video and audio clips posted on Vimeo, and photo galleries can be posted on Flickr.

Occasionally introducing one-time features such as contests, forums and special events will keep readers coming back to the site for fresh content. Contest giveaways such as free yearbooks or free newspaper subscriptions would be appropriate prizes. Or, online advertisers could be tapped for gift cards or certificates.

❝❝ WORDS of WISDOM

With the popularity of mobile devices, social networking and instant sharing, teens are used to constant communication. While the traditional yearbook model creates some disconnect with delayed gratification, new digital models present an opportunity for yearbook staff to maintain an ongoing relationship with their audience. During a major school event such as homecoming, for example, the yearbook staff can post photos on a Facebook page as the event takes place, allowing for a multi-user conversation through comments, likes and shares.

Using social media has become a critical component of the reporting and creation process. Tools like Facebook and Twitter enable reporters to pose questions, find sources, post survey links and connect quickly to others in the school community. Students live online, and it makes sense to connect with them using the most relevant and popular methods. Using digital tools like social media or a publication website also help from a sales and marketing standpoint, as students promote the publication and point readers to where they can order yearbooks, buy advertising space or purchase a photo they liked.

Adding or expanding an online presence also adds value to the book. Student journalists have the opportunity to tell more stories by producing multimedia content, including slideshows or other aspects not possible in a traditional book. This serves to complement – not replace – the print publication. In some cases, yearbook staff have thousands of unused photos. Creating a website is an easy and inexpensive way to showcase those images, and it provides valuable training in technology skills like using a content management system. Staff can use Flickr to create photo galleries or a free Tumblr blog as a way to offer readers something new, giving them something to click on and share – which matches much of teens' online activity. The key is to treat the online content with the same respect as what goes in the printed publication, expecting nothing less than high-quality images with accurate and detailed reporting. My kids publish content on Pinterest (http://pinterest.com/detailsyearbook/) and also have a "behind the scenes" Tumblr blog about the yearbook staff (http://www.detailsyearbook.tumblr.com/).

Sarah Nichols, Adviser, Details Yearbook, Whitney High School, Rocklin, Calif.

FIGURE 14.9 *The Rider Online*, Legacy High School, Mansfield, Texas. Screengrab of home page, May 18, 2012. Reproduced by permission of Leland Mallett.

a *Rider Online* showcases news with a flashing banner of content at the top of the site. **b** Major navigation links across the top of the page contain sub-navigation listings that drop down, linking to more specific content. "Extra" includes student-produced content from non-staff members, a link to coverage of live events, a chat room and links to paid game sites. A header entitled, "I Am Legacy" showcases videos and slideshows, and an area for daily photos keeps fresh content on the site. A link to "Print Edition" appears in the navigation bar.

FIGURE 14.10 *HiLite*, Carmel High School, Carmel, Ind. Screengrab from May 18, 2012 issue. Reproduced by permission of Jim Streisel.

The *HiLite* website provides a list of QR code links for the issue, for readers who may not have smartphones. Making content easily accessible is important to users who may get frustrated searching for online content.

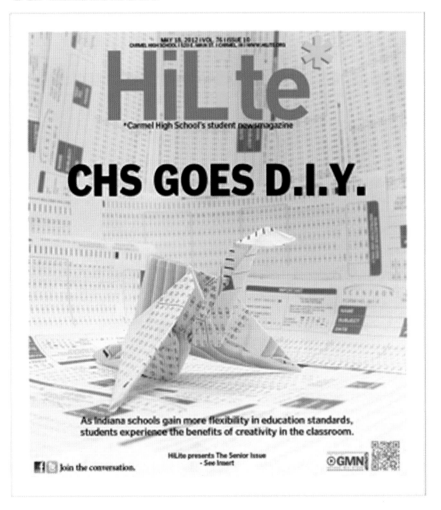

Our Latest Issue

Links to QR codes from our latest issue

▸ **Feature: HiLite religion stories**

▸ **Feature: HiLite Pinterest page**

▸ **Student Section: HiLite Twitter Page**

▸ **Sports: Spring sports previews**

▸ **Perspectives: Caroline & Monica's food blog**

▸ **15 Minutes of Fame: Sophomore Ella Spoerle is a professional dancer**

▸ **Prom King & Queen: Rafael Miranda and Amber O'Connell are the 2012 prom king and queen**

Ten things to think about before you design or redesign your newspapers website:

Brand your site

Within a newspaper's website are many different areas of content; headlines, subheads (deck heads), body copy, sidebar copy, photos, video, audio, graphics, plus others. Your goal should be to create a unified feel throughout the site, from page to page, so that it is clear to the reader that they have not left the site. Branding your publication will create an emotional connection for your reader.

Grids, grids, grids

Websites today are designed around an industry standard computer display of 1024x768 pixels, which essentially is the whole monitor screen. A web design of 960 or 978 pixels wide fits perfectly in a browser window. Using the 960 pixel grid (http://960.gs/) or the 978 pixel grid (http://978.gs/) can help you divide your page into a header, main-bar, sidebar and footer. These grid systems can help you maintain a similar visual look from page to page.

Use white space

Common thought tends to be that design is about the mark on the page, when in reality it's about the white space around that mark. The less white space around marks, the more cluttered the page will look. Give designs room to breathe. The 978 pixel grid system works better, in my opinion, because it allows for more white space in the design.

Proximity

We tend to group similar items based on how close they are to one another, which is called proximity. Making sure similar information is grouped together is key to a good website. This also means grouping similar pages together in the navigation.

I want a big screen TV

Humans are very visual, that is why we like to see big pictures. Include a big picture at the top of the page that introduces the best story of the day. Most news websites trend toward smaller pictures but use the limitless space the web offers.

Usability

Whenever I buy a new clock radio I need to look at a page of instructions (in small type) so I can set it. Websites don't have instructions, but things are familiar from using other websites such as underlined text, text that's a different color, items that change color when you mouse over them. You know that these items are interactive. It's important that you don't make something look interactive if it's not or it becomes confusing to the user.

Don't reinvent the wheel

Why do most websites have a site ID (logo) in the upper left page corner and primary navigation across the top or down the left side? Because a website loads from the top left corner of a browser window. If the site ID was on the right and the navigation was on the bottom, a user opening the page on a lower resolution monitor might not be able to see these important pieces of information. Help can be found by looking at major corporate websites to see how they place information on a page.

No hidden navigation

When creating a navigation menu bar that has more navigation when you mouse over it, such as a drop-down menu or a fly-out menu, give the user clues to the additional information that is initially hidden. Add an arrow or plus sign to any navigation link that has more navigation when you mouse over it.

HTML Web standards

When designing a site it is important to follow the common uses of HTML tags. A search engine needs to be able to find and understand your content. Common tags like H1, H2, H3 for headings, P for body copy and ASIDE for sidebar copy will provide a clear understanding of content by search engines, which will enable the site to be ranked higher.

Create designs for multiple devices

Once you've created the design for a computer screen you now need to think about designing it for a tablet and a smartphone. More people are viewing content on tables and smartphones, and you don't want your design to be shrunk down to fit on those smaller screens. You want the design to work with the screen size. Designers are designing to at least three screen sizes, 1024, 768 and 300 pixels wide.

Darren A. Sanefski, Assistant Professor of Multimedia and Design,
The Meek School of Journalism and New Media,
University of Mississippi

COOPERATIVE EFFORTS

As more schools develop websites and online content, school publications can form partnerships with other publications in their regions and states. Some states have already established networks allowing schools to share information and news reports. Linking to other publications' sites can provide student readers with other perspectives on issues of common concern. Linking to state and national press associations (see Appendix) gives readers the opportunity to compare their own paper's coverage to that of other publications. Student writers can also access information about other schools in their state and beyond when researching stories. Many newspapers include summary reports of news from other schools. My High School Journalism (myhsj.org) offers a news service with free content and a weekly national edition.

Journalists from several schools can also arrange for joint interviews through Internet services such as Skype, which allow the subjects to respond to questions in real time. Interviewers can follow up with questions in response to comments from other interviewers or from the subject being interviewed.

A different form of cooperative interviewing is video conferencing. Through video-conferencing software such as Adobe Connect or Go To Meeting (gotomeeting.com), students can interview people in distant locations and can actually see and talk to them through video hook-ups. These possibilities broaden the resources and possibilities available to student journalists.

CONCLUSION

The future of multimedia online journalism can evoke both excitement and trepidation. With all the new and evolving technologies available, student journalists can take advantage of better research and reporting opportunities to tell compelling stories, both visually and verbally.

Enhancing print content with frequently updated web material bridges gaps in publishing schedules and offers opportunities to stay connected to student readers with innovative multimedia and interactive content.

Student journalists will help shape the future of the media landscape. School publications may soon develop their own mobile apps, just as many professional publications have done. Eventually, parts or all, of the printed yearbook may also become a tablet magazine. And who knows what other communications channels will emerge?

SUMMARY

- A website is crucial for all publications to stay connected with readers and to offer unique and expanded content.

- A web editor and staff should work alongside the print editor and staff to identify ways in which appropriate visual and verbal content can be generated for the website.

- Print content should link to the website's coverage through appropriate page and story weblinks and QR codes.

- Staff without websites can use free online resources such as WordPress or *my high school journalism* (my.hsj.org) to create and manage their site and content.

- The website should seek, and actively involve, appropriate non-staff contributors.

- Yearbook staff should be proactive in establishing websites to interest potential buyers and to utilize multimedia content to expand coverage in the print edition.

- The website's design should make navigation easy and should encourage usability and readability through appropriate color, type and organization.

KEY TERMS

citizen journalists

compression formats

computer-assisted
   reporting

content banners

digest service

footer bar

header bar

JPEG format

navigation content
   headers

open content

open source content
   management systems

photo releases

QR code

sub-navigation links

web editor/manager

EXERCISES

1   Visit the website of your local newspaper, if it has one, or of a larger, regional newspaper. Analyze its effectiveness by answering these questions:

   (a) Is the site visually interesting and easy to read?

   (b) Is color used effectively?

   (c) Is the site easy to navigate? Is it easy to find specific information on the site?

   (d) Is it easy to contact staff members for questions or to leave comments on content?

   (e) Is the content different from that of the printed publication? Is it fresh and updated frequently? Is it easy to find timely content?

   (f) Is multimedia used effectively on the website? Is it appealing and informative?

   (g) Are graphics and other multimedia forms used effectively in presenting information?

2   Visit the Student Press website at http://studentpress.org. Once at the site, click on "NSPA," the National Scholastic Press Association website. Then click on "Best of the high school press." The site maintains links to winners of the national press association's annual contest for newspaper, yearbook and online websites. Visit several newspaper and online websites and analyze the effectiveness of their design and content. Which sites are your favorites? Why? What is a feature you particularly like? Watch a video and comment on its interest level to readers.

3   If your school or student publications have a website, evaluate its effectiveness using the criteria in Exercise 1. In class, discuss the site's strengths and weaknesses. Compare these sites with those of a nearby school and student publication.

4   On paper, outline and sketch an online site for yourself. Choose a name and design for the site. What colors would you use? How would you divide your site's content into navigation links? What content would you add to the site?

5   Visit the website of a metropolitan city newspaper and view an online multimedia presentation. Does the presentation offer interesting content and information?

6   Visit the website of the Newseum (newseum.org) and click on Today's Front-Pages. Click on the websites of three of the newspapers and compare the way the information is presented with the printed front-pages. Note stories that have been updated and added to since the print edition was published.

7   Invite the school's media specialist or a local media specialist to discuss online search engines and efficient online searches. Prepare a list of five general topics from five different sections of the newspaper to use as sample search topics.

VISUAL STORYTELLING: PICTURES, ART AND GRAPHICS

15

> *The best storytelling happens when words, pictures (moving or still) and presentation combine like a symphony. Together they'll achieve a higher state than each can alone. Consider how each medium can tell the story and recognize that they don't have to mirror each other. Words can tell a story one way, pictures another and the design can add yet another voice while unifying the entire presentation. Engaging an audience is the goal; the more dimensional your presentation, the more likely you'll achieve that goal.*

Mike Davis, Independent Picture Editor, Owner, One28 Media, Former Picture Editor, The Oregonian *and*

The Albuquerque Tribune

LEARNING OBJECTIVES After completing this chapter you will be able to:

- understand the importance of visuals in storytelling
- recognize the qualities of content and composition that make a strong photograph
- understand the importance of ethics in photojournalism
- tell stories through a variety of visual forms including illustrations and infographics
- write a good caption for a photograph
- edit photographs and archive them for use in publications
- enhance web content through slideshows and videos.

WITH THE ADVENT OF SMARTPHONES and mobile devices, almost everyone can *take* a picture. But not everyone can *make a picture*. The difference is often dramatic.

Close your eyes. Think about a picture that has significant personal meaning to you. Maybe it represents a special personal experience. Perhaps it was taken by a close friend or relative. Recall the smallest details of the picture's content – from the subjects' expressions to the clothes they are wearing.

Keep your eyes closed. Concentrate on a famous, well-known picture you've seen or studied. Recall the significant details of the picture's content. A photojournalist or illustration photographer with training and experience may have *made* that memorable picture. So even though you don't have a personal connection to the content and weren't present when the image was taken, the quality of the image's information makes the picture memorable.

Amazing, isn't it? Almost everyone can recall the content of a favorite personal image and a famous historical image just from memory. Such is the power of visual images. Details as minor as facial expressions, clothing and other circumstances of the pictures can be vividly recalled. These bits of information are stored deep in the hippocampus, the brain's permanent storage area.

Just as images are important and powerful in everyday life, so are they important in student publications. Distracted readers bombarded with many information resources have to limit their media consumption. Images with stopping power – those that readers find interesting and meaningful – are more likely to be viewed and remembered. Websites allow photographers to add visual slideshows and videos to supplement their work. Web content also allows more people and events to be seen by a broader audience. Online content can be shared on social media sites, reaching people beyond the school campus such as alumni and other interested individuals.

WWW

WEBLINK Check out

www.poyi.org/

Pictures of the Year International includes winners from this annual international photography competition in both still and multimedia photography. The site also includes good links to other photography sites and educational information.

THE IMPORTANCE OF VISUALS

In a student publication or on a website, images can be used for a variety of reasons: to identify, to report, to entertain, to inform and to amuse. But most importantly, pictures are a key part of the storytelling process. They shouldn't be used to fill space, to decorate pages, to hold type or for other extraneous reasons. Rather, pictures and other visuals should be used because they add to the verbal reporting. They provide a different kind of interest and information to the publication, and they appeal to, and attract, the interest of readers in different ways.

FIGURE 15.1 *Globe*, Clayton High School, Clayton, Mo. Reproduced by permission of Erin Castellano.

Without pictures to help tell this story, readers would have no reference point for the swimmer highlighted in this story on her success as a nationally ranked swimmer who doesn't swim for her school. Both pictures help readers visualize her training regimen. The dominant photo also holds the main headline and provides a wider angle in the lanes of the pool at a pivotal moment in her stroke. The photographer also places her at a far right position allowing her room to swim into the left. The second, smaller photo is cropped tightly to her face and arm providing additional information.

❝❝ WORDS of WISDOM

One of the biggest challenges for student multimedia storytellers is knowing what the story is. What is the purpose of your story and what are you trying to show and say? This takes a bit of time in the early stages of creating a multimedia piece, but once you figure this out, it will guide you in figuring out what to photograph, what questions to ask and what to shoot for video. You will make the most of your time, and editing becomes a lot easier.

When it comes to gathering media, make sure you understand what each form of media can do to enhance your story. Stills freeze a moment in time to emphasize a decisive moment, video can give the viewer an experience and audio can be the driving force in the narrative as well as relaying a sense of environment with natural sound.

When you get to the edit, make sure you play on the strength of what you've gathered through the various forms of media. Keep the story in mind and avoid redundancy. When you think you're done, get feedback from the people who can give you an honest critique. Evaluating your own work is one of the hardest things to do.

Most students who produce multimedia work are coming from the visual side of things. Most people have experience taking pictures and video, but very few come in knowing how to record audio in the field, whether natural sound or an interview. Because of this, audio tends to take a back seat in every step of the gathering and editing process. Make an effort to learn how to collect and edit audio as a single form of media and your multimedia stories will be that much better.

Sung Park, Instructor of Photojournalism/Multimedia School of Journalism and Communication, University of Oregon ❞❞

Yearbook and newspaper photographers should constantly be shooting pictures and videos around the school – in classrooms, in hallways, before school, after school, at sports events, at club meetings and at special school events. Photographers are the visual documentarians of the school. They should carry cameras to class with them so the students become accustomed to having their pictures taken and will react naturally to the camera. The widespread use of smartphones has helped this process. Pictures are taken all the time in today's world, not just on special occasions.

Experienced photographers will help novice photographers by mentoring them through the process of shooting, especially in large gatherings where they may be intimidated by the size of the crowd. During sports events, mentors can remind inexperienced photographers to cover all aspects of the event – from the crowds in the stands to the action on the court or field. Shooting as partners will enable the photographers to feel more comfortable and less conspicuous, and will result in the photographers moving around, getting closer to their subject matter.

WWW

WEBLINK Check out
www.the37thframe.org

The 37th frame posts
photojournalism work
from veteran and emerging
photojournalists. It's particularly
helpful for learning about
long-form picture stories.

Photographs aren't the only form of visual storytelling. Cartoons, art, illustrations and infographics may be better ways to provide visual interest to stories and enliven page layouts. Staff should look beyond their own members in seeking illustrators and cartoonists to add variety to layouts. Identifying strong illustrators from the school's art department is a good way to start this process.

The use of effective graphics in design also adds to attractive layouts. Rule lines, screens, colors and text details give the designer many tools for effective layout (see Chapter 12 for more information).

PHOTOGRAPHS

Photographs should be used in design both for their content and for their technical strengths. Good publication staff create parameters for the technical quality of photos and adhere to those standards throughout the publication. Selecting content, on the other hand, is more subjective. A student trained as a good picture editor can prove invaluable in working with photographers and editors to select the pictures for publication that do the best job of providing meaningful content.

Technical parameters

A good photograph has several qualities. First, it's always in focus so the important content can be seen and understood. Second, the picture should have a range of good exposure. Areas of the picture known as the shadows should be rendered in shades of black or rich, dark tones. Midtones should show as shades of gray in black-and-white photos, or have a range of tonalities in color photos. **Highlights** should be the lightest areas of the picture, but are not necessarily white. Generally, the highlight areas should retain some detail. When using more than one picture on a page, it's important that the tones in the pictures are consistent. A poorly exposed, washed-out picture will lose all appeal next to a picture with good tonal values.

When taking a picture, good photographers are careful to correctly expose the digital image using the camera's light-metering system. In the traditional darkroom, photographers learn to use advanced printing skills that enable them to "**burn in**," or darken, areas that would reproduce without tone in the publication, or "**dodge**" areas that would reproduce too darkly and with solid tonality.

In today's electronic environment, the tools of the traditional darkroom are available to photographers through the electronic toning features of programs such as Adobe Photoshop or Photoshop Elements.

Good photographers must take the publication's printing method into consideration when preparing pictures for publication. Many newspaper and yearbook printers have a difficult time reproducing photographs in which the **contrast** – the range of tones – is too extreme. Pictures with a little less contrast will often reproduce more effectively. Photographers must therefore make adjustments to their finished pictures to ensure the tones will be reproducible. Many tools are available for improving picture tonality, but correct initial exposure will ensure pictures have the data necessary for tonal adjustment. Working with the printer, doing exposure tests to calibrate computers or using print profiles will ensure correct picture reproduction.

Digital camera equipment should be kept clean and be protected to ensure that problems do not occur. Digital chips in SLR cameras attract dust through static charge and may need to be cleaned professionally from time to time. "**Point-and-shoot**" digitals are immune to this problem.

Good electronic filing systems are particularly important to the digital photographer. A protocol needs to be established to ensure that consistency is maintained in the electronic storage of images. Consistency is also important in ensuring that every photographer is saving images with set guidelines determined by the publication. Adobe's Photoshop can be set to "batch" images with a sequence of actions that can be applied to each image in a file for basic uniformity. Using Adobe Lightroom and Bridge for editing images will give photographers a method of organizing and editing images from each shoot. Electronic archives should be created through a logical system of organization. Archives should be built for storing raw files (unaltered images) as back-up. Designs can be built using lower resolution images, which will load faster

FIGURE 15.2 *The Indian*, Shawnee Mission North High School, Overland Park, Kan. Reproduced by permission of Shawnee Mission North Principal Richard Kramer.

A technically strong photograph was made from a composite of three strong portraits of students displaying their tattoos in this yearbook spread. The photographer took time to shoot each portrait in interesting, strong, directional side lighting placed to illuminate each tattoo. Each student's position in the portrait is also carefully chosen to spotlight the tattoo. The perspective sizes of the students in the composite adds depth and dimensionality.

when designing the initial layout. The final toned, high-resolution images can then be placed in the page layouts before going to print. Images on websites only need to be 72 **dpi** (dots per inch), though print images will often need to be 200 to 300 dpi.

Content and composition

Good photographs have strong content. While evaluation of content is somewhat subjective, certain qualities are universally agreed upon. A good picture uses good compositional techniques, which photographers should keep in mind when shooting. Using some of the following traditional rules of composition will improve the content.

- **A center of interest**. The reason why a photograph was taken should be obvious to the viewer. In most pictures, the content will be immediately visible and strategically placed in the frame. Beginning photographers who stand too far away from their subjects may create images in which the viewer is left to search for the photograph's meaning. Photographers who fill the frame with meaningful content will produce images of higher visual interest. With **standard lenses**, photographers may need to be as close as five–seven feet from their subjects in order to fill the frame. Longer lenses, called **telephotos** or **zooms**, can bring content into the frame from a greater distance. A telephoto lens (also known as a "long lens") can be useful when a photographer cannot get physically close to a subject. A zoom lens accommodates a range of focal lengths, allowing a photographer to use any focal length within the range.

- **Rule of thirds**. Photographing a subject by placing it directly in the middle of the frame usually results in a less interesting and static picture. Long a rule in art and architecture, the "**golden mean points**" dictate that meaningful content be placed in areas of the frame other than the center. When looking through the **viewfinder** of the camera, the window that enables the photographer to see the content, the photographer can visually divide the space into thirds, both vertically and horizontally. The intersections of these thirds result in the golden mean points. These points are the most powerful areas for placing primary visual information in the frame. When using the rule of thirds, photographers should make sure that what is next to the subject is adding to the visual context of the photograph.

WWW

Weblink Check out

lightbox.time.com

Lightbox, *Time* magazine: Curated by *Time* magazine photo editors, this site includes current and archived work. It also links directly to the archive of *Life* magazine with its vault of classic picture stories.

FIGURE 15.3 *Wingspan*, Enochs High School, Modesto, Calif. Reproduced by permission of Tamra McCarthy.

There is no mistaking the subject of this picture's center of interest. In a tie-dyed shirt that matches the purple of the hula hoop framing her, this student is also caught in the fun of her event displayed in her expression. The photographer used shallow depth of field to keep the background softly out of focus. The photographer's tilted angle adds to the motion of the action and helps block out the two faces behind the girl. The yearbook staff chose wisely in making this picture a dominant on this spread. The girl's face and head also point the reader to the headline and into the spread's content.

- **Leading lines.** Lines in photographs can lead the viewer directly to the primary subject matter. These lines can be obvious, such as a road or path someone is walking on, or can be subtle, such as geometric lines repeated in a stairwell or in architectural details.

- **Framing.** Framing in a picture takes advantage of foreground or background detail to provide a partial border or frame around the subject matter. Portrait photographers often use parts of flowers or tree branches to subtly frame their subjects to provide texture and contrast. Photographers shooting scenic images often include nearby trees in the image's foreground to show distance and scale.

- **Grounds.** Though photographs compress three dimensions into two, they can still show depth and indicate spatial differences. Placing meaningful content in the foreground, the middle ground and the background of the image will take advantage of this principle. If the information in any of the areas is not contributing to the contextual information, the photographer can often use a technique known as shallow depth of field to improve it.

- **Depth of field** refers to the range of focus from the foreground to the background of the image. Photographers control the depth of field through three factors when taking the picture: the lens used, the size of the **aperture** or lens opening and the distance from their subjects. Longer lenses such as telephotos will render shallower depth of field than shorter ones such as wide angles.

A photographer seeking to eliminate a distracting background could change camera position to effectively "clean up" the information behind the subject, eliminating it completely or rendering it in softer focus. If changing position isn't possible to completely eliminate the distracting elements, the photographer could use **shallow depth of field** to make the background information less focused and less distracting. Viewers will concentrate on areas of sharp focus. When using shallow depth of field, the information in the frame isn't necessarily blurry, indicating camera movement when the picture was taken. Rather, it's soft and indistinct in focus.

A long, telephoto lens will always have a shallower depth of field than a shorter lens, such as a wide angle which usually has good depth of field. Large **f-stops**, such as 2, 2.8 and 3.5, will always provide shallow depth of field or **selective focus**. F-stops are the settings on the lens which control the size of the opening allowing light to expose an image on the camera's sensor. The smaller the number the larger the opening. Getting close to subjects forces the camera to hyperfocus, also providing shallow depth of field.

FIGURE 15.4 *The Decamhian*, Del Campo High School, Fair Oaks, Calif. Reproduced by permission of Jim Jordan.

Placing the subject of this spread at the right intersection of the rule of thirds gives the photograph interesting space used by the yearbook designer for supporting information in this spread on students' life habits. The photographer's low angle adds to the interest as do the repeating yellow lines of the bleacher edges. Keeping the face and head cropped out of the image adds mystery and focus to the habit displayed.

FIGURE 15.5 *The Hornet*, Bryant High School, Bryant, Ariz. Reproduced by permission of Margaret Sorrows.

Emerging from the stadium tunnel through a spirit banner, football players are framed as they jog onto the field at the beginning of a game. The photographer's low angle shooting from behind them adds interesting light to the scene as they emerge from the darkness into the stadium's illumination. The yearbook designer used the photo in a dramatic way by making it bleed on three sides of the spread and giving it dominance in the design.

These factors are all relative to each other. So a photographer seeking shallow depth of field would stand closer to the subject using a longer lens set to a wider aperture.

- **Lighting.** Interesting lighting can make a picture more appealing. Silhouettes – images that show shape against a light background – are one example of interesting lighting. Dramatically lighted skies or sunsets after storms can also create lighting that adds to a

FIGURE 15.6 *The Image*, Dos Pueblos Senior High School, Goleta, Calif. Reproduced by permission of John Dent.

By moving in close to the action and using a longer, telephoto lens, this photographer creates depth in this fun photo. The combination of closeness to the subject and the long lens helped the photographer achieve really shallow depth of field in the background. The muted, darker tones provide a clean, simple background to the image. The boy's face is in the foreground in sharp focus as the girl, in the middle ground of the photo, squirts him with whipped cream. The use of all three grounds adds depth and dimensionality.

FIGURE 15.7 *The Harbinger*, Shawnee Mission East High School, Prairie Village, Kan. Reproduced by permission of C. Dow Tate.

Silhouettes make interesting images through their combination of solid outline shapes against interesting background light and are one example of interesting lighting. In this photo with a layered sunset in late afternoon, the photographer wisely took advantage of the situation by photographing a soccer player from a low angle. Note that the details of her face, hair and arms holding the soccer ball provide all necessary information. Silhouettes also work well for holding type, especially when shot using the rule of thirds with empty space on one side of the image.

picture's appeal. Pictures shot with light coming into the camera from side angles result in **side light** that emphasizes texture and form. **Outline light**, strong light from behind the subject, can provide a halo effect, which is sometimes useful when shooting people, since the sun will be away from their faces. Pictures of people shot in bright sunlight with the sun behind the photographer will result in **flat light,** or light that flattens the shadows and eliminates any detail. The photographer will also have problems with squinting subjects whose eyes may be almost shut. Shooting outdoors on overcast days will also result in flat light, where no shadows or texture detail will be present.

SPORTS

Inside

Lowell High School
March 23, 2012
Page 13

■ Reporter follows
career of rising star
Jeremy Lin.
Page 17

Cardinals blow competition out of water

CHRIS LEE

Junior **Dylan Westover** swims the butterfly on March 2 against Wallenberg. Both varsity teams beat the Bulldogs 25-0 at Sava Pool. Both the JV boys and girls won, 129-6, 128-13.

By Samantha Wilcox

THE STARTING GUN signaled the passionate cheering from spectators as swimmers launched off the blocks and began to power through the water. With hearts pounding to the rhythm of the swimmers' rapid strokes and jagged breaths, the Cardinals proudly plunged into their new season.

Over 30 JV and varsity swimmers returned to the team this season, so the Cardinals are boasting a 61-man team. This is massive compared to other schools in the Academic Athletic Association, such as the Wallenberg Bulldogs, who only have a 13-man of JV swimmers.

The Cardinals routed the Galileo Lions with ease on March 15. With Varsity boys and girls winning 144-25 and 128-0, this is just another standout victory for the Cardinals. JV girls and boys also blew the Lions out of the water 123-31 and 125-15.

After dominating the first meet of the season over the Wallenberg Bulldogs on March 2, when confronting the Balboa Buccaneers on March 9 the Cardinals took home the win for all divisions. Varsity boys went home with a shut-out with 25-0, while varsity girls took home a massive win of 25-6. JV boys and girls also joined in the festivities with scores of 99-58

and 113-43.

The team's head coach, Jonathan Riley — better known to swimmers as "Jo-Jo" — is expecting a great season for the team. "I've coached for the Cardinals for five years," Riley said. "I started swimming at Sava at 10 years old and while at Riordan."

The Cardinals work hard for their reputation in the world of AAA swimming. "Junior varsity teams are divided into two groups, each practicing three times a week," freshman JV swimmer Eva Heyert said. "We typically swim about 4,000 yards each practice." Four-thousand yards are 160 laps. Varsity swimmers practice five days a week at Sava Pool, as well. Their practices are similar to the JV team practices, but the intervals are accelerated. Intervals are the time given for swimmers to complete a set.

Practices are long and tiring, but worth it to the teammates. "Although the practices are hard, I know that they are making me a better swimmer overall," Heyert said.

Clocking in numerous hours a week at Sava Pool, swimmers have improved immensely thanks to intense work and dedication. "I've been swimming for eight years," freshman JV swimmer Jordan Jiang said. "My goal for this season would be to get a time under 24 seconds on my 50-yard freestyle." A

50-yard freestyle is two lengths of the pool.

Although the Cardinals had many successes, each group does not always win the championship, hence the teams have stepped up their efforts.

Last year, varsity boys, girls and JV girls all took home the win in their divisions, with only the JV boys losing to the Lincoln Mustangs. "There is some stiff competition in the AAA this season," Riley said. "Lincoln and Washington are both great competitors, and in those upcoming meets, we need to make sure our lineups are set properly to score as many points as possible."

The Cardinals are always looking to improve on their skills. "We have been working on our "under waters" quite a bit this season to gain more speed off of our starts and turns." Riley said. "Our goal every season is to improve with faster times at Championships, to win all AAA divisions, hopefully break a few records and most importantly, to have a safe season."

The Cardinals are very proud of their accomplishments as a team. "Our strengths this season are our team unity and senior leadership," Riley said.

Bring your school spirit today at 3:30 p.m. at Sava Pool to see the Cardinals face off against the Lincoln Mustangs.
A VERSION OF THIS STORY FIRST WWW.THELOWELL.ORG

Taylor "TK" Takao wins the 145-pound All-City Championship on Feb. 25 at Lincoln High School.

JOE FIORELLO

Wrestling takes third

By Sean Wang

AFTER MONTHS OF DETERMINATION, hard work and relentless drilling, the wrestling season has finally ended, with mixed, but gratifying, results.

On Feb. 25, the Cardinals placed third overall at the annual Athletic Academic Association All-City championship at Lincoln High School. Five Lowell wrestlers were amongst the top three finishers in their weight classes, four of which made the finals. Senior captain Taylor Takao and sophomore Rostyslav Tolochko were crowned All-City champions in the 145 and 220-pound weight classes, respectively. "Compared to last year we did much better, and we're a sophomore-heavy team, which means we're in great shape for the future," senior co-captain Emilio Wise said, who placed third in the 132-pound weight class. (See "The Logistics of Wrestling" for weight class explanation, *The Lowell*, Jan. 2012).

The team's champions, Takao and Tolochko, went on to Bakersfield during the weekend of March 9-10, but did not place in the State finals.

Two female wrestlers, senior captain Ivy Ouyang, a competitor in the 146-pound weight class, and junior Alondra Barajas from the 132-pound weight class, advanced on to their own State Invitational Championships, held at Lemoore High School in Lemoore from Feb. 24-25. Because the AAA section for girls is so small, the California Interscholastic Federation required female wrestlers from San Francisco to compete at the Central Coast Section Championships. There Ouyang took the wrestling title and Barajas placed fourth in their respective

See WRESTLING on Page 18

FIGURE 15.8 *The Lowell*, Lowell High School, San Francisco, Calif. Photographer Chris Lee. Page design by sports editor Joseph Fiorello. Reproduced by permission of Sharn Matusek.

The strong impact of this swimming shot engages the reader's attention. The photograph shows peak action with the swimmer's arms spread across the water. A fast shutter speed on the camera freezes all the water splashing from the swimmer's arms as he breaststrokes through the pool. The photographer also shot the subject on the right rule of thirds points. A strong horizontal crop and the large use of the photo spanning the text columns add to the impact on this newspaper sports page.

- **Impact**. Impact is the photograph's stopping power. A viewer may be attracted to an image because of its dramatic content. Pictures of conflict often fall into this category. Dramatic images of peak action in sports have strong impact because they capture action that is often impossible to see on the field when the event is actually taking place. Or pictures shot at peak moments may show players' bodies at diagonals to the ground, indicating the intensity of the moment. This diagonal motion is also visually interesting because it's dramatic.

  Impact can result when strong emotion or reaction is present in a picture. High schools offer many opportunities for photographers to capture emotion. Competitions are held for clubs and organizations. When someone is named a winner or a loser of such a competition, strong emotion is bound to result. Sporting events are full of emotion, with players, fans, cheerleaders and parents all invested in the outcome. Even classrooms can be arenas for emotion or reaction when students are asked to perform a dissection in biology, present a speech or act out a literary classic.

  Impact can also result from humorous or surprising incidents. If a group of cheerleaders practicing a pyramid tumble into disarray, with flailing arms and intense laughter, a photographer may want to capture the fun of the moment. A photograph of a student holding a baby for the first time in a child development class could elicit viewer response if the interaction between the student and the baby is striking.

  Meaningful relationships will create interesting content with impact. Schools are full of relationships, including those of older and younger students, peers, friends, boyfriend/ girlfriend, teachers and students and athletes and coaches, to name just a few. Focusing on the interactions between people is important to good storytelling. It also means that most photos will contain more than one person.

TELLING STORIES THROUGH IMAGES

Often, a well-chosen, single image will be effective in presenting information to a viewer. The single image can be used by itself as a **stand-alone** photograph, or it can accompany a story. A stand-alone image requires a complete caption to give the reader the necessary detail and to provide identification for the people pictured. Many newspapers use stand-alone images in a particular design style, with a small headline or **catchline**, above the image, and a complete caption underneath. These stand-alone photos are often set off in the design by rule lines or boxes to indicate their singular storytelling function. Stand-alone pictures can be news pictures, pictures of events or activities or feature-oriented images chosen for their striking content.

Single pictures used to accompany text should be carefully chosen. The content should amplify that of the verbal text. Designers should vary the sizes and placements of single pictures throughout publications so the design doesn't become predictable and static. The images should be cropped to strengthen content and eliminate distracting elements. The picture's size and shape should be determined by its strengths and should not be compromised because of a predetermined picture shape on the layout.

Picture packages or groups

When more than a single image is needed to tell a story, a **picture package** or group can be used. Usually consisting of two or three images, a picture package is edited to make sure each image adds to the reader's understanding of an event. Therefore, each photo should contribute different information. For instance, one picture might be a wide shot, giving the reader a general feel for the event. Another shot might be a close-up, where the photographer has used a longer lens to isolate a few individuals participating in the event or some other detail. An additional shot might show the outcome or result of the event or activity, capitalizing on emotion.

A special type of picture group is a **picture sequence**, used to show a series. A speaker with an interesting visual speaking pattern could be shown in two or three shots with different expressions and gestures. A sports sequence is appropriate to show a pivotal play or series of plays in a game. Or a sequence could show how to do something, such as how to throw a pot on a wheel in a ceramics class. How-to sequences showing the main steps of

FIGURE 15.9 "Nailing It," from *Blue & Gold*, Findlay High School, Findlay, Ohio. Reprinted with permission.

This stand-alone photo is used without an accompanying story on a news page. Photographing classroom projects and situations is a good way to show events of interest throughout the school without printing a story that might be dated due to the time delay between publishing cycles. The newspaper has a specific style of displaying a stand-alone photo by using a catchline headline and a deck above it, enclosing it in a rule-lined box and including a longer, storytelling caption with a label headline to provide the details without a story.

FIGURE 15.10 *Northwest Passage*, Shawnee Mission Northwest High School, Shawnee, Kan. Reproduced by permission of Susan Massey.

A package of four pictures offers readers more visual information about this aspiring musician in a two-page layout. The right page's dominant image effectively introduces the reader to the musician in his music-oriented environment. The column of smaller photos on the left page contributes visual scenes and information from the mixing board and computer the student uses in his pursuit of music. Using combinations of photos helps readers understand more about the subject.

doing something, such as how to carve a pumpkin or how to throw a football, sometimes include numbered steps in their captions.

Picture stories

Picture stories are just like verbal stories except told with images rather than just words. A picture story should have a beginning, middle and end. Subjects for picture stories are abundant in schools. They should be broad enough to offer a range of picture possibilities, but narrow

FIGURE 15.11 *Blue & Gold*, Findlay High School, Findlay, Ohio, p. 6, Oct. 22, 2010. Reprinted with permission.

A picture story or essay is a strong way to cover a major event or activity in a school and many newspapers designate a page devoted to this content every issue. In addition, on news websites, photo galleries, slideshows and photo soundslides – galleries with added sound – add strong visual coverage and interest for viewers.

On a page labeled, "Big Picture," this newspaper's back page covers homecoming week through six carefully edited images that show a range of activities. A dominant image at the top anchors the coverage accompanied by three vertical and two horizontal images.

A fun and appropriately feature-oriented headline anchors the top of the page, and a small amount of text provides context. Each picture includes a complete caption with a catchline lead-lin.

FIGURE 15.12 *The Harbinger*, Shawnee Mission East High School, Prairie Village, Kan. Reproduced by permission of C. Dow Tate.

Yearbook spreads are traditionally designed around picture stories on activities, topics, subjects, sports and other areas of coverage. In addition to having a variety of people on these spreads, the pictures should be carefully edited to show a variety of content avoiding visual redundancy. This yearbook tennis spread anchors coverage with a dynamic dominant image in which the tennis player seems to be hitting the ball off the page. Additional images show the reader a range of other action tennis players are involved in during matches.

FIGURE 15.13 *Crusader*, Mt. Kapaun Carmel Catholic High School, Wichita, Kan. Reproduced by permission of Ashley Watkins.

In many high schools, natural illumination without flash will provide the best lighting for photos for publications. With window light coming from one side of the room, as many high schools offer, and overhead light, a balanced lighting exposure can often be achieved with a shutter speed of 1/60th of a second metered with an appropriate f-stop. In each of these evenly illuminated classroom shots, no harsh flash shadows mar the images.

enough to be able to tell the story in about five–seven well-chosen pictures. Picture stories can be used on single pages or on double trucks in the school newspaper. Yearbook spreads are often built around picture stories. Backstage commotion during a play production, a weekend debate tournament, a student demonstrating a special skill or a team having a good or a difficult season would all be possible picture stories.

Picture stories take time and planning. A photographer may want to observe and research a topic before embarking on the shoot. A photographer might work in conjunction with a reporter so that a verbal story can appear with the picture story to complete the presentation. Good,

WWW

WEBLINK Check out

www.alexiafoundation.org

The Alexia Photo Competition includes winning work from the annual competition named in honor of a college photo student killed in the bombing of Pan Am 103 over Lockerbie, Scotland. The documentary work from professionals and students is archived on the site.

Quick Exercise

From your own publications, exchange publications or online at www.issuu.com, find a picture story in print and discuss its focus, use of dominance and supporting images. How does it provide a narrative? Does it use images in a variety of shapes and sizes? Are there different camera angles including close-ups, wide shots, medium shots and long shots? Are people pictured in different sizes and in varying group sizes?

Test your knowledge

What are the major differences between a picture sequence, picture story and a picture package?

detailed captions should also be a part of the presentation. In a picture story, a dominant picture, at least two to three times larger than any other, should establish the event for the reader. In addition to being the largest photo in the layout, the dominant image should be the most compelling, but it doesn't necessarily have to be the first picture in the narrative story.

The other pictures accompanying the dominant image should be carefully edited to make sure that each is contributing new information to the reader's understanding of the event. Careful attention should also be paid to make sure each picture is a different size and shape, with emphasis on strong verticals and horizontals. Pictures should be edited so that people in the images are different sizes. The number of people pictured in each photograph should also vary.

Picture stories should not be confused with picture sequences – "how-to" narratives in which the reader is shown how to do something sequentially as previously defined.

Designers should avoid collaging pictures together in a scrapbook style, with edges fused into each other or a page of pictures all the same size and shape. Both are weak uses of multiple pictures. Occasionally, a grid arrangement of pictures might work for some content. This technique is often used by yearbook staff.

Visual slideshows added to a website offer the use of additional images from edited shoots. Particularly when space is limited in print, images can be organized into galleries, scrolling "pictures of the day" on home pages and multimedia presentations with sound and image. Galleries and scrolling picture displays should allow for full captions with each image. These forms should supplement print content.

DIGITAL SHOOTING

When photographers are learning to use equipment, they may find it easier to work with simple digital 35 mm single lens reflex (SLR) cameras, long a staple of the journalism world. Simple 35 mm cameras have working light meters that require the photographer to take light meter readings and change both f-stop settings and shutter speeds. Learning how to use these settings will help photographers learn to control depth of field to eliminate a distracting background or to use a fast shutter speed to capture moving action. Other students may use simple point-and-shoot cameras with automated exposure. At a pinch, even smartphone cameras provide quality that is good enough for websites, social media sites and small images in the newspaper or yearbook.

More experienced photographers will feel comfortable with more advanced cameras, those with sophisticated, multimode exposure systems and automatic focus. These cameras often use dedicated flash systems to determine and set correct exposure. Beginning photographers using sophisticated automatic cameras may be intimidated by the equipment until they learn to work all the bells and whistles on the camera. Training photographers to use equipment should be an important part of mentoring, or taught in photo classes.

Similarly, videographers can choose from simple, point-and-shoot cameras, sophisticated video cameras or 35 mm digital SLRs that also shoot video and record sound. Sound can be recorded from camera microphones or from hand-held microphones and recorders.

Simple and advanced digital 35 mm cameras enable the staff to purchase a range of lenses for shooting. In addition to traditional 50 mm lenses – which become 32 mm lenses on a digital camera and reproduce subject matter in normal view – staff need additional lenses so the content of photographs can vary, avoiding visual redundancy.

Lenses

A **wide-angle lens**, starting somewhere in the range of 28 mm and encompassing lenses as wide as 18 mm, will enable the photographer to shoot wide shots, which show a greater range of subject matter horizontally in the frame.

Extremely wide lenses, sometimes called "fisheye lenses," are novelty lenses with uses too limited for normal shooting. More extreme fisheye lenses produce pictures that show a 360-degree range and produce images that are completely round.

❝❝ WORDS of WISDOM

The most important thing a high school shooter must understand is the important role they play on their high school publication as visual historians. It's critical that a photographer understand that charge.

The essential part of being a good photographer is about building skills and this starts with an understanding of basic camera controls. The most critical of these is learning how to make proper exposures. I recommend working in the manual mode though it's fine to use a preset mode from time to time. Most of all, learn how to use your camera's light meter and the manual exposure mode. It takes a bit of time and practice, but once you gain this ability your images go to a new level. Once photographers are comfortable with making good exposures, this allows them to concentrate on what's happening in front of their lens. This is the difference between being a photographer and a photojournalist. A photojournalist shoots moments that tell stories.

On assignment, look for good visual opportunity. Every assignment has them! I had a photo editor who used to say there are no bad assignments only bad photographers. If an assignment looks boring it's up to the photographer to find an interesting way of covering it. This could mean using a unique angle or finding an engaging expression in reactions. Remember good photographers go to ordinary assignments and bring back extraordinary images.

Lastly, think of covering the complete spectrum of the assignment which means shooting the action as well as reactions. Think variety. Shoot wide, mediums and close-ups. This will help to tell a complete visual story and improve layout options. Also, shoot both horizontals as well as verticals. Above all, always avoid setting up photos. Being a patient photographer means shooting real life as it's happening, not recreating it.

Mike McLean, McLean Photo (McLeanphoto.com) Dallas, Texas

Beyond the standard lenses, photographers can benefit from a range of short telephoto and zoom lenses. Short telephotos, beginning at about 70 mm, will enable photographers to shoot portraits, for instance, without being right in the subject's face. In a classroom, a short telephoto will enable a photographer to bring action into the camera lens when he or she can't move in close to the subjects. Short telephoto lenses work well in capturing certain angles in some sports, particularly on courts, such as in volleyball or basketball.

Zoom lenses incorporate a range of focal lengths in one lens. Popular with many publication staff, zooms have some limitations. Owing to their combination of multiple focal lengths, they

Test your knowledge

What role do shutter speeds, ISOs and f-stops play in exposure?

aren't always as "fast" as **fixed focal length lenses**. A fast lens is one with a large maximum f-stop or lens aperture, such as f:1.8, f:2 or f:2.8. Fast lenses are often important in high school shooting because the light conditions in the school are often dim. Lenses with larger maximum f-stops will enable the photographer to shoot without resorting to flash or artificial light. Zoom lenses are sometimes heavier to hold because of the range of focal lengths incorporated into their design. This heaviness can cause photographers to move when shooting, resulting in camera "**blur**" or movement that will be visible in the picture. A staff considering a zoom lens should shop carefully for one with minimum limitations. Zoom lenses can be an economical way to get a versatile lens and are popular choices for limited budgets.

Medium telephotos provide a focal length of about 150–200 mm. These lenses are useful in classrooms and in many sports shooting situations, especially for court sports such as tennis, volleyball and basketball.

Long telephotos range from 300 mm lenses and longer in focal length. Few schools can afford to buy really long, "fast" telephoto lenses because they often cost thousands of dollars. Instead, many schools opt to purchase slower lenses, those with maximum f-stops in the range of f:3.5 or f:4. These slower lenses may be adequate for the school's shooting needs, but setting cameras at high **ISOs** will create greater grain in film and greater pixelation in digital formats. In film, ISOs refer to numbers that rate the sensitivity of the film to light. The higher the number, say 1600 or 3200, the more sensitive the film is to light. Or, low numbers such as 100 or 200 will have finer grain structure when the film is developed. In the digital world, the ISOs refer to the sensitivity of the film sensor. So, low numbers will result in images with finer grain structure. Higher numbers result in images with more visual noise.

Other quality factors will also be lessened at high ISOs. Poorly lit football stadiums will render lenses with small maximum f-stops mostly inadequate, even with fast ISOs, if the maximum shutter speed isn't fast enough to freeze the action on the field. A sports photographer will usually need to shoot at shutter speeds faster than 1/500 of a second to stop sports action. With sophisticated cameras offering faster shutter speeds, such as 1/2000, faster lenses become even more of an important factor. Or, the chosen ISO may result in images that have too much visual noise for quality reproduction.

A better option might be for the school to occasionally rent or borrow a long telephoto lens. Many large camera stores rent equipment. Renting such a lens a couple of times a season might be adequate. However, using a long telephoto lens for the first time will prove difficult for most photographers without any previous experience. The lenses are heavy, difficult to use and difficult to stabilize. Long telephoto lenses should be used with a **monopod**, a single-legged support system that screws into a thread in the lens and provides stability.

Many schools have mentoring programs with local professional newspaper photographers and other photographers in their communities. These professionals often shoot the school's athletic events. The mentor might occasionally be willing to let the school's photographers use the lens during a game, and might provide instruction on its use. Many local newspaper photographers started out as high school photographers and remember the limitations of shooting sports without the right equipment.

Some photographers buy lens doublers that will double the range of the lens. For instance, a 75 mm lens will now shoot 150 mm. Lens doublers may be a good choice, but they can reduce the maximum f-stop of the lens, and may lead to images that aren't sharp.

Low-cost options for obtaining lenses include pawnshops, garage sales or Internet sites such as eBay and Craigslist.

WWW

WEBLINK Check out

www.worldpressphoto.org

World Press Photo: The winners in this international annual competition are showcased in galleries on this site. The work includes both still and multimedia.

Flash

Another essential accessory is a flash to use in shooting low-light situations. Photographers shooting in these conditions may want to avoid aiming the flash directly at their subjects (**direct flash**). Photographs shot with direct flash will have harsh, dark shadows and will often reproduce with washed out or faded highlights, or bright image areas. Photographers will have a hard time eliminating these artificial effects, which are distracting when reproduced in the yearbook or newspaper.

Newer camera models often sell companion flashes called **dedicated flash systems**. These sophisticated systems provide automatic exposure for pictures when the flash is used.

Flash will be more natural when it is bounced off a low white ceiling or wall. Photographers using flashes with pivoting heads can aim the head at an angle so the light will hit the wall or ceiling and bounce light back to the subject. This technique requires that the flash be used at a stronger intensity setting. The photographer must set the distance for the flash, adding the flash-to-ceiling and ceiling-to-subject distance to get a correct exposure. The technique also requires a wall or ceiling no more than about 10 feet away from the camera. The **bounce flash** technique provides a shower of light on the subject that is very pleasing, rather than harsh. The photographer can combine bounce flash with a small white card placed on the flash head. This card will kick light back into the subject's face and eyes.

Flash can also be used separately from the camera, in a technique called **indirect flash**. The photographer can throw the shadows behind the subject or out of camera range by holding the flash away from the camera and aiming it out of the picture range, while still illuminating the subject.

Flash may also be used outdoors in what is called the **synchro-sun** technique. This technique will help reduce the shadows provided by natural light, or can provide stronger, more interesting light on overcast days.

Camera bodies

Even though many digital camera models are now competitively priced, good ones offering a range of options and sophisticated shooting settings are still beyond the budgets of many photographers. Many will settle for simple digital cameras with limited options.

Point-and-shoot cameras, with simple operation, will enable almost anyone on the staff to produce usable images, but the limited lens options will prevent these cameras from working in all shooting situations. They are excellent choices for loaning to clubs and organizations, whose members may be attending a field trip or competition that staff photographers will be unable to attend. Loaning such cameras to chaperones or club sponsors accompanying the groups will also be a good way to get pictures that otherwise might not be available to the staff. Encouraging this cooperative camera arrangement is a good way for staff to expand their coverage.

Before loaning out cameras, some yearbook staff offer training sessions for contributing photographers to teach them basic compositional skills. Offering printed photo credits for non-staff contributors to the yearbook or newspaper is an appropriate form of recognition.

Occasionally, pictures can be obtained from local media outlets, including community newspapers. Yearbook staff often get a certain amount of professional photography as part of their yearbook portrait contract. In all cases, it is better if students take their own pictures for their own publications, but seeking the help of outsiders is sometimes necessary to ensure good coverage.

CAPTIONS AND CUTLINES

Every picture, with few exceptions, will need a caption. Captions are often complete sentences that provide details about pictures. Complete names should always be provided. People in pictures should be named from left to right, but it isn't necessary to include "left to right" since that's a normal reading pattern. When pictures are being named in some other arrangement, such as clockwise, it might be necessary to state the naming pattern. Staff should make sure the names are spelled correctly by double-checking them against an official list of students provided by the school's registrar or through a staff resource file. Many schools with computerized records may be willing to give the publication staff a digital list of student names. Each year, the staff can delete the graduating seniors and add freshmen and new students to the list. Staffs may also want to further identify students by using their year of graduation or grade in school (freshman, sophomore, etc.) after their names.

Captions can start with small-sized **catchlines**, brief summaries that provide visual entry into the caption information. These catchlines should be printed in a contrasting typeface, possibly a bold or a bold italic, in one or two point sizes larger than the caption type. In yearbooks, sections

Quick Exercise

Using a camera and a flash unit take pictures using these techniques: direct flash, bounce flash, indirect flash and synchro-sun. Compare the highlights and shadows in each of your techniques. If your lighting isn't working well, keep practicing with different flash settings.

Test your knowledge

What is a flash technique that can be used to eliminate shadows?

FIGURE 15.14 *Featherduster*, Westlake High School, Austin, Texas. Photos by Barrett Wilson and Karen Scott. Writing by Selah Maya Zighelboim and Monica Rao. Reproduced by permission of Deanne Brown.

Captions are strong reader entry points into visuals and verbals. On a page about raging local wildfires near their school, the "*Featherduster* staff" provided multi-sentence captions full of specific information detailing the extent of the fire damage. The staff included localized information about a teacher's escape from serious damage and included a quote from him.

Below: A scorched car sits in a yard hundreds of feet from a leveled house. Bottom Left: A charred tree trunk continues to burn alongside a Bastrop road almost five days after the wildfires ignited.

Karen Scott

Karen Scott   Barrett Wilson

Barrett Wilson

Above: Austin firefighters assess the speed and direction of the fire which broke out west of Austin Sept. 3. Some 24 homes were destroyed and 30 homes suffered damage. A total of 125 acres were burned in the Steiner Ranch subdivision. Left: These burned trunks are all that are left of the grove of trees along the road in Bastrop. The fires in Bastrop were the worst across Texas with 1,554 homes burned and 34,068 acres destroyed. Teacher Kevin Yeoman was one of the lucky few whose home suffered only minor damages even though it was directly in the burn zone. In describing his return to the subdivision after the danger passed, he said, "All of our neighbors were there, and my wife and I got to walk through the front door of our house. Everybody else was sifting through ashes."

WWW

WEBLINK Check out

www.viiphoto.com

This site is the work of photographers who are members of VII, a photo agency. It includes current work from some of the world's top photographers.

will often be designed to coordinate the graphics in the page headlines to the design of the catchlines. Catchlines are commonly used in newspapers with stand-alone photos. Often, the catchline appears above the picture.

Captions can begin with different parts of speech to avoid a redundancy in their grammatical construction. For instance, on a yearbook spread with seven pictures, if all captions begin with names or with prepositional phrases, readers will become bored. Details and specific nouns should be used to add to the reader's understanding of the story. Captions can be more than one sentence in length. Often, a second sentence is used in yearbook captions to add outcomes or results to the first sentence's description of the pictured information.

Because captions describe what is going on when the picture was taken, the information should be in present tense, especially in the first sentence. Follow-up information may be written in past tense to indicate the passage of time.

Good captions require good reporting. If photographers don't provide basic caption information for the designers, reporters should talk to the people shown in the pictures to find out what was going on in the photograph and possibly to obtain quotes. In this case, trying to write a caption without talking to the subjects will usually result in inaccurate information, threatening the credibility of the staff. On the other hand, caption information should not be obvious, nor should it merely repeat what the viewer can tell from looking at the picture.

In naming people pictured in group shots, the rows should be designated as "front," "second," "third" and so on, until the back row. Using "first," "second" and "third" without "front" and "back" is confusing. In group shots, complete names should be used in the captions. Again, it isn't necessary to specify the naming pattern unless it isn't left-to-right.

To add dimension to captions, quotes can be included. Reporters can ask questions of the people pictured to get their reactions to the situation. Quotes will often add rich texture and personal understanding to captions.

Ideally, captions should be placed adjacent to the pictures they describe, either under the pictures or next to them. If the picture bleeds across the gutter, the caption should not bleed unless the picture is on a double truck or centerspread. In that case, the caption should be placed under the picture on the widest side, beginning on the margin of that page. In placing long captions under wide, horizontal pictures, the designer may want to break the captions into columns to keep the line lengths from being wider than comfortable reading patterns allow.

Some publications include the photo credit (for the person who took the picture) at the end of the caption. This information can also be placed at the bottom right edge or on the right side of the photograph. No matter where it appears, a picture credit is needed for each photograph. The picture credit can appear in a type size a point or two smaller than the caption information, and it can be in a contrasting typeface, such as italic.

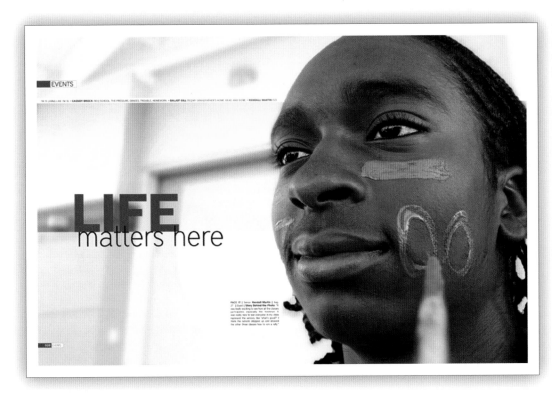

FIGURE 15.15 *Titanium*, Antelope High School, Antelope, Calif. Reproduced by permission of Pete LeBlanc.

Strong cropping creates a dramatic moment in this close-up of a girl whose face is being painted. Cropping the photo directly to the face and hand get the reader's immediate attention. The photographer's low angle and placement of the girl on the right rule of thirds create a clean background and leave space for verbal information on the left side. The impact of this photo is enhanced by the use of the photo bleeding on all four sides of the yearbook spread.

Cropping photographs

Cropping is both a visual and a physical process. On a visual level, cropping improves the content of the photograph by eliminating distracting or extraneous elements. Good cropping should result in photographs with stronger impact in the design and can also correct certain photographic flaws, such as subjects being too small because the photographer was too far away. Cropping is not a solution for poor photographic composition.

In sports shooting, cropping can make pictures more dramatic by removing parts of the photograph that are not essential to the action. For instance, in upper-body sports, such as volleyball and basketball, cropping out the legs of an athlete and concentrating primarily on the athlete's arms can make the interaction of the arms and the ball more dramatic. In cropping sports shots, designers must also be aware that cropping out the ball or eliminating the opponents removes the visual context of the action and could weaken its meaning. In sports action shots, the ball should definitely be part of the image.

Digital photographs will be placed directly in page layouts. Designers will be able to see the effects of their cropping and picture placement decisions on the computer screen. Pictures imported into layout and design programs should not be stretched vertically or horizontally from their original proportions. Designers should carefully check the measurements palette when the pictures are imported, to make sure the x and y scaling coordinates remain consistent.

PHOTO EDITING

Visual redundancy results when the same information is repeated in photographs, just as verbal redundancy results when information is repeated in print. A good picture editor working carefully with the other photographers and designers can make a big difference to a publication. Unfortunately, many staff appoint a photo editor without training that person to do the job.

Photo editors should be present at all staff meetings and contribute to the discussion of story development and planning. They should help writers develop photo assignments that will contribute to the story development. These assignments should be realistic for photographers to complete and should avoid staged, posed or predictable images. Photo editors should tailor

Quick Exercise

Using archived picture files, open pictures in a photo-imaging software program such as Adobe Photoshop. Locate the cropping tool and practice cropping the pictures. Try out a variety of crops to determine which crop works most effectively. The software will allow you to save different versions of your crops for comparison and will also enable you to undo as you work.

IN ACTION

Preparing images for print or web

After the pictures have been made, the images edited and the layouts drawn, hopefully in that order, a photographer's work isn't done. Next comes preparing the image files for publication in print or on the web. Here are some tips for the process. Remember that mastering camera exposure will eliminate the need for extensive toning and will save time.

1   File Management: Set Photoshop color to North American Pre-Press 2 (under Edit/Color Settings/North American Pre-Press 2), click okay. Your working color space will then be Adobe RGB (1998). Reset the color space on your digital camera to Adobe RGB (1998). Default color space on most digital cameras is sRGB and is not recommended.

2   Open the file with the existing profile and save it as an "S," source file. Immediately save a second file labeled as "W," a work file in the Photoshop format. Keep both files together in a folder.

3   Apply Meta Data (File/File Info) to include your name, a description or caption information, give the image a star rating and include key words to help you search your files at a later date (varsity football, the opponent's name, etc.)

4   Crop your picture, but as little as possible to avoid destroying data. Cropping can be an additive process in which you start with a loose crop and add to it after seeing how effectively it's working with your image.

5   Retouch your image only to adjust burning (darkening highlights) and dodging (lightening dark tones in areas that need detail). No retouching like cloning should be done to alter the content of a journalistic photo.

6   Adjust contrast and density through layers for brightness and contrast, levels and curves. Set black-and-white

points in levels in each RGB channel. Monitoring calibration is vital for matching monitors to color workflow or offset printing. Consult your printer if your images are not printing correctly.

7   Sharpen focus in your image using the unsharp masking filter. Try this setting to start out: Unsharp mask/amount 200–250/radius .1/threshold 3. Then Edit/fade unsharp mask/100%/luminosity.

8   Image size for screen is 72 dpi. For print the rule of thumb is twice the line screen your printer uses. In yearbooks you'll probably need files at about 300 dpi. Newspapers use lower line screens on coarser paper so files around 150–250 dpi will usually be adequate. Consult your printer for specifics. If your picture was shot raw or at maximum resolution settings you'll have more options for using it larger in your print publications. Enlarging images by increasing file size will be degraded.

9   Save your file according to your publication's file management system and naming convention.

10 Consult your printer about converting RGB files to CMYK for color printing. RGB space is much larger than CMYK. Your printer may want to work with your RGB files and do CMYK conversion on their end. If your color files will be printed in black-and-white, you'll want to tone them in grayscale instead of RGB. Always consult your printer if you have questions. They have to work with your files and they can give you guidelines to make the process better.

Information includes guidelines for Multimedia, Photography and Design classes, Newhouse School of Communications, Syracuse University, Tony Golden, author.

WWW

WEBLINK Check out

http://lens.blogs.nytimes.com

The Lens, the *New York Times's* photography blog, showcases work from the paper's photography department staff in still and multimedia. The site maintains an impressive archive of work

assignments to the photographers, taking into consideration their individual strengths. They should discuss the assignments with the photographers and suggest possible picture angles and images. They should make sure the photographers have the right equipment to effectively shoot the assignments. Photo editors should make sure photographers are provided with detailed information about the events or activities they will shoot, including the time and place they will occur and the possible use of the pictures in the publication. Many photo editors use a formal photo assignment process, either electronically or on paper.

After photographers shoot an assignment, photo editors should individually sit down with the photographers afterwards, helping edit their shoots directly in Adobe Lightroom, Bridge or Photoshop. Photo editors can offer photographers advice on cropping, composition and on technical problems such as improper exposure. As mentors, photo editors can help younger photographers improve their photographic vision and their abilities to tell compelling stories. Occasionally, inviting in local professional photographers, perhaps those who have graduated from the school in previous years, will also assist novice photographers as they develop their skills. These professionals can offer both technical and artistic advice.

Photo editors should make sure photographers are trained to complete the digital work. A consistent, clear and easily understood method of preparing the images for layouts should be used. Photographers should use picture-editing software to complete basic picture alterations such as toning, burning, dodging and cropping. Other alterations may be used to correct crooked horizon lines or redeye.

Photo editors should look at layouts with designers when complete to make sure visual variety has been achieved in chosen photographs with photo angles, lens use, the number of people in each picture, cropping and in the actual content in the images. The photo editor can also check for consistency in toning.

Photographers should make sure to provide complete caption information for each image. Photographers are journalists, too. During assignments, they should carry a reporter's notebook in which they record the names of the people they photograph, as well as other details. Alternatively, this information can be electronically recorded on a phone or tablet. When covering a game, the photographer should get a copy of rosters or programs so names can be easily matched to numbers on uniforms. Also during sporting events, photographers can occasionally shoot a frame of the scoreboard so the progression of important plays during the event can be referenced.

Digital picture files can be downloaded and viewed in a variety of software editing programs, such as Adobe Photoshop, Bridge or Lightroom or Photo Mechanic. As photos are viewed, the best ones should be tagged to indicate that they will be kept. Untagged files, or those of lesser quality, can then be eliminated in the editing process.

Lastly, photographers should use a filing system to archive the images for later use by page designers. Labeling computer folders with appropriate subject matter such as "varsity football," "homecoming" or "fall play" might be particularly helpful for yearbook staffs, which may not be using the photographs right away. Individually, additional files should archive each game labeled with specific tags such as the game date and/or opposing team's name in sports. Keeping archives current will ensure that photographers become more competent and will prevent photographers from facing unrealistic amounts of work at deadline times. It also ensures that photographers have ample time to reshoot if necessary.

Archiving photo files in two places is always a good idea, especially during deadline time. Also, original, raw images should be carefully stored for retrieval in case images go missing. An organized system of storage and retrieval will prove invaluable in meeting deadlines and in maintaining historical files for future use. It will also ensure that images are easy to find.

For the yearbook staff, this collection of edited pictures shot during the year and stored in files should be used when choosing photos for designing layouts. A second edit should be done in a collaborative process by designers and either the photographer or the photo editor. When choosing pictures for spreads, designers should make sure each picture is chosen because it contributes new information, shows different action and people and increases the range of sizes and shapes used in the layout.

Abuse of images

Because photographs are so important in the design process, designers should be careful not to abuse or distort them in their layouts. Following are some examples of abusive design decisions that can weaken the impact of photographs:

- **Creating cutout shapes**. Removing the background of the photo in digital image alteration programs is quite quick and easy. However, unless the picture was shot in a photo studio or planned as a cutout, removing the background by cutting it out can result in a loss of contextual information that distorts meaning. Cutout shapes are visually active and should be grounded in design by using lines or borders or a soft shadow of the image. Cutout images with hard edges always need to be grounded by a line or edge.

- **Creating cookie-cutter shapes**. Editing photos into shapes such as circles, triangles or ovals compromises their content in the same way as cutting out the images. Contextual information is removed or cropped. Readers have a hard time understanding the meaning of incomplete visual information. Pictures designed to be placed in shapes should be carefully shot by photographers in studios where the backgrounds can be controlled.

FIGURE 15.16 *Echo*, St. Louis Park High School, St. Louis Park, Minn. Reproduced by permission of Lori Keekley.

Cutting out images from their contextual backgrounds can cause a loss of important visual information, especially if the cutout images are not intact. In this case, the partial cutout preserves the bottom of the photo which shows the action involved between these two players and the ball. The upper background of the photo has also been removed in a way that maintains the details of the shapes without losing information.

People follow Coach Andy Ewald on Twitter. Follow him at twitter.com/CoachEwald **22** **Sports** Tuesday, September 1, 2009 **O5**

Soccer, football shift sections

Some teams will be playing smaller schools during the upcoming fall season

Abby Bongaarts | Staff writer

Junior Courtney Frakes (in blue) fights for the ball against Junior Emily Casey during practice at the Jr. High Aug. 25.

This fall some Park teams will no longer be competing in the big leagues.

Football will move from class 5A to class 4A and boys' and girls' soccer will move from class 2A to class 1A. This means that rather than compete against the biggest schools in the state during sections, Park will play schools with a more similar enrollment.

According to football coach and athletic director Andy Ewald, the high school has no say in this decision.

"It's out of our hands," Ewald said. "It is set down by the High School League." The Min-

nesota State High School League uses a formula every two years to calculate an enrollment number for each school. They use this number to divide up classes based on the number of schools who participate in each sport and the size of each school. Each sport uses a different method to divide up classes, so no other Park sports will be affected this year.

Despite the boys' soccer team's success last year in 2A, head coach Chato Alvarado sees changing classes as a positive.

"I think it's great we moved down," Alvarado said. "On paper it gives us a better chance to make it to state. 2A is more competitive, they have a bigger pool to choose from. We don't have that luxury."

Senior soccer captain Caitlin Doyle also believes the change will benefit Park.

"Before our chances were one in a million [to make state], now we have a chance," she said.

However, Ewald believes smaller schools do not always mean less competition for Park teams.

"To make it to state in any sport you need a good team and some luck," he said. "It's never a cake walk getting to state."

Alvarado agrees with Ewald and hopes his players won't underestimate any teams this season.

"The thing I'm worried about is that our players think it's going to be an easier year and then because of attitude, not perform as well," he said.

However, senior soccer captain Mohamed Dirshe won't take this season lightly, as he hopes to return to the Metrodome one more time.

"Everybody has to work hard and believe in themselves," he said. "We have to work as a team, not as individuals, that's what it will take to make it to state."

The class changes allow Park to face smaller schools, but teams will have to prove themselves in any class.

Photo | Abby Bongaarts

Graduate has shot to make Olympics

Abby Bongaarts | Staff writer

Park graduate Laishema Hampton threw her way to two school records and the state tournament in high school, and now aims for the Olympics.

Hampton, who graduated in 2008 and now attends Iowa State University, threw shot put and discus while at Park. She holds the school record in both events. Hampton placed first in shot put in the state tournament in 2006. She was also part of a school record breaking 4x100-meter relay team.

Recently, she placed second in shot put at the USA Junior Championships, which brought her to Trinidad to represent the United States in the Pan American Junior Athletics Championships.

The competition was from July 31-Aug. 2 and Hampton placed fourth in the shot put. For Hampton, her favorite part of the trip was representing the United States.

"Putting on the USA jersey made everything real, that I'm here in Trinidad. It just hit me when I put on the USA uniform," Hampton said.

Hampton may get the chance to represent the United States again, only next time at the Olympics.

"I feel like I have a good chance [to make the Olympics], but it's still up in the air. If I don't make it in 2012, I still have another four years," she said. "If I make it I want to come out with something. I want to make the podium and hear our national song."

Brad Brubaker, social studies teacher and Hampton's high school coach, also believes she has a chance at making the Olympics.

"I think her chances went up this year, but it's still going to depend on her im-

Laishema Hampton practices her shot put throw while still in high school. Hampton won the state tournament for shot put in 2006 and placed second in 2007 and 2008.

File photo

provement," he said. "She is one of the best three juniors in America so it stands to reason that she may be in the mix."

Laishema's improvement during her freshman year of college enabled her to make it to the Pan American Junior Championships. She threw more than 50 feet this season bettering her high school mark by ten feet.

"It's so surprising her huge improvements at Iowa State. You don't usually see that kind of improvement in one season," Brubaker said. "This is the highest level I've ever had an athlete compete at. I don't take credit for it but it's fun to follow someone internationally."

While Brubaker does credit himself for Hampton's success, he recognizes him as being one of her biggest influences.

"My parents, they help me a lot and my high school coaches, I love them. [Coach Amy] Rechem and Brubaker have helped me a lot getting to where I am. I have lots of respect for them," Hampton said.

According to Brubaker, Hampton has all the attributes needed for success in shot put.

"She was a natural, strong and fast," he said. "She could go from goofy to game face when she needed to compete. She was a nice kid, good leader, good captain and fun to coach."

Junior Emma Nichols, who used to practice with Hampton believes she has the ability to compete in the Olympics.

"I can definitely see her going to the Olympics. She has what it takes," said Nichols. "I expect her to get there someday."

Who: Kathryn Ostrom, 9
Sport: Swimming

How did you get involved in swimming?
My sister because she did, and my cousin swam all the way through college swimming. I just kind of followed.

If you didn't swim, what sport would you play?
Soccer. Swimming got more intense so I had to quit.

What is your biggest accomplishment as a swimmer?
Making it to Speedos for club swimming. It's a big, intense meet. You have to make a certain time, and then you get to race against people from other states.

Does having your older sister on the team change the way you compete?
Yeah, it makes us closer because we have something to talk about. It's both good and bad- good because you can always rely on her for help, bad because you fight with her when you're in the same lane at practice.

Name: Greg Hynes, 12
Sport: Football

How did you get involved in football?
I started playing in fourth grade. My parents just asked me if I wanted to play and I said sure so they signed me up for the fourth grade team.

Do you have any rituals you go through before a game?
Usually a couple of friends come over and hang out before the game. We have spaghetti for a good pre-game meal.

If you could have the power of a Greek god to help you when you play, which one would you choose?
Whichever one runs really fast.

What is your most embarrassing sport moment?
When I was a freshman I went into the varsity game for the first time and the running back went the wrong way so it looked like I messed up. I looked like an idiot.

What do you consider your biggest accomplishment?
Being one of the captains of the team this year. Also, last year's season when we won four games after the year before going 0-9.

● **Collaging and overlapping pictures.** Placing pictures so they overlap or touch each other without separation can also compromise content. If the pictures have areas of dead space where they can overlap, it's generally a good indication that they need tighter cropping. Overlapping the images also runs the risk of creating connections between

FIGURE 15.17 *The Lowell*, Lowell High School, San Francisco, Calif. Article and photos by Joseph Fiorello and Sean Lee. Page design by features editor Sean Lee. Reproduced by permission of Sharn Matusek.

A fun surprise to a typical sports page takes advantage of collaging, image alteration, shaped cutouts and cookie-cutter-shaped photos. While these techniques don't work for everything, in this case the design creates an action comic book look with appropriate type to tell the story of obscure sports. Surprising readers with fun content and appropriate design is a good way to mix things up.

pictures where there may be no real connection. If tones are similar, the photo content can actually merge. Blurring images' edges together through image manipulation software to create a **collage** can occasionally be effective if it is done for a specific purpose and its use is limited.

- **Duotoning images.** Applying a single color to a black-and-white image can often be effective. For instance, duotoning black-and-white images with brown will give them the effect of sepia-toned prints, a classic brown-toned bath applied to pictures to give them the look of antiquity. This technique can now be achieved digitally in Photoshop. However, using garish or inappropriately bright colors on images of people will make the pictures distracting or misleading. Rather than viewing the content, viewers will try to find meaning in the colors.

- **Tilting photos.** Photos turned so they are positioned slightly off a straight horizontal baseline can be playful and quirky. Tilting should be applied only if it's appropriate to the content of the image. A tilt of less than 12 degrees will maintain stronger readability for the image.

- **Creating highly stylized images.** Particularly on yearbook staff, designers often draw layouts before the pictures have been taken. Planning for a highly stylized form of picture use, such as overlapping large image areas, extreme shapes or sizes or other stylized devices, can create compromises in image quality and content. Designers intent on creating such styles should consult carefully with photographers and photo editors to see if these styles will be possible, and to make sure the photographers are looking for images that will accommodate the designers' needs, if possible.

- **Creating photo patterns and grids.** A recent yearbook trend in using pictures is positioning them in patterns, modules or grids composed of similarly sized shapes and with the images touching or separated only by thin hairline rules. A pattern needs visual contrast in photo tones and in content or it will be viewed as one large, continuous image.

- **Creating postage stamp-sized images.** Especially trendy in yearbook design, the use of multiple images in small sizes needs careful attention. Pictures need to be carefully cropped and edited to make sure they will still be "readable" in such small sizes. Maintaining quality across multiple small images may be difficult (see Chapter 13 In action, "The Nickel Rule").

- **Flipping or flopping images.** A photograph should be reproduced as it was seen in the camera. Designers sometimes create layouts in which the content of the photo leads eyeflow off the page. In these cases, some designers resort to electronically flipping, or reversing, the image. Doing so is considered ethically dishonest since it reverses the content of the original photo.

  If writing or numbers appear in a flipped picture, they will be backward, immediately alerting the viewer to the picture's changed orientation. Even without numbers or words, people in the pictures will be aware of a change in details, such as a part in their hair, or jewelry or watches appearing on the wrong arm or hand. Rather than flipping images, designers should work to arrange pictures so the eyeflow faces naturally toward the gutter. This is another reason page designs and templates should be flexible, particularly if they're created before the pictures have been taken and the best ones have been edited and selected for use.

- **Creating visual clichés.** A good photographer avoids visual clichés, images that are common and often overused. In basketball, for instance, the cliché shot is one that features a single player shooting a basket. Because high school photographers rarely have the restrictions on shooting positions that college and professional sports enforce, they should move around to capture a variety of angles. Moving out from under the basket will enable photographers to depict defensive as well as offensive action.

  Taking pictures of teachers standing at the blackboard or administrators talking on the phone results in visual clichés. People often pose this way, thinking this is what the photographer wants.

NEWSFLASH

Code of Ethics, National Press Photographers Association
NPPA Code of Ethics

Preamble

The National Press Photographers Association, a professional society that promotes the highest standards in visual journalism, acknowledges concern for every person's need both to be fully informed about public events and to be recognized as part of the world in which we live.

Visual journalists operate as trustees of the public. Our primary role is to report visually on the significant events and varied viewpoints in our common world. Our primary goal is the faithful and comprehensive depiction of the subject at hand. As visual journalists, we have the responsibility to document society and to preserve its history through images.

Photographic and video images can reveal great truths, expose wrongdoing and neglect, inspire hope and understanding and connect people around the globe through the language of visual understanding. Photographs can also cause great harm if they are callously intrusive or are manipulated.

This code is intended to promote the highest quality in all forms of visual journalism and to strengthen public confidence in the profession. It is also meant to serve as an educational tool both for those who practice and for those who appreciate photojournalism. To that end, The National Press Photographers Association sets forth the following.

Code of Ethics

Visual journalists and those who manage visual news productions are accountable for upholding the following standards in their daily work:

1 Be accurate and comprehensive in the representation of subjects.

2 Resist being manipulated by staged photo opportunities.

3 Be complete and provide context when photographing or recording subjects. Avoid stereotyping individuals and groups. Recognize and work to avoid presenting one's own biases in the work.

4 Treat all subjects with respect and dignity. Give special consideration to vulnerable subjects and compassion to victims of crime or tragedy. Intrude on private moments of grief only when the public has an overriding and justifiable need to see.

5 While photographing subjects do not intentionally contribute to, alter or seek to alter or influence events.

6 Editing should maintain the integrity of the photographic images' content and context. Do not manipulate images or add or alter sound in any way that can mislead viewers or misrepresent subjects.

7 Do not pay sources or subjects or reward them materially for information or participation.

8 Do not accept gifts, favors or compensation from those who might seek to influence coverage.

9 Do not intentionally sabotage the efforts of other journalists.

Ideally, visual journalists should:

1 Strive to ensure that the public's business is conducted in public. Defend the rights of access for all journalists.

2 Think proactively, as a student of psychology, sociology, politics and art to develop a unique vision and presentation. Work with a voracious appetite for current events and contemporary visual media.

3 Strive for total and unrestricted access to subjects, recommend alternatives to shallow or rushed opportunities, seek a diversity of viewpoints and work to show unpopular or unnoticed points of view.

4 Avoid political, civic and business involvements or other employment that compromise or give the appearance of compromising one's own journalistic independence.

5 Strive to be unobtrusive and humble in dealing with subjects.

6 Respect the integrity of the photographic moment.

7 Strive by example and influence to maintain the spirit and high standards expressed in this code. When confronted with situations in which the proper action is not clear, seek the counsel of those who exhibit the highest standards of the profession. Visual journalists should continuously study their craft and the ethics that guide it.

◀ **NPPA Statement of Principle**

8 Adopted 1991 by the NPPA Board of Directors

9 In the early days of the electronic revolution that swept through our profession, it was evident that digital photography would be very beneficial but at the same time posed a real threat to the integrity of our images. NPPA adopted this Statement of Principle to affirm unequivocally our commitment to honesty and accuracy in this new environment. It is a strong admonition aimed directly at the practice of digital manipulation but also sums up the NPPA Code of Ethics in a matter of a few sentences.

10 As journalists we believe the guiding principle of our profession is accuracy; therefore, we believe it is wrong to alter the content of a photograph in any way that deceives the public.

11 As photojournalists, we have the responsibility to document society and to preserve its images as a matter of historical record. It is clear that the emerging electronic technologies provide new challenges to the integrity of photographic images … in light of this, we the National Press Photographers Association, reaffirm the basis of our ethics: Accurate representation is the benchmark of our profession. We believe photojournalistic guidelines for fair and accurate reporting should be the criteria for judging what may be done electronically to a photograph. Altering the editorial content … is a breach of the ethical standards recognized by the NPPA.

Photo alteration

With the growth in image-altering software programs, it is now easier than ever to manipulate photos and other images by combining parts of them, by moving objects around in the images or by editing out parts of the images and replacing them with other images. To do so may be unethical and could cause legal problems for the staff.

Photographers must protect the truth and accuracy of their images, just as writers must check the accuracy of their reporting. In news and feature pictures, readers expect the content to be accurately represented. Altering news and feature images should not be allowed in a publication. Allowances can be made for alterations to the basic tonality and quality of the image: toning, burning, dodging, adjusting contrast and cropping.

Increasingly, however, artistically altered images are being used for illustrative purposes. As long as the photographer is altering only his or her own images, and not combining them with others without permission, these illustrative uses of photo manipulation may be acceptable. They should be labeled as photo illustrations or photo enhancements, rather than with traditional photo credits, to help the reader understand that they are illustrative, not accurate portrayals of news or feature events. It is important for students to understand the need to protect the readers' belief that what they see in a picture really happened.

The National Press Photographers Association, the association to which most professional photojournalists belong, adopted a code of ethics when image manipulation software problems were emerging in the professional world. This code of ethics is one that student photojournalists should seek to understand, adapt to their needs and practice (see Newsflash, "Code of Ethics").

ART AND ILLUSTRATIONS

In addition to pictures, **illustrations** can be effective visuals in publications. Art and illustrations should be used when designers are seeking to show something different from what a photograph will show or when a photograph is inappropriate or impossible to get. Using a variety of illustrative forms will also surprise readers and keep the visual content fresh and interesting. Illustrations in a range of styles – from cartoons to artistic renderings – can effectively coordinate with story content.

Illustrations don't have to be created solely by staff members. Just as professional publications do, staff can seek outside artists with differing talents and styles to add dimension to visual presentations. Allowing the illustrator to read the story or text will result in illustrations that tell stronger visual stories. Combined with strong headline presentations, these illustrations can be refreshing and fun.

Illustrative style possibilities are endless. Collage, three-dimensional art, watercolor, pen and ink drawing and caricature could all effectively showcase verbal content. Staff can coordinate with art teachers and outstanding art students.

WWW

WEBLINK Check out

www.nppa.org

The National Press Photographers Association (NPPA) is the primary organization for news photographers. Their site features a wealth of information including a student link. The site also links to winners of Best of Photojournalism, the organization's annual photography competition.

FIGURE 15.18 *The Lowell*, Lowell High School, San Francisco, Calif. Page layout by features assistant editor Jenna Fiorello. Reproduced by permission of Sharn Matusek.

Print visuals don't always have to be photos. When appropriate content calls for a unique approach, using art work helps break up the content and approach and can provide a stronger visual-verbal connection. In this story on cafeteria food, presented as a behind-the-scenes expose, the combination of "kidnap note" typography, the police caution tape and the art surrounding the design all create an interesting visual approach.

WWW

WEBLINK Check out

www.pdnonline.org

Photo District News is a magazine and online site primarily for advertising and illustration photographers. It includes links to information on camera gear, a classified link, a blog and feature articles.

On the web, interesting animations can be used to tell stories. Students trained in 3- and 4-D animation software, as well as motion graphics software can use their skills to expand informational content beyond still and video photography.

Good artwork should be detailed and provide dimension. Single-dimension artwork can often seem uninteresting. Artists should make sure to be inclusive in representing the full range of the school community.

Choosing a visual strategy

- *Photographic*. Use if large and dominant photo(s) are high quality and would attract the reader's attention. Ask the question: What photos would help tell the story? Avoid set-up, posed or clichéd shots.

- *Illustrative*. Use if the story lends itself to illustration rather than photographic treatment; keep in mind that illustrations should be visually strong and dominant in size. Give your text to an artist so they can make visual connections with the words in the story. On a website, use animations and motion graphics to supplement the content.

- *Typographic*. If you don't have strong photographic or illustrative material to choose from, consider using a typographic treatment. This could include large primary heads with detail-oriented deck heads; varied headline positions; typography that matches the mood or tone of the story; emphasis type; large initial caps; and other type-as-illustration techniques.

Choosing an alternative verbal strategy

- *Factoids/summary boxes*. Use if the story contains policy changes or suggests a strategic approach. Can also be used to summarize the major points made by speakers. Consider small bullets to draw in the reader's eye.

- *Profile box*. Is the story primarily about an individual or a group? If so, consider a profile box with relevant information headers in bold type. Set the profile in a typeface contrasting in weight and stroke to the primary story.

- *Harper's Index/Q&A*. Use if the story is full of facts and figures that could use simplification. Also use for elections.

- *Timelines*. Use for stories that are sequential in organization of information, that trace historical significance or that show change over a period of time.

- *Sidebars*. Use if there is an angle or dimension to the story that is particularly interesting or could use more detail. Sidebars can be written in first person to amplify a particular detail of the main story.

- *Infographics/locator maps*. Use if the story has a complex set of numerical or other data that can be better understood through visual presentation. An infographic should be based on visual icons. Avoid straight pie charts and encyclopedic charts. Look to *USA Today*, *Time*, *Newsweek* and other popular publications for interesting ways to clarify information through visual means.

- *Story or paragraph captions with a picture package*. Telling part of the story through a package of two or more pictures that show different aspects of the story can be valuable. Make sure the captions add information using either a few sentences or paragraphs.

Other visual options

- *Callouts*. **Callouts** (often pull quotes) showcase compelling quotes or significant information from the story. These are displayed in a point size larger than the body text but smaller than the headline text (preferably about 18–24 points), with a distinctive design strategy that readers will recognize. If an interview subject is particularly quotable, or the story controversial, consider a box of quoted material. This can also be used as a pro/con box to present conflicting viewpoints.

- *Logos*. Develop a visual strategy based on icons that immediately relate to a story or lend it a graphic strategy. It can also be used to visually tie together a series of stories, particularly over a course of time or in different parts of the newspaper.

- *Text heads*. Break up the story by inserting subheads at natural junctures to help guide eyeflow. Choose type in bolder weights.

Keep in mind

- Combining two or more visual forms may help the reader understand the story more clearly. If so, determine which are appropriate and avoid duplication of information.

- To avoid reader confusion, make sure information presented in alternative story forms looks different from the main story. Consider using a sans serif typeface if the story is in a serif typeface. Consider using a different weight of text if typeface choices are limited. Consider varying the line widths of alternative copy. All of these techniques will help indicate to the reader that the information is separate from the primary story.

- Make sure your visual-verbal forms are helping the reader clarify and process the information being presented. Keep your reader in mind at all times. Don't add visual-verbal forms unless they do clarify information.

- Create multiple entry points for the story. Make sure the reader is getting valuable information regardless of whether he or she enters the story through the body text.

- Remember your time frame. What can realistically be produced in the amount of time you have before publication? Consider your resources. Do you have someone with the ability to produce complicated or stylistic art? Do you have time to work with a photographer to produce top quality photographs that add to the reader's understanding of the story?

- Keep the writer's angle or focus in mind at all times. Connecting visuals with verbals reinforces the story and makes it more vivid for the reader. Make sure every person working with the story understands where the story is going. If it changes, or if team members discover new or interesting angles along the way, rethink the visual-verbal strategies. Add to or adjust as necessary. Don't repeat information.

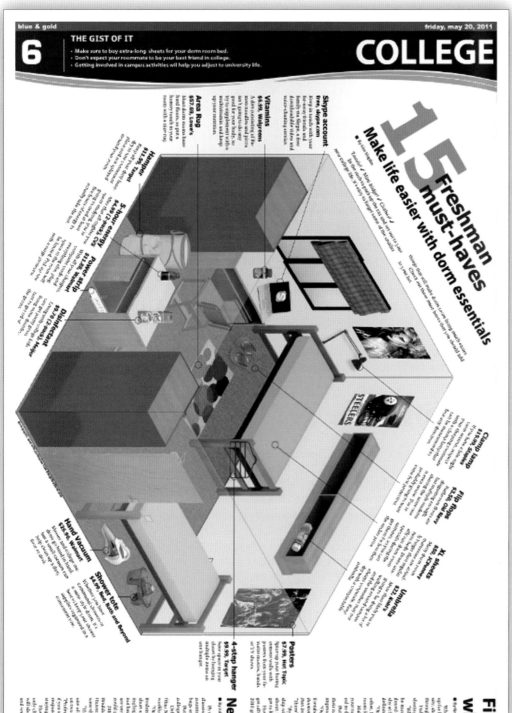

FIGURE 15.19 "Freshman must-haves for dorms," *Blue & Gold*, Findlay High School, Findlay, Ohio, p. 6, May 20, 2010. Reprinted with permission.

Information graphics in the form of visual charts and diagrams can add interest and clarity to written information. In this full-page story on freshman must-haves for dorm life, the addition of a cutaway graphic with information called out of the diagram and linked to lines with details simplifies the information and allows readers to view each of the 15 must-haves in any order. This vertical, broadsheet page was turned horizontally in print to maximize use of the space for the illustration.

INFORMATION GRAPHICS

An additional form of visual presentation is information graphics – information presented in visual ways. Information graphics utilize visuals as a way of breaking down complex information and making it understandable. Information graphics can appear in a variety of forms, including pie charts, graphs, bar charts, locator maps, diagrams and sequence maps. Good information graphics can be designed with the help of statistical charting software programs for better accuracy. Sources of information used in the graphics should be provided. Or, if using the results of a student poll, the size of the sample should be presented at the bottom of the graphic.

Information graphics should be used to help readers process and understand complex information, especially numbers, trends and statistics. They can also help readers understand how something happens or where it happened and who the key players were.

Staff artists are logical resources for information graphics, or if the school offers a class in computer graphics those students can be recruited to help create information graphics. Working with a statistics class or other appropriate subject-area content source could be helpful in gathering information and presenting it to readers.

Accuracy is crucial in presenting information visually just as it is in presenting information verbally. Numbers, representations of numbers and comparisons should be checked for accuracy and clarity.

On websites, combinations of information can result in dynamic audio/visual presentations, which can bring life to static information.

OTHER GRAPHIC FORMS

In addition to creating visual interest through photographs and illustrations, designers have other graphic tools at their disposal. These include the use of rule lines, boxes, screens of color, isolation elements and text display elements.

Rule lines can be used singly or in a combination of various widths. Rule lines can separate, connect, frame or box content and are sometimes used to create visual connections between separate pages when they are designed as a single visual unit.

Designers can use screens, shades of solid color, to isolate and separate content, to connect visual elements and to bring the reader's eyes to a particular area of the page. These can also be designed as graduated screens of color when appropriate. Colors in boxes holding type should always be designed so type is still readable and in a color that provides contrast with the background.

FIGURE 15.20 *HiLite*, Carmel High School, Carmel, Ind. Reproduced by permission of Jim Streisel.

Type in colored backgrounds, whether in print or online, should never interfere with readability. Dark colors requiring all the type be reversed to white can slow down the print reader and discourage readability. On top of a full page, double truck image, the page designer has created a translucent textbox background to add some opacity to the picture. The translucent background creates enough separation between the photo and type to allow for easy reading.

Isolation elements, primarily created through increased white space, can separate visual from verbal or main story from sidebar. They can help move the reader's eyes from one page area to another.

Designers have a wealth of text display options for creating interesting visual displays of text. For example, headline designs, arranged as strong visual units on the page, can utilize size and shade contrasts as well as changes in typography to create interesting displays (see Chapter 11 for more information on using type).

The use of drop cap letters, large initial letters beginning paragraphs or text heads throughout the story will add contrast and break up large passages of gray text. Pull quotes can be lifted from the text and placed in display-size type to draw interest to the text. Matching the color and typography of the primary headline in drop caps or text heads will create visual unity. Designers can use other devices such as white space between story transitions or between natural junctures in the story to vary the density of the text.

Graphics work best when they are subtle. Overdone graphics should be avoided as they distract the reader from the overall page or story content. The ultimate goal of good visual communications is to contribute to the storytelling process.

CONCLUSION

Visuals are among the most important and fundamental components of newspapers, yearbooks and websites, attracting primary visual attention and directing readers to verbal content. When visual and verbal content is harmonious, readers are engaged in storytelling and focused on the information. Readers want to see pictures of people engaged in a variety of activities. The web is a great tool for including additional content beyond what is printed. Slide shows can provide extensive content and variety. Multimedia content on the web also allows for both sound and image.

SUMMARY

- Good photographers make strong visuals by waiting for key action and using the tools of good content and composition.

- Technically strong photos will ensure quality reproduction.

- Photographs can be used in a variety of presentations including stand-alone, picture packages, picture stories, slideshows and multimedia.

- Photographers can access a variety of lenses to improve content and eliminate visual redundancy.

- When necessary, photographers can utilize flash units to improve lighting.

- Every picture should include complete caption information answering readers' questions.

- Good cropping ensures photos tell the best story by eliminating distracting and unnecessary elements.

- An effective photo editing process can improve photo quality and improve photographers' shooting ability.

- Designers should avoid abusive photo uses by respecting the storytelling qualities of the images.

- Art, illustrations and infographics can be effectively used as visuals in addition to pictures.

- Graphic strategies including use of color, rule lines, boxes and backgrounds should be used to improve design and content.

KEY TERMS

aperture	fast lens	picture package
blur	fixed focal length lens	picture sequence
bounce flash	flat light	picture story
burn in	flipping/flopping	point-and-shoot camera
catchline	framing	rule of thirds
center of interest	golden mean points	shallow depth of field
collage	grounds	side light
contrast	highlights	stand-alone photograph
cropping	illustration	standard lens
dedicated flash system	impact	synchro-sun flash
depth of field	indirect flash	telephoto lenses
direct flash	ISO	viewfinder
dodge	monopod	visual redundancy
dpi, dots per inch	outline light	wide-angle lens
duotone image	overline	zoom lenses

EXERCISES

1   In small groups, develop a set of parameters for the quality of images that should be used in a publication at your school. Consider whether staff should use pictures that are out of focus; that show the backs or tops of people's heads; that are marred by poor practices; that are of the same people; that are flipped or flopped; that are of staff members' friends. Consider digital effects in your list. Justify your reasons for each decision. Refer to the NPPA Code of Ethics.

2   Using digital files of pictures from the yearbook or newspaper staff, find a picture that would be a good stand-alone shot. Design a style for how the picture could be used in the newspaper. Write a catchline and/or caption for the picture.

3   Cut out five examples of information graphics from professional publications. Find examples of a pie chart, a bar graph, a diagram, a locator map and a 3-D illustration. Examine the content and determine whether the forms have been used effectively.

4   Find examples of these picture techniques: a cutout image, an image cut into a cookie-cutter shape, overlapping or collaged images, a photo pattern, grid or module and a photo cliché. Attach each example to a sheet of paper and write an explanation of how each was used in print. Was it effective in its presentation?

5   Visualize picture stories that could be developed for each of the following five topics: prom, graduation, homecoming, a field trip and a debate tournament. Make lists of possible pictures that could be taken and indicate what kind of lens might be appropriate for each picture. Go through your list and add compositional qualities that would improve the pictures.

6   Using a digital camera, photograph an event or activity in your school. Download the pictures onto the computer and edit them using the computer software program your school uses. Write captions for each of the images and design a picture package. Make sure one of the pictures appears in a dominant shape and size in the package.

7 Cut out five different pages from professional publications in which artwork or illustrations have been used instead of pictures. Attach each to a sheet of paper and explain its effectiveness in visualizing the story it illustrates. Underline passages in the story that relate directly to elements of the art or illustration. Explain how the illustration utilizes detail and color. What style is used in the art?

8 Cut out examples of the following features: rule lines; color used to separate and isolate content; headline units using color, contrast or visual detail; white space used for visual or verbal separation; and pull quotes and text heads in a story. Attach each example to a sheet of paper and label it. Evaluate the effectiveness of each example.

ADVERTISING IN NEWSPAPERS AND YEARBOOKS

16

> " *Even on student newspapers wholly funded by the school, students need to learn salesmanship, audience appeal, graphic design and business. The solicitation and creation of advertising allows students to gain a complete journalistic experience.*
>
> Mitch Ziegler, Redondo Union High School Newspaper Adviser, Redondo Beach, Calif.

"

LEARNING OBJECTIVES After completing this chapter you will be able to:

- understand the goals of creating an advertising program
- prepare for an advertising program
- prepare for an advertising sales call
- explore the considerations of an advertising policy
- design an advertisement.

IT'S A FAVORITE AMERICAN TEEN pastime – spending money – someone's, anyone's.

There's Andrew, who just had to spend his $340 check from lifeguarding at the city pool. Then there's Holly who begs her mother to buy her brand of cereal. Teens and tweens have become a powerful buying force in America. The two groups have grown to represent an estimated $450 billion market. Consider all the ways businesses focus their advertising on teens. The Disney Channel has created a business empire of pop stars, television shows and movies by catering to the tween market. Companies buy advertising space on school buses, lockers and gym walls. School newspapers and yearbooks offer advertisers a direct link to America's 30 million-plus teenagers.

The communication link that publications provide between businesses and readers can create a beneficial relationship for both groups. Advertising in school publications has a number of important functions. These include:

1 *Providing income for the publication.* Nearly all media – newspapers, magazines, news websites, radio and television – derive most of their income from advertising. School publications with little funding find advertising a necessity. Even those publications with school district funding may find advertising a great way to raise money for such items as additional computers or camera equipment or more expensive printing options.

2 *Providing a service to businesses.* Because the school newspaper, website and yearbook are read by teens in a limited geographic area, businesses can reach a specific audience with focused messages about products and services. The news website provides a direct link to students as well, but offers expanded opportunities to reach adults in the community and beyond. Advertising can create brand or business name recognition, sell products or services or publicize job openings.

3 *Providing readers with information about products and services.* Students are always searching for new restaurants, weekend jobs or the latest sales on athletic shoes. Advertising can make students aware of all of these things. Informing students about services such as an SAT prep class or a driving school will also help meet student needs.

4 *Forging a bond between the business community and the student body.* Advertising in a high school newspaper not only makes good financial sense, but it also signals that businesses are investing in their communities. Building mutual respect between the student body and businesses strengthens the sense of community. When a pharmacy buys a full-page yearbook ad, parents and students may shop there, in part, to show their appreciation for the business's investment in the student endeavor. The community as a whole is stronger for such an exchange.

CREATING AN ADVERTISING PROGRAM

Advertising can be a vibrant, fun part of scholastic journalism programs. From the preparation stages to the sales visits to the design and placement of ads, each stage of creating an advertisement is creative and interactive. (The many possible career choices in the field of advertising are explored in Chapter 19.)

Preparation

An informed salesperson is a successful salesperson. The advertising salesperson must fully understand information about the school, the publication and the business. The **advertising director**, the staff member chosen to lead the advertising program, should collect and organize such information to arm and train advertising salespeople.

One of the first steps is understanding the **market** or, in this case, the student audience. The best salespeople know the make-up of their audience, as well as that audience's buying power and habits. Students spend large amounts of money. Sometimes it's their money. Sometimes it's their parents' money. Conduct your own **market survey**, and you may be surprised by how much students spend, and what they purchase and where they shop. Lakota East High School's *Spark*

Market survey tips

A good first step for any school publication's advertising program is to conduct a survey of student spending. Keep the survey short to encourage students to complete the form. A one-page questionnaire with ranges of answers to circle may help. A few questions you could include in your own survey are:

→ How much do you spend in one week?

→ How much do you spend for clothes each school year?

→ In what stores do you buy these clothes?

→ What do you do for entertainment each week?

→ How much do you spend on this entertainment each week? How much for movies? Concerts? Video games? Other activities?

→ How much do you spend per week on food? Outside the school cafeteria, where do you buy this food?

→ How much do you spend on school supplies each school year? Where do you buy them?

→ How much do you spend on transportation? Do you own a car?

→ Which stores do you buy from the most? Why?

→ Which stores do you buy from the least? Why?

found that seniors spend an average of more than $130 a month. Multiply that average by the more than 1,500 students at Lakota East, and you will see that *Spark* reaches an audience with sizable spending power.

In addition to knowing the buying power and habits of the readers, a good salesperson needs to know how many people are in the school and what communities the school draws from.

The advertising staff should take all this information and incorporate it into a set of professional-looking sales aids. The **sales aids** can include a rate card, a flyer and sales charts or graphs.

Although it can be many sizes or shapes, the **rate card** is typically a small brochure containing all the basic information about advertising in the publication. It should also include information about the publication itself and the market. The rate card should be well designed and anticipate most of a potential advertiser's questions (Figure 16.1).

The card could include some of the following information:

- Publication dates
- Deadline dates for space reservation and copy
- Basic publication information such as address, phone number, fax number and email address
- Reasons to buy an ad in the publication
- Readership information, such as number of readers or website hits, buying power and habits
- Policies on what ads the publication will and won't accept
- Billing and payment policies, such as discounts, acceptance of checks and billing dates
- Design information, such as a requirement that logos must be on a white background
- Additional costs, such as fees for providing photographs or other graphics for an ad.

Don't overwhelm the advertiser with information. Make the rate card easy to read and use.

WWW

WEBLINK Check out

http://www.tru-insight.com

Teenage Research Unlimited studies teenage buying habits and offers press releases with the results of some of their polls that could be helpful for advertising salespeople.

FIGURE 16.1 *Spark*, Lakota East High School, Liberty Township, Ohio. Reproduced by permission of Dean Hume.

High school publication staff can improve their professional image by preparing a well-designed rate card. *Spark* staff regularly update their rate card with the latest ad rates and deadlines. Their card does a good job of providing specifics such as the formats the ad can be submitted in, the results of a student buying habit survey and available design services – all in an organized, attractive color brochure.

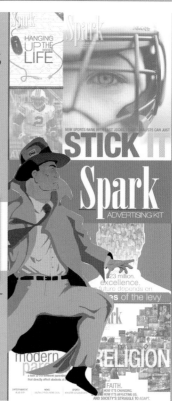

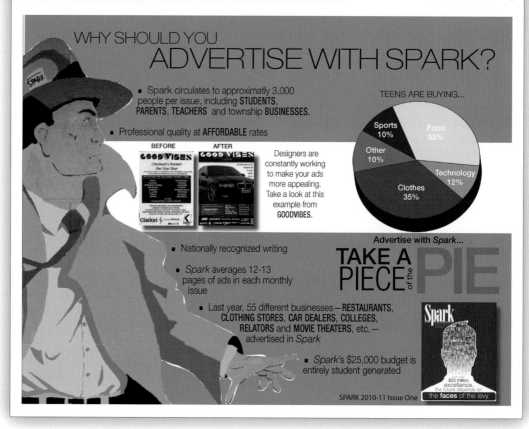

FIGURE 16.2 *HiLite*, Carmel High School, Carmel, Ind. Reproduced by permission of Jim Streisel.

Creating business cards such as this one from the *HiLite* staff at Carmel High School in Carmel, Ind., can help ad staff establish a professional relationship with advertisers. The cards should be designed to connect visually with the other marketing material the staff uses. The business card gives the salesperson something to leave after a sales call, and is especially useful when the manager wants to call back for more information.

CARMEL HIGH SCHOOL HILITE AD SALES STAFF 520 East Main Street Carmel, Indiana 46032-2299 (317) 846-7721, Ext. 1143 Fax: (317) 571-4066 Web: www.hilite.org	Art Bortolini • 506-1030 • abortolini@hilite.org Jon Campbell • 575-9276 • jcampbell@hilite.org Stacie Feldwisch • 848-2821 • sfeldwisch@hiite.org Nichole Freije • 848-1789 • nfreije@hilite.org Chase Graverson • 844-3240 • cgraverson@hilite.org Dave Hoffman • 843-1980 • dhoffman@hilite.org Quinn Shepherd • 844-2408 • qshepherd@hilite.org Jon Titus • 571-9744 • jtitus@hilite.org Jake Wilson • 844-5437 • jwilson@hilite.org

The **sales graphs and charts**, presentations about the publication, its market or advertisers, can be as varied as the publication's sales needs. For example, compare the percentage of students who read your publication with the percentage who read the closest major daily. Display all the tuxedo rental businesses that have advertised in your publication as a way to encourage other formal-wear businesses to do the same. List the dates of upcoming dances and special events along with survey information about the amount of money students spend getting ready for these events. This information can be condensed into a one-page **flyer**, an easy-to-understand summary of relevant sales information to leave with prospective advertisers. Both flyers and sales graphs and charts can serve as quick reference material for a salesperson.

A professional packet of sales aids, typically uniform in design, serves several purposes. The packet gives the salesperson something to work from during a **sales call**, a salesperson's visit to a business to sell ad space. If the businessperson is busy or uninterested, the salesperson can leave the packet for later review. The business owner may come back to the packet and will have the prices and phone number handy when he's ready to call and purchase an ad.

The advertising director should also make sure each salesperson has billing forms, proofing forms and an assortment of sales and thank you letters. The additional forms can help establish trust between the business and the salesperson, increasing the likelihood that the business owner will buy an ad. More advanced publication programs will make the packet and additional advertising forms available on their website (Figure 16.3).

A good salesperson should not have to refer to sales aids for basic information such as advertising rates and deadline dates. The numbers should be as familiar to the salesperson as his or her birthdate. The salesperson needs to know the number of subscribers to the newspaper, the number of hits to the website or the number of yearbooks sold. It's also helpful to have memorized the number of students in each class (freshman to senior) and the percentage of boys and girls. A basic understanding of the publication enhances a student salesperson's image as a professional.

Advertising policy

A written **advertising policy**, or guidelines for advertising-related decisions, will help salespeople address any circumstances that arise in the course of their work. The policy might address issues such as ad sales for political campaigns, health centers where pregnancy tests or abortions are performed or businesses that get a majority of their income from liquor sales. For example, a pizza place that students frequent might have a logo with the words "Friends of wine and beer." Does your policy prohibit running the ad with the logo as is? Do you ask for a modified logo, or ask for permission to crop the logo out?

The policy may also need to address some of the following questions:

- Must an ad sell a product or service? What happens if a person buying space in the newspaper is promoting a personal viewpoint that may be offensive to certain groups or populations in the school? Do you accept congratulations ads? Do you accept political ads?

- What about sex-related advertising? Will your yearbook run an ad for a store that sells condoms? Do you advertise R-rated movies? What about a tanning salon ad with a photo of a woman in a revealing swimsuit?

- The advertising policy may also deal with minimum advertising sizes. A 1 × 1-inch or a 1 × 2-inch ad may disrupt layouts and is often an inadequate amount of space in which to advertise a product or service.

Test your knowledge

List two of the four major roles that advertising plays in a high school publication.

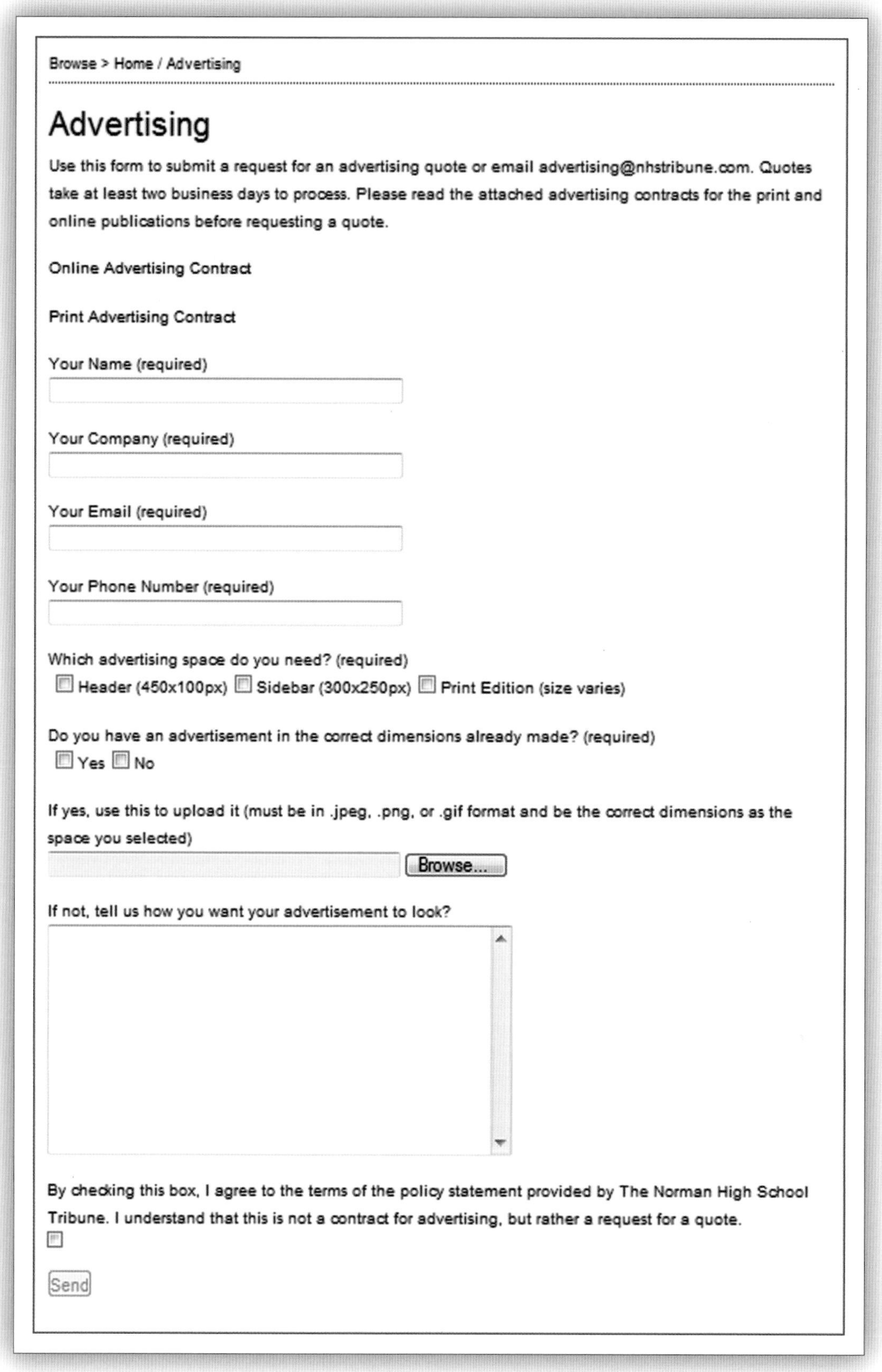

FIGURE 16.3 Use of form from www.nhstribune.com/advertising. *NHS Tribune*, Norman High School, Norman, Okla. Reprinted with kind permission.

Publications have begun providing advertising contracts online as a way to make them more accessible to advertisers. The *NHS Tribune* staff provide their contracts online and prompts potential advertisers to read them before filling out an online request for more information. Other publication staff offer online copies of their rate cards and other sales aids as a service to advertisers.

Browse > Home / Advertising

Advertising

Use this form to submit a request for an advertising quote or email advertising@nhstribune.com. Quotes take at least two business days to process. Please read the attached advertising contracts for the print and online publications before requesting a quote.

Online Advertising Contract

Print Advertising Contract

Your Name (required)

Your Company (required)

Your Email (required)

Your Phone Number (required)

Which advertising space do you need? (required)
☐ Header (450x100px) ☐ Sidebar (300x250px) ☐ Print Edition (size varies)

Do you have an advertisement in the correct dimensions already made? (required)
☐ Yes ☐ No

If yes, use this to upload it (must be in .jpeg, .png, or .gif format and be the correct dimensions as the space you selected)

[Browse...]

If not, tell us how you want your advertisement to look?

By checking this box, I agree to the terms of the policy statement provided by The Norman High School Tribune. I understand that this is not a contract for advertising, but rather a request for a quote.
☐

[Send]

- Some schools also have policies on what can be included in senior yearbook ads. Messages with innuendos or inside jokes, such as those sometimes included in senior wills, could raise libel and ethics concerns.

Business knowledge

Good salespeople must observe and understand the businesses of prospective advertisers. They should know when a sporting goods store has new school team T-shirts to sell. They should be aware that students from their school often go out for Frappuccinos and slushies. Information such as what products or services students buy from the area clothing stores, movie theaters and restaurants will make a salesperson a valuable ally for the business owner.

Salespeople should collect as much of the following information as possible before they make a sales pitch:

- Who is the store manager?
- Who handles the business's advertising?
- What products or services does this business have that is of interest to your readers?
- What medium does the owner prefer advertising in? What sizes of ads does this business buy regularly? What products or services is the business currently promoting?
- What upcoming events in the community, school or store could increase the impact of an ad?

Preparing for the sales call

Creating a smooth sales pitch can be a challenging task that requires combining information about the school publication and the prospective advertiser. Practice helps. The advertising director can organize an ad meeting in the summer. Invite a professional salesperson to discuss tips for selling ads. Role-play a typical ad sales call to practice the approach. The more times a person talks through a sales approach, the more at ease he or she will feel.

The role-playing should be realistic. More experienced salespeople will know the scenarios that you may face in the sales call. Some examples are:

- The business owner who doesn't have time
- The business owner who doesn't advertise in high school publications
- The manager who uses the "I already donated money to the band" excuse.

When role-playing a sales call, be creative. Will the owner question the image of your school? Will the owner be abrupt and angry because she had to fire an employee that morning? Will the owner agree to buy an ad only if you also pass out flyers for him? The more situations you face in role-playing, the more comfortable you'll be in dealing with situations as they arise in real sales calls.

Before going out to sell, salespeople should be assigned a specific territory to cover. The advertising director can organize the territories regionally. A salesperson may feel more at ease if covering an area in his or her neighborhood, with businesses he or she frequents. Good rapport between the salesperson and the business owner is crucial for successful sales calls. Another way to learn the sales call is to shadow a more experienced salesperson.

The sales call

There's one sure way to fail in a sales call: walk into a business and mumble, "Do you want to buy an ad?" You'll get a predictable response. "No." Don't let this happen. Give the business owner a reason to buy. A salesperson should know that because businesses differ, the reasons they want to purchase ads vary. The salesperson must communicate the information that fits the needs of the particular customer and the special type of store. An advertiser convinced of the value of advertising in the school publication can be spoken to differently from one who is skeptical.

Quick Exercise

Make a list of possible advertisers for your school publication.

HELPFUL TIPS

Tips for making an effective sales call:

→ Dress in appropriate clothing.

→ Begin with a reason why the business owner would want to advertise in the school yearbook, website or newspaper.

→ Be prepared with other reasons why a business owner should advertise.

→ Anticipate all possible objections a business owner might raise and plan valid rebuttals.

→ Remind advertisers that the most effective ads are not one-time propositions. Emphasize that regular advertising builds an image in the minds of readers, which brings product and store recognition. A store running an ad only once has a poor chance of leaving a lasting impression. After all, consider the number of McDonald's ads you've seen in the last year.

→ Go armed with a predesigned ad for the business. The time you take to develop a concept and design an ad will show the business owner that you care about his or her business. Even if the sales call does not end in a sale, you can be successful in earning the respect of the business.

→ Keep notes to analyze the results of successful or unsuccessful sales presentations with businesses. A file on a business will help the salesperson keep up with the account. For example, a business owner may say, "I really want to advertise before prom." A good salesperson will write down the owner's comment and return six weeks before prom.

→ Understand that many chain businesses rely on corporate offices to purchase advertising. Some student salespeople have been successful by persistently calling corporate offices to make the sale. A publication can join certain agencies that sell advertising to corporations on behalf of a large group of school publications, primarily newspapers. In other cases, salespeople have encouraged local managers of chain businesses to use community-relations funds to buy advertising for their products or services or for hiring purposes.

→ Tactful persistence pays off. Most sales are made after at least five calls. Rapport and respect take time. Coming back to the business owner to show new designs or to see if he or she needs anything will frequently pay off.

Quick Exercise

Pair up with another student for a role-playing exercise. One will play the salesperson for your high school publication, the other the business owner in these scenarios.

1 A car repair shop owner whose ad had a misspelling in it two years ago and he hasn't bought since.

2 A dress shop owner who hadn't thought about advertising with a high school publication.

3 A tuxedo shop owner who wants to advertise but wants a discount and wants to use student models.

A new business owner may need information about your school's location and size as well as the total buying power of your readers. A previous advertiser may need a reminder that prom is only four weeks away.

A salesperson may have made contact with the business owner before making the sales call. Some salespeople phone first and make appointments. If the salesperson is not comfortable with the business to begin with, a brief face-to-face visit to set up the appointment may be better. While this initial visit may be more time-consuming – because many managers or business owners may not be in or are unavailable – meeting face to face will help establish a rapport with the business owner. A long-time Dallas newspaper advertising salesperson suggests that the business owner must like the salesperson as much as the publication in order to want to buy an ad.

The creation and sale of advertising requires thorough preparation and a professional demeanor. When the salesperson initiates the sales call, he will be more at ease if armed with the sales aids discussed above. Remember that the salesperson is a skilled individual who helps business owners communicate with students through a school publication.

Test your knowledge

List three things you should do to prepare for a sales call.

Ad Script -- A typical day on the job

(The setting is Papa John's Pizza. Phil is a **SPARK** *ad salesman. His job is to make money. This could be the middle, end or beginning of the year. Regardless, Phil does not return without a filled out ad contract for fear of bodily harm from the hands of Amy Silver or Catherine Matacic. The time is 4 p.m. The salesman is dressed professionally. He is calm, cool, and collected. He has some background on the business: their competitors, previous advertisements with SPARK, their competitors advertisements in SPARK, and their prime target audience. Phil is just being himself and flashing them a handsome smile. Advertisers like to be secure with and trust the people they send their checks to. That trust and security hinges on the moment he walks in their store. Phil must make a good first impression.)*

Phil: Hi! May I speak with the manager?
Papa John's Delivery Boy: He isn't in right now.
Phil: Well, may I speak with the assistant manager?
Papa John's Delivery Boy: Hold on one second. *(Delivery boy goes and fetches the assistant manager, who is on the telephone. Phil has to wait a couple of minutes. John Deluca approaches the counter.)*
John: Hi! How may I help you?
Phil: My name is Phil Tork, and I'm from Lakota East High School's nationally acclaimed student newsmagazine **SPARK**. I've come here to tell you about a great opportunity your company has been missing out on. That opportunity is the local teenage, pizza hungry market. The easiest way to hit them and their parents is through their school. **SPARK** distributes to over 1,000 students, parents, teachers, and community members. We are one of the largest high school publications in the state and have been in operation for over five years. We would like you to consider advertising with our paper. Here is a copy of our ad information, publication dates, ad sizes and also a placement sheet. We do inserts and would gladly print out coupons with your ad. Coupons are a really good idea because those indicate to you whether the ad is working and whether you are satisfied with the job we are doing. Here is a list of other companies in the area who have advertised with us. I'm pretty sure Pizza Hut and Dominoes are on the list. Our space fills up pretty quick. So are you interested?
John: Do I have to give you the money now? *(Looks unsure about what he is getting into.)*
Phil: You can but you don't have to. After each publication is distributed, we will send you a bill through the mail. If we make any mistakes on your ad, we will gladly give you a free ad in our next issue. If you buy more than one ad a year, we can easily change the ad to say something else, but you would need to send us the new information.
John: Okay. I'll purchase a quarter page for the October, December and May issues. *(Phil fills out the required spaces on the placement sheet, informs John of the total price and writes down the company's name, address, and telephone number.)*
Phil: We have the technology to do camera-ready ads. Do you have any material that you would like to see placed in the ad, such as your logo or coupons? *(John hands him what he wants on the ad.)* Would you like us to design the coupons for you?
John: Sure.
Phil: What would you like them to say? How about ... *(The lights and sound fade out on the scene. Phil has just received a lot of stringbook points toward his quarter grade and a lot of gratitude from the business department. And all it took was to become a salesman for a day.)*

> **NOTE:** NOT ALL ASSISTANT MANAGERS OR MANAGERS ARE AUTHORIZED TO PURCHASE ADS. IF THEY CAN'T, ASK WHO TO TALK TO, OR WHEN THE OWNER WILL BE IN, THEN STOP BACK ON THAT DATE. DON'T GET FRUSTRATED IF YOU DON'T SUCCEED IN EVERY STORE YOU WALK INTO. JOANN TIEMANN TWO YEARS AGO WENT TO OVER 12 STORES IN ONE DAY AND ONLY TWO STORES BOUGHT ADS.

Spark Journalism Handbook   20   Lakota East High School

FIGURE 16.4 *Spark*, Lakota East High School, Liberty Township, Ohio. Reproduced by permission of Dean Hume.
Young salespeople often need guidance in what to say when making a sales call. At Lakota East High School, *Spark* newsmagazine staff members are given this script to help think through a sales call ahead of time. Good salespeople will know what they want to say going into a call but will keep the interaction with the client smooth, relaxed and conversational.

Telephone sales

In some schools where administrations are reluctant to allow students to leave campus to sell ads, a phone campaign may be necessary. A well-written phone script may help. However, the script should not be read mechanically or sound as if it is being read from a sheet of paper. The tips above for effective sales calls also apply to telephone sales. A face-to-face meeting after school or on a weekend prior to a call is preferable and will help establish a rapport with the business owner. A telephone call may also suffice as a follow-up when the salesperson has already made the sale and is trying to extend it for another issue.

CREATING AN ADVERTISEMENT

WWW

The Advertising Media Internet Community website estimates the average person will be exposed to 245 ads each day. Clearly, consumers are exposed to a great deal of advertising that competes for their attention. Faced with advertising images on billboards, television, websites and T-shirts, the reader will not give much notice to a plain business card reprinted at the bottom of a page in the high school newspaper. The quality of the ad concept and design is critical.

Advertising must have a message that fosters name recognition, evokes a feeling about the product or service or informs the reader about its benefits. One ad for athletic shoes might promote a cool, go-all-out image for the brand. Another ad might seek to convince students to buy roses from the corner florist for their prom dates. Still another ad for a neighborhood restaurant might offer a 15 percent discount on burgers and fries for students showing their school IDs.

Define the message

The advertiser will often know what aspect of the business he or she wants to advertise. Other times, the advertising salesperson may help develop the message. Either way, the point conveyed by the ad should be simple. The message can be as specific as "Rent your tux for homecoming from us" or as abstract as "the Pizza Shack sells fun." Both are simple, clear messages that can and should be visually and verbally communicated in interesting ways. The message should clearly define what makes this particular business different from all other businesses of the same type.

In the book *Hey Whipple, Squeeze This: A Guide to Creating Great Ads*, Luke Sullivan explains what a good ad must accomplish:

> It's as if you're riding down an elevator with your customer. You're going down only 15 floors. So you have only a few seconds to tell him one thing about your product. One thing. And you have to tell it to him in such an interesting way that he thinks about the promise you've made as he leaves the building, waits for the light and crosses the street. You have to come up with some little thing that sticks in the customer's mind.

> *Luke Sullivan*, Hey Whipple, Squeeze This: A Guide to Creating Great Ads, *Hoboken, New Jersey: John Wiley & Sons*

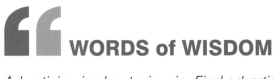 **WORDS of WISDOM**

Advertising is about win-win. Find advertisers that win by advertising in your program. Help your audience win by selling advertising that gets them an advantage. And, please don't re-create business cards; design aggressively to showcase the company and appeal to the teen audience.

Mark Newton, Mountain Vista High School Adviser, Highlands Ranch, Colo.

Sullivan provides a wealth of suggestions for delivering the message creatively through a print ad. Here are a few of his suggestions:

- Find the central truth about your whole product category. The central *human* truth. Hair coloring isn't about looking younger. It's about self-esteem. Cameras aren't about pictures. They're about stopping time and holding life as the world moves on.

- Avoid style; focus on substance. Remember, styles change; typefaces and design and art directions, they all change. Fads come and go. But people are always people. They want to look better, to make more money; they want to feel better, to be healthy. They want security, attention and achievement.

- Quiet your mind. And ask, "What would make me want to buy this product?"

- Get to know your client's business as well as you can.

- First, say it straight. Then say it great. To get the words flowing, sometimes it helps to simply write out what you want to say. Make it memorable, different or new later. First just say it.

- Try this. Begin your headline with: "This is an ad about …" And then keep writing …. Whatever you do, just start writing.

- Remember notebook paper is not made solely for recording gems of transcendent perfection. A sheet of paper costs about one squillionth of a cent. It isn't a museum frame. It's a workbench. Write. Keep writing. Don't stop.

- Think of the strategy statement as a lump of clay. You've got to sculpt it into something interesting to look at. So begin by taking the strategy and saying it some other way, any way. Say it faster. Say it in English. Then in slang. Shorten it. Punch it up. Try anything that will change the strategy statement from something you'd overhear in an elevator at a sales convention to a message you'd see spray painted on an alley wall.

- Try writing down words from the product's category. Let's say you're selling outboard engines – I start a list on the side of the page: Fish, Water, Pelicans, Flotsam, Jetsam, Atlantic, Titanic, Ishmael. What do these words make you think of? Pick up two of them and put them together like Tinkertoys. You have to start somewhere. Sure it sounds stupid. The whole creative *process* is stupid.

- Allow your partner to come up with terrible ideas. The quickest way to shut down your partner's contribution is to roll your eyes at a bad idea. Don't … just say "that's interesting," scribble it down and move on.

- Don't look for what's wrong with a new idea; look for what's right.

- Stare at a picture that has the emotion of the ad you want to do.

- Come up with a lot of ideas. Cover the wall.

- Quick sketches of your ideas are all you need during the creative process … Just put the concept on the paper and continue moving forward.

- Get it on paper, fast and furious. Be hot. Let it pour out. Don't edit when you're coming up with ads. Then later, be ruthless. Cut everything that is not A-plus work.

" WORDS of WISDOM

Developing a creative concept for an ad from scratch should be seen as an opportunity to help a business communicate an ownable and differentiating message in an engaging and memorable way.

Jen Cunningham Augustyn, The Dealey Group partner, Dallas, Texas

FIGURE 16.5 Drake University, Des Moines, Iowa. Reprinted with permission.

The Drake University ad conveys a simple idea: "make your mark at Drake." The designer created visual-verbal reinforcement with the use of the fingerprint image. By reviewing the copy, the reader will see that Drake wants its students to make their "mark" by writing a play, designing homes or helping find a cure for a disease.

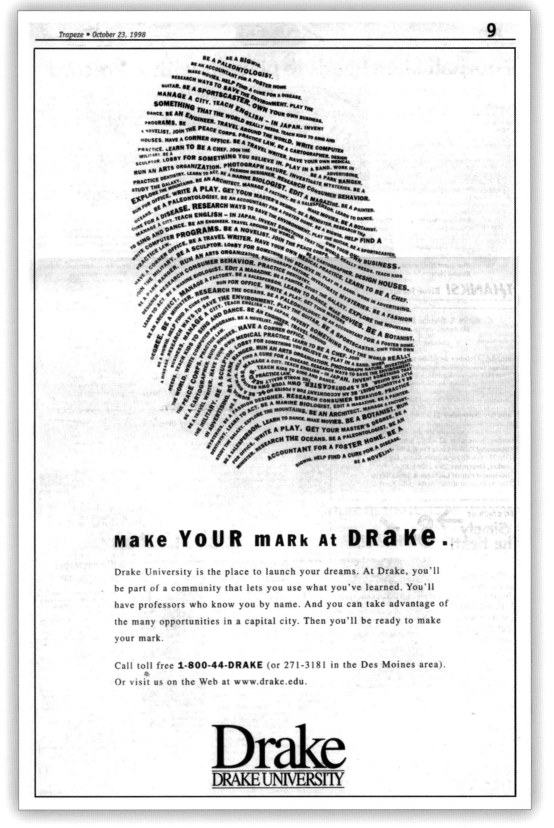

Creating the advertisement, one step at a time

Taking the ideas from the brainstorming process to the computer screen is the next step. Each advertising design can be broken down into four elements: illustration, headline, body copy and logo. The elements should work together to communicate the clear message that was developed in the steps above. In Figure 16.5, all the elements work together to deliver their message: that Drake University will help you be somebody.

The illustration, a photo or artwork, is usually the dominant feature of the ad. In the visual hierarchy, discussed in Chapter 12, the illustration is typically more prominent than the other elements. The advertising designer should seek to demonstrate the practical value of the product, service or business, as well as a particular feeling inherent to the brand. People are visual. Good dominant visuals, placed in the **optical center**, a point slightly above the exact center of the page, grab the reader's attention.

The headline is rarely used as the dominant visual element in an ad. However, the headline is still critical to effectively communicating the ad's message. It should rarely be simply the name of the store. Instead, the headline should describe the benefit of the product or service and complement the ad's illustration. The type selection should enhance the feeling that the ad seeks to evoke. A well-written headline, created in a clean and easy-to-read serif or sans serif type, is preferable to illegible novelty type. Ad headlines should also be short and punchy. A secondary headline in many retail ads, or ads that advertise a specific store, may include the store's name. Often, however, an advertiser has a logo they wish to use.

The **copy** is the written text of the ad and should reinforce the message of the headline and illustration. The text should be specific and vivid, helping to sell the product or service by personalizing its benefits. In the Drake University ad (Figure 16.5), the headline states that readers can make their mark at Drake. The copy lists specific ways this can be achieved (for example, by being part of a hands-on learning community, and by having the personal attention of professors).

If the ad is a **retail ad**, which advertises a specific business, the copy will usually include basic information such as the address, phone number and store hours. The local retail ad is also more likely to include prices for specific products. Try to limit the copy. Keep it short and snappy. In the visual hierarchy of the design, the body copy typically is secondary. The designer should choose much smaller type sizes and weights. Clean, easy to read serif and sans serif types are preferable.

The **logo** is the trademark of the company. Typically company-provided, the logo is given larger display than the body copy, but not usually larger than the headline and illustration. Make sure that the logo is on a white or light background if you have to scan or reproduce it. A logo on dark-colored paper will muddy and become unreadable in the reproduction.

As already mentioned, the illustration is usually the dominant element in the design. The reader's eyes are attracted to the illustration, and from there the eyes must make a clear and logical movement through the ad. The eye movement is sometimes called **gaze motion** and is usually left to right. But if an ad features a dominant image of a football player on the right side of the ad, looking toward a headline on the left, this will surely draw the reader's eyes from right to left – or from illustration to the headline. Use visual hierarchy to move the reader's eyes through each element of an ad. A larger headline under a dominant illustration will create logical gaze motion. The last thing the reader should see is the logo. This advertising strategy can be likened to the last song you hear on the radio before getting out of your car in the morning: it sticks in your mind throughout the day. The art director hopes the same thing happens with the last visual element you see: the logo. This will create familiarity and comfort with the logo the next time you see it, and may even cause you to seek it out. When presented with a row of restaurants, the advertiser wants you to stop at the one you recognize from an ad.

White space is also a consideration in ad design. White space can help frame and give emphasis to elements. Elements should not be crammed into a space. Avoid the use of decorative dingbats and big, overwhelming borders. A simple one-point rule often suffices. Let the four elements defined earlier – illustration, headline, body copy and logo – attract the reader's attention.

WEBLINK Check out

www.oneclub.org

The website offers the winners of their national advertising production and design awards that students can study for their creativity, design and execution.

FIGURE 16.6 *Cub Tracks*, Humboldt High School, Humboldt, Kan. Reproduced by permission of Humboldt High School.

This Humboldt High School public service announcement uses a compelling headline visual as its dominant illustration to tie texting and driving with death. The font is bold and strong to display a powerful message. The inclusion of the cracked windshield with the blood splatter is subtle but strong. The use of the red spot color was judicious to make sure we see the word "Dead" as well as to reinforce the blood but to avoid overwhelming the reader.

Some other considerations in ad design

Advertising is a service business. The professionalism should not start at the sales call and end in the ad design. If a publication wants to keep its advertisers, the following considerations will help to provide a satisfied repeat customer:

- Once you've completed an ad design, try it out on some friends. Ask them what message they got from the ad to see if it matches the desired one. If an ad needs explanation, it fails.

- After the ad is designed, the process is not over. Providing the business owner with an ad to proof after proofing the ad yourself is critical to doing good business. Make sure

Test your knowledge

What is gaze motion?

NEWSFLASH

Two types of advertising

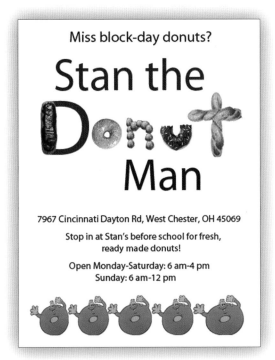

Sidebar 16a *Harbinger*, Shawnee Mission East High School, Prairie Village, Kan. Reproduced by permission of C. Dow Tate.

Display advertising is exactly what its name suggests: advertising that displays, through type and illustrations, the product or service a merchant wants to sell. Well-designed display ads use typefaces appropriate to the product or service and effective illustrations and borders. Such ads help to make news pages attractive and direct readers' attention to the ads.

Classified advertising typically appears in its own section of a paper and classifies products and services under appropriate headings. These might include such categories as "Jobs Wanted," "Used Books" and services available primarily for teenagers. Few school papers have classified ad columns, yet this section could be a source of revenue and perform a real service to readers. Personal ads in newspapers are discouraged because they can create ethical and, in some cases, legal problems for the school. Make sure all ads sell a service that is legal.

Sidebar 16b Classified Ad.

FIGURE 16.7 Advertisement. *The Harbinger*, Shawnee Mission East High School, Prairie Village, Kan. Reproduced by permission of C. Dow Tate.

The Shawnee Mission East High School student designer asked the advertiser if he could redesign this tailor's ad so that the ad made an emotional impression along with providing name recognition. The designer developed a concept built upon a stock photo image (which the student got the business owner to purchase) and accentuated that image with good font choices to create a stylish feel.

the ad contains a correct address, fax and phone information and a cleanly reproduced logo. Also, make sure the ad contains an updated coupon date, if applicable.

- Do not put coupons on back-to-back pages in the newspaper.

- Once the advertisement runs, the advertising salesperson should deliver a copy of the newspaper or the yearbook page to first-time advertisers to encourage repeat business. A **tear sheet**, or copy of the reproduced ad, serves as proof of the business's purchase.

- Make sure all billing is prompt.

- A satisfied advertiser is a repeat advertiser.

FIGURE 16.8 Bishop Snyder High School newspaper. Prom issue, 2011. Designed by Emily Corrigan. Reprinted with permission of *The Cardinal Chronicles*, Bishop Snyder High School, Jacksonville, Fla.

The Bishop Snyder newspaper staff uses two strong techniques to draw students to this tuxedo shop ad for the prom issue. The staff used real students as models for the tuxes, something that will most assuredly grab the reader's attention. The inclusion of a coupon also increases the ad's value for the reader. Some of the better newspaper staff look for creative ways such as these to tie the advertiser directly to the student body.

FIGURE 16.9 Website advertisement. *The Pinnacle*, Klein Forest High School, Houston, Texas. Screengrab from homepage of website: http://kfpinnacle.com/. Reprinted with permission.

Pinnacle staff place ads near their banner on their website. *The Pinnacle* charges a different rate for static ads, which don't change, and rotating ads, which share the space with other ads. Many online publications charge advertisers by the month, while some offer online ads a bonus for advertisers who buy a print edition ad at a certain rate or for a certain period of time.

Quick Exercise

Choose three of your favorite TV commercials. Explain what product benefit each ad is trying to communicate and how the ad communicates the message. Decide which ad is the most creative and explain why.

CONCLUSION

Advertising pays the bills. The adage speaks to the fact that most publications wouldn't exist without the money that advertising brings in. While the ads bring in the money needed for publishing, advertising is also a service for businesses and the public alike. The spending power of teens has grown such that high school publications need to see the value that advertising in their publication has for the community. High school journalists who value their own advertising should then understand the professionalism with which they'll want to handle advertising sales and design.

SUMMARY

- Advertising provides income for publication, sales to businesses and products and services information to readers.

- High school publications should do a market survey of their readership to better understand the buying habits and spending power of their school.

- High school publications should prepare a professional set of sales aids that includes a rate card, flyer and business card. The sales aids will help to create a knowledgeable sales staff that will be better prepared to handle potential advertisers' question.

- Advertising sales representatives should think through and practice a professional presentation before making a sales call. Sales representatives should remember their role is to communicate the proper information that fits the need of the business.

- Advertising must have a message that fosters name recognition, evokes a feeling about the product or service or informs the reader about its benefits.

- The design of an advertisement should deliver the message to the reader through a thoughtful and sometimes clever concept. The advertising delivers the concept through a strong visual–verbal connection.

KEY TERMS

advertising director	gaze motion	retail ad
advertising policy	logo	sales aids
classified advertising	market	sales call
copy	market survey	sales graphs and charts
display advertising	optical center	tear sheet
flyer	rate card	

EXERCISES

1 Evaluate the ads in Figures 16.10–16.12. Do they really sell a service or a product? Is the concept creative? Are they effectively designed? If not, how might they have been improved? Is the copy effective? If not, why not? In your discussion, use all the principles of ad creation you studied in this chapter.

FIGURE 16.10 Advertisement produced by *Hillcrest Hurricane*, Hillcrest High School, Dallas, Texas. Reprinted with permission.

FIGURE 16.11 Advertisement produced by *Hillcrest Hurricane*, Hillcrest High School, Dallas, Texas. Reprinted with permission.

FIGURE 16.12 Advertisement produced by *Hillcrest Hurricane*, Hillcrest High School, Dallas, Texas. Reprinted with permission.

2   Write a carefully composed critique of an ad from a recent issue of your school publication. Discuss the kind of advertising it represents, the layout, the copy and the placement on the page. Is the advertising professional? Is the business getting its money's worth? Redesign the ad, if necessary.

3   Design a market survey of the purchasing power and buying power of your student body. In small groups, discuss what areas you need to survey in order to collect information that would help an advertising salesperson. You could distribute the poll later through homeroom classes or during an activity period.

4   Select a product or service that you know well and believe would be appropriate for an ad in your school publication. In small groups, discuss what the possible message for the product or service would be – the benefit it provides, or the feeling it conveys. What makes it better than similar products or services? Design an ad using the message you selected.

5   From newspapers or magazines, clip, mount and label three ads that you think are especially effective in layout. Beneath each, discuss the reasons for its effectiveness.

6   Select five area businesses and decide what information an advertising salesperson would need to know about the businesses to sell them an ad. Vary the business types.

7   Use sticky notes to label the prices of 10 ads in your yearbook and newspaper to prepare for a sales call. Are there extra costs for photography? Are there discounts available?

8   Prepare a sales pitch for the following businesses. Role-play in front of the class with another class member playing the business owner. Have the class discuss the demonstration.

   (a) A flower shop that you hope will buy an ad in the issue before homecoming.

   (b) A new sporting goods store.

   (c) A new multiscreen theater that is trying to hire employees

   (d) A restaurant that offers 20 types of burgers.

STUDENT PRESS LAW

ROY S. GUTTERMAN

17

> *It can hardly be argued that either students or teachers shed their constitutional rights to freedom of speech or expression at the schoolhouse gate.*
>
> *Justice Abe Fortas,* Tinker v. Des Moines *(1969)*

LEARNING OBJECTIVES After completing this chapter you will be able to:

- understand the United States legal system and the way it affects student journalists

- recognize certain legal issues that affect student journalists

- be your own first advocate for a student speech and press rights under the First Amendment

- use the law, particularly the First Amendment, to facilitate your newsgathering and production and better inform your readers and the community

- understand the First Amendment rights associated with public records and open meetings laws.

Scholastic Journalism, Twelfth Edition. C. Dow Tate and Sherri A. Taylor.
© 2014 John Wiley & Sons, Inc. Published 2014 by John Wiley & Sons, Inc.

STUDENT JOURNALISTS ARE, FIRST AND foremost, journalists. In reporting and disseminating the news within a school or community, student journalists perform the same important democratic function as the institutional press or the professional media, known as the "**Fourth Estate**." However, while student journalists report, write and publish, broadcast or disseminate the news, they do so in an environment with fewer legal protections under the **First Amendment**. The press, the only business mentioned anywhere in the Constitution, is protected from government censorship. But for decades, courts have found the school setting has many distinctive characteristics that potentially justify more limited rights for student journalists.

James Madison, primary author of the First Amendment, questioned government censorship:

Nothing could be more irrational than to give the people power, and to withhold from them information without which power is abused. A people who mean to be their own governors must arm themselves with power which knowledge gives. A popular government without popular information or the means of acquiring it is but a prologue to a farce or a tragedy, or perhaps both.

The Writings of James Madison, ed. Gaillard Hunt. 9 vols. New York:
G. P. Putnam's Sons, 1900–10

Whether Madison and the Framers of the Constitution envisioned the student press in its conception of the Fourth Estate is lost to history. But there is no question that the First Amendment does recognize the rights of students and the student press.

WHO, WHAT, WHERE, WHEN AND HOW – AND STUDENT PRESS LAW

The First Amendment applies to government action. This means that students in public schools are afforded some level of rights to speak, publish and complain about government in both in speech and their student media – newspapers, broadcasts, magazines, yearbooks and even blogs. Under major Supreme Court precedent, public school students may have stronger First Amendment rights with regard to extracurricular media or media created off-campus on their own time than they may have with a student newspaper produced in a class or through the school. Students in private schools have fewer guarantees to First Amendment rights.

The law

The law is really just a set of rules and regulations dictated by society. The law affords citizens rights among themselves and with the government, which has the authority, in our democracy, to enforce these laws and rights. Most importantly, in a civil society, laws allow citizens to resolve disputes and afford individuals protection from harm. The laws are written by legislatures (Congress, state legislatures and local governing bodies such as city, town or village councils or school boards). Laws are enforced by the executive branch (the President, state governors or local mayors). And, laws are interpreted by courts (the Supreme Court, federal District Courts and state courts, usually county courts or superior courts).

As a means of dispute resolution, courts offer parties opportunities to have a neutral entity, a judge or jury, with government backing, resolve cases and controversies. Think of the most common disputes resolved in court under doctrines of civil liability. Torts or civil wrongs allow a plaintiff to bring a lawsuit and press a cause of action against a defendant to seek damages, monetary payments or a cessation of behavior by a defendant. A defendant, in turn, has a chance to defend him- or herself in a public setting. Ultimately, a jury may have to render a verdict, deciding what happened in this dispute and how it should be resolved.

Civil lawsuits or litigation often involve mundane issues of liability or civil responsibility, such as negligence or property damage, among private parties and businesses. Sometimes, the courts are called in to resolve broken promises in a business setting, or to resolve a dispute between parties to a contract.

In the criminal sphere, courts serve as a public place where people charged with crimes are formally accused and confronted. This is where charges are publicly unveiled and evidence is presented. Ultimately, a jury would again render a verdict of guilty or not-guilty. The judge acts as a referee, interpreting and applying court procedure and matters of evidence as well as matters of law – the template under which a case is brought. The judge will also deliver the sentence to a guilty party.

The court system itself can be an intimidating and confusing place. Most legal disputes are handled locally – either by municipal courts, for minor violations such as speeding or parking tickets, or by superior or county courts, for more serious civil disputes and criminal prosecutions. These trial courts are usually at the county level and their names vary from state to state. For example, the trial courts in California are the Superior Courts while in New York they are the State Supreme Court. In Ohio, they are Common Pleas but in Florida the Circuit Court.

HELPFUL TIPS

Can I use this?

Questions often arise as to whether you can publish a piece of intellectual property created or owned by someone else. **Copyright law** protects original works of authorship in a fixed, tangible format. This encompasses everything from books, movies, photographs, music, plays to even dances and pantomimes (17 U.S.C.A. §106).

Printing, reprinting, broadcasting or otherwise publishing someone else's work can not only lead to accusations of plagiarism but also liability for copyright infringement. Plagiarism is an academic offense. But copyright infringement can have financial consequences. Simply providing a credit line or attribution might not be enough to stave off an infringement claim.

This is why careful scrutiny for potential copyright infringement is important. In many instances, a student newspaper is not likely to be sued for copyright infringement. But web-based publications have an international audience, which would make discovery of an infringement just a Google search away and a lot more likely to generate litigation than it would have been years ago.

Your defense could hinge on several important doctrines and factors. First would be the built-in statutory defense in the Copyright Act: fair use. This is an affirmative defense, which means if you are sued and invoke fair use, your use will be evaluated based on the following four statutory elements:

1   the purpose and character of the use, including whether it is a commercial use or for non-profit educational purposes;

2   the nature of the copyrighted work;

3   the amount and substantiality of the portion used in relation to the copyrighted work as a whole;

4   the effect of the use on the potential market for or value of the copyrighted work (17 U.S.C.A. §107).

The fact that a work is not yet published will neither ensure nor bar a finding of fair use.

Tips:

→ Look for work that is in the public domain.

→ Use rights-free work, like free music or images.

→ Use materials, particularly photographs, from press packets or press materials.

→ If you are using intellectual property, such as a photograph or a digital clip, try to use it as part of the story.

→ Facts cannot be copyrighted.

→ Parody and satire are protected.

→ Ingredients for recipes.

Quick Exercise

Fair use or infringement? Compile a list of ways a publisher might use copyrighted materials – text, digital images, video, music, characters – and discuss whether it might be permissible under the doctrine of fair use to copyright or an unfair infringement.

Test your knowledge

How do laws affect what you do as a student journalist?

There are also federal District Courts in every state, which handle federal matters, such as copyright infringement or prosecution of federal crimes by the United States Justice Department or a United States Attorney. In civil settings, a case may end up in federal District Court through what is known as diversity jurisdiction, which involves parties from two different states in a dispute worth more than $75,000.

A plaintiff seeking redress for a violation of a constitutional right, such as a government body's abridgment of First Amendment rights, may bring a claim in either a state court or federal District Court.

Even though a jury or judge may render a verdict, that does not necessarily signal the end of the road for a court case. Parties dissatisfied with the decisions of a trial court can seek further redress on appeal for matters of law, procedure or constitutional violations rendered at the lower level. States have intermediate appellate courts, often called appellate divisions. At the state level, litigants have one more court to bring an appeal to, the state's highest court. An appeal in federal courts would go to the Court of Appeals. There are 12 federal circuit courts, each of which covers a specific region of the country. For example, New York is in the Second Circuit while California is in the Ninth Circuit.

The court of last resort is the United States Supreme Court. The Supreme Court hears cases asserting a constitutional violation. Of the more than 8,000 petitions seeking review or a writ of certiorari that the court receives every year, the Supreme Court accepts fewer than 90. When the Court grants certiorari or cert, the party seeking constitutional redress is called the petitioner and the party defending the lower court action is the respondent. Parties file briefs, persuasive papers arguing matters of law. A month or two later, the parties convene at the Supreme Court to present oral arguments. Months later, the Supreme Court renders an opinion, thereby setting new precedent.

THE FIRST AMENDMENT

The Framers of the Constitution provided a blueprint for the American governmental system with three co-equal branches of government – legislature, executive and judiciary. They also sought to provide a set of rights for the people. The civil rights created in the Bill of Rights include such protections as freedom from unreasonable search and seizure (Fourth Amendment), due process (Fifth Amendment), the right to counsel (Sixth Amendment) and freedom from cruel and unusual punishment (Eighth Amendment).

For Framers such as James Madison, perhaps nothing was more important than the right to publish, speak and petition government. The press is the only business or industry mentioned anywhere in the Constitution and Bill of Rights, and it is singled out for protection.

The Virginia Declaration of Rights, co-authored by Madison, included a strong pronouncement about the rights of the people with regard to censorship, declaring that the people's right to "publish their sentiments; and the freedom of the press, as one of the great bulwarks of liberty, shall be inviolable."

The Constitution's **First Amendment**, ratified on Dec. 15, 1791, states: "Congress shall make no law respecting an establishment of religion, or prohibiting the free exercise thereof; or abridging the freedom of speech, or of the press; or the right of the people peaceably to assemble, and to petition the Government for a redress of grievances."

These rights of freedom to publish, express opinions and speak out, have been vital to the democratic development of the United States. Madison and the Framers emerged from an era of rigid control of the press through licensing and seditious libel laws intended to punish dissent or criticism of the government – the royal family, parliament, the church or other government officials. With no protections, publishers engaged in self-censorship and also faced government censorship and harsh punishments.

The First Amendment not only encouraged freedom of expression, but protected it. First Amendment rights are not absolute, though. Despite First Amendment protections, there is a range of limitations. The courts in the past two centuries have applied the First Amendment to a range of government actions and a range of media entities from the big metropolitan newspapers to television stations to websites and blogs, and student media. Student journalists follow in the fine tradition of the media in exercising their First Amendment rights.

Unprotected speech

Despite strong protections under the First Amendment, there are categories of speech that are not protected. Some types of speech outside the scope of the First Amendment are defamation and obscenity. Without First Amendment protection, these categories of speech may be subject to punishment under tort law, such as civil damages paid to someone who had been defamed in a newspaper, or prosecution by the government on obscenity charges.

In a student journalism scenario, speech that falls outside the First Amendment would most likely be legitimately censored by a teacher, adviser or school administrator.

Defamation

Defamation, publishing a false statement of fact about someone, is comprised of two similar torts (civil wrongs): libel and slander. **Libel** is the printed form while **slander** is the spoken form.

Libel is a printed false statement of fact about someone that causes damage and harm to his or her reputation. This applies to words, text, photographs or artwork in a printed or permanent format, whether it is a traditional newspaper, yearbook or an Internet-based publication. The long-standing criteria for libel require the false statement to expose a person to shame, hatred, ridicule, disgrace or harm to his or her reputation in the community, often injuring the plaintiff's livelihood.

A publisher is liable or responsible for the content it publishes or disseminates. Thus, a newspaper could be liable for publishing a defamatory letter to the editor or a defamatory quote from a source of a story.

Libel requires proof of four elements:

1 A false statement of fact
2 Published (to at least a third party) with either knowledge of falsity, reckless disregard for the truth **or** a high degree of negligence (**depending on who the plaintiff is**)
3 About or of and concerning the plaintiff
4 Causing harm or damage to the plaintiff's reputation.

Within defamation law, there are four categories of false statements that are considered libel per se, or libelous on their face. With libel per se, general damages are implied, meaning the plaintiff will not have to prove harm because the nature of the false statement is already so harmful.

The four categories of libel per se are:

1 imputing criminal activity
2 imputing dishonesty in business or trade
3 imputing a loathsome disease (STD or HIV)
4 unchastity of a woman.

Potential defenses against a libel lawsuit include the following.

Truth. This will always be a publication's best defense, which means a legal defense begins at the front end, when gathering facts and information and writing, arranging, editing and checking the facts. The "**provable truth**" defense is usually strongest, even if there is damage to the plaintiff's reputation from the story. Believing something is true without sufficiently checking it out will not be sufficient.

However, courts often hold journalists to a "sting of the truth" or "gist of the truth" standard. Reporters are not held to an unreasonable, 100 percent, all-or-nothing standard for truth. But publishers, both in traditional print newspapers, magazines or books, as well as online or even broadcast, are responsible for defamatory comments made by sources or third parties, such as letters to the editor, advertisements or quotes from sources.

The Internet and social media sites have created another interesting area of liability. See sidebar on the Internet and the law.

Privilege. Depending on where a potentially libelous statement came from, you might have a defense under privilege. Certain communications, depending on the circumstances, might have immunity from libel liability. Reporters are allowed to publish fair and accurate accounts of official proceedings, such as a school board meeting, city council meeting or court or judicial

The Internet and the law

The Internet has created a new world of online and digital content that presents a number of potential legal issues. Whether it is an online version of a student newspaper or a modern social media site, web-based entities are subject to the same legal concerns as "old" or traditional media (newspapers, magazines, books and even radio and television).

Thus, it is possible to defame an individual or invade someone's privacy on a website. Copyright infringement is also a concern. In some cases, if you produce and post or publish content on a website, you are fulfilling the same function as a traditional publisher, and face many of the same liabilities.

In certain narrow settings, a website may be considered nothing more than a distributor of content posted by third parties. For example, sites like Facebook, Twitter or YouTube, which thrive on content generated by its users, may be considered protected from liability for defamation under a federal law, the Communications Decency Act, §230. Under this federal law, many websites have immunity for allowing users to post content. However, there is no immunity for infringing on a copyright, and if such a site is hit with a "take down" notice from an intellectual property owner, then it would be wise to take down the infringing content.

The protections under §230 may extend to the online comments section to a story, if it is not moderated or edited by the staff. However, staff-generated content, even for an entirely web-based entity may create legal liability for the publisher.

Using web-based sites for newsgathering is also rife with potential risk. Attributing content or allegation made on or in social media or websites with questionable provenance can be risky. Reporters should make use of web-based content for stories, but this should only supplement traditional reporting techniques.

---

proceeding. This privilege also attaches to government records and documents. When reporting on a controversy discussed at a government meeting or in public records, the journalist does not have to independently verify the statements contained in those communications. Because privileges are matters of state law, the names of the privileges vary from state to state. Some states call this a qualified, conditional privilege or record-libel privilege.

Actual malice. Invoking the actual malice defense is contingent on the plaintiff's status. There are three basic types of plaintiffs: private figures, public officials and public figures. Public officials and public figures will have to prove that the statement was published with actual malice, a legal term of art which means it was published either with known falsity or reckless disregard for the truth.

The Supreme Court established the actual malice rule in the landmark case *New York Times v. Sullivan* (1964). The ruling was designed to allow for democratic debate. It also protects the press from libel suits brought by public officials who can command a role in public affairs and also have non-judicial resources to repair their reputation in the face of public criticism.

A public official is someone who works in government and who has substantial responsibility for, or control over, the conduct of government affairs. Public officials include elected and most appointed government officials. In a school setting, public school principals, superintendents and school board members are all public officials. Teachers, in some states, may be considered public officials.

Public figures are also held to the actual malice standard because they, too, command media attention, which can be used to repair their reputations. Public figures are people who thrust themselves into the limelight or inject themselves into the public sphere. In a school setting, public figures may include a student who voluntarily runs for student government or a student's parent who circulates a petition to ban books from the school library. There are also subcategories of public figures:

- voluntary or all-purpose (actors and athletes)
- vortex or limited purpose (people who thrust themselves into a public controversy to influence the outcome)
- Involuntary (victims, some criminals or people associated with newsworthy events).

Fair comment. This is also known as the critic's privilege or defense, which allows journalists and critics to express opinions or publish critiques about a matter of public concern. This includes reviews of movies, books, television shows, music, plays, concerts, restaurants, sporting events, video games and performance of elected officials. Journalists must be commenting on a

NEWSFLASH

Sunshine laws

Public or government meetings and public records and documents can provide a backbone for some interesting and important stories for students. Student journalists have just as strong a right of access to meetings and records as do the working press and general public.

The business done by school boards and municipalities and even state and federal agencies may be important to your readership. Do not be intimidated by government officials or government records.

In many cases, government officials are there to help the public. But the sad reality is, sometimes they are not. Don't fret. The law is on your side. Every state has a version of a Sunshine or Open Meetings Law, which requires government bodies to publicly announce their meetings and publish their agendas – the items the body will consider and vote on. When a quorum, or the majority of the body, meets, the discussions, debates and votes must be held in public. (This is true in all cases except for narrow settings, discussed below.) The public's business is the public's business, and the press, even the student press, has a right to observe and report on this business.

Similarly, every state has a freedom of information law, which requires a government body – school board, city, town or village bodies and state and federal agencies – to turn over information upon request. Freedom of information laws are subject to exceptions, meaning that the agency may withhold information if it can prove the information fits into one of the law's exceptions.

For example, the Federal Freedom of Information Act (FOIA), which would be used to obtain records from a federal agency, includes nine exceptions. If the agency can prove the documents fall under one of the following exemption categories, the agency can withhold the information. The nine exemptions are:

1 national security
2 internal agency rules
3 statutory exemptions
4 trade secrets
5 internal agency memos
6 personal privacy
7 certain law enforcement records
8 bank reports
9 oil and gas well data.

The exemptions under open meetings laws closely mirror those under FOIA, with the addition of certain personnel matters, pending litigation and the sale or purchase of real estate.

Because every state has its own version of these laws, the language may vary from state to state. Ultimately, if a government official denies a records request, you may have to file a lawsuit.

Tips for reporting on government meetings

- Get your paper on the contact list for agendas and meeting notices.
- Start attending and covering the meetings regularly.
- Understand the nature of "executive session" and the legitimate grounds for going into executive session. Discussion of certain personnel issues or sale or purchase of real estate are legitimate grounds. The body must announce why it is going into executive session.
- Members of the student press have the same rights as the public.

Tips for freedom of information requests

- Identify the records, information or data you are seeking.
- First, ask the appropriate official for the materials.
- Be polite but persistent.
- Upon a verbal denial, write a FOIA letter to the appropriate agency or official.
- Your letter should identify the records you seek, cite FOIA statute for your state; note that you are a student journalist working on a story and the fees should be waived or limited. If you are denied a record, ask to whom you appeal the denial.
- You do not have to explain why you want the documents or what your story is going to be about.

---

real matter of public interest and their views must be presented as opinions, not statements of fact. (The opinions must be based on certain stated facts.) Fair comment generally requires proof of the following:

1 that the criticism was on a legitimate matter of public concern;
2 that the criticism was based on facts either stated or otherwise known to the reader;
3 that the criticism represented the actual opinion of the critic; and
4 that the criticism was not made solely for the purpose of causing harm to the person criticized.

Professor Charles Davis of the University of Missouri and co-author of the book, *The Art of Access – Strategies for Acquiring Public Records*, offers a list of types of public records that could enhance stories for a student newspaper:

- School budgets
- Safety inspection reports
- Civil lawsuits involving your school district or employees
- Parking tickets or police citations
- Criminal records
- Crime data
- School bus driver licenses and records
- Certain personnel or personnel disciplinary records (varies from state to state)
- School directories
- Arrest reports
- 911 police logs
- Arrest warrants
- Code enforcement
- Crime logs
- Environmental hazards reports and investigations
- Fire incident reports
- Sex offender registries
- Food safety inspections
- Water quality studies
- Census data
- Property records
- Development programs
- Dog bites
- Drug houses
- Party violations
- Liquor licenses and violations
- Noise complaints
- Odor complaints
- Park plans
- Property taxes
- Road plans
- Street maintenance
- Traffic accidents

→ Zoning documents

→ Government audits

→ Government calendars

→ Contracts with government agencies

→ Corporate filings

→ Discrimination reports or investigations or claims

→ Elections

→ Government emails or correspondence

→ Expense reports

→ Meetings minutes

→ Telephone records.

Opinion privilege. In the vein of fair comment, matters of pure opinion will also be afforded immunity from libel. However, pure opinion cannot be a statement of fact following the clause, "I think …" or "I believe …" Protected opinion is a statement that is recognizable as the writer's opinion and something that could not be proven true or false. The Circuit Court of Appeals for the District of Columbia established a useful four-point test for determining whether a statement is an assertion of fact or the speaker's opinion. In *Ollman v. Evans* (D.C. Cir. 1984), the court established:

1 Can the statement be proved true or false?
2 What is the common or ordinary meaning of the words?
3 What is the journalistic context of the remark? (front-page vs. opinion page);
4 What is the social context of the remark?

Thus, a column on the editorial page or a critique in the features section would likely be protected.

Parody/satire. Likewise, content that is recognizable as parody – for example, a humor column – will be protected. This closely follows the rationale under the opinion privilege that no reasonable reader could look at this content and expect to read something factual. For example, in broadcasting, when you watch Jon Stewart, Steven Colbert or Jay Leno, you know you are watching a comedian and the jokes are just that – jokes.

Although a libel case against a minor, or a defendant under the age of 18, would be rare, minors could still encounter some liability or responsibility for publishing defamatory content. Writers, reporters, photographers, artists and editors all may encounter some liability. The school, acting as the publisher, may also be held liable.

Obscenity and indecency

Publishing graphically sexual content in a student publication would most likely be censorable under the tenets of student speech precedent. It could also meet the definition of obscene content established by the Supreme Court.

Graphically sexual content that passes a three-part test set by the United States Supreme Court in *Miller v. California* (1973) could be deemed obscene, thus losing First Amendment protection. The three-part test is as follows:

1 the material, as judged by a contemporary community, appeals to a prurient interest;
2 the material is patently offensive;
3 the material lacks serious literary, artistic, scientific or political value.

Test your knowledge

What are the elements of a defamation case? What are the defenses to a defamation lawsuit?

Indecent content often focuses on sexual content, but in a less graphic manner than obscenity does. **Indecency** is often more of a concern than obscenity for broadcasters. Indecency standards tend to focus more on language, specifically the use of profanity and curse words, which would not be appropriate in most newspapers or magazines, anyway.

Invasion of privacy

Invasion of privacy is also an area of tort law and legal liability that should concern student journalists. Where defamation law protects an individual's reputation, **invasion of privacy law** protects the image or likeness of and information about an individual. This tort also guards against certain damages incurred during the newsgathering process, such as trespass. The state common law invasion of privacy tort consists of four categories of invasion of privacy:

1 **Misappropriation of an image or likeness** – Using someone's image or likeness without permission for commercial gain.
2 **False light** – Publication that shows or depicts the plaintiff in a false way, which is highly offensive to a reasonable person.
3 **Intrusion upon solitude** – Similar to trespass, intentionally intruding on someone's seclusion or solitude or private affairs or property;
4 **Publication of private or embarrassing facts** – This requires a public disclosure of a private fact that would be offensive, outrageous or objectionable to a reasonable person and lacks legitimate public concern.

Because each state defines its own law on invasion of privacy, the tort varies from state to state. For example, many states, including New York, do not recognize false light as a viable cause of action.

Invasion of privacy issues can arise in a variety of newsgathering scenarios ranging from recording a person without consent in certain circumstances to embellishing content or using "b-roll" footage.

When it comes to recording someone, roughly a dozen states require the consent of all parties. Some of these states include California, Connecticut, Massachusetts and Pennsylvania. States like New York, Ohio and Texas are known as "single-party consent" states, meaning as long as one party (which could be the reporter) knows he or she is being recorded, then there is viable consent.

The law of privacy has been supplemented by numerous laws related to data and information security. For instance, medical records are generally kept private under the Health Insurance Portability and Accountability Act (HIPAA) while academic records and grades are kept private under the Family Educational Rights and Privacy Act (FERPA), known as the Buckley Amendment. Liability for breaking these laws, however, rests with the guardians of information. Similarly, lots of computer user information and financial records are protected under a range of federal and state laws. While officials in charge of information may legitimately withhold it, reporters who obtain it through other sources without breaking the law may publish it without violating privacy laws.

FERPA governs academic records, which would prevent a school administrator from disclosing a student's grades or other academic information to a third party.

Incitement

Speech inciting a riot or "imminent lawless action" also falls outside the First Amendment in non-school settings. The standard that emerged from several Supreme Court cases dating as far back as 1919 is the "clear and present danger" test that in a matter of proximity and degree creates a risk of imminent lawless action. The clear and present danger standard is embedded in the *Tinker* standard (see below) for material and substantial disruptions in school activities.

THE SUPREME COURT AND SPEECH IN SCHOOL

The First Amendment emerged from an era of rigid governmental control of the press, at the time primarily newspapers and books. Publishers needed government licenses, paper was taxed and printers operated under the fear of not only censorship – **prior restraint** – but fear of significant penalties and severe punishments for printing critical or unapproved news. Criminal libel and seditious libel laws were accompanied by severe penalties for even minor or incidental offenses.

First Amendment rights of students in public schools are governed by a quartet of cases starting with *Tinker v. Des Moines* (1969), *Bethel School Dist. No. 403 v. Fraser* (1986), *Hazelwood School District v. Kuhlmeier* (1988) and *Morse v. Frederick* (2007). *Tinker, Fraser* and *Frederick* relate to the levels of protection students have with regard to expression and speech in and around public schools. *Hazelwood* is controlling for the rights and limitations of student media, specifically student newspapers.

Tinker

Public school students have First Amendment rights. In *Tinker v. Des Moines Independent School District* (1969), the Supreme Court held that a school district violated three students' First Amendment rights after they were suspended for wearing black armbands to school in protest of the Vietnam War.

While a public school does have special characteristics for educational purposes, which would allow a school district to censor or even punish certain speech that would otherwise be permissible in a non-school setting, the Supreme Court adopted a standard that could be both objective and subjective. Speech that "materially and substantially" disrupts the school setting can be subject to sanctions – from prior restraint or censorship, to a range of punitive actions from detention to suspension.

Despite allowing for some controls on student speech, Justice Abe Fortas, wrote for the court in one of the most quoted passages on this point: "It can hardly be argued that either students or teachers shed their constitutional rights to freedom of speech or expression at the schoolhouse gate." Public schools play an important role in educating students, molding future responsible citizens and fueling the marketplace of ideas, the court wrote.

The three students in *Tinker* decided to protest the war by wearing black armbands to school. The district had adopted a policy against wearing protest symbols to school, but the court determined that the policy was aimed solely at the armbands. Students wearing buttons with other political messages were not punished. Furthermore, the court acknowledged that the school's policy was content-specific and aimed at suppressing "pure speech." School rules regulating expression such as length of skirts, hair style or other behavior would not be construed the same way as those regulating "pure speech," the court held.

The court added, "In the absence of a specific showing of constitutionally valid reasons to regulate their speech, students are entitled to freedom of expressions of their views." The government's role in speech is to protect it. But reasonable restrictions on speech must be related to "carefully restricted circumstances." These controls extend beyond the classroom, reaching into other areas, including the school cafeteria and athletic fields. The armband protest

WORDS of WISDOM

Students in school as well as out of school are "persons" under our Constitution. They are possessed of fundamental rights which the state must respect, just as they themselves must respect their obligations to the state. In our system, students may not be regarded as closed-circuit recipients of only that which the state chooses to communicate. They may not be confined to the expression of those sentiments that are officially approved. In the absence of a specific showing of constitutionally valid reasons to regulate their speech, students are entitled to freedom of expressions of their views.

Justice Abe Fortas, Tinker v. Des Moines *(1969).*

generated no disruptions, threats or violence. More importantly, the court viewed the armband protest as pure speech, which is entitled to protection even in a school setting.

Fraser

The Supreme Court applied *Tinker* in a case involving a student's speech laced with sexual innuendo and language that was deemed offensive, inappropriate and disruptive in *Bethel School District No. 403 v. Fraser* (1986).

Here, the Supreme Court reversed two lower court decisions, holding a school district was within its authority to sanction a student who gave an offensive nominating speech for a student government election in front of 600 students, many young teens.

The student had been warned about giving the speech and was later suspended. He challenged his suspension under §1983, seeking damages from the school district for violating his First Amendment rights.

The Supreme Court distinguished Fraser's speech from Tinker's, which had a substantial political message. Devoid of a political message, Fraser's speech did not touch on unpopular political views or manifest a political protest.

Chief Justice Warren Burger wrote for the court:

> Surely it is a highly appropriate function of public school education to prohibit the use of vulgar and offensive terms in public discourse. Indeed, "the fundamental values necessary to the maintenance of a democratic political system" disfavor the use of terms of debate highly offensive or highly threatening to others. Nothing in the Constitution prohibits the states from insisting that certain modes of expression are inappropriate and subject to sanctions.

It is well within the authority of a school to determine the appropriateness of speech within classes and school assemblies. The speech in question here was offensive to students and teachers.

Morse

The Supreme Court's most recent pronouncement on student speech came in *Morse v. Frederick* (2007), commonly referred to as the "Bong hits for Jesus" case. Here, Joseph Frederick, then a high school senior in Juneau, Alaska, was suspended from school for 10 days after he unfurled a banner bearing the phrase "BONG HiTS 4 JESUS" on a public street while the Olympic torch paraded through downtown Juneau. The school's principal believed the message violated the school district's anti-drug mission, confiscated the banner and took administrative action against Frederick.

Frederick sued the school district in federal court, alleging the school district violated his First Amendment through the principal's actions and his subsequent suspension. The lower court dismissed his action and the Court of Appeals for the Ninth Circuit reversed, ruling that Frederick's First Amendment rights were violated.

The United States Supreme Court took the case by granting certiorari to decide whether Frederick had a valid First Amendment claim and the right to display his banner. Building on *Tinker*, the Court had to decide whether a reasonable reading of the banner could be seen as promoting illegal drug use, and whether that message "materially and substantially disrupt[ed] the work and discipline" of the school.

The court ruled that the "special characteristics" of the school environment combined with the government's interest in preventing illegal drug use justified the sanction against the student because, despite the student's argument that the banner was both nonsensical and humorous, the court believed a reasonable reader would view the content as endorsing illegal drug use.

"The concern here is not that Frederick's speech was offensive, but that it was reasonably viewed as promoting illegal drug use," Chief Justice John Roberts wrote for the court. The court wrote:

> School principals have a difficult job, and a vitally important one. When Frederick suddenly and unexpectedly unfurled his banner, Morse had to decide to act – or not act – on the spot. It was reasonable for her to conclude that the banner promoted illegal drug use – in violation of

established school policy – and that failing to act would send a powerful message to the students in her charge, including Frederick, about how serious the school was about the dangers of illegal drug use. The First Amendment does not require schools to tolerate at school events student expression that contributes to those dangers.

In an eloquent dissent, Justice John Paul Stevens reprised *Tinker* in writing:

> Most students, however, do not shed their brains at the schoolhouse gate, and most students know dumb advocacy when they see it. The notion that the message on this banner would actually persuade either the average student or even the dumbest one to change his or her behavior is most implausible. That the Court believes such a silly message can be proscribed as advocacy underscores the novelty of its position, and suggests that the principle it articulates has no stopping point.

Hazelwood

In 1988, the United States Supreme Court set the seminal precedent for applying the First Amendment to student journalism. *Hazelwood School District v. Kuhlmeier* (1988) established that a school district may censor a student newspaper for a variety of reasons.

This case emerged from a journalism class in the Hazelwood East High School, outside St. Louis, Missouri. In the spring of 1983, the class produced a student newspaper called the *Spectrum*, which planned to publish news stories on teen pregnancy, teen sex, divorce, runaways and juvenile delinquency. The newspaper, published every three weeks with a circulation of 4,500, was part of the Journalism II class, and financially underwritten by the school district.

As was normal practice, the faculty adviser submitted page proofs to the principal for review before publication. The principal objected to the content of the pregnancy story, even though it used pseudonyms to maintain the privacy of the students who were interviewed. References to sexual activity and birth control, the principal felt, were inappropriate for the school's audience. The story on the effects of divorce on high school students was deemed unfair and unbalanced by the principal because it did not contain interviews with parents named in the story.

The principal censored six articles in the *Spectrum*, withholding two full pages from publication. The students objected to the censorship and brought a lawsuit in federal court. Seeking a judicial declaration that their First Amendment rights had been violated, the students also sought an injunction preventing the censorship and monetary damages.

Though unsuccessful at the district court, the federal appellate court – the Court of Appeals for the Eighth Circuit – ruled that the principal and school district had violated their First Amendment rights.

The United States Supreme Court, however, voted five–three in favor of the school district. Justice Byron White wrote the opinion for the court, applying some of the rationale from *Tinker v. Des Moines* (1969) and *Bethel School District No. 403 v. Fraser* (1986).

Though students have some First Amendment rights in public schools, because of the "special characteristics of the school environment," teachers, principals and school district administrators retain authority to censor student publications that are part of the curriculum. This decision also applies to other forms of school-sponsored speech such as yearbooks, magazines, television and radio programs and theater productions.

Although public education is a public or governmental function, a school newspaper is not necessarily going to be considered a public forum like streets, parks or other traditional public spaces. The *Spectrum* was a school-sponsored publication. As part of the educational curriculum, school administrators had authority to censor the paper to promote responsible, ethical journalism and ensure topics were appropriate for a school setting.

The court's public forum-analysis is critical to determining the level of control school administrators can exert on student publications. First Amendment rights vary among the three traditional arenas:

1 traditional public forums
2 limited public forums
3 non-public forums.

First, it is important to note that this analysis is only relevant to public school settings. There are no First Amendment rights in a private school. On the other end of the spectrum, in a traditional public forum, speakers, even students, would be afforded the highest level of protection under the First Amendment. Determining where a student newspaper falls on this spectrum of rights requires a detailed analysis of a number of factors:

1 Whether the students produced the newspaper as part of a high school curriculum
2 Whether the students receive credits and grades for completing the course
3 Whether a member of the faculty oversaw the production
4 Whether the school deviated from its policy of producing the paper as part of the educational curriculum
5 The degree of control the administration and the faculty adviser exercise
6 Applicable written policy statements of the school administration.

When a school newspaper is part of the school curriculum, such as a production of a journalism class, the school district may be considered the publisher because it is paying for the production as well as an instructor, teacher or adviser. In this scenario, a school district's censorship may be considered a legitimate function of both its role as an educator and role as a publisher. Teachers and administrators are empowered to make determinations based on the "emotional maturity" of students and the appropriateness of the content, the court said. Thus, sensitive topics may be material that a school administrator can legitimately censor.

The court wrote:

These activities may fairly be characterized as part of the school curriculum, whether or not they occur in a traditional classroom setting, so long as they are supervised by faculty members and designed to impart particular knowledge or skills to student participants and audiences.

***

A school must be able to set high standards for the student speech that is disseminated under its auspices – standards that may be higher than those demanded by some newspaper publishers or theatrical producers in the "real" world – and may refuse to disseminate student speech that does not meet those standards.

Distinguishing its opinion from *Tinker*, the court noted the difference between punishing speech and not promoting speech. The key factor for upholding an act of censorship, the court wrote, was that it must be "reasonably related to legitimate pedagogical concerns."

The First Amendment is implicated only when the censorship is not related to a pedagogical concern. *Hazelwood* allows the school district to censor stories based on content that is:

1 Ungrammatical
2 Poorly written
3 Inadequately researched
4 Biased
5 Prejudicial
6 Vulgar or profane
7 Unsuitable for immature audiences.

In a school setting, inappropriate content could range from a story about the existence of Santa Claus to information about teenage sex or drug use or anything that would "associate the school with anything other than neutrality on matters of political controversy."

Applying this analysis to the facts in *Hazelwood*, the court determined that the principal "acted responsibly" in censoring the pregnancy and divorce articles. The other articles, which were on the same pages, were caught in the crossfire.

The pregnancy article, school administrators feared, would identify students. The students' anonymity was not adequately protected. The article, which included "frank talk" about sex and

NEWSFLASH

Student Press Law Center – fighting for your First Amendment rights

Founded in 1974, the Student Press Law Center (SPLC) has been at the forefront of fighting for student press rights. Staffed by lawyers and part of a national network, the SPLC assists high school and college journalists in matters of censorship and other legal disputes, from access to meetings and records to fending off libel suits.

Inspired by the 1974 book *Captive Voices: High School Journalism in America*, a report by the Robert F. Kennedy Memorial Foundation's Commission of Inquiry into High School Journalism, SPLC was created to fight high school censorship. The commission wrote: "Censorship, more than any other factor has a greater adverse effect on the quality and relevance of high school journalism."

"Where a free, vigorous student press does exist, there is a healthy ferment of ideas and opinion with no indication of disruption or negative side effects on the educational experience of the school," the report stated.

The Commission recommended the creation of an organization aimed at safeguarding the First Amendment rights of students, and the SPLC was formed under the joint auspices of the Robert F. Kennedy Memorial and the Reporters Committee for Freedom of the Press. SPLC has been an independent non-profit corporation since 1979, based in Arlington, Virginia.

"SPLC's work ranges from operating a hotline for legal questions to lawyer referrals to workshops and lobbying efforts on behalf of free press rights for high school and college students," said Executive Director Frank LoMonte.

LoMonte, both a lawyer and former newspaper journalist who got his first taste of journalism in middle school, has been SPLC's executive director since 2008.

"This is a job that carries the opportunity to practice law at a very high level, working with cutting-edge legal issues, plus working with cutting-edge inquiring journalists," he said. "This combines all of my interests and passions. Not a day goes by when you don't appreciate what you're doing."

"If we weren't speaking up for student journalists, nobody would be," he added.

For example, the telephone hotline regularly fields more than 2,000 phone calls a year with questions ranging from copyright fair use to libel. However, the majority of the inquiries typically involve questions of censorship, LoMonte says, "The principal is telling us we can't publish XYZ because it will make the school look bad."

Whether through workshops, speeches or public education efforts through editorials, SPLC seeks to educate students, the public and lawmakers on the value of a free, vigorous and protected student press.

LoMonte points to the March 2011 legislative effort in West Virginia in which the legislature rewrote the state's shield law to extend the reporter's privilege to student journalists.

"No one flagged 'what does this do for student journalists,'" LoMonte said, adding that the SPLC wrote op-ed articles to educate lawmakers. "This was literally re-written with our model language on the senate floor, solely because we were vocal. West Virginia went from the worst state to the best for students."

SPLC's vision
The Student Press Law Center will improve the climate for student journalism in all forms, by:

- breaking down barriers that prevent students from gathering, publishing or airing news and commentary,
- reducing censorship of students' journalistic work,
- educating students about their responsibilities as journalists, and
- improving students' access to essential documents and meetings, and teaching them to put the knowledge gained to productive use.

Student Press Law Center
1101 Wilson Blvd., Suite 1100
Arlington, VA 22209–2275 USA
Telephone: (**703) 807–1904**
www.splc.org

the use and non-use of birth control, was deemed "inappropriate" in a school-sponsored publication. The divorce article, which quoted a named student, the principal felt was unfair because it did not provide the father of one of the students an opportunity to respond to allegations.

Justice William Brennan wrote a dissent which was joined by Justices Thurgood Marshall and Harry Blackmun: "In my view, the principal broke more than just a promise. He violated the First Amendment's prohibitions against censorship of any student expression that neither disrupts classwork nor invades the rights of others, and against any censorship that is not narrowly tailored to serve its purpose."

The *Hazelwood* case laid out the protections student journalists have under the First Amendment. But *Hazelwood* also speaks to the significant restraints on the student press. The holding empowers teachers, principals and school administrators to rein in the student press. After *Hazelwood*, school districts can censor the student press on objective grounds such as grammar, profanity, defamation or poorly researched news content. In addition, it gives these administrators authority to censor under subjective standards of appropriateness and pedagogical interest.

Post-Hazelwood cases

While the *Hazelwood* decision provided some clear areas of legitimate censorship, such as allowing a school to reject stories that may contain defamatory statements or poorly-reported or ungrammatical content, the landmark case has also led to school administrators, teachers and student newspaper advisers making both legitimate and illegitimate calls on censorship. There is no accurate way to determine how heavily censored student newspapers are. While the Student Press Law Center (SPLC) receives thousands of calls to its hotline, it is fair to say that the vast number of censorship cases do not get reported.

In the decades since *Hazelwood*, a number of lower court decisions applied and tested the precedent in state and federal courts, at both the trial and appellate levels. Subsequent judicial interpretations provide guidance for the modern application of *Hazelwood*. In recent years, *Hazelwood* has been applied to a variety of traditional school journalism cases. But the precedent has also been used to guide school districts with advertising content in student newspapers and yearbooks, access to school space by religious or controversial student groups and even content of student theatrical productions, student government elections and school mascots.

The following case summaries show how recent courts have applied *Hazelwood* in some high-profile student journalism controversies.

Dean v. Utica Community Schools, 345 F. Supp. 2d 799 (E.D. Mich. 2004)

A Michigan school superintendent pulled an article from the high school newspaper about a dispute and litigation concerning the district's bus garage that was the subject of a nuisance and pollution lawsuit by neighbors.

The school newspaper, *The Arrow*, had a history of covering controversial topics including teenage sex, suicide, drug and alcohol abuse and sexual orientation. But it was a story about the dispute surrounding the bus depot that raised the superintendent's eyebrows because she thought it was an inappropriate topic and based on questionable scientific reporting.

The student journalist, Katherine Dean, challenged the censorship in federal court, and won. With *Tinker* and *Hazelwood* as guides, the court reviewed the precedent, especially through the lens of the First Amendment. Applying both *Tinker* and *Hazelwood*, the court determined that school speech falls into three categories:

1 speech that happens to occur on school premises
2 government speech, which may be subject to viewpoint-based regulation because the school may determine speech it thinks is appropriate
3 school-sponsored speech (*Hazelwood*).

The court's public forum analysis also noted the differences between a traditional public forum and a limited public forum. A limited public forum could be subjected to more regulation.

The Arrow was considered a limited public forum, the court held, because it was designed and created to foster a public dialogue and inform the public. The court evaluated the status of the newspaper, weighing: (1) whether the school intended to create a limited public forum; and (2) the context for the forum. Then, the court applied the eight *Hazelwood* factors, finding:

1 *The Arrow* was published as part of the high school curriculum.
2 Students received credit and grades for their work on *The Arrow*.
3 The newspaper was supervised by a teacher/adviser.
4 The school's policy encouraged "sustained" participation in the class with the purpose of producing a newspaper.
5 The school administration did not actively censor or regulate the newspaper prior to the 2002 edition.

Quick Exercise

Go to the Student Press Law Center website and take the online quiz. www.splc.org.

6 The school district did not have any documents or policies indicating the paper was not a public forum, while the paper had a published statement of purpose, which stated among other things that it was intended to "inform the students, faculty and community of school related news."

7 The paper's actual practice had been journalistic since its founding in 1977.

8 The paper was clearly expressive conduct.

Under *Hazelwood*, the Dean court held that the censorship was unreasonable and unsupported by any legitimate pedagogical concerns. Furthermore, the article in question did not raise any privacy concerns or include discussion of sexual content. The reporter sought to interview multiple parties and offer a variety of viewpoints on the controversy and the pending lawsuit.

In the 25-year history of the *Arrow*, the paper had one adviser and the paper was never subject to pre-publication review by the administration.

As far as other legitimate grounds for censorship – grammar, writing quality, poor research, or prejudice or bias – the court found no grounding in this any. The use of pseudonyms was not convincing, nor were there legitimate questions about the story's accuracy.

The court wrote:

Dean's article properly and accurately attributes its quotations to their sources. The article qualifies any statement made by its sources. The article does not present the author's own conclusions on unknown facts. In other words, Katy Dean had a right to publish an article concerning the Frances' side of the lawsuit so long as it accurately reported the Frances' side of the lawsuit.

...

The newspaper class at Utica High School is intended to teach journalism. A core value of being a journalist is to understand the role of the press in a free society. That role is to provide an independent source of information so that a citizen can make informed decisions. It is often the case that this core value of journalistic independence requires a journalist to question authority rather than side with authority. Thus, if the role of the press in a democratic society is to have any value, all journalists – including student journalists – must be allowed to publish viewpoints contrary to those of state authorities without intervention or censorship by the authorities themselves. Without protection, the freedoms of speech and press are meaningless and the press becomes a mere channel for official thought.

...

The freedoms of student journalists are by no means unfettered by legitimate concerns for school administration and education. However, the First Amendment undoubtedly protects the freedom of student journalists, under circumstances such as those presented in this case, to maintain their school-sponsored publications as limited public forums for the expression of viewpoints that question, endorse or deviate from the official viewpoints of state authorities.

In short, the court believed the superintendent censored this story because she had "difference of opinion with its content."

R.O. v. Ithaca City School District, 645 F.3d 533 (2d Cir. 2011)

A school's censorship of a cartoon depicting stick figures in sexual positions prompted an unsuccessful First Amendment challenge by the student author. Both a federal district court and later the Second Circuit Court of Appeals, found the school district legitimately exercised its control over a school-sponsored student newspaper under *Hazelwood* as well as the content deemed lewd, inappropriate and offensive under *Fraser*.

The Ithaca High School newspaper, *The Tattler*, was deemed a limited public forum because it bore the imprimatur of the school, employed a faculty adviser and was otherwise sponsored and supported by the school district. The school district could legally employ a range of restrictions, including outright censorship. The newspaper was educational and related to a legitimate pedagogical purpose.

WWW

WEBLINKS Check out

There are a number of online resources available to provide information and support on legal issues. Here are some useful weblinks:

Student Speech/Student Press Law

Student Press Law Center (SPLC)
www.splc.org

Foundation for Individual Rights in Education (FIRE)
http://thefire.org

The First Amendment Center
www.firstamendmentcenter.org

The Tully Center for Free Speech
http://tully.syr.edu

Reporters Committee for Freedom of the Press
www.rcfp.org

The Freedom Forum
www.freedomforum.org

Citizens Media Law Project
www.citmedialaw.org

Intellectual Property Law

United States Copyright Office
www.copyright.gov

United States Patent and Trademark Office
www.uspto.gov

Freedom of Information Law

Freedom Info.org
www.freedominfo.org

National Freedom of Information Coalition
www.nfoic.org

New York Committee on Open Government
www.dos.state.ny.us/coog

General legal

Findlaw
www.findlaw.com

Scotusblog
www.scotusblog.com

Oyez.com
www.oyez.org

Cornell Law School Legal Information Institute
www.law.cornell.edu

Journalism

Investigative Reporters & Editors (IRE)
www.ire.org

Society of Professional Journalists (SPJ)
www.spj.org

The Poynter Institute
www.poynter.org

"Under *Hazelwood*, school-sponsored speech may be censored 'so long as the censorship is reasonably related to legitimate pedagogical concerns,'" the court wrote.

The student also attempted to self-publish and distribute the newspaper on campus himself. But school authorities refused his request, again finding the content offensive and inappropriate for a school audience based on *Fraser*.

Romano v. Harrington, 725 F. Supp. 687 (E.D. N.Y. 1989)

The adviser to a student newspaper, fired for allowing the newspaper to publish an editorial critical of the Martin Luther King federal holiday, sued the school district on First Amendment grounds.

The student-written column published in *The Crow's Nest* in Port Richmond, New York, criticized the proposal for the federal MLK holiday. The main question before the court was whether the extracurricular student newspaper fell under the control of the school district under *Hazelwood*. If the paper was considered a school-sponsored or educational endeavor, the adviser's termination would have been justified.

Key factors here included: student reporters, writers and editors published the newspaper as an extracurricular endeavor outside of class; students received no formal classroom instruction from the adviser and did not receive academic credit or a grade; students received feedback and critiques from the adviser and readers, but no formal grades.

"Because educators may limit student expression in the name of pedagogy, courts must avoid enlarging the venues within which that rationale may legitimately obtain without a clear and precise directive," the court wrote in holding that the plaintiff had a legitimate First Amendment action.

The school district would have fewer rights to censor an after-school or extracurricular student newspaper, such as *The Crow's Nest*. Incidentally, after this controversy, the school district created a journalism course in which students produced the newspaper and earned academic credit and grades for their performance.

Desilets v. Clearview Regional Board of Education, 647 A.2d 150 (N.J. 1994)

Censoring a student's reviews of two R-rated movies violated the First Amendment and the state constitution, the New Jersey Supreme Court held.

Though the student newspaper here, *The Pioneer Press*, was not a public forum, the school district enforced a policy that was considered vague. Further, the school was unable to prove that the censorship was reasonably related to a legitimate pedagogical purpose.

The court wrote:

> The school board's position with respect to the policy that applied to student publications, specifically as related to matters such as movie reviews, was vague and highly conclusory. It conceded that it had no specific policy regarding movie reviews of R-rated films; nevertheless, it argued that the action taken by the principal and superintendent complied with that "policy." Further, how any "policy" was applied to the student's R-rated movie reviews remains unclear.
>
> The school authorities assert that the publication of [the student's] R-rated movie reviews violated its official policy because those reviews constituted "material which advocated the use or advertised the availability of any substance believed to constitute a danger to student health." However, no one explained how such R-rated movie reviews posed a danger to student health. Moreover, if such R-rated movie reviews did violate that policy, the evidence strongly suggests that the policy was often ignored or applied inconsistently because R-rated movies were discussed in class, referred to and available in the school library, and, in fact, reviewed and published by the student newspaper.

While ruling that the district acted inappropriately in censoring the student's reviews of the movies *Mississippi Burning* and *Rain Man*, it did say that in other cases similar censorship might be within a legitimate pedagogical interest.

Draudt v. Wooster City School District, 246 F.Supp. 2d 820 (N.D. Ohio 2003)

Student journalists in Wooster, Ohio, sued their school district after the principal censored the student newspaper and confiscated its entire press run over an article quoting a student who admitted to underage drinking.

Although the newspaper, *Blade*, was a bi-weekly newspaper written and edited solely by the students (some of whom earned grades and academic credit), the paper included commentary by members of the community and the paper was distributed both on and off campus, the district acted within its legal authority under *Hazelwood*, the federal court held.

While declaring the newspaper a limited public forum under *Hazelwood*, the court backed the school district because the principal had a "reasonable belief" the article contained potentially defamatory material. The student had spoken on the record to the student journalists about drinking alcohol at a party. However, throughout a subsequent investigation about the drinking, the student denied that she had been drinking at the party. The principal and school officials testified that the student had denied drinking at the party.

Fearing the article contained false, defamatory statements, the school district withheld the newspaper. The court wrote:

> In sum, though the *Blade* meets some *Hazelwood* intent factors weighing against finding a limited public forum, it differs from the *Hazelwood* newspaper in three critical respects. First, outside columnists from the community write columns and letters for the *Blade*. Also, the school widely distributes the *Blade* in the community and prints it at the town's newspaper. Finally, unlike the *Hazelwood* school district, the District has not, in practice, exercised much editorial control. Although the paper's administration is subject to an adviser's approval, the adviser testified that, in practice, the students have broad reign. Further, unlike the *Hazelwood* principal, the Wooster principal usually never reviews the content of the paper before publication.

NEWSFLASH

State statutes

A number of states have adopted laws providing student journalists with greater protection and more rights.

State	Title	Law	Key provisions
Arkansas	Arkansas Publications Act	Ark. Stat. Ann. Sections 6–18–1201–04 (1995)	Students have right to freedom of expression in school-sponsored publications regardless of whether the publication is supported financially or otherwise by the school. Unprotected speech includes obscenity, libel, slander, invasion of privacy or speech that incites unlawful acts on school property or that materially disrupts school activity.
California	California Student Free Expression Law	Calif. Ed. Code Section 48907 (1977)	No prior restraint except in cases of libel, slander, speech that poses a clear and present danger of breaking the law or disrupting school activity. In these exceptions school administrators must provide timely justification for prior restraint. Each school district is instructed to draft a school publications codebook. School employees are not to be dismissed, suspended or otherwise retaliated against for protecting a student journalist engaging in protected speech.
Colorado	Colorado Student Free Expression Law	Colo Rev. Stat. Sec 21–1–120 (1990)	Content is not subject to prior restraint unless it is deemed obscene, libelous, slanderous, defamatory, a false expression about a non-public figure or poses a clear and present danger to the school or materially disrupts school activities. Particular attention is given to speech regarding gang activity. Furthermore, the board of education publishes a written publication codebook to be distributed at the beginning of each school year.
Iowa	Iowa Student Free Expression Law	Iowa Code Sec. 280–22 (1989)	Right to freedom of speech for student journalists without prior restraint unless said speech is deemed obscene, libelous, slanderous or encourages students to commit unlawful acts, violate school policies or materially disrupt school activity. School media advisers may supervise student journalists to maintain professional English and journalism standards. This section does not apply to rules governing oral communications.
Illinois	College Campus Press Act	110 ILCS 13 (2007)	Pertaining to college "campus media" not intended for distribution solely in the classroom. All "campus media" are considered a public forum and are not subject to prior restraint by school officials. Students or advisers may seek injunctive or declaratory relief and attorney's fees may be awarded to a prevailing party. Institutions are granted immunity from any lawsuits arising from expression made in campus media.
Kansas	Kansas Student Publications Law	Kan Stat. Ann. 72.1504–06 (1992)	Student publications are protected so long as speech is not libelous, slanderous or materially disrupts "normal school activity." Administrators may regulate the content of school publications in keeping with the standards of English and journalism.
Massachusetts	Massachusetts Student Free Expression Law	Mass. Gen. Laws. Ann. Ch 71, Section 82 (1988)	Right to freedom of speech and expression is protected unless it causes a "disruption or disorder" in the school. Expression includes the right to peaceably assemble at a time and place to be determined by administrators ahead of time. Student media is not an expression of school policy and school officials are not liable for student speech.

State	Title	Law	Key provisions
Oregon	Oregon Student Free Expression Law (Public Secondary Schools)	Oregon Rev. Stat. sec. 336.477 (2007)	Freedom of speech and expression for student journalists in school-sponsored media regardless of whether the media is sponsored or supported, financially or otherwise, by the school. Student journalists are free to determine content consistent with exceptions for libel, slander and speech that materially disrupts normal school activity. The act does not prevent faculty advisers from regulating content in keeping with professional standards of English and journalism.

Administrative Codes

State	Title	Law	Key provisions
Washington	Washington Administrative Code: Student Rights	Washington Administrative Code 392–40–2115 (1977)	Students granted the right to freedom of speech and the press, as well as the right to peaceably assemble. Students granted right to privacy and freedom from unreasonable searches and seizures. Includes the right of each student to pursue an equal educational opportunity.
Pennsylvania	Pennsylvania Administrative Code: Student Rights and Responsibilities	Pennsylvania Administrative Code 22 Pa. Code Section 12.9 (2005)	Freedom of speech and expression in schools is protected unless it materially interferes with "the educational process" or threatens harm to the school or community, encourages unlawful activity or interferes with the individual rights of another. Students may be required to submit publicly posted materials for prior approval. School-sponsored speech may be regulated by the faculty adviser but school officials may not censor material simply because it is critical of the school or administration. The statute lays out specific rules for different venues of expression including bulletin boards, newspapers, wearable expression and the distribution of materials.

Thus, the court denied the students' request for both an injunction and suit based on the First Amendment.

The forum analysis was critical in this case because the paper was a limited public forum, and the decision greatly expanded the legitimate pedagogical standard.

Planned Parenthood of Southern Nevada v. Clark County School District, 941 F.2d 817 (9th Cir. 1991)

The court found that a school's denial of Planned Parenthood advertisements in school publications – newspapers, yearbooks and athletic programs – was a valid exercise of the school district's authority to develop content in school-sponsored activities.

Comparing this case to *Hazelwood*, the court wrote:

Because both are school cases and the publications are school-sponsored, we do not write on a clean slate. *Hazelwood* instructs that we are to invest high school educators with greater control over expressive activities that bear the school's imprimatur than other forms of speech or use of government facilities. Thus, in striking a balance between the school's interests and Planned Parenthood's, we must assume that school-sponsored publications are non-public and that unless the schools affirmatively intend to open a forum for indiscriminate use, restrictions reasonably related to the school's mission that are imposed on the content of school-sponsored publications do not violate the First Amendment.

This case raises troubling issues because few things are so fundamental as our right to speak out, student or adult, pharmacist or Planned Parenthood. It is the more so because few things are so significant to our society, or reflect such deeply held and widely divergent views crying out for expression, as family planning, sex education, birth control and teenage pregnancy.

CONCLUSION

While the First Amendment provides journalists with a range of freedom to gather and disseminate news, student journalists fall into a different category. The Supreme Court has repeatedly stated that students, even student journalists, have First Amendment rights, it has also empowered school districts, teachers, principals and advisers, with the power to censor student publications that are part of the school curriculum.

Student journalists may have more concerns than professional journalists when it comes to censorship. However, student journalists are also subject to many of the same possible restrictions that the working press faces with regard to legal liability for defamation, invasion of privacy and copyright infringement.

The First Amendment, nevertheless, provides student journalists with some protection to be viable members of the important institution called the Fourth Estate.

SUMMARY

- Student journalists have legal rights under the First Amendment.

- Student journalists are subject to some of the same legal restrictions as working journalists and could be held legally responsible for defamation, invasion of privacy or copyright infringement.

- The Supreme Court has held that student journalists may be subject to censorship depending on how the publication is produced.

- Publications produced as part of a class may be subject to more control by school administrators than publications produced as extracurricular activities.

- Student journalists can attend government meetings and use public records for news stories.

KEY TERMS

actual malice	indecency	prior restraint
copyright law	intrusion upon solitude	privilege
defamation	invasion of privacy law	provable truth
fair comment	libel	publication of private or embarrassing facts
false light	misappropriation	
First Amendment	obscenity	public official/public figure rule
Fourth Estate	opinion privilege	
incitement	parody/satire	slander

EXERCISES

1 Compile a list of public records that are relevant to stories you want to report and publish. Ask the appropriate government agency or official for those documents, most likely a school superintendent, obtain the documents and use them as materials for your stories. If you are denied the documents upon request, draft a written request under your state's freedom of information law and follow up on this request.

2 Attend and cover your school board: obtain the school board agenda, look for items that are relevant to your readership. Attend the meetings and publish stories about what transpires, the votes and the details of new policies and practices approved by your school board.

3 Organize a meeting with a First Amendment, media law or Student Press Law Center lawyer in or near your community who can come to your newspaper, discuss legal issues and be on call if a legal emergency occurs.

4 As a class, find a recent United States Supreme Court case dealing with First Amendment, free speech or free press issues or a recent lower court case dealing with student speech or student press issues; read the case and discuss the merits. Or conduct a mock trial or appellate argument with students adopting a variety of stances. Have students serve as a panel of judges or seek a local lawyer to serve as a judge.

5 Research the current justices on the Supreme Court and analyze how they might have voted on the *Hazelwood* case from 1988. Explain how and why each justice would vote and the rationale behind a prospective vote.

6 Public or private. As a class, create a list of people and sources and discuss whether for libel purposes they would be considered a private person, public official or public figure.

7 As a class, discuss the legal and ethical issues involved if a crime involving a juvenile occurred on your campus. Consider the rights and concerns of the accused, the victims and the community. Do you name the accused? Do you name the victims? Can you name them?

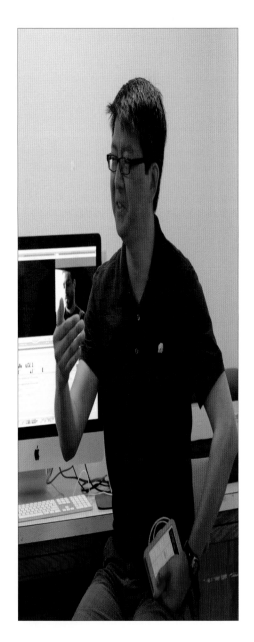

ETHICS FOR STUDENT JOURNALISTS

ROY S. GUTTERMAN

18

> *The way you do journalism in middle school and high school becomes the way you will do it professionally. As an adult, you may get better at it. But the ethical foundation of how you do it, whether you're fair, whether you show compassion, the way you collect it, those things start pretty early.*

Tom Rosenstiel, Director, The Project for Excellence in Journalism

LEARNING OBJECTIVES   After completing this chapter you will be able to:

- understand the nature of journalistic ethics

- apply professional journalistic ethics to your school publication, newspaper, television station or web-based news site

- envision the range of potential ethical quandaries you and your staff may encounter

- distinguish between ethical and unethical behavior in a journalistic setting and understand the difference between the law and ethics.

AS HUMAN BEINGS, WE ARE judged by our actions. From the way you behave in the hallways to how you comport yourself in a restaurant, your conduct reflects on you. Consider all the situations in which you've been advised to just, "Do the right thing." This standard for living your life should apply to journalism, as well. In fact, it might be even more important because of journalism's societal role. Gathering information and disseminating it to a wider audience is an immensely important function in a democracy. The press is made up of private institutions that must serve the public, and no outside body, not even the government, can police its conduct. There is an extensive body of law, starting with the First Amendment to the Constitution, that governs and protects the right to free speech and the press, especially with regard to journalism. However, the law cannot, should not and does not govern every sticky situation a journalist may encounter. That is where journalistic ethics come into play. Ethics should guide how all journalists work, even student journalists.

Truth, accuracy, objectivity and independence are the hallmarks of good journalism. Journalists seek the truth. But ascertaining the truth is often difficult. Sometimes the right people are tough to find and unable or unwilling to be quoted. Some news subjects are sensitive. Some topics are controversial and may elicit strong emotions.

Journalists have serious responsibilities to the public – both their sources and their viewers or readers. Readers expect accuracy in the information they receive. The press must act as an independent agent of unbiased, objective truth. That means that the press must not be controlled or manipulated by government, business or other powerful interests. Such ethical concerns will reflect on the credibility of the information published or broadcast, which only has as much integrity as the journalist and the sources.

Ethical decision-making should inform how a journalist gathers the news. Things like lying to get information, using anonymous sources, surreptitious recording or being rude or unnecessarily hostile to sources all raise ethical issues. But ethics have applications far beyond the newsgathering process. Ethics should play a role in the editing and production of the news. It should inform the structure of news stories to avoid sensationalizing events, misquoting sources or distorting facts through the use of inaccurate headlines, questionable photo captions or misleading photographs.

Even after publication or broadcast, ethical responsibilities persist when handling corrections or complaints from readers or sources. Thus, journalistic ethics transcend any one story and any individual publication.

WWW

WEBLINK Check out

www.journalism.org

Pew Research Center's Project for Excellence in Journalism: A non-partisan journalism think tank's website focusing on a wide range of media issues, including journalism ethics.

WHAT IS ETHICS?

Ethics is the branch of philosophy that studies the principles of right and wrong or good and bad. It is a system of moral conduct. The word *ethics* comes from the Greek word *ethos*, meaning disposition or character, or what a person does to develop good character. The development of ethics goes back more than 2,500 years to ancient Greece, where the philosopher Socrates strove to develop universal ethical standards by asking fundamental questions about the nature of society, value and human conduct.

Ethics or morals are also associated with each culture's systems of beliefs and socially approved customs. Over the centuries, ethics have changed and developed to reflect different societal values and structures. We develop our own sense of ethics, our so-called "personal ethics," from a variety of sources: parents, peers, schools, role models, religion, law and society. These sources help us navigate our lives, influence our propensity to do good or bad, to help or harm – in other words to do the right thing or the wrong thing.

ETHICS, THE LAW AND THE FIRST AMENDMENT

The First Amendment provides journalists with a range of protections for gathering and publishing news. Freedom of the press and speech are fundamental democratic principles which have been protected by the courts, including the Supreme Court. The First Amendment also extends some protections to student journalists.

Under the First Amendment, the law provides a legal structure for the press on a range of subjects – from defamation (publishing false statements about someone) to the legality of recording an interview (which varies from state to state and sometimes depends on the circumstances). Supreme Court cases have also touched on topics including anonymous sources, invasion of privacy and the use of quotation marks.

The law establishes basic standards for what journalists *can* legally do. Journalistic ethics establish standards for what journalists *should* do. Sometimes what a journalist can do and should do are very similar. Sometimes there is a razor-thin margin between the two. Sometimes ethical lapses can even lead to prosecutions, lawsuits or other legal actions.

Test your knowledge

What is ethics? How does ethics differ from "the law"?

MEDIA ETHICS

Because the media are a largely unregulated profession, ethics must guide journalists in areas where the law is silent or unclear. Journalism is not like other professions such as medicine or law. Doctors and lawyers are highly regulated professionals, who require a specialized education, certification based on rigorous exams and a license, which can be revoked if certain professional and ethical standards are not upheld. Although many journalists in the modern era have college degrees in the field, higher education is not a necessary requirement. In short, anybody can be a journalist.

In recent years, journalists have not been viewed as particularly trustworthy professionals. A 2009 Gallup Poll found that 27 percent of the public placed journalists in the "low" and "very low" categories when asked to rate the honesty and ethical standards of 21 professions. The public's perception of journalists and the media in general could be worse, but it could be a lot better, too.

The public's perception of the media may be based on a sense that it is intrusive, nosy or insensitive. The work of journalism requires that reporters ask painful and controversial questions, which can have a profound impact on the lives of both readers and sources. Whether you are a journalist for a national newspaper, a television network, an online publisher or a small-town school newspaper, you are engaging in an inherently important and sensitive endeavor – gathering and disseminating information and news. In the absence of licensing guidelines and ethical codes, journalists are left to their own devices to develop standards and responsible practices.

What is the right way to get a story? What is the responsible way to tell a story? Will this hurt someone? Is this account accurate? Is this story balanced and fair? These are some of the questions reporters, editors and managers should ask at various times during the reporting and production of news.

Ethical lapses in journalism raise questions about the profession itself. News is not developed in a vacuum – it both involves and affects the community in which it is produced.

Ethicists call parties with an interest in a situation or outcome, or people affected by an action, "stakeholders." In journalism, the stakeholders are:

- **The sources:** the people the journalists interview for the story. Sources and reporters engage in an exchange of information based on trust – that the information is accurate and it will be accurately portrayed in the story.
- **The subjects:** the people the story is about.
- **The audience:** the people who read, view or consume the news. In a school setting, this means peers, classmates, teachers, administrators and members of the community.
- **The journalists:** the reporters, editors, designers and photographers whose credibility and integrity should be reflected in every piece they produce, and the journalism profession itself because the actions of one rogue, ethically-challenged journalist can cast doubt on the entire profession.

When an ethical quandary arises in a journalistic setting, reporters and editors should discuss the challenges, risks and potential solutions. Student journalists also have the benefit of working with upperclassmen and faculty advisers and teachers who may be well-versed in responsible journalistic practices and ethical decision-making. Many professional news organizations can also be a resource to help answer ethical questions.

The Potter's Box

Developed by Harvard Divinity School Professor Ralph B. Potter, Jr., the "Potter's Box" guides the user through four interrelated questions. Many journalism ethicists find the "Potter's Box" a useful tool for ethical guidance. When an ethical question arises, it may be useful to work the situation through this flowchart.

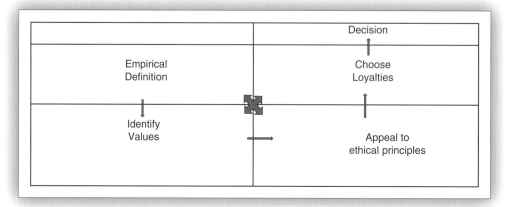

The Potter's Box. Developed by Harvard Divinity School Professor Ralph B. Potter, Jr., the "Potter's Box" guides the user through four interrelated questions.

Newsgathering ethics

Reporters use a variety of resources to gather news. A well-balanced news story draws on a diversity of human sources, documents, public records and sometimes even descriptions of the scene, setting and parties. How a reporter gathers this information and the transparency in newsgathering, is sometimes just as important as the information a reporter gets. The value of the information a journalist publishes is dependent on the credibility of the newsgathering process. Thus, a reporter who lies to get information may later be accused of having a bias, casting doubt on the news itself. A reporter who mis-states or exaggerates elements in a story may undermine the story as well as the credibility of the entire publication. A reporter who does not include multiple sources or tell "both sides" of a story may be accused of bias.

Journalists may go to great lengths to get information, but they are still subject to ethical guidelines, as well as the law. Newsgathering tactics that violate laws might include trespassing, wiretapping or hacking into someone's cellphone or private email account. A reporter who breaks the law to gather news may be subject to criminal prosecution or civil litigation. But beyond possible legal sanctions, these actions would also violate most conceptions of journalistic ethics. Either way, the reporter's behavior counts. When in doubt, journalists must ask themselves, "How would an explanation of my actions look in print?" "Can I explain the legitimacy of my behavior?" The answers to those questions may assist journalists in deciding whether their conduct is ethical.

Interview ethics

Ethical behavior also plays a role in your interaction with sources, most commonly in an interview setting. How a reporter behaves in an interview is also a matter of ethical concern. A responsible, ethical reporter is well-prepared; he or she performs advance research, shows up on time and asks intelligent, well-reasoned and probing questions, not leading or badgering questions. The responsible, ethical reporter wears professional attire and treats sources, even hostile or recalcitrant ones, professionally and respectfully. Addressing sources with honorary titles – Mr., Ms., Dr., Prof. – goes a long way and plays into both personal and professional ethics.

The mechanics of an interview also play into ethics. For example, allowing a source time to answer questions is important. Not arguing with, ambushing, talking over, cutting off a source, especially in an interview for broadcast or video, is important.

HELPFUL TIPS

Ask These 10 Questions to Make Good Ethical Decisions

Over the course of his career as a former television reporter, Professor Bob Steele, journalism ethics expert at the Poynter Institute, now a distinguished professor at DePauw University, developed a series of 10 questions for ethical decision-making.

→ What do I know? What do I need to know?

→ What is my journalistic purpose?

→ What are my ethical concerns?

→ What organizational policies and professional guidelines should I consider?

→ How can I include other people, with different perspectives and diverse ideas, in the decision-making process?

→ Who are the stakeholders – those affected by my decision? What are their motivations? Which are legitimate?

→ What if the roles were reversed? How would I feel if I were in the shoes of one of the stakeholders?

→ What are the possible consequences of my actions? Short term? Long term?

→ What are my alternatives to maximize my truth-telling responsibility and minimize harm?

→ Can I clearly and fully justify my thinking and my decision? To my colleagues? To the stakeholders? To the public?

Arriving on time, being punctual, courteous and well-prepared for an interview is vital. Of course, a breaking news situation may create obstacles to being well-versed or well-prepared for an interview. But this is another situation where a reporter's demeanor may be the difference between getting information and having a door slammed in your face.

Breaking news – crimes, disasters, accidents, fires, tragedies – are tense and dramatic. People are usually at their worst and then the reporters show up. This is where a reporter's demeanor and compassion can play a role in the newsgathering process. Getting information is the reporter's job. But the reporter must also be sensitive to people and the nature of the situation.

Human sources

Reporters encounter a range of people who may be possible sources for a story. The choices they make about whom to interview and quote have important ethical implications. Reporters should ask themselves if they are interviewing the appropriate person. Does this source have a hidden agenda? Is there a relationship between the source and the reporter that will not be obvious to readers? Are they friends or family members? Are they in the same clubs? Do they sit at the same lunch table? Whether the journalist is interviewing an expert or a layperson, other issues, such as diversity, may also play an important role.

Some people deal with reporters for a living or are in high-profile or public positions that expose them to frequent media attention. Other people may not be as comfortable talking to the media. Some people who have been swept into a breaking news situation will not be comfortable or confident answering reporters' questions. Journalists must show particular sensitivity in dealing with these private individuals.

In no cases should reporters pay sources for interviews or accept money from sources for any reason.

Recording

Recording an interview is often helpful for reporters who want accurate quotes and documentary proof of statements made by sources. For broadcasters or multimedia reporters, recording audio and video is essential. But recording an interview can sometimes raise ethical concerns. A majority of states (38 plus the District of Columbia) allow the recording of interviews or conversations as long as one party is aware of the recording. These are known as "one-party consent" states. This means that in such states, a reporter may record an interview without obtaining the permission or consent of the other parties.

Thus, it might be perfectly legal to record someone without their knowledge or consent. But would this be ethical? In many cases, the answer is no. Recording someone without his or her knowledge outside of a one-party consent state could create legal liability, most likely under invasion of privacy statutes. But beyond the potential for breaking laws, recording someone using hidden cameras or recorders is ethically questionable and can aggravate the public's mistrust of the media. Many newsrooms do not allow their reporters to engage in surreptitious reporting or use hidden cameras or recorders.

There are, however, some situations in which such tactics may be legitimate. Many investigative television news magazines and some traditional television stations occasionally use hidden cameras to gather vital information when there are no other reasonable or feasible means to do so. Information obtained in this way should usually be of pressing civic importance or involve criminal behavior or public safety. When surreptitious or "undercover" newsgathering techniques are used, those means become part of the story, and the journalist has an obligation to explain to viewers how and why the techniques were employed. Journalists should engage in serious discussions about the ethics and legality of using these surreptitious techniques before employing them.

Test Your knowledge

How does ethics play a role in gathering or reporting information?

Publishing ethics

Putting together that story requires making sure it is balanced, meaning all the relevant parties have had an opportunity to tell their side of the story. However, sometimes reporters are unable to get comments from one or more parties with a vested interest in the story. In that case, it is important that the parties' unavailability or refusal to comment is stated in the story. Here, care should be taken to make sure this lack of information is presented accurately and neutrally. There is a difference between "Smith had no comment," and "Smith could not be reached for comment." A description of efforts to reach a source should maintain a neutral tone. Thus, there is a difference between "Smith could not be reached for comment," and "Smith could not be reached for comment after three telephone calls, two emails and a fax."

Transparency – explaining the methods and sources on which each story is based – is a cornerstone of journalistic ethics. Establishing that efforts have been made to reach all of the subjects – especially those who are involved in a scandal or accused of wrongdoing – is an important practice of journalistic transparency. A reporter has an obligation to give subjects the opportunity to respond to criticism or tell their sides of the story. Reporters should never assume that subjects will not talk to them, and must make every possible effort to get even a potentially hostile subject to comment.

Fact checking

Reporters and editors must be careful to verify and double-check the factual assertions they intend to publish. It is also important that the story accurately reflects the information at hand or what the reporter actually observed. Many investigative reporters see their primary role as collecting evidence – solid, verified information that backs up claims of the story.

In addition to the story, the headline, photographs and captions, infographics and artwork should accurately reflect the facts as they were reported. Exaggerations and distortions undermine the truthfulness of a story and erode journalistic credibility.

If truth is a primary goal of good reporting, then reporters should do anything and everything to ensure they are publishing or broadcasting truthful information. This means checking the facts and verifying that information. Magazines, which operate with longer deadlines, have dedicated fact-checking departments. In all publications, editors, copy editors and fact checkers should refer to almanacs, encyclopedias, books, websites and databases to verify facts included in stories.

Fact checkers and journalists sometimes verify direct quotations by calling the sources for confirmation. As a rule, though, journalists should not submit articles to sources for pre-publication review, even if the sources request it.

Sometimes tension arises between editors – who are verifying, proofreading and otherwise editing copy – and writers. The editing process is a delicate dance, and writers and editors must keep in mind the ultimate goal of publishing accurate and truthful information. Errors in copy, even minor spelling errors, can not only raise questions about the veracity of other data in the story, but also about the quality and integrity of the publication, website or broadcast program.

Fairness and balance

Journalists have an obligation to tell all sides of the story. If there are only two sides to a controversy or debate, this task is usually easier. Often, though, there are multiple sides to the story, sometimes with competing or adversarial interests. Thus, the ethical reporter has an obligation to obtain all opposing viewpoints. This is especially critical for stories making accusations or dealing with controversial topics. It is never easy to approach sensitive and controversial topics, people in vulnerable situations or people accused of wrongdoing. Reporters are sometimes met with hostility, rudeness, even threats of violence or lawsuits. But the job of a reporter is to collect information and tell stories. Sometimes people accused of wrongdoing simply want the chance to tell their side of the story. Sometimes they do not. But fairness demands the reporter seek those comments.

A reporter must make every effort to contact all possible subjects of a news story and convey their sides in the account. When all efforts fail, it should be transparent in the story and explained to the reader.

Post-publication ethics

The journalist's ethical obligation to sources, subjects and the audience continues after publication. It is not uncommon to learn about mistakes after publication. Mistakes happen. Reporters and editors working under tight deadlines sometimes err. Even *The New York Times* makes mistakes and runs corrections. Many publications have a designated place in the newspaper or magazine where corrections appear. Internet-based publications and the web-based entities of established traditional media can immediately fix errors online, though even these corrected mistakes should be noted (usually at the top or the bottom of the story).

Journalists consider their work to be a "first draft of history." Thus, every newspaper can be considered a "paper of record." Your student newspaper is a paper of record for your school and community. That means that readers rely on the truthfulness of the information included in your pages: the facts and figures, game scores and even the time and date of a concert. In the future, historians, scholars and curious readers will look to your paper, news site or digital archives to learn about what happened.

When mistakes are brought to the attention of writers and editors, the publication has an obligation to correct the record. Sometimes publishing a correction may even stave off a lawsuit because it could mitigate damages for defamation and demonstrate the publication's good will and concern for the truth.

There are several ways to fix mistakes:

Corrections – statements that "correct" the journalistic record. An error such as a misspelled name, a misidentified source or an incorrect fact or figure should be recast and corrected in a published explanation. Some publications also note how the error occurred, using phrases such as "in an editing error" or "in a reporting error." Some publications also include a gratuitous, often superfluous, statement that the publication "regrets the error." Corrections should run in the next edition of a newspaper or be appended to online versions as soon as possible. Corrections for yearbooks are often done with inserts or errata pages.

Retraction – a withdrawal of an entire story or other piece of content. A retraction might be necessary in the case of a particularly egregious error where corrections will not be sufficient. A retraction would most effectively be published as a brief paragraph, similar to a correction. However, in a particularly controversial issue, a retraction might be published as a story along with comments from the editor or adviser.

Apology – an expression of regret or sorrow by a publication for an error in judgment or lapse of journalistic ethics. In some cases of extreme or outrageous behavior or mistakes, a publication may publish an apology. This may be addressed to a specific source or subject of a story, or to readers or viewers in general.

Test Your knowledge

How does the way you publish your news implicate ethical concerns?

Test your knowledge

What is the best mechanism for handling an ethical lapse that affected something you published or broadcast?

Clarifications – a post-publication explanation for something that was published that may raise questions about the story or the means through which the story was acquired. Clarifications may help readers better understand certain elements of the story, either through a clearer language or the addition of information.

Editor's note – an introductory paragraph or paragraphs to introduce a story or series or to provide background on the topic or the newsgathering process. Sometimes the editorial staff will provide such a note in the interest of journalistic transparency. For example, such an explanation may be necessary if a story relies on anonymous sources, questionable reporting techniques or a special newsgathering process – Freedom of Information Act requests, computer-assisted-reporting techniques or extensive research in archives.

COMMON ETHICAL ISSUES JOURNALISTS FACE

Gathering the news and the practicalities of dealing with a wealth of information creates a range of ethical concerns. From the use of quotes to anonymous sourcing to conflicts of interest, the journalist's behavior may raise concerns. This, too, is a place where the law may provide a baseline, but the journalist's ethics will fill in the gaps.

Quotes

Quotes are the lifeblood of a news story. Even though quotation marks are generally a topic for elementary school grammar classes, these punctuation marks can raise unique ethical concerns for journalists. Using quotation marks indicates that the words appearing within those marks are the actual, verbatim words of the speaker. The bond between a publication and its readers requires that readers can depend upon the absolute integrity of quoted material in a story.

Every news story needs direct quotes. The best news stories use multiple quotes from numerous sources to illuminate the story and give life to its subjects. Reporters are not stenographers. It is difficult to conduct an interview and simultaneously get down every word the subject utters. Sometimes audio and video recorders malfunction, too. On top of those difficulties, not all sources are comfortable speaking with reporters. Not every source speaks perfect English, and sometimes sources speak ungrammatically, in incomplete sentences or with inappropriate profanity, which cannot be printed in many publications.

Sometimes, practicality requires the reporter to use a partial quote or **paraphrase** some statements – putting the speaker's words into your own words without using quotation marks, but with proper attribution.

Though paraphrasing can be appropriate, altering direct quotes is never acceptable. Altering a direct quote not only raises ethical concerns about the integrity and credibility of the reporter and publication, but in some situations, putting words in a source's mouth could even lead to legal liability for defamation.

This issue was the subject of a Supreme Court case, *Masson v. New Yorker Magazine* (1991), which reaffirmed the legal significance of quotation marks. This case also gave journalists some wiggle room to alter the words inside quotation marks in certain narrow circumstances to avoid legal liability. The Supreme Court held that writers can alter the words within quotation marks to fix grammar, syntax or spelling. This case represents another nexus between the law and journalistic ethics.

Some journalists and publications adhere to a strict policy of never altering direct quotations, even for grammar, syntax or correction of an obvious error. Each publication should develop a policy for handling questionable quotes. Re-interviewing the source might be the most responsible course of action. But deadlines and availability of sources may be an issue. Thus, it might be more responsible to use a partial quote or a paraphrase if the direct quote is problematic.

A number of punctuation marks may also provide assistance in cleaning up quotes or providing the reader with a clearer picture of the speaker's words or intended words. For example, use of brackets [] or parentheses () with the missing words inside may clear up a quote. The use of ellipses … to break up a long quote may also help. Even though this may be helpful, some editors try to avoid inserting these punctuation marks because it may still be construed as putting words in the speaker's mouth.

Anonymity and confidentiality

Using **anonymous sources** is a complicated issue even for professional journalists. Granting a source anonymity, meaning that you do not identify the source in published accounts, can be fraught with both ethical and legal concerns. Because of some high-profile incidents of fabrication in news stories, anonymous sources can sometimes raise questions about the veracity and credibility of an account. Anonymous sourcing also raises questions about whether the source has a hidden agenda that would become apparent if he or she were identified. Because of these difficulties, many news organizations shy away from using anonymous sources.

Courts have found reporters and sources create a verbal contract when they agree to exchange information confidentially. This contract may protect reporters from being forced to divulge information obtained from those sources, or the sources themselves. Conversely, in some narrow settings, reporters have been compelled by courts to either reveal the identity of a confidential source or face jail time for contempt of court.

Journalists should be cautious and reluctant when granting sources anonymity or **confidentiality**. Student journalists granting anonymity may find themselves in an even more complicated predicament with regard to school administrators. However, there may be times when there is no other way to get the story or the right source.

Anonymity can come in a variety of forms. Reporters covering governmental institutions have developed a range of agreements that they may set up with their anonymous sources. There are no set parameters for these agreements, which should generally be set up before any interviewing takes place. Interviews with reporters are considered "**on the record**," or available for publication, unless otherwise specified. A source cannot say something and later tell you, "That's off the record, don't use that." See Newsflash sidebar.

NEWSFLASH

On and off the record

The multiple ways reporters exchange information "on the record" and "off the record" can put a reporter in both legal and ethical difficulties. Many professional news organizations have rigid rules regarding anonymous sources, especially when quoting them directly.

In 1998, Stephen Glass, a young reporter for *The New Republic* magazine, was found to have fabricated sources and information for multiple stories he published in the magazine, many of which extensively quoted anonymous sources. Adam Penenberg is a journalism professor at New York University and a former Forbes.com reporter who exposed Glass's elaborate deceptions.

As the principal author of the *NYU Journalism Handbook for Students – Ethics, Law and Good Practices*, Penenberg writes: "There is so much murkiness about what 'off the record' means that it is essential that the reporter and source agree on a definition before beginning an 'off the record' portion of an interview."

Penenberg's handbook offers the following useful explanation of these terms:

- **On the record** – means anything your source says can be reported, published or broadcast. All interviews are considered on the record unless the source expressly requests, and the reporter expressly agrees, to go "off the record." The reporter should clearly mark notes to reflect when they went off the record.

- **Off the record** – restricts the reporter from using the information the source is about to deliver. Sometimes the information is offered as an explanation to assist the reporter in understanding an issue or event. If this information can be confirmed by someone on the record, the reporter can use the information.

- **Not for attribution** – means that the reporter agrees not to identify the source by name. The reporter and source often agree on how the source will be identified, such as "a high level administrator" or "high-ranking official in the State Department." These types of exchanges tend to be a staple in high-level government reporting. Reporters must try to be as specific as possible when using a not for attribution source and must steadfastly maintain those confidences.

Conflicts of interests

Reporters must be scrupulous about their independence. Readers and viewers have a right to expect that the journalism they consume is truthful, impartial and objective – that the reporter has no bias and has not been influenced or compromised by outside parties. The audience expects that reporters and sources have no outside relationships, whether familial, business, social or romantic. Journalists should not interview friends or family members.

Professional journalists are particularly aware of **conflicts of interest**, both real and perceived. The appearance of a conflict of interest is enough to cast doubt on a reporter's integrity and credibility. Different types of reporters have specific conflicts of interest they should watch out for:

- **Political reporters** should not participate in political rallies, donate to political campaigns, wear promotional items, sign petitions or compose policy materials or speeches for candidates or campaigns.
- **Sports reporters** should not cheer for the teams they cover, accept gifts from teams or gamble on games or sports they cover.
- **Business reporters** should not trade stocks or commodities based on inside information or accept gifts or gratuities from the businesses they cover.
- **Entertainment reporters** should not accept free tickets for shows, concerts or movies or trade favorable coverage for access to celebrities.
- **Travel reporters** should not accept free trips and then write about them.

These are just a few of the real-life situations that may raise ethical questions about a reporter's integrity and independence. The appearance of a conflict of interest not only jeopardizes the journalist's reputation but could cast a shadow on the entire publication. Who is going to trust your publication if readers think the reporters are compromised in any way – whether they are friends with a source, "being bought" by special interests or simply too close to the subjects?

Student journalists are not immune from conflict of interest concerns. In fact, student journalists often find themselves in closer proximity to their sources and audience than professional journalists. Student journalists are classmates, friends and teammates with many of their news subjects. In some cases, student journalists may be members of a group being covered by the publication – a clear conflict of interest. Thus, a student journalist who is also a member of the Student Government Association (SGA) should not also cover the SGA or even edit stories involving it. The same standards would apply to Model UN, the Spanish Club, sports teams and other student groups and activities.

Similarly, it is not acceptable to interview friends or family members. When these situations arise, it is important for the journalist to be recused and find someone without a relationship to the sources to cover the story.

Another potential conflict of interest could arise if the entities that advertise in your publication become part of the news you have to cover. Advertisers should receive no special treatment in your news pages.

Test your knowledge

Consider the implications of using an anonymous source and how you may incorporate that source or information into your story.

Crimes, victims and the suspect

Schools are not immune from crimes, which are often newsworthy and need to be covered. The public has a right to know when crimes occur or if the school is unsafe. Reporters have an obligation to investigate and report these stories, but crime reporting may raise ethical issues. Topics that may need to be considered before reporting on a crime include:

- **Victims**   Some publications have policies that require reporters to withhold the identities of victims of crime. Sometimes the identification of the victim is an essential part of the story. Sometimes certain details of crimes should be left out of the stories to assist law enforcement or to respect the privacy of victims and their families.

- **The suspect** Sometimes a publication's policy may be to withhold the identity of a suspect until the person has been formally charged with a crime. But there is no clear ethical standard for naming or not naming a suspect. The public might very well have an interest in knowing the suspected criminal's identity. A solid news story may also help dispel myths and rumors surrounding a major crime in your school or community.

- **Victims of sex crimes** Identifying rape victims or victims of sex crimes is not only an ethical concern for news organizations but also raises legal concerns. In the United States, most news organizations do not name the victims of sex crimes unless the victims themselves wish to be identified.

- **Minors** Many news organizations have a policy against naming minors involved in a crime. In many states, juvenile court proceedings are kept confidential and the names of minors accused of crimes are withheld from the public. Law enforcement will sometimes release the names of minors who are accused of serious felonies such as murder. But reporters might learn the minor's identity from basic reporting, which raises the ethical question of whether to print or broadcast that name. The Supreme Court ruled in *Smith v. Daily Mail* (1979) that reporters who lawfully obtained and truthfully reported the identification of a teenage murder suspect would be legally permitted to publish the juvenile's name.

WWW

WEBLINK Check out
www.rcfp.org
Reporters Committee for Freedom of the Press: A comprehensive website for legal and ethical issues for the journalism industry.

Photo integrity

News photography should be grounded in the truth, just like a news story. Remember the adage "seeing is believing." Photographs are taken as visual proof. As a result, the publication staff may have a strong obligation to let images speak for themselves, without alteration or editing. Similar to reporters, photographers face numerous ethical concerns in their newsgathering process, especially with regard to intrusive behavior and privacy concerns.

How photographs are used in publications, websites, broadcasts and even yearbooks can present questions of fairness and accuracy. Whether a photograph accurately depicts an event is a perennial concern. Special considerations include:

- **Photo editing.** Affordable and widely-used computer programs allow even a novice the ability to edit and alter digital photographs. News photographs should never be altered.

- **Photo illustrations.** Many magazines and feature sections employ photo illustrations, which are artistic, staged or posed photographs or combinations of photographs. Photo illustrations may be useful tools to add life and color to a feature or in-depth story or package. Photo illustrations should always be labeled as such, usually in the cutline or caption.

Using someone else's photographs or artwork

This is another area where the law and ethics converge. Photographs may be protected by copyright law. Using a photograph that is copyrighted without permission (or a "license") could constitute copyright infringement. But the likelihood that a student newspaper will be sued for infringement is slight. Furthermore including such images may be fair use – the legal defense for many infringement disputes. But even if your use of these images is legal, it may not be ethical (see Chapter 17 for more information).

Test your knowledge

What are the ethical implications of reporting, photographing and publishing a story involving a crime?

ETHICAL LAPSES – GAFFES, QUANDARIES AND JOURNALISTIC FELONIES

When a journalist engages in ethically questionable behavior, it tends to be a highly-publicized affair, even a scandal. Journalism is a very public endeavor and breaches of the public trust are often just as public as the underlying journalism. Ethical breaches can end a journalist's career and cast doubt on the journalism profession.

Fabrication

There is no greater breach of trust between reporters and readers than **fabrication** – making up facts, figures and people in news stories. There is no wiggle room here. Writing fiction and passing it off as truth is considered a "journalistic felony" that shatters the audience's trust. In recent years, there have been several famous cases of journalists fabricating stories and sources and passing them off as the truth.

There are no shortcuts in journalism. Responsible newsgathering takes time. Good reporters can spend days or even weeks researching their topics and identifying the best sources. Sometimes reporters will interview a dozen people or more just to find the right source.

NEWSFLASH

Rogues' gallery

For as long as there has been independent, objective journalism, there have been journalists who have violated the trust of editors and readers. Whether it was outright hoaxes, such as The New York Sun's 1835 report that there were winged humanoids inhabiting the moon, or more subtle deceptions, such as the composite character a Washington Post reporter created and chronicled in a series that won the 1981 Pulitzer Prize, there have been numerous examples of journalistic fabrication over the centuries.

Contemporary journalism is rife with high-profile liars, cheats, thieves and fabricators who violated the trust between the press and readers, passing off phony stories and characters as truth.

This is the rogues' gallery:

Janet Cooke In 1980, Cooke, a reporter for the Washington Post, wrote a series of stories about an eight-year-old heroin addict named "Jimmy." The stories won the highest honor in journalism, the Pulitzer Prize. After the stories turned out to be totally fictitious, the reporter was forced to resign and the paper had to return the award.

Janet Malcom In a long-form profile for the New Yorker magazine in 1983, the reporter fabricated five quotes attributed to the subject of the article. The two-part story was based on more than 40 hours of taped interviews. Five quotes published in the piece were alleged to be fabricated. This led to a protracted lawsuit, an appeal to the United States Supreme Court and two trials and liability for fabricated quotes.

Stephen Glass In 1998, Glass, a 25-year-old rising star at The New Republic was found to have fabricated entire stories for the magazine. Glass went so far as to create phony interview notes, a bogus website and voicemail system and a cast of colorful, but completely phony, characters. A subsequent investigation determined that Glass had fabricated elements or complete stories in 27 of his 41 bylines in The New Republic.

Jack Kelley In 2003, after a 21-year career as one of USA Today's star reporters, Kelley was fired for fabricating facts and anecdotes in a decade's worth of stories. A team of journalists charged with investigating his work found Kelley lied to editors, manufactured scripts for sources to read, lifted quotes and details from other publications, lied on expense reports and fabricated eyewitness accounts of dramatic accounts including witnessing a suicide bombing. Despite the fact that Kelley was a finalist for the Pulitzer Prize, the paper later withdrew his work from contests.

Jayson Blair A young New York Times reporter on the national desk plagiarized and fabricated details in dozens of news stories. Blair lifted quotes and details from other newspapers on major national stories including the 2003 sniper attacks in the Washington, D.C. area, and numerous stories about the domestic effects of the wars in Iraq and Afghanistan. He also lied on his expense reports and recreated descriptive scenes by viewing photos online. Blair's misdeeds also led to the resignation of the paper's executive editor and managing editor.

Brian Walski A Los Angeles Times photographer manipulated two news photos, digitally grafting photos together into one altered image of an Iraqi man carrying a child and being directed by a gun-toting British soldier. Attributing his "complete breakdown in judgment" to stress and fatigue, he was fired in 2003 after a 20-year career.

NBC News A 1993 Dateline NBC report, "Waiting to Explode," looking at the hazards of gas tanks in General Motors trucks, used video footage of rigged tests showing fires. The report went forward despite the reporter's objections, and the footage was labeled "unscientific."

Every time a journalist fabricates a source or piece of information, it undercuts the entire profession and casts a vast shadow over the journalism profession. A reporter who fabricates will get caught. Editors are not the only people out there fact checking stories. Today's modern media allows every reader to independently verify facts. A reporter caught fabricating will be exposed as a fraud, a liar and a cheat.

Fabricating news is career suicide for a journalist. For student journalists, it not only undermines the integrity and credibility of their work and the publication as a whole, but it could also be considered an act of academic dishonesty. Because many student newspapers are part of a journalism class or an off-shoot of some organized student activity, student journalists caught fabricating could face additional academic sanctions.

Plagiarism

Plagiarism is taking someone else's work and passing it off as your own. Plagiarism is theft and is considered a journalistic felony.

Plagiarists are motivated by many of the same reasons as fabricators. The pressures to find the perfect source, quote or anecdote may sometimes compel a journalist to lift, borrow or steal someone else's work. There is no excuse for plagiarism.

Part of the fun and thrill of journalism is going out and finding the story, interviewing people and digging for documents or other materials. Breaking an original story that is all yours is not only thrilling but an essential element of journalism.

Modern technology has made plagiarism as easy as a Google search and a "right click" on the mouse. Sloppy research techniques, ignorance of the rules or lack of intent to plagiarize are not adequate excuses. Sometimes, a simple attribution for a quote or a paraphrase is enough to avoid a plagiarism situation. "According to an article in …" or "Smith told *The New York Times*" may provide you with the transparency that journalistic ethics demand.

Lies, deception and undercover reporting

We have discussed the concept of transparency in reporting. Many journalism ethicists and codes of ethics recommend that reporters should always identify themselves as such. The days of reporters wearing fedoras with press cards stuck in them are long gone. But many reporters carry press passes and sometimes wear them when they are in the field reporting. (Preparing official identification cards for your staff might be a worthwhile endeavor and would professionalize your operation.)

When interviewing a source, reporters should identify themselves. But if you are attending a rally with hundreds or thousands of people or a public forum such as a school board meeting, is it necessary to stand up and identify yourself as a reporter? Many ethicists would say, in those situations, no.

There are few situations where deception is vital to getting the story. The use of hidden cameras, surreptitious reporting technology and outright lies are controversial and rarely used techniques, even by professional journalists. So-called undercover reporting raises ethical questions about transparency and fairness. But it also treads particularly close to breaking the law in some situations.

In the 1990s, ABC's *Primetime Live* got in hot water for its hidden camera story about the Food Lion supermarket chain. Two reporters lied on job applications and spent two weeks working at the supermarket chain while secretly recording what they did to show unsafe practices in the chain's deli and butcher sections. Food Lion sued for trespass and fraud, and a jury awarded the supermarket chain $5.5 million in damages. This was eventually reduced by an appellate court to a $1 award of nominal damages and some minor fees for processing costs because the reporters submitted phony job applications. ABC's legal fees, however, reached into the millions of dollars.

These surreptitious techniques are sometimes a last resort. A decision to use these techniques would have to be based on serious discussions within the newsroom.

Stolen materials and unauthorized access

Reporters should never break the law to acquire information. The First Amendment does not protect reporters who steal information, trespass or commit other crimes in the newsgathering process. In recent years, technology has facilitated reporters breaking the law. Reporters have been caught illegally hacking into voicemail systems and email accounts. It is one thing to work hard and aggressively pursue a story. It is quite another to violate someone else's legal protections to obtain information.

However, good reporters develop sources who sometimes "leak" confidential or privileged information to reporters. Sometimes these leaks involve the illegal transmission of information or materials, including top-secret documents and illegally intercepted or recorded conversations. Reporters should not encourage sources to break the law.

But the Supreme Court has held that journalists who are given confidential or illegally obtained information may use that information as long as the reporter played no role in the commission of the crime.

Identification of groups/stereotyping/sexist/racist/personal details

Whether a publication adequately represents the community and uses appropriate descriptions of its sources and subjects also becomes an ethical concern. Details are important for stories, but reporters also have to be sensitive about how they use certain types of descriptions regarding race, ethnicity, religion and physical descriptions. When using these types of descriptions, it should be vital to the story. Because these types of editorial decisions are based on journalistic judgments, reporters and editors may have to incorporate ethical standards into their decision-making on these topics.

News vs. opinion

Journalists strive for objectivity. Providing unbiased, impartial and objective news to readers and viewers is one of journalism's core functions. There are some who believe that complete objectivity is illusory. Every editorial decision is based on some subjective bias, whether it is choosing the appropriate adjective, the leading quote in the story or the walk-off ending.

Journalists must divest themselves from their personal beliefs when reporting and writing. Again, because this is an area in which editorial discretion is applied, the nuances between opinion and news could raise ethical concerns. This also plays into how the story is framed, whether quotes are in context and fairly represent the truth.

Obscenity, profanity and vulgarity

Journalistic ethics dictates an adherence to certain professional standards. Most professional news organizations refrain from using profanity within their news and editorial pages. In a school journalism setting, curse words may also be legitimately censored or edited out as inappropriate language under the legal precedent set by the Supreme Court in the *Hazelwood v. Kuhlmeier* (1988) case. Even professional news organizations wrestle with the occasional situation where profanity appears in a direct quote. The stylebook of the Associated Press, the world's largest news organization, suggests: "Obscenities, profanities, vulgarities – Do not use them in stories unless they are part of direct quotations and there is a compelling reason to use them. Try to find a way to give the reader a sense of what was said without using the specific word or phrase."

Broadcast entities, in most settings, are barred by Federal Communications Commission from broadcasting some vulgar and profane curse words.

Web reporting

The Internet has been both a blessing and a bane for journalists at all levels. The proliferation of data and the facility of search engines have put a seemingly infinite amount of data at our

WORDS of WISDOM

Journalists must strive to uphold certain ethical standards. The editorial process from the assignment to the reporting and gathering of information to how the story is published must adhere to certain standards. Professor Stephen J.A. Ward, an esteemed journalism ethicist at the University of Wisconsin offers these six points:

Traditional objectivity

1 ***Factuality*** *– reports are based on accurate, comprehensive and verified facts.*

2 ***Fairness*** *– reports on controversial issues balance the main rival viewpoints, representing each viewpoint fairly.*

3 ***Non-bias*** *– prejudices, emotions, personal interests or other subjective factors do not distort the content of reports.*

4 ***Independence*** *– reports are the work of journalists who are free to report without fear or favor.*

5 ***Non-interpretation*** *– reporters do not put their interpretations or opinion into their reports.*

6 ***Neutrality and detachment*** *– reports are neutral. They do not take sides in a dispute. Reporters do not act as advocates for groups and causes.*

Prof. Stephen J.A. Ward, The Invention of Journalism Ethics – The Path to Objectivity and Beyond *(McGill-Queens University Press 2004), p. 19.*

fingertips. Telephone directories, online encyclopedias, expert listings, property records, news and government information are now only a Google search away. Email and social network websites have connected us with people around the world in real time.

The Internet is a great starting point for research and for finding sources. But journalists must be cautious about some online publications and the veracity of online contacts. For instance, interviewing a source via email or instant messaging can raise serious credibility questions. How do you know that the person writing back to you is really who he or she claims to be? An email interview should be a last resort for other reasons, too, because it deprives the reporter of an immediate opportunity to ask follow-up questions and interact with the source. Nevertheless, a verifiable email interview is better than no interview at all. But it should be noted in your copy that the source provided the comments or quotes in an email.

Veracity of data on websites is also a concern. For instance, some widely read websites such as Wikipedia may have credibility gaps because anyone can contribute or edit content. Thus, journalists should be extremely wary of quoting hard data from such sites.

Surfing websites, including social media sites, may sometimes enhance a story and play a critical role in research. But the web should not replace good old-fashioned "shoe leather" reporting – going to the scene of the event, meeting, concert, crime scene or disaster.

FIGURE 18.1 Code of ethics used by the Society of Professional Journalists (www.spj.org/ethicscode.asp).

WWW

WEBLINK Check out

http://www.ojr.org/ojr/wiki/ethics

This website includes articles and posts on ethical issues facing contemporary and digital journalists.

Code of Ethics

PREAMBLE
Members of the Society of Professional Journalists believe that public enlightenment is the forerunner of justice and the foundation of democracy. The duty of the journalist is to further those ends by seeking truth and providing a fair and comprehensive account of events and issues. Conscientious journalists from all media and specialties strive to serve the public with thoroughness and honesty. Professional integrity is the cornerstone of a journalist's credibility. Members of the Society share a dedication to ethical behavior and adopt this code to declare the Society's principles and standards of practice.

SEEK TRUTH AND REPORT IT
Journalists should be honest, fair and courageous in gathering, reporting and interpreting information.

Journalists should:

▶ Test the accuracy of information from all sources and exercise care to avoid inadvertent error. Deliberate distortion is never permissible.

▶ Diligently seek out subjects of news stories to give them the opportunity to respond to allegations of wrongdoing.

▶ Identify sources whenever feasible. The public is entitled to as much information as possible on sources' reliability.

▶ Always question sources' motives before promising anonymity. Clarify conditions attached to any promise made in exchange for information. Keep promises.

▶ Make certain that headlines, news teases and promotional material, photos, video, audio, graphics, sound bites and quotations do not misrepresent. They should not oversimplify or highlight incidents out of context.

▶ Never distort the content of news photos or video Image enhancement for technical clarity is always permissible. Label montages and photo illustrations.

▶ Avoid misleading re-enactments or staged news events. If re-enactment is necessary to tell a story, label it.

▶ Avoid undercover or other surreptitious methods of gathering information except when traditional open methods will not yield information vital to the public. Use of such methods should be explained as part of the story.

▶ Never plagiarize.

▶ Tell the story of the diversity and magnitude of the human experience boldly, even when it is unpopular to do so.

▶ Examine their own cultural values and avoid imposing those values on others.

▶ Avoid stereotyping by race, gender, age, religion, ethnicity, geography, sexual orientation, disability, physical appearance or social status.

▶ Support the open exchange of views, even views they find repugnant.

▶ Give voice to the voiceless; official and unofficial sources of information can be equally valid.

▶ Distinguish between advocacy and news reporting. Analysis and commentary should be labeled and not misrepresent fact or context.

▶ Distinguish news from advertising and shun hybrids that blur the lines between the two.

▶ Recognize a special obligation to ensure that the public's business is conducted in the open and that government records are open to inspection.

MINIMIZE HARM
Ethical journalists treat sources, subjects and colleagues as human beings deserving of respect.

Journalists should:

▶ Show compassion for those who may be affected adversely by news coverage. Use special sensitivity when dealing with children and inexperienced sources or subjects.

▶ Be sensitive when seeking or using interviews or photographs of those affected by tragedy or grief.

▶ Recognize that gathering and reporting information may cause harm or discomfort. Pursuit of the news is not a license for arrogance.

▶ Recognize that private people have a greater right to control information about themselves than do public officials and others who seek power, influence or attention. Only an overriding public need can justify intrusion into anyone's privacy.

▶ Show good taste. Avoid pandering to lurid curiosity.

▶ Be cautious about identifying juvenile suspects or victims of sex crimes.

▶ Be judicious about naming criminal suspects before the formal filing of charges.

▶ Balance a criminal suspect's fair trial rights with the public's right to be informed.

ACT INDEPENDENTLY
Journalists should be free of obligation to any interest other than the public's right to know.

Journalists should:

▶ Avoid conflicts of interest, real or perceived.

▶ Remain free of associations and activities that may compromise integrity or damage credibility.

▶ Refuse gifts, favors, fees, free travel and special treatment, and shun secondary employment, political involvement, public office and service in community organizations if they compromise journalistic integrity.

▶ Disclose unavoidable conflicts.

▶ Be vigilant and courageous about holding those with power accountable.

▶ Deny favored treatment to advertisers and special interests and resist their pressure to influence news coverage.

▶ Be wary of sources offering information for favors or money; avoid bidding for news.

BE ACCOUNTABLE
Journalists are accountable to their readers, listeners, viewers and each other.

Journalists should:

▶ Clarify and explain news coverage and invite dialogue with the public over journalistic conduct.

▶ Encourage the public to voice grievances against the news media.

▶ Admit mistakes and correct them promptly.

▶ Expose unethical practices of journalists and the news media.

▶ Abide by the same high standards to which they hold others.

The SPJ Code of Ethics is voluntarily embraced by thousands of journalists, regardless of place or platform, and is widely used in newsrooms and classrooms as a guide for ethical behavior. The code is intended not as a set of "rules" but as a resource for ethical decision-making. It is not — nor can it be under the First Amendment — legally enforceable.

The present version of the code was adopted by the 1996 SPJ National Convention, after months of study and debate among the Society's members. Sigma Delta Chi's first Code of Ethics was borrowed from the American Society of Newspaper Editors in 1926. In 1973, Sigma Delta Chi wrote its own code, which was revised in 1984, 1987 and 1996.

Web-based reporting:

- **should not** replace human sources – people interviewed face to face, often in their own offices, classrooms or homes
- **should not** be a substitute for attending actual events or public meetings, such as student government or school board meetings
- **should** supplement traditional reporting

- **should** facilitate finding multiple, diverse and appropriate experts and lay people who can add valuable information to stories
- **should** assist reporters in locating government officials and public records.

Affordable computer software has made production and reproduction of textual material as simple as a "right click" of the mouse. Technology has made reproduction of photos, music and video just as simple, and it is just as easy to copy your own original materials for personal use as it is to illegally copy or pirate the works of others. In a journalistic setting, intellectual property law may provide a viable defense for using some text and images without permission. Using copyrighted material for a feature or entertainment piece might not be legal without the owner's permission, even if you provide credit.

In online video or multimedia packages on the publication's website, using music without permission may also violate copyright laws.

The use of copyrighted material also raises ethical issues. The old adage of putting yourself in someone else's shoes is applicable here. Imagine how you might feel if an organization posted content you created and own on its website without your prior permission or compensation?

JOURNALISM CODES OF ETHICS

Many newspapers, television stations, news organizations and trade groups have codes of ethics. However, some news organizations do not have their own codes – sometimes for legal reasons, so when breaches occur, their codes cannot be used against them in court. Although codes of ethics are aspirational, non-binding and cannot cover every situation, they still provide a useful framework for journalists at all levels – from students in a middle or high school setting to a reporter at a major national or international news organization.

Some ethics codes are more explicit than others. For example, *The New York Times*'s "Policy on Ethics in Journalism" specifies that, in accordance with the paper's duty to its audience and its adherence to neutrality, sports reporters may not serve as scorers, and entertainment and travel reporters must pay their own way. Gannett's policy states that a reporter's private interests cannot interfere with the interests of the company. *The Detroit Free Press* emphasizes telling the truth, correcting mistakes, not stealing work of others and maintaining fairness in stories. *The Los Angeles Times* strives to achieve fairness, access and precision.

The Society of Professional Journalists (SPJ), one of the oldest journalism trade groups in the United States, has perhaps the "gold standard" of ethics codes. Among the code's highlights are that: journalists should seek truth and report it; minimize harm in newsgathering and dissemination; act independently; and be accountable to readers, viewers and the profession.

CONCLUSION

Journalism at all levels is rife with potential ethical concerns – from how you get the story to how you package and publish it. While some ethical decisions are fluid, others require judgments and decisions at the moment the ethical dilemma emerges, such as how you go about reporting a story. Many ethical decisions lie in a "gray" area between the firm or "black-and-white" answers of good or bad behavior. However, other ethical standards are rigid. There is no "gray" area when it comes to lying, cheating, stealing, plagiarizing and fabricating in a news setting. Ethical behavior requires the journalist to assess the situation and decide what the "right thing" or the appropriate course of action will be.

Test your knowledge

What are the six characteristics Professor Ward cites as central to objective reporting?

WWW

WEBLINKS Check out

There are a number of professional organizations and journalism trade groups that can help you sort out an appropriate course of action.

http://www.spj.org/ethicscode.asp

Society of Professional Journalists

http://www.studentpress.org/nspa/pdf/wheel_modelcodeofethics.pdf

National Scholastic Press Association Model Code of Ethics

SUMMARY

- Ethics provide a framework for behavior.

- Professional ethics, specifically journalistic ethics, fill in the gaps in the law.

- The law is what you *can* do, ethics is what you *should* do.

- There may be a host of questionable behavior – such as using confidential sources, altering quotations, using illegally-gathered materials – that may be perfectly legal, but ethically questionable.

- Journalists can seek guidance on ethical quandaries from journalism ethics codes, professional journalists, trade groups or other professionals.

KEY TERMS

anonymous source	conflict of interest	paraphrase
apology	correction	plagiarism
balance	editor's note	retraction
clarification	ethics	source
confidentiality	fabrication	

EXERCISES

1   Work with your adviser or school administrators or a professional journalism organization to create and produce "press passes" or press cards for your staff.

2   As a class, create and discuss a range of potentially sticky situations. Discuss and debate what the appropriate course of action should or could be.
To get you started, for example:

(a) Your opinion editor wants to run for Student Government.

(b) Your features editor is best friends with the director of the drama club.

(c) Your sports editor is also on the varsity soccer team.

(d) A staff writer's parent is on the board of education; your main advertiser calls your office and demands a front-page article about its business.

(e) A student was arrested, accused of committing a serious crime. Even though the police are refusing to name the student, you have confirmed the student's name. Do you publish the student's name?

(f) An anonymous source provides you with a package of confidential documents that are integral to a story you are about to publish. Do you use these materials?

3   Meet with a local media lawyer, members of journalism trade groups or press clubs and

discuss ethical quandaries and draft
your own ethics policy.

4   Fact check your last issue or an edition
of a local newspaper.

5   Role play – as a staff, create a series of
potentially sticky situations where
different people assume roles of
"stakeholders," and discuss the ethical
concerns and possible solutions.

Create your own situation, but to get
you started here are a few:

(a) Interview a grieving victim.

(b) Interview a suspected criminal.

(c) Interview an anonymous source.

(d) Engage in a discussion between an
editor and a reporter who wants to
use stolen documents for a news
story.

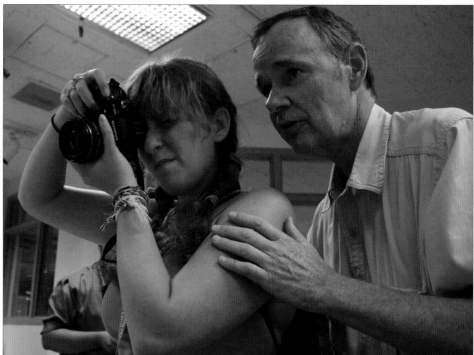

CAREERS IN THE MEDIA

19

Many people get into journalism because they love writing – but that's a mistake. Journalism isn't about writing. It's about knowing and showing. And in the last decade or so, the ways of accomplishing both have increased by leaps and bounds, which means there's a place in journalism for everyone – the writers, the photographers, the graphic designers, the journo-programmers.

In the distant past, if you wanted to give people the news, your options were limited – you could present it in print, on television or on the radio. Now you can create a blog, make an app, design an interactive graphic, in addition to the more "traditional' ways of doing things. Journalism gives you a chance to explore yourself as much as you'll explore the world around you.

Wasim Ahmad, Assistant Professor, School of Journalism, Stony Brook University

---

LEARNING OBJECTIVES After completing this chapter you will be able to:

- understand how the skills and knowledge you acquire by participating in high school journalism can be applied in your future career

- appreciate the value of media skills in college and beyond

- distinguish the varied media careers available and what it takes to succeed in each.

Scholastic Journalism, Twelfth Edition. C. Dow Tate and Sherri A. Taylor.
© 2014 John Wiley & Sons, Inc. Published 2014 by John Wiley & Sons, Inc.

STUDYING MEDIA IN HIGH SCHOOL

Few high school athletes will ever play professional sports. Few high school choir members will ever appear on stage at Carnegie Hall later in life. Few high school drama students will ever appear on Broadway stages. But student journalists not only earn money for their work in high school and in college, but can pursue many career opportunities that employ their journalism skills after high school.

Many of the skills high school journalists know and use will help them in a media landscape in which **convergence** is the future. No longer is it enough to possess skills in only one form of media. Media companies produce multimedia content that is disseminated by print, web, tablet, social media and forms that have yet to be invented. Students with broad skills across delivery platforms will be valued.

In addition to learning tangible skills that transfer directly to later life, high school journalists also develop strong skills in critical thinking, logic, organization and interviewing. "High School Journalism Matters," a research study conducted in 2008 for the Newspaper Association of America by Jack Dvorak, Ph.D., director of the High School Journalism Institute and a professor of the School of Journalism at Indiana University, affirms this. Among the study's findings:

- Students with high school journalism experience earned higher scores than non-journalism students in overall high school grade point averages, ACT composite scores, ACT English scores, college freshman English grades and college freshman grade point averages.
- Students with high school journalism experience also had higher grades in high school math, social science, science and English courses than non-journalism students.

Students who become editors and managers of their publications develop critical leadership and people-management skills that will help them throughout life. High school publications provide a strong sense of accomplishment for the individuals working on them since those publications are seen by the community at large and usually include bylines or credits for the work. Student journalists develop self-confidence through interaction with fellow staff members as well as the subjects of their stories and photographs. Meeting frequent deadlines helps student journalists with organizational skills beyond journalism.

Student journalists can win individual and staff awards for their work, can earn college scholarships and can compete for internships. Once in college, former high school journalists can use their **portfolios** of work to get paid positions on college publications or jobs as writers and photographers for college departments – even if they aren't pursuing journalism or media as a career.

The skills learned on high school publications will prove valuable in other ways. Professional design software skills will help students produce more polished presentations for class and personal work. Photographic skills will improve even family snapshots and could be useful in many careers. Advertising skills will arm students with persuasive arguments as well as sales and marketing skills. Writing skills will help students research and write coherent and well-organized papers, and quickly compose their thoughts. Design skills will prove useful for all manner of projects requiring brochures or flyers that may be needed in college or the larger community.

In addition to working for school publications, many students seize opportunities to expand their portfolios by contributing to neighborhood newsletters, youth sections in the local paper and school public relations materials. School publications staff often help produce district newsletters, design programs for theatrical productions, produce athletic programs and sell advertising to support these endeavors.

Almost all school districts have public relations and sports offices that distribute information online and in print. For instance, the athletic director's office may be in charge of publishing a program for major sports events or other sports publications. The school's public relations director may publish a newsletter for parents, or may maintain a website for the school district. These offices provide opportunities for students who might obtain internships or earn school credit. If credit isn't available, students can still gain experience and items for their portfolios.

Figure 19.1 *YO!* (youthoutlook. org) is an award-winning literary journal of youth life with participants between 14 and 25 years old. *YO!* publishes a magazine 10 times a year, with a national distribution of 25,000. It also maintains an online site. The participants also produce *YO! TV*, a monthly program and distribute news through the Pacific News Services wire. The program is funded by private grants and organizations and supported by New America Media, an organization made up of more than 2,000 ethnic news organizations.

Some professional newspapers have youth sections or pages for student writers, and have training or **internship** programs for students who are interested in journalism careers. Although few pay the student writers who become correspondents, these opportunities offer student journalists a chance to improve their skills and build their portfolios, supervised by professional journalists. Student contributions are frequently published or posted online. Students can usually find time to work for both a professional news organization and their own student publications by using good organizational skills.

In some larger cities, independent teen newspapers and online sites publish youth news through cooperative efforts of teens across the region. *YO!* (Youth Outlook), in the San Francisco Bay Area, *VOX* in Atlanta and *LA Youth* in Los Angeles are youth organizations funded privately by grants and contributions.

Teen and youth publishing provides students with opportunities to report, film and photograph significant events from a youth perspective. Youth journalism programs may even provide opportunities for student reporters and photographers to attend professional events. Another advantage of working on community publications is that they allow students to begin **networking** by interacting with professional journalists. In this way they can not only improve their skills by working with professionals, but also explore careers in media and get advice on building a career in journalism.

Small- or medium-sized community or local newspapers often hire trained student journalists as stringers, particularly in sports departments. **Stringers** are non-staff member writers or photographers who periodically contribute stories or photographs to a publication, often covering local high school news. Stringing for a professional newspaper during high school can develop relationships that lead to paid internships during college, or to permanent positions after college.

Many students choose to work for more than one student publication or website during high school to expand their skills. Writing or taking pictures for both the yearbook and the newspaper

Quick Exercise

Visit the website of *YO!*, *VOX* or *LA Youth* to view content including stories, photographs and videos. Identify stories you find interesting. Discuss with other class members how a story was covered, who was interviewed for it and how the story was presented visually. Would the story be appropriate for your staff to tackle in your publication or online site?

Test your knowledge

How can working for multiple high school and other publications better prepare you for a media career?

gives students the chance to have more of their work published and to hone their skills. Or, students may prefer to play different roles on different staffs, broadening their skills and giving them a chance to see where their true interests lie. Developing a broad range of skills will prove beneficial in college and beyond.

AFTER HIGH SCHOOL

Opportunities abound for working on college publications. Yearbooks, magazines, newspapers, online publications, administrative and departmental publications all provide students with opportunities to pursue their interests in media careers. Many college publications offer paid positions or pay by the story or photograph. Working on college publications offers opportunities to cover interesting speakers, well-known entertainers, competitive sporting events and breaking news.

Majoring in journalism or media-related studies will provide students with the training they need to prepare for professional jobs. Large colleges with communications or journalism programs may offer a range of majors within the communications field. Within these majors, career-specific concentrations may be offered. For instance, in some schools, advertising majors can choose between tracks in creative advertising or advertising management. Creative advertising prepares students for jobs as creative directors, copywriters or art directors. Advertising management prepares students for careers as account managers or media buyers. In smaller communications programs, students may need to choose between broader tracks, such as editorial and advertising/public relations.

In addition to classes in their major or career concentration, journalism students should take classes that will expand their knowledge of the field as a whole. For someone on an editorial track, this may include taking classes such as design, photography and online journalism. Media majors should also take classes in other departments to expand their general knowledge base and skill set. A minor course of study in college often helps students focus on areas that they might want to report or photograph or that complements their major interest.

In college journalism programs accredited by the Accrediting Council on Education in Journalism and Mass Communications, students are required to take no fewer than 65 hours in arts and sciences or liberal arts education. This standard ensures that students will be well-rounded in their course of study.

Working on college publications is rarely required, even when a student is majoring in communications. However, students who choose to supplement their classroom education with hands-on work for college publications will find more opportunities for summer internships and job possibilities after college. College publications also provide opportunities for gaining leadership and management experience. Membership of college press associations or student chapters of professional organizations provide opportunities for networking with media professionals, as well as the chance to win awards, scholarships, internships and name recognition. These associations also host annual national conventions that are attended by media professionals, featuring panel discussions on such topics as ethics and job hunting.

Students preparing for careers in media need good websites with portfolios of work and résumés to present to prospective employers for internships and jobs after college. The portfolio is a compilation of work published in college publications or online, as well as work from internships or other professional opportunities. Almost all media organizations offer formalized internship programs in areas ranging from advertising and editing to web journalism and photography. Competitive internship programs have early deadlines, usually near the end of the fall semester. College students often do one or more internships during college, some for college credit or for pay.

Quick Exercise

Identify a national organization for a media field in which you have an interest. Visit its website to learn about internships or other opportunities for college students. Look for job listings on the site. Find a job you would be interested in pursuing. What are the skills required for the job?

Colleges often require students to obtain junior standing in school before completing an internship for credit. This ensures the student will have taken the basic courses in their field of study so they will be prepared for the work they will be asked to do in the internship. Starting out at smaller media organizations is a good way to get an initial internship. Many students complete a second internship at medium- to large-sized media organizations.

As newsrooms continue to diversify their staff and do a better job of representing the voices of their communities, they provide many opportunities for minority students interested in media

Competitions in college media

The **College Photographer of the Year** competition is sponsored by the University of Missouri School of Journalism. The winners of the competition receive equipment, internships and prizes. (cpoy.org).

The **National Press Photographers Association** (nppa.org) offers scholarships; a quarterly clip and multimedia competition; and names a NPPA Student Photographer of the Year, who has accumulated the most competition points over the course of the year.

The **Hearst Journalism Awards** college competition is sponsored by the William Randolph Hearst Foundation (hearstfdn.org) and offers students in accredited journalism schools awards in such categories as writing, broadcasting, still photography and multimedia. Scholarships are awarded to the winners and matching grants are provided to their college communications programs.

The **Society of Professional Journalists** (spj.org) recognizes outstanding student chapters and college journalism in its annual Mark of Excellence Awards competition.

The **Association for Women in Communications** (womcom.org) presents the Clarion Awards, which includes a division of competition for college entries.

The **Society of News Design** (snd.org) gives scholarships and awards to student media designers in its annual college competition hosted by the University of Missouri. **Michigan State University's SND** chapter also sponsors an annual design contest for college students.

Advertising students can participate in several competitions, including the **American Advertising Federation's National Student Advertising Competition** (www.aaf.org) in conjunction with a national corporate sponsor. Students can also compete in the student area of the **One Show College Competition** (www.theyoungones.org/).

Public relations students can become members of the **Public Relations Student Society of America** (www. prssa.org) and win chapter awards or enter its annual Case Study competitions.

---

careers. Syracuse University, in conjunction with the Newhouse Foundation, offers a minority fellowship and apprenticeship for graduate study in newspapers; this is available to students interested in journalism careers who haven't majored in communications as undergraduates. The Dow Jones Newspaper Fund (www.newsfund.org) offers summer internship programs for students and provides links on its websites to a variety of minority-focused internships and scholarships.

Minority journalists have their own professional organizations, such as the National Association of Black Journalists (www.nabj.org), Asian American Journalism Association (www.aaja.org), National Association of Hispanic Journalists (www.nahj.org) and Native American Journalists Association (www.naja.org). Some of these organizations belong to an umbrella organization called Unity (unityjournalists.org), an alliance with a membership of more than 10,000. Unity hosts an annual national convention, among its many other initiatives.

Students can also obtain updated internship and job bank information online from professional organizations such as the Society for News Design (www.snd.org) and the National Press Photographers Association (www.nppa.org), or directly from media organizations.

Test your knowledge

Why is it important for someone aspiring to a media career to take classes in arts and sciences?

AFTER COLLEGE

Students who have had good internships and have built competitive portfolios during college will have an advantage when pursuing entry-level jobs after college graduation. Even without an undergraduate communications degree, a student with a solid liberal arts education, a competitive portfolio and internship experiences may be able to obtain a job in media. With the growth of non-traditional media forms, students with a broad range of technical skills will also have opportunities to pursue a career in media.

Advertising

Jobs in advertising range from creatives who come up with the advertising designs, art direction and copy writing concepts, to account managers, who work with client accounts. Copywriters and art directors create concepts and campaigns in a variety of print, digital and broadcast forms for advertising clients. On the management side of advertising, account managers, account

WWW

WEBLINKS Check out

http://www.journalismjobs. com/career_advice.cfm

This site includes good career advice for a wide range of media careers, provides answers to very specific concerns such as creating resumes, and answers questions about preparing portfolios.

NEWSFLASH

Getting a good internship

Students seeking career-building internships need to know how to land the dream internship. The first step is crafting a strong cover letter and strong portfolio of work for creative jobs in photography, design or advertising. Here's some advice from Chip Maury, former director of photographer at the Indianapolis Star and Providence Journal on writing a good cover letter and portfolio.

Keep the cover letter just that, a **cover** letter. Short, sweet and to the point. Do not expound on your hopes, dreams, beliefs and so on.

Your work should smack a prospective employer between the eyes so you let the portfolio speak for you.

Remember that "less is more" and build your body of work around the really great images and drop the poor or marginal work.

WWW

WEBLINKS Check out

www.aef.com/industry/ careers/career_advice/ landing

For students seeking careers in advertising, this is a great site that offers career advice, and answers most questions about the advertising industry. It also includes a link to career advice from advertising pros.

WWW

WEBLINKS Check out

www.prsa.org/jobcenter/ career_resources/career_ level/entry_level

The Public Relations Society of America offers an extensive career center with advice and resources for entry level public relations practitioners on this site.

planners and strategists, media planners and buyers work as agency specialists and liaisons with the advertising accounts. Some advertising agencies also employ people in related agency endeavors such as public relations, production and branding.

Those interested in advertising can also find opportunities within larger media organizations such as newspapers and magazines and within the parent companies of media operations. Many newspapers and magazines are owned by **media conglomerates**, companies that own a variety of media forms. Freelancers also find opportunities in advertising, working with a variety of clients on an as-needed basis.

Public relations

Public relations departments are a part of almost every corporate agency, including healthcare systems, professional sports teams and major entertainment businesses. It is the job of public relations practitioners to bring together organizations and individuals with their key audiences. Companies without internal public relations departments may hire public relations agencies, often called **full-service agencies**, for their capability to handle everything from crisis communications to public relations campaigns. The agency might work on a campaign or strategy for a short- or long-term project, or work continuously with the client's ongoing needs.

Public relations departments or agencies employ a variety of communicators to manage strategy for their clients. These include writers for press releases and campaigns, designers to create print or digital communications, web designers, social media specialists and account strategists and managers. Freelance photographers are often contracted to shoot photographs for annual reports or to produce photographs or videos for various campaigns and initiatives.

Basic photographic and video skills can be quite helpful to people working in internal public relations departments. Often, the company will not be able to hire a photographer to shoot pictures of every corporate event that the office may want to use in publicity.

News organizations

Newspapers have undergone major changes in response to the emergence of digital delivery. Jobs have been cut, printing has been scaled back and online and mobile delivery of news has become the primary focus of many publications. Many newspapers have ceased operation or merged. In response, news organizations have built paywall models offering subscriber-based access to information to help replace lost print revenue by privatizing online content. Some newspaper organizations or previously family-owned newspapers have splintered and many have been sold, some to non-traditional, private owners, many of whom have little history or experience in the news business. What does this mean to students who might like to work for news operations in coming years?

The delivery of news continues to be a vital media career. New models of delivering news and information have emerged on many fronts. *The Huffington Post* (www.huffingtonpost.com),

ProPublica (www.propublica.org), *Politico* (www.politico.com), *The Daily Beast* (www.thedailybeast.com), *Bloomberg News* (www.bloomberg.com) and other online organizations delivering niche news are among the sites competing with traditional media. Some of these sites collect information and reprint it in digest form, while others feature a combination of blog posts and original reporting. *Politico* and *The Huffington Post* have recently won Pulitzer Prizes for original reporting. Most news organizations are migrating content to mobile and tablet delivery, and will continue to evolve with changing technologies.

Traditional, legacy news organizations are trying to do more with less, but even a small staff can maintain an online presence. News websites started out as operations relying on some original reporting and some reposting of information. Regardless of their web presence, news organizations still need good writers, editors and photographers along with ad staff and research departments. Some still maintain state, national or international bureaus where small staff report from important locations such as state capital offices, the nation's Capitol or large cities around the world. However, most now rely on wire or online services for this information saving revenue by shutting down these costly operations.

Newspapers, especially small ones, need people with wide-ranging visual skills – those who can design interesting page layouts, maintain web content, create coherent and useful informational graphics and shoot compelling photographs and video, all under deadline pressure.

Presentation directors are often the managers or overseers of newspaper design departments. They work with illustrators, graphic artists, motion graphic designers and page designers to prepare each day's print, online and mobile editions and to manage the overall visual direction of the newspaper.

With newspapers becoming more invested in online and mobile news delivery, entire areas of newsrooms have expanded to provide content for the newspaper's website on a 24-hour basis. Websites may have additional staff of writers, editors, photographers, designers and producers, along with web tech staff. Individuals with multiple skills will be valuable assets to website operations. Web and mobile designers are often focused on improving user experience.

Many news organizations are members of larger media operations that provide broadcast, digital and print content to member subscribers. Gannett, which still owns more than 80 daily newspapers and provides news to more than 11.6 million readers daily, is located in McLean, Virginia. Its flagship national newspaper is *USA Today*. Gannett created a new design model for its member publications by centralizing print and web design into regional operations. Each regional operation handles the print, web and mobile design for several member publications.

Smaller, local news organizations, many of which might be family or independently owned, often hire students as writers and photographers. With limited resources, small newspapers also need writers who can occasionally take photographs or produce and edit video. Knowledge of still and video photography will prove helpful to young journalists seeking entry-level jobs in small news operations.

Students who have experience gathering and processing large amounts of data can find interesting jobs in news content operations and research libraries. With the growth in computer-assisted reporting, news organizations need people who can conduct information research and who can make sense of the information they find. They often work hand-in-hand with reporters to develop stories, and graphic designers to develop visual content. Students who have studied statistics and statistical research methods can use their skills in these jobs.

Magazines

Traditional, large circulation print magazines have experienced some of the same problems as newspapers, as their readers turn to websites and mobile devices. Shrinking circulations have caused print magazines to cut back their published editions and migrate more content online. Some magazine publishers have shut down titles or have created new online- and mobile-only magazines. Making matters more complicated, some struggling print news organizations have turned to magazine publishing – creating sports, lifestyle and other special interest magazines – to compete with traditional print magazines sold on newsstands.

Many magazines hire freelance writers with established reputations for feature-length articles, which appear in the magazine's well, its primary feature section usually in the middle of the magazine. However, magazines employ a full staff of editors, writers, designers and managers to

WWW

WEBLINKS Check out

www.gannett.com

The flagship site of one of the nation's leading media organizations provides news and information about its operation and a link to Gannett careers.

WWW

WEBLINKS Check out

www.hearst.com/magazines

The corporate website of the Hearst Corporation provides individual links to each of its magazine titles as well as information about the corporation. It also links to its other media including print and broadcast.

NEWSFLASH

Esquire magazine: experiment and innovation

Esquire magazine has established itself at the forefront of media innovation, by applying new designs and new technologies to its print edition. Using special e-ink (electronic ink), *Esquire* embedded a moving image on the cover of its limited-edition 75th anniversary issue in 2008. The covers were embedded with a special battery that enabled a panel to flash content. (*Esquire* later provided instructions on how to preserve the battery's life – which involved refrigerating the magazine.)

In February 2009, *Esquire* published a window in a flap on its cover, featuring an illustration of President Barack Obama. Readers were encouraged to "open here" to expose the content, a series of quotes from the issue's articles. Opposite the quotes, an ad for a Discovery Channel program featured a photo of an escape artist who seemed to be crammed into the small flap.

In May 2009, *Esquire* published an "origami" cover, which encouraged the reader to tear perforated cover panels. These featured the faces of President Obama, singer and actor Justin Timberlake and actor George Clooney. The flaps allowed the reader to mix parts of the three faces together.

Finally, in December 2009, *Esquire* published an "augmented reality" issue. Augmented reality is a field of computer research which deals with the combination of real world and computer-generated data. Readers were encouraged to download free software and then hold the print magazine in front of a webcam or other built-in camera. The software enabled the computer to read a certain symbol, or marker, which was similar to today's QR codes. By tilting the magazine forward in front of a computer, still content came to life in video. It included a 3-D cover featuring Robert Downey, Jr., a weather-changing fashion portfolio, a joke told by a beautiful woman, a song, a photo slideshow and an ad for Lexus. Each video feature included a code that activated the content when viewed on a computer

---

handle the day-to-day operations. Magazines may also contract or hire copy editors and fact checkers, those whose responsibility it is to check the accuracy and writing quality of the stories before they go to print.

Magazine designers are often known as art directors. They are responsible for the design of the feature-length articles, as well as the overall design, look and typography of the publication. From time to time, the publication's design might need to be updated, a process known as a **redesign**. Redesigns are often led by art directors and staff designers, although occasionally outside design consultants are hired to work with the magazine's staff. Many design consultants own their own companies and specialize in updating a publication's visual presentation.

Most magazines contract with freelance photographers to provide the primary photographs for the feature-length articles. Many times they seek photographers with expertise in specialized kinds of photography such as fashion, food and portraiture. Magazines also hire freelance illustrators to create art for articles. Visuals might also be bought from stock agencies, which buy work directly from photographers and artists and sell rights to use it.

Many large magazines are produced and published in New York City and are owned by large magazine publishing companies, such as Condé Nast. As of 2012, Condé Nast publishes 18 consumer magazines, four business-to-business magazines, 27 websites and 50 plus applications for mobile and tablet delivery. As with news organizations, magazines maintain websites where content is restricted to those who subscribe online or through a combination of print and online subscriptions. Many magazines have also developed content delivery methods for mobile devices. Magazines often offer additional digital content, sometimes linked to QR codes printed in the magazine, including video and photo galleries, infographics and motion graphics.

Magazines and their publishing companies have advertising staff, circulation staff and other departments to support their missions.

Multimedia photography

While some photographers shoot primarily in digital still format, many others have transitioned to multimedia photography by also shooting and editing video.

In addition to photojournalism, a career practiced primarily by photographers who work for news organizations and some magazines, photographers can specialize in commercial photography, which includes photographs for advertising and illustration. Photojournalists who work for news organizations shoot a variety of assignments on a daily basis. These assignments are generated by the news organization's various editors. Advertising photographers are hired by

An interview with Leslie White of *The Dallas Morning News*

Figure 19.2 Leslie White, Director of Photography, *The Dallas Morning News*. Reproduced by permission of Leslie White.

Leslie White is Director of Photography at *The Dallas Morning News*, where she has worked for 20 years.

When did you decide to pursue photography as a career?

I decided between high school and college. I was a reporter/yearbook editor in high school and found that I didn't really enjoy the written reporting duties – I was attracted to the visual aspects of journalism. Thus, a career as a photojournalist was born.

How did high school help you with your career?

It opened my eyes to the different types of specialties involved in being a newspaper journalist – photographer, reporter, editor, designer, artist. Being a high school journalist gave me the chance to "try on" the different disciplines and find the best fit. It also gave me a pretty accurate picture of what the life of a journalist would be. Choosing to be a journalist of any sort isn't just choosing a job – it's choosing a way of life.

What other jobs/internships did you have?

I did three different internships before landing my first real job as a staff photographer at The Times-Picayune *in New*

Orleans. I've also been a photo editor and a web designer at the DMN at different times in my career.

What's the best part of your job?

Knowing that I went the extra mile to make the work of the photojournalists that work with me a little easier – getting them the right equipment, time to work on a story, get the display that they need, etc. These may sound like mundane things (and as tasks go, they are), but little bits of help or encouragement can make all the difference to a photojournalist doing his or her job. Making their job easier and better is my job.

What are your job responsibilities?

As Director of Photography, I am responsible for setting the direction for the newspaper's photo report as well as the video, photography and staff-produced multimedia content on DallasNews.com, apps and digital platforms. I manage a staff of 25 individuals who edit photos and manage photographers, shoot stills and video, tone photographs, archive photographs, edit video and create rich, photo-based multimedia projects. I'm also responsible for buying photo equipment, computers and software to serve content across all platforms – often inventing technology workflows within the department to meet the needs of all platforms.

What is the importance of photojournalism as a career?

We are history's witnesses. The world sees through the eyes of photojournalists.

What do you consider your biggest accomplishment in your career?

Being on board from the beginning with all the changes to newspapers and journalists as a result of the digital age. The old ways of doing things are great when reminiscing with coworkers, but clinging to those ways going forward is bad for the journalism business. Our job is to serve and inform the readers – the platform, device or delivery system of the journalism is irrelevant. Storytelling is storytelling. Period.

---

clients who need product advertising, or by advertising agencies hired to produce ads or campaigns for clients. The creative vision and skills of advertising photographers help them secure jobs. Illustration photographers are often hired to illustrate feature-length magazine articles or special publishing projects such as books. Specialized careers in photography include those focused on weddings, portraiture, outdoor adventures, still life and art.

Many photographers prefer documentary photography, a form of visual storytelling used by magazines such as *National Geographic* and multimedia sites such as MediaStorm (www.mediastorm.com) and VII (www.viiphoto.com). Documentary photographers are concerned with in-depth or sociological photography, and their work can take them all over the world to document different cultures, conflicts, natural phenomena and current events. These photographers work primarily as freelancers, and can spend many years building their reputations before being hired by professional magazines, companies or agencies.

Freelance documentary photographers may also find work with non-governmental organizations or agencies, or advocacy networks such as Doctors Without Borders or the Nature

Conservancy. These photographers often partner with public relations writers hired to promote the organization's mission.

Photographers can seek funding for independent projects through websites such as kickstarter (www.kickstarter.com), which offers artists of all types a platform to promote their vision and generate project funding. Grants and funding are also offered by private foundations such as the Open Society Foundation, founded by George Soros (www.soros.org) and The Alexia Foundation for World Peace and Cultural Understanding (www.alexiafoundation.org). The Alexia Foundation awards competitive grants to professional and college photographers and was founded by the parents of Alexia Tsairis, a college photography student who was killed in the bombing of Pan Am Flight 103 over Lockerbie, Scotland in 1988. The National Press Photography Association (www.nppa.org) also provides grants to photographers to help fund projects.

Most publications also hire picture editors, whose responsibility is to manage photographic operations. Picture editors rarely shoot though they may have started their careers as photographers. They spend their time making assignments, editing photographers' shoots and providing advice about how the photographs should be used in print or online.

Wire services

Wire services are agencies that provide information to various news organizations from across the world. Publications pay subscriber fees to access data feeds from wire services. Set up in bureaus in worldwide locations, wire services offer stories, photographs, graphics, multimedia and broadcast material to member publications. The Associated Press (www.ap.org), Agence France-Presse (www.afp.com), Reuters (www.reuters.com) and Getty Images (www.gettyimages. com) are among the largest of the world's wire services. Specialized wire services such as SportsShooter (www.sportsshooter.com) and a variety of entertainment and other wire services also offer specialized content to their members.

Wire services hire writers, editors, photographers, graphic designers and managers in various locations to develop content and cover news and events happening in their areas. Wire services enable news organizations to close far-flung bureaus, which are often expensive to operate, while still receiving content from important global locations.

NEWSFLASH

An interview with John Moore of Getty Images

Figure 19.3 John Moore, staff photographer, Getty Images

John Moore is a senior staff photographer for Getty Images, a wire service and leading provider of digital media worldwide. In 2008 he was awarded both Magazine Photographer of the Year from Pictures of the Year International and Photographer of the Year from the National Press Photographers Association.

His exclusive photography of the assassination of Benazir Bhutto in Pakistan earned him top awards from World Press Photo and the Robert Capa Gold Medal for courage in photojournalism given by the Overseas Press Club. He was a member of the 2005 AP team which was awarded the Pulitzer Prize for Breaking News Photography for coverage of the Iraq War and for Getty Images, he was a finalist for the 2012 Pulitzer for his coverage of the Arab Spring uprisings in Egypt, Libya and Bahrain.

Where are you based?
I work as a staff photographer in the editorial photo division of Getty and I have been based in New York City since the beginning of 2012. I joined Getty in 2005, after working for 14 years for the Associated Press.

Where were you before that?

Well, I've been based a lot of places, most of them abroad. In fact, I lived outside the United States for 17 years, so here's the chronological list – Nicaragua, India, South Africa, India, Mexico, Egypt, Pakistan, then Denver, Colorado and now New York City. The longest I lived in one place was in Mexico City for five and a half years and the shortest Johannesburg, South Africa, where I was based for about 10 months. From those bases I traveled out on assignments. I think I've worked in more than 70 countries, if that seems possible, which I consider a great honor.

When did you decide to pursue photography as a career?

I took an introductory photojournalism class at Irving High School in Irving, Texas and had a pretty good idea from then on, at age 16, that I wanted to be a photojournalist. Of course I had no idea that I would spend much of my career doing international work, but I fell in love with photography immediately, and the ability to tell a story with photographs still makes this rewarding for me, even the tough stories.

Where did you go to college? What did you do in college to help you with your photography career?

I went to college at the University of Texas at Austin. I knew that UT had one of the strongest daily newspapers in the country, The Daily Texan, and I knew that's where I could get early experience to learn how to do this work. My parents helped me the best they could financially, but still, I was working full time while in school, shooting photos for the college yearbook, newspaper, the athletic department, part time for the AP, really, whoever would pay. Several semesters I dropped below full-time status in my courseload, because of my work schedule, so it took me five and a half years to finally graduate. My 11 semesters shooting at The Daily Texan was a record at the time, and I imagine it still is.

How did high school help you with your career?

My first photography course in high school got me hooked on photojournalism in general. Then working as chief photographer and photo editor for both the high school newspaper and yearbook, I learned a rather obsessive work ethic that I think has served my career well over the years.

What internships did you have?

I interned at four newspapers around the country, my first after my sophomore year of college, at the Idaho Statesman in Boise, ID, then the Sacramento Bee in California, the Pittsburgh Press in Pennsylvania and then a final internship after graduation at the Albuquerque Tribune in New Mexico. These internships really gave me the real world experience in the newspaper business to learn from some great photographers and build my portfolio, which eventually landed me my first job as an AP photographer in Nicaragua.

What are your job responsibilities at Getty Images?

My job is to cover news assignments and do feature projects which are distributed on the Getty photo wire service to our subscribers in the United States and internationally, which includes most of the major newspapers, magazines and online publications. I travel about half the time, both inside the United States and outside, and work on news assignments in New York when I am home. In the last ten years, I have covered quite a bit of conflict, from the American wars in Afghanistan and Iraq, to the Arab Spring in Libya, Bahrain and Egypt. I've also photographed disasters such as the famine in Somalia and the earthquake in Haiti. Domestically, I did a long-term project in Colorado on the American foreclosure and eviction crisis and another photo essay about illegal immigration and border security issues in Arizona.

What's the best part of your job?

I have a lot of freedom to photograph the stories that I come up with. This is rare in this business and I don't take it for granted. This profession allows me to get to know so many people I would never normally meet, and step into their lives for a brief time to tell their story. I'm always grateful that people open themselves up to me, and I do my best to photograph them with respect. The idea that I'm often a witness to history isn't bad either.

What is the importance of photojournalism as a career?

Photojournalism informs people about what's happening in the world. At its best, it can change the world, but most often than not, it simply informs, occasionally changing people's misguided opinions. But that's ok, too. The challenge now is that the profession has not kept up with the times, in terms of business models. Newspapers, which have been traditionally the biggest employers of photojournalists, have cut staff, so it's been a hard time for the profession in general.

What do you consider your biggest accomplishment in your career?

I have been doing this for more than 20 years and have been fortunate to cover many stories that have been dear to me. I don't think I can come up with a single accomplishment that was the biggest. I try to treat every story as important.

What has it been like for you to be involved in photographing some of the most turbulent worldwide situations?

Covering world conflict requires a cool head when things around you are very chaotic. I think I do a pretty good job of that. I've been in some very risky situations, and had very close calls in places like Somalia, Iraq, Israel and Pakistan and Libya. Despite the dangerous locales, I try to minimize the risk as much as I can and am fine with missing photographs for safety's sake. Still, I feel very strongly that I should cover the tough stories and am still willing to go there.

Broadcasting

Radio and TV broadcasters hire staff to write, produce, photograph, edit and anchor shows, as well as designers to produce on-air graphics. Students with good design skills and knowledge of standard software packages can transfer their skills to broadcast editing equipment to produce graphics for story content.

TV stations and networks often have dedicated digital staffs that produce content and promote special programming throughout the year. These digital efforts require writers, producers, photographers and editors. Broadcast outlets also sell advertising.

Videographers provide content for broadcast sites. Although National Public Radio (NPR) is a radio operation, its website supplements stories through the use of text, sound, pictures and video presentations.

Freelancing

Freelancers, or workers who contract independently, can work for many clients, and can be hired by different companies and organizations. Because freelancers work for themselves, they have to be good financial managers, schedulers and promoters, or they have to hire people to do these jobs for them. They can pick and choose from among the jobs they are offered. Freelancers rely on their professional reputations to get work, or they hire reps to help them get hired for various jobs.

Freelancers must maintain their own offices and equipment and are responsible for their own transportation. Since they work for themselves, they often have to set up their own retirement accounts, purchase individual health plans and pay taxes quarterly.

Freelance work for multimedia companies and web production companies is in growing demand as these forms of media skyrocket. Freelance web designers often move from finished project to new project, working for different companies for various periods of time. Or, they may own their own companies where they are hired to work on multiple projects at the same time.

Other opportunities

In addition to the growth in multimedia, web and tablet design, other career opportunities benefit from people with media experience. Book publishers, most primarily located in New York City, hire editors and designers to work in their print and e-book publishing operations.

Online media has created an entirely new area of communications growth. Companies specializing in creating and maintaining websites for corporate clients hire people with diverse media skills.

Web design companies often create websites for corporate clients and continue to maintain and periodically update them. Or, they may create the websites and turn them over to the company, often providing training for the client's staff in maintaining and updating the site using a content management system.

Web designers might also be involved in creating web advertising, either working directly with clients or through an advertising agency.

Multimedia designers work on projects such as books, magazines, catalogs and promotions. They can work for multimedia production companies, be employed by individual media companies or can work freelance for a variety of clients.

Companies that publish in print or online and through mobile devices need people who can photograph, write and design for many platforms. **E-commerce**, selling directly online, is now an accepted and growing form of doing business for many companies. Marketing for such companies may involve **email blasts** – email ad campaigns sent to large customer bases of people who seek to receive electronic contacts from the company.

Beyond the professional world, students who have journalism skills and experience may want to use their skills in a public service setting. Journalists can perform public service work that helps special interest groups, political causes or philanthropic organizations.

Quick Exercise

Choose an area of communications you would be interested in pursuing as a possible career. Find someone you admire in the field, either locally or nationally. Do an online search to learn about that person's career path, including schools attended, majors, internships and jobs.

Test your knowledge

What jobs would be suitable fits for the skills that you possess? What skills would you like to learn to become a stronger fit for your dream job?

CONCLUSION

Communications skills will be even more valuable as news delivery tools continue to evolve and change. Technological advances will continue to increase the volume of communications and create new types of communication and social media outlets. Media forms will converge and overlap. Students with broad skills and knowledge will have an advantage in the media job market.

Regardless of the format messages take, individuals with strong and diverse media skills will find they are valued in a job market where multimedia information is instantaneously reported and received.

SUMMARY

- Skills learned in high school journalism prepare students in multiple ways for studying communications in college.

- Skills learned in high school journalism such as writing, editing and photography will be useful throughout life.

- Portfolios of work from high school will help students obtain media jobs in college.

- Many college communications programs emphasize liberal arts foundations with broad course offerings that will help students develop diverse skills and knowledge.

- Strong portfolios of college work and internships will help students obtain jobs in desired careers.

KEY TERMS

convergence	internship	redesign
e-commerce	magazine well	stringers
email blasts	media conglomerates	wire service
freelancer	networking	
full-service agencies	portfolio	

EXERCISES

1 Plan a journalism career day or week for your class. Divide the class into various groups based on media forms. Have each group contact professionals or professional organizations to book speakers. Each group should plan and coordinate their speaker's visit to the class. Groups should prepare the class for the visits by providing brief biographical information about the speakers in advance. This information can be obtained from online resources or from questionnaires sent to the speakers.

Students should be encouraged to generate questions for each speaker. If possible, shoot videos of the speakers for future use.

2   Make a list of your strengths and interests with regards to journalism. Review this chapter and determine what careers and which potential employers best match your list.

3   If your local newspaper publishes a youth page or has an outreach program for school journalism programs, contact the youth page editor or program coordinator and invite them to speak to your class. Find out how students from your school can get their work published or how they can contribute to the newsgathering process. Discuss story planning and ideas. Would the editors of the publication be willing to make room on their website for school news? How does the newspaper develop story ideas? Could their process serve as a model for creating content for your newspaper or yearbook?

4   Invite back former staff members now in college during a school holiday or break to speak to the class about opportunities for getting jobs on college publications. Or, if your town has a local college, invite some of its journalists to your class. If possible, arrange a follow-up visit to the local college for a tour and to observe the newsroom in action. Arrange for students with specific interests to talk to people specifically involved in those areas.

5   Contact local not-for-profit organizations to see if they need help with publicity for a special event, a website, a photo gallery, a video, a newsletter or other outreach efforts. Organize a team of students to work on the organization's project(s).

6   If your school allows absences for job shadowing, arrange to spend a day or part of a day with someone who works professionally in media. Observe them and take notes. When you return to school, discuss what you learned from your shadowing experience.

PROFESSIONAL AND STUDENT ORGANIZATIONS

American Copy Editors Society
7 Avenida Vista Grande
Suite B7 #467
Santa Fe, NM 87508
P (800) 393-7681
E **info@copydesk.org**

American Press Institute
4401 Wilson Boulevard, Suite 900
Arlington, VA 22203
F (571) 366-1195
E **api@naa.org**

American Society of Magazine Editors
810 7th Avenue, 24th Floor
New York, NY 10019
P (212) 872-3700
F (212) 906-0128
E **asme@magazine.org**

American Society of News Editors
Reynolds Journalism Institute
Missouri School of Journalism
Suite 209
401 S. 9th St.
Columbia, MO 65201
P 573-882-9854
F 573-884-3824

Asian American Journalists Association
5 Third St., Suite 1108
San Francisco, CA 94103
P (415) 346-2051
F (415) 346-6343
E **national@aaja.org**

Associated Collegiate Press
National Scholastic Press Association
2221 University Avenue, SE, Suite 121
Minneapolis, MN 55414
P (612) 625-8335
F (612) 626-0720
E **info@studentpress.org**

Associated Press Media Editors Association
450 W. 33rd Street
New York, NY 10001
P (212) 621-1838
F (212) 506-6102
E **apme@ap.org**

Association for Education in Journalism and Mass Communication
234 Outlet Pointe Road
Columbia, SC 29210
P (803) 798-0271
F (803) 772-3509
E **aejmc@aejmc.org**

Association for Women in Communications
AWC National Headquarters
3337 Duke Street
Alexandria, VA 22314
P 703-370-7436
F 703-342-4311
E **info@womcom.org**

The Association for Women in Sports Media
161 W. Sylvania Ave.
Neptune City, NJ 07753
E **info@awsmonline.org**

College Media Advisers
David Swartzlander
CMA President
Doane College
1014 Boswell Ave.
Crete, NE 68333
P (402) 826-8269
E **david.swartzlander@doane.edu**

Columbia Scholastic Press Association
Columbia University
Mail Code 5711
New York, NY 10027-6902
P (212) 854-9400
F (212) 854-9401
E **cspa@columbia.edu**

Scholastic Journalism, Twelfth Edition. C. Dow Tate and Sherri A. Taylor.
© 2014 John Wiley & Sons, Inc. Published 2014 by John Wiley & Sons, Inc.

Dow Jones Newspaper Fund
PO Box 300
Princeton, NJ 08543-0300
P (609) 452-2820
F (609) 520-5804
E djnf@dowjones.com

The Freedom Forum First Amendment Center
1207 18th Avenue South
Nashville, TN 37212
P (615) 321-9588
F (615) 321-9599
E info@fac.org

Investigative Reporters and Editors
141 Neff Annex
Missouri School of Journalism
Columbia, MO 65211
P (573) 882-2042
E info@ire.org

Journalism Education Association
103 Kedzie Hall
Kansas State University
Manhattan, KS 66506
P (785) 532-5532
F (785) 532-5563
E jea@spub.ksu.edu

National Association of Black Journalists
1100 Knight Hall, Suite 3100
College Park, MD 20742
P (301) 405-0248
F (301) 314-1714
E nabj@nabj.org

National Association of Hispanic Journalists
1050 Connecticut Avenue NW 10th Floor
Washington, DC 20036
P (202) 662-7145
F (202) 662-7144
E nahj@nahj.org

National Association of Science Writers
P.O. Box 7905
Berkeley, CA 94707
P (510) 647-9500
E info@nasw.org

National Federation of Press Women
P.O. Box 34798
Alexandria, VA 22334-0798
P (800) 780-2715
F (703) 534-5751
E presswomen@aol.com

National Institute for Computer-Assisted Reporting
141 Neff Annex
School of Journalism
University of Missouri
Columbia, MO 65211
P (573) 882-0684
F (573) 884-5544
E info@nicar.org

National Lesbian and Gay Journalists Association
2120 L St, NW Suite 850
Washington, DC 20037
F (202) 588-1818
E info@nlgja.org

National Newspaper Association
P.O. Box 7540
Columbia, MO 65205-7540
P (573) 882-5800
F (573) 884-5490
E info@nna.org

National Press Photographers Association
3200 Croasdaile Drive, Suite 306
Durham, NC 27705
P (919) 383-7246
F (919) 383-7261
E info@nppa.org

Native American Journalists Association
University of Oklahoma
Gaylord College
395 W. Lindsey St.
Norman, OK, 73019-4201
P (405) 325-9008
F (405) 325-6945
E info@naja.com

Online News Association
P.O. Box 65741
Washington, DC 20035
P (312) 881-6477
E support@journalists.org

Poynter Institute for Media Studies
801 Third Street S.
St. Petersburg, FL 33701
P (888) 769-6837
F (727) 821-0583
E info@poynter.org

Project Censored
Media Freedom Foundation
P.O. Box 571
Cotati, CA 94931
P (707) 874-2695
E mickey@projectcensored.org

Quill and Scroll Society
University of Iowa
School of Journalism and Mass Communication
100 Adler Journalism Building
Iowa City, IA 52242
P (319) 335-3457
F (319) 335-3989
E quill-scroll@uiowa.edu

Radio and Television News Directors Association
The National Press Building
529 14th Street, NW, Suite 425
Washington, D.C. 20045
P 800-807-8632
F (202)-223-4007

PROFESSIONAL AND STUDENT ORGANIZATIONS   **487**

Society for News Design
424 E. Central Blvd. Suite 406
Orlando, FL 32801
P (407) 420-7748
F (407) 420-7697
E **snd@snd.org**

Society of Professional Journalists
3909 N. Meridian Street
Indianapolis, IN 46208
P (317) 927-8000
F (317) 920-4789
E **questions@spj.org**

Southern Interscholastic Press Association
College of Journalism and Mass Communications
University of South Carolina
Columbia, SC 29208
P (803) 777-6284
F (803) 777-4103
E **ebdickey@gwm.sc.edu**

Student Press Law Center
1101 Wilson Boulevard, Suite 1100
Arlington, VA 22209
P (703) 807-1904
E **splc@splc.org**

Tully Center for Free Speech
426A Newhouse Three
S.I. Newhouse School of Public Communications
Syracuse University
Syracuse, NY 13244
P (315) 443-3523
F (315) 443-3946
website **http://tully.syr.edu/**

GLOSSARY

Academics section the part of the yearbook covering classroom and learning activities both at school and outside of school

Actual malice a specialized legal doctrine which means libel was published either with known falsity or reckless disregard for the truth

Advance story announcement-type story for coming event

Advertising director the staff member chosen to lead the advertising program; person who collects and organizes advertising information repeats to arm and train salespeople

Advertising policy a written policy that details the publication's guidelines concerning ad sales and use in the publications

Advocacy editorial editorial that interprets, explains or persuades

Agate type the smallest point size in type a publication uses; traditionally used for sports scores and classified ads

Air white space ("fresh air") around type and illustrations

Align instruction to bring type into straight line

Alignment bringing lines of type or design elements into common starting and/or ending points

Alley see **internal margin**.

Alternative copy space use of a different form of content, often visual or presented in a different form from a traditional prose story

Ampersand symbol for *and* (&)

Anchorperson principal person in charge of newscast

Anecdote interesting short stories that help bring an experience to life

Angle point of view from which something is written

Anonymous source source whose name is changed or omitted in a story to protect the source from harm or because the story's subject is sensitive or controversial

Aperture the size of the opening on a camera lens

Apology type of correction published in cases of extreme or outrageous behavior or mistakes

Art illustration(s) to accompany stories or ads

Art head specially designed headline that may break away from consistent typefaces or styles used in the rest of the publication

Ascender stem or loop that extends above x-height of letters; includes the letters *b, d, f, h, k, l* and *t*

Assignment book (sheet) record of reporters' assignments kept by editor

Associated Press cooperative wire news service owned by its member newspapers and radio and television stations. See **wire service**.

Attribution a statement assigning the source of information in a story

Audience the people who read, view or consume the news

Auto leading computer setting that adds a percentage of the point size of the active typeface to the space between lines

Backgrounding the process of reading and doing research in preparation for asking questions and interviewing sources for a story

Balance in writing, refers to facts in stories being given proper emphasis, putting each fact into its proper relationship to every other fact and establishing its relative importance to the main idea or focus of the story; in design, refers to the weight of the page appearing even

Banner (streamer) one-line head that extends across top of page

Bar thick rule used for decoration or to reverse a line of text

Baseline the imaginary line upon which all type letters sit

Beat (run) reporter's specified area for regular news coverage; scoop or story obtained before other media can print or air it

Beat system (beats) a plan to cover routinely all potential news sources in a specific area

Big on the body typefaces with large x-height proportions to capital letters

Biweekly publication that appears once every two weeks, as distinguished from semiweekly (twice a week)

Black letter type commonly known as Old English typefaces, these types are of Germanic origin and are used primarily in newspaper nameplates or flags

Bleed illustrations and type extended beyond regular page margins to outside page edges

Blog online commentary, usually dealing with a specific area of knowledge, and appearing on a regular basis

Blur in a photograph, indicates movement by the photographer during the exposure

Body copy the text that verbally tells the story on the page

Body type type used for main text, as distinguished from headlines; generally between nine and 12 picas in height

Boldface (bf) heavier, blacker version of type style

Book in magazine terminology may mean magazine (as in "back of the book")

Border line or frame that surrounds elements in design

Bounce flash diffused flash softened by aiming the direction of the flash at a low, light ceiling or wall and allowing the flash to shower the subject with light

Breaking news coverage of an event as it is actually happening

Broadsheet full-size newspaper, often measuring 14×21 inches

Budget list of content for newshole (non-advertising space) of newspaper

Bullet visual or typographic device, usually at beginning of paragraphs or before items in list

Burning in in a traditional darkroom or through computer imaging software, adding tone to an area of a print that would print without detail

Byline author's credit printed with the story

Callout see **pull quote**.

Call to action concluding statement of an editorial that helps readers understand what action they should take on the issue

C and lc capital and lowercase letters

Canned material filler material, usually not local, used as time copy

Caps (uppercase) capital letters

Caption lines of text describing illustrations and photographs; also known as *cutline*

Caption lead-in see **catchline**.

Catchline headline for cutline or caption, usually used between photo and cutline; also known as *caption lead-in*

Centered type type set to the middle of an alignment

Center of interest a photographic compositional quality that makes it obvious why a photograph was taken

Center spread two facing pages at centerfold of publication that are designed as one page

Chronological story form a time sequence story form

Citizen journalist non-professional contributor such as a blogger or reviewer or photo contributor

Civic journalism journalism that works to stir public conversation and problem-solving by framing issues in ways to promote understanding and compromise, rather than hostility and intolerance; also known *as public journalism*

Clarification a follow-up item published after a story has been printed that offers a clearer explanation of facts

Classified advertising advertising in the section of a publication that classifies products and services under appropriate headings

Cliché overused, trite expression that weakens the overall content of a story; also refers to overused photographic content or composition

Closed-ended question question that should be avoided in interviewing because it can be answered with a "yes" or "no" response

Clubs section the section of a yearbook in which school organizations and their activities are covered

Cluster caption all the captions for a set of images grouped together in a single block

CMYK the four-process printing colors: cyan (blue), magenta (red), yellow and black

Coaching writing a discussion and working relationship between a writer and editor to improve the writing process

Coastline the shape made by drawing lines around type set in capital and lower case letter (c/lc) display to indicate the shape made by the ascender and descender letters

Collage art produced by combining multiple elements into a single composition

Color separation process of separating color originals into process printing colors for reproduction in print

Column (design) see **grid**.

Column (opinion) a type of story written to express the views of one writer, appears on editorial or opinion pages and under a title and byline; often includes photo of the author to help establish that the story represents an opinion of that person.

Column inch unit of space one inch deep and one column wide, used primarily in measuring advertising space

Column rule thin line separating columns of type

Commendation editorial an editorial that praises the actions of a person or group of people

Community feature a feature story that relates the school to parts of the community with ties to students

Comparison lead a lead that compares time, size or culture, for example. See **contrast lead**.

Compression formats electronic formatting option that makes files compact enough to open easily and quickly

Computer-assisted reporting (CAR) the process of using online database research to supplement traditional reporting methods

Condensed type narrow or slender typeface taller than its width

Confidentiality protecting the identity of a source because of real danger that serious physical, emotional or financial harm will come to the source if his or her name is revealed

Conflict a news value based on interest created from people who have differing opinions

Conflict of interest a reason to disqualify a reporter or a photographer from covering an event in which he or she has substantial personal involvement

Content banner scrolling or interactive banners of pictures, headlines and short summaries that appear on a website

Contrast the range of tones from pure white to pure black with all gray tones in between in a photograph

Contrast lead a lead that contrasts time, size or culture, for example. See **comparison lead**.

Convergence the evolution and blending of traditional media forms with emerging technology

Copy written text or story; also called body copy

Copy editing the process of tightening and improving writing, checking for accuracy and style

Copy editor person who works with the writer to correct or generally improve material intended for publication

Copyright law a legal protection for original work that prohibits its use by someone other than the creator without permission

Correction a revision published in the next edition of a publication after a story containing an error in fact has been printed

Counter the open space inside enclosed letters such as in *a, d, e, g, o, p* and *q*

Courtesy title the use of *Mr., Ms., Mrs.* or *Miss* along with the name of a person

Coverage the range of pictures and verbal stories throughout a publication

Credit line line giving source of picture or story

Crop to eliminate areas of a photograph

Cursive type resembling handwriting but with letters not connected

Cutline see **caption**.

Cutoff rule line across column separating text and advertising or between stories

Cutout background electronically cutting a photograph into the shape of its content and removing the background

Datebook a master calendar of all school activities

Dateline line at beginning of news storytelling the point of origin (date is seldom included)

Deadline time at which copy must be presented in order to be printed

Death euphemism indirect reference to death, such as "passed away" and "Death's call"

Deck a more detailed headline, smaller in size than the main headline which provides details about the story. See **secondary headline**.

Dedicated flash a flash that coordinates with an automatic or program camera to determine correct flash settings electronically

Defamation unprotected expression that is publishing a false statement of fact about someone; libel is the printed form while slander is the spoken form

Delete to remove text (letter, word, sentence, paragraph or story)

Departmentalization grouping contents of publication by subject matter

Depth of field the range of focus from the foreground to the background present in a photograph

Depth reporting see **in-depth reporting**.

Descender part of letter that descends below x-height; includes the letters *g, j, p, q* and *y*

Descriptive lead a lead that describes the story's setting or gives details leading up to the story itself; also known as *background lead*.

Designer headline headline often used for features that establishes the mood through choice of type; often created by adding graphics or manipulating type size

Detail small, specific facts that help make a larger point or impression

Dialogue the use of quotes and conversation in writing

Digest short burst of content such as news briefs or quick-read information

Digest service brief story summaries or previews accompanying headlines on a website

Digital words, pictures and graphics expressed in numerical form for use and output by computers

Direct address lead a lead that temporarily speaks directly to the reader by using the second-person pronouns *you* and *your*

Direct flash flash aimed directly at the subject from camera position

Direct quote information from sources used in quotation marks because it contains their exact words

Display advertising advertising that displays, through type and illustrations, the product or service a merchant wants to sell. See **retail ad**.

Display type type larger than body type used in headlines and ads; usually 14 point and above

Display space use of a space, often a column grid, to create a visual area for a typographic element or a picture element

Divider page in a yearbook, a page or spread that introduces a new section of the book to the reader

Dodging in a traditional darkroom or through computer imaging software, holding back light from an area of a print that would have blocked detail

Dog leg design columns of type extending down a page, in uneven vertical lengths not lining up on common type baselines

Dominant element the largest element with the most impact on a page; a minimum ratio of 2:1 should be maintained in size to command dominant reader interest

Dominant image the largest image in size on a page or spread; larger than the next largest photo, generally by a ratio of 2:1 or greater

Double spread (truck) the center spread of the publication, where the pages are actually printed on one sheet of paper; two facing pages designed as a single unit

Down style newspaper form of capitalization using minimum capital letters, primarily for the first letter and only for proper nouns following the first letter

DPI dots per inch

Drama a news value that can create interest in a story because of events that create passion or emotion

Drop cap large initial letter set in larger size than rest of text; appears at the beginning of text or at junctures throughout text

Duotone image use of a black-and-white image plus one additional color such as brown or sepia tone to make a picture suggest antiquity

DVD a high density compact disk for storage of large amounts of data, especially high resolution, audio-visual material

Echo interview an interview technique where the reporter repeats key information in his own words to the source to see if the interpretation is correct

E-commerce selling content directly online

Editorial the opinion of the newspaper as it appears on the editorial page; it appears without a byline and represents the views of the editorial board

Editorial board on a high school publication, an editorial board is usually made up of editors of the publication who meet to make decisions about the publication's editorial policies

Editorial cartoon distinctive art combined with a few words or a sentence or two that commends, criticizes, interprets, persuades or entertains as other editorial page content

Editorial lead the editorial introduction in which the writer either establishes the opinion first, directly or by giving the sense and reasoning of the overall argument, or gives background on the issue first and then transition to a statement of stance

Editorializing inserting a reporter's or editor's opinion in a news story

Editorial of criticism see **problem–solution editorial**.

Editor's note introduces a story or series or explains certain background information about the newsgathering process that readers should know

Em a unit of measuring type on the web in which the value is absolute in context to screen resolution; equal in size to a letter m in a typeface size and weight

Email blast email ads sent to databases of people who seek to receive electronic contacts from the company

Emotion a news value that adds interest to news because of passion or strong feelings

En one-half em or the width of a letter n in a typeface size and weight

Endsheet decorative and functional heavy paper that holds pages into book binding and that can be used for design elements such as yearbook themes or contents listings; end paper

Ethics codes of conduct that guide journalists in the pursuit of truth and the news-gathering process

Evergreen refers to feature news lacking a strong timeliness factor; news that could be printed today, a week from now, next issue or even later without losing importance or relevance

Expanded type typeface wider than standard type of the same design (extended)

External margin white space borders framing the page on all four sides

Eyeline an area of alignment that continues across facing pages that helps connect the pages into a single visual unit

Fabrication creating a person, a situation, a dialogue, statistics or any pivotal or incidental information and passing it as real

Factoid list or summary of facts

Fair comment a defense against libel that allows a reporter and others in journalism to express an opinion about a matter of public interest

False light invasion of privacy by showing or depicting the plaintiff in a false way that is highly offensive to a reasonable person

Fast lens a lens with a large maximum f-stop, usually in the range of f/2.8 or larger; this lens allows more light to reach sensor during exposure

Feature story story that goes beyond factual news reporting with emphasis on human interest appeal; element in story highlighted in lead; item in newspaper such as cartoon and syndicated material supplied by "feature" services

Feature fact the most important fact and the one that makes the best beginning for the lead of the story

Featurized news a news story with characteristics of a feature story

Filler item, usually short, used to fill holes around stories and ads

Filter a censorship restriction placed on Internet access

First Amendment the part of the Constitution that guarantees freedom of the press

Five-color printing requires the page to pass through an additional color press after four-color (CMYK) to apply one or more special colored inks or varnishes such as Pantone inks. See **pantone; matching system**

Fixed focal length lens a camera lens with only one focal length as opposed to a zoom, which encompasses a range of focal lengths

Flag nameplate (or logo) of newspaper. See **masthead**.

Flat single side of a printed signature containing half the pages of the signature

Flat light light shining directly on subjects from in front that tends to flatten out the dimensions and details of the subject

Flexographic press inexpensive and simple method of printing that uses rubber plates and water- or solvent-based inks in a two-roller system; usually web-fed

Flipping/flopping in photography, printing the picture opposite from its natural orientation usually so it faces into the page gutter rather than off. This process should be avoided.

Flush left or right instructions to set type even with margins, left or right

Flyer (sales) an easy to understand summary of relevant sales information

Focus graph/graf see **nut graph/graf**

Folio line type on each page giving publication name, date and page number which could include additional information such as page topic or visuals in yearbook design

Follow-up question a question in response to a source's statement to evoke more specifics or a clearer explanation

Follow-up story a story that reports on an event after it has taken place; provides important information to questions that the first story didn't answer

Font see **typeface**.

Footer bar area near the bottom of a website that often includes a privacy policy and site copyright information

Force justify an alignment pattern that causes type to spread across a line width and leave awkward white spaces between letters or words

Format size, shape and general physical characteristics of publication

Four-color process cyan, magenta, yellow plus black (CMYK), which reproduce full-color spectrum

Fourth estate term for journalism or journalists, attributed to Edmund Burke and first used in the House of Commons (the three original estates were nobles, clergy and commons)

Framing using objects in the foreground or background to provide a natural frame around subjects in photographs

Freedom of Information (FOI) laws federal and state laws that allow all citizens access to a vast array of information

Freelancer journalist or photographer who contracts independently and works for many clients, can be hired by different companies and organizations

F-stop the size of the opening on a lens that allows light to reach a camera's sensor during exposure

Full-service agencies public relations or advertising agencies that can handle multiple client needs

Future (book) editor's calendar of upcoming events

Future story information to be developed, discussed and possibly used for a story in the future

Game story a sports story in which the significant details, game summary and highlights, and player and coach analyses are presented on a timely basis

Gatekeepers of information the role journalists serve for readers in choosing to report and include information in print or online

Gathering assembling folded signatures in proper order. See **signature**.

Gaze motion a clear and logical pattern of eye movement through a design

Glyph special character sets historically accurate to the typeface; can include fractions, ligature pairs (conjoined letters such as *fi, fl, ff*), ornaments, old style figures (non-aligning numbers) and other choices

Golden mean points the intersections created when a composition is divided into the rule of thirds. See **rule of thirds**.

Graf/graph paragraph

Graphic visual design device such as line, screen or art that enhances text and overall page appearance

Gravure printing a printing method which uses a raised or sunken surface into which the image has been etched

Gray out a page appearance relying on heavy use of text lacking visual components

Grid geometric pattern that divides page into vertical and horizontal divisions and provides underlying layout/design structure; also known as *column*

Grounding anchoring visual or verbal content on the page so it isn't floating

Grounds the three dimensions present and seen through the eyes that are compressed into two dimensions in photographs

Gutter space between columns

Gutter margin the space between two facing pages

Hairline fine line stroke of type character (modern roman) or thinnest printing rule (usually 0.25) used for borders

Halftone printing plate made by exposing negative through screen converting image into dots

Hammer headline a short phrase or single-word headline with an accompanying, smaller headline underneath it

Hanging punctuation punctuation such as quote marks on the left that line up outside the alignment of the type

Hard news important factual information about current happenings

Hardware equipment that makes up computer system, as distinguished from programming for system (software)

Headbands colored strips of fabric attached to the top and bottom of book binding to finish it

Header bar landing area at top of publication's website that includes the school's name and location; often includes nameplate or logo of the print publication

Headline the largest displays of type on a page or spread that focus the reader's attention into the page content

Highlights the lightest areas of a photograph

Historical feature a feature story that brings the past to life through coverage of a timely event

Historical present use of the present tense in a headline to describe past events

Human interest news value which places emphasis (usually) on persons and seeks emotional identification with reader

Hyperlocal news news of importance to a newspaper's immediate and local audience

Illustration drawing, art, map or other form of non-photographic material used in a publication

Impact a news value based on the idea that something that affects a larger number of readers gives a story more importance

Imposition software software that places page forms in order to be printed on single sheet to form signature with numbered pages

Incitement unprotected expression defined as speech capable of inciting a riot or "imminent lawless action"

Indecency expression that is similar to obscenity but less graphic; tends to focus more on language, specifically the use of profanity and curse words

Indent setting used to indicate a paragraph's beginning

In-depth reporting single story, group of related stories or series resulting from detailed investigation of background information and multisource interviewing; also known as **long-form reporting**.

Index a complete, alphabetical listing of each person, club, event, advertiser and subject in the yearbook

Indirect flash flash used off camera and aimed off subject so shadows fall outside the subject area

Indirect quote a paraphrase of information from a source. It does not require quotation marks

Infographic/infograph short for *information graphic*; any chart, map, diagram, timeline, etc., used to analyze an object, event or place in the news

Informative feature story a feature story in which readers are given information about ordinary topics that they may deal with each day, in and outside of school

Ink jet printer printer that sprays ink to create a printed page

Inset picture or design carried within natural boundary of another reproduction

Internal margin space also known as *alley* that appears between columns of type and in the gutter

Internet system of computer networks all over the world that are linked together through telecommunications systems

Internship working relationship in which student is hired for short period of time to perform professional responsibilities for publication or other media organization

Interpretative article/feature see **news analysis**.

Interviewing asking people questions to gather information

Intrusion upon solitude invasion of privacy by intentionally intruding in someone's seclusion, solitude, private affairs or property

Invasion of privacy law legal protection of the image or likeness and information about an individual

Inverted pyramid form of news story with most important facts first and remainder in order of descending importance; form of certain headline decks

ISO International Standards Organization, an organization which provides guidelines for camera settings used to correctly expose photographs based on how much light is in a scene

Isolation elements visual or verbal elements that are separated or surrounded by white space as a way to attract the reader's eye

Italic variation of roman letters that slant to right

JPEG (jpg) a format derived from Joint Photographic Experts Group which is a standard for compression of digital images. JPEG format is a compression that loses small amounts of data with each opening

Jump coverage to continue story in another column or page

Jump headline headline for portion of story from another page

Justified type adjustment of spacing between words and word divisions so that all lines of type are of equal length and align on both the left and right sides

Kerning adjusting the space between letter pairs, primarily in display (headline) type

Keyword use of specific words in Internet searches that will yield necessary information

Kicker short line above larger headline

Kill delete (remove) paragraph story or advertisement

Label attaching an identifying phrase to a story to help focus attention on the importance of the information; i.e. special report, in-depth report, centerspread, front-page feature, special section, etc.

Ladder diagram a chart showing a page-by-page delineation of a yearbook's content

Laser printer a printer that uses a computer language to digitally render type and images on paper

Layout the process of combining elements into finished pages

lc lowercase letters

Lead (*leed*) opening words of story written to grab the reader's attention

Leading (*ledding*) spaces between lines of type

Left-aligned type starts on a common left margin but features uneven or ragged arrangement on the right

Legibility extent to which typefaces are easily read. Compare with **readability**.

Letterpress form of printing in which ink surface of type or plate is pressed on paper

Letterspacing spacing between letters of words

Libel malicious defamation of person made public by any printing, writing, sign, picture reproduction or effigy tending to provoke him or her to wrath or expose him or her to public hatred, contempt or ridicule

Ligature two or more letters cast together (e.g., *fj, ff, fi, ffi*)

Light meter a meter usually built into a camera that determines correct exposure based on available light and the ISO setting

Localizing news making important international, national or state news relevant to the immediate audience by establishing a local connection

Locator map graphic map that helps readers identify the location of a place or event mentioned in a story

Logo a visual brand or identifier

Long-form reporting single story, group of related stories or series resulting from detailed investigation of background information and multisource interviewing. See **in-depth reporting**.

LPI lines per inch

Magazine well the pages in a magazine usually in the middle that begin the feature story presentations

Market audience of publication, i.e. student readers

Market survey a poll conducted by a publication's advertising staff to determine the buying habits of its readers

Masthead identification statement of newspaper's staff members and editorial policies, usually on editorial page

Measure width of line of type or page, usually expressed in picas

Media conglomerate a large media company that owns smaller diversified media companies

Misappropriation invasion of privacy by using someone's image or likeness, without permission, for commercial gain

Miscellaneous type type that can't be simply categorized due to its unusual structure or quality. See **novelty type**.

Modified news lead a soft or indirect lead that can be more creative and less "formulaic" than traditional news leads

Modular design layout/design style that uses vertical and horizontal four-sided shapes, balanced informally, for all page elements. See **module**.

Module unit or component of page set off by box rules or white space on all sides

Mondrian page utilizing rectangles of harmonious shapes and sizes

Monopod a single leg support used for stabilizing cameras when photographing with extremely long lenses or long exposure times

Montage composite of several pictures, or parts of pictures, blended together

Morgue newspaper reference library

Mortise placing pictures so they overlap or touch

Mug shot a small identifying picture usually cropped to show only the face or head and shoulders of a writer or person identified in a story

Nameplate the name of the newspaper or publication as it appears on the front-page or cover

Narrative storytelling method of story development

Navigation content header link to other pages of a publication's website, such as news, feature, sports, entertainment, editorial or opinion, etc.

Negative negative image on transparent material used for printing positive picture

Networking interacting with journalism professionals to improve skills, explore careers and learn the paths to media jobs

New journalism writing style using fictional techniques applied to reporting

News analysis effort to explain "news behind the news." It approaches editorial form but does not involve deliberate value judgments; also known as *interpretative article*

News brief a short article that reports the basic facts of timely news stories

Newsgroup site on the Internet where persons with similar interests can gather electronically and enter messages about related topics

Newshole space left for news after ads have been positioned

News lead see **straight news lead**.

Newsmagazine a publication traditionally 8.5 × 11 inches in size

News peg that which is new, changed or different about the topic; often used following feature leads

Newsprint paper made from wood pulp and used by newspapers

News story an objective story or report emphasizing the timely impact of the story for its readers

News value a range of elements which give information important to readers including timeliness, proximity, prominence, audience impact, surprise or oddity, human interest, conflict and drama and visual impact

Novelty lead see **oddity lead**.

Novelty type typefaces whose appearance is visually augmented or quirky. The appearance may connect to the typeface's name; also known as **miscellaneous type**.

Nut, focus or wrap graph/graf summary paragraph located near the beginning of a story, usually identifies subject; also known as *wrap* or *focus graph/graf*

Obit abbreviation for *obituary*

Obituary a written notice of a person's death, usually including full name, identification, age, date of death, cause of death, biographical details, survivors, date, time and place of funeral and memorials

Objectivity goal in newswriting of converting news event into precise, unbiased description

Obscenity unprotected expression defined as content that is judged by a contemporary community to appeal to a prurient interest, depict in a patently offensive way and lack serious literary, artistic, scientific or political value

Oddity lead a creative lead that succeeds in attracting readers because it is different, often using humor, a startling statement or an allusion; also known as *novelty lead*

Offset lithography; process in which image on plane-surface plate is transferred to rubber blanket roll from which impression is made on paper

On-demand printing single or limited number of copies printed at a time as requested

Op-ed opinion-editorial; refers to page opposite editorial page, usually devoted to analyses, opinion columns, reviews and special features

Open content information available to anyone without charge

Open-ended question question preferred during an interview because it elicits detailed answer and provides information for quotes

Open meeting laws (sunshine laws) laws that require certain government agencies to open their meetings to the public

Open source content management systems website systems allowing for content changes in which the source code is developed through public collaboration and is available for use or modification as users or developers see fit

Opinion privilege defense against libel that allows journalists to express matters of pure opinion in a statement that is recognizable as the writer's opinion and not be proven true or false

Optical center point about 10 percent of page height above mathematical center, fulcrum for page balance

Orphans last lines of paragraphs that are pushed to the top of the next column of type separated from the rest of the paragraph in the previous column

Outline light light coming from behind a subject in a photograph that can provide a "halo effect"

Overline headline over illustration. See **catchline**.

Overrun copies printed in excess of distribution needs

Pace the rhythm in writing created by word choice, sentence length and construction and paragraph lengths

Packaging an arrangement of information on a page that may include visuals and alternative story forms accompanying a main story and designed as a coherent unit

Padding use of A, and, the, their in a headline

Page dummy usually scaled-down layout showing preliminary format and appearance of publication

Page proof proof of entire page for checking before printing

Pagination electronic design and eventual production of newspaper pages by newsroom editors

Pantone Matching System a patented color process allowing the selection of very specific shades and tones of color for adding colors beyond the four-process colors. See **four-color process**.

Paraphrasing see **indirect quote**.

Parody/satire defense against libel that follows the rationale under the opinion privilege that no reasonable reader could read recognizable parody or satire and expect something factual

Pasteup composite page of proofs, artwork and the like, ready to be photographed for offset reproduction

PDF portable document format, a native file format for Adobe Systems' Acrobat. In PDF format, data can be viewed independently of the original application software, hardware and operating system

Perfect bound a binding method in which strips of glue are applied along a flat gutter to hold the pages together

Photo cutout cutting a photograph into the shape of some of its content and removing the background; also known as COB, cutout background

Photoengraving process of making printing plates by action of light on film

Photojournalist reporter who covers news and features with camera

Photo poll A form of information in which quotes appear near small photos or head shots of the people who provide the quotes

Photo release form for obtaining signed approval from person appearing in commercial picture or for picture possibly not privileged as news

Phototypesetting preparing printing surface for offset reproduction by photographing letter images on film or paper, usually electronically, at great speed

Pica printer's unit of measure, six picas to one inch

Picture credit photographer's byline appearing with photograph

Picture editing the process of selecting pictures for use in a publication

Picture package a combination of two or three images from a single event or situation used with a caption to show different aspects of the event or situation

Picture sequence a series of sequential pictures of a singular subject or action

Picture story a visual narrative told primarily through pictures with a short amount of text, full captions and a complete headline

Pixel short for picture element, a pixel is a single point in a graphic image

Pixelation breaking up of a webcast image showing the pixels. Also used when printing a low resolution photo reveals the pixels

Plagiarism taking someone's words, art and other original work and passing it off as one's own

Plate piece of metal or plastic carrying printing image on its surface

Point unit of measure used principally in measuring type sizes in which 72 points equal one inch (12 points in one pica); printer's terminology for any punctuation mark

Point-and-shoot camera camera with mostly automated functions that is simple to use and produces consistent exposures

Poll respondents individuals who have been selected to participate in a survey

Poll story a story based on a survey of a specific population

Portfolio compiled work published in college publications or online, as well as work from internships or other professional opportunities

Portrait section a yearbook section featuring mug shots of individuals and school faculty and staff

PostScript computer language invented by Adobe Systems

Precise writing choosing accurate and specific language

Presentation director the designer in charge of the overall publication's design and look

Press release stories prepared by individuals and organizations seeking publicity

Primary audience the target audience, i.e. the students, staff and teachers within the school

Primary colors in light: red, green and blue

Primary headline headline that is largest in the design and often created as a visual design unit

Primary source an eyewitness to an event or the creator of an original work – physical or intellectual property

Print a photograph

Printer spread an arrangement of pages as they will be printed in a flat or signature

Prior restraint/review reference by court of law prohibiting any future news or comment on case

Privilege a second defense against libel that allows reporters to publish fair and accurate accounts of official proceedings, such as school board meetings and court proceedings, and reports, such as court records, without being overly concerned about libel

Problem–solution editorial an editorial used when the publication's staff wants to call attention to a problem or wants to criticize someone's actions; also known as *editorial of criticism*

Process colors the four ink colors needed to reproduce color in a publication: cyan (process blue), magenta (process red), yellow and black

Profile/profile box a type of feature story in which the writer captures a central focus of someone's life that others might find interesting or entertaining

Progressive margins margins that are most narrow at the gutter and increase in size at the top, sides and bottom of the page

Prominence a news value in which a person's position or job creates interest in news that pertains to that person

Proofreading the process of checking for accuracy and necessary corrections in finished copy or pages before they are printed

Proportion a design principle using size to create contrast and attention for content

Provable truth the best and only absolute defense against libel

Proximity a news value indicating importance of information when it occurs near and affects people in a particular location

Publication of private or embarrassing facts invasion of privacy by publicly disclosing a private fact that would be offensive, outrageous or objectionable to a reasonable person and lacks legitimate public concern

Public official/public figure rule a defense against libel that allows reporters to publish stories about public officials or public figures in which actual malice would have to be proven by the persons bringing legal action against the reporters. See **actual malice**.

Pull quote quote or short amount of text taken from the body of a story and reinserted, often in a contrasting way, to break large areas of text or to simply highlight it; also known as *callout*

Put to bed completing work of putting paper on (bed of) press for printing

Pyramid ad arrangement on page, with wider ads at bottom and with peak of pyramid usually on the right

Q and A copy that features questions and answers in a dialogue format

Question lead a lead that asks a question, often hypothetically

Quick response code (QR code) a printed symbol that can be read by software on a smartphone that connects to and opens content on a website

Rail Narrow column of white space that provides additional visual separation for primary packages

Rate card (schedule) list of prices for ads of various sizes and length of run in a newspaper used as an aid by an ad salesperson

Readability quality of type that determines ease with which it can be read in quantity; how well written something is, how easily read. Compare with **legibility**.

Reader advocate a neutral party who investigates reader complaints and issues brief reports that will be published in a subsequent edition of the publication

Readership measure of number of readers attracted to story or publication

Reader spreads the natural flow of pages in a publication as viewed by a reader

Redesign process of updating a publication's design and typography

Refer cover or front-page teaser that refers readers to inside content

Retail ad an ad for a specific business. See **display ad**.

Retraction printed statement withdrawing content or correcting error made in earlier story (in libel case can help establish absence of malice)

Reverse type that prints white with background in black

Reviews student critiques of entertainment in which writers offer their opinions about events that have already occurred or about new releases or issues

Review writing a type of story in which the writer evaluates a product for an audience

Revise second proof of galley in which errors made in first proof have been corrected

RGB mode red/green/blue; the way in which color appears on computers, mobile devices and televisions

Rhythm in design, refers to the visual flow of a page; often used in writing terms to refer to pace

Right-aligned type with a common right arrangement, but a ragged left alignment

Rivers of white space holes of white space appearing between words or letters in text in poorly typeset copy; a problem often caused by bad hyphenation or justified text without hyphenation allowed

Rising caps oversized letters that sit on the first baseline of text and rise into white space above the text

Robot used by a search engine to locate websites on the Internet that fit a specific criteria and are then added to the search engine site database or list. See **search engine**.

Rollover a web connection or link that changes color or typeface when the mouse is positioned over it

Roman type style of book-weight upright letters characterized by serifs. Compare with **italic**.

Rule of thirds a photographic compositional framing technique in which the photographer divides the viewfinder into thirds both vertically and horizontally and places the subject along the intersection of the thirds points

Running quote multiple paragraphs of quoted material in succession with closing quotation marks omitted until the end of the quote

Run of the press (ROP) color printing using whatever color the printer happens to have on the press, providing a less expensive color use

Saddle-stitching a binding method in which staples are applied through the gutter of the publication

Sales aid summarized information on the market readership; can include a rate card, a flyer and sales charts or graphs

Sales call a meeting between the publication's ad salesperson and a potential advertiser

Sales graphs and charts presentations about the publication, its market or advertisers to aid in ad sales calls

Sampling error degree of confidence in the accuracy of the poll; defines the difference between those actually interviewed and the opinions of the entire group

Sans serif type style without serifs

Scale in design, the use of grids or columns that guide the designer in placing text and visuals

Scanner input device for a computer that turns pictures and art into digitized images for editing and pagination on the computer

Scoop (beat) important story released in advance of other media coverage

Scoreboard a complete listing of a team's season including the opponents and outcomes of the games or competitions

Screen pattern available on software or as an acetate transfer sheet that is used as background or is placed over type or another page element; glass plate or film with etched crosslines placed between negative and plate when making halftone; number indicating number of lines per inch in halftone (e.g., 65-line screen, 150-line screen)

Screened color a percentage of color ranging between 10 and 100 percent used to lighten or darken the color

Script typeface that resembles handwriting. See **cursive**.

Search engine used on the Internet to find information electronically through keywords

Secondary audience the untargeted audience, often a wide network of interested readers from surrounding communities, interested alumni, other school journalists and friends and relatives of the school community

Secondary headline a headline unit in a smaller type size than the main headline that provides details and amplifies the main headline for the reader. Also known as *deck*

Secondary source a person with some knowledge of information but not from personal involvement; a published work that cites the words of others, work that has already been published in a primary source

Section template a style sheet for the design of an individual section of a publication; can include a basic column structure, a headline style, an alternative copy style and a format for the layout

Series reporting stories broken into parts and presented over the course of several issues

Serif type with small finishing strokes at the ends of main strokes of letters

Set solid body text set with leading equal to the point size of the type; can result in letters touching

Shadows the darkest areas of a photograph

Shallow depth of field a photographic technique that allows one area of a photograph to be in focus while other areas are not, bringing the viewer's eye to the content

Sheet-fed press a press that prints a single sheet of paper at a time

Shopper publication with newspaper format devoted to advertising with very little news

Sidebar a companion story to a main story; usually provides specific information about a narrowly defined topic related to the main story and is placed in a layout adjacent to the main story

Side caps large, display initial letters that appear in narrow margins to the left of the beginning of the text

Side light light that illuminates the subject from the side and provides good texture and form

Side-stitching a method of binding in which staples are placed in the sides of the pages, but not in the gutter of the publication

Signature large sheet of paper printed with (usually) four, eight or 16 pages on either side and folded to form one unit of a book or other publication

Single-use camera inexpensive camera with fully automated operation that is recycled by manufacturer after development

Slab serif types see **square serif types**.

Slander malicious defamation of person made public through speech

Small cap a letter set to the posture of an uppercase letter, but to the height of a lowercase letter

Smythe-sewing a book-binding method in which signatures of pages are connected by a heavy thread sewn across the forms and then glued to a gauze strip

Soft news news in which the primary importance is entertainment, although it may also inform, and is often less timely than hard news

Source information obtained from an interview with a person

Special edition an irregular section or edition of a newspaper published because of some important event or news coverage

Special section a published report of from one to several pages usually reserved for late-breaking news or special kinds of content

Speech story story written when someone knowledgeable speaks to a group about a timely and relevant issue

Sports feature story focused on what lies behind or beyond the game, often the human interest angle or something unusual or surprising

Sports news story a type of story used to keep the reader informed on the latest issues tied to the sport but often beyond the field or arena

Sports section the section of a yearbook in which organized or individual in-school and out-of-school athletic events are covered

Spot short commercial or public service announcement over radio or television

Spot color the use of a single color in addition to black on a printed page

Spot news timely, important news

Spread two facing pages often designed as one visual unit

Spread unity elements that visually connect two facing pages

Spring supplement a printed addition to the yearbook that covers events and activities that occurred between the last printing deadline and the end of the year

Square serif types typefaces with wide, blocky serifs attached to the stems of letters. See **slab serif types**.

Stand-alone photograph a photograph that appears with caption information, but not necessarily with a story

Standard lens a lens in the 50 mm range that reproduces a subject exactly as seen through the camera

Standing head head that appears consistently in publications issue to issue, and identifies content such as briefs and columns

Straight news lead a lead written to give the reader the most important information in the story; answers the most important 5 W's and H within the first sentence then answers the remaining questions as soon as possible.

Stringer person who works casually or freelances for publications rather than working as a paid staff member

Student life section often the first main section of the yearbook following the opening section. Provides coverage of social activities and discussion of issues of concern to teenagers

Style manual a list of writing conventions including abbreviations, punctuation and word selection that guides writers and maintains consistency in writing style throughout the publication

Style sheet definition of type styles set for various information in a publication and applied consistently to type through a computer layout and design software program

Sub-navigation link organized under major navigation links, including related links to additional information or areas of the site such as blogs or columns

Subscription database an information source providing data for a price

Summary lead hard news lead that gets readers immediately to the main point of an article. See **straight new lead**.

Surprise or oddity news value based on the idea that unusual, odd or mysterious content can result in intrigue and add interest to a story

Symposium interview a feature story in which panels of students discuss timely topics of interest to readers

Synchro-sun flash flash used as a fill light to balance shadows cast by natural light outdoors

Syndicate company that provides nonlocal feature material

Tabloid newspaper format that is about 11 × 17 inches

Tear sheet sample of newspaper page, proof of publication to an advertiser

Teaser graphic that often appears above the paper's nameplate on page 1 that promotes inside stories. Usually it is made up of a headline that teases the reader and some simple art or a photo.

Teaser headline A headline that is a play on words to pull the reader in by arousing curiosity or providing entertainment

Teen section special interest newspaper section targeted toward student readers, often with contributions from student reporters and photographers

Telephoto lens a camera lens that brings content distant from the photographer into the camera's range of view

Teller headline straightforward headline that gains the reader's attention by summarizing the story clearly and concisely; often used on websites

Template a skeletal page structure stored electronically in a page layout program allowing the designer to structure the page; can include type style sheets

Text head short, summary headline of from two to five words dropped into natural junctures in longer stories to help break up the text

Theme a visual or verbal unifier that creates continuity throughout a yearbook

Theme copy copy that introduces the yearbook theme and its relevance to the school year; also unifies the different sections to the theme

Theme development the development of specific pages of the yearbook in which a word and/or visual theme appears in some repetitive form to link the designs

Third-party source information used from a printed or published article attributed to the original source by lifting the information from the original source

Thirty (30 dash) symbol for end of story or almost anything else in journalism, including reference to journalists' obituaries

Thumbnail miniature rough sketch of layout

Timeliness a news value in which information is important due to its current occurrence

Time sequence a chronological story form

Tint block background of color for type or picture

Tombstoning use of similar headlines side by side

Tracking uniform kerning in a range of text

Transcribe to write down word for word what a person said in a taped conversation, interview or speech

Transition word or phrase that ties together paragraphs and develops story continuity

Transpose (tr) to exchange the position of two letters, words or lines

Trend sports story a sports story in which the writer covers a highlighted trend of a team since the time of the last publication

Trim to shorten copy considerably by deleting unnecessary words

Tripod headline a headline combining a large word or phrase followed by a two-line headline set in type half its size; both lines of the second part equal the height of the larger, opening words

Typeface a range of type used for all the characters in one size and weight; also known as **font**

Type family a range of text in weights and postures for a particular typeface

Type wrap type that contours to the shape of a picture; also known as **type runaround**

Typo typographical error

Unity in design, refers to a sense of continuity in use of type and column grids throughout a publication for consistency

Up style copy for heads and body type set with maximum possible capitals

Viewfinder the window that enables the photographer to see the content as it is being photographed

Vignette cut in which background screen gradually fades away

Vignette lead an anecdotal lead that describes a personal example of the issue at hand

Visual continuity design factors that keep a section of a publication coherent and unified

Visual entry points a series of visual devices used by readers to enter content or pages

Visual hierarchy an organized method of displaying information on a page, allowing a reader to understand the importance of the information by the size and weight of its headline(s) and its placement on the page

Visual impact a photograph's power to stop viewers and engage them in its content

Visual redundancy weak picture editing in which two pictures provide the reader with the same or similar content or meaning

Visual-verbal separator use of a column as an isolation element

Voice tone and feel of writing, derivative of the writer's combination of pace, word choice and use of examples, dialogue and details

Washed out a photographic print in which no pure black areas have been produced or in which tones reproduce without contrast

Web as in World Wide Web or the Internet

Webcasting broadcasting by streaming live viewing of games through their publication website

Web editor, manager the editor of an online publication

White space the area of a page not filled with content; needed for balance in page design

Wide-angle lens a camera lens in the range of 35 mm to 24 mm that gives a wider angle of view of a subject

Widow last lines of type in paragraphs that end in less than half a line of type's width

Wire service agency that provides information to member publications from across the world

Wordprocessing computerized method of typing and editing

Word theme yearbook theme or unifier that is verbal and chosen because it is tied to specific events or issues related to the school community or to teenagers in general

Wrap to continue type from one column to the next, as in "wrap around pix"

Wrap graph/graf see **nut graf/graph**

5 W's and H the what, who, where, when, why and how information that forms the basis for all stories

X-height height of lowercase letters in proportion to the capital letters

Yearbook theme the unifying concept for the book

Zoom lens a camera lens that allows a photographer to use the lens between a minimum and maximum focal length range built into the lens

Z pattern the pattern a reader's eyes follow as they move through a page entering at the top left, moving across, diagonally down to the left and exiting at the bottom right of the page

INDEX

Page numbers in *italics* refer to illustrations.

A-Blast, The 8, *282*, *295*, 356, *353*, *359*
abbreviations 228–229
  in headlines 254, 255
Abstract, The 277
academic section, yearbooks 85
academic writing 85–86
accuracy
  checking facts 456–457
  in-depth reporting 211
  names 227
  in newswriting 65
Adobe
  InDesign 328
  Photoshop/Photoshop Elements 374, 389,
    390, 391, 394
  PostScript 281, 286
  typefaces 281
advance stories
  news 12
  sports 143–144
advance story 12
advertisements
  color 317
  copy 417
  creating 414–421
  defining the message 414–416
  design 414–415, *416*, 418–421
  newsmagazine 311
  newspaper 316
  yearbook 336
advertising 405–424
  careers 474, 475–476
  classified 419
  display 419
  functions 406
  policy 409–411
  programs 406–414
advertising sales
  calls 411–413, *413*
  preparation 406–409
  telephone calls 414
advertising salespeople
  business knowledge 411
  materials needed 406–409, *408*
  preparation 411
  publication knowledge 411
agate type 156, 265
Agence France-Presse 480
Alexia Foundation for World
    Peace and Cultural
    Understanding 480

alignment
  baseline 276, 280
  type 265, 272–273, 319
almanac 219
alternative copy 101–106
alumni, identifiers 226
American Advertising Federation's
    National Student Advertising
    Competition 475
American Copy Editors Society 485
American Press Institute 485
American Society of Magazine Editors 485
American Society of News Editors 350, 485
anecdotes 36, 124–125, 127
angle, news 15
anonymous sources 209–210, 458, 459
aperture, camera 376
apology 457
apostrophes 231
appearance, describing 235
Apple Leaf, The 68, *70*
art directors, magazine 478
art heads 278
artwork 396–399
ascenders 265
Asian American Journalists
    Association 237, 475, 485
Associated Collegiate Press 485
Associated Press (AP) 480
  style manual 219, 226, 229, 232
Associated Press Media Editors
    Association 485
Association for Education in
    Journalism and Mass
    Communication 485
Association for Women in
    Communications 475, 485
Association for Women in Sports
    Media 485
athletics
  in-depth reporting 193
  see also sports; sportswriting
attribution 17
  interviews and 34
  in news writing 75, 76
audience
  impact 9–10
  importance 11
  primary 11
  secondary 11
Audiobook 45

back issues 47, 219
backgrounding 30
balance
  in design 299
  in writing 456, 457
baselines 265
  alignment 276, 280
beat reporting 12–15
Bethel School District v. Fraser
    (1986) 437, 438, 439
bias 454
Bill of Rights 430
binding 283–284
biographical dictionary 219
Black and White 54
black letter typefaces 271, *272*
Blair, Jayson 462
bleeding copy 328
bleeds 325, *332*, 333
blogs 46, 176
Bloomberg News 477
Blue & Gold 264, *399*
  design *300*, *311*
  news leads *59*
  photography *381*, *382*
body copy 325
body text 265, 280
book printing and binding 283–284
book publishers 482
Boston Globe, The 279
boxes 276, *300*, 301, 306, *307*,
    316, 317
broadcasting
  careers 482
  online 354
broadsheets 292, *295*
  grids and columns 301
Broadview, The 200
bubbles, conversation 172
bullets 265
business cards, advertising
    staff *409*
business records 46
business reporters 460
businesses, local 412
  advertising sales 411–413
  knowledge about 411
bylines 167

C/lc 266
callouts 398

cameras
  digital 374, 384–387
  point-and-shoot 387
Campanile, The 95–96
capitalization 227–228
  of headlines 254
captions 387–389
  design 316, 319
  lead-ins 333, *336*
  with picture packages 398
  typefaces 280
  yearbooks 325, 333, *333*, 387
careers, media 471–484
cartoons 374, 396
  editorial 172–175, *175*, *313*, 316
catchlines 380, *381*, *382*, 387–378
catchphrases 327
  see also themes, yearbook
censorship
  law 428, 430, 436–437, 439–440
  news 23
Center for Integration and Improvement 237
center of interest, photos 375
center spreads *see* double trucks
Central Times 318
Charger, The 15, 16
Chicago Tribune 279
Chronicle, The 93, *93*, *94*, *146*, *173*, *174*,
    195, *309*
citizen journalists 354
civic journalism 97–99
clarifications, publishing 458
Clarion Online 252
clarity 218, 220
clichés 34, 59
  in editorials 176
  in sportswriting 140, 142
  visual 394
clips, video 363
  audio 363
clubs and organizations
  in-depth reporting 194–195
  yearbook page design 330, 335, *336*
coaching writing 216–218, 237
coastline 266
code of ethics
  journalism 463, 466, 467
  National Press Photographers
      Association 395–396
collages 393–394, 396
College Media Advisors 485
College Photographer of the Year 465
college publications 473–474
colons 230
color
  in newspaper design 317
  printing 285, 286
  run of the press (ROP) 317
  typefaces 273, 274
  websites 361–362
  in yearbook design *333*, 343
Columbia Missourian 142
Columbia Scholastic Press Association 485
columns
  newspaper design 299, 302–306
  opinion *see* opinion columns

width 302, 319
  yearbook design 326, 327–331, *328*
commas 230, 255
commentary *see* opinion
community
  businesses *see* businesses, local
  feature stories 131
  in-depth reporting 193
competitions in college media 475
computer-assisted reporting 348
computer-related terms 232
computers
  calibration 283
  headline writing 247
  photo alteration 396
conciseness 218, 220
Condé Nast 478
confidentiality 459
conflict stories 10
conflicts of interest 460
continuity, design 327
contrast
  in photos 374
  type *270*, 274–277, *277*
controversial topics 192, 209, 453
convergence 472
Cooke, Janet 462
cooperative efforts 203, 368
copy
  advertisement 417
  alternative 101–106
  bleeding 328
  body 325
copy editing 215–243
  clarity and conciseness 218, 220
  coaching writing 216–218
  details 220–222
  fact checks 218–220
  resources 219
  symbols *224*
copy editor 216
  skills 233
copyright 429, 432, 467
corrections, publishing 457
counter 266
court records 46
court system 428–430
cover, newsmagazines *293*
creative writing, student 85, 358
crime news 460–461
crime reports 46
crime victims 461
critical analysis 237
cropping photographs 310, 315,
    316, 389
Crusader 383
curriculum coverage 193–194
  see also academic writing
cursive typefaces 269–271, *270*
cutlines 325, 387–389
cutout photos 336, 391
cyberbullying 68–69

Daily Beast, The 477
Dallas Morning News, The 254, 255–256, 479
Dart, The

profile story *126*
  sports packaged coverage *155*
dash 232
dates, format 229
deadline 40
Dean v. Utica Community Schools
    (2004) 442–443
death coverage 87, 88–90
Decamhian, The 330, *377*
deck 250
defamation 431–436
Deka 324
depth of field 376
descenders 266
design
  abuse of images 391–394
  advertisements 414–415, *416*
  careers 477
  double trucks/center spreads 316
  editorial pages 312–316
  elements of 292–301
  feature pages 311–312
  front-page 310, *311*
  inside pages 310–311
  modular *see* modular design
  multimedia 482
  newspaper 291–321
  pacing 317–319
  packaged sports coverage 154, *155*
  picture use 316–317
  points to remember 319
  preparation for 306–310
  principles 299–301
  sports pages 316
  typography 263–289
  using color 317
  web site 361–362
  yearbook 323–345
Desilets v. Clearview Regional
    Board of Education (1994) 445
desktop-publishing software
  production 281
  style sheets 278
  typography 272, 273, 274, 276
  yearbook design 328
DeSoto Eagle Eye 114
Details 362
details
  copy editing 220–222
  in feature stories 117–118
Detroit Free Press, The 467
Devil's Advocate The 195, *272*
dialect 126
dialogue 118
  see also quotes
dictionaries 219, 256
DIGG 352
digital cameras 374, 384–387
digital photographs 334
  altered 396
  editing/cropping 389, 391
  filing systems 375–376, 391
  in newspaper layout 308
directories
  online 46
  school 219

discussion forums, online 353
display space 328
display type 266
disruption of school activities 436, 437, 438, 441
divider pages 325
Doctors Without Borders 479
documentary photography 479–480
dog leg design 306
dominant images 325, 332, 384, 389–396, 461
dot matrix printers 281
double trucks 284
  design and layout 316
  in-depth articles 192, 200
  typefaces *273*
Dow Jones Newspaper Fund 475, 486
down style 254, 266
Drake University ad *416*, 417
drama 10
Draudt v. Wooster City School District (2003) 445–447
drop caps 266, 292, 325
duotoning images 394
DVDs 341–342

e-commerce 482
Eagle Edition 176, 205
Echo 392
Echoes 91
Edge, The 277, 279, 307, 357
editing
  ethical aspects 457
  photo 332, 389–396
  see also copy editing
Edition 250
editorial board 167, 172
editorial cartoons 172–175, *175, 312*, 315, 316
editorial lead 169, 170–172
editorializing 72
editorials 167–168
  argument development 172
  idea development 168
  page design 312–316
  role of 168–169
  writing 169–170
Editor's note 458
El Estoque 87, 88, 147, *196*
email 48
  blasts 482
  interviews by 33
emotion
  in photos 380
  in writing 6, 10, 118
emphasis
  italics for 232
  words, headlines 274
entertainment reporters 460
entry points, visual *see* visual entry points
errors *see* mistakes
Esquire magazine 478
ethics
  interview 454–455
  in journalism 451–469
  lapses in 461–467
  media 453–458

personal 452, 454
  in photography 395–396, 461
  post-publication 457–458
  professional 453, 454
  publishing 456–457
  see also code of ethics
ethnic language 236–237
ethnic minority groups *see* minority groups
euphemisms 87
examples, in feature writing 118
executive sessions 433
expert sources 46
extracurricular areas, in-depth reporting 194–195
eye contact 33
"eyeflow" 333

f-stops 376
fabrication 462–463
Facebook 45, 46, 352, 360
factoids 398
facts
  accuracy 44–45, 456–457
  checking 40, 42, 44, 218–220
  feature 54
  opinion vs. 169
faculty members, identifiers 226
fair comment, defense against libel 432–433
fair use, copyrighted material 441
fairness, in newswriting 457
Falcon, The 352
Falconer 10, *73*
Family Educational Rights and Privacy Act (FERPA) (Buckley Amendment) 436
Feather, The 357
Featherduster 267, 315, 388
feature fact 54
feature stories 111–137
  community 131
  deaths 87, 88–90
  elements 116–124
  examples 113
  headlines 255–258
  historical 131
  human interest 126–130
  idea 112
  informative 130–131
  interpretative 131
  page design 311–312
  profiles 124–126
  sports 151–152, *153*
  symposium interview 131
  types 124–126
  writing process 113–116
featurized news 15
federal court system 428, 430
FHN Today 207
film clips, online 354
firsthand reporting 116
first-person pronouns 175
fisheye lenses 384
"five W's and H" *see* reader questions
five-color printing 285
flash photography 384, 386–387
flexographic printing 283
Flickr 352

flipping/flopping, photos 333, 394
focus graphs (paragraphs) *see* nut graphs
focus paragraph 115
folios
  newspapers 280, 310
  yearbooks 326, 327
follow-up question 35, *36*, 40
fonts *see* typefaces
Foothill Dragon Press *134*
four-color printing 285, *285*
  newspapers 317
  yearbooks *342*
Fourth Estate 428
framing, photo 376, *376*
Freedom Forum First Amendment Center 486
freedom of information 47, 433
Freedom of Information Act 458
freelancing 482
front-page
  design 310, *311*
  starting in-depth reports on 198
full-page coverage, in-depth reports 198–200
full-service agencies 476
future story 12

game stories, sports 142, 146–149, *148*
gaze motion 417
gender-neutral terms 234
Getty Images 480
gifts, accepting 460
Globe, 190, 193, *372*
glossary 488–497
glyph 266
golden mean points 375
Google 44, 46, 47
Google Drive *223*
government meetings/records 433
grammar handbook 219
graphics 374, 400–401
  in-depth reports 200
  information *see* information graphics
  yearbook design 335
  yearbooks 326
  see also illustrations; visuals
gravure printing 285
"gray out" 292, 316
grids
  editorial pages 312
  narrow 302, *309*, 328, *329*
  newspaper design 299, 302, *307*, 308, 310, 312
  yearbook design 326, 327–328, *328*
grounds, photos 376
group photographs 380–381
  captions 388
  yearbook design 335, *336*
groups, identification 464
Guidestar 47
gutter 283
  double trucks 316
  margins 284, 326
  type spanning across 333–334

halo effect 378
hanging punctuation 266

Harbinger, The 7, 11, 69, 115, 130, *185, 251, 298–299, 357, 378, 383, 419*
Harper's Index/Q & A 398
Hauberk 328
Hawk, The 270
Hawk Eye, The 38
Hazelwood School District v. Kuhlmeier (1988) 437, 439–442, 443, 444, 445, 447, 464
headlines 245–61
  advertisement 417
  appearance 248–250
  construction rules 253–255
  designer 246, 250
  feature 255–258
  fitting into page 246–247
  four-line 249, *249*
  graphics 400–401
  importance 246
  jump 250, *250*
  news website 248
  newspaper design 292, 302, 306, 319
  one-line 248, *248*
  special stylized (art heads) 278
  teaser 246, 247
  teller 246, 250, 252
  three-line 249, *249*
  two-line 249, *249*
  typefaces 264, *267, 268, 270,* 270–274
  yearbook design 327, 333–334
Health Insurance
health writing 82–85
Hearst Journalism Awards 475
Helvetica 268
Hey Whipple, Squeeze This: A Guide to Creating Great Ads (Sullivan) 414–415
high school, studying media in 472–474
Highlander 336
HiLite 64, 210, 297, 351, 366, 400, 409
Hillcrest Hurricane 423
historical features 131
Hornet, The 377
Huffington Post, The 476–477
human interest
  feature stories 126–130
  news stories 10, 126–130
hyperlocal news 4
hyphens 231–232

I voice 175
identifiers 226–227
illustrations 374, 396–399
  in advertisements 417
  photo 396
  text wraps (runarounds) 276, *279*
illustrators
  information packaging 301
  magazine 478
images *see* visuals
immediacy, of news 12
impact
  audience 9–10
  news 9–10

photos 380
  visual 10
importance, of news 4
imposition software 283
in-depth reporting 189–213
  checking for accuracy 211
  design 201–204
  getting started 198–204
  news story 64
  topics 192–197
  writing the story 204–211
  in yearbooks 189, 203
incitement 436
InCopy 225
indecency 435–6
indexes, yearbook 337–340
Indian, The 204, 251, 325, 375
informants *see* sources
information
  freedom of 433
  layering 211
  packaging 301, 319
  stolen 464
information graphics (infographics) 374, 398, 400
information resources 219
  Internet 44–47, 348
  see also sources
informative feature stories 130–131
ink jet printers 281
inserts, yearbook 340–341
inside pages, design 310–311
interactive coverage, yearbooks 341–342
Internet
  law and 432
  polls 45
  research 44–45
  search tips 46–47
  see also websites
internship programs 473, 475, 476
interpretative features 131
interviews 30–40
  checklist 33
  conducting 33–40
  email 33
  ethics 454–455
  for health writing 83, 84
  organization 32
  phone 33, 454
  Q & A format 103
  setting up 32–33
  at work 38–39
invasion of privilege 436
inverted pyramid form 54–55, *55, 56,* 69
Investigative Reporters and Editors 486
isolation elements 400, 401
italics 231, 232

jargon 71, 141
job designations, gender 234–235
journalism
  careers 475
  civic or public 97–99
  ethics 451–469
  functions of 452
  online 347–369

skills 472, 482
  style 226–237
  training 473–474, 475
Journalism Education Association 486
JPEGs (Joint Photographic Experts Group) 334, 362
jump coverage
  in-depth reports 198
  yearbooks 330
justified type 265

kerning 265, 274, *275*
kickstarter 480
Kirkwood Call, The 57–58, 76, 177

LA Youth 473
labels, group 236–237
Lair, The 101, 102–103, 105, 115
Lance 5
language
  in news stories 71
  racial and ethnic 236–237
  sports 141–142
laser printers 381
law
  copyright 432
  court system 428–430
  freedom of information 47, 433
  Internet and 432
  media 427–449, 452–453
  privacy 436
  state statutes 446–447
  sunshine 433
  unprotected expression 431–436
layering information 211
layout
  newspaper 291–321
  yearbook page 323–345
layout designers
  careers 477
  newspaper 292
  yearbooks 327–331
lead, news 6
leading 266, 273
leading lines, photos 376
leads
  contrast 59–61
  copy editing 217
  descriptive (background) 62–63
  editorials 170–172
  feature stories 113–116
  in-depth reports 204–209
  news stories 54–59
  question 114
  speech stories *93*
  sports stories 152–154
  startling statement 114
  vignette 61–62
Legend 104
legibility, typefaces 272–274
lens doublers 386
lenses, camera 384–386
letterpress printing 285
letters to the editor 315, 431
libel 431–436
libraries 47

lighting, in photos 378–379, *383*
LinkedIn 46
Lion 100
listening 37, 42
literary works, student 358
localizing wider issues
　in-depth reporting 195–197
　in news lead *56*
　in news stories 17, 25
logos 398, 417
Los Angeles Times, The 467
Lowell, The 180, *199*, *294*, 355,
　　379, *393*, *397*

magazines
　binding 283–284
　careers 477–478
　printing 283
　see also newsmagazines
malice, actual 432
maps, locator 398
margins 306
　external 306, 326, *326*
　gutter 284, 326
　internal 306, 326
　yearbooks 327
Marquee, The 150–151
Masson v. New Yorker Magazine
　　(1991) 458
masthead *313*, 316
media conglomerates 476
media
　careers 471–484
　law 427–449, 452–453
　working for multiple 474
MediaStorm 479
meetings
　access to public 433
　minutes 47
men, courtesy titles 227
mentoring, photographers 373, 386
Michigan State University's SND 475
Microsoft Word *223*, 225
Miller v. State of California
　　(1973) 435
Mini-themes 327, 336
Minneapolis Star-Tribune 279
minority groups 236–237
　media careers 475
minors 461
minutes of meetings 47
misappropriation 436
mistakes
　common editing 225–226
　correcting 220, 457, 467
modular design
　newspapers 306, *307*
　yearbooks *328–9*, 334
morgue 31
Morse v. Frederick (2007) 438–439
movie reviews 432
multimedia designers 482
multimedia photography 478–480
multiple-grid formats 301
Murmur, The 13
My High School Journalism *349*, 350

name blocks, portrait pages 335
nameplates 271, *272*, 310, 361
names
　changing, for anonymity 210
　in headlines 254
　in news stories 17
　in photo captions 387
　style 226–227
narrative form *see* storytelling form
National Association of Black
　　Journalists 237, 475, 486
National Association of Hispanic
　　Journalists 237, 475, 486
National Association of Science Writers 486
National Federation of Press Women 486
National Geographic 479
National Institute for Computer-Assisted
　　Reporting 486
national issues, localizing *see* localizing
　　wider issues
National Lesbian and Gay Journalists
　　Association 237, 486
National Newspaper Association 486
National Press Photographers
　　Association 475, 480, 486
　Code of Ethics 395–396
Native American Journalists Association 237,
　　475, 486
Nature Conservancy 479–480
navigation content headers 352
NBC News 462
New York Times, The 94
　headlines 253
　nameplate 272
　style manual 219, 226
New York Times v. Sullivan (1964) 432
Newhouse Foundation 475
news
　analysis *see* interpretative reporting
　angle 15
　breaking 6, 15
　　coverage, factors affecting 22–25
　featurized 15
　localizing 17
　origins 6
　prominence 8–9
　proximity 7–8
　timeliness 6–7, 10, 15
　understanding 3–27
　value 6–10
　vs. opinion 464
news organizations 476–477
news peg 59
news stories 17, 51–79
　advance 12
　body 66–69
　checklist 75
　deaths 87, 88–90
　development 63–69
　ethical aspects 454–456
　flow and organization 69
　focus 65
　inverted pyramid *see* inverted
　　pyramid form
　online coverage 74–75
　proximity 7–8

　questions after publication 458
　sports 146, *147*
　storytelling form *see* storytelling form
　updating 6, 12
　see also news writing
news writing 51–79
　checklist 75
　quotes 75
　leads 54–59
　tips 70
　weaknesses in 69–74
newsmagazines 292
　advertisements 311
　color in *315*
　cover *293*
　　front-page 310
　grids 301
　as information sources 20
Newspaper Association of America 472
newspapers
　advertising 405–424
　back issues 47, 219
　careers 476–477
　design and layout 291–321
　printing 283
　sizes 292
　teen sections 473–474
　websites 352
nickel rule 335
nicknames 231
North Star 193, *297*, *314*, *360*
Northwest Passage 381
not for attribution 459
note-taking
　during interviews 34, 40
　during speeches 91–92
novelty typefaces 271, *272*, 273
numbers 229
　in headlines 254
numerical distortions in news writing 72–73
nut graphs (paragraphs) 61, 62
　feature leads 59
　feature stories 114, 115

obituaries 87, *91*
objectivity, news stories 67
obscenity 435–436, 464
observation 40
　in profiles 124–125
　reporting 115
Octagon, The 21–22, 314
oddity 10
"off the record" 459
offensive material 435
offset lithography 283, *283*
Old English typefaces 271
Ollman v. Evans (D.C. Cir. 1984) 435
On-demand printing 286
"on the record" 34, 459
One Show College Competition 475
"one-party consent states" 456
online journalism 347–369
Online News Association 486
op-ed page 168, 183
open meetings laws 433
Open Society Foundation 480

open source content management systems 350
OpenType 281
opinion
vs. fact 169
vs. news 464
packaged coverage 183
opinion columns 168, 175–176
page design 311, *313*
opinion privilege, defense against libel 435
opinion writing 165–186
optical center 417
organizations, contact details 485–487
see also clubs and organizations
orphans 266

pace
feature stories 118, 123
newspaper design and 317–319
packaging
information 301, 319
opinion coverage 183
picture 380–381, *381*, 398
sports content 154, *155*
page dummies 306
page numbers 326
see also folios
Paladin 249
Pantone Matching System 285
paragraphs *see* leads; nut graphs
paraphrasing 34–40, 76, 458
parody/satire, defense against libel 435
pdf files 281
perfect binding 283, 284, *285*
photo editors 390–391
photo illustrations 396
Photo Mechanic 391
photo polls 315
photo releases 352
photocopying 285
photographers 372
information packaging 301
mentoring 373, 386
photo editing 389–396
picture credits 388
yearbook 99, 330, 333–334
photographs 372–374, 374–380
abuse of 391–394
altered 396, 461
captions 387–389
collages 392–393
color 285, 317
content and composition 375–380
cookie-cutter shapes 391
cropping 310, 389
cutlines 387–389
cutouts 336, 391
digital *see* digital photographs
dominant *324*, 325, *328*, 332, *332*, 334, *339*, *342*, 343, 384
duotoning 394
editing 332, 389–396, 461
ethical use 395–396, 461
flipping or flopping 333, 394
group *see* group photographs
illustrations 461

in newspaper design *293*, 310, 316
online publication 354, 362
packages 380–381, *381*, 398
patterns 394
picture stories 381–384, *382–383*
portrait *see* portraits
postage stamp-sized 394
printing 283, 285, 375, 390
sequences 380–381, 384
stand-alone 388
storytelling with 380–384
stylized 394
technical parameters 374–375
text wraps (runarounds) 276, *279*
tilting 394
in yearbook design 99, 330
photography
careers 477, 478–480
documentary 479–480
equipment 384–387
ethics 395–396
flash 384, 386–387
freelance 476
multimedia 478–480
photojournalism 395, 478
Photoshop/Photoshop Elements 374, 389, 390, 391, 394
pica 266
picture editors 480
picture packages 380–381, *381*, 398
picture sequences 380–381, 384
picture stories 381–384, *382–383*
picture use 316–317
pictures *see* photographs
Pilot 334
Pinnacle, The 421
pixelation 156
pixels 166
plagiarism 463
Planned Parenthood of Southern Nevada v. Clark County School District (1991) 447–448
Poh, Carolyn 256
points, typeface 266
policy, advertising 409–411
political activity 23, 25
political reporters 460
Politico 477
poll story 94–97
polls, online 352, *352*
Portability and Accountability Act (HIPAA) 436
portfolios, published work 474
portraits
framing 376
yearbook page design 335
position statement 170
PostScript 281, 286
Potter's Box 454
Poynter Institute for Media Studies 486
Pre-press production 281
precision, in feature writing 117
presentation director 292
press associations, student membership 474
printer spreads 283
printers 281

printing 283–286, *285*
digital toning for 281–283
prior restraint 436
prison registries 46
privacy 456, 460, 461
privilege defense, libel 431–432
problem words 236
production 281–286
profanity 464, 436
profile box 398
profiles, feature 124–126
Project Censored 486
prominence, of news 6, 8–9
pronouns 70, 175
proofreading 286
proportion, in design 301
ProPublica 477
Prospective, The 42–43, 85
Prospector, The 17, 18–20
provable truth defense, libel 431
proximity, news stories 7–8
public figures
libel 432
privacy 436, 455
public forum, student print publication as 439–440
public journalism 97–99
public meetings, access to 441
public officials, libel 432
public records, access to 441
Public Relations Student Society of America 475
public relations, careers 472, 474, 476
punctuation 229–231, 458
in headlines 255

QR code (Quick response code) 348
question and answer (Q&A) sidebar 103
question leads 114
questions
follow-up 35, *36*, 40
interview 31–32
poll (survey) 95–97
reader *see* reader questions
Quill and Scroll Society 486
quotation marks 230–231, 255
quotes
accuracy 455–456
in captions 387
direct 17, 34, 76
ethics 458
in feature stories 118
indirect 17, 34–40
in news stories 75
paraphrased 76
in profiles 125
running 207
in speech stories 91–92, 97
in sportswriting 143, 149, *150*
in yearbooks 105

R.O. v. Ithaca City School District (2011) 443–444
racial language 236–237
Radio and Television News Directors Association 486

radio broadcasting 482
rails 301, *309*
Rampages 247
rate cards, advertising 406–407
readability
    page design and 292, 302
    typefaces 267, 269, 272–274, 310
    websites 361
reader questions (5 W's and H)
    in interviews 31, 32
    inverted pyramid form 54–55, *55, 56*
    in leads 54, 55–56, *55*
reader spreads 283
recording, interviews 33–34, 455–456
    see also note-taking
records, access to public 441
redesign 478
religious beliefs 23
religious groups 236
ReMarker 24, 60, 178, 194, *206,*
    275, 313
    descriptive lead *63*
    follow-up questions *36*
    informative feature *132–133*
    packaged opinion coverage *182*
    profile writing *125*
    sports feature story *153*
reporting
    beat 12–15
    in-depth 189–213
    observation (firsthand) 115
    undercover 463
    web 464–467
    work 38–39
research
    conventional 47
    in-depth reports 198
    Internet 44–45
    online 348
    see also information resources
resources, information *see* information
    resources
retail advertisement 417
retraction 457
Reuters 480
reverse type 317
review writing 178
    tips 178–180
rhythm, in page design 299
Rider Online, The 365
rivers of white space 265
Rock, The 41
Role-playing, sales calls 411
Romano v. Harrington (1989) 444–445
Royal News, The 270
RSS (Really Simple Syndication) 352
rule lines 400
rule of thirds, photos 375
runarounds, text 276, *279*
run of the press (ROP) color 317
running quotes 207

saddle-stitching 283, 284
Saga 281, 342
sales aids 407
sales, advertising *see* advertising sales

sampling error, polls 95
sans serif typefaces 268–269, *269*
scale, in page design 299
school governing boards 193
School Newspapers Online 350, *350*
School Tube 353
science writing 84–85
screened type 319
screens 390, 400
script typefaces 269, *270*
search engine 248
searches, internet 46–47, 348
secret meetings 441
semicolons 230, 255
sensitive topics 192–193, 209
sentences, writing 54, 74, 75
series reporting 200
serif typefaces 267–268, *268*
sex crimes, victims of 461
sex offender registries 46
sexist details 464
sexist language 234–235
sexual orientation 25, 236
sexual stereotypes 236
sheet-fed printing presses 283
shock value, leads with 62
sidebars 101–106, 398
side-stitching 284
signatures 283
silhouettes 377, *378*
Silver Chips 53, 115, *148*
single lens reflex (SLR) cameras 384
slab serif typefaces 269, *270*
slander 431
slang 141–142
small caps 266
Smith v. Daily Mail (1979)
Smythe-sewing 284
Society for News Design 475, 487
Society of Professional Journalists 466, 467,
    475, 487
Soros, George (www.soros.org) 480
Soundcloud 45
sources
    anonymous 209–210, 458, 459
    beat system 12–15
    confidentiality 461, 464
    ethical issues 455
    in-depth articles 205–210
        news 17–22
        primary 17–18
    reliability 42
        secondary 20–22
        third–party 17
    see also information resources
Southern Interscholastic Press
    Association 487
space
    alternative copy 328
    display 328
    fitting headlines into 246–247
    in-depth reports 198
    in newspaper design 306
    see also white space
Spark, The 8–9, 115, 356, *359*
    advertising 407, *408, 413*

cover *293*
    design and layout *293*
    news story *66*
    opinion writing *167*
special edition 23–25, 203
special section 25, 203
specialty stories, writing 81–108
speech stories 87–94
spellings 232–234
    checking 219
    names 227
Spoke, The 175
sports
    packaged coverage 154, *155*
    page design 316
    photography 373, *379,* 380
    in yearbooks 335
sports briefs package 156
sports reporters 460
sports webcasting 155–158
SportsShooter 480
sportswriting 139–162
    advance stories 143–144
    clichés 140, 142
    feature leads 152–154
    feature stories 151–152, *153*
    game stories 142, 146–149, *148*
    in-depth reports 193
    language 141–142
    news stories 146, *147*
    trend stories 145–146
    using statistics 142–143
spot color
    in newspaper design 317
    printing 285
spread unity *326*
spreads, yearbook 284, 326
Squall, The 145
square serif typefaces 269, *270*
St. Petersburg Times 118–124
staff listing 308, 316
staff, webcast 156–158
stakeholders 453
standing heads 299, 312, 317
state regulatory boards 47
statistics, in sportswriting 142–143, 148
stereotypes 464
    identification 464
    negative 236
    racial, ethnic, religious 236
    sexual 236
Stinger 98
stolen information 463, 464
Storify 45
storytelling form
    multiple 74
    news 11
storytelling, visual 371–403
straight news lead 54
stringers 473
Student Government Association
    (SGA) 460
Student Press Law Center (SPLC) 441, 487
students
    creative writing 85, 358
    identifiers 226–227

style, journalism 226–237
style sheet 226–237
  typographic 278, 308, 331
  use by copy editors 219
stylebooks (manuals) 219, 226
Sullivan, Luke 414–415
summary boxes 398
summary lead 148
sunshine laws 433
surprise 10
surveys 94–95
suspects 461
symposium interview features 131
Syracuse University 475

tablet magazines 359
tabloid format 292, *294*
tabloid printers 281
teen sections, newspapers 473–474
telephone
  advertising sales calls 414
  books, local 219
  interviews 33
telephoto lenses 375, 385
television (TV), careers in 482
templates
  newspaper design 306–310
  section, yearbooks 329
tense, in headlines 254
Teresian 86
text
  body 267, 280
  breaking up 292
  color 317
  line width 272
  wraps (runarounds) 276, *279*
  yearbook design 333
text heads 292, 398
"the" in headlines 253
themes, yearbook, page design 326, 335
thesaurus 219
thirds, rule of 375
tickets, accepting free 460
tie-ins *see* nut graphs
Tiger 2011 337
tight writing 71
timelines 398
timeliness
  news 6–7, 10, 15
  feature stories 114
*Tinker v. Des Moines Independent
    Community School District*
    (1969) 427, 436, 437–438, 439, 440, 442
Titanium 389
titles
  abbreviations 228
  accompanying names 226
  capitalization 227, 228
  courtesy 227
  of works 231
tmwired 355
Tonitrus 329, 340
Tower, The 303
training, media careers 473–474
transportation, accepting free 460
travel reporters 460

trend story, sports 145–146
Triangle, The 296
TrueType 281
Tully Center for Free Speech 487
Twitter *44*, 45, 46, 352, 353
type
  agate 156, 265
  categories (races) 267–272
  color 273, 274
  display 266
  family 266
  justified 265
  posture 269, 271
  reverse 317
  screened 319
  terms 265–266
typefaces 264–265
  black letter 271, *272*
  choosing 272–281
  consistency 277–281
  contrast and creativity *270,* 274–277, *274*
  cursive 269–271, *270*
  feature pages 312
  headlines 264, *267,* 268, *270,* 270–274
  mixing 278
  nameplates 271, *272,* 310
  novelty 271, *272,* 273
  sans serif 268–269
  script 269–271, *270*
  serif 267
  sizes 278
  square (slab) serif 269, *270*
  website 361
typography 263–289, 299

U.S. Constitution, First Amendment 352, 428,
    430–436
  ethics and 452–453
  rights 430, 437
U.S. Court of Appeals 430, 435, 438,
    439, 443
U.S. Supreme Court 428, 429, 430, 432,
    435, 436–448
unity 475
  design 299
  spread *326*
updating, news stories 4, 6, 12
USA Today 477

vagueness in news writing 69
Valkrie 114
verbs
  in headlines 253–254
  in news writing 74
victims 460, 461
video clips 363
  online 350, 354
video conferencing 368
videographer 157
vignette leads 61–62
VII 479
Vimeo 352, 363
visual continuity 327
visual entry points
  newspaper design 310, 316
  yearbook design 336

visual hierarchy
  in newspaper design 292, *294, 300,* 301
  using typefaces 280, 281
  in yearbook design 327
visual impact 10
visual redundancy 389
visual reporting *see* information graphics
visual storytelling 371–403
visual-verbal separators 328
visuals
  in advertisements 417
  double trucks 316
  editorial pages 316
  in newspaper design *318*
  see also artwork; cartoons; illustrations;
      information graphics; photographs
vocabulary, pretentious 71
voice
  active and passive 74, 220, 253
  in editorials 176
  in feature stories 118–124
VOX 473
vulgarity 464

Walski, Brian 462
Washington Post, The 462
Wavelengths 114
web editor 353
web manager 353
web presses 283
web publications
  creation of 348–357
web reporting 464–467
webcasting, sports 155–158
websites
  assembly 351–353
  careers 477
  content 353, 354–357
  cooperative efforts 368
  creating 348–357
  design 361–363
  hosting 350
  as information sources 44–47
  involving readers 354, 358–359
  law governing 432
  multimedia content 354
  newspaper 352, 477
  privacy policies 350
  yearbook 360–361
  see also Internet
  personal 47
  company 47
white space
  ad design 417
  columns and 306
  double trucks 316
  feature pages 312
  layout planning and 312, *312,* 316
  newspaper design 292, 293–296, *295–297,*
      301, *305*
  yearbook design 331
White, Leslie *479*
wide-angle lenses 384
Wikipedia 465
William Randolph Hearst Foundation
      student competition 475

Wings 104, *334, 342*
Wingspan 376
wire services 480
women, courtesy titles 227
wordiness in news writing 71
WordPress 350
wordprocessing 225
words
  choosing 71, 218
  problem 236
wrap graphs *see* nut graphs
wraps, text 276, *279*

X–height 266, 272

yearbook design 323–345
  page design 331–335
  preparation for 327–331
  terminology 324–327
  use of color *342*, 343
yearbooks
  academic section 85
  advertising 405–424
  back issues 219
  binding 284
  captions 325, 333, *333*,
    387–388
  death coverage 87, 88–90
  DVDs and interactive
    coverage 341–342

  In-depth reports 190, 192
  photo cropping 389
  photographs for 99, 387
  printing 283
  sizes 327
  theme 99–101, *100*
  unique story angles 101
  writing 99–106
YO! (Youth Outlook) 473
YouTube 46, 352

zoom lenses 375, 385–386